THE APPRAISAL
OF REAL ESTATE

THE APPRAISAL OF REAL ESTATE

Seventh Edition

Prepared by the
Textbook Revision Subcommittee

AMERICAN INSTITUTE OF REAL ESTATE APPRAISERS,
430 N. Michigan Avenue • Chicago, Illinois

Foreword

This seventh edition of *The Appraisal of Real Estate* has been more than 40 years in the making. The material was first presented as a collection of monographs in the 1930s and then rewritten and supplemented in 1951 to produce the first textbook version. Each succeeding edition has contributed important clarifications, revisions, and new material. Thus *The Appraisal of Real Estate* continues a proud tradition of keeping pace with change without losing sight of the past and the unchanging fundamental principles set forth in the first edition.

The reader who is familiar with earlier editions will find many new additions as well as helpful clarification of traditional subjects in this edition. Attention is directed to the neighborhood analysis chapter, which is extensively revised, and also to the reorganized and expanded chapters dealing with the income approach to value. Another new feature is the "math for appraisers" appendix. Added by popular demand of appraisal teachers and students, this material no doubt will be appreciated also by veteran appraisers as a handy reference.

The Appraisal of Real Estate combines the work of numerous contributors over many years. Although it would be impractical, if not impossible, to name all contributors, the American Institute of Real Estate Appraisers deeply appreciates each and every contribution. John D. Dorchester, Jr., MAI, and Peter D. Bowes, MAI, deserve recognition for their leadership in guiding this seventh edition to completion. Mr. Dorchester was chairman of the Institute's Division of Publications in 1977 and was succeeded by Mr. Bowes in 1978.

Major credit goes to Chairman Richard L. Lodge, MAI, and his Textbook Revision Committee: Vice Chairman George A. Stauss,

Ph.D., MAI, and committee members John C. Albertson, MAI; David W. Craig, MAI; John A. Doerr, MAI; and Robert J. Weiler, Ph.D., MAI. Mr. Lodge and his committee are to be commended for their dedicated service and valuable contributions. Janet Seefeldt, Director of Publications, Institute staff, provided professional advice and assistance.

Finally, a special commendation is accorded to Walter R. Kuehnle, MAI, past president of the Institute, who personally directed the creation of the second, fourth, fifth, and sixth editions of this work. In recognition of his countless contributions to prior editions of this great work, I hereby dedicate this seventh edition to Walter R. Kuehnle, MAI.

> Charles B. Akerson, MAI
> 1978 President
> American Institute of Real Estate Appraisers

Contents

1

Nature and Purpose
of Appraisals

A substantial portion of the private, corporate, and public wealth of the world consists of real estate. The very magnitude of this fundamental resource in our society creates a need for informed appraisals to support decisions pertaining to the use and disposition of real estate and the rights inherent in ownership. Appraising these rights is the art of solving an identified problem by finding and assembling facts, analyzing the facts, and forming a conclusion.

In the past real estate appraisals were simply opinions of value expressed by owners or others involved in the sale or management of real estate. In today's complex economy such "appraisals" are overly simple and could be unreliable and misleading.

Professional appraisals are more than opinions. They require selective research into appropriate market areas; assemblage of pertinent data; the application of appropriate analytical techniques; and the knowledge, experience, and professional judgment necessary to develop a conclusion that is appropriate to the problem.

Professional judgment is a critical factor. Although a scientific method is applied throughout the appraisal process, appraising is not an exact science. The making of a judgment in the formulation of a conclusion is based on and supported by facts developed from research. The competent appraiser gathers and selects relevant information, applies expertise to the processing of the information, maintains complete objectivity and high ethical standards, and develops a valid conclusion.

In forming the conclusion, the appraiser recognizes and clearly identifies the difference among personal opinions, observed facts, and professional judgment. An estimation of market value reflects market attitudes and actions; personal positions are out of place.

VALUATION AND EVALUATION

Estimations of market value have been the most frequent type of appraisal assignment, and the public perception of appraisal activity is probably limited to such assignments. However, because of their specialized training and experience, appraisers are called upon to provide a wide range of additional appraisal services—from consultation to key roles in decision-making situations related to real estate.

To reflect the broad scope of appraisal activity and to distinguish between the specific field of market value estimation and the expanding area of other related assignments, a distinction is now recognized between valuation and evaluation.

Valuation is the act or process of estimating the market value of an identified interest or interests in a specific parcel of real estate as of a given time. Any other type of appraisal assignment is evaluation.

Evaluation is a broad term that is applied to studies of the nature, quality, and utility of any parcel of real estate or any interest in, or aspect of, real property including value estimates other than market value. The purpose is to provide solutions to real estate problems that do not necessarily include market value. Land utilization studies, supply and demand studies, economic feasibility studies, highest and best use analyses, marketability or investment considerations for a proposed or existing development, and similar research-related studies are examples of evaluation assignments. They are generally of an economic nature and often involve some aspect of value.

Because confusion about the type of assignment can arise, and because certain types, such as market value estimation, require special definitions and processes, the appraiser clearly identifies the nature of the assignment during the appraisal and in final reports. Standards of professional practice and codes of ethics also have been developed to guide the appraiser's action.

The principles of valuation discussed in this book are essential background for all appraisal assignments. In general, they will relate primarily to estimates of market value because of the importance of such estimates in the appraisal profession and in the structure of economic life in the United States.

FORCES INFLUENCING REAL ESTATE VALUE

The market value of real property reflects and is affected by the interplay of basic forces that motivate the activities of human beings. These forces, which produce the variables in real estate market values, may be considered in four major categories: social ideals and standards, economic changes and adjustments, governmental controls and regulations, and physical or environmental changes. Each force is dynamic, exerting pressure on some facet of human existence. Combined, as cause and effect, they influence every parcel of real estate. They are complex, and there are many constantly changing factors encompassed by each force.

Some of the social forces are:

1. Population growth and decline
2. Shifts in population density
3. Changes in size of families
4. Attitudes toward education and social activities
5. Attitudes toward architectural design and utility
6. Other factors emerging from human social instincts, ideals, and yearnings

Economic forces, including the resources and efforts of people to achieve social ideals, are made up of factors such as:

1. Natural resources—their quantity, quality, location, and rate of depletion
2. Commercial and industrial trends
3. Employment trends and wage levels
4. Availability of money and credit
5. Price levels, interest rates, and tax burdens
6. Other factors that have direct or indirect effect on purchasing power

Governmental regulations created by political forces include:

1. Zoning laws
2. Building codes
3. Police and fire regulations
4. Rent controls, national defense measures, priorities, allocations, special use permits, and credit controls
5. Government-sponsored housing and guaranteed mortgage loans
6. Monetary policies that affect the free use of real estate, including all forms of taxation

Physical or environmental forces can be created either by nature or by people. They encompass:

1. Climate and topography
2. Soil fertility
3. Mineral resources
4. Community factors such as transportation and proximity to schools, houses of worship, parks, recreation areas
5. Flood control and soil conservation
6. Characteristics of soil and subsoil
7. Technological advances affecting land use

Each of these social, economic, governmental, and physical forces affects cost, price, and value. The impact of each force—sometimes direct, sometimes indirect—is considered in estimating the cost, the probable price, or the value of real property. These four forces, with the factors comprising them, constitute the basic material for estimating real property value. Any decision or action in the real estate market is based on an appraisal, whether or not it is prepared by a professional appraiser or presented in a formal written report.

PURPOSE OF AN APPRAISAL

The purpose of an appraisal is to provide an estimate of value. Everyone at some time is affected by an appraisal of the value of real estate. Everyone uses real estate and pays for its use by purchase or rent. Any decision about payment involves a decision about value. When based on personal opinion unsupported by market research or knowledge, the quality of the decision may be questionable.

Professional expertise and an understanding of the application of appropriate methods and techniques are necessary for meaningful estimates of market value, as well as for studies of marketability, feasibility, highest and best use, land utilization, and other aspects of the use and value of real estate.

DEFINITION OF AN APPRAISAL

An appraisal is an estimate of value or the act of estimating value. This definition permits application of the term to any such estimate, whether it is an informed conclusion based on evidence or simply a personal opinion. In this book use of the term *appraisal* implies that some level of professional expertise is employed in developing the value estimate. The reliability of an appraisal depends on the basic competence and integrity of the appraiser, the availability of pertinent data, and the skill with which the data is processed. An appraisal is *an opinion of value for an adequately described property, as of a specified date, supported by the analysis of relevant data.*

An opinion is a conviction founded on acceptable evidence but less than positive knowledge. Anyone may have an opinion; but to have meaning, the opinion must be supportable. A professional appraisal goes beyond any personal feeling of the appraiser. It reflects market evidence in a conclusion of value, derived by appropriate analysis in conformity with standards of professional practice.[1] Personal opinions, which may or may not conform to current market activity, may be proper only when an appraiser is acting in the position of a consultant.

The conclusion may be transmitted orally or presented formally in written form. Further discussion of an appraisal report format and content is provided in Chapter 26.

LEVELS OF REAL ESTATE APPRAISAL

There are three levels of activity related to real estate value decisions. People who use and own real estate or invest in it beyond indi-

---

1. Regulation No. 10 of the American Institute of Real Estate Appraisers' Code of Professional Ethics and Standards of Professional Conduct establishes such standards for members of the Institute.

vidual residential and business needs make decisions on the first level. Their decisions relate to asking prices, offers to buy, mortgages, leases, insurance programs, casualty losses, and land development projects. They make decisions about contemplated construction programs; remodeling, rehabilitation, or modernization projects; and other actions that involve substantial sums of money. When confronted by any of these problems, individuals may make independent decisions or turn to a professional appraiser for assistance. In either case, an intelligent decision is predicated on some form of appraisal or feasibility study. Because the quality of the decision reflects the dependability of the analysis on which it is based, the desirability of professional assistance is apparent.

An understanding of the forces that influence real estate value is the result of acquired knowledge. Not every individual can be expected to understand many essential appraisal procedures. Too often people rely on emotions or their own unfounded judgments and make costly mistakes. For example:

1. A buyer pays more for a property than is justifiable in the market.
2. A seller takes less for a property than it is worth.
3. A landlord signs a lease, the terms of which adversely affect the value of his interest in the real property.
4. A tenant signs a rental contract that prospective business income will not support.
5. An owner undertakes an unsound modernization or rehabilitation project.

Opinions of value—based on sound valuation—are safeguards against such commitments. Not everyone on this first level of activity needs to understand and utilize valuation techniques; but individuals faced with a decision about real estate should recognize what constitutes an adequate valuation, sufficient in scope to meet their requirements.

The men and women in the general real estate vocation— salespeople, brokers, investors, subdividers and builders, property managers, and mortgage lenders, as well as those concerned with tax assessments, right-of-way proceedings, and other governmental

functions—make decisions the second level of real estate appraisal. Although these people usually are not professional appraisers,
they deal with problems involving real estate value as part of their
everyday work. Frequently the general public asks them to express
an opinion of real estate value. It is entirely proper that they give
their opinions of value up to the limit of their qualifications. However, they should be aware of their limitations and recognize
situations in which they are not qualified to act. The services of a
professional appraiser should be used whenever the situation calls
for market research, expert advice, or third party objectivity.

The work of professional appraisers is the third level of value estimation. The members of this group may devote their time exclusively to real estate appraisal assignments or they may also carry on
a practice in other branches of real estate activity. They are highly
competent in knowledge, skill, and integrity and are identified by a
recognized professional designation.

The need for appraisal services on the professional level has long
been recognized by banks, trust companies, savings and loan associations; insurance companies; governmental agencies; universities and other institutions having the responsibility of investing
endowment and trust funds; public utilities, chain stores, and many
other concerns and individuals who make decisions based on estimates of real estate value. Investors, private companies, and institutions that have real estate problems are increasing their demands
for professional appraisals. Governmental agencies are employing
greater numbers of professional salaried appraisers and professional
fee appraisers.

USES OF AN APPRAISAL

The fundamental purpose of an appraisal assignment is to assist in
making reasoned real estate decisions. The value most commonly
sought is market value. However, there are other concepts of value,
depending on the use for which the client requires an appraisal.

The need for an appraisal of market value may arise from many
situations.

1. Transfer of ownership
    a. To help prospective buyers decide on offering prices
    b. To help prospective sellers determine acceptable selling prices
    c. To establish a basis for exchanges of real property
    d. To establish a basis for reorganization or for merging the ownership of multiple properties
2. Financing and credit
    a. To arrive at the essential security offered for a proposed mortgage loan
    b. To provide an investor with a sound basis for deciding whether to purchase real estate mortgages, bonds or other types of securities
    c. To establish a basis for a decision regarding the insuring or underwriting of a loan on real property
3. Just compensation in condemnation proceedings
    a. To estimate market value of property as a whole—that is, before the taking
    b. To estimate value after the taking
    c. To allocate market values between the part taken and damage to the remainder
4. A basis for taxation
    a. To separate assets into depreciable items, such as buildings, and nondepreciable items, such as land, and to estimate applicable depreciation rates
    b. To determine gift or inheritance taxes
5. A basis for rental schedules and lease provisions
6. Feasibility in relation to a renovation program
7. A basis for corporations or third-party companies to purchase homes of transferred employees
8. Other situations in which a decision about real estate is necessary

Other needs may require an appraisal for other than market value.

1. Insurable value—a concept of replacement cost to serve the needs of insured, insurer, and adjuster.
2. Going concern value—a concept of value that includes tangible assets plus intangibles such as goodwill or going business value. It may be used in corporate mergers, the issuance of stock, or revision of book value.

3. Liquidation value or price—for forced sale or auction proceedings.
4. Assessed value—a uniform schedule for tax rolls in ad valorem taxation. This schedule may not conform to market value but usually bears some relation to a market value base.
5. Value in use—a concept reflecting the economic contribution of the real estate to the enterprise of which it is a part, particularly applicable to real estate for which no rental or sale market can be identified.

Although this list does not include all of the needs for appraisals, it indicates the broad scope of the professional appraiser's activities.

An appraisal is an answer to a question that may be as limited as "What is the market value of this parcel of real estate today?" However, there are more complicated and sophisticated considerations that may involve interests, equities, historical and future values, and other conditions. The answer to any question involving the value of an interest in real estate, under any assumed conditions, may be undertaken by the qualified appraiser, provided the question and the conclusion are fully and clearly stated.

THE IMPORTANCE OF THE APPRAISER TO THE COMMUNITY

The professional appraiser provides essential services that contribute to the growth and stability of the community or city in which assignments are executed. Decisions concerning substantial investments are based on valuations and other market studies or feasibility reports. These studies, including research leading to judgment decisions by the appraiser, are essential for new construction, large renovation or development programs, and major changes in land use.

The appraiser is frequently regarded by lenders and the public as the expert in evaluating a neighborhood's strength and weakness. Accordingly, the appraiser must exercise this responsibility with care and be certain that a considered judgment about a community's trend is supportable by objective facts. An appraiser must never let emotional arguments or advocacy affect the presentation of demonstrable facts. Through its regulations, by-laws, and appraisal review procedures, the American Institute of Real Estate Appraisers contributes to assure conformity with acceptable practices, unbiased judgments, and complete integrity within its membership.

Professionally designated appraisers who have demonstrated their competence find that their services are in demand and that theirs is a rewarding and satisfying profession.

2

Nature of Real Property and Value

Land is an indispensable accompaniment to human life and activity, but it has significance only as it satisfies human needs and desires. Utilization gives it character, and desire gives it value. The measure of a property's value is the degree of its utility and the scarcity of comparable utilities. Land that is so remote from human activity that people cannot use it has no monetary value. Such land may have rich soil; it may abound in precious minerals; it may be located in an agreeable climate and have scenic beauty; but it will remain valueless until its use is economically feasible.

Land acquires value when it is desired and has a feasible use, but the value imputed to a particular parcel of real estate is not limited solely to the individual whose desire created it. Effects of that value have significance for every other person whose welfare is or can be affected by its utilization.

"Under all is the land." The ramifications of this statement are as extensive as it is brief. Land is vital to human existence. It is the source of food and the foundation for the structures necessary to social and economic activities. Because all people use land, whether or not they own it, an understanding of the concept of real property is based on a comprehension of land utilization.

LEGAL CONCEPT OF LAND

The legal concept of land is more comprehensive than is generally realized. The legal theory holds that land:

. . . includes not only the ground or soil, but everything which is attached to the earth, whether by course of nature, as trees and herbage, or by the hand of man, as houses and other buildings. It includes not only the surface of the earth, but everything under it and over it. Thus, in legal theory, a tract of land consists not only of the portion on the surface of the earth, but is an inverted pyramid having its tip or apex at the center of the earth, extending outward through the surface of the earth at the boundary lines of the tract, and continuing on upward to the heavens.[1]

The concept that ownership of land extends from the center of the earth to the periphery of the universe conveys the idea of full and complete ownership, but it is neither established law nor a rule of property. Examples of the limitation of ownership of air space are shown by acts of Congress, beginning in 1926, declaring that the United States has complete and exclusive national sovereignty in the air space over the nation and granting to any citizen "a public right to freedom of transit in air commerce through the navigable air space of the United States."[2] Navigable air space is defined as "air space above the minimum safe altitude of flight prescribed by [the Civil Aeronautics Authority]."[3] The Authority fixed these altitudes at 1,000 feet over congested areas and 500 feet over other areas, including the necessary area for safe takeoff and landing.[4]

Since these early limitations on air space ownership, there have been recurring legal interpretations further refining the private ownership concept. A Supreme Court opinion in 1972 stated:

It is ancient doctrine that at common law ownership of the land extended to the periphery of the universe. . . . But that doctrine has no place in the modern world. The air is a public highway, as Congress has declared. Were that not true, every transcontinental flight would subject the operator to countless trespass suits. Common sense revolts at the idea. To recognize such private claims to the air space would clog these highways, seriously interfere with their control and development of the public interest, and transfer into private ownership that to which only the public has a just claim. 328 U.S., at 261.[5]

---

1. Robert Kratovil, *Real Estate Law*, 6th ed. (Englewood Cliffs, N.J.: Prentice-Hall, Inc. 1974), p. 5.
2. The Air Commerce Act of 1926 (formerly 49 USC § 171 et seq.); and Civil Aeronautics Act of 1938 (formerly 49 USC §401 et seq.); and the Federal Aviation Act of 1958 (see 49 USC §401).
3. 49 USC §180.
4. 49 USC 1301 (24).
5. *Laird* v. *Nelms*, 406 U.S. 797 (1972).

This developing modification of the rights of ownership illustrates that ownership of land is subject to various limitations, which are discussed later in this chapter under the bundle of rights theory.

Distinction between Real Estate, Real Property, and Personal Property

To avoid misunderstanding about the meaning of these terms, they have been defined as follows:

REAL ESTATE—This refers to the physical land and appurtenances, including structures affixed thereto. In some states, by statute, this term is synonymous with real property.[6]

REAL PROPERTY—This refers to the interests, benefits, and rights inherent in the ownership of the physical real estate. It is the bundle of rights with which the ownership of real estate is endowed.[7]

PERSONAL PROPERTY—Generally, movable items; that is, those not permanently affixed to and a part of the real estate. In deciding whether or not a thing is personal property or real estate, usually there must be considered:
 1.   The manner in which it is annexed
 2.   The intention of the party who made the annexation — that is, to leave permanently or to remove at some time [frequently revealed by terms of a lease]
 3.   The purpose for which the premises are used. Generally, but with exceptions, items remain personal property if they can be removed without serious injury either to the real estate or to the item[s] [themselves][8]

As these definitions indicate, real estate, real property, and personal property are three totally different concepts. The distinctions among them are subtle. Being concerned with all three, the appraiser acquires a thorough understanding of the distinctions and their significance.

---

6. American Institute of Real Estate Appraisers and Society of Real Estate Appraisers, *Real Estate Appraisal Terminology*, ed. Byrl N. Boyce (Cambridge, Mass.: Ballinger Publishing Company, 1975), pp. 171-172.
7. *Ibid.*, p. 172.
8. *Ibid.*, pp. 157-158.

The chief characteristics of *real estate* are its immobility and tangibility. It is comprised of land and all things of a permanent and substantial nature affixed thereto, whether by nature (trees, the products of the land, natural resources) or by people (objects—buildings, fences, bridges—that are erected on the land). All equipment or fixtures such as plumbing, electrical, heating, built-in cabinets, elevators, which are installed in a building in a more or less permanent manner, usually are held to be a part of the real estate.

Real property may be considered a composite term because it embraces the tangible (physical) elements of real estate plus the intangible attributes that are the rights of ownership. *The appraiser is concerned with real property in estimating the value of the rights and benefits to be derived from the ownership of real estate.*

The chief characteristic of *personal property* is its mobility. Furniture and furnishings, office equipment, livestock and farm machinery, mortgages, and securities of every type—practically anything the owner can move about at will—are personal property.

Sometimes the distinction between personal property items and real estate is so fine that a court opinion has been required to resolve the issue. The necessity for classification or distinction has given rise to the law of fixtures wherein the basic theory holds that a fixture is

... an article that was once personal property, but that has been installed in or attached to land or a building in some more or less permanent manner, so that such article is regarded in law as a part of the real estate.[9]

The distinction between personal property items and real estate is important to the appraiser, for if a fixture remains an item of personal property, its contribution to value may not be considered in estimating the value of the real property. But if the fixture has become part of the real estate, its contribution to value is included in the real property value estimate.

Because the distinction between real estate and personal property items is not always evident and because it is important in the valuation of real estate, the appraiser should be familiar with the law of fixtures as it applies in the locality of the property being appraised. When the law is not clear concerning an item, the appraiser may abide by local

---

9. Kratovil. *op. cit.,* p. 11.

custom. However, in an appraisal report, the appraiser's assumptions concerning what constitutes real property and personal property are clearly identified.

Although personal property generally consists of tangible items, an intangible personal property right may be created by a lease. Such rights may have economic value (see Chapter 23).

Bundle of Rights Theory

This theory holds that the ownership of real property may be compared to a bundle of sticks wherein each stick represents a distinct and separate right or privilege of ownership. These rights are inherent in ownership of real property and guaranteed by law, but subject to certain limitations and restrictions. They are the right to use real property, to sell it, to lease it, to enter it, to give it away, and the right to refuse to exercise any of these rights.

Although the legal definition of land implies complete ownership of land and everything attached to it, under it, and over it, legal title to land in fact does not convey absolute fee simple title to real property and the unrestricted exercise of the entire bundle of rights. These rights and privileges are limited by four powers of government:

1. The power of taxation.
2. The power of eminent domain—the right reserved by government to take by condemnation private property for public benefit provided it pays just compensation therefor. This right has been extended to quasi-public bodies such as housing authorities and to public utilities. There is an apparent trend toward a broader interpretation of these rights and powers of government as the concept of what constitutes public benefit broadens.
3. The police power—the right to regulate property for promoting the public's safety, health, morals, and general welfare. Zoning ordinances, building codes, traffic regulations, and sanitary regulations are based on the police power of government.
4. Escheat—the right to have titular ownership of the property return to the state if the owner dies leaving no will and no known or ascertainable heirs.

In addition to governmental restrictions on property, legal private agreements also may impose restrictions. These could limit the use or manner of development, or even the manner in which ownership can be conveyed. These are called deed restrictions, and a purchaser of a property so encumbered may be obligated to use the property subject to such restrictions. Other private restrictions include easements, rights of way, and party-wall agreements. For example, an owner can sell or lease the mineral rights while retaining the rights to use the surface area of the property. An absentee property owner can rent surface rights to one party and lease the subsurface rights to another. Air rights, whether for construction or avigation, can be sold or leased. Thus some of the rights may have been severed from the property by sale, lease, or gift to other parties before a property is acquired.

The remaining rights in the bundle, subject to the limitations imposed by governmental and private restrictions, can also be sold, leased, transferred, or otherwise disposed of. Therefore, an appraisal of a property's value involves consideration of the rights remaining with the property and the effect of the loss of any of these private rights on its value as a whole. Knowing exactly which rights are under consideration is fundamental in appraising. Their precise definition customarily is a matter of documentation. In the absence of such definition, it may be necessary to obtain a legal opinion. The appraiser, however, should be generally familiar with the broad range of property rights, their more common characteristics, and the usual manner in which they are utilized and transferred.

Federal, state, and local fair housing laws guarantee persons the right to buy, sell, lease, hold, and convey property without being subjected to discrimination on the basis of race, color, religion, sex, or national origin. These laws have nullified private deed restrictions which limited occupancy on racial or religious grounds. They have also operated to prohibit other types of discrimination in the sale and rental of housing, so that equal housing opportunity is now regarded as a basic civil right.

MEANING OF VALUE

Value is the key word that links different segments of the real estate business. Value plays an important part in all real estate activity. A buyer or seller bases the offering or asking price on his or her opinion of value. The broker's and manager's concern with value is important for their own interests, as well as for advising their clients about realizing sale prices and rental rates. The builder who is not cognizant of the value involved cannot know what to build, where to build, and when to build. The lender must have knowledge of value to ensure sound mortgage investments. The appraiser is directly concerned with value because all problems in appraising involve value-related decisions.

The significance and importance of value to the real estate vocation would imply that its meaning is precisely and clearly defined, thoroughly understood, and so utilized in all real estate activities. Unfortunately, this ideal condition does not exist. Value as a broad concept is given many interpretations, but there is common agreement as to the specific nature of many types of value.

The existence of many types of value in real estate is not difficult to understand when even a modest-sized dictionary may list as many as 10 definitions for the word *value.* It means one thing to the artist, another to the musician, still another to the scientist. This tendency to interpret value in terms of specific social and economic activities is so widespread that to find it in the real estate field is not strange. Lenders may use the term *loan value;* brokers may use the term *sales value;* others may use the term *condemnation value,* when in each case *market value* is implied. The assessor refers to *assessed value,* and casualty insurance companies refer to *insurable value.*

Learning terminology is an important facet of an appraisal student's curriculum. Proper use of terminology improves communication and is the medium through which an estimate of value is expressed. Terminology must be understood and correctly used, and definitions or explanations in a report must be presented clearly and concisely. The appraiser also recognizes that the terminology of the real estate appraisal profession is not static. Changing circumstances or development of new techniques may involve modification in the usage of terminology or in the wording of existing definitions.

Evolution of Value Theory

Concern with the meaning of value has intrigued scholars, writers, philosophers, and economists for centuries. From the time of Aristotle until the middle of the 16th century, views expressed on value were often incidental to the philosophical discussion of other subjects. Thereafter, value theories were accorded greater consideration by economic theorists. The history of the evolution of value theory, particularly after the 16th century, can be found in many books on economics.[10] Contributions made by the more significant schools of economic thought are summarized below.

The Mercantilists (1500-1800).   The objectives of the mercantilists, in an era of emerging national states, was to increase national wealth as a means of improving individual economic well-being. This was considered possible only in a strong economic state with strict control of productive agencies, land, and means of transportation. A favorable balance of trade was essential, and export of gold was prohibited.

The mercantilists contribution to value was recognition of *desire* as a factor creating value. Their understanding of the effect of supply and demand on price led to a concept of value in exchange.

The Physiocrats (1750-1800).   The Physiocrats belonged to an agrarian-oriented French philosophic school. They took a strong position that individual rights should not be subordinated to advancement of the national state. Theirs was a *laissez-faire* doctrine of natural order under a benign Deity, in which the chief function of government was to protect the life, liberty, and property of the individual.

The Physiocrats established the foundation for our concept of economic rent attributable to land. Value created in excess of the cost of production was attributed to land since land was held to be the elemental productive agent.

The Classical School (1775-1885).   Adam Smith, a Scottish moral philosopher, in *The Wealth of Nations,* published in 1775, contended that mercantilism or planned economy operated outside a moral framework because the individual was denied freedom of choice and that it failed to achieve its intended goal because people are more

10. For example, see L. H. Haney, *History of Economic Thought,* 4th ed. (New York: The Macmillan Company, 1949); Arthur M. Weimer, "History of Value Theory for the Appraiser," *The Appraisal Journal,* October 1960, pp. 469-483; Paul A. Samuelson, *Economics,* 9th ed. (New York: McGraw-Hill, 1973).

productive when free than when coerced. Smith went beyond an agricultural base. He introduced the concept of capital and recognized the cost of capital as an essential part of value.

In a capitalistic economy he saw profit as the incentive and competition as the regulator, while growth was inherent in the system. He still based value primarily on cost of production, recognizing land, labor, and capital as three elements of cost. He added a profit incentive to complete the four agents in production as we now know them. Within this cost of production concept, he conceived what he called "normal price," a level toward which market prices would gravitate because of competition.

David Ricardo (1772-1823). Ricardo contributed to the evolution of the value concept with his theory of economic rent. Rent was defined as that portion of the produce of the earth which is paid to the landlord for the use of the original and indestructible powers of the soil. He regarded capital as stored labor, thus reducing all costs to the cost of labor. Accordingly, he concluded that value is determined by scarcity and the quantity of labor involved in production.

Under Ricardo's theory of economic rent, as long as land is available for no cost, no rent will be paid. With increasing population and higher prices for farm products, better land becomes scarce, and increasingly, poorer land comes into use. As the process continues, the better land commands increasingly higher rentals, and land that has no margin of productivity beyond the value of the labor and capital expended has no rental value. Operation of this marginal land determines cost, and the better grades of land command a level of economic rent in proportion to their margin of productivity.

Thomas Robert Malthus (1766-1834). Like Ricardo, Malthus subscribed to the marginal theory of rent; but he placed additional emphasis on the influence of supply and demand and contended that as population increased, so would land values. He is best known for his essay on population published in 1798. Unlike Adam Smith, who. had predicted a growing and improving world, Malthus anticipated that populations would increase until, within a foreseeable future, they would exceed the ability of land to produce food, and starvation would be inevitable.

John Stuart Mill (1806-1873).   Mill accepted and reformulated Adam Smith's classical doctrine governing the production of wealth, but he thought government should have a hand in its distribution. He stressed value as being power in exchange and in 1848 published his theory of the unearned increment of land value. He proposed that the government make a periodic revaluation of all land, urban or rural, and collect, through taxation, any increased value. No provision was made for a decrease in value. Present inheritance laws may reflect some influence of this type of thinking which, if continued long enough, would result in eventual government confiscation of all land.

Karl Marx (1818-1883).   Publication of *Das Kapital* in 1867 was the culmination of Karl Marx' writings, begun in 1848. Considered by some as the founder of modern socialism, his labor theory of value (which was not original but which he espoused with zeal) regarded value as a mere summation of human labor. He reflected a period in which philosophic thinking began to consider human desires and social benefits in relation to property ownership and value. How much the times contributed to Marx or he to the times is a subject of controversy. Although his theories have gained considerable acceptance in various national applications, they have undergone many conceptual changes and interpretations in the process. An interesting note is that he felt the United States, with an emphasis on human liberties, would be among the first nations in which his theories would receive general acceptance.

The Austrian School (late 19th century).   In the writings of this group of economists, the theory of price in relation to value reached its first complete development. Utility was the keystone to value, and "normal value" was the level of value attained when supply and demand were in perfect balance. Price, considered to be a function of marginal utility, was established as that point at which the seller would not accept one cent less and the buyer would not pay one cent more.

The Neo-Classical School (late 19th to early 20th century). Economists of this school emphasized the cyclical nature of business activity and gave impetus to increasing public and private research in this area and related fields. They compared the presssures of supply and demand to two blades of a scissors. They held that market forces tend to move toward a state of equilibrium where value is at a maximum and market price and market value come together. Government intervention was conceived as a means of effecting economic or social changes. John Maynard Keynes evolved the concept of increased government spending in periods when the private sector of the economy lagged and decreased government spending when activity in the private sector revived—actions designed to maintain a reasonable level of equilibrium in the national economy. Misapplication of this concept is considered by many to be responsible for much of the inflation of recent years.

The Historical and Institutional Schools.   These two schools emphasize the study of economics in broad historical perspective and in terms of contemporary human situations and human behavior. Neither has, to date, made any major contribution to our present concepts of value.

This brief summary of the history of value theory demonstrates that *value* is a word with many meanings. Because it is the symbol of ideas, it cannot be defined precisely. Oliver Wendell Holmes, Associate Justice of the Supreme Court, emphasized this concept when he said:

> A word *(value)* is not a crystal, transparent and unchanged; it is the skin of a living thought, and may vary greatly in color and content according to the circumstances and the time in which it is used.[11]

FACTORS THAT CREATE VALUE

Value pertains to the relationship between a thing desired and a potential purchaser. The important word in this statement is *relationship*. It implies that value is not inherent in an object, existing independently as in a vacuum. Value is created by, and varies with, changing factors in this relationship. Four essential factors involved in this value relationship may be identified: (1) desire, (2) utility, (3) scarcity, and (4) effective purchasing power.

Desire for an object contributes to its value. This desire, which may

---

11. *Towne* v. *Eisner*, 245 U.S. 418.

exist in the absence of actual "need," is not sufficient to create value without the presence of some other factor or factors. The belief that desire or need alone creates value would imply that value is a characteristic inherent in the object itself. If this concept were true, bread would be intrinsically valuable because it is needed to satisfy hunger. But hunger is limited. If bakers were to produce twice as much bread as needed to satisfy all normal hunger, half would have little, if any, value. The value of the bread, then, is not intrinsic but depends on a relationship between bread and hunger.

Utility is the ability to satisfy a human need or desire. Utility depends in most instances on the usefulness of the object, but utility encompasses more than mere usefulness. A useful object may and may not have utility at the same time, depending on the desires of different individuals. For example, bread has great utility to a hungry person but may have little or no utility to one who is not hungry.

Scarcity must accompany desire and utility before value can exist. For example, air has the highest possible utility, but air is not scarce. No object, including a parcel of real estate, can have value unless it possesses some degree of utility and scarcity.

Effective purchasing power to implement desire for an object that has utility and scarcity produces value. Purchasing power, or the ability to participate in the market, enables an individual to satisfy desire.

The appraiser's understanding of value can be summarized as follows: Value is not a characteristic inherent in real property itself. Value arises from the relationship of the real property to those who constitute the potential market and varies from person to person and from time to time. Real property cannot have value unless it has utility. A degree of scarcity must also exist to create value. Utility and scarcity together do not confer value unless they arouse the desire of a purchaser who has the purchasing power to buy. Thus utility, scarcity, desire, and purchasing power together are prerequisites to value.

Attempts to estimate the value of real estate are complicated by its permanent character. Unlike goods which are rapidly consumed and whose utility is obtained at once, the benefits of real property are realized over a long time. Land and its improvements have a useful life extending over decades. The value of real property, consequently, is equal to the present value of the future benefits forthcoming from the property. Estimating the market value for the highest and best use is the paramount problem in the valuation of real estate. Any such estimate must take into consideration social and economic trends which may influence the value for its highest and best use. A clear understanding of current conditions and the perception to recognize the forces that modify and change these conditions are essential.

In considering these factors, the appraiser is really interpreting the reactions of typical users and investors. Appraisers do not make value; they interpret it, chiefly from market evidence.

VALUE IN EXCHANGE AND VALUE IN USE

The concept of value has been a subject of investigation and discussion among economists and, before them, philosophers and lawmakers for many centuries. Their thinking has resulted in separating the general concept of value into two categories: (1) value in exchange (market value), and (2) specific use value for which there may be no identifiable open market demand.

Value in exchange, or market value, reflects the actions of buyers, sellers, and investors in the market and typically represents the primary concern in an appraisal of real property. Unless there is no identifiable market, existing or potential, for the property being appraised, the usual concept of the value sought is market value. This has been defined in various ways in different parts of the United States because most definitions have been taken from decisions in eminent domain cases. The most widely accepted definitions of market value include:

1. The highest price in terms of money that a property would bring in a competitive and open market under all conditions requisite to a fair sale, the buyer and seller each acting prudently and knowledgeably and assuming the price is not affected by undue stimulus
2. The price at which a willing seller would sell and a willing buyer would buy, neither being under abnormal pressure
3. The price expectable if a reasonable time is allowed to find a purchaser and if both seller and prospective buyer are fully informed

Certain conditions or assumptions implicit in the market value definition are noted in *Real Estate Appraisal Terminology* as follows:

1. Buyer and seller are typically motivated.
2. Both parties are well informed or well advised, and each acting in what he considers his own best interest.
3. A reasonable time is allowed for exposure in the open market.
4. Payment is made in cash or its equivalent.
5. Financing, if any, is on terms generally available in the community at the specified date and typical for the property type in its locale.
6. The price represents a normal consideration for the property sold unaffected by special financing amounts and/or terms, services, fees, costs, or credits incurred in the transaction.[12]

The factors of utility, scarcity, desire, and purchasing power are inherent in the definition. The implication that buyer and seller are working under equal pressure is seldom completely true, although typical motivation for each does imply a reasonable balance for a market value transaction. Unusual financing or other factors that might result in a price deviation from market value are also excluded. However, if the availability of other than conventional financing (such as FHA or VA loan terms) is sufficiently extensive to constitute a market within which the property being appraised is expected to sell, the typical purchaser may be expected to take advantage of this available financing, and the market value of the property reflects the probable sale price in this market. In market valuation assignments the appraiser first identifies the market in which the property being appraised will be exposed and sold. The market value of the property is then identified within parameters that reflect conditions in this market.

There is a distinction between *market value* and *market price*. The price asked for a property and the price at which a property sold are historical facts and may or may not bear any specific relationship to market value, either currently or as of the date of sale. An estimate of market value may be justified by market evidence, whereas a sale price may reflect caprice, unequal motivation or negotiating position, unusual terms, or other factors that cause price to deviate from value. Most real estate, whether a single family home or investment prop-

12. *Real Estate Appraisal Terminology, op. cit., p. 137.*

erty, has value in use *and* value in exchange. The value in exchange demonstrated by market evidence provides a measure of use value as viewed by the individuals comprising the market. Properties may be valued through rental and sale market research and application of the three accepted approaches to value (cost, market data, and income). However, real property improved to meet the demands of a specific use (e.g., places of worship; schools; libraries; public buildings; single-use industrial facilities including steel mills, cement plants, breweries, refineries, wharves, and docks) cannot be similarly valued because no adequate sale or rental market can be identified in which to make comparisons. A value-in-use analysis is indicated.

The concept of value for such properties reflects the potential use limitations and represents the amount an owner of the operation using the property would be warranted in paying for assurance against being deprived of its use but without premium for immediate availability.

There are types of properties that are designed for a single use but for which a rental value may be estimated by allocation of income produced by the business operation of which the real estate is a part. An example of this type of real estate is a hotel or motel. Although rental or sale data may be limited and, when found, may require allocation between components of the sale price (i.e., going business, chattels, and real estate), these properties may be valued using the three approaches. A value-in-use analysis is appropriate only when no rental or sale market can be identified or when a rental value cannot be estimated by allocation from the earnings of the enterprise of which the real estate is a part. Value-in-use computation is generally appropriate when:

1. The property is fulfilling an economic demand for the service it provides or which it houses.
2. The property improvements have a significant remaining economic life expectancy.
3. There is responsible ownership and competent management.
4. Diversion of the property to an alternate use would not be economically feasible.
5. Continuation of existing use by present or similar users is practical and assumed.
6. Due consideration is given to the property's functional utility in support of the purpose for which it is being used.

Under these circumstances, the appraiser may consider the propriety of giving an opinion of value in use. The cost approach, duly reflecting existing functional lack of utility and reflecting economic depreciation as well as physical deterioration, may be applied in such situations. All measures of the economic contribution of the real estate to the total going-concern situation are relevant. Since cost is not synonymous with value, only the part of the property that can be effectively or profitably used has value, the measure of which, under the principle of contribution, depends on the extent of that use. Accordingly, *value in use* may be defined as *the value of a property for a specific use or to a specific user, reflecting the extent to which the property contributes to the utility or profitability of the enterprise of which it is a part.*

A property may have one value in use and quite a different value in exchange. The design and specialized installations of a building can so affect its utility that its economic value might be realized only through a special use. However, in many instances there is no current competitive demand for such a specialized building.

A common assignment in the industrial real estate field is to estimate the value in use of a given parcel of real estate as a basis for asset valuation in a merger, or in a going-concern situation, such as a security issue, or simply as a value judgment of the worth of a property to its present owner.

There are many qualifications of the word *value* as it pertains to real property. Common phrases include *assessed value, value in use, going-concern value, insurable value, liquidation value, rental value, leasehold value.* These qualifiers reflect the character or the proposed use of the value estimate and include concepts that may not be directly concerned with the estimation of market value.

Varied interpretations of value are also reflected in the decisions and opinions of various courts. Not all courts subscribe to identical definitions of value, but generally they rely on prices paid for comparable properties as the major evidence. There have been exceptions occasionally in the field of condemnation and in public utility valuation generally. A legal determination may settle a controversy, but that determination should not be regarded as having unquestionable validity beyond the particular situation to which it was applied.

The problem becomes complicated when property is not commonly exchanged in any identifiable market and does not fall into a rental category where sufficient rental data exists to constitute a basis for analysis using the income approach to value. When this situation exists, a value-in-use analysis is proper. However, in the absence of a market, the conclusion of value cannot be defined, or referred to, as market value.

People often use the word *value* carelessly, with no agreement among those using the word as to the precise meaning implied. Appraisers, dealing in value, are specific concerning value concepts and recognize the close relation between the objective of an appraisal assignment and the specific value concept appropriate to that objective. The definition of this value concept is an important part of an appraisal assignment.[13]

BUYER-SELLER SUBJECTIVE VALUE CONCEPTS

Whereas the real estate appraiser is primarily interested in market value, the courts, accountants, engineers, architects, and other professions have other criteria of value. These include value in use, capital value, intrinsic value, replacement value, scrap value, residual value, and book value. However, all of these value denominations relate to the basic economic concept that value is not inherent in an object but depends on the relation of the object to unsatisfied human needs or desires. Thus there are two aspects of value: (1) the supply and availability of an object, and (2) the effective demand for the object, demand being a direct reflection of usefulness or utility to present or prospective owners or users. In many business transactions characterized by specific conditions of ownership or operation, the value assigned to certain parcels of real estate by owners or prospective purchasers may differ from that indicated by the potential price obtainable in the open market.

Although this text is primarily oriented to market value of real property, there is no disposition to exclude the possibility and indeed the desirability of expanding the application of the appraiser's expertise to other related fields of valuation.

Probably the most significant difference between the real estate appraiser's approach to value and that of most other professions in the wide field of valuation is that the appraiser estimates and provides an opinion of market value in the type of market in which the

---

13. See Definition of Value in Chapter 4.

property to be appraised has an indicated demand. This may differ from its value to one particular owner or user, unless it can be shown that this is indeed a typical owner or user in the market.

Only a small portion of all real estate is placed on the market. Some of it never has been on the market, and much of it may not be within the foreseeable future. This does not imply that it has no value. It may have a value to the community at large, contributing something to each parcel of real estate in that community—for example, a forest preserve. It may have no calculable realistic contribution to make to any particular piece of real estate in its immediate vicinity or even in the nation, but may be of value because of its present or prospective service to the community as a whole.

Graphic representations are useful to illustrate value concepts and to form bases for statistical study of economic phenomena. Figure 2.1, The Buyer-Seller Subjective Value Concept, may at first seem similar to the familiar supply and demand curve. It is, in fact, quite different, reflecting another type of relationship. Since the buyer-seller relationship is necessarily subjective, it must be considered as a tendency, rather than a mathematical conclusion.

Curve *YS* represents the subjective value estimates at various times for a parcel of real estate as assigned to it by the owner of the fee or owner of the right to use the property. The curve *OB* represents the subjective value estimates at various times, as assigned to the property by a prospective buyer who is assumed to be a typical buyer in the market. This curve need not pass through *O* but may have its origin at any point along *OY*. The curves *YS* and *OB* intersect at *I* where the value estimates of the owner and the prospective buyer coincide. At this point neither the buyer nor the seller would gain from a transfer at the expense of the other. They would simply be trading dollars. Each may be evaluating different attributes of the land, the building, or the property as a whole; or each may be using a different rate of capitalization, but the results of their valuations are the same.

Between *IB* and *IS* (the shaded sector) a market exists; here the real estate appraiser's activity centers. Here a willing buyer and willing seller can adjust their estimates to agree on a market price. This is an area of negotiation within which adjustments to the "trading dollars" price at *I* are made and within which market value is found. The seller must be convinced that a lower price is acceptable,

Figure 2.1   Buyer-Seller Subjective Value Concept

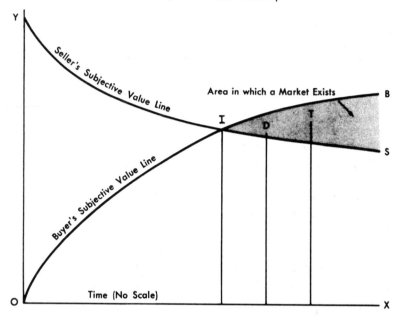

Source: Thurston H. Ross, *Some Economic Aspects of Urban Land Valuation* (Los Angeles: University of Southern California, 1933).

or the buyer agree to pay a higher price; and the appraiser must be satisfied, after taking into consideration all factors influencing the market, that an opinion of market value can be certified to at some point in this area, say at *D* where a sale can be made; or if the opinion allows additional waiting time, Point *T* could be reached.

This concept is not presented as new. It illustrates the fact that at any given period of time, the great majority of properties are not available for sale at a price at which many buyers will purchase. A transaction is consummated usually only when the owner lowers the asking price or the prospective purchaser raises the level of an offer.

Many factors may influence either buyer or seller. For example, there may be several competitive properties that could be purchased and the prospective buyer may consider them in comparison with the subject offering. The buyer compares the cost of capital assembly and is influenced by available interest and amortization rates and terms of prospective financing. Capital capacity even within a small group of sophisticated purchasers may vary greatly and their effective costs of money may influence their decision as to the price they will pay. Tax advantages are also important factors and depreciation allowances often are dominant elements in value estimates. Immediate need is also a factor, as are many other considerations.

The seller may be influenced by personal factors including the specific profit, capital reinvestment costs, capital gains or other forms of income tax, selling costs, and various options for continued use of the property.

All these considerations on the part of prospective buyers and sellers are subjective. The function of the appraiser is to analyze all such factors that are apparent in the marketplace and resolve them to an estimate of market value; this would be the price most reasonably expected for a typical buyer to pay and a seller to accept at any one specified period of time.

SUMMARY

Land is essential for all human activity, but its value is dependent upon its usefulness, including all its improvements, together with appurtenant property rights. Real property is distinct from personal property.

Land ownership is limited by governmental powers and frequently by private restrictions and agreements.

There are many uses of the term *value*, but the real estate appraiser is usually interested in market value. The field of economics has long been concerned with analysis and interpretation of value concepts, classifying them in two broad categories: value in exchange and value in use.

The legal definition of market value becomes a most significant guide for the real estate appraiser who is responsible for making an analysis and formulating an opinion of value (usually market value). This opinion falls within a negotiating range between buyers and sellers, each of whom has subjective reactions to the individual offering.

In arriving at any market value conclusion, the appraiser takes into consideration all the factors that influence the conditions of the market and make an impact on its buyers and sellers. The significance of the real estate appraiser's opinion depends on skill and thoroughness in the analysis of the actions of buyers and sellers in the marketplace and ability to interpret these actions in terms of the property being appraised.

3

Basic Principles of
Real Property Value

Wealth is the composite of economic goods in or on the land, subject to public or private use. Property is the right to use economic goods. Appraising, as considered in this text, is the valuation of rights of use or ownership, of real estate.

The principles of land utilization are founded in economics. Because appraising is the estimation of value of the rights of use of real property, basic economic concepts underlie the valuation procedures. A comprehension of these concepts is essential to an understanding of the procedures of valuation.

ANTICIPATION

The principle of anticipation affirms that value is created by the expectation of benefits to be derived in the future. The future, not the past, is important in deriving opinions of value. The primary value of past experience arises from its significance for the estimation of possible future trends and conditions. A buyer of income property invests in anticipation of future benefits to be achieved through possession, operation, or in the form of capital gain. Examination of a property's income experience may reveal factors, favorable or unfavorable, that have enabled this property to produce a net income. The assembled data is then analyzed, and appropriate factors are weighed in order to form an opinion concerning whether the net income stream may be expected, under typical management and business conditions, to continue, to decline, or to increase.

Value is defined as the present worth of the rights to all prospective future benefits, tangible and intangible, accruing to ownership of real estate. In most cases the quantity, quality, and durability of future benefits may be estimated in the light of past experience as disclosed by results of operation of the property being appraised and comparable properties.

Recent sale prices of comparable properties indicate the attitudes of informed buyers and investors in the market concerning the present value of these anticipated benefits of ownership of a particular property. The value of an individual property is not necessarily established by its past selling price or by the cost to create it.

SUBSTITUTION

The principle of substitution holds that when several commodities or services with substantially the same utility are available, the one with the lowest price attracts the greatest demand and widest distribution. The importance and application of this principle can be found in many segments of the economy. In real estate, for example, if two apartments offer approximately the same advantages, the prospective tenant will select the one with the lower rent.

The principle of substitution applies within each of the three approaches to value as follows:

1. The cost approach. No rational person will pay more for a property than the amount at which a property of equal desirability and utility can be obtained, through purchase of a site and construction of a building, without undue delay.

2. The market data approach. The value of a property replaceable in the market tends to be set at the cost of acquiring an equally desirable substitute property, assuming that no costly delay is encountered in making the substitution.

3. The income approach. Value tends to be set by the effective investment necessary to acquire, without undue delay, a comparable substitute income-producing property offering an equally desirable net income return.

Properties such as schools, churches, transportation terminals, and hospitals exist in a limited number because of their specific use characteristic. Comparable substitute properties in the sale or rental markets are difficult to find; therefore, use of the market data or income approaches in the valuation of such a property is rarely appropriate. The cost approach is usually the most effective method to obtain a value indication for this type of property. The cost approach principle stated above can be applied by estimating the current cost to produce a comparable new property affording equal utility and benefits. Then, because the property being valued is not new, the cost new figure must be adjusted to reflect the estimated loss in value due to physical, functional, or economic depreciation. A value estimate derived in this manner is referred to as a value in use.

CHANGE

The principle of change affirms that change is inevitable and is constantly occurring. Change is the law of cause and effect at work. In real estate it affects individual properties, neighborhoods, and cities. Changes can be evolving so slowly that their movement is almost indiscernible. The real property and its environment, with the probability and rate of change, should be examined to detect not only the obvious, but also the subtle indications leading to change. These may be apparent only to the experienced observer.

The appraiser recognizes economic and social forces at work and weighs the present and future effects of these forces on the value of real property. The more trends influencing the real estate market that the appraiser can identify and interpret, the more effectively their impact on the market value of a parcel of real estate can be estimated. Individual properties, districts, neighborhoods—sometimes entire cities and towns—may follow a pattern of growth in desirability, passive existence, and eventual decline in desirability and usefulness.

In the market the value of a property is not based on a price paid for it in the past or the cost of its creation, but rather on the prospective benefits that buyers and sellers believe it will provide. The actions of the market (sales) reflect informed investors' opinions of the probable future benefits of ownership. The attitude of the market toward property in a specific neighborhood reflects the probable future trend of that neighborhood.

The principle of change implies that properties and their environments are in a continuing state of transition. Accordingly, a value estimate is valid only as of a specific point in time.

COMPETITION

The principle of competition implies that when net income exceeds the requirements of labor, capital, coordination, and land, the excess constitutes profit and encourages competition. Profit as applied to real property in this context is not the same as profit obtained from the operation of a business. Normal business profit is the monetary return for capital investment in the business. Similarly, the normal return on investment in land and buildings consists of an allocation of net income representing a fair return on the amount of this investment. In the analysis of a real property, profit implies some net return after all costs of operation and adequate returns to land and buildings have been satisfied. Thus it is income in excess of that necessary to satisfy the four agents in production, which are:

1. Labor (wages)
2. Capital (the investment in buildings and equipment)
3. Coordination (management or entrepreneurial contribution)
4. Land

Profit encourages competition, and excess profit tends to breed ruinous competition. The first merchants locating in an area where their services are needed may make large profits. Competing merchants are attracted to the district and these newcomers share in the total amount of available business. Thus the volume of business initially enjoyed by the pioneer merchants declines and so do their net incomes. This process may continue until few, if any, merchants make a satisfactory return. Competition, by dissipating the net return, has reduced net yield to land, and thus its value. Eventually, all profit can disappear if the expansion of competitive services continues beyond the point of economic demand.

However, excess profit may result in increased land value. For example, a store in a new and expanding district has a five-year percentage lease with a minimum rental of $6,000 per year. Suppose this percentage rent is $2,000 the first year, and $4,500 the second year, then drops off to $2,500 and $2,000, and finally to $1,500 per year because of increasing competition. Perhaps the base rental at the end of the initial five-year lease should be increased to $7,500 per year. This reflects a higher level of economic rent which is currently applicable to the property. After a recomputation of operating expenses and return on a current building value, the net income attributable to land reflects an increase in land value which has occurred as the district expanded and business volumes in the area increased. A proper return to the four agents in production may now account for the net income produced by the property, and a condition of balance has been restored.

Competition is one of the most familiar and easily recognized forces present at all levels of economic activity. Reasonable competition stimulates further creative contribution; but in excess, it can destroy that which it attempts to create. The appraiser not only recognizes its presence in normal situations, but perceives the situations in which it is weakening and, if unchecked, may destroy value. Competition is a product of supply and demand; a proper study of the highest and best use of a property includes current supply and demand factors.

BALANCE

The principle of balance affirms that a proper economic balance between types and locations of land uses in an area creates and sustains value. Land in an area is most efficiently utilized when usage is related to the number of services or activities that can be supported by the population. When there are too many drug stores in a community, for example, either some are successful at the expense of others, or none yield an adequate return on investment.

A desirable balance in land utilization may be assisted by good zoning laws. When more land is committed to commercial use than the population of the area can support, the commercial land value is adversely affected. Conversely, too little land available for such use may temporarily increase the commercial land value while adversely affecting the value of residential or apartment land that is inadequately provided with retail services. If the lack of commercial land results in strong competitive facilities being located elsewhere, even the existing commercial land value may be restricted in potential value.

The concept of balance may be extended to apply to an individual property. A proper balance among the agents in production is essential if maximum net return is to be produced and maximum land value developed. Improper balance may be reflected in an under- or over-improvement of a site (as explained in the discussion of the principle of surplus productivity). Because land has last claim on the gross income produced by the proper apportionment of the four agents, the land value is residual. This concept is utilized in estimating land value by the land residual method (see Chapter 8). Thus the concept of balance underlies the process of estimating highest and best use in appraisal practice. Three subelements of balance are increasing and decreasing returns, contribution, and surplus productivity.

Increasing and Decreasing Returns

The principle of increasing and decreasing returns affirms that larger amounts of the agents in production produce greater net income up to a certain point (the law of increasing returns). At this point, the maximum value has been developed (the point of decreasing returns). Any additional expenditures do not produce a return commensurate with these additional investments (the law of decreasing returns). The fertilization of farmland affords a simple example of this principle. Increasing the use of fertilizer results in a greater yield, up to a certain point. Beyond this point, however, increasing the use of fertilizer does not produce an additional return sufficient to warrant the additional cost.

It is frequently necessary to determine the character and size of the structural improvement that will enable the land to produce the greatest net yield. To ascertain this point, hypothetical combinations of probable income and expense factors and capital requirements for improvements of various types and sizes are analyzed. This process of developing hypothetical improvements to obtain the combination of the agents in production that will return the greatest net yield illustrates the principle of increasing and decreasing returns as used to develop an opinion of highest and best use.

Contribution

The principle of contribution states that the value of an item in production is measured by its contribution to the net return of the enterprise. This is the principle of increasing and decreasing returns applied to a portion or portions of a property. Enterprise in this sense means the combination of all items in production such as land, buildings, and other improvements.

The value of any part of a structure or a service provided to the occupants must be economically justified by its influence on the structure's productivity (income or occupancy) and utility. Any remodeling project of an existing building must so justify itself. For example, the expenditure of $15,000 to convert a basement into an apartment or to add a recreation room to a home is justified only if the result is the production of additional value in excess of the amount spent. Similarly, the installation of modern automatic elevators in place of old ones should increase the net income—by either a reduction in operating expense or an increase in rentals—to some amount in excess of a fair return on, and a recapture of, the cost of installation.

The principle of contribution is applicable in valuing lots of varying depths. It is necessary to know the value, if any, the additional land contributes to its parcel over and above the value of the standard-depth lot in the area. In the reverse situation where a lot is shorter than standard, its value would reflect this loss of contribution by the value of that portion by which it falls short of conformity to the standard.

With a practical bearing on many valuation problems, the application of this principle is fundamental to any consideration of the feasibility of remodeling or modernization.

Surplus Productivity

Surplus productivity is defined as the net real property income remaining after the costs of labor, capital, and coordination have been paid. This surplus may be attributed to the land and constitutes a key to the value of the land in its present use. Surplus productivity is dependent on the principle of balance, the law of increasing and decreasing returns, and the proper apportionment of labor, capital, coordination, and land.

Therefore, maximum value is achieved when the agents in production are in economic balance. In each property there is a theoretical point of balance that will produce the greatest net return. An imbalance exists when a building represents an underimprovement or overimprovement of its site. It is present also when the cost and amount of special services to the tenants are too little or too much as related to the character of the building and its rent schedule. These conditions illustrate the principle of balance, affirming that disadvantage or loss in value attends any excess or deficiency in the contribution of the four productive agents.

Goods and services resulting from the use of these agents produce gross income. Labor has the first claim on gross income. The costs of capital are next. These costs include interest on, and amortization of, funds invested in the buildings, equipment, and furnishings. The source of these funds will shrink and eventually disappear if the costs of capital are not paid. The costs of coordination have the third claim. In classical economic theory land has the last claim on gross income. Any income remaining after labor, capital, and coordination have been satisfied can be credited to the land for its contribution to gross income.

In appraisal practice recovery of all or part of the capital invested in land is not provided as an allowance, such as a depletion allowance for natural resources, set aside for that purpose. As developed in succeeding chapters, any uncertainty concerning the future value of urban land is reflected in the rate of return necessary to attract investment capital. For example, an investor might consider 12% to be a reasonable rate of return for land with a somewhat uncertain outlook, but a 7% rate might be considered sufficient if the land were in a well-stabilized location.

CONFORMITY

The principle of conformity holds that maximum value is realized when there is a reasonable degree of architectural homogeneity and where land uses are compatible. Thus conformity in use is usually a desirable feature of real property because it tends to create and maintain value; and it is maximum value that affords an owner a maximum return.

The elements of conformity are not preconceived standards of development; they have evolved as cities grew and land uses multiplied. Homeowners recognized the advantages of living in neighborhoods designed and developed to provide facilities or amenities that added to the benefits of ownership, and they protected those assets by maintaining conformity through zoning.

After World War II leaders of industry discovered the advantages of locating in areas that were exclusively industrial or parks designed and developed to provide industry's required facilities. Many industrial parks further restrict occupancy to either light or heavy industry.

Harmony or conformity of use is also apparent in the grouping of stores in certain retail districts. Generally, merchants realize the most satisfactory volumes if their stores are located in close proximity to those of other merchants who sell the same type and quality of merchandise. In many areas zoning protects retail locations from nonretail commercial uses. Therefore, conformity is one of many important factors considered in the selection of a store site.

The principle of conformity also implies some degree of harmonious similarity in architectural style or design, but it does not mean monotonous uniformity. Generally, the most satisfactory use of land is realized when it conforms to the standards governing the area in which it is located.

The standards of conformity are subject to the principle of change. For example, racial homogeneity was once considered a sign of social conformity and neighborhood stability. Conversely, racial integration was once considered a sign of social nonconformity and neighborhood decline. Social perceptions and attitudes have changed. The idea that racial or ethnic homogeneity is a requirement for maximum value is without empirical support. Many strong and stable neighborhoods are composed of residents of varied and diverse racial, religious, and cultural backgrounds. The appraiser is alert to changing social perceptions and attitudes and avoids preconceived concepts that are not supported by market evidence.

Other signs of change may be observed in the fields of architectural design and urban planning. Design and equipment changes may be expected to meet new energy conservation standards. The trend toward multipurpose urban structures and a deliberate mixing of land uses reflects an increasing awareness of the interdependence of land uses.

Certain effects of a violation of the principle of conformity may be observed. For example, an overimprovement, underimprovement, or misplaced improvement lacks conformity between a property and its environment. The value of an overimprovement sometimes declines (regresses) toward the value level of the conforming properties; and conversely, an underimprovement sometimes increases toward the value level of adjacent and otherwise conforming properties. The principles of regression and progression relate to the principle of conformity.

The concept of *regression* maintains that between dissimilar properties or things in the same classification, the value of the superior property or thing is affected adversely by the presence of the inferior. For example, in a residential block where the average value of a home is $42,000 to $45,000, there is a high-quality home which would be valued at $60,000 if it were located in an area of similar high-quality homes. In its present location the value would tend to approach that of neighboring properties. People in the market for homes in the $42,000-to-$45,000 range look for them in neighborhoods where that price range predominates. They might appreciate the additional features and amenities of the $60,000 house, but be unable or unwilling to purchase it. A few might pay somewhat more for it; but rarely would the owner be able to obtain the full $60,000 for the property. Typically, a person seeking a $60,000 property would look in neighborhoods with houses in that range where neighbors would be expected to have similar backgrounds and interests.

The concept of *progression* is the opposite of regression; that is, the value of a lesser object is enhanced by association with better objects of the same type. If the situation in the preceding example were reversed and it were a $42,000 house among homes of $60,000, the $42,000 house probably could bring a somewhat higher price in the market. A person who aspires to live in that neighborhood, but is unable to afford a $60,000 home, might pay more for this $42,000 house in a neighborhood of better houses.

SUPPLY AND DEMAND

The principle of supply and demand affirms that increasing supply or declining demand tends to affect adversely the price obtainable in the market. The opposite is also true, although the relationship may not be directly proportional in either case, owing to collateral considera-

tions in a specific situation. There is a point at which supply and demand are, at least theoretically, in balance. At this point market value tends to reflect cost of reproduction or replacement.

Demand for a commodity is created by its usefulness and affected by its scarcity. Demand is unlimited in the social sense; that is, there is no limit to the things people desire—from a cottage to a castle in Spain. But effective demand is limited in the economic sense by the financial ability of people to satisfy their desires. For example, many people share a longing for expensive things, which they are financially unable to buy. The strongest desire is ineffective unless it is accompanied by the buying power to gratify it. Although this inability to satisfy desire does not reduce the intensity of the desire, it does affect the intensity of the demand for an object. Because demand is influenced by desire, the forces that arouse, intensify, or create desire also affect demand. Two major creative forces are education and advertising. Without knowledge that an object exists, people cannot desire it, and there would be no demand for it.

Land scarcity is a shortage in the amount of land available in a stated area for a specific use. Obviously, the greater the scarcity of land available for a specific purpose, the greater is the economic desirability of that land. This is shown by historically increasing land values in the central business districts of rapidly growing cities. Usually cities are surrounded by land that is not available, due to location, for convenient and profitable use. Thus value is influenced by land scarcity in relation to its utility.

Technological and zoning changes, particularly with reference to some types of commercial property, often have the effect of increasing land area by adding floor levels to buildings. Faster elevators, improved communications and security facilities, and higher ratios of net rentable area may give land increased utility, and resulting value, by enabling more square footage of usable floor area to be created on each square foot of ground. These higher ratios result from advanced architectural design as well as from improvement in construction materials and their uses.

Among the factors affecting supply or demand for real property are population changes, purchasing power, price levels, wage rates, taxation, building codes, and government controls. The supply of housing, for example, is controlled in part by rentals and sale prices—that is, it is increased or decreased according to whether these rentals and sale prices conform to the temper of the market. A certain combination of factors must be present in the housing market to stimulate additions to the housing supply. This occurs when simultaneously there is a shortage in the supply of housing units, a strong demand for housing, and an effective purchasing power to satisfy the demand at the rentals and prices offered. But those rentals and sale prices must be high enough to encourage builders to construct new units. If demand is very strong and purchasing power is increasing faster than the ability of the supply to satisfy it, the rentals and sale prices for available units will rise. When increased rentals or prices continue to find a ready market, more builders enter the market, thus accelerating the pace at which additions to the supply are made.

Other factors also influence the real estate market. Scarcity of labor, accompanied by high wage rates, can affect the supply by increasing its cost beyond the purchasing power of the market, thus discouraging builders from adding to the supply. Taxation, by increasing the cost of home ownership or increasing apartment or commercial rentals above the means of owner or tenant, can affect the supply by restricting demand. Rent control, imposed in a market affected by a shortage of rentable units, discourages the new construction that would otherwise provide new units to increase the supply and eliminate the shortage. Restrictions on the supply of money, zoning, and other governmental regulations influence supply and demand by imposing limitations.

HIGHEST AND BEST USE

Fundamental to the concept of value is the theory of highest, best, and most profitable use. Land is valued as if vacant and available for its highest and best use. Highest and best use for land is *the use that, at the time of appraisal, is the most profitable likely use.* It is the use that will provide the greatest return to the land after the requirements of labor, capital, and coordination have been satisfied. Thus it may also be defined as *the available use and program of future utilization that produces the highest present land value.*

The most profitable likely use cannot always be interpreted strictly in terms of money. Return sometimes takes the form of amenities. A wooded urban site, for example, may have its highest and best use as a public park; or the amenities of living in a private dwelling may represent to its owner satisfaction that outweighs a monetary net rental yield available from rental to a typical tenant. In this time of increasing concern over the environmental effects of land use, environmental acceptability is becoming an addition to the highest and best use concept.

Land has no value until there is a use for it, but the amount of the value depends on the character of the intended use. The owner of real property typically desires to reap the greatest possible return from the property and hence selects a use intended to achieve this objective. Since change is ever present, the existing use of land may no longer conform to what has become its highest and best use, and the highest and best use of improved property may differ from the highest and best use of the site if vacant. In the central business districts of most large cities there are parcels of land devoted to surface parking lots. In an area usually characterized by scarcity of land and high use-density, utilization as a parking lot would seem to be the antithesis of highest and best use. However, consideration of all factors involved may indicate that such use is, in this case and at this time, a most profitable interim use because the supply of land already devoted to characteristic central business district uses exceeds current demand.

Parking lot use or construction of a "taxpayer" improvement is an interim use during a period of waiting until the time is right for development. During this period the land may be valued for its prospective highest and best use, and this valuation may then be discounted at an appropriate rate for the remainder of the projected interim period.

Many tall buildings are razed, and their sites are developed as parking lots or with single- or two-story structures. At the time the change in use is made, the net return to the land from the proposed new use is higher than had existed under the former use. Hence the value of the improvements is inextricably related to the principle of contribution, inasmuch as existing improvements are tied to the land, and their value will rise or fall accordingly.

Under the law of eminent domain, in most jurisdictions admissible value evidence requires the appraiser to consider a property's highest and best use in formulating an opinion of its market value. In most takings the highest and best uses customarily are the ones physically feasible and permitted by zoning ordinances or private restrictions. If the land manifests more valuable use potential than allowed by law and if there is a reasonable probability that a change in its use will be permitted, the value of the land may be enhanced to the extent that a buyer or a seller might recognize this potential, after giving due consideration to time and expense factors involved in the change.

When existing improvements do not constitute the highest and best use of a site, the highest and best use for the property, as improved, constitutes a separate consideration. Present highest and best use for the property may be affected by a substantial existing improvement or by a long-term lease involving the property as presently developed. The basic concept—highest and best use is the available use or program of future utilization that produces the highest present value as applied to land—is similarly applicable in the analysis of improved properties. The appraiser considers alternate use possibilities leading to selection of the program of use that best meets the objective of the concept.

Use Density

Use density is the relationship between the supply and demand for land adaptable to a particular use. This relationship is an important factor in a highest and best use analysis. When the supply of land adaptable for a particular use is in balance with the demand for such use, the quantity of that type of land has reached its highest or ideal density of use.

Most metropolitan areas contain older residential neighborhoods that include multifamily properties. A conclusion that such a neighborhood is in transition and is ripe for development as an apartment area could be right or it could be wrong. The appraiser relates existing apartment development to demand and to the supply of such units in other areas. If research reveals a short supply and strong demand for apartments and other factors, including location, are favorable, the conclusion may be that the neighborhood is ready for a higher density and more profitable use.

Use density relationships are frequently affected by zoning regulations—for example, a restriction limiting the number of apartment living units per acre affects use density and may not permit the highest and best use of a site. Highest and best use frequently is at variance with zoning regulations. Long arterial streets zoned for commercial use may exemplify this situation. All such frontage rarely, if ever, can be developed to profitable commercial use at the same time.

CONSISTENT USE

Consistent use affirms that a property in transition to another use cannot be valued on the basis of one use for land and another for improvements. This would be inconsistent with the economics of valuation. Improvements must add to the value of the land in order to have value attributed to them. A building that may have many years of remaining physical life may not enhance the value of the land that has a higher use, except as an interim-use taxpayer while the land itself is in transition. Following the concept of appraising the land as though vacant for immediate use, the land value vacant may exceed the value of the property as presently improved. The improvements may represent a burden to land value to the extent of the net cost of their removal.

Where the transition to highest and best use is deferred, the element of interim use should be considered. The improvements may represent only a temporary enhancement of site value, measured by comparable market data and by consideration of the net income produced during the interim period.

SUMMARY

The concepts discussed in this chapter have been treated separately, but with a recognition of the relationship and interdependence among them. For example, demand creates profits; profits arouse competition; competition adds to the supply; additional supply decreases profits; decreased profit weakens demand; weakened demand reduces the supply. These forces and factors are related in a cyclical cause-and-effect movement. This is a broad generalization; in actual experience other factors could modify the pattern at different intervals or points in the cycle. Familiarity with each of these concepts and their relationships assist an appraiser in study of real property.

Although the fundamental economic principles discussed in the chapter form a basic background for real estate valuation, their practical application in appraisal practice necessitates the use of various techniques. Selected techniques are applicable to specific properties in a well-recognized market and subject to manifold financial arrangements. Economic connotations are frequently identified by appraisal terminology and sometimes in terms relating to accounting and financial usages.

In brief, the concepts discussed in this chapter are:

Anticipation
1. The principle of anticipation affirms the definition that value is the present worth of the rights to all prospective future benefits accruing to ownership and use of real property.
2. Recent sale prices of comparable properties indicate the market value of such rights and benefits.

Substitution
1. The value of a replaceable property tends to be indicated by the value of an equally desirable substitute property.
2. The value of a property tends to coincide with the value indicated by the actions of informed buyers in the market for comparable properties.

Change
1. Change is inevitable and is constantly occurring.
2. Cities, neighborhoods, and individual properties undergo the process of change.
3. The effect of prospective changes is reflected in the market.
4. Change is fundamentally the law of cause and effect.

Competition
1. Competition arises from profits; profits create competition.
2. Excess profit breeds ruinous competition.
3. Competition is a product of supply and demand.
4. Profit denotes an excess or surplus over and above satisfactory returns to labor, capital, coordination, and land.
5. Competition tends to dissipate the major portion of excess profit, although some part may remain and contribute to increased land value.
6. A certain portion of profit may be temporary; therefore, it is not

capitalized in the estimate of the value of land. For its duration, it is treated as a short-term annuity.
7. The value of land is dependent on the use that yields the best return.

Balance
1. The value of a property depends on the balance of the four agents in production: labor, capital, coordination, and land.
2. Disadvantage attends any excess or deficiency in the supply of the agents in production.
3. Equilibrium (balance) in character, amount, and location of essential uses of real estate creates and maintains value.
4. Balance in land use may be assisted, or adversely affected, by zoning regulations.

Increasing and Decreasing Returns
1. The application of larger and larger amounts of the agents in production produces greater and greater net income (increasing returns) up to a point (surplus productivity).
2. The point of maximum contribution of agents in production (point of decreasing returns) attests to the proper combination of agents resulting in highest and best use.
3. Any further increase in the amount of agents in production decreases the margin between cost of agents and gross income they will produce, resulting in decreased net income returns.
4. The principle of increasing and decreasing returns applied to a proper improvement of the land indicates its highest and best use.

Contribution
1. The principle of contribution is the principle of increasing and decreasing returns applied to a portion or the whole of an improvement.
2. The value of an item in production is measured by its contribution to the net return of the enterprise.
3. Application of this principle is basic to any feasibility study or remodeling or modernization program and in the valuation of lots of varying depths.

Surplus Productivity
1. Surplus productivity is defined as the net income remaining after the costs of labor, capital, and coordination have been paid.

2. Land has the last claim on the surplus productivity of the agents in production.
3. The principle of contribution is related to surplus productivity in that the value of an individual agent in production depends on how much it adds to, or detracts from, the income because of its presence.

Conformity
1. Conformity is the result of a reasonable degree of architectural homogeneity and compatible land uses.
2. The standards of conformity have changed over the years, reflecting changes in market attitudes, societal trends, economic conditions, and public policy.
3. The highest and best use is generally realized under circumstances of harmony or reasonable conformity in land usage.
4. Zoning regulations and private restrictions operate to maintain conformity.

Supply and Demand
1. Utility creates demand, which is desire for possession.
2. Demand is effective when supported by purchasing power.
3. Value is increased,if supply is reduced by effective demand, resulting in scarcity. The converse is equally true.

Highest and Best Use
1. Highest and best use of land is the most profitable likely use at the time of appraisal. It may also be defined as the available use and program of future utilization that produces the highest present land value.
2. Existing use may or may not conform to highest and best use.
3. Highest and best use may comprise a combination of a profitable interim (transitional) use and a deferred, more profitable potential use.
4. Highest and best use may be limited by zoning or deed restriction.
5. The principle of increasing and decreasing returns affirms the proper apportionment of land and improvements to achieve maximum land value.
6. The concept of highest and best use may be extended to improved real estate for various decision-making situations, but

such applications should not be confused with the underlying concept of highest and best use of land only.

7.   Balance and consistent use are important collateral considerations in the selection of highest and best use.

Consistent Use

1.   A property cannot be valued on the basis of one use for land and another for improvements.
2.   Improvements must add value to the land in order to have value attributed to them.

4

The Valuation Process

Valuation is a problem-solving process in which the influences of sociological, economic, governmental, and physical forces are analyzed in relation to a real property. The finished product provides the basis for a decision relating to the property being appraised.

Characteristics of real estate differ widely. This does not mean, however, that there is a wide variation in the orderly procedure for solving the appraisal problem. The best experience in the appraisal field is crystallized in the *valuation process*. This process is an orderly program by which the problem is defined; the work necessary to solve the problem is planned; and the data involved is acquired, classified, analyzed, interpreted, and translated into an estimate of value. The valuation process is a concise, logical, and thorough procedure that leads to a supportable conclusion of value. It also can serve as the outline of the appraisal report. The step-by-step procedure of the valuation is illustrated in Figure 4.1, The Valuation Process.

By extension and by special adaptation, the valuation process may also be generally applied to other types of appraisal assignments. Thus the valuation process may be viewed as an example of a systematic problem-solving process.

DEFINITION OF THE PROBLEM

The first step in the valuation process is to develop a concise statement of the problem, thus eliminating any ambiguity about the objective of the assignment. To understand the precise nature of this process, five basic factors are identified:

51

Figure 4.1. The Valuation Process

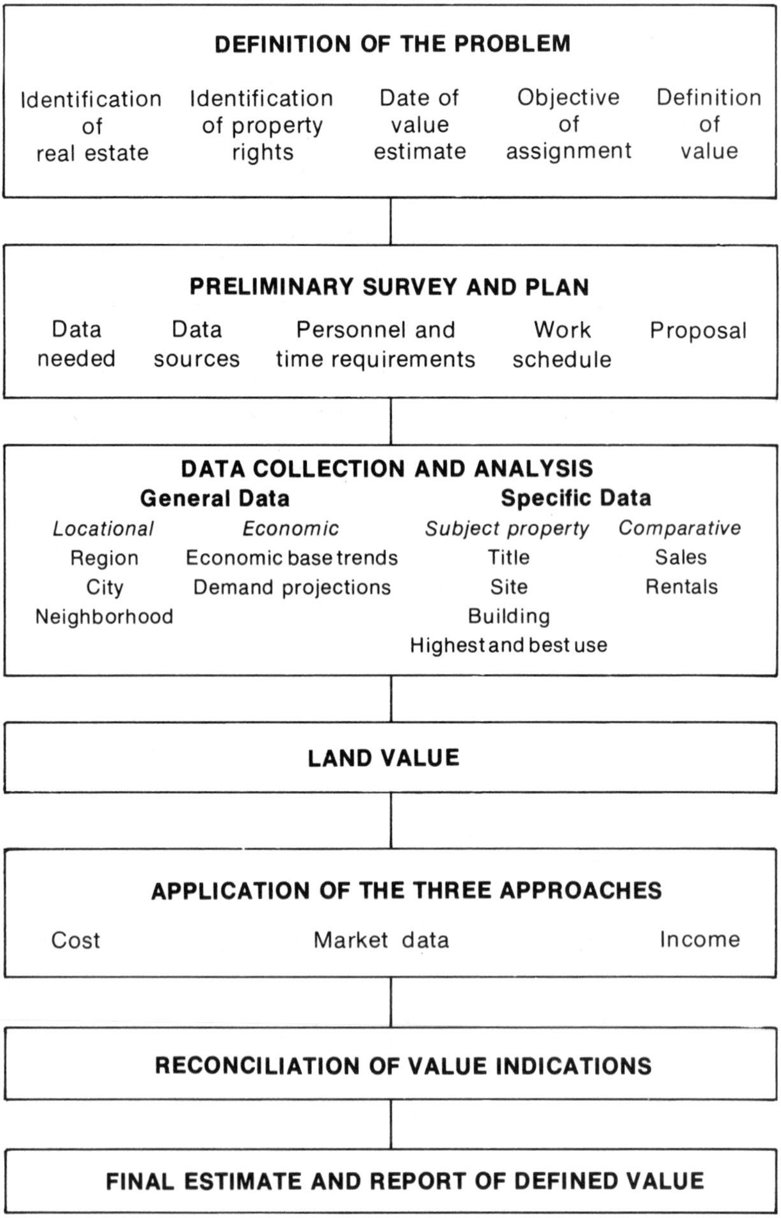

DEFINITION OF THE PROBLEM

Identification of real estate	Identification of property rights	Date of value estimate	Objective of assignment	Definition of value

PRELIMINARY SURVEY AND PLAN

Data needed	Data sources	Personnel and time requirements	Work schedule	Proposal

DATA COLLECTION AND ANALYSIS

General Data **Specific Data**

Locational	*Economic*	*Subject property*	*Comparative*
Region	Economic base trends	Title	Sales
City	Demand projections	Site	Rentals
Neighborhood		Building	
		Highest and best use	

LAND VALUE

APPLICATION OF THE THREE APPROACHES

Cost	Market data	Income

RECONCILIATION OF VALUE INDICATIONS

FINAL ESTIMATE AND REPORT OF DEFINED VALUE

1. The real estate to be appraised
2. The property rights involved
3. The date as of which the estimate applies
4. The objective of the appraisal
5. The defined value to be estimated

Identification of Real Estate

A property is first identified physically by means of a mailing address or other descriptive data, which enables anyone to locate the property or to refer to it by recognized landmarks. A property might be identified:

132 South Ninth Street, Central City, State of Ohio, fronting 100 feet on the west side of the street, 50 feet north of Main Boulevard. The site is 150 feet deep, improved with a two-story and basement retail building.

More precise identification is provided by a legal description. This description can be obtained from the existing deed, from a title policy, from the public records, from an existing mortgage, or from an accredited survey. After the legal description has been obtained, it can be checked carefully to make certain that it describes accurately the precise property to which it is intended to apply. Whether a complete legal description is included in the body of an appraisal report is a matter of judgment in each case. A lengthy legal description may be made part of the appraisal addenda.

Legal descriptions of real estate are basically derived from land surveys and are preserved in public records in accordance with laws applying in the area where the property is located. Land surveying is a highly technical procedure. The appraiser need not be a surveyor, but should be familiar with the specific system or systems commonly employed in the area. Described in detail in Chapter 7, several systems of legal description in use are:

Government survey
Lot and block
Metes and bounds
Geodetic survey, prepared by the United States Geological Survey, Department of the Interior

Identification of Property Rights

The second factor in defining the appraisal problem is the determination of the property rights to be appraised. An appraisal of a real property is not solely a valuation of the physical land and improvements. It includes a valuation of the rights that one or more individuals may have in the ownership and/or use of the land and improvements. An appraisal of all of the private rights usually attached to a specific real property may be desired; or the appraisal of only limited rights in the property may be required. Partial or fractional interests may be divisions of the benefits accruing from the use of the entire property through partnership interests in fee ownership or through land trusts or corporation stock. They may also be contractual interests including fee, leasehold, easement, and use restrictions. Ownership of a property may be held by an individual, a partnership, a corporation, or a group of heirs. When ownership is vested in more than one interest, each may hold an equal or unequal share.

The property rights or interests to be appraised may be the value of rents to be received plus a reversionary right at the end of a lease term. It may be a reversionary right that becomes effective upon the death of a designated individual. It may be the air rights over a specified area, or it may be designated subsurface rights. It may be the value of a tenant's interest in an existing lease. It may be an easement, a right of way, or a fee subject to an easement. Because the value of real property is not limited to the physical land and the improvements, the appraiser cannot define the problem precisely without knowing exactly what property rights may be involved. Without this information, an estimate of value may be developed that is not relevant to the objective of the assignment. Accordingly, the appraiser ascertains at the outset exactly which rights are to be valued. This knowledge relates to the character and complexity of the appraisal assignment, the extent of research required, the amount of time necessary to accomplish the assignment, whether additional specialized personnel will be needed, and probable costs. For example, the appraisal of the fee simple interest held by one person in a ranch may be an uncomplicated assignment; but if it involves the valuation of mineral deposits held by a lessee under a 15-year lease of the subsurface rights of a property, it could become complicated and might require consultation with an engineer or a geologist. The subject of partial interests is more fully covered in Chapter 23.

Date of Value Estimate

The third factor in defining the problem is the date as of which the value estimate applies. The specific date is important because the factors that increase or decrease value are always in the process of change, causing the value of real property to fluctuate. Thus an opinion of value is valid only for the point in time for which it is formulated. Usually an appraisal assignment involves a current value estimate. The character of the data and the time and effort involved usually follow a familiar pattern. They concern conditions that can be observed at the time valuation is made.

In many cases, however, a valuation is required as of some date in the past. Such valuations may require retrospective valuations as of dates varying from months to years earlier. Retrospective appraisals may be required for inheritance tax (date of death), insurance claims (date of casualty), or federal income tax. It has frequently been necessary to establish value of a property as of March 1, 1913, the date of the inception of the federal income tax, to establish the capital gain on property owned since that date. Another example is valuation of Indian treaty lands. Practically the entire area of the continental United States for years has been the subject of suits by the various Indian tribes who conveyed their lands to the United States by treaty for a consideration. This has required retrospective appraisals as of dates from the time of the Revolutionary War through most of the 20th century.

In condemnation appraising, depending on local legal procedure, the appraiser may be required to make a market value estimate either as of the date on which the petition to condemn was filed or some other date as fixed by the court.

Objective of the Assignment

The fourth factor in defining the problem is to develop a clear understanding of the objective of the assignment. Basically, an appraisal is an answer to a question. Such a question may be simple. In valuation assignments it is: What is the market value of the property? In other types of assignments other questions may be asked: What is the rental value of the property? For what amount should the improvements be insured? The questions, however, may become much more involved. The appraiser may answer any question the client presents, provided the entire question asked by the client, with the conclusion, is clearly stated in the appraisal report.

A valuation provides a basis for a decision concerning real property. The nature of the decision affects the character of the assignment and subsequent report. The purpose is to estimate a value, but the definition of the value sought dictates the type and character of data to be gathered, the methods to be employed, the factors likely to wield the most influence, and the type of report required. The uses for which a valuation may be needed vary. The arrangement of the report and the data that is given the most weight in formulating the final estimate of value reflect the objective of the assignment, the specific question for which the valuation is to provide an answer. Therefore, in defining the problem, the appraiser usually develops an understanding of this objective that is clearly acceptable to both the client and the appraiser. This avoids misunderstanding and misdirected effort.

Definition of Value

The fifth major factor in defining the problem is the definition of the value to be estimated. Whereas a property has only one market value as of a given date, there are occasions when other types of value are sought. If the value estimate is to be based on a special set or alternate sets of circumstances, these assumptions should be stated with the definition of value.

Although market value is sought in most appraisal assignments, this may not be the answer sought in all instances. If the owners of an industrial concern require an appraisal of their plant for negotiating a merger or for the sale of a partial interest, the appropriate value concept may be value in use or it may be going-concern value. However, if the same owners wish to sell the property and seek an opinion of its market value, many of the highly specialized features of the plant that are necessary to the owners' operation may have little, if any, value to another user. In fact, some features could be liabilities in adapting the property to another type of industrial operation. The estimate of its market value will reflect the price expected if the property were offered in the market for a reasonable period.

The possibility that uninformed people may not understand the exact meaning of terms commonly used by appraisers is another reason to include a written definition of value in the appraisal report. An exact definition of the value sought delineates the question to be answered for both client and appraiser. It explains the choice of data considered and the methods used to process that data, thus supporting the logic and validity of the final value estimate.

PRELIMINARY SURVEY AND PLAN

The appraiser's survey of the basic problem leads to a definite plan for developing the report. This usually involves an outline of the proposed contents, indicating the main divisions or sections of the report and the data and processes pertinent to each. Such an outline permits intelligent and orderly assemblage of data and the judicious allocation of time to the steps involved. It also indicates the subject classifications for a plan of work. After deciding on the type and scope of the data to be assembled, the appraiser is ready to consider the problem of its availability.

Selection of the approaches that develop the most rational value indication also affects the type of data to be assembled. Because the majority of assignments involve an estimate of market value, the market data approach is basic to most value estimates. Nevertheless, in nearly all appraisals, application of all three approaches is fundamental. This means that cost and income data also should be developed except when application of one or both of these approaches is not pertinent or is impractical.

The selection of the dominant approach may depend on the question to which the client seeks an answer. An appraisal to estimate the value of a property for insurance purposes might require emphasis on the cost approach. The most relevant consideration in the appraisal of a property taken by condemnation is market value, as indicated by the application of the market data approach, which may be supplemented by the cost and income approaches. The income approach—using comparable income data from the market—is particularly indicative in the appraisal of income-producing, investment-type properties. An opinion based primarily on a value indication derived from the use of the cost approach is seldom acceptable, except where the type of property is so specialized that it is not customarily traded in the market.

Data Needed

Once the problem is defined in terms of the five essential factors stated above, the appraiser is ready to make a preliminary survey. The purpose of this survey is to estimate the character, the scope, and the amount of work necessary to solve the problem. These depend largely on the type of property being valued—for example, a great deal more information is required in the valuation of a large motor hotel than in the valuation of a residence.

Data Sources

Some data sources are used in practically every appraisal, and others are used only occasionally or for specific types of improvements. Data pertinent to the appraisal of a hospital differs from data assembled to appraise a truck terminal, theatre, or bowling alley. Although the valuation of special purpose or single-use properties may involve specific areas of research, several customary sources of essential data in a community are consistently employed. These can be divided into public and private categories.

Public records.   A major source of title information is legally on record in the courthouse or hall of records. Some recording systems are well classified and maintained, so a title check can be made with greater reliance on the accuracy of the records and with a minimum expenditure of time and effort. The city and county offices are the customary sources of information about zoning, traffic regulations, water and sewer lines, and public health and welfare regulations. Information about transfers, leases, and assessed values is published and sold in some cities. A large volume of general data pertaining to the city, region, and neighborhoods in which the appraiser operates can be compiled. When data of this character is pertinent in numerous assignments, a permanent filing system and an office procedure for its maintenance may be established for convenient reference.

Private sources. Data pertinent to the physical cost analysis of buildings may be found in cost manuals published by several reputable organizations. These manuals usually can be purchased separately or as a part of a continuing service providing current data at regular intervals. Local cost indexes are published for the larger cities. The appraiser may also maintain current data on the local cost of construction materials, labor wage scales, and copies of contractors' cost breakdowns for specific structures. Multiple listing systems, real estate brokers' records, classified advertising, and newspaper items are additional sources of information.

Data personally compiled by the appraiser gradually accumulates into what is called an appraisal plant or library. The accumulation of general and specific property data, classified by location and type of property, makes the data plant progressively more useful. This data plant may also include various publications devoted to appraising and to related business and industrial fields as well as those in which building materials, costs, and trend information are reported.

In the preparation of a specific report, appraisal plant data is usually augmented by current research. The appraiser's investigations may be extended to include other appraisers, real estate brokers active in a particular market, mortgage lenders, property managers, data banks or similar services—all in addition to the public or private record sources noted above. A great deal of specific and general data is available from local chamber of commerce offices, newspaper publishers, title companies or abstract offices, and utility companies.

Personnel and Time Requirements

Orderly planning and scheduling of all steps in a valuation result in an efficient application of the time and effort necessary to complete the assignment. Time and personnel needed for any particular assignment vary with the amount and complexity of the work entailed. Some assignments may require only a few days. More complex situations may warrant weeks or months for gathering and processing all pertinent data and may require the services of professional assistants to supplement the appraiser's staff.

Outside assistance may be engaged when a report should be augmented by the professional opinion of an expert in some specific area. This might be an engineering opinion about matters such as soil bearing, structural, or functional considerations. The ability to recognize areas in which work can be delegated improves efficiency and leaves the appraiser free for important decisions.

Work Schedule

A planned schedule of work to be performed is helpful, particularly for larger, more complicated assignments. Sound working habits for both the appraiser and assistants, combined with a clear and definite understanding of the exact nature of the work to be done by each person, also help to expedite efficient handling of an assignment. The appraiser, with overall responsibility, should be able to see the assignment both totally and in detail, to recognize the nature and volume of work entailed, and to schedule and delegate the work to take full advantage of staff capabilities. A completion flow chart often helps to make the work systematic.

PROPOSAL

The proposal to a client may be oral or written and should cover the appraiser's understanding of the problem, including:

1. Identification of the property
2. Statement of rights to be appraised
3. Date as of which the estimate is desired and date on which the appraisal report is to be delivered
4. Questions to be answered by the appraisal
5. Definition of the value to be sought
6. Form of report and number of copies required
7. Quotation of the fee, either specifically or within a range, and a clear understanding of the nature and terms of the contract for employment
8. Understanding concerning responsibility and compensation for any other services, such as testimony or recertification of the value after completion of proposed construction

Acknowledgment that the client understands and approves the conditions may be indicated by nothing more formal than his or her signature on a copy of the letter. Such a commitment from the client is evidence that client and appraiser agree on the nature of the problem. It also promotes harmonious relations between client and appraiser and avoids misunderstandings when the report is delivered.

Fee Proposal

An appraiser may be asked to quote a firm fee before receiving a commitment to proceed with an assignment. The fee may be on a per-hour or per-day basis, or it may be a specific fee or a range within which the fee will fall. The appraiser's experience and familiarity with typical expenses permits estimation of a base figure to cover the actual cost of typical assignments. This requires consideration of the extent of research and personnel needed and the time and work schedules for completion of the report—all according to a preliminary survey and plan. This figure may be adjusted to include any additional or unusual expense necessary for the specific assignment. The appraiser's own remuneration, reflecting both the time involved and the complexity of the problem, is added. The total is the fee quoted to the client. For a complex assignment the fee should be determined after consideration of the probable time to be spent by the appraiser and assistants in research, office and field work, and conferences. It should also cover any consultation fees the appraiser may incur for engineering, architectural, and other specialized services, in addition to the cost of overhead, travel, and clerical help.

The amount any particular appraiser may command for appraisal services varies, reflecting the reputation, experience, judgment, and special expertise of the appraiser and the extent of the confidence felt by clients in the finished product. In this regard the real estate appraisal profession is no different from any other. The appraisal report itself is only paper, but with the appraiser's signature, it acquires tangible value in proportion to the appraiser's reputation for professional competence, judgment, and integrity.

DATA COLLECTION AND ANALYSIS

The guiding principle in the collection and analysis of data in connection with any specific appraisal assignment is that it should have a bearing on the value of the property being appraised and the appraiser's conclusion. Data should not be included in a report without some analysis pointing out its general or specific impact on the valuation conclusion. Appraisal data that is pertinent in a specific assignment may be divided into two classifications: general and specific.

General Data

General data includes regional, city, and neighborhood characteristics. These categories represent influences originating outside the property (described in Chapter 1 under the social, economic, governmental and physical forces influencing value).

Population trends are important for almost all types of real estate, and reference to regional or local practices and attitudes toward family structuring is usually appropriate. Increasingly important are governmental and societal attitudes concerning land use, density, transportation, and environmental issues. If the location is rural, its proximity and accessibility to cultural and educational facilities such as universities, museums, concert halls, places of worship, sports arenas, or other amenities should be mentioned. If the location is urban, reference should be made to the availability of recreational facilities and "open-space" environment. (Chapter 6 provides additional information.)

Economic data.   Trends in the national, regional, and local economies are pertinent to the appraisal problem to the extent that they relate to the property being appraised. Included typically are local unemployment rates, building costs, market and economic base analyses, financial trends, absorption and vacancy rates. Also important are demand studies of location, type, pricing, timing, quality, and quantity of demand within identified market segments. Dependence on a single industry or employer should be noted. The appraiser becomes a business analyst to the extent of projecting a continued level of demand for the property being appraised in the light of its highest and best use. (Chapter 5 discusses additional factors, such as building cycles, purchasing power, and interest rates.)

The research involved in developing economic and general background information may be extensive, but the increasing use of computers has expanded the availability of statistical data and made historical patterns accessible for appraisal applications. Statistical inferences developed through use of simple averaging or multiple regression analysis may improve short-term trend projections, particularly in the market and income approaches.

Specific Data

Specific data relates to the property being valued and is also substantially applicable to comparable sale properties.

Subject property data. Specific data about the property being appraised includes information about the title, improvements, and site. Pertinent data may include identity of ownership, type of ownership (warranty deed or other), existing easements and encroachments, zoning regulations, assessed value and taxes, and deed or other restrictions. Information about the site includes a description of the land (size, shape, topographical features) and public improvements (paving, walks, curbs, water, sewers, gas, electricity). Additional data for consideration may pertain to factors such as corner influence, building orientation, advertising value, or accessibility of the site, depending on the type of property and the problem to be solved. Site data in an appraisal of an industrial or commercial property, for example, may include considerations that are irrelevant to a single-family homesite.

Building data includes a complete description of the physical improvement; its condition; and an analysis of its layout, style, and design.

The final step in the analysis of specific data is to ascertain the highest and best use of the site. The work done in this step may constitute the background for later consideration of market value. Often the highest and best use of a site is its existing use, which may conform to the use permitted under the current zoning regulations. However, the appraiser may find evidence that the existing use does not constitute the highest and best use, that a higher use is permitted within current zoning restrictions, or that a change in zoning represents a reasonable expectancy that would be recognized by an informed purchaser. Investigation may reveal that the prospective change is to a more restrictive zoning with consequent adverse effect on land value. In either case a factual finding may have substantial impact on the final estimate of defined value.

Comparative Data.   This includes data on sale prices and rentals of properties that are reasonably comparable to the property being appraised. Because the purpose of analyzing these sales is to obtain an indication of the amount for which the property being valued would sell if offered on the market, such sales should ideally be sales of identical parcels. However, since no two properties are identical, available sales of reasonably comparable properties are used and adjustments are made that reflect the probable differences in their market values. The subject of comparable sales and the treatment of market data are discussed more fully elsewhere in this volume.

A comprehensive program of market research is basic to the assemblage of this, or any, data in the appraisal process. The total process of data collection and analysis represents the foundation for a sound appraisal. Moreover, the conclusion can be no better than the reliability of the data considered or the competence of the analysis and reasoning applied to it.

LAND VALUE

Land value is an essential component of the cost approach and frequently is used in application of market data and income approach techniques. The four basic procedures for the valuation of land[1] are:

1. The market data (comparative) approach. Sales of similar vacant parcels are weighed, compared, and related to the land being appraised.
2. The allocation (abstraction) procedure. Sales of improved properties are analyzed, and the prices paid are allocated between land and improvements. This allocation is used either to establish a typical ratio of land value to total value (allocation), which may be applicable to a property being appraised; or to derive from the portion of the sale price allocated to land, a land value estimate for use as a comparable land sale (abstraction).
3. The anticipated use (development) procedure. The total value of undeveloped land is estimated as if the land were subdivided, developed, and sold. Development costs, incentive

---

1. See Chapter 8.

costs, and carrying charges are subtracted from the estimated proceeds of sale, and the net income projection is discounted over the estimated period required for market absorption of the developed sites.

4. The land residual procedure. The land is assumed to be improved to its highest and best use, and the net income imputable to the land after all expenses of operation and return attributable to the other agents in production is capitalized to derive an estimate of land value.

At this point the background has been completed for development of each of the three approaches to the final estimate of defined value.

APPLICATION OF THE THREE APPROACHES

The three approaches—cost, market data, and income—are based on three facets of value:

1. The current cost of reproducing or replacing a property less loss in value from deterioration and functional or economic obsolescence (accrued depreciation)
2. The value indicated by adjustment of recent sales of comparable properties in the market
3. The investment value that the property's net earning power will support, based on a capitalization of net income

For a particular property or type of property, the value indication from one approach (or two) may be most significant; yet when possible, all three are used to check against each other. There are appraisal problems in which all three approaches cannot be applied. For example, the cost approach is impractical in the valuation of vacant land; the market data approach is similarly inapplicable for specialized property, such as a garbage disposal plant; and only rarely is the income approach helpful in the valuation of an owner-occupied home. All three approaches are, however, pertinent to the solution of many appraisal problems. Their use is well established in appraisal practice and generally accepted as part of fundamental appraisal procedure.

Despite this general acceptance of the three-approach concept in appraisal practice, appraisers recognize the close interdependence that may be involved in the application of the approaches. They may be interrelated to such an extent that some appraisers prefer to combine approaches, avoiding separate presentations of a cost approach, a market data (direct sales comparison) approach, and an income (economic) approach. The chosen format for the appraisal report is less important than the requirement to utilize all the recognized appraisal concepts and techniques that will contribute to a solution of the problem or to a proper valuation of the property being appraised. Many appraisers feel that recognition of three approaches provides a better opportunity to confirm one value indication by the evidence of a second or third conclusion when such procedure is practical and when at least some degree of independent analysis can be achieved.

Cost Approach

In the cost approach[2] the appraiser obtains a preliminary indication of value by adding to the estimated value of the land, an estimate of the depreciated reproduction cost of the building and other improvements.

To obtain financing for a proposed development, a valuation of the land and the projected improvements is essential. Such an appraisal requires an estimation of the probable cost of the improvements from a set of plans, to which is added the value of the site. The cost approach also plays an important part in the effort to determine highest and best use based on cost estimates for hypothetical improvements.

The appraiser follows five steps in executing the cost approach:

1. Estimates the current reproduction or replacement cost of the existing structure(s)
2. Estimates accrued depreciation from all causes
3. Deducts accrued depreciation to derive an indicated current value for the existing structure(s)

---

2. See Chapter 14.

4. Estimates the current depreciated value of accessory improvements (minor structures, parking areas, etc.)
5. Adds the indicated current value of all improvements to the estimated land value to develop an indicated property value

Reproduction cost new.   The cost approach is based on the assumption that the reproduction cost *new* normally tends to set the upper limit of value, provided the improvement represents the highest and best use and is not subject to substantial functional or economic depreciation. A newly constructed building is also assumed to have advantages over an existing building. The first step in analyzing the improvements, therefore, is the development of their estimated *reproduction* or *replacement* cost new. Methods of deriving this figure are discussed in Chapter 12, where the difference between these two terms is explained.

Depreciation.   The appraiser next considers the effect on value of any disadvantages or deficiencies of the existing building as compared with a new building. The measure of this deficiency is called depreciation.[3]

Depreciation may be one or all of three kinds:

1. Deterioration, or the physical wearing out of the property
2. Functional obsolescence, or a lack of desirability in utility, style, or design as compared with that of a new property designed to serve the same function
3. Economic obsolescence related to a loss of value from environmental causes

Cost Estimating Methods.   Obtaining reliable construction cost figures on which to base the estimated reproduction cost is one of the practical problems encountered in applying the cost approach. The quantity survey method (detailed cost estimates of labor and materials) is a comprehensive method of estimating reproduction cost.

---

3. See Chapter 13.

Such an estimate entails considerable time and money, and a decision to compile one depends on the significance of the cost approach in the appraisal. In most appraisals a highly detailed estimate of reproduction cost is not necessary. A reasonable estimate of reproduction cost obtained by applying square-foot or cubic-foot reproduction cost units to the area or volume of the building usually is sufficient.[4]

Limitations.   A well-developed cost approach is basic to the understanding and solution of most appraisal problems, but its applicability and importance may vary widely among individual cases. The cost approach value estimate is valid if the land value estimate is sound, if the reproduction cost has been estimated accurately, and if the estimate of depreciation from all causes is correct. But physical deterioration and functional and economic obsolescence cannot be measured as precisely as a physical object. Measurement—or better, estimation—depends largely on the experience and judgment of the estimator. Therefore, a final estimate of value based solely on reproduction cost less depreciation plus the value of the land may be subject to serious limitations when accrued depreciation is substantial. Whenever possible, it should be supported and reconciled with the market data and income approaches.

Market Data Approach

The market data approach[5] is essential to almost every appraisal of real property. The value estimated by this approach is variously defined in Chapter 2. These definitions are essentially based on the threefold assumption that there is a market for a particular property, that both buyer and seller are fully informed about the property and the state of the market for that type of property, and that the property would be exposed on the open market for a reasonable time.

In applying the market data approach the appraiser does five things:

1.   Seeks similar properties for which pertinent sales, listings, offerings, and/or rental data are available

---

4. See Chapter 12.
5. See Chapters 15 and 16.

2. Ascertains the conditions of sale, including the price, motivating forces, and its bona fide nature
3. Analyzes each of the comparable properties' important attributes in relation to the corresponding attributes of the property being appraised under the general divisions of time, location, physical characteristics, and terms of sale
4. Considers the dissimilarities in the characteristics disclosed in Step 3, in terms of their probable effect on the sale price
5. Formulates, in the light of the comparisons made, an opinion of the relative value of the property being appraised

The application of this approach produces an estimate of value for a property by comparing it with similar properties that have been sold recently or are currently offered for sale in the same or competing areas. Procedures used to estimate the degree of comparability between two properties involve sound judgment decisions concerning their similarity with respect to many value factors such as location, construction, age and condition, layout, equipment, design, utility, and desirability. The sale prices of properties judged to be most comparable tend to set a range within which the value of the subject property will fall. Further consideration of the comparative data should lead to a logical estimate of the probable price for which the property could be sold as of the date of the appraisal. This is the market data value indication.

Pertinent data. The data involved in the application of this process applies to the comparable properties as well as to the subject property and varies with the type of property. Three categories of data are sales, asking prices, and offers. These may be analyzed on the basis of four areas of comparison:

1. Date of sale, listing, or offer
2. Location of each property
3. Physical characteristics of land and improvements for each property
4. Conditions influencing each sale

In specific cases—for example, income property—gross or net income figures for the comparable properties as well as for the subject property are essential; in a farm appraisal the acreage of various soil types and production figures may be important considerations.

The market data approach has been referred to as the comparison approach because it utilizes the process of comparison. However, since comparisons are made in each of the three approaches, the entire appraisal process is in one sense a series of comparisons, which are made in three categories: cost, income, and market.

Limitations.   Although the market data approach has wide application as a method of estimating value and is of primary importance where applicable, there are factors that may limit its usefulness. Examples of these limitations include the following:

1. No provision is made for arriving at an estimate of value in cases where there are no current sales of comparable properties or there is no active market.
2. No two properties are identical, since they vary in location even if alike in other respects. All differences must be considered in the comparative process, with adjustments made for the degree of variation. The more factors to be compared and adjusted, the greater the number of decisions and judgments necessary. Minimal adjustment tends to increase reliability.
3. Amenities, which may be intangible qualities, are difficult to compare.
4. Learning the exact conditions attending each sale is essential so that the validity of the sale as comparative data may be established. If the owner were not an "informed" seller or the buyer were not an "informed" buyer, either being unaware of the current market, the sale price may not reflect the property's value in the market. Many motivations lead to the transfer of real property at figures unrelated to the property's market value. Tax situations may affect the sale price. Transfers of property between relatives or at auctions may not give a true indication of market value.
5. The adjustment process is subject to many interrelationships among the factors considered and may over- or underaccount for dissimilarities. Thus the precision of an adjustment grid may imply an accuracy that does not exist.

In spite of its limitations, the market data approach has broad application in all appraisal work. The value estimate found by the use of this approach is usually considered particularly significant because it is an expression of the value established by actions of buyers and sellers in the market.

Income Approach

In using the income approach[6] the appraiser is concerned with the present value of the future benefits of property ownership. This is generally indicated by the net income a fully informed person is warranted in assuming the property will produce during its remaining useful life. After comparison of rates of return for investments of similar type and class, this net income is capitalized to an estimate of value.

Selecting the capitalization rate is one of the most important steps in the income approach. A variation of only one half of one percent can make a difference of thousands of dollars in the capitalized value of the income. For example, the difference between an annual net income (after provision for recapture) of $64,000 capitalized at 8% and at 8.5% is over $47,000.

In assembling and processing income data the appraiser:

1. Obtains the rent schedules for the property being appraised and for comparable properties for the current year and for several past years. From this information gross rental data and trends for comparison and adjustment are extracted to develop the potential gross income expectancy.
2. Obtains and analyzes occupancy data for the property and for similar properties in the market. In the light of supply and demand trends, projects a vacancy and collection loss deduction from potential gross to derive an effective gross income projection.
3. Obtains and analyzes data on taxes, insurance, and other operating costs for the property being appraised and for comparable properties. Considers indicated trends and deducts a projected expense estimate from the effective gross income to derive a net income projection.
4. Estimates the remaining economic life of the building to establish the probable duration of its income or, alternately, esti-

---

6. See Chapter 17.

mates a probable period of ownership and income stream pattern.
5. Selects an appropriate capitalization method and technique.
6. Selects or develops the appropriate capitalization rate reflecting the rate of return necessary to attract capital.
7. Completes the necessary computations to derive an economic value indication by the income approach.

The income approach, like the cost and market data approaches, involves the appraiser in extensive market research. This research is not limited to the items of data specifically itemized in the above tabulation. Specific data is essential, but the analysis of this data is against a background of basic research in which supply and demand relationships are analyzed. This primary research provides rationalization for trends identified in the specific data patterns.

The income approach has its greatest usefulness in the valuation of income-producing property because the average investor in such property purchases it to receive future benefits (the income). The investor in an apartment building, for example, anticipates an acceptable return on the investment in addition to return of the invested funds. The level of return necessary to attract investment capital fluctuates with changes in the money market and with the levels of return available from alternate investments. The appraiser is alert to changes in investor requirements as revealed by evidence in the current market for investment real estate and to changes in the more volatile money markets that may indicate a forthcoming trend.

RECONCILIATION OF VALUE INDICATIONS

The final step in the appraisal process is the consideration of the indicated value resulting from each of the three approaches to derive a final estimate of the defined value.[7] Under no circumstances are these "averaged." To do so would be as illogical as asking three persons for the right time and averaging the three replies. The appraiser considers the relative dependability and applicability of each of the three approaches in reconciling the three value indications into a final estimate of defined value.

_____
7. See also Chapter 25.

After examining the range between value indications, the appraiser places major emphasis on the one or ones that appear to produce the most reliable and applicable solution to the specific appraisal problem. The objective of the appraisal, the type of property, and the adequacy and relative reliability of the data processed in each of the three approaches influence the weight to be given to each approach. For example, in the case of an owner-occupied factory, if the appraisal were being made for insurance purposes, the greatest weight might be assigned to the cost approach. In the case of an old and obsolete income-producing property, greater weight would be assigned to the market data and income approaches. In the absence of conclusive market data, more reliance might have to be placed on the income approach.

A well-presented valuation analysis is concise and enables the reader to understand the problem and the factual data and then to follow the reasoning leading to the appraiser's conclusion of value. This value estimate is the appraiser's opinion, reflecting the application of experience and judgment to a consideration of all of the assembled data.

THE FINAL ESTIMATE AND REPORT OF DEFINED VALUE

With the final estimate of defined value, the appraiser has achieved the immediate objective of the appraisal process. However, an appraisal assignment is not completed until this conclusion has been stated in a formal report for presentation to the client. This presentation of the defined value—or the answer to the question—is usually written and includes the data considered and analyzed, the methods used, and the reasoning followed in achieving the final estimate or conclusion. This report is the tangible expression of the appraiser's service. It is the instrument that fulfills the contract with a client and for which the fee is paid. For these reasons alone, the manner in which it is written, the organization and presentation, and the overall appearance are important elements in its preparation.[8]

---

8. See Chapter 26.

5

Economic Trends

Value is affected by the interplay of social, economic, governmental, and physical forces, which are continually changing, often in a cyclical pattern. Although the value of real estate may seem relatively stable in comparison to the value of stocks or commodities, it is still subject to the multitude of pressures and influences created by this interplay. Recognition and understanding of the resulting economic trends affecting the value of real property are prerequisite to an appraisal analysis. Accordingly, a more detailed examination of the economic aspects of the actions of these four great forces is in order.

To know that changes have taken place or are taking place is not enough. The direction of the changes, and their probable extent and impact, are considered in order to identify a trend and to permit a reasonable projection of that trend. *A trend may be defined as a series of related changes brought about by a chain of causes and effects.* An economic trend being projected in an appraisal analysis may be rooted in social or governmental causes and effects.

GENERAL ECONOMY

The appraiser's immediate concern is with the economic factors in the community and area as they relate to purchasing power. However, basic trends reflected by national and international economic indicators, such as balance of foreign trade, rates of foreign exchange, commodity price levels, wage levels, interest rates, industrial production levels, and retail sales, also merit the appraiser's consideration.

The interplay of economic forces affects all levels of the economy.

Therefore, any change, good or bad, at any level in the economy can be compared to a stone dropped in a pond. As the circle widens, the ripples lose intensity and strength.

The sensitive interweaving of the many factors affecting regional or national economies extends to influence the general economy. The economic health and well-being of one nation may affect many nations, directly and indirectly. The greater the intensity of the change and the longer it endures, the wider is its influence.

NATIONAL ECONOMY

The state of the national economy is basic to any appraisal analysis. However, the character and magnitude of an appraisal assignment may affect the extent to which consideration of this level of the economy is treated in a report. The national economy may be prosperous and expanding or depressed and declining. Its state depends on conditions within various sectors of the whole, including the status of domestic industrial, commercial, and agricultural activities. The strength of each economic segment contributes to the strength and health of the total economy.

REGIONAL ECONOMY

The national economy reflects the economic state of the nation's geographical regions. The economic health of a region depends on the status of economic activities within the region. These activities are the aggregate of the economic activities of the individual areas and communities within its geographical boundaries.

Although minor disruptions may seriously affect a local economy, if the regional and national economies are strong, the overall effect may be minimal. However, if the general economy is not well supported in all its segments, the effect of a change in one area could spread, undermining the economy of adjacent areas until the condition of the entire nation is affected.

The extent to which the appraiser is concerned with the economy of the nation or region, as opposed to the city or neighborhood economy, depends on factors such as the size and type of property being appraised. For example, a large regional shopping center serving a trade area of 500,000 people or an automobile assembly plant employing 5,000 workers is more sensitive to the general state of the economy than a medical-dental office building or a retail service operation in a suburban residential area.

POPULATION

A direct relationship exists between the value of real property and population growth. Because land is fixed and the amount of land cannot be changed in response to changing demand, population changes affect the value of the existing land. Scarcity of land of a particular type in demand results in a higher value for that which is available. The effective demand for land is in direct proportion to the number of people able and willing to buy, sell, or use it. Consequently, increasing land value generally reflects population growth. Today's births lead to tomorrow's demands, structuring the succession of future needs, including the amount of children's goods and services, education, recreation, and housing. These children progressively enter and leave the new markets, adding to or subtracting from demand.

Demand exists for specific parcels for specific purposes, rather than for land in general. Population changes combine with industrial development and, in a broad sense, with the entire spectrum of human activity to influence the value of real property. Value rises or falls in step with the changing geographic pattern of industrial expansion or contraction and with the shifts in population that occur in response to these alterations in the pattern of industrial and other activities.

Property values are affected by the number of people in a region and community and by impending changes in the size or purchasing power of this population. Pertinent information may be obtained from private fact-finding agencies or from detailed reports of government agencies, such as the Bureau of the Census. This latter data, reported for geographically outlined districts called census tracts, indicates trends within an entire metropolitan area and its components. Also shown are the type of population as well as its rate of increase or decrease in any area in relation to the rate of change for any other community in the state and for the nation.

An investigation of the demographic composition of the population is important to the appraiser investigating the anticipated need for single family residences as opposed to apartments or condominiums. Reference to statistical studies is helpful in such cases (see Table 5.1).

Table 5.1. Population Growth in 1960s and 1970s Concentrated in Young Adults

	1950-1959	1960-1969	1970-1979	1980-1989
Change in population, all ages (millions of persons)	4.7	7.2	10.3	9.0
Percent of total change Age of Males				
18-24	5%	53%	24%	−20%
25-34	−11	13	51	31
35-44	23	−6	9	63
45-54	30	15	−4	14
55-64	18	15	10	−4
65 or older	35	10	10	16
All ages	100%	100%	100%	100%

Source: U.S. Bureau of the Census, "Current Population Reports," Series P-20, No. 418 and Series P-25, No. 448. Compiled by the Mortgage Bankers Association.

Data like that shown in Table 5.1 is sometimes available every five years instead of every 10 years, and current computer-generated statistics on population characteristics and other statistical information in support of appraisal projections can be secured in most urban areas.

PURCHASING POWER

An important by-product of population growth is purchasing power, or the economic ability of the population to satisfy its desires and needs. A multitude of factors affect the purchasing power of the population, which in turn affects the value of real property. These factors include the number of people employed in basic industries and in service industries; farm prosperity and the level of farm subsidies; the current level of commodity prices; the figure for gross national product per person; violent storms, floods, or earthquakes; strikes; the availability of credit, interest rates, and the purchasing power of the dollar.

The ability to purchase a thing desired has been described as one of the elements of value. The appraiser understands that the value of residential real estate depends in part on individual purchasing power. Accordingly, all developments that tend to affect the ability of an individual to purchase real estate are considered in an appraisal analysis.

Although purchasing power depends on income, it does not equal income because a part of income must go for taxes. The balance, termed disposabie income, is spent for many commodities and services. The manner in which it is expended affects the value of the real property involved in providing those commodities and services. A major share of disposable income is expended on the necessities of living, which include housing. The remainder could be spent for nonessential commodities and services, or part could be saved. This residual portion of disposable income has the most direct effect on property value. The larger the portion, the greater is its effect. For example, the amount available for the purchase of automobiles can tax the industry's capacity to produce. This necessitates the construction of new facilities which in turn increases the value of new property and enhances the values in adjacent areas. However, it can have the reverse effect when the margin of disposable income shrinks to a point sufficient to cover only necessities.

The appraiser is concerned with the status of disposable income in the community. The stability of property values depends on local purchasing power. Any increment in value depends on the amount and duration of the marginal disposable income.

Thus population growth coupled with sustained purchasing power acts to maintain and enhance real property values. The outward pressure of urban population growth plus its disposable income cause the conversion of farm acreage into suburban communities. Within these, certain areas increase in value as they become shopping centers, industrial parks, or residential developments.

Among pertinent statistics pertaining to purchasing power are those relating to employment and to disposable income. Newspapers and chambers of commerce frequently make regional studies of employment; and federal and state agencies often prepare statewide, regional, and citywide studies. A variety of statistical material is available.

Studies relating to disposable income are reported annually in many businesses and government publications. These studies list, by city or trading area, the amount of money the average family has to spend after paying income taxes. Trends over a period of years are frequently tabulated. Changes in disposable income per family are reflected in the volume of retail sales. This in turn helps to establish the level of rent merchants can pay and influences the value of the real estate occupied by the merchants.

PRICE LEVELS

The value of real property is affected when general price levels rise or fall, quite apart from the level of supply and demand for land and buildings. The reason is that physically a building is merely an accumulation of materials. If the prices of steel, sand, gravel, cement, and lumber decline, their dollar values decline, whether they are piled in a building supply dealer's yard or assembled in a building. The converse also applies.

The cost of living index, which is widely used in business summaries and for the adjustment of wage contracts, is an important appraisal tool. Records of the wholesale price index, other selected price indexes, and price movements, which indicate whether the current prices of commodities are static, rising, or declining, are available. Studies of the causes and effects of these movements may be useful in projecting their probable impact on real estate values.

EMPLOYMENT AND ECONOMIC BASE ANALYSIS

The prudent investor or lender making a substantial commitment to real property is sensitive to the economic base of the area in which the property is located. A healthy economic base with broad support is a favorable factor. A one-industry town or a community economically dependent on the presence of a large military installation is less attractive to a lender or investor than a community that has a diversified employment base.

Ideally, a city or region provides a variety of employment opportunities so that a curtailment of activity in one segment will not initiate a decline in the other components of the local "labor" structure and it alone will not create a substantial decline in local employment.

One of the methods used to analyze economic trends within a city or region is an economic base analysis. This is a study to identify sources of employment within the area and to divide this employment into basic and nonbasic categories. Activities that export goods and services and bring into the community funds with which to purchase other goods and services constitute basic employment on which the rest of the community depends. One job in basic employment may support several jobs providing services to the community, and a specific relationship may be developed.

An economic base study reveals the relative importance of various local sources of income to the community and includes a consideration of their future potential. Estimates of future population changes may be based on the potential changes in basic employment as revealed by an economic base analysis. Within a community, there is a close relationship between population, purchasing power, price levels, and the economic base. The appraiser exercises judgment concerning the degree to which a particular appraisal problem warrants in-depth economic base analysis.

Location, climate, the presence of significant institutions or government bodies, major sources of employment, and similar factors affect local economy. Chicago is an example of a city that originated and grew because of a desirable location as a natural transportation route. Chicago is a major air and rail traffic center, and its physical attributes seem to be so permanent that one can hardly envision Chicago by itself suffering long-term economic distress. Florida and Southern California will continue to attract people unless pollution or some unforeseen condition destroys their climatic and scenic advantages. The cities of Palo Alto, California, and Cambridge, Massachusetts, will be appealing as long as Stanford and Harvard universities exist there. State capitols, and to a lesser degree county seats, represent a high degree of economic stability. Conversely, complete shutdown of Lockheed's Missile and Space Division, which employs 17,000 people, could cause economic disaster to Sunnyvale, California, and neighboring cities. Other communities where major sources of employment could be significantly affected by governmental action require careful analysis and may involve considerations of nuclear power plant production, strip mining, shipbuilding, and the manufacture of road building equipment.

The long-term national trend reflects a decline in the percentage of population engaged in the primary sector of agriculture, mining, lumbering, and fishing, while the industrial and construction and the sales and service sectors have increased. Since 1900 the latter has accelerated dramatically, and both these increasing sectors are city builders.

A comparison of sources of employment, as revealed in economic base analyses since 1945, continues to reflect a substantial decline in the number of persons employed in agriculture and in heavy industry, while the number of people employed in "clean" industry and office work, both private and governmental, has increased. Such trends may continue nationally or regionally, and the appraiser considers carefully whether an identifiable trend will have any significant effect on a particular appraisal problem. Cities with an economic base dependent on tourism, gambling, or health facilities may be affected only indirectly by the above trends.

BUILDING CYCLES

Business cycles are periodic movements within long-term economic trends. Efforts to curtail the production of items that cannot be produced at a profit and concurrent efforts to accelerate the production of items that can be produced profitably are responsible for the cycles of overproduction and underproduction—for example, in the automobile, textile, and building industries. There are also clearly established cycles of production in agriculture. The duration of both the industrial (urban) and the agricultural (rural) cycles is affected by the length of time required to create and reduce surpluses.

The building industry has an important influence on business cycles. Real estate is one of the primary supports of national prosperity. A high rate of building activity is accompanied by a correspondingly active demand for all the commodities and furnishings involved in housing and related activities. Conversely, reduced construction activity serves as a brake on prosperity.

Overexpansion in the building industry is directly reflected by an excess supply of improved property and a consequent adjustment in real estate prices. Conversely, a period of curtailed building activity is ultimately reflected by a shortage and consequent increase in demand, which in turn is reflected by higher property values.

Probably no other period in history has been so affected by

technological developments as the third quarter of this century. The effects of technology on real estate are exemplified by the development of air conditioning and advanced systems of heating and ventilation which provide comfort in homes, offices, factories, and stores. Many areas that were formerly considered undesirable for year-round living now have residential development.

The airplane and the automobile, shifting retail emphasis from downtown districts to suburban centers, have changed the focus of city planning. Central business district uses in large cities, including many department stores and retail specialty shops, hotels, and office buildings, have decentralized to strategic suburban areas accessible to superhighways and airports.

The increasing cost of energy has become an important consideration affecting the marketability of existing properties. Both cost and availability promise to become increasingly important factors affecting market value and the design of new projects. The development of new techniques for the assembly and analysis of data, including use of computers and data storage banks, has placed new demands on the real estate appraiser and broadened appraisal activity.

Since World War II there has been a very definite trend from what was generally considered to be a free-moving capitalistic economy toward a political economy largely controlled by a multitude of government commissions and study groups. These are often oriented toward social, political, and environmental considerations, rather than toward the conventional economic objectives, which were formerly considered standard business practices.

This trend has resulted in restrictions on the productivity of real estate which have a pronounced effect on its value in the market. The long-time effects of this transition are not yet fully apparent. Some governmental regulations undoubtedly will continue to produce a favorable social dividend; others may not. The effectiveness of such regulations will undoubtedly contribute to both social and economic welfare in direct proportion to their timing and the intelligence with which they are devised and enforced. Furthermore, most regulations involve costs, which have an impact on value. Only where costs of governmental regulation contribute directly or indirectly to an increase in, or maintenance of, real estate values are they economically warranted in terms of value of real estate and its productivity.

As the 21st century approaches, an estimate of future conditions and trends necessitates an interpretation of cyclical movements by considering how the government probably will act on the matter of imposing or lifting controls.

ECONOMIC INDICATORS

The importance of supply and demand is presented in Chapter 30. In estimating the future demand for all types of real estate, consideration must be given to the trend of factors that influence supply and demand.

Demand factors include:

1. Population, rate of increase or decrease, and age distribution
2. Geographic factors, such as climate, topography, and natural or manmade barriers
3. Land use and city growth
4. Types, services, and costs of transportation; and highway systems
5. Sources and levels of employment and rate of unemployment
6. Average wage rates and disposable income levels
7. Financial aspects such as personal savings, mortgage lending, and insurance rates
8. Cultural institutions
9. Educational facilities
10. Health and medical facilities; fire and police protection
11. Tax structure and assessments

Supply factors include:

1. Volume of new construction
2. Availability and price of vacant land
3. Construction costs
4. Volume of available houses (new and old)
5. Owner-occupancy versus tenant-occupancy
6. Causes and amount of vacancy
7. Impact of building codes and zoning ordinances on construction volume and cost[1]

---

1. These demand and supply factors are from Jerome Knowles, Jr., "City and Neighborhood Data and Analysis," *The Appraisal Journal*, April 1967, p. 261.

Other factors include the increase of leisure time, size of households, and environmental controls.

TAXES

Real estate taxes are on an ad valorem basis or an amount of dollars per year related to assessed value. If the tax rate is $60 per $1,000 of valuation and the assessed value of a property is 50% of its market value, this parcel is taxed in the amount of 3% per year of its worth.

$$\frac{60}{1,000} \times 50\% = 3\%.$$

In another example, if the gross annual rental income is 12.5% of the market value and if annual real estate taxes are 2.5% of market value, one-fifth of the gross income must be allocated for payment of taxes.

In some communities the trend in real estate taxes is an important consideration. In cities with an increasing trend of public expenditures for schools and municipal services, a heavy burden of taxation may adversely affect the level of real estate values. Under these circumstances, new construction may be discouraged in such an area. Appraisal services may be required where ad valorem real estate tax assessments bear an established or provable relationship to market value and in the resolution of tax appeals.

Income taxes are not treated as an expense in the appraisal process, except in certain specialized situations. Among these exceptions are cases where various properties are included as an integral and essential part of technological operations (such as a public utility) and where the net income of the entire operation is being capitalized, usually because separating the real estate from the business operation is impossible or impractical. Increasing in importance is the influence of tax regulations on the price and value of real estate in certain situations. Accordingly, although this is the specialized area of the accountant or the income-tax expert, the appraiser should have some general knowledge of the substance and trend of federal and state income-tax regulations as they tend to affect equity cash flow rates and real estate values.

BUILDING COSTS

The cost of reproducing a building tends to follow general price levels established over a long period. However, they vary from time to time and from place to place. Building costs generally decline in times of deflation and increase with inflation. A comparison of the cost of living index and adjusted construction cost index covering 1960 to 1976 illustrates the effects of change on the economy and on building costs (Table 5.2). Figure 5.1 (see p. 86) shows construction cost trends from 1913 to 1977.

Table 5.2 Construction Cost Compared to Cost of Living

Year	U.S. Department of Commerce Composite	American Appraisal Co. Index[a]	Cost of Living Wholesale Price Index
1960	83	80	94.9
1965	93	91	96.6
1970	122	124	110.4
1975	189	189	174.9
1976	198	206	182.9
	100=1967		

Source: U.S. Bureau of the Census, *Statistical Abstract of the United States* (Washington, D.C.: 1977).

---

[a]Materials and labor, four industrial types (frame, brick, concrete, and steel).

INTEREST RATES

Real estate activity is closely related to the supply and availability of money. Most real estate is purchased subject to financing; transactions, then, are dependent on the availability of mortgage money and the current lending policies of insurance companies, mortgage firms, and other sources of funds. An understanding of the money market involves familiarity with the sources of money being loaned on the various types of real estate in which each lender specializes.

The source of savings and loan associations' funds, for example, is the pooled financial resources of individuals and private organiza-

Figure 5.1.   1977 Construction Cost Trend Chart

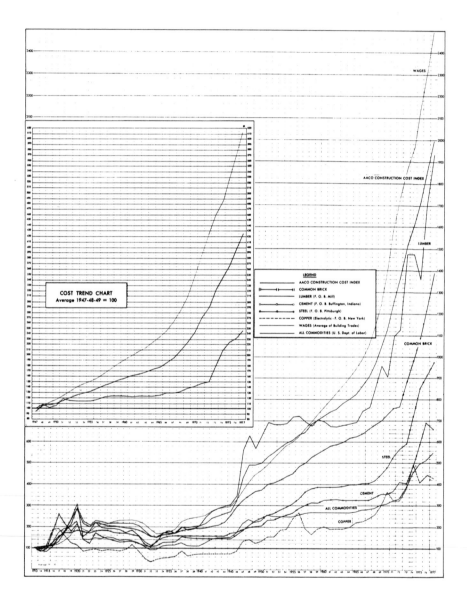

Source: *Copyright, The American Appraisal Company, 1978.*

tions together with vast sums of money these associations may borrow from federal government agencies. Commercial savings banks receive funds for deposit, and credit is created in the banking system. Life insurance companies administer large sums of money which they collect as premiums on insurance policies as well as from incomes on their investments and from capital gains on their securities, real estate, or other assets. Real estate investment trusts secure funds from investors who purchase stock in the trusts.

Availability of financing depends largely on the ability and willingness of individuals and private organizations to save and to conserve their resources. Since premiums paid by policyholders are the primary source of insurance company money, the availability of this important source of mortgage money is controlled by the ability and readiness of people to buy insurance.

The appraiser's study of financial trends covers the activities of related federal agencies, including those that provide a secondary mortgage market. Public financing of construction projects results in building activity that otherwise might not exist. Such government initiative can stimulate demand for real estate.

Interest rates on funds borrowed in the money market fluctuate upward or downward in accordance with a number of factors, including the existing supply of, and demand for, funds.

All investments in real estate or real estate equities are competing—in regard to both rate of interest and advantages offered—with all other real estate or non-real estate investments. Therefore, the rates of interest on real estate investments fluctuate with interest rates and relative risks and advantages of categories of competitive investments.

OTHER TRENDS

As an appraiser becomes active in counseling clients, the importance of a broad grasp of economic and related trends increases. The extent to which this knowledge is necessary to complete a specific appraisal assignment depends on the nature and scope of the appraisal problem involved. The information assembled, including some that may be irrelevant, can become so voluminous that efficient application of the appraisal process is impeded.

A principal index of real estate activity is the number of deeds filed. County recorders' offices frequently keep a count of the number of deeds filed for record in a month and in a year. Generally, an increase in the number of deeds filed indicates an increase in sales (unless they are foreclosures). This, in turn, usually signals a strong market. Study of such information leads to a better understanding of business cycles.

Economic trend information is also available from sources such as the regional surveys of the Federal Reserve Bank, U.S. Department of Commerce, Bureau of the Census; universities; publications of real estate and other trade associations; savings and loan associations and banks. Their statistics include retail sales indexes for department stores and retail specialty shops. Such sales volume figures are significant because they reflect economic trends.[2]

SUMMARY

There are many available sources for all aspects of economic trends. Subjects include price levels, purchasing power, population figures, rental and operating trends, building cycles, government regulations, construction costs, and interest rates. A general knowledge of the history of the reasons for these economic phenomena is useful to understand the implications of current observable trends. The appraiser's analysis of observed or projected trends is objective and free from preconceived ideas or concepts. The final value estimate should reflect all elements with a demonstrable impact on market value and none that are conjectural, remote, biased, or speculative. The appraiser should be able to establish that factors affecting market value are measurable by objective means.

---

2. See, for example, *Editor and Publisher Market Guide* (New York: Editor and Publisher, annually).
   Joint Economic Committee of Congress, *Statistical Indicators* (Washington, D.C.: U.S. Government Printing Office, monthly and weekly).
   Financial and Operating Results of Department and Specialty Stores (New York: National Retail Merchants Association, Controllers Congress, annually).
   Economic Indicators (Washington, D.C.: U.S. Department of Commerce, Office of Business Economics, monthly).
   Statistical Abstract of the United States (Washington, D.C.: U.S. Department of Commerce, Bureau of the Census, annually).
   Survey of Current Business (Washington, D.C.: U.S. Department of Commerce, monthly). Biennial supplement is *Business Statistics*.

6
Neighborhood Analysis

A parcel of real estate is an integral part of its environment and cannot be treated as an entity unaffected by its surroundings. The value of real property is not intrinsic, resulting exclusively from its physical characteristics. An analysis of the economic, social, physical, and governmental forces currently influencing the neighborhood is prerequisite to understanding their present and probable future effects on the value of the property being appraised. Because all properties share the future of the neighborhood in which they are located, their values may fluctuate, reflecting the action of environing forces.

The depth of analysis will vary according to the need, but a neighborhood must be defined in terms of some common characteristics and trends in order to interpret market evidence fairly.

In neighborhood analysis the appraiser should avoid reliance on the racial, religious, or ethnic characteristics of the residents. Racial and other ethnic factors are not reliable predictors of value trends, and use of those factors by the appraiser in neighborhood analysis can be misleading. People's reactions and preferences are so diverse and variable that they are not readily quantifiable in the course of the appraisal process.

In the appraisal process neighborhood analysis precedes, and provides background for, valuation. For appraisal purposes, information that has no bearing on value is irrelevant. This does not suggest that neighborhood analysis can or should be reduced to a detailed reckoning of neighborhood influences in some final equation of value. Misuse of neighborhood analysis can lead to double counting and false conclusions.

Assume, for example, that after complete neighborhood analysis the appraiser delineates the neighborhood and obtains an indication of value based on recent prices received for similar properties in the same neighborhood. In such a case, it would be incorrect to adjust value for neighborhood influences, since it can be assumed that these market influences are reflected in the observed market prices.

NEIGHBORHOOD IDENTITY

A neighborhood is seldom easily or clearly defined. It may be part of a larger community or it may be an entire community. Every city began as a small community or neighborhood. The reasons for establishing the original communities may help in understanding modern neighborhoods. Some of these reasons may have included:

1. A need for the safety afforded by numbers
2. A desire for companionship
3. A desire to take advantage of opportunities to engage in trade or commercial pursuits
4. A desire to take advantage of the greater availability of commercial or service facilities
5. A desire to enjoy greater cultural advantages

As a community grows, a tendency toward the grouping of land uses—residential, retail, commercial, warehousing, manufacturing—becomes evident. The areas devoted to these varied uses become physical neighborhoods; as these areas expand, they ultimately become many neighborhoods, each with its own characteristics and physical delineation. *A neighborhood, then, may be more specifically defined as a grouping of similar or complementary land uses.* The neighborhood may be part of a larger community or it may be an entire community defined in terms of some common characteristics or interests that relate the inhabitants to the neighborhood or to each other.

Commercial or industrial neighborhoods are areas in which the predominant land use is devoted to these activities. A downtown commercial district usually can be clearly mapped, with its main streets, mass transportation lines, and traffic arteries fanning out to the residential neighborhoods. The string type of store district is likely to develop along major arteries, punctuated by more intensive groupings at important traffic intersections or former transportation transfer points. A modern commercial neighborhood or a regional shopping center is a cluster of retail trade and service establishments supported by a primary trading area composed of a residential neighborhood or neighborhoods.

Industrial neighborhoods once tended to be concentrated along waterways or railroads, ribbon fashion. More recently they have been developed in the form of industrial centers or parks on the peripheries of cities. Related industries generally are grouped in a geographical area to which they have been attracted by abundant natural resources, availability of trained labor, interlocking interests, or a combination of these.

Farm communities are characterized by size of operation, type of ownership, soil, crops grown, or land use. The boundaries of farm communities may cover several counties or larger areas.

Residential neighborhoods are frequently more flexible than commercial and industrial neighborhoods. They are sometimes composed of a narrow range of income levels and social groupings, but there is a growing preference for heterogeneity within neighborhoods. The criteria for neighborhood analysis are clearly changing, reflecting changes in our social structures and attitudes. Obsolete standards of conformity have no place in modern neighborhood analysis. Broad federal and state fair housing laws have made discrimination on the basis of racial, religious, or ethnic factors unlawful in the sale, rental, and financing of housing. These laws and changing social standards have contributed to the establishment and maintenance of many stable, integrated residential areas. The increasing mobility of people in this country also tends to make neighborhoods less static than they once were.

The social nature of people provides a force that tends to strengthen neighborhoods. People of similar ages with growing children often tend to gather in a specific subdivision, establishing a neighborhood identity. Common interests, which provide conversational bonds, represent a strong aspect of the desirable living appeal of many single family neighborhoods. The nature of these common interests is not permanent; and some of the former religious, racial, or ethnic considerations have become less important common denominators than economic patterns, business interests, investments, sports, recreational activities, vacation patterns, civic action, school or children's activities, and other facets of today's life. In many large cities, particularly in multifamily neighborhoods, neighbors may hardly know each other. Bonds that help strengthen neighborhood ties in one location may be nonexistent in another. The combined effect of all these changes is to make racial, religious, or ethnic characteristics unreliable as indicators of value trends in neighborhood analysis.

NEIGHBORHOOD BOUNDARIES

Neighborhoods may be of varying sizes, but generally they are considered to be homogeneous in some respect. Sometimes neighborhood boundaries may be clearly defined (for instance, by a distinct change in land use, type of buildings, or in the economic status of the inhabitants). Sometimes boundaries are natural barriers, such as topographical features, lakes, rivers, or streams; or manmade barriers, such as canals, railroad rights of way, or traffic arteries. The boundaries of a given property's neighborhood encompass not only the improvements adjacent to it, but extend to include similar or complementary improvements that relate to or support the value of the immediate location. This characteristic is most applicable to a commercial property. Its neighborhood consists not only of the store district, but also of the extent and character of the trading area from which it draws its economic support.

Identification of neighborhood or district boundaries is important because this is where growth occurs and where pressure from adjacent neighborhoods may be encountered.

Neighborhoods within a larger community are not isolated districts, and each is dependent on all the other districts, the city itself, and its entire economic area.

SHIFTING NATURE OF NEIGHBORHOODS

Neighborhoods are not fixed. They are always changing, some very slowly, others rapidly. Often they work against one another. In any relatively stable city, for example, the rapid growth of one district may mean the decline of a competitive district. A city's growth may reach the point where accessibility to the center is difficult from the more remote districts. In these instances, the establishment of new business centers better serves the needs of these outlying neighborhoods. Thus commercial subcenters come into being and the city pattern becomes complex. The suburban business centers may adversely affect the central business district. The newer residential areas may affect the old. The added supply of new homes may induce shifts from old to new, thereby placing older homes on the market, increasing the supply with possible consequent effect on market value. If the location of a neighborhood makes it ripe for conversion to a more intensive use, the existing improvements may be torn down to make way for redevelopment.

The growth of the city results in changes in the utility of parcels of land and their improvements. Utility may be increased or decreased, and changes in value result. No neighborhood is absolutely static. Changes may be proceeding at a slow pace (which is usual), but they are always present.

THE IMPORTANCE OF OBJECTIVITY IN NEIGHBORHOOD ANALYSIS

Consideration of observable neighborhood conditions and trends is an important aspect of neighborhood analysis and will typically include observation of factors that detract from or enhance property values. In identifying and discussing these conditions, trends, or factors, objectivity is essential. For instance, general reference to a presumed "pride of ownership" (or the lack thereof) may be too vague and too subjective to be indicative of an actual contribution to or detraction from property values. The presence of special amenities or detrimental conditions should be noted and described with particularity.

The appraiser's findings with respect to neighborhood conditions and the effects of these conditions on property values are considered by buyers, sellers, brokers, lenders, courts, arbiters, public officials, and other decision makers or advisors. Because of this broad influence, the appraiser is often called upon to provide specific evidence of neighborhood conditions and trends and to elaborate the findings of a written appraisal report. The use of photographs and detailed field notes enables the appraiser to recall important evidence and verify the facts considered in the analysis.

The appraiser should avoid generalization with respect to the desirability of particular types of neighborhoods. Older urban neighborhoods, as well as newer suburban subdivisions, can attract a wide range of residents. Neighborhood trends do not necessarily depend on the age of the neighborhood or the income of neighborhood residents.

ANALYZING THE RESIDENTIAL NEIGHBORHOOD

A brief analysis of the nature of the typical residential neighborhood discloses that retail stores, service establishments, schools, churches, theatres, libraries, and parks may be considered necessary because they serve the needs of the inhabitants. This is particularly so in older, built-up areas.

In neighborhood analysis, the consideration of discernible patterns of urban growth, structure, and change is of major importance. Just as a dwelling is influenced by the surrounding residential neighborhood, the neighborhood is influenced by the surrounding metropolitan area. Each metropolitan area responds to its own local demands for urban space, but careful analysis can reveal the general trends and directions of growth, decay, and renewal. Residential neighborhoods typically pass through three stages:

1. Growth—a period during which the neighborhood gains public favor and acceptance
2. Stability—a period of equilibrium without marked gains or losses
3. Decline—a period of diminishing demand

Although the concept of neighborhood life cycle describes the stages of neighborhood evolution in a general way, it should not be overemphasized as a guideline to neighborhood trends. Many neighborhoods exist in a stable stage for very long periods of time, and decline is not imminent in all older neighborhoods. There is no preset life expectancy for a neighborhood. Unless caused by the advent of some specific adverse influence—for example, a new high-way changing traffic patterns—decline may be at a barely perceptible rate and subject to interruption by changing use or revival of demand.

After a period of decline, there may be a period of transition to other land uses, or the neighborhood life cycle may be repeated. Neighborhood rejuvenation is often the result of organized rebuilding or restoration, but it may also be the result of a natural rekindling of demand. The rebirth of an older inner city neighborhood, for example, may occur without a planned renewal program, simply because of changing preferences and lifestyles.

An understanding of neighborhood trends and their influence on value involves considering the relevant physical, social, economic, and governmental factors. Each of these categories may include various considerations.

Physical
1. Relation to the rest of the city
2. Street patterns and width of streets
3. Convenience to public transportation
4. Quality of, and convenience to, schools
5. Quality of, and convenience to, stores and service establishments
6. Convenience to parks and recreation areas
7. Pattern of land use, shape and size of lots
8. Visual aspects, geographical and topographical features, and climate
9. Availability and quality of utilities
10. Nuisances and hazards, such as fog, smoke, smog, and industrial noises and vibrations

Social
1. Community or neighborhood organizations (e.g., improvement associations, block clubs)
2. Density of population
3. Extent or absence of crime or litter

Economic
1. Degree of thrift and homeownership
2. Rent and income levels
3. Vacancy of residential units

4. New construction and vacant land
5. Attitude of financial institutions
6. Growth of the neighborhood
7. Changing use

Governmental
1. Special assessments
2. Tax burden
3. Zoning and building codes
4. Other regulations restricting design or use

Physical Considerations in Neighborhood Analysis

Although it is not always essential to delineate definite boundaries for the neighborhood being analyzed, it is highly desirable to know the extent of similar land use radiating in all directions from the property being appraised. If the area is of considerable size, the possibility of adverse effect from undesirable developments in adjacent neighborhoods decreases as distance from the outer edges of the neighborhood increases.

Well-planned city streets discourage inter-city and inter-neighborhood traffic from penetrating a residential area. Curvilinear and dead-end streets reduce traffic hazards. Curving streets and wide boulevards usually make a neighborhood more aesthetically attractive. The street pattern is one of the factors that attracts buyers to a neighborhood. The relationship of the neighborhood's street pattern to main traffic arteries and to the overall local transportation situation must be considered; equally significant is the neighborhood's distance from employment centers and shopping centers.

Transportation. Time consumed in traveling to desired destinations, cost of transportation, and frequency of service are important considerations in making comparisons between areas. The modern trend to superhighway and limited-access highway systems and the extension of public transportation are bringing the city and its satellite areas closer together, permitting wider population dispersion without proportionate increase in travel time. The most suitable type of transportation facility depends largely on the income level of the people being served. It is not enough to note that transportation exists; the kind of service given and how it relates to the needs of the passengers are also pertinent.

Adequate public transportation to the downtown area and to principal centers of employment still is a major consideration in valuation, despite the increased dependence on privately owned transportation. Public transportation is important to the many people who do not have automobiles or who prefer not to use them for daily transportation to places of employment, to avoid traffic congestion, inconvenient parking, or the increasing cost of daily parking in downtown areas. Residential properties located in remote sections or having slow and infrequent public transportation tend to command lower rentals and prices than do properties more conveniently located or having better service. Distance from public transportation is considered in relation to the people who are to be served by it. Although in the past public transportation in areas where most families own two or more cars was used mostly by domestic help, current emphasis on its ecological advantages and convenience make it an important consideration in such areas. Urban apartment dwellers dislike traffic noise, but usually prefer to be within convenient walking distance from public transportation. For most of them, to be too far away is less desirable than to be too close.

A study of a neighborhood's transportation facilities takes into consideration the territory through which users of these facilities must pass. People dislike walking along poorly lighted streets and through rundown areas. Another factor is the type and adequacy of transportation to schools and other centers of activity. Generally, it may be concluded that almost everyone—whether living in homes or in apartments, owning two cars or none—is interested in transportation. Ordinarily, the closer to good public transportation, the wider is the market for a property.

Balance in land use. Families are attracted to a neighborhood by good schools of their choice. Access to elementary schools either by walking or by school bus is of more importance than to higher level schools. A well-regarded parochial or private school nearby will frequently enhance the market appeal of a neighborhood.

Most people prefer to live within reasonable walking distance of convenience stores and service establishments, although this may become less important in suburban areas, due to an increasing number of multi-car families. Despite the widespread desire to be near sources of supplies and services, residential properties bordering on shopping centers or in proximity to commercial districts may have less salability because of traffic, noise, floodlighting, or unsightliness. Most people require adequate and convenient shopping—but not adjacent to their homes. Modern shopping centers, whether neighborhood or regional, usually provide a neighborhood with a sufficient range of goods and services. Some of a neighborhood's recreational facilities are commonly associated with its schools, but it is to a neighborhood's advantage to offer ample, well-supervised parks, beaches, pools, ice rinks, baseball diamonds, tennis clubs, or other similar facilities. Some of these provide broad appeal for adult patronage and help to keep children constructively occupied.

The highest efficiency in the use of urban land is the result of a proper balance between different types of use. Such a balance is attained when the right amount and kind of land is used for residential purposes; when the proper areas are zoned for commercial and industrial use; and when land is correctly allocated to other forms of use, such as parks and playgrounds.

Value is maximized when the land-use pattern is ideally balanced; value is reduced when uses are imbalanced. Unfortunately, practice has not conformed to principle. The incompatible land-use patterns that exist in many major cities exemplify lack of ideal balance. However, progress is being made through the increased activity of city and regional planning agencies which implement sound land-use principles.

Natural and manmade environment. A neighborhood may be well designed and developed, but its desirability is reduced if it must be approached through unattractive and overcrowded districts. Consideration must be given to the appearance and the condition of streets, sidewalks, lawns, landscaping, buildings, and vacant lots. The architectural styles in a neighborhood also have a bearing on its desirability. Prevalence of a currently popular design is a favorable influence; and good maintenance of older buildings, prompted by a pride of ownership and occupancy, attests to the character of the residents.

The presence of a lake or river, a bay or swamp, or a hilly area in or contiguous to a neighborhood may constitute an advantage or disadvantage. Such features may endow an area with a scenic advantage uncommon in other sections. A hill may mean little in a rugged section, but an elevated or wooded section in a predominantly flat area could enhance the value of property. A river subject to severe flooding would be a negative factor, and the value of homes along its banks would reflect risk from such a hazard.

Topographical conditions can endow a neighborhood with protection against wind, fog, or flood; or they can expose it to danger or damage from these forces. A geographical feature, such as a river, lake, or park, may serve as a buffer to protect a residential district from encroachment by commercial or industrial enterprises.

The invasion of commercial or industrial usages generally constitutes a depreciating factor in a residential neighborhood. However, the value of the site occupied by the new use frequently increases. This increase might partially or even entirely offset the decreased value of a specific property, but the encroachment of nonresidential uses can injure the neighborhood as a whole.

Exposure to odors, smoke, dust, and noise from commercial or manufacturing enterprises limits a neighborhood's desirability. For example, the physical presence of a nuisance depreciates the value of a home that is located across the street from a tavern. Some areas are liable to hazards such as the possibility of floods, landslides, or perhaps so common a problem as an excessive volume of automobile or truck traffic. Not every hazard is readily apparent; but the possible existence of any threat to value should not be overlooked.

Provisions for gas, electricity, water, telephone service, and storm and sanitary sewers are essential to meet the standard of living in municipal areas. The adequacy of these services affects a neighborhood's desirability. A deficiency in any one tends to decrease value. If water and sewage facilities have not yet been installed, the value of land is regularly less than the value of the same or similar land after installation has been accomplished. The availability of utilities affects the direction and timing of new neighborhood growth or development.

Social Considerations in Neighborhood Analysis

Consideration of social factors in neighborhood analysis is necessarily a subjective process. It is difficult, if not impossible, to ascertain and quantify accurately the real opinions and preferences, with respect to social factors, of the many people who comprise a given market, and then attempt to relate these opinions and preferences to an effect on value. Accordingly, the appraiser should exercise caution in placing too great a reliance on social factors when arriving at a value conclusion. From an appraiser's viewpoint, the social characteristics of a residential neighborhood are significant only to the extent that they are considered by the buying public and can be objectively and accurately analyzed by the appraiser. While the appraiser must be sensitive to social changes, neighborhood analysis, like any other part of the appraisal process, must be unbiased.

It was once common practice to examine the racial composition of a neighborhood in an effort to detect any signs of nonconformity or change. Such practice is now regarded as misdirected. This evolution in appraisal practice reflects corresponding evolution in social attitudes and public policy (see Conformity in Chapter 3).

Another example of social change of direct concern to the appraiser is the growing preference for social heterogeneity in some neighborhoods. In such areas the traditional social groupings have little or no relevance in the appraisal process. In a changing society, there can be no universal set of social standards, and the factors that are relevant in one neighborhood may be irrelevant in another. The objective of the analysis should, therefore, be to identify factors that are relevant and can be objectively measured, without attempting to assess deviation from some presupposed social norm.

Economic Considerations in Neighborhood Analysis

The higher the percentage of homeownership in a neighborhood, the more pride is visible in the appearance of its properties and the more community responsibility is felt by its citizens. Pertinent statistics regarding the percentage of homeownership may be available from census data and city directories or may be obtained by spot-checking an area.

Rental data provides clues to the financial capability of a neighborhood's occupants. Their income levels also are revealed by census information, newspaper surveys, and private studies. Such information indicates the price levels the residents can afford for the rental or purchase of property.

Vacancy statistics frequently are compiled by newspaper and other fact-finding agencies. Other significant statistics include the quantity of classified newspaper advertising for rent or for sale. This data helps the appraiser to estimate the strength of housing demand and the extent of supply.

The existence of vacant lots or acreage suitable for development may forecast much construction activity, or it may indicate a lack of demand. Current construction creates trends that affect the value of existing improvements. Careful study of these factors is helpful in rating the probable future desirability of an area.

Block-by-block information helps to pinpoint directional trends of growth. A neighborhood may be developing, it may be static, or it may be declining. This may be a local phenomenon or it may affect the entire community. A change in the economic base on which a community depends (e.g., the addition or loss of a major industry) is frequently reflected in an impact on the rate of population growth or decline. Sales demand and rental occupancy levels tend to remain strong when population is growing and to lag when the population of a community is declining.

Governmental Considerations in Neighborhood Analysis

Tax burdens are greater in some areas than in others. Where these areas are in the same community, variations in taxes are significant in making comparisons. Sometimes special assessment levies in a certain location become so heavy that they seriously affect the marketability of property. The benefits resulting from special assessments frequently do not enhance the obtainable sale price in proportion to their cost; nevertheless, the costs must be offset. As a rule, properties that are otherwise comparable to those not subject to special assessments can be expected to bring a lower sale price. For example, assume that two identical properties, located in the same block but on different streets, are each worth $35,000 if free of encumbrances. If however, one were subject to a $1,000 special assessment lien, its value, subject to this lien, may be $34,000. Market evidence may indicate that typical purchasers are not discounting for the lien.

Divergent tax rates may similarly affect value. Local taxes may favor or discriminate against certain classifications of property. It is advisable to examine the local structure of assessed values and tax rates to compare the burdens created by various forms of taxes and their apparent effect on the value of different classes of real estate.

Sound judgments about neighborhoods or individual properties cannot be made without adequate data concerning public and private restrictions. These include zoning and fire ordinances; building, plumbing, and sanitary codes; and other governmental controls.

The federal secondary market organizations have developed an appraisal form that effectively summarizes relevant neighborhood factors. The Federal Home Loan Mortgage Corporation (FHLMC) and the Federal National Mortgage Association (FNMA) each year purchase billions of dollars in conventional single-family mortgages. Consequently, the standard appraisal form they require for loans submitted to them is gaining wide use (see Figure 6.1).

Among the principal factors that may tend to improve value in residential neighborhoods are:

1. Convenience to activity centers such as educational, religious, and recreational facilities
2. Neighborhood organizations (block clubs, improvement associations, etc.)
3. Visual appeal
4. Satisfactory transportation facilities and good approaches
5. Natural topographical and geographical advantages
6. Good planning and adequate utilities
7. Conformity in land use and sensible zoning

The appraiser's minimal task is to analyze the neighborhood in accordance with these advantageous factors as well as those that may tend to depreciate value. Among the latter are:

1. Declining rentals or sale prices of surrounding properties
2. Abnormal vacancy level
3. Vandalism or litter
4. Movement of commercial or industrial uses into the area
5. Pollution from smoke, noise, or heavy traffic
6. Miscellaneous factors, such as lack of zoning protection, in-

Figure 6.1. Neighborhood Analysis Section — FHLMC Form 70/FNMA Form 1004

					Good	Avg.	Fair	Poor
Location	☐ Urban	☐ Suburban	☐ Rural	Employment Stability	☐	☐	☐	☐
Built Up	☐ Over 75%	☐ 25% to 75%	☐ Under 25%	Convenience to Employment	☐	☐	☐	☐
Growth Rate ☐ Fully Dev.	☐ Rapid	☐ Steady	☐ Slow	Convenience to Shopping	☐	☐	☐	☐
Property Values	☐ Increasing	☐ Stable	☐ Declining	Convenience to Schools	☐	☐	☐	☐
Demand/Supply	☐ Shortage	☐ In Balance	☐ Over Supply	Adequacy of Public Transportation	☐	☐	☐	☐
Marketing Time	☐ Under 3 Mos.	☐ 4–6 Mos.	☐ Over 6 Mos.	Recreational Facilities	☐	☐	☐	☐

Present Land Use ____ % 1 Family ____ % 2–4 Family ____ % Apts. ____ % Condo ____ % Commercial

____ % Industrial ____ % Vacant ____ %

Change in Present Land Use ☐ Not Likely ☐ Likely (*) ☐ Taking Place (*)

(*) From _____ To _____

Predominant Occupancy ☐ Owner ☐ Tenant ____ % Vacant

Single Family Price Range $ _____ to $ _____ Predominant Value $ _____

Single Family Age _____ yrs to _____ yrs Predominant Age _____ yrs

	Good	Avg.	Fair	Poor
Adequacy of Utilities	☐	☐	☐	☐
Property Compatibility	☐	☐	☐	☐
Protection from Detrimental Conditions	☐	☐	☐	☐
Police and Fire Protection	☐	☐	☐	☐
General Appearance of Properties	☐	☐	☐	☐
Appeal to Market	☐	☐	☐	☐

Note: FHLMC/FNMA do not consider the racial composition of the neighborhood to be a relevant factor and it must not be considered in the appraisal.

Comments including those factors, favorable or unfavorable, affecting marketability (e.g. public parks, schools, view, noise) _____

NEIGHBORHOOD

creasing taxes, lack of adequate planning, congestion, mixture of architectural styles, lack of trees or landscaping, or lack of community spirit as evidenced by the level of maintenance

ANALYZING THE APARTMENT DISTRICT

Apartment districts differ to some degree from single family residential areas, but are influenced by many of the same factors that affect private homes. A residential neighborhood is usually a geographical area of considerable extent. In large cities an apartment district usually covers an extensive area, but in smaller cities it may be quite limited in size, dispersed, or not defined. Apartments may be of multistory, garden,[1] row or town house design,[2] and may take on the character of individual homes in the form of cooperatives[3] or condominiums.[4]

The factors and amenities that affect the apartment neighborhood may be outlined in the same way as for the private dwelling district, but with some change of emphasis. In an apartment area, desirability and value may be influenced by:

1. Convenience to places of employment
2. Adequacy of transportation service
3. Convenience of access to shopping centers, theatres, and cultural institutions
4. Presence or absence of convenient school facilities and their significance to the tenants
5. Reputation of the neighborhood
6. Residential atmosphere, appearance of the neighborhood, and adequate protection against unwanted commercial and industrial intrusion
7. Proximity to parks, lakes, rivers, or other natural advantages that make residence more desirable; this involves the extent to which others' enjoyment of these natural advantages impinges on the privacy and quiet of the residents

1. American Institute of Real Estate Appraisers and Society of Real Estate Appraisers, *Real Estate Appraisal Terminology*, ed. Byrl N. Boyce (Cambridge, Mass: Ballinger Publishing Company, 1975), p. 99.
2. *Ibid.*, p. 208.
3. *Ibid.*, p. 51.
4. *Ibid.*, p. 47.

8. Supply of vacant apartment sites that are likely to be built on, with the potential effect of making present accommodations either more or less desirable
9. Sufficient parking for tenants and guests
10. Economic status of tenants
11. Amount of vacancy and tenant turnover rate

These factors and other pertinent data form the background for the appraiser's study of rental housing property. In some cities statistics are available concerning the supply of apartments, vacancy, and rent levels. Where statistics are not available, the appraiser may make a personal survey of the area.

ANALYZING THE COMMERCIAL DISTRICT

The commercial district and its property values are influenced by the factors that affect the value of the residential property surrounding it. In appraising a commercial property, then, the neighborhood is defined as the grouping of stores plus the area the stores serve.

Is the store district purely a local grouping along a business street or freeway service road? Is it a development adjacent to a public transportation intersection? Is it a regional or neighborhood center? Is it the downtown central business district? Depending on the type, the appraiser will seek answers to various questions, although the primary concern will be the competitive outlook. Nowhere does the principle of change have greater application.

In the analysis of the commercial district, the emphasis is on the quantity and quality of purchasing power available to the shopping area.

Desirability and value are also influenced by:

1. The 100% location or core of the grouping of stores
2. The direction of visible growth
3. Enterprise of retailers; their investment in inventory and leasehold improvements
4. Availability of land for expansion and customer parking
5. Character and location of competition, existing or anticipated
6. Buying power of the trading area and the economic trends of the contributing residential neighborhood

7. Pedestrian or vehicular traffic count
8. Physical factors such as visibility, access, medians, traffic signals

When analyzing strung-out local retail groupings, the appraiser also examines the zoning policies that govern the supply of competing sites.The reasons for vacancy and business failure are studied, and the level of rents compared to current rent levels for stores in new buildings is considered.

Commercial establishments located at public transfer points have been adversely affected by the increasing use of the automobile and the decline in use of public transportation. Business from these areas has been lost chiefly to regional and neighborhood centers with adequate parking space. This does not mean that every such commercial center is in a state of decline. Where surrounded by well-developed apartment neighborhoods, businesses may continue to prosper.

Central Business Districts

Central business districts of a number of large cities have been the subject of study in past business surveys.[5] The general pattern shows a tendency toward fewer stores and less increase in sales than for the metropolitan area as a whole. Downtown merchants endeavor to counteract this trend of retail decentralization, usually through improved public transportation, more parking, better access, and coordinated sales promotion programs. The downtown district embraces more than retail trade. Offices, wholesale uses, and entertainment may be additional balancing influences. The appraiser makes a point of understanding the direction of downtown trends by studying available factual data.

Regional Centers

The regional center, with an extensive parking facility and from 40 to more than 100 stores, constitutes a quite different category of commercial neighborhood. The major tenants consist of one or more

---

5. *Survey of Current Business* (Washington, D.C.: U.S. Department of Commerce, monthly). Biennial supplement is *Business Statistics.*

department stores offering a full range of merchandise. While the emphasis is on apparel stores, balance is usually achieved by including a larger number and a greater variety of the same type of stores found in the neighborhood center. In addition, there may be banks; service establishments; medical, dental, and business offices; and sometimes a theatre. The trade area for a regional center may include several neighborhood centers. Despite competition for certain segments of economic support, neighborhood centers provide services to their immediate areas and may be considered supplementary to, rather than competitive with, the major shopping services provided by the large regional center.

Regional centers not only develop a substantial value for the land occupied; they also have a substantial impact on values in surrounding locations. They affect adjacent or nearby land favorably by creating a demand for satellite stores, office buildings, and other commercial uses. Beyond this immediate area, they increase demand for new single or multifamily residential development.

Neighborhood Shopping Centers

In most localities there is a steady demand for the neighborhood shopping center, which typically includes 10 or more stores with parking. The success of this center is keyed primarily to supermarkets, drug stores, variety stores, and service establishments. These centers serve the day-to-day needs of a limited surrounding and supporting area and are seldom seriously affected by the advent of a new regional center. The emphasis is on prominent exposure and adequate parking, although public transportation and location are important factors.

Community Centers

When a neighborhood center expands to include a department store branch or when the number or size of the stores exceeds that which can be supported by the neighborhood, it may be referred to as a community center. Because of its dependence on the ability to attract customers from beyond the local environment, such a center may be vulnerable to regional center competition. It may be too small to compete with the big regional center and too large for the neighborhood to support.

In the appraisal analysis of any center, care is essential in making a feasibility study or marketing survey. Helpful statistics may be found in various publications. Business and population census data form the basis for statistics such as the disposable income per family in a trading area and how this income is divided among food, general merchandise, automobiles, and other classifications. Such information is essential to the appraiser in gauging the amount of business a trading area will support. However, the available business still must be allocated among competing centers of trade. Patterns of customer buying are studied carefully by analysts employed by the major chain stores.

Shifts in Retail Groupings

A study of the history of business districts clearly shows that there is a constant shifting in a dynamic economy. A business district may expand and encroach on land devoted to other uses when the community and its surrounding area are growing. An entire business district almost literally may leap to a totally different location if room for expansion is lacking. Such a shift is usually in the direction of the better residential sections of the community where the purchasing power of the inhabitants is highest. The original location is left with no business activity and eventually will drift into a less profitable use.

ANALYZING THE INDUSTRIAL DISTRICT

Values of land and buildings in an industrial district are influenced by considerations such as the character of the district, the available labor supply, the adequacy of transportation, the economy of bringing in raw material and of distributing finished products, the political climate, and the availability of utilities. To arrive at an informed conclusion about the value of any industrial property, the data pertinent to these categories should be obtained.

Characteristics of the Industrial District

Industrial districts vary from heavy industry, such as steel plants, foundries, and chemicals, to assembly or other "clean" operations.

In most urban areas heavy- to light-use districts are established by zoning ordinances, which may limit not only uses but also air pollution, noise levels, and the operations that may be carried on outside of buildings.

So-called manufacturing or warehouse districts vary from older districts where typical units are obsolete multistory elevator buildings, with limited parking and expansion area, to the newer type industrial districts and parks with modern one-story buildings. In each such district there tends to be a value pattern reflective of the reaction of the market to its location and the character of sites and improvements. For example, the market for older multistory buildings tends to stabilize at a certain price per square foot of gross floor area, rather than at their physically depreciated reproduction cost. Similarly, prices for modern one-story buildings in a good district tend to be influenced by replacement cost.

An important item influencing land value in industrial districts is the availability of public utilities including sanitary and storm sewers and municipal (or well) water. Prevailing levels of real estate and personal property taxes also influence desirability and may be reflected in real estate values.

Availability of labor.   No industrial district is desirable unless there is an adequate labor supply available in the categories required by its manufacturing plants. Labor requirements of plants vary from unskilled to semi-skilled and lower management and supervisory levels. The dependence of industry on an adequate labor supply of a suitable character frequently is the reason that these districts are located close to the residential areas of the workers. Often special inducements, such as a company cafeteria and other employee facilities, or social programs of the company are provided to attract employees to a particular plant. The park-like atmosphere of the plant with landscaped grounds may be an inducement to prospective employees. A study of the available labor supply is a necessary step in the analysis of a particular industrial district.

Availability of materials.   Manufacturing operations require a convenient and economic source of raw or semi-finished materials and facilities for convenient and economic distribution of their manufactured products. Depending on the type of product, the desirability of a district or a site is influenced by means of access to their unprocessed raw material.

Distribution facilities.   The adequacy and acceptable economy of shipment facilities by air, rail, truck, or waterway vary with the size, weight, and character of the commodity and the distance of shipment. For many industrial operations, the former importance of rail facilities has diminished with more extensive use of truck shipment. Accessibility to major highways, adequate ingress and egress, and on-site parking and maneuver areas constitute important considerations for most manufacturing or warehouse operations.

FARM NEIGHBORHOODS

A neighborhood is described as being in some sense a homogeneous area. Some farm neighborhoods, because of a certain homogeneity, can extend over several counties. The type of soil, the crops grown, the typical land use, the size of the typical operation and whether it is run by the owner or tenant are factors that usually help to define the neighborhood.

Grain farm neighborhoods usually are characterized by soil types and topography conducive to the growing and harvesting of corn, wheat, and other grain crops. Orchards are another type of farming in which the soil and climate combine to create a distinct economy. Areas that are not capable of producing cash crops may be adapted to production of particular grasses. The boundaries of these areas are related to altitude and climate. Generally these grasslands are used for livestock production. Dairy neighborhoods are located where the soil type is best for the production of pasture grasses and hay. These areas are traversed by good highways leading to primary marketing centers for the farm's products. As in any neighborhood, the standard of the farm community is dependent on government services such as roads and schools, availability of utilities, and proximity to cultural institutions, markets, and shopping centers.

REDLINING AND THE APPRAISER

A discussion of redlining may seem inappropriate in an appraisal text, but it is included to acquaint appraisers with a subject that is becoming increasingly relevant to neighborhood analysis particularly in connection with residential neighborhoods.

Since the attitudes and decisions of lenders and insurers may affect the marketability of homes within a particular neighborhood, an understanding of redlining will be helpful for many types of neighborhood analysis problems.

Redlining refers to the reluctance of lenders, investors, or insurers to make loans, invest, or issue insurance on usual terms in a particular geographic area because of some feature or characteristic in the area that is perceived as adversely affecting the utility or security and hence the value of individual parcels of property in the area.

The word *redlining* originated many years ago to describe a practice, once engaged in by both private and governmental organizations, of drawing a red line on a map around the borders of areas considered to contain such adverse features and regarded as unsuitable for lending, insuring, or investing purposes. The term is now applied figuratively whether or not an actual map or red pencil is used. The word *greenlining* is sometimes used to describe a policy on the part of a lender, group of lenders, or other organizations to affirmatively seek out loans in specific neighborhoods. The word *greenlining* is also sometimes used to characterize strategies employed by homeowners or activist groups to protect a neighborhood from the effects of redlining.

Redlining can be a rational response to a real risk that exists in an area. For instance, property located in a floodplain, in a slide area, or in close proximity to a geologic fault may present a level of risk that would be unacceptable to a mortgage lender or insurer. Redlining practices are said to gain an impropriety, however, when the perceptions of risk on which they are based are unrealistic, inaccurate, or arbitrary, or when the boundaries of affected areas are overbroad so that the practices result in negative decisions being made with respect to whole neighborhoods that may contain many sound properties and might otherwise be stable and viable.

The term *racial redlining* refers to the practice of basing loan, insurance, or investment criteria on the racial characteristics of the people who live in a particular neighborhood, presumably because of a perception of risk arising from the racial or social composition of the population or changes in this composition. Racial redlining has been held to be unlawful by the courts and by several federal agencies which have regulatory authority over lending institutions, including the Federal Home Loan Bank Board, the Federal Reserve Board, and the United States Department of Housing and Urban Development. In addition, the major secondary market organizations that purchase home loans (FHLMC and FNMA) have stipulated that the racial composition of areas must not be considered in appraisals for home loans submitted for purchase by these organizations.

SUMMARY

A neighborhood may be a segment of a city, town, or village; or it may be an entire community. Its character may be residential, commercial, industrial, or agricultural.

In the analysis of neighborhoods—whether for private dwellings, apartments, commerce, industry, or farming—many factors may be pertinent. They may include population growth; economic status; occupations; community interests; convenience to transportation; educational, religious, and recreational facilities; road pattern; municipal services; employment opportunities; and business centers. The relative importance of these factors changes over time, reflecting changes in lifestyles, social customs, and economic conditions. There is a difference in the emphasis on the applicability of each factor, depending on the type of neighborhood being analyzed. Neighborhood analysis is not a fixed process, and neighborhoods are not fixed in their characteristics. They are always changing—some slowly, others rapidly. Such neighborhood changes affect the utility of parcels of land and the improvements thereon. Because a property is an integral part of a neighborhood, its value is affected by shifts in the economic, social, and physical forces creating the environment. In some instances utility is increased; in others it is decreased, resulting in changes in value. The valuation process, in arriving at a well-reasoned and credible conclusion of the value of a property, should include an analysis of the effect of the neighborhood and neighborhood trends. The form and depth of the analysis may vary according to the need, but the objective of the process should be to fairly and accurately represent the considerations of buyers contemplating the purchase of property in the neighborhood.

7
Land or Site Analysis

The basic principles of real property value apply to land valuation. The potential value of a parcel of land is measured in terms of the income imputable to it after the other agents in production have been satisfied. This surplus productivity is attributed to the land. The greater the surplus, the higher is the land value. The principle of substitution also is applicable because the value of the land tends to be limited by the price at which an equally desirable substitute parcel can be purchased.

The value of unimproved land is enhanced by improvements to the land such as grading and installation of streets or utilities. With the addition of these improvements, raw land may be transformed into lots or sites ready for the addition of buildings or other improvements thereon. Although raw land may be platted, the words *lot* and *site* in this book refer to land that has been improved to the extent that it is ready for its intended use or development. In applying the principle of substitution to derive a market value estimate for the land component of property value, this distinction between raw land and an improved site is important. Sales of raw land and improved land require adjustment for the cost of improvement before valid comparison is possible.

In estimating the value of improved real estate, the appraiser analyzes two distinct entities: the land and the improvements on the land. Although the two are joined physically, it is often desirable and necessary to value the land separately. The buildings and other improvements are subject to deterioration; they are a wasting asset. The value of land may change, but land is presumed to exist indefinitely.

PURPOSE OF LAND OR SITE VALUATION

Separate valuations of the land may be required for specific purposes, such as:

1. Local tax assessments
2. Estimation of building depreciation
3. Application of appraisal techniques
4. Establishment of ground rent
5. Condemnation appraising
6. Estimate of casualty loss
7. Valuation of agricultural land

Local Tax Assessments

In many sections of the country, local ad valorem real estate tax laws require that land and buildings be valued separately in order to achieve assessment uniformity. Special assessments for public improvements, such as streets, water lines, and sewers, are levied, frequently based on their probable effect on land values.

Estimation of Building Depreciation

Under federal income tax regulations, the owner of an improved property can provide for an annual expense deduction to cover estimated depreciation only on the improvements. Accordingly, for this purpose the owner must allocate the original cost of an acquired property between land and improvements.

Site valuation is useful in estimating the degree of economic obsolescence of existing improvements. Assume, for example, that an analysis reveals that the highest and best use is as a store location and that the value of the land for this purpose is $100,000. Suppose further that the land now is improved with an apartment building, but that the value of the entire property, improvements included, based on the net income from the apartments is only $75,000. It is apparent that the land is not being put to its highest and best use, and that the apartment structure is an underimprovement with little or negative value.

Assume a case where the obsolescence is less severe. Suppose the improvement were a store and apartment building which, on a $80,000 parcel of land, would be worth $400,000. The valuation would be divided:

Land value	$ 80,000
Depreciated building value	320,000
Total	$400,000

If located on a parcel of land that would be worth $200,000 when developed to its highest and best use, the above building would be a misplaced improvement, partially obsolete but still joined with the land for years to come.

In applying the cost approach, the total value of the property is still only $400,000. However, since the value of the land is $200,000, the depreciated value of the building based on reproduction cost less depreciation (physical, functional, and economic) represents the difference, and a separate valuation for the land is basic. It is shown thus:

Land value	$200,000
Depreciated building value	200,000
Total	$400,000

Application of Appraisal Techniques

Separate site valuation is important in applying the building residual technique in the income approach to value. In this technique a reasonable return on the land value is deducted from the net income earned by the total property. Hence a separate land value is needed.

A separate land value may be required also where properties subject to long-term leases are involved and it is necessary to project what the land may be worth at the end of the building's useful life or at the end of the long-term lease. In such circumstances this projected value is usually considered equivalent to the present value unless there are reasons for an assumption that the land value will either increase or decrease during the projection period.

Establishment of Ground Rent

Ground rentals under long- or short-term leases are generally based on a relationship to the land value. Hence an estimate of land value is usually a prerequisite for establishing the rental figure.

Condemnation Valuations

In some states valuations made for condemnation purposes require that land and buildings be valued as a unit without separation. In other states testimony concerning separated values of land and improvements is expected.

Estimate of Casualty Loss

In the case of the destruction of the improvements by fire, a separate value of the land and the buildings may be required to establish the value of the improvements destroyed.

Valuation of Agricultural Land

In agricultural property valuation the value of the land is usually the dominant factor. Except in unusual circumstances, the value of structures on the land depends on their utility and contribution to the productivity of the land. Minor structures may be included in the agricultural land value.

With loss of fertility or repeated removal of sod and topsoil, agricultural land may depreciate in a physical sense, although the existence of the land as an area of the earth's surface remains as a permanent asset. This loss in value is in contrast to the typical concept of land, particularly urban land, as being imperishable and, despite value fluctuations, not subject to depreciation.

Frequently in recent years improved agricultural property is purchased, and the improvements and a small tract of land are sold for residential use. The remainder of the land continues to be farmed, usually as part of a larger assemblage.

DATA REQUIREMENTS

An adequate land study requires that pertinent types of data be assembled and considered.

Title and Record Data

Essential facts include data relating to taxes, special assessments, zoning, restrictions, easements, other pertinent legal matters, and the legal description of the property.

Taxes. Taxes are intended to pay for services that make owner-ship more desirable. But net benefits obviously decrease when taxes are out of proportion to income. Therefore, the appraiser compares the tax status—assessed values, tax rates, and tax burdens—with that of competitive or comparable sites.

In many communities the assessed value of land for taxes bears a reasonable relation to market value, particularly when a recent reassessment has been made. In other communities this may not be true, or assessments may not be current.

Unit-foot depth and corner premium tables may be used to establish uniformity in valuations made by assessors for tax purposes. The purpose of such tables is to express equivalent values for 1 foot of frontage applicable to sites of varying depth. The standard unit of land represented is 1 foot of frontage for a typical lot width and a specified depth. For a lot of any stated type or location, this standard depth is established. It originally was fixed in most localities at 100 feet.

If the adopted standard depth is 100 feet, a lot 50 x 100 feet with a value of $2,175 would have a unit-front-foot value of $43.50. Another lot, 50 feet wide with a depth of 150 feet, might have a value of $2,500, or $50 per front foot, with the same unit-front-foot value of $43.50—that is, it would be equivalent in value to $43.50 per front foot for a depth of 100 feet, times a depth factor of 115%. The percentages are designed to provide a uniform system of measuring the additional value that accrues because of added depth.

Depth tables are neither universally applicable nor infallible. The validity of any depth or corner table as indicating the effect of depth on value is dependent on its applicability to each location, situation, or type of use. Depth tables vary for different types of property. A depth table developed to apply to conditions in one city may not apply to conditions existing in another city. Since real estate is a local product, its value is founded on local conditions and usage.

One of the first depth rules was the 4-3-2-1 rule: the front quarter of a lot contributes 40% of the value; the second quarter, 30%; the third quarter, 20%; and the fourth, or rear quarter, 10%. Because this left too wide a margin for assessment purposes, the deficiency usually has been overcome by the establishment of more specific depth tables expressed in percentages for every foot, or at least for every 10 feet of depth, in order to reflect the conditions applicable in a certain locality or to certain types of property (residential, business, industrial, commercial).

Similarly, corner influence (premium) tables have been developed for ad valorem tax purposes, in order to establish the amount by which the market value per unit foot of an inside lot is increased for a lot with a corner location. Such tables are also related to localities and types of land for which they are prepared.

Both depth and corner premium tables have their most practical use in mass appraising for local ad valorem tax purposes.[1] The objective of such tables is to approximate the effect of depth and corner influence on the value of specific properties in a mass appraisal project, in order to arrive at value estimates approximating those obtainable by individual appraisal of any single property in the class to which these tables are applied. In a valuation, averages are seldom appropriate, and a specific analysis of the effect of depth and corner influence on the utility of the property is in order.

Special assessments.   Unlike general property taxes, special assessments apply only to specific districts and only for definite periods. Sometimes a property falls under the jurisdiction of several districts, each of which has the power to levy special assessments. Thus a property could be inequitably burdened and consequently lose desirability. However, special assessments actually are installment payments for improvements such as streets and utilities which usually enhance value. A property so encumbered could be valued subject to the payment of the remaining installments; or the amount of the remaining special assessment installments could be deducted from the value estimate derived from comparable sites that are free of such liens.

Such special assessments are often computed similarly to valuation for ad valorem tax purposes. They are usually based on the benefits (increase in value) anticipated as a result of the improvements for which the special assessments are levied.

Zoning.   Zoning is a legally imposed restriction on the uses of a

---

1. Mass appraisal, such as a uniform system of valuation for local real estate tax assessment purposes. See Walter R. Kuehnle, *Valuation of Real Estate for Ad Valorem Tax Purposes* (Chicago: Author, 1954), p. 16

site, but the site's highest and best use may not necessarily be any of the uses designated by a zoning ordinance. Changes in uses permitted by zoning may substantially increase or decrease the value of the property in accordance with the permitted use. Properties are frequently bought and sold subject to the success of obtaining a zoning change, such as residential to more intensive apartment use, or residential to industrial or business use.

Sometimes zoning changes, in creating a condition of monopoly, allow the older, nonconforming properties a land utilization with which new buildings cannot compete. Over the past half-century there has been a trend to reduce the percentage of the lot that the building is permitted to occupy. Thus properties with buildings constructed in the past, under more liberal land coverage provisions, may give the land a monopoly value for the life of the existing improvements. This is disclosed by examination of the latest zoning maps and zoning ordinances. Citations from these are often included in appraisal reports to substantiate the appraiser's interpretation of permissible usages. Sometimes a legal interpretation may be required. Differences of value opinion in court may have their source in misunderstanding of permissible use under the terms of zoning ordinance.

When more land is allocated to one kind of use than is economically sound, the principle of balance is violated, and the potential value of the land may be adversely affected.

Value may be similarly affected by a change in zoning that, because of a lower classification, reduces the allowable intensity of use. Such down-zoning is encountered with increasing frequency in some areas.

Restrictions and easements.   There are two kinds of restrictions: public and private. Public restrictions (in addition to zoning ordinances) are those imposed by law. They include limitations set by fire ordinances; building, plumbing, and sanitation codes; housing acts; and other legislative enactments. Public restrictions usually are not so stringent as private restrictions, although both deal with essentially the same matters. Both are concerned with permissible building uses and designate the permitted type of building materials, building heights and volume, ground coverage by buildings, and setback lines.

When legal private and public restrictions conflict, the more stringent prevails. For instance, if public zoning regulation permits only single family homes and private agreements permit business, the latter are nullified by the former.

Private restrictions are contractual limitations. They are usually imposed by the deeds used to convey title. Sometimes they are imposed by means of a general plan of restriction for an entire tract recorded by the developer of the land. Then, whenever a lot is deeded to a purchaser, the deed provides for the title to be conveyed subject to the recorded restrictions. Legal private restrictions are of greatest significance when there are no public controls.

At one time racial and religious restrictive covenants were not unusual in single family subdivisions. In the 1930s and early 1940s the Federal Housing Administration sometimes required such restrictions as a condition of granting mortgage insurance. Restrictions of this kind have been unlawful for many years following a 1948 decision of the Supreme Court and would now violate many federal, state, and local fair housing laws. Occasionally, deeds containing such racially restrictive covenants still appear, but they are not enforceable by property owners. In some areas recorders of deeds cannot accept documents that contain racially restrictive clauses.

Title reports are the usual source of data concerning private restrictions. Recorded deeds may mention that restrictions are imposed, but usually do not specify them.

Reservations retained by grantors in the chain of title, such as easements on and rights of way across a property, restrict the rights of subsequent owners. An easement for ingress and egress in favor of parties other than the owner may decrease a property's utility and value. However, an easement attaching to adjacent property may be beneficial to ownership of a property. Rights of way, party-wall agreements, and other agreements that run with the land can either restrict or enhance the land's utility and value.

Restrictions and easements that affect property rights may be contracts that bind only the contracting parties, rather than covenants that run with the land and bind all parties in the subsequent chain of title.

An estimate of the value of an easement or right of way independent of the fee title to the land is an appraisal of one or more but not all of the bundle of rights constituting the entire property. Depending on how comprehensive are the rights included, the value of an easement may range from a small percentage of the value of the easement area to the value of the whole. There may be additional value loss to adjacent land in the same ownership owing to creation of the easement. Pipelines, electric transmission lines, cable lines, railroad rights of way, airport approach patterns, avigation easements, and often roadways are examples of easement ownerships that involve substantial interests in the bundle of rights of the land they traverse.

Of growing importance in the valuation of land is the effect of environmental studies that consider the impact of a proposed land development on wildlife, flora, or surrounding properties. These studies involve time for preparation and additional time for approval; they may result in restrictions on potential development that adversely affect the value of a site.

Legal description. The legal description identifies a property in such terms that it cannot be confused with any other parcel. Explained in the next few pages are several systems of legal description that have long been in use.

Government Survey System. This rectangular system resulted from the work of a committee headed by Thomas Jefferson and was adopted by the Continental Congress in 1785. This plan, dividing the land into a series of rectangles, provided only for townships six miles square. Since these areas proved too large, Congress passed an act in 1796 directing that these townships be divided into 36 sections. In 1800 Congress passed an act directing the subdivision of sections into halves. By the Act of February 11, 1805, Congress further provided for division into quarter sections. Not until 1820 did Congress, by another act, provide for half-quarter sections; finally in 1832 Congress directed the subdivision of all public lands into quarter-quarter sections (40 acres), the smallest statutory division of regular sections.

The government—or rectangular—survey system ideally provides for a unit of land approximately 24 miles square, bounded by base lines running east and west, and meridians extending north and south, as shown in Figure 7.1. The north boundary of the square is slightly shorter than the south boundary because the east and west boundary lines are true meridians of the earth and thus tend to converge toward

Figure 7.1.   Government Survey System

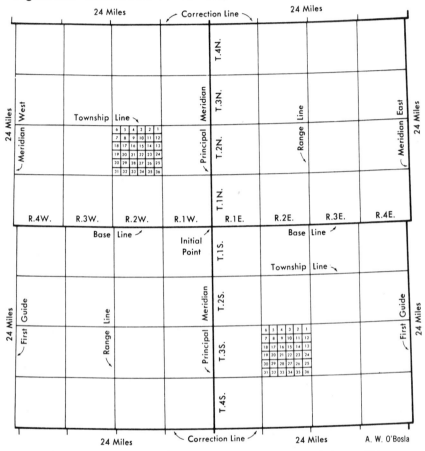

Source: John S. Hoag, *Fundamentals of Land Measurement* (Chicago: Chicago Title Insurance Company, n.d.).

the north in this hemisphere. The 24-mile-square unit is divided into areas six miles square, called townships. A tier is an east-and-west row of townships between two parallels of latitude six miles apart. A range is a north-and-south row of townships between two meridian lines also six miles apart. Ranges and tiers are assigned numbers from principal meridians and base lines. A township is divided into 36 sections, each one mile square.

The sections are numbered consecutively beginning with the sec-

Figure 7.2. Division of a Section of Land

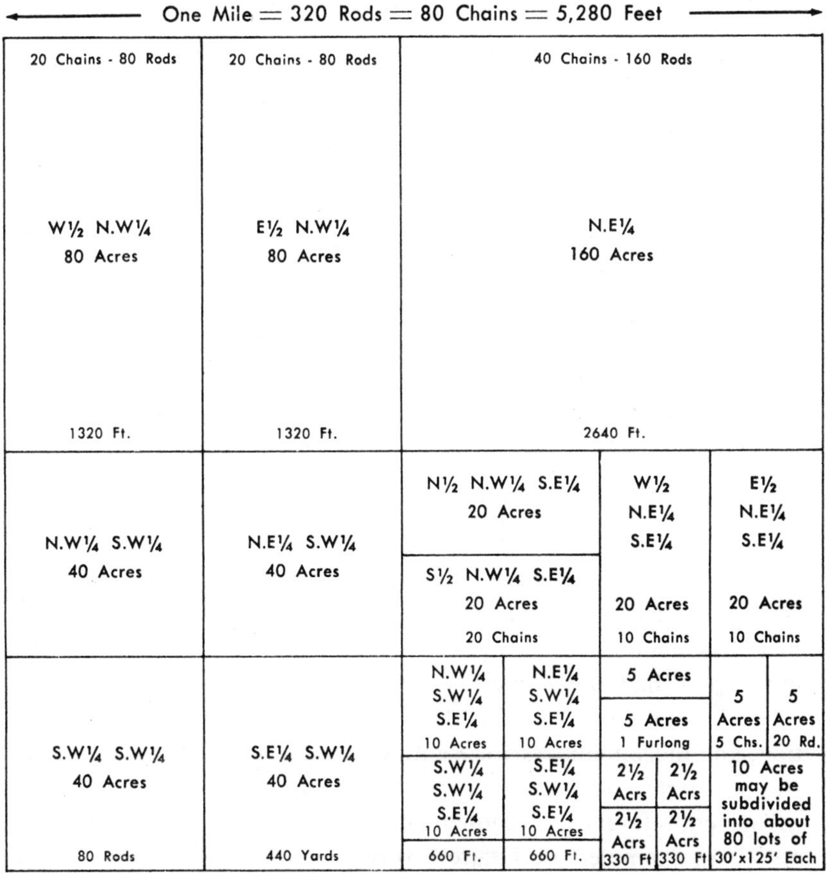

⟵——————— One Mile = 320 Rods = 80 Chains = 5,280 Feet ———————⟶

20 Chains - 80 Rods	20 Chains - 80 Rods	40 Chains - 160 Rods			
W½ N.W¼ 80 Acres	E½ N.W¼ 80 Acres	N.E¼ 160 Acres			
1320 Ft.	1320 Ft.	2640 Ft.			
N.W¼ S.W¼ 40 Acres	N.E¼ S.W¼ 40 Acres	N½ N.W¼ S.E¼ 20 Acres		W½ N.E¼ S.E¼	E½ N.E¼ S.E¼
		S½ N.W¼ S.E¼ 20 Acres 20 Chains		20 Acres 10 Chains	20 Acres 10 Chains
S.W¼ S.W¼ 40 Acres	S.E¼ S.W¼ 40 Acres	N.W¼ S.W¼ S.E¼ 10 Acres	N.E¼ S.W¼ S.E¼ 10 Acres	5 Acres 5 Acres 1 Furlong	5 Acres 5 Chs.	5 Acres 20 Rd.
		S.W¼ S.W¼ S.E¼ 10 Acres	S.E¼ S.W¼ S.E¼ 10 Acres	2½ Acrs	2½ Acrs	10 Acres may be
				2½ Acrs	2½ Acrs	subdivided into about
80 Rods	440 Yards	660 Ft.	660 Ft.	330 Ft	330 Ft	80 lots of 30'x125' Each

Courtesy of Chicago Real Estate Index Co.

tion at the northeast corner of each township and continuing west to the northwest corner. Then the sequence of numbers drops down one row and returns eastward. This process continues—east to west and west to east—until the entire township is numbered, with Section 36 in the southeast corner. As mentioned above, the township's northern boundary is not exactly six miles in length because.of the convergence of the meridians. This discrepancy, and others due to errors in measurement or alignment, are allowed for in the most westerly half mile of the township. Shortages or overages in acreage of sections thus are usually found on the west and north sides of townships. Fractional sections also resulted when they were bounded or bisected by navigable waters. Figure 7.2 illustrates the scheme of the government survey system.

Units of Measurement

1 Link is 7.92 inches.

1 Foot is 12 inches.

1 Yard is 3 feet or 36 inches.

1 Rod is 16½ feet, 5½ yards or 25 links.

1 Chain is 66 feet or 4 rods of 100 links.

1 Furlong is 660 feet or 40 rods.

1 Acre may be divided into about 8 lots 30 × 125 feet.

1 Mile is 8 furlongs, 320 rods, 80 chains or 5,280 feet.

1 Square rod is 272¼ square feet or 30¼ square yards.

1 Acre contains 43,560 square feet.

1 Acre contains 160 square rods.

1 Acre is about 8 rods by 20 rods long, or any two numbers (of rods) with a product of 160.

Lot and Block System. This system, derived from the rectangular survey system, applies in most urban communities. It originated in the manner in which these communities grew. The early land developers had their tracts surveyed and platted in rectangular blocks and lots. Each block and lot was then numbered for identification, and these numbers were entered on the plat map of the tract. Copies of this plat were filed in the county recorder's office for permanent reference. The lot and block system is simple and convenient. An example (see Figure 7.3) reads:

> Lots 23 and 24 in Block 8 in Tremont Ridge, a Subdivision of the Southwest Quarter of the Northwest Quarter of Section 18, Township 38 North, Range 14, East of the Third Principal Meridian in Cook County, Illinois.

Metes and Bounds System. This system identifies a property by delineating its boundaries in terms of a series of directions and distances from an identified initial point or place of beginning. Followed in many parts of the world, this system was introduced into the original 13 colonies and the southern states. Still widely encountered in the United States, it was in general use before the introduction of the government survey system.

Figure 7.3. Lot and Block System

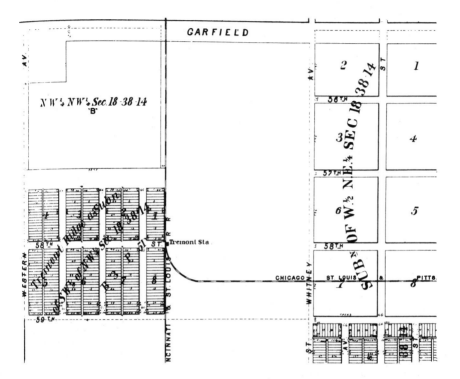

Landmarks, such as fixed features of landscapes and "witness trees," were originally used as points of reference in the metes and bounds system. A custom introduced from Europe, reportedly often used in colonial days, was that of the witness or "flogging fee." A young boy was given a fee to be taken to the witness tree to submit to a sound thrashing in the presence of an assembled group. While the efficiency of this method may be open to question, the theory was that during his entire life, he would never forget the location of that landmark. The metes and bounds system, which may also be used with the government survey system or the lot and block system, is illustrated in Figure 7.4.

Figure 7.4. Metes and Bounds System

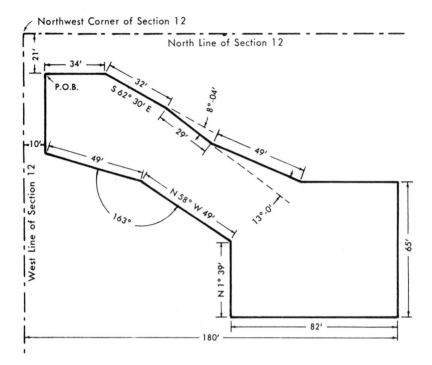

Description of Tract: Commencing at the Northwest corner of Section 12 thence South along the section line 21 feet; thence East 10 feet for a place of beginning; thence continuing East 34 feet; thence South 62 degrees, 30 minutes East 32 feet; thence Southeasterly along a line forming an angle of 8 degrees, 04 minutes to the right with a prolongation of the last described course 29 feet; thence South 13 degrees, 0 minutes to the left with a prolongation of the last described line a distance of 49 feet; thence East to a line parallel with the West line of said Section and 180 feet distant therefrom; thence South on the last described line a distance of 65 feet; thence due West a distance of 82 feet; thence North 1 degree West 39 feet; thence North 58 degrees West a distance of 49 feet; thence Northwesterly along a line forming an angle of 163 degrees as measured from right to left with the last described line a distance of 49 feet; thence North the the place of beginning.

If the parcel is not situated in a recorded subdivision, as frequently occurs in nonurban areas, a point of beginning must first be established. This may be accomplished by relating it to the government survey system. The parcel is then specifically identified by a metes and bounds description which starts from this point and, following the boundaries of the property, returns to conclude at this point. Such a survey is referred to as a traverse and, when encountered, it should be checked to ascertain that it does, in fact, "close" by returning to the point of beginning.

Geodetic Survey System. Another method of land survey is the United States Coast and Geodetic Survey System. It was initiated to identify tracts of land owned by the federal government, but gradually it has been extended throughout the nation. These survey maps are prepared by the United States Geological Survey Division, Department of the Interior. They show, among other things, height contours, latitude and longitude, existing rivers and streams, buildings and railroads. These printed maps are available on various scales by named quadrangles (see Figure 7.5).

This system is as exact as the science of measurement can reasonably be, and it integrates all real estate in the country into one unified system. The skeleton of this method is a network of "bench marks" which cover the entire country. Each is located by its latitude and longitude.

RELATION OF SITE TO LAND PATTERN

The utility of a parcel of land may be affected by forces and factors external to the land itself. Analysis of a site is not complete without careful examination of its relationship to surrounding land use patterns. This requires a study of the influence of such factors as abutting and nearby streets, contiguous and nearby sites, alleys, and traffic conditions.

Utility is also affected by physical attributes of the land that may prevent development to its highest and best use. Thus it is also important to accumulate data concerning physical factors pertaining to a site such as frontage and width, depth, shape, area, topography, drainage, landscaping, soil and subsoil conditions. The analysis of this data supplements the study of neighboring land use factors.

Figure 7.5.   United States Department of the Interior Geological Survey

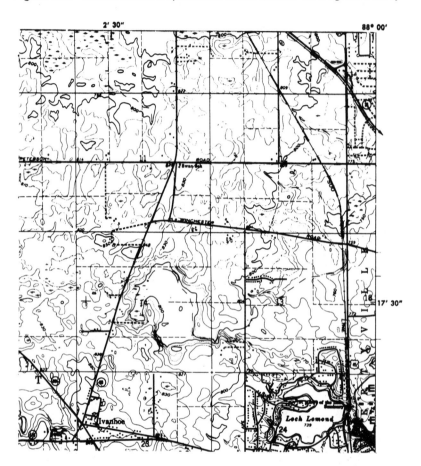

Mapped, edited, and published by the Geological Survey
Control by USGS and USC&GS

Topography by photogrammetric methods from aerial
photographs taken 1958. Field checked 1960

Polyconic projection. 1927 North American datum
10,000-foot grid based on Illinois coordinate system, east zone

This Map Complies with National Map Accuracy Standards
For Sale by U.S. Geological Survey, Washington, D.C.
And by the State Geological Survey, Urbana, Illinois

A Folder Describing Topographic Maps and
Symbols Is Available on Request

Reduced from original scale 1:24,000
Contour Interval 10 Feet
Dotted Lines Represent 5-Foot Contours
Datum is Mean Sea Level

APPROXIMATE MEAN
DECLINATION, 1960

Abutting Lots

The gridiron pattern of most cities may cause one side of a lot to abut on the rear lines of another. When all adjoining lots are improved with structures, the view from the abutting side is of backyards and garages. This usually results in decreased value.

The gridiron pattern also used alleys to separate rows of residential lots on opposite streets. Sometimes an alley may be laid out between a row of homes on one street and a row of store properties on another. Good residential development avoids such situations.

Width and Frontage

Although these terms are often used synonymously, their meanings differ. *Width* is the distance between the side lines and may vary at different distances from the front, as in the case of a triangular lot. A lot that is wider than another may possess greater usefulness and value because a larger building or several types of buildings may be erected on it. Width alone, however, does not indicate the presence of utility. Without proper depth, a site may not have sufficient area on which to build a satisfactory structure. Units of land measurement that relate to width alone are not adequate and may be misleading. The front foot is such a unit. It conveys nothing about depth or width at points away from the front line. Nevertheless, the front foot is a useful unit for making comparisons between sites, if its limitations are recognized. Most lots have one or more boundaries that provide exposure to a street or other thoroughfare.

Frontage refers to the length of boundary contiguous with the thoroughfare right of way. Frontage frequently is more important than average width because the extent of frontage provides an indication of prominence and accessibility. In practice, comparisons made in land analysis include both frontage and area.

Sometimes greater width results in decreased unit value. In an area where residential lots typically are 50 feet in width and frontage and worth $100 per front foot, an 80-foot lot might be worth only $6,400 or $80 a front foot. The reason for this is that the utility of the wider lot is not proportionately greater than that of the typical lot. Added width is accompanied by increased taxes and cost of maintenance without proportionately increased desirability or income-producing possibilities. Similarly, a 35-foot lot in the same district might be worth $2,625 or $75 per front foot, because it does not offer sufficient area to accommodate a building typical for the neighborhood.

To a certain extent, utility varies in direct proportion to width, if the width is uniform through the depth of the lot. Value varies in a like manner. However, simply because one lot is twice as wide as another does not mean that its value is twice as great even though the depth may be the same in each case. Certain widths are more adaptable to buildings intended for certain purposes. For example, a narrow lot may not be well adapted for use as an apartment site. A lot that is suitable for this use might be worth three or four times as much per foot of width or frontage, even though it is only twice as wide as the narrow lot. Similarly, the wide lot might be worth more than the combined value of two or more lots that, taken together, equal it in width, assuming that the smaller lots were in the hands of different owners. As separate lots, the smaller parcels might be worth $100 per front foot, but when combined in one parcel, the front foot value might be $150. This increment in unit value is called plottage value, which reflects the potential for a more profitable use owing to assemblage into a larger site.

Depth

Custom in different communities suggests the units to be used in estimating land value. In most large communities commercial land is valued in terms of a dollar amount per square foot. Industrial land generally is valued in terms of dollars per square foot or per acre. Single-family residential land is usually valued in terms of front feet; apartment sites in terms of front feet, square feet, or in terms of so many dollars per (zoned) allowable dwelling unit. Farmland is normally valued in dollars per acre. Units of land value typically follow these rules.

1. As the depth of a lot decreases from the typical, the value per unit of frontage tends to decrease, but the square-foot, or acreage, unit value tends to increase.
2. As depth increases beyond the typical, the value per unit of frontage tends to increase, but the square-foot or acreage unit value tends to decrease.

Both of these rules are modified to the extent that the value of a lot is less if it is too shallow to be developed for an appropriate use. In like manner, following the principle of contribution, if the lot is too deep, the incremental value of the back land is lower.

Corner Influence

A location at the intersection of two streets may be advantageous for some uses. The intersection of an alley may also involve some advantages. A corner location usually provides more light and air and may afford more prominence, features that could enhance value. However, a corner location may also have higher taxes because of increased street frontage. It may also be subject to more noise and more passing traffic. Whether a corner location is advantageous or disadvantageous to a site can be judged in terms of its best or intended use and other considerations.

A corner location has greater influence on value in a business district than in other areas. Corner location is usually a positive influence for business and apartment sites, owing to increased prominence, accessibility, light and air, and special zoning advantages. However, corner location may not be a positive value influence in single family residential lots because research indicates that there is approximately as much demand for an inside lot as for a corner lot. Because of the suburban trend toward larger residential lots, owners of inside lots find that they too enjoy ample light and air, plus the advantages of more privacy, which may be ensured by careful planning.

Plottage

Plottage value is the increment in the value of an assembled site in excess of the sum of the values of the individual parcels comprising the assemblage. It reflects the potential for a higher and more profitable use for the assembled plottage than that available to the smaller parcels individually developed. Without this potential, the whole cannot be worth more than the sum of its parts.

To accommodate a substantial building development, small plots may have to be assembled, often from different owners. This procedure usually entails extra costs, and the price of key parcels may be more than their independent land value either because they are already improved or because of negotiating disadvantage. The completed project must support these excess land costs in addition to the other capital costs involved. Cost of assembly does not create plottage value, and size alone is no guarantee of a plottage value increment. In an effort to avoid cost of assemblage, increasing use has been made of air rights, railroad yards, reuse areas, and other available land peripheral to central areas of large cities.

The importance of plottage for agricultural land has increased with the increasing amount of land that can be farmed with the same number of man-hours. The typical farm has increased in size, and as in urban land assemblage, a premium may be involved in the purchase of additional land to achieve a more economically efficient whole. Without adjustment, prices realized in such sales may not be indicative of value for typical parcels of similar agricultural acreage.

The concept of a plottage increment accruing to large sites is not always valid. Without the potential for a more intensive use, plottage increment does not accrue to large parcels of land. A large tract in a location where typical development does not require a large site, or where development of the tract as a single site would be inconsistent with existing surrounding development, may be more valuable divided into several smaller parcels with improved marketability. In the context of maximizing land value, the value increment in this situation is achieved through subdivision rather than assemblage.

Shape

The utility of a specific parcel of land may be affected by its shape. Two lots identical in area could possess entirely different utility and value because one is 30 x 300 feet and the other is 60 x 150 feet. The latter would be the more valuable for almost any conventional improvement.

In many cases irregularity of shape may prove to be a serious drawback. This is particularly true in commercial zones where, under existing laws, the entire ground area may be covered by a building. Because of a site's irregular shape, construction costs could run so high that it would be impractical to erect a building that otherwise would represent the best use. Irregular commercial and industrial lots might accommodate a satisfactory building erected at a practical cost, but still not provide for efficient parking, ingress-egress, or yard storage.

However, if a site offers sufficient area and is adequately proportioned to accommodate a single family dwelling suitable to its surroundings, it could retain its utility even though it does not conform to the usual pattern of lot width and depth.

Value of irregularly shaped parcels is usually indicated in dollars and cents per square foot of area or in dollars per acre. This may be misleading because it implies that all portions are equally useful and that every square foot is equal in value to every other square foot. This situation rarely exists. Value usually does not vary in direct proportion to depth and sometimes not in direct proportion to width.

Value per square foot, rather than per front foot, is applied to most industrial properties and to many types of commercial or apartment properties. But square foot comparisons may be misleading if used to make direct comparisons of sites that have different widths or depths. This also applies to front-foot value. The application of any comparative value unit requires individual adjustment to the shape and size of the site under consideration, particularly where it is irregular.

Contour and Topography

Land tends to have a lower value if it is costly to improve because of topographical conditions. A lot that is higher or lower than the abutting street level may require additional costs for cutting or filling to achieve an acceptable grade level, to provide drainage, improve accessibility, or prevent erosion. Sometimes, however, difficult conditions are offset by advantages such as view or privacy.

In the appraisal of agricultural property, topographical factors are analyzed to ascertain their effect on utility. Considerations may include the availability of irrigation, problems of drainage or of erosion, accessibility of the fields for planting or removal of grain or livestock, and possible difficulty in the use of equipment.

In any appraisal of sites located within government-designated flood or mud slide areas, this fact is noted. The effect, if any, on the value of the site may reflect local restrictions on development or other factors the appraiser investigates and considers.

Soil and Subsoil

The character of surface and subsoil has a definite bearing on the cost of preparing a site for building. It can also influence the design of the structure to be erected on the site. The cost of improvements is increased if it becomes necessary to blast, or if unstable soil or quicksand is found. Soil conditions are usually determined by an engineering study of the bearing quality of the soil and its suitability as support for foundations of different types of structures. Extra expense is entailed for foundation walls and the sinking of piles if a site must be filled in. A sandy or rocky soil requires the expense of topsoil for lawns and landscaping. Underground tunnels could present a hazard in mining districts. Site analysis must include consideration of all such possibilities. The additional cost of the proposed improvements usually is a measure of reduced land value.

A study of soil characteristics also constitutes an essential step in agricultural land analysis. The type and depth of soil and subsoil are critical to the types of crops that can be grown successfully. Descriptive data on soil types, with locational maps, is available generally through agricultural agencies of the government.

Landscaping

Trees and shrubs may be considered as improvements or simply as part of the land itself. Landscaping may be treated separately. The influence of these features varies with the best use of the property. Trees on a residential lot may add to its value, while trees in a tillable field to be used for cropping may be considered a liability, with the cost of their removal reflected in a lower land value.

Lawns, shrubbery, gardens, and manmade plantings in general improve the appearance and desirability of residential, commercial, or industrial properties. However, because plantings are a matter of individual taste and deteriorate rapidly without constant care, property buyers are inclined to discount the cost of replacing the plantings. Although such improvements are usually regarded as an asset, their contribution to the value of the property varies with their extent, location, and character.

Utility Connections

While considering the physical features, the appraiser also ascertains the availability of adequate utility connections for sewers, water, electricity, gas, and telephone. Proximity to, and accessibility of, utility lines of adequate capacity are highly important.

Electricity is a primary requirement for raw land, to provide for pumping water, lighting, and other needs. Electric requirements for household appliances and industrial uses have precise voltage and wiring specifications. Therefore, the mere presence of electric service does not ensure that the property is adequately served.

The availability of water is also a critical factor. Value is influenced by the chemical content, the adequacy of the pressure, and the location and cost of a waterline connection to the property.

Storm sewers must be installed to relieve damp or swampy soil conditions. Water that formerly sank into the ground must be conducted away from roofs and paved surfaces. The storm sewer and the connection to it must be large enough to care for anticipated runoff. Sanitary sewage is disposed of either by septic tanks or municipal lines. The desirability of a property is influenced by the adequacy of public sewers and availability of branch connections. Otherwise, septic systems can be installed, if—and as—permitted by law, provided percolation tests indicate soil conditions are suitable.

The existing and future availability of natural gas or other sources of energy is of increasing importance in real property valuation and is an essential consideration in the initial development of new land areas.

Telephone connections usually are available except in some remote areas.

Public Transportation, Traffic Patterns, and Controls

The need for public transportation varies with the character and demands of the highest and best use of the land.

Road patterns and automobile traffic are influences to be considered in analyzing neighborhoods and in appraising an individual site. Wide roads lend prominence to frontage and develop consequent demand for service station locations and other uses that can capitalize on advertising display value. However, extremely heavy auto traffic can destroy that display value.

Limited access highways, one-way traffic regulations, newly located traffic signals, median strips—any of these can be influencing factors. The existence of these controls, or their anticipated existence, are reasons for the appraiser to include in the report an opinion of their potential effect on value.

Climatic Conditions

In some regions climatic conditions may increase the value of lots that face in a certain direction. For example, prevailing winds may favorably or adversely affect lots according to their relation to the direction of the wind.

Local shopping habits and pedestrian traffic patterns may affect the value of commercial land for retail use. For example, if shoppers tend to avoid the sunny side of the street, stores located on that side do less business. Because, consciously or subconsciously, more people avoid unnecessarily crossing heavily traveled streets, the shops located on the long side of a rectangular block usually receive the most patronage. Thus land on the short side tends to become less desirable.

HIGHEST AND BEST USE

To have value, land must have a utility that is in demand by prospective purchasers—that is, utility that will produce amenities or net income to the user. The objective of land analysis is to gather the data that tends to indicate the highest and best use for the land and to estimate its value in terms of this use.

Highest and best use is the use that fully develops the land's potential.[2] This use may change with time and conditions. Zoning of a particular site might be for a single family house. However, because of shifting economic and social patterns, the highest present utilization of this site might be achieved by conversion to commercial uses;

---

2. Highest and best use is that which, at the time of appraisal, is the most profitable likely use to which a property can be put. It may also be defined as that available use and program of future utilization that produce the highest present land value (see Chapter 3).

or it may be possible to anticipate developments that will bring about a change in highest and best permitted use, and endow a property with future value even though there is no current demand for such use. The term also is employed to designate a program of utilization that is to produce the greatest future benefit to the owner. This may include more than one potential future use, each foreseen to be the most profitable use at a stated time.

The concept of highest and best use is well established in condemnation law.[3] The power of the government to take property from a private owner is incontestable if the purpose is for public benefit. Usually compensation is awarded by the courts on the basis of market value. As a rule, the owner is allowed to establish the highest and best use of a property regardless of present use, if such potential use is reasonably probable, not speculative.[4]

Uses permitted by zoning regulations may be less valuable than the potential use to which the land is adapted, as previously noted. Courts customarily take the position that testimony may be heard only as to the highest and best use permitted by law at the present time. The appraiser risks being put into an equivocal position in giving testimony concerning highest and best use because purchasers of land will sometimes pay more for a parcel for its potential use than could be supported by its legally permitted present use. Such purchasers buy in anticipation of a reasonably expected change in the permitted use. Accordingly, a market value estimate takes into account not only current zoning, but the market's estimate of the added value with the probability of a zoning change permitting the highest and best use.

Estimating the future highest and best use depends on many factors in addition to the site's physical features. These may be legal, contractual, or economic restrictions on the use of the site; or they may relate to market conditions such as supply and demand.

In making market value estimates, appraisers should limit themselves to highest and best use considerations that have a strong probability of achievement. Not every large vacant tract is a potential shopping center site; nor is every tract along the railroad a future

---

3. "Legal Aspects of Highest and Best Use," *Condemnation Appraisal Practice,* Vol. 1 (Chicago: American Institute of Real Estate Appraisers, 1961).
4. "The Meaning of Just Compensation," *ibid.*

industrial park. Courts have held that projected highest and best use should not be "remote, speculative or conjectural."[5]

SUMMARY

The potential utility of land is measured in terms of the income imputable to it after the other agents in production have been satisfied. Whereas land and building are usually appraised as a unit, separate valuation of the land may be required for appraisal, legal, and accounting purposes. An adequate site study made in connection with the valuation of land requires the analysis and consideration of various types of data, which include:

1. Title and record data
   a. Assessed value and taxes
   b. Special assessments
   c. Zoning—classification of use, setbacks, heights, ground coverage
   d. Public restrictions—same as zoning, plus building, fire, sanitation, and other ordinances
   e. Private restrictions—same as zoning and public restrictions
   f. Easements, such as rights of way and party-wall agreements
   g. Legal description
2. Relation to land pattern
   a. Abutting lots
   b. Width and frontage
   c. Depth
   d. Corner influence
   e. Size and plottage
   f. Shape

---

5. See, for example, McGovern v. New York, 229 U.S. 363, 57 L. Ed. 1228, 33 S. Ct. 876.
Pacific Gas & Electric Co. v. Hufford, 311 P. 2d 936.
Trunkline Gas Co. v. O'Bryan, 21 Ill. 2d 95, 171 N.E. 2d 45.
Dillenbeck v. State, 193 Misc. 542, 83 N.Y.S. ed. 308, aff'd 275 App. Div. 871, 88 N.Y.S. 2d 389.
Melton v. State, Texas, 395 S.W. 2d 426.
Muscoda Bridge Co. v. Grant County, 200 Wis. 185, 227 N.W. 863.

    g. Contour and topography

    h. Soil and subsoil

    i. Landscaping

    j. Utility connections—electricity, water, storm sewer, sanitary sewer, gas, telephone

    k. Public transportation, traffic patterns, and controls

    l. Climatic conditions

3. Highest and best use

    a. Present

    b. Anticipated

8

Land or Site Valuation

Several procedures for the valuation of land are available to the appraiser.

1. *The market data (comparative) approach.* Sales of similar vacant parcels are analyzed, compared, and adjusted to derive an indication of value for the land being appraised.
2. *The allocation (abstraction) procedure.* Sales of improved properties are analyzed, and the prices are allocated between land and improvements. This allocation is used either:
   a. To establish a typical ratio of land value to total value (allocation), which may be applicable to a property being appraised, or
   b. To derive from the portion of the sale price allocated to land, a land value estimate for use as a comparable land sale (abstraction)
3. *The anticipated use (development) procedure.* Undeveloped land is assumed to be subdivided, developed, and sold. Development costs, incentive costs, and carrying charges are subtracted from the estimated proceeds of sale, and the net income projection is discounted over the estimated period required for market absorption of the developed sites to derive an indication of value for the land being appraised.
4. *The land residual procedure.* The land is assumed to be improved to its highest and best use, and the net income imputable to the land after all expenses of operation and return attributable to the other agents in production is capitalized to derive an estimate of land value.

MARKET DATA APPROACH

The market data approach, which is generally preferred, requires the gathering, recording, and comparing of sales data for comparable parcels. The greatest weight should be placed on actual sales of similar land made at times relatively concurrent with the date of the appraisal and subject to comparable conditions. These and other facts assembled for comparison constitute the market data.

Sometimes market data is too meager to support any significant conclusions; then a study of comparable properties being offered for sale may be helpful. However, offering prices usually have limited validity as market data because a seller can offer a property at any price, no matter how unrealistic.

The appraiser may also consider offers by prospective purchasers. These offers, however, may tend to be less than the land value unless the prospective purchaser has a current need for the land. Courts usually do not give much weight to evidence based on offers to purchase. The reason for this attitude may be found in the definition of market value.

Prices paid by federal or state governments or other condemnors are not usually accepted as market data because of the possible compulsion to complete a sale when the parties face condemnation (law suit), as opposed to the willing buyer-willing seller concept in the definition of market value. The price paid may reflect market value, but may not qualify as a free market transaction under this concept.

If weight were to be given to value indications other than actual comparative sales, the testing of the material would be the same as for sales data. Accordingly, the following discussion is concentrated on comparative sales data.

Sources of Data

Market data may be obtained from many sources. These depend on the character of the property, the local methods of reporting and recording real estate transactions, and the contacts the appraiser has developed. Completed real estate sales are shown in the public records by the recorded deeds of conveyance.

An appraiser who is not personally familiar with the details surrounding a transaction may interview the grantor, the grantee, the broker, or all three. Interviews enable the appraiser to obtain firsthand information about the unrecorded conditions surrounding the sale, which might have influenced either or both parties to the transaction, and to verify the sale price. Although news stories may be in error about prices, the figures they cite serve as a starting point for market price investigation. The lender or the sale closing agency are also potential sources of data.

Qualified local opinion may be relevant as a background study of contemporary value. Although bankers and others who loan on, or negotiate transactions in, real estate are not appraisers in the professional sense, their views, when properly interpreted, reflect market opinion on questions of value.

Market data may be found in public records—transfer maps or books, the index of deeds, and the deeds themselves. From these or similar sources the appraiser can obtain certain pertinent information, including:

1. Name of the grantor (seller)
2. Name of the grantee (purchaser)
3. Date of sale
4. Legal description, to identify location, to verify size and shape
5. Stated consideration (may be a nominal figure)
6. Encumbrances (usually taxes not due and payable, zoning ordinances, and restrictions of record)
7. Mortgage indebtedness (if assumed by purchaser)
8. Sale price as indicated by tax stamps, if the state has a law requiring that stamps be affixed to the deed to cover the tax at a certain rate on the consideration. The "actual consideration" indicated by tax stamps attached to the deed may have been deliberately overstated or inaccurate. In trades the indicated consideration may not represent value in the minds of buyer and seller. However, the price inferred from tax stamps is a starting point that requires verification.

Court opinions differ concerning the point at which hearsay ends and knowledge begins. In some places the price must be verified by testimony of grantor, grantee, or both. In other courts the statement of the broker is sufficient. In all appraisal work the appraiser uses prices that are believed to be reliable. If reported prices do not conform to an existing market pattern, every effort is made by the appraiser to verify the price and conditions of sale before concluding that a new value level is indicated.

Analysis of Data

Information assembled on numerous sales of land in the general vicinity of the site being appraised is of limited value if it is presented simply as a list of transactions. The sales listed should be classified and analyzed in terms of similarity to, and differences from, the property being appraised so that the relevant transactions can be segregated for further study.

Although legal interpretations vary from state to state, most courts require that a comparative transaction meet four tests: the sale must be voluntary, bona fide, similar to the property being appraised in physical and locational characteristics, and recent. Accordingly, the appraiser usually eliminates forced sales and purchases, negotiated purchases by condemnors, credit sales, transfers of convenience, trades, and jury decisions and awards.

A bona fide sale should have terms that are reasonably typical. The sales data may then be considered in respect to these points:

1. Date of sale
2. Locational features of property
3. Physical characteristics

In respect to location, the most comparable sales may be at a considerable distance from the property being appraised, even in another city or state. Distance may affect the weight to be accorded to a comparable sale but not its pertinence; and other factors being equivalent, more weight is accorded to the closer sales. The less data available, the farther the appraiser must search. He or she must decide why location of the comparable parcel is superior to, equal to, or poorer than the location of the property being appraised and whether the comparable sale provides a valid indication of the probable price at which the subject property would sell. A sale that is not thus indicative serves no purpose.

To constitute a valid indication of the value of the parcel being appraised, a comparative sale should be reasonably similar in characteristics and reflect the current market. Prices constantly fluctuate, not only in terms of the economy, but also in relation to the location and the type of property. Individual sales consummated in past years may be adjusted to a present market value indication on the basis of a time relationship, established through research of past and present market data. A study of prices over a period of time in a neighborhood may show prices moving up or down, requiring plus or minus adjustments to show what the comparable property would sell for on the date of appraisal.

Presentation of Data

In a typical situation, the appraiser might thus analyze and weigh a comparative land sale transaction:

Location:	1221 East Third Street, Blankville
Grantor:	A. B. Jones
Grantee:	Ray Brown Optical Co.
Date:	March 19, 19___(one year previous)
Size:	100 feet front, 80 feet rear, 130 feet deep, 11,700 square feet
Shape:	Narrows to rear
Public utilities:	Sanitary sewer, storm sewer, electricity, gas, water, telephone
Street and sidewalk:	36-foot wide blacktop, concrete curbs and sidewalks; good condition
Soil and subsoil bearing capacity:	Typical; adequate for proposed use
Zoning:	B2—Business
Contour:	Level and at street grade
Location:	Corner
Other:	
Indicated price:	$15,000
Actual price:	$14,700 (verified by Mr. Jones)
Motives:	Purchaser constructing a single-story commercial building. On market six months prior. Purchaser paid cash.
Unit price:	$14,700 ÷ 100 = $147 per front foot; $14,700 ÷ 11,700 = $1.26 per square foot.

Comparisons may be made in several ways. For example, if a square-foot basis is used locally, the comparison of the above sale with the property being appraised may be made on a unit basis as follows:

Time factor (in terms of market change):
market is improving.   add 5%
Location: in same block as subject   no adjustment
Physical factors:
Shape: subject is rectangular   add 5%
Depth: subject is deeper   add 10%
Land pattern: subject is not a corner   deduct 10%
Other: same contour, public utilities,
zoning, streets, sidewalks, etc.   no adjustment
All factors   add (net) 10%

Estimates may be made in actual dollars rather than percentages. Comparison may also be indicated by narrative description. However, regardless of the method, the indication of value for the property being appraised would tend to be $1.26 per square foot plus 10% ($1.26 x 110%), which equals $1.39 per square foot. Whichever method is used, it is logical to work from the known to the unkown— that is, from the sale price of the comparative property to an indication of the probable selling price for the property being appraised. A number of such comparisons may be presented in a chart. Adjustments may be explained in great detail, or a short statement may be used to summarize how the adjustments were derived and applied. Even if the explanation is short, the appraiser should keep on file the complete reasoning process leading to the final conclusion. Whether shown in detail or retained in field notes, this conclusion should be supported by an analysis of the pertinent factors' effects on the value.

LAND VALUE BY ALLOCATION OR ABSTRACTION

Allocation

Since the principles of balance and contribution affirm that a ratio tends to exist between the agents in production—land and improvements—the portion of property value attributable to land may be developed through analysis of typical and similar improved property sale prices to establish a ratio applicable to the property being appraised. That such a general relationship does exist in single family homes is substantiated for example, by reports of the U.S. Department of Housing and Urban Development (see Table 8.1).

Table 8.1   Average Value of Improved Lot Compared to Average Sale Price of Home

Year	Sale Price	Market Price of Site	Site Value as % of Sale Price
1955	$12,113	$1,626	13.5
1960	14,662	2,477	16.7
1965	16,825	3,442	20.0
1970	23,056	4,982	21.2
1975	32,342	6,382	18.8
1976	34,608	6,954	19.2

Source: *1976 Statistical Yearbook of the U.S. Department of Housing and Urban Development* (Washington, D.C., 1977), p. 106.

As the age of the improvement increases, the ratio of land value to the total value tends to increase where site characteristics are similar. If the property being appraised includes a lot of unusual size or of undesirable contour or shape, the typical ratio might be affected. Building costs may also influence the ratio.

Although a distribution or allocation of a price or value between land and improvements by statistical ratios can be useful at times, the procedure has limitations. For example, if typically 20% of the total sale price of a new home tends to represent the price at which comparable vacant lots have sold, 20 to 25% of the sale price of an existing home might represent a fair allowance for land.

The allocation procedure also has applications in other classes of property. In a new apartment project, for example, a fair allocation to land might be, say, 20% of building cost or, alternately, a land value per apartment unit. The advantages are that a sense of proportion is retained. If the neighborhood is improved chiefly by certain types of properties that can afford only a certain land value, the typical vacant lot probably will not be improved by a much higher and better use. Where no vacant land sales are available, this allocation procedure does afford an indication of land value.

Abstraction

In this use of the allocation procedure, comparable land sales data is abstracted from sales of similar improved properties. From the total sale price of a comparable property, the portion that could reasonably be assigned as building value is estimated and deducted. The remainder, except for intangibles, must be the land. For example, a 10,000-square-foot garage sold for $120,000. The appraiser estimates the depreciated cost of such a garage at $9 per square foot, or $90,000. The remainder of $30,000 may indicate a residual price of the land, assuming that the garage building represents typical or highest and best land use and that no intangible considerations were involved in the transaction. The portion of the sale price allocated to land is then treated as if it were the price obtained in an actual sale of vacant land.

Although perhaps applicable where there are no sales of vacant land or even where vacant land does not exist, the result of this procedure may not be conclusive and collateral confirmation may be needed.

LAND VALUE BY ANTICIPATED USE OR DEVELOPMENT

This procedure involves the comparison of undeveloped land to be appraised with a developed parcel or parcels for which individual lot sale prices are known. If available, data on sales of comparable raw land to developers is the best evidence of value. When such market data is lacking, however, the anticipated use or development procedure may be applicable to raw unsubdivided land, potential residential subdivisions, new neighborhoods, reuse neighborhoods, or industrial centers or parks. In some circumstances this procedure may be the only one available for valuing raw land.[1]

For example, a 20-acre parcel of undeveloped land is presently suitable for development as a single family subdivision and is appropriately zoned. Sales of comparable parcels are lacking, but the value of residential lots in similar subdivision developments can be ascertained. A typical appraisal procedure follows:

---

1. *Educational Memorandum No. 1, Subdivision Analyses,* rev. ed. (Chicago: American Institute of Real Estate Appraisers, 1978).

1. Identify the economic bracket of the residents and check the range of sale prices of typical new homes in the area.
2. By distribution, or comparison with lot sales in similar subdivisions, decide what figure represents a typical lot value in this category of development.
3. Study and lay out a subdivision plan to develop typical lots.
4. Project the total probable gross sale price for these lots.
5. Estimate development costs to include:
    a. Engineering or other fees
    b. Cost of streets and utilities
    c. Advertising and cost of sales
6. Estimate overhead and administrative costs to include:
    a. Taxes and inspection fees
    b. Financing fees and carrying costs
7. Deduct these direct expenses for development from the figure derived in Step 4.
8. Deduct an adequate profit allowance to provide incentive for the developer so that the calculated value of the raw land is exclusive of development profit. (Alternatively, profit may be provided for in the rate used for capitalization in the discounting process.)
9. Deduct for time lag by discounting, at an appropriate risk rate, the annual net income flow over the time needed for completion and market absorption of the project.

The sum of these discounted cash flows represents the price at which the land could reasonably be expected to sell and reflects the price a developer would be justified in paying for the raw land under the assumptions made. A critical assumption is the projection of the probable time required for market absorption of the developed sites.

Frequently the services of an engineer are required to establish a subdivision plan permissible under an existing building code. Evidence to support the projected cost of streets and utilities may involve obtaining formal estimates from contractors.

There are variations of this procedure for processing the income and expenses from the hypothetical development, including a discounted cash flow analysis. The important factors in the anticipated use procedure are projected time for sale of the developed lots, estimation of development costs, and discounting of income from sales for the estimated waiting period before receiving this income.

LAND VALUE BY LAND RESIDUAL TECHNIQUE

In the absence of land sales, to establish the value of a site by the market data approach, the value of land may be indicated by the land residual technique of the income approach. In this approach the net income of the site improved to its highest and best use is estimated. From this net income is deducted a fair interest return and provision for recapture of the estimated cost of the building and/or other improvements. The residual net income is ascribed to the land. Capitalizing this net income at an appropriate risk rate results in an indicated value for the land by use of the land residual technique.

Selecting the highest and best use is the first and most important step in the income capitalization approach to site valuation. The type of improvement that seems best suited to the land commonly is suggested by the present land-use pattern. But the problem is to ascertain the optimum quality or size of the improvement (principle of balance). To derive a use and program of future utilization producing the highest present land value a series of gross and net income yields from hypothetical buildings of various types and sizes may have to be processed. In other words, through the projection of a series of hypothetical buildings on the site, one is selected that would produce the greatest residual return imputable to the land, which therefore represents highest and best use. The procedure reflects an application of the principle of surplus productivity.

For example, the appraiser might test for a two-story building with a net income of $21,500 (net to land of $3,200); for a four-story building with a net income of $30,400 (net to land of $5,600); and for a six-story building with a net income of $50,000 (net to land of $4,000). That the four-story building will yield the greatest residual return to the land becomes apparent. The net income hypothetically assigned to the land in this income capitalization approach is the amount remaining after payment of all expenses plus interest on, and recapture of, the building investment. The land earnings are the final consideration and therefore are residual.

In appraising a site the land residual technique should be used with special care, because assumptions of highest and best use may produce a considerable difference in the residual net income imputable to the land. Any such difference is magnified by the process of capitalization. Further, the divergencies in the final result may be substantial even if the estimated rate or rates of capitalization vary only nominally.

The land residual technique produces more satisfactory results when the number of estimates made by the appraiser are held to a minimum. The number of estimates involved in developing replacement cost and net income for a hypothetical one-story building may be materially fewer than for a multistory office building, and fewer judgment decisions involved in the analysis will probably result in a more reliable conclusion of land value.

Applied generally to income-producing property, the land residual technique is useful either as a check against the market data approach or as an alternate means of estimating land value when the market data approach is inconclusive. Further details on the application of this technique are explained in the chapters on capitalization.

SUMMARY

The same fundamental principles underlie all site valuation. However, the key factors that influence the utility and value of a given site vary with the type of property being appraised. For example, a factor, such as heavy pedestrian traffic, that tends to create value in a business site might detract from the value of a residential site. Aesthetic considerations, which are of paramount importance in a residential site, might have different significance in a business site.

Major factors influencing the value of a site vary with different types of land use. Examples of such factors are convenience of location and other amenities for residential sites; location in the trading area, the community's purchasing power, and the relative availability for business sites; zoning regulations, the convenience of location to shipping facilities and labor sources, and the degree of proximity to related industries for industrial sites.

Factors that affect the value of single-use or service properties are legal, physical, and locational adaptability to the intended use. The value of a park site, for instance, depends on its relation to the existing city plan; of a golf club, on its convenience to the people to be served; of cemeteries, on matters of license (governmental permission) or institutional sponsorship.

Of the four procedures for site valuation, the market data or comparative process is basic. After obtaining pertinent sales data, the appraiser decides whether the sale was voluntary and bona fide. If so, it is compared with the property under appraisal in terms of time, location, and physical characteristics. Adjustments are made to derive an indicated value for the site being appraised.

Other procedures are useful in the absence of comparable sales or when circumstances indicate their application. The allocation or abstraction procedure is helpful in older neighborhoods and as an aid to the market data approach. The development (subdivision) procedure is helpful when applied to tracts of land ripe for improvement. The land residual technique is applicable principally to income-producing sites, either to check a conclusion derived by the market data method or as the major consideration when adequate market data is not available.

The major factors influencing site values vary with the highest and best use of the land.

9
Residential Styles and Functional Utility

The primary concern in valuation analysis of any residential property is its degree of marketability, or acceptability, when offered for sale. Because amenities constitute an important aspect of residential marketability, the residential appraiser keeps informed of changing standards in design, materials, styles, and functional utility. This knowledge provides a basis for judging the relative value of amenities in the study of each property. The appraiser's analysis is then extended to include a study of the market in which the property is to be sold because this is where the final test of marketability takes place.

ARCHITECTURE

A maximum contribution to the degree of marketability is made by factors generally included in the term *good architecture*. Rarely the result of fortuity, good architecture is characterized by the natural, unpretentious use of appropriate materials, in the proper scale, and in harmony with the setting. An expert combination of mass, materials, openings, and detail is inherent in good architecture, which, however, is not limited to elements of exterior style or design. It also includes consideration of functional utility, which can be achieved only through sound planning. These characteristics, suitably combined, create, and sustain the market value of a residential property.

Many architectural styles have widespread acceptance throughout the country.[1] Some are related to classic architectural designs; others have an historical heritage from later periods; and some styles are influenced by climate, geographical factors, availability of local construction materials, and public acceptance. However, regardless of style, almost any new home that is not totally inappropriate will sell because of the appeal of its newness. When it is no longer new, a house lacking a fundamentally appropriate design loses marketability.

Good architecture does not mean that every residence need be individually designed by an architect. A subdivision developer may have an architect design five or six styles of homes suitable for the range of lots in a new development and then build dozens of homes of each style, modified to suit individual purchasers or specific lot topography. Many successful builders or developers have acquired the ability to construct acceptable residences from stock plans designed by architects.

CHANGING DEMANDS IN STYLE

Attitudes demonstrated in the market dictate both style and design. The value of a residence decreases if prospective buyers do not like the design, no matter how authentic it may be.

Public taste in residential styles goes through long cycles, with extensive changes, not all of which reflect sound judgment and economic considerations. The popularity of different house styles is constantly changing, reflecting current economic conditions, lifestyles, family sizes, and average age of the population.

Attitudes toward energy use have an impact on design and style considerations. The current trend toward energy conservation has led to the use of building designs, material, and equipment previously considered unacceptable. It has also led to higher insulation standards and to the exploration of new energy sources, with the solar-heated home one innovative outcome. Market preference is shifting from residences with large rooms and/or separate special-purpose rooms to

---

1. Henry S. Harrison, *Houses: An Illustrated Guide to Construction*, rev. ed. (Chicago: Realtors National Marketing Institute, 1976).

those with smaller multi-purpose rooms. Consideration is also being given to placement of the residence on the site in relation to energy needs. The structure is positioned to take advantage of the varying angles of the sunlight occurring during the year.

The appraiser is concerned with the acceptability of different styles by the market in the neighborhood in which the property is located. Unusual or radical house styles should be carefully studied to estimate marketability.

USE OF MATERIALS AND DESIGN

The basic design for a residence is deficient if it combines incompatible architectural styles or too great a variety of materials. Other liabilities include a number of distracting features, poor or incorrect proportions, or a lack of balance. After selecting at random an attractive entrance from one style of house, a beautiful roof and eave design from another, a charming bay window from a third, and a graceful chimney from a fourth, a buyer may wonder why the attempt to build a dream house produced an unbalanced monstrosity.

A house designed to be built of one material seldom can be built of another without altering the desired effect. If a builder substitutes brick in constructing a house designed for exterior horizontal wood siding, the long horizontal lines and shadows of the wood siding are lost; so may be the sense of breadth that the architectural design was intended to convey. A similar loss may occur, perhaps in an attempt to reduce cost, if asbestos shingles or board-and-batten siding are substituted. Such substitution often destroys the architectural balance between height and breadth.

RELATION TO SITE

Architectural style and execution should be related to the site, or all effort to achieve good design may be lost. The house planned for a 40- or 50-foot lot may not utilize the advantages or justify the cost of a lot 50 to 70 feet wide. A rambling ranch house designed for a suburban lot might look completely out of place on a small urban site. A house that presents a charming appearance on a wooded slope might be totally unsuited to a level lot devoid of trees. A house skillfully designed to blend into its location between a Georgian house and an English style might be entirely inappropriate elsewhere. Relating the design to the site is fundamental to good architectural practice.

The crowded appearance that characterizes so many older neighborhoods in urban areas is the direct result of building houses on lots too small to accommodate them properly. It may be apparent to an appraiser that the lots were divided or compressed because of the high cost of installing utilities or because of limited available raw land within practical reach of public transportation, whereas the houses were built to accommodate the limits of their buyers' purses and to conform to zoning laws and other restrictions. The dimensions may also reflect the contractor's desire to realize a profit on as large a house as potential buyers in the area could afford.

These factors still exist. Lots are larger in many areas, but the dimensions of the houses have also increased, with the result that many subdivisions of large functional homes look overcrowded. In general, however, the land-to-building ratio has improved in response to demands imposed by home buyers and lenders of mortgage money.

In some areas zoning is criticized for requiring such large lots that the building density is too low. Some lot-size requirements are said to prevent the construction of low- and medium-priced houses. Rising costs and scarcity of land have contributed to high density housing, such as cluster housing, row houses, and patio houses. These also have the ecological and economic advantage of utilizing less land per family than typical single family suburban lots.

FUNCTIONAL UTILITY

Marketability is the ultimate test of functional utility. If a property is sufficiently useful and desirable to attract buyers and if it can be sold and resold without a substantial discount in price, it possesses the necessary degree of functional utility to sustain marketability and value.

A high degree of functional utility is the result of good planning. Consider, for example, two houses, side by side, on similar-sized lots, with the same number of rooms and the same total floor area. The two houses are new, erected by the same builder with the same crew; and the cost to build was the same. Here the similarities end because the two houses were built from different plans. The first house reflects excellent layout and design. The room sizes and shapes are good, and the arrangement is convenient, providing ample light and air. There is a good pattern of traffic flow; the areas of different use are separated; and the closet space is ample. The sum of the house's advantages makes it comfortable, attractive, and readily marketable at a price commensurate with its cost.

The second house is poorly designed. The rooms are badly proportioned, dark, and arranged so that furniture placement is difficult and areas of different use interfere with each other. In addition, the hall is too long and too narrow, and storage space is inadequate. The house is hard to heat and ventilate. Prospective buyers regard it as undesirable, which results in a loss of value. This loss is in reference to the norm, represented by the functionally acceptable home. The finest materials, structural soundness, and superior condition may not offset a loss in value due to functional inutility.

Because acceptability of a property when offered for sale is the final test, the appraiser must understand the market and know how to measure the effect of deficiencies noted during an inspection of the property. Its functional utility is considered good, despite a number of theoretical deficiencies, if these do not adversely affect its marketability.

The appraiser weighs the amenities afforded by a specific residential property in the light of current market standards of functional utility. The characteristics and customs of the nearby residents are considered in estimating the extent to which a design meets the needs or desires of those who comprise the probable market. The appraiser keeps in mind that considerations that seriously influence the market value of a high-priced house may have little or no bearing on the value of a house in a lower price range. The opposite also is true. An example of a theoretical deficiency is the location of a bedroom off the dining room of a 60-year-old house in a lower-middle-class neighborhood. The lack of an entry hall and the traffic pattern through living and dining rooms in this house result from poor planning and violate functional utility. Though the typical purchaser of the 60-year-old house would probably not object to these deficiencies, they would lower the value of a new house because they would be unacceptable to prospective buyers of a new house.

Judgment is needed to evaluate the floor plan of a particular house. Whether a residence possesses functional utility probably can be decided only after its good points and faults are weighed in the light of numerous considerations, such as price range, style, design, age, and location. Because these factors affect minimum requirements, they are omitted from the following comprehensive checklist. Despite wide general applicability, specific items may be altered or eliminated in a particular application due to regional or local circumstances or public preferences.

I. Floor plan and layout
    A. Room sizes and shapes
        1. Adequate size and usable shape
            a. Living room
            b. Kitchen
            c. Dining room or dining area
            d. Master bedroom
            e. Other bedrooms
            f. Family room or recreation area
        2. Wall space in relation to furniture requirements
    B. Circulation
        1. Entry hall: direct access to kitchen, living room, dining room, bedrooms
        2. Rear entry to kitchen
        3. Direct access from garage to house
        4. Mud entry for young children
        5. Room relationship
            a. Bedrooms to bath
            b. Living areas to bath
            c. Kitchen to dining room and living room
            d. Bedrooms separated from work and living areas
    C. Privacy
        1. Access to bedrooms
        2. Access to bathrooms
    D. Doors
        1. Location (convenient)
        2. Swing (not objectionable)
        3. Adequate size
            a. Front and rear entrances (to move appliances)
            b. Rooms (to move furniture)
            c. Closets and bathrooms

E. Light and air
    1. Single exposures
    2. Cross ventilation
    3. Windows (type and material)
    4. Screens and storm windows
    5. Glass area in relation to room size
    6. Exterior obstructions
        a. Porches
        b. Roof overhangs
        c. Adjoining buildings
    7. Patio door (view)
F. Halls
    1. Area in proportion to house size
    2. Location and appearance
    3. Lighting
G. Stairs
    1. Upper floors
        a. Location and appearance
        b. Width and steepness
        c. Tread and riser size and proportion
    2. Basement
        a. Width, steepness of stairway, handrail, and head room
H. Storage (adequacy and location)
    1. Bedroom closets
    2. Hall closets
    3. Guest closet
    4. Linen closets
    5. Basement storage area
    6. Other storage area in house
    7. Garage storage area
I. Laundry facilities
    1. Location and space
    2. Plumbing and electrical connections
    3. Vent for dryer
    4. Space for clotheslines in basement

II. Equipment
    A. Heating
        1. Type of unit and fuel
        2. Local acceptance
        3. Adequacy

      4. Automatic controls
      5. Insulation
      6. Other (humidifier, air cleaner)
      7. Air conditioning (type and adequacy)
B.   Electric
      1. Adequacy of service, distribution panels, and circuit wiring
      2. Adequate number of convenience outlets, fixtures, switches
      3. Adequate wiring for appliances
C.   Plumbing
      1. Adequate supply and drainage piping
      2. Bathrooms and powder rooms
          a. Number
          b. Quality of fixtures
          c. Finish of wainscot and floors
          d. Vanities, mirrors, linen closets
          e. Ventilation
          f. Bathroom heater
      3. Hot water heater
      4. Basement floor drains
      5. Exterior hose connections
D.   Kitchens
      1. Finish of floors, walls, splash areas
      2. Wall cabinets
      3. Base cabinets, sink and counter top
      4. Built-in appliances
          a. Garbage disposal
          b. Dishwasher
          c. Ventilating fan and hood
          d. Range and oven (type of fuel)
          e. Other
      5. Pantry
      6. Lighting
E.   Other appliances (built-in or connections)
      1. Washer
      2. Dryer
      3. Refrigerator
      4. Freezer
      5. Power tools
      6. Vacuum cleaner system
      7. Other

F. Hardware
    1. Suitability for property
    2. Quality, condition, and finish
G. Fireplaces
H. Special equipment
    1. Bell and call system
    2. AM-FM radio and intercom
    3. Mail boxes
    4. Burglar alarm or ADT system
    5. Sump pumps
    6. Fire or smoke alarms
    7. Elevator (type, capacity, specifications)
    8. Incinerator
    9. Other

III. Garage
A. Style compatible with house
B. Size and capacity
C. Location
    1. Detached
    2. Attached
    3. Doors exposed to street
    4. Doors not exposed, but garage wall a part of house front
D. Doors (type, size, automatic)
E. Utilities (electricity, water, heat)

IV. Site
A. General
    1. Balance (relation of lot to house)
        a. Adequate size lot
        b. House suited to lot
        c. Property compatible with neighborhood
    2. Light, air, and view
    3. Nuisances (noise, odors, appearance)
    4. Privacy (proximity of other buildings)
        a. Side yard, especially for bedrooms
        b. Rear yard (space for patio, garden, recreation)
    5. Setbacks, proximity to traffic
        a. Pedestrian
        b. Vehicular
    6. Landscaping
        a. Lawn

          b. Trees
          c. Foundation planting
      7. Service facilities
      8. Drainage
          a. Grading
          b. Downspouts
B. Yard improvements
      1. Walks (material)
      2. Fences, garden wall, retaining wall
      3. Patio or terrace
      4. Garage driveway
          a. Material
          b. Width, turning radius, grade
          c. Location with respect to house entries
          d. Ingress and egress (alley)
          e. Traffic hazard at street
      5. Underground improvements
          a. Sewers
          b. Electric service
          c. Telephone service
C. Topography
      1. Placement of house
      2. Steps to entrance (number, railing)
      3. Driveway (grade)
      4. Grading and drainage
      5. Usable yard area

Experience teaches that public taste and market acceptability are subject to constant change. Extremes in architectural style or floor plan often prove to be poor investments, since designs or layouts in favor at one time may be in disfavor at another. A good design and layout based on public acceptance, a degree of conservatism plus reasonable individuality, a proper regard for the character of the surrounding development and neighborhood — all combine to produce a residence with an inherently stable market value.

Sound Planning for Houses

The appraiser acquires a familiarity with local conditions and with the basic types of residential design, construction, and floor layout. The one-story, single family house may be large or small, of costly or inexpensive construction, and with infinite variations in floor plan and layout.

Government agencies have underwritten the financing and construction of many small homes, one of the benefits of which has been the widespread acceptance of low downpayments and amortized long-term monthly mortgage payments. This easier financing has contributed to a large increase in small-home ownership. In the 1940s and 1950s many homes were erected in accordance with minimum government standards. The typical small, competitive or subdivision house included a living room, kitchen, two bedrooms, and a bath. If there was no basement, a utility room was provided. There was usually an attached or basement garage or an attached carport. The dining space often was included in a larger living room or kitchen, but often the space was arranged to include a modest dining room. These homes were in demand and served their purpose well. There was generally a good use of space, fairly large living rooms; efficient kitchens equipped with cabinet sink and base and wall cabinets; and adequate dining closet space. Time, however, showed that lack of a basement tends to affect adversely resale value in cold climates and that one medium-sized and one small bedroom were inadequate for growing families.

When the one-story, medium-sized ranch house on a larger lot first became popular, the layout usually included a third bedroom and an additional half or full second bath. In the higher price ranges formal dining rooms were included; but for the medium-sized ranch house, the space ordinarily used for dining was sometimes made part of a family room or recreation room. Additions were readily made to this design, which resulted in L- or U-shaped layouts, maximizing available light and ventilation. Patios, porches, breezeways, and garages were often included in the floor plan.

The reproduction cost of comparable areas of living space is highest for a one-story house, because basement, foundation, and roof do not serve two or more levels, as they do in a multistory house. As indicated by market acceptance, people who can afford the extra cost prefer the single-story plan, because it eliminates stairs and simplifies maintenance and housekeeping. Because the long, low fronts appear impressive, the garage wall is sometimes added to the facade dimension, with an entrance at the side or rear. The availability of larger lots and the less-dense zoning in suburban areas has made this trend possible.

The story-and-a-half house represents a better utilization of living space. Often two-story houses are designed to look like one-and-a-half story houses, to achieve long, low, sweeping roof lines. The Cape Cod home usually provides one or two bedrooms on the first floor, but uses attic space with dormers for additional bedrooms and bath.

In northern regions of the United States, a popular style of dwelling has two stories and six rooms, three of which are bedrooms. Usually the house provides a full basement, with living room, dining room, and kitchen on the first floor. All but the lowest in cost include a first-floor lavatory, eating area in the kitchen, and a small entry hall with good traffic pattern. The three bedrooms on the second floor are medium to large in size, with cross ventilation and good closet space. This compact two-story house provides the greatest amount of living space per housing dollar invested. Some decline in favor resulted from the dislike of stairs at a time when larger lots became obtainable in new suburban communities. There has, however, been a trend back to two-story homes and even to townhouses and row houses. Some of these have a third level for a basement and recreation area.

The larger two-story house provides four or more bedrooms, two or more baths, and usually a family room on the first floor. The preference is now for a private bathroom for the master bedroom and another bathroom centrally located to serve the other bedrooms. At least a half-bath is conveniently located on the first floor. Dressing rooms have become less popular; if present, they are smaller and may be part of a two- or three-section bathroom, consisting of toilet and tub, vanity lavatory and mirror wall, and large walk-in closet. Servants' quarters are less important because domestic help seldom "lives in." Rooms formerly used for that purpose are now considered as extra bedrooms or guest rooms. Garages are generally attached and usually accommodate two or even three cars.

The split-level home, built in increasing numbers since the 1950s, has the advantages of short stair flights, excellent utilization of space, and substantial economy in construction cost. The design is well adapted to sloping sites, and is suitable for lots where construction of a single-story ranch house is impractical. The exterior appearance of the split-level home is considerably different from that of one-and-a-half stories. When attractive and appropriate to the site, many variations in split-level design have been well received.

Sound Planning for Apartments

In the analysis of an apartment building, an accurate room count is important, because it provides a basis of comparison for the various designs and layouts found in the locality. The apartment is often rated and rented on the basis of its room count, as well as on the total square-foot area.

The minimum room sizes for apartment units, as recognized by the Federal Housing Administration, are shown in Table 9.1.

Large, modern apartment houses are usually designed to obtain a degree of privacy while affording maximum light and air. Space and location requirements imposed by elevators and orientation may dictate the decision for a central main lobby entrance or for several stairway-lobby entrances. The need for security measures may make it desirable to design one main entrance with interior access to other stairways. Modern garden apartments located on a slope may have at least one entry to the second floor, limiting stairs to one flight up or down. When compatible with climate, garden apartments may have individual entrances off exterior corridors resembling balconies.

Except for higher priced units, the modern apartment offers less flexibility in layout because standardization is now a primary aim in apartment house planning, design, and layout. The objective is to provide one or more windows for each room, while wasting as little space as possible. The areas of the dining space, kitchen, and baths are frequently kept to a minimum, with the other rooms planned to be as spacious as possible. Efficient use of space for utility rooms or storage facilities can eliminate basement area and locker storage. A utility closet may contain an individual heating unit, hot water heater, or a central heating and air-conditioning unit.

Laundry facilities are often included, with coin-operated equipment in central areas of lower- or medium-priced apartments. Connections for washer-dryer units in utility rooms are included in medium- and higher-priced apartments. Garages usually are found only in medium- or higher-priced units, and the entire basement or

Table 9.1. Minimum Room Sizes

A. Minimum Room Sizes for Separate Rooms

Name of Space[b]	Minimum Area (sq. ft.)[a]					Least Dimension
	LU with 0 BR	LU with 1 BR	LU with 2 BR	LU with 3 BR	LU with 4 BR	
LR	NA	160	160	170	180	11′ 0″
DR	NA	100	100	110	120	8′ 4″
BR (primary)[c]	NA	120	120	120	120	9′ 4″
BR (secondary)	NA	NA	80	80	80	8′ 0″
Total area, BR's	NA	120	200	280	360	—

B. Minimum Room Sizes for Combined Spaces

Combined Space[a,d]	Minimum Area (sq. ft.)[a]					Least Dimension[e]
	LU with 0 BR	LU with 1 BR	LU with 2 BR	LU with 3 BR	LU with 4 BR	
LR-DA	NA	210	210	230	250	
LR-DA-SL	250	NA	NA	NA	NA	
LR-DA-K[f]	NA	270	270	300	300	
LR-SL	210	NA	NA	NA	NA	
K-DA[g]	100	120	120	140	160	

Source: *HUD Minimum Property Standards: One and Two Family Dwellings* (Washington, D.C.: U.S. Department of Housing and Urban Development, 1973) pp. 4-8 & 4-9.

[a]The floor area of an alcove or recess off a room, having a least dimension less than required for the room, shall be included only if it is not more than 10% of the minimum room size permitted and is useful for the placement of furniture.

[b] *Abbreviations*

LU = Living unit	K = Kitchen
LR = Living room	NA = Not applicable
DR = Dining room	BR = Bedroom
DA = Dining area	SL = Sleeping area

0 BR = LU with no separate bedroom

[c]Primary bedrooms shall have at least one uninterrupted wall space of at least 10 feet.

[d]For two adjacent spaces to be considered a combined room, the horizontal opening between spaces shall be at least 8 ft., 9 in., except the opening between kitchen and dining functions, may be reduced to 6 ft., 0 in. Spaces not providing this degree of openness shall meet minimum room sizes required for separate rooms.

[e]The minimum dimensions of a combined room shall be the sum of the dimensions of the individual single rooms involved, except for the overlap or combined use of space.

[f]A combined LR-DA-K shall comply with the following: the food preparation-cooking area shall be screened from the living room sitting area; the clear opening between the kitchen and dining area shall be at least 4 ft., 0 in.

[g]These required minimums apply when the only eating space is in the kitchen.

first story may be used for this purpose. Garden apartments usually have surface parking areas on the site and may provide necessary parking for tenants and guests.

Most new apartment buildings do not have living quarters for janitorial help, and in the older units these facilities are seldom used for their original purpose. Gas or electricity for heating requires almost no supervision, and the cleaning and maintenance formerly required of resident janitors may be handled by individuals under contract to a number of buildings.

Beginning in the 1960s, nearly all new apartments had (or provided for) air conditioning, usually a combination heating and air-conditioning unit for each apartment; and the kitchens were equipped with appliances, dishwashers, and garbage disposers. This trend is growing even in some northern states where air-conditioning needs are less critical.

Because many apartments built before World War II do not meet existing building-code requirements, substantial expenditures may be required to make them conform. Like single-family dwellings, many older apartment buildings with deficiencies that would not be acceptable in newer structures, may be considered entirely adequate by the tenant who can afford to pay only the lower rents in their neighborhoods or by tenants who are willing to forego, for example, an elevator in favor of high ceilings, a fireplace, and so on. Older apartment buildings should be compared to similar ones and penalized only for faults uncommon to their vintage.

EQUIPMENT

Items of equipment, including utility systems, fixtures, appliances, cabinets, and other built-in features, seem to represent increasingly higher proportions of the total cost of a residential unit each year. The quality, character, and extent of these items can affect marketability as much as the functional aspects of architectural design and layout.

The appraiser should study the heating system, the water piping, the air conditioning, the electrical system, the bathrooms, the kitchen, and all the other systems or areas that include the various items of equipment and fixtures. Other factors being equal, the more modern and complete the equipment, the greater the market acceptability.

The growing tendency is for appliances, formerly considered personal property, to be built in. Wall ovens, countertop ranges, dishwashers, and disposal units contribute to sales appeal.

Bathroom equipment, fixtures, and finish are other major considerations for a purchaser who easily recognizes new styling and utility. Value and acceptability are increased by ceramic tile, medicine cabinets, shower stalls, vanity lavatories and counters, modern lighting, and an adequate linen closet. Many owners of older residential properties have found that here cost does not always equal value. In the bathroom, as in the kitchen, often it is not economical to replace a good, serviceable item for the sake of modern style or utility. The owner may pay for a complete kitchen remodeling project, only to discover that the cost cannot be fully reflected in the subsequent sale price. Although the modernized kitchen does make the property more salable, some of the cost must be "lived out" as an amenity of ownership, being more fully appreciated by the person making the expenditure than by a prospective buyer.

This is a difficult phase of the analysis for an appraiser and also for an owner who is considering the sale of a residence. When items of equipment are worn out, do not operate properly, or are broken, there is little question that they are replacement items and should be treated as such. But where a fixture, cabinet, or appliance is merely old, old-fashioned, or out of style, it may be better to maintain it. A new owner may decide to replace it and to enjoy the increased amenity value resulting from the expenditure.

Modernization and the replacement of equipment, utility systems, and fixtures must be carefully considered. In most cases, the cost of replacement is not fully reflected in value, but some percentage of the cost should be regained. Consideration of the other elements and aspects of functional utility may also influence the role of the equipment in the measure of marketability and acceptability.

As in valuing single family houses, the market acceptability of apartments is reflected in the effect that the presence or absence of an item of equipment has on rent obtainable from typical tenants. To be considered also are laundry facilities, carpeting, draperies, shades or blinds, stoves, refrigerators, and elevators.

The principle of balance, as it may apply to interior or exterior aspects of a residence, deserves careful study by the appraiser.[2]

---

2. See section on Balance in Chapter 3.

Prevailing circumstances, customs, and requirements help to explain and refine the relationships that represent proper balance in a specific situation. A lack of balance, in which the size or cost of the improvement or any of its individual parts is too great or too small and hence out of proportion for the neighborhood, the site, or the remainder of the structure, implies a probable lack of market acceptability, with a resulting loss of value for the improvement.

Some houses and apartment buildings are designed in a manner to make later additions or modifications practical. Because this often helps to keep a property closely in step with current construction developments, it should add to value. Examples are the house built with a sunroom or breezeway that can be incorporated into a living room, the unfinished area in a grade-entrance basement that can be converted into a family room or playroom, and the unfinished area in a story-and-a-half house with dormers that can be finished as bedrooms and a bath. In all these examples, the principle of balance should be kept in mind. The cost of such an addition or modification (extra initial cost and later finishing cost) may be reasonable and economic to the individual planning it. However, the cost, layout, type of finish, or design may not suit a prospective buyer and may be heavily discounted to arrive at his or her opinion of market value.

A home built to the specifications of individuals for the occupancy of their family usually exhibits the particular tastes and requirements of that family. For a given total area, a childless couple might desire a large dining room and living room, but only two bedrooms. A large family might prefer a large kitchen, more bedrooms, an extra bathroom, a large family room, a small living room, and no dining room. Either of these two homes might encounter a limited market with a loss in acceptability and consequently a lower value—except to a similar user. Because value is affected by such considerations, potential loss is taken into account by the appraiser.

The ideal plan for a single family house or apartment probably has never been achieved. Family needs or desires change, and what is considered essential today may become nonessential tomorrow. However, experience has shown that the living unit planned and constructed to meet the most typical demand—the average requirements of the largest number of families—achieves maximum market value.

SUMMARY

The primary concern of the appraiser in the analysis of a residential property is to weigh all the factors governing its acceptability to prospective purchasers or renters. The architectural design should be appropriate to the site, with good proportions and no distracting features. The plan should be functional, efficiently meeting the requirements of typical purchasers or renters in the price range and location. Equipment and other features of the design should be similarly functional and acceptable in the local market. The property should comply with the principle of balance. The appraiser extends this analysis to include the community, in order to consider the architectural style in the light of local trends, climatic conditions, and social factors, because these considerations are influential in the final test—the acceptability of the property to buyers and prospective tenants.

10
Commercial and Industrial
Functional Utility

Functional utility, as related to commercial or industrial properties, pertains to their efficiency and desirability for their intended uses. *Functional utility* is broadly defined as the sum of a property's attractiveness and usefulness, the ultimate test of which is reflected in its marketability. If a property is sufficiently useful and desirable to attract buyers at a reasonable price, it possesses functional utility. The word *functional,* in appraisal practice, refers to the physical characteristics of a building with reference to the design and ability to perform some useful purpose. The term *functional inutility* implies a loss in desirability or usefulness arising from some inherent physical characteristic that is measurable by a loss in market value.

Architectural style is not so important for commercial and industrial buildings as for residential property. Although there are striking differences in architecture from one period to the next, commercial and industrial buildings of a particular age tend to maintain relatively consistent designs. Changes generally result from the development of new materials and methods of construction or from new and added functional requirements. The floor plan and layout are of major importance in the commercial building or industrial facility because they are closely related to usefulness and efficiency. The relationship of the site area to that of the building is also significant.

The appraiser's knowledge, understanding, and skill are developed here, as in other areas, through experience and by keeping informed of current trends and developments. Almost every merchant, operator, or manufacturer is a source of current information on changes in space and design requirements pertinent to their type of business or operation. Accordingly, a building's owners or tenants may be excellent sources of information. Is the building well-adapted to the occupant's operation? What can be done to make it more useful or suitable? How does it compare with a new, modern, functional building? What are its deficiencies? Building superintendents and maintenance personnel are frequently in a position to provide valuable information pertaining to adequacy and quality of building components and equipment.

Current periodicals, technical bulletins, case studies, experience exchange reports, and other published material, available for many types of commercial and industrial properties, are a means of keeping informed about the trends of equipment and design.

RETAIL STORE BUILDINGS AND SHOPPING AREAS

The appearance and character of retail store buildings has changed substantially over the years, reflecting changes in merchandising patterns and building materials. The typical downtown or central business district and strip-type outlying retail subcenters have been supplemented by the modern shopping center and freestanding suburban shopping facilities. All four of these retail types are in use.

Shopping centers may often present the physical standards with which older store buildings are compared. The large shopping center is designed to enable a group of merchants to offer a complete range of products and services to their supporting community. Problems of the developer of the shopping center include how best to group the stores in relation to each other; how to plan circulation to make the maximum number of stores accessible, with display windows visible to the shopper; and how to provide maximum parking at a minimum distance. Current designs for larger centers usually include completely enclosed malls, which are heated and air conditioned to provide all-weather shopping. Additional amenities frequently include patios or landscaped public areas. Larger centers often include other freestanding buildings such as banks, supermarkets, auto service, office buildings, medical buildings, bowling alleys, theatres, and restaurants. Desirable locations for shopping centers are near intersections of major highways, which afford rapid access to the population providing economic support.

Many retail store buildings that were typical of central retail locations or strip-type, outlying shopping areas are still in use. They have changed little in appearance or character over the years. Columns or bearing walls were spaced at 14- to 20-foot centers, related to the load capacity of ceiling joists. Usually there was a basement to accommodate a heating plant, toilet, sink, and merchandise storage. When the structure included a balcony in the rear, it was used for office and storage. The store front was glass above a bulkhead under the show window, and the front door was recessed. The rear door opened to an alley or rear yard. The driveway, if any, was narrow. Access from the alley made possible deliveries from the rear.

The rapid growth of chain stores and improved building methods have brought about many changes. The modern store building is larger, and the use of new techniques with steel beams and bar joists allows bays of 30 to 60 feet, providing large uncluttered space and flexibility in placement of dividing curtain walls. Some basement area may be included, depending on the needs of the tenant. The store front may be a floor-to-ceiling glass-and-metal treatment, sometimes tilted or on a slight diagonal leading to the door; and there may be a protective canopy. The rear door usually opens on a delivery dock with sufficient access area to permit truck traffic. Lighting is generally high intensity and includes spot and decorative lighting. Convenient electrical outlets and power capacity are provided for showcases, displays, and appliances. Heating is by unit heaters with freestanding air-conditioning units or all-weather central systems with concealed duct distribution. Long, unbroken wall surfaces permit maximum display. Storage areas are well-lighted and conveniently arranged. Floor surfaces may be terrazzo, vinyl tile, or carpet. Ceilings are generally of acoustic material. Ceiling and roof insulation is becoming increasingly important because of high energy costs, which are also responsible for some movement away from the extensive use of glass and some tendency to reduce nonessential high-intensity lighting.

Obsolescence in an old building may be partly curable, because many modern features can be installed. Incurable obsolesence is caused by things that cannot be remedied, either because of physical limitations or because the change would be too expensive to be economically practical. Such items may include close column spacing, fixed partitions or bearing walls, uneven floor levels, poor delivery access, shallow depth of store, inadequate utility service, and lack of adequate and convenient parking. In studying the existing functional utility of a building, both curable and incurable items should be noted, with their cost to cure and an estimate of their negative influence on value.

Parking accommodations needed by a retail store facility vary according to location and type of business. Parking areas generally are surfaced with blacktop and include drainage, lighting, marking, and bumpers. Adequacy of parking may seriously influence the value of retail store properties. In some cities building or zoning codes now include minimum requirements.

Recent research indicates that some formerly accepted standards for shopping center parking may be subject to an adjustment. A 1965 Urban Land Institute study resulted in wide acceptance of 5.5 parking spaces per 1,000 square feet of leasable area (approximately a 2.2 to 1 area ratio) as a reasonable standard. A 1977 Urban Land Institute study reveals that an acceptable ratio for large centers may be 5 spaces per 1,000 square feet of leasable area and, where employee vehicles can utilize off-site parking during annual peak shopping periods, the ratio may be reduced to about four spaces.[1] These levels appear to provide adequate parking for all but the highest demand periods which are of brief duration on a limited number of days in a year. This trend may partially reflect new land uses—for example, theatres—that do not conflict with peak retail parking demands or involve lower parking requirements per unit of area within the center. Parking requirements are also minimized by efficiency of design and use combined with improved control of employee parking.

In older shopping areas parking may be located at the rear of stores, accessible by driveway or alley, or on nearby lots, maintained as a community project. Merchants prefer to have parking in front for convenience and display value, and the desirability of front parking

1. Barton-Aschman Associates, Inc., "Parking Demand at the Regionals," *Urban Land* (May 1977), pp. 3-11.

has been demonstrated by numerous surveys. The development of the freestanding store on an individual site as a satellite to a nearby shopping center is an outgrowth of the demand for more convenient parking. The parking ratio is usually equal to, or greater than, that of the shopping center. Such stores, which complete the variety of products and services available in a prime location, may have great customer drawing power and special parking needs. Included are supermarkets, discount department stores, furniture stores, hardware building supplies, automobile supplies and accessories, and restaurants.

OFFICE BUILDINGS

A primary measure of the efficiency of an office building plan is the ratio of net rentable area to gross area. The net rentable area of office space extends from the inside of the exterior wall to the inside of the corridor wall for multiple-occupancy floors. Corridors, rest rooms, elevator lobbies, elevator shafts, stairways, and vertical facility duct space are excluded. For single-occupancy floors, the gross area includes all except the perimeter walls, the stairwells, elevators, and vertical duct space.

The efficiency (ratio of net rentable to gross area) of multiple-occupancy buildings formerly approximated 76 to 80%. This provided corridors sufficient to permit leasing the entire floor to numerous small tenants. Exceptions to the standard multiple-occupancy buildings are "one-sided" buildings, tower buildings, and buildings with large lobbies, wide corridors, and light wells. Buildings on awkwardly shaped lots may cost more per square foot to build but have less rentable area and therefore a lower efficiency than a conventional building. For a single or major-occupancy tenant, such as a corporate headquarters, the building that produces as much rentable area per floor as possible may be more than 90% efficient.

Many office buildings involve a mixture of multiple- and full-floor occupancies. In multiple-occupancy buildings, a depth of 30 feet is about the maximum that efficiently accommodates small tenants. Elevator lobbies are usually 12 or more feet wide on the first floor, with a typical width for upper-floor corridors of 6 or more feet.

Before the advent of air conditioning and high-intensity lighting, space could not be deeper than 30 feet for two reasons: many cities required a fixed ratio between floor area and exterior window glass; and depths other than 30 feet were generally uneconomic to build. To comply with the required ratios, buildings were erected in various "alphabet" shapes. These second-era (1919 to 1945) buildings initially provided only about 25-footcandles intensity of illumination at desktop level,[2] included no air conditioning, and the heating was usually a two-pipe steam system with cast iron radiation. Men's and women's rest rooms were frequently on alternate floors.

Office buildings built since 1945 represent a different type of structure. They may be conventional with punched windows or with glass exterior walls. The latter type is more flexible, because the mullions are set on the modular lines, and each exterior private office may have a full window. The most efficient module dimensions are from 4½ feet to 5 feet, but there are variations. Probably 95% of modern buildings have fixed glass, although there are certain cleaning advantages to pivoted windows. Lighting intensity may approximate up to 85 or 100 footcandles in office work areas. Floor loads are as high as 100 pounds per square foot owing to the desire on the part of corporate tenants to utilize the space to its maximum capacity. Acoustic tile ceilings with flush fluorescent lighting are common.

Experimental architectural features—for example, walls without windows or extreme setbacks of glass line in efforts to reduce air-conditioning costs—sacrifice rental area and obstruct view. If not economically practical, such features may result in functional inutility. Round, cross, and other odd-shaped buildings have not been generally satisfactory because of economic factors, including layout problems. An efficient design for square or rectangular floors involves a central mechanical core with service facilities available from the interior of the core.

Records have shown the larger and higher buildings have made the best return over the years. However, small office buildings are frequently in order. They subscribe to the specifications of the larger buildings, although records indicate that for office buildings with a typical floor area of less than 10,000 square feet, the ratio of square

---

2. Intensity is measured in footcandles of illumination. A footcandle is a unit of illumination on a surface that is everywhere one foot from a uniform point source of light of one candle, and equal to one lumen per square foot. For office buildings, intensity of illumination is measured at desktop height.

feet to vertical facilities is disadvantageous, and generally the operating costs per square foot are higher.

In large cities there may be reduced necessity for providing parking space, but in the majority of other cities, where public transportation is meager or nonexistent, it would be most impractical to build a large office building without owned parking facilities immediately adjacent to the office building or within it. The presence or absence of owned parking in any office building and the practicability, efficiency, and economic effect of the inclusion of parking garage facilities within, or adjacent to, a large office building affect its functional utility.

The standard ceiling height for modern office space is 9 feet, but many buildings have been successfully rented with ceilings that are only 8½ feet high. Only a few buildings have been built with ceilings in excess of 9 feet to meet unusual requirements. The larger the floor areas, the closer to 9 feet should be the ceiling.

The exterior fascia of the modern office building may be stone, poured or precast concrete, marble, porcelainized steel, porcelainized aluminum, sheet bronze, mosaic, glass, brick, or terra cotta. In the regions of severe frost conditions, terra cotta has proven unsatisfactory because water gets into open joints, freezes, and cracks the terra cotta tile. It is seldom encountered today except on older structures. There is a growing tendency to set the building back from the lot line and to install arcades, which tends to "open up" the downtown area. Many ordinances are written so that this design is almost a necessity if an owner seeks maximum development. In some cities, where temperature extremes are encountered, a trend to second-level or sublevel pedestrian walkways connecting central business district structures is evident with substantial economic consequences for the properties involved.

To estimate the extent of obsolescence and functional inutility in an office building, factors to be considered in relation to current standards include:

1. Ratio of net rentable area to gross area
2. Corridor widths
3. Ceiling heights and waste space
4. Floor load design
5. Conventional or glass wall construction

6. Type of window with respect to vertical section, and whether of fixed glass
7. Allocation of lobby space
8. Efficient use of first-floor store or office space
9. Flexibility in layout of office space
10. Number, location, and size of rest rooms
11. Elevator design, capacity, and probable remaining life before replacement is necessary
12. Adequate wiring for lighting, office machinery, and power demands
13. Quality and design of heating and air-conditioning systems or adaptability for an installation of adequate equipment
14. Ability to comply with OSHA standards
15. Parking adequacy and convenience
16. Location with respect to centers of business or tenant-related activities in the community
17. Public acceptance of architectural design

INDUSTRIAL BUILDINGS

Before 1925 most factories were built in urban centers. The employees either walked to work or used public transportation. Unlike steel mills and large assembly plants, most factories were centrally located on high-priced land, which resulted in multistory construction. The mill-type factory building had heavy masonry bearing walls, timber columns and beams, heavy wood floors, 10- to 15-foot ceiling heights, elevators, and rail or truck docks. Column spacing provided for 10- to 20-foot bays (space between columns).

The multistory reinforced concrete building appeared about 1910. It generally provided a concrete floor with columns 16 to 20 feet on center and 9- to 12-foot ceilings.

Beginning about 1925, widespread use of automobile transportation made it practical to decentralize industrial locations. Utilization of less expensive land permitted one-story design plus adequate parking.

For work-in-process, horizontal transportation by conveyor is usually less expensive and more efficient than vertical transportation by elevator. A production line or assembly process is generally more efficient at one level. Almost all new factory construction is single story, including mezzanine or upper-floor office space, and partial basements

The predominant requirement today is for a single-story building on a large site with ample parking. The availability of rail service is an important consideration for many industrial operations, but for most plants, good truck service facilities and accessibility to major thoroughfares are the essential considerations. The adequacy of truck or rail docks and other loading or unloading facilities is often an important factor in building utility.

Ceiling clearance is now typically 16 feet or higher. The increased use of forklift equipment permits industry to utilize higher ceilings and encourages larger clear-span bay areas. Bay size has increased from 20 feet to 50 feet or more. Modern office areas are well-finished, lighted, and air conditioned, varying in extent with plant size and type of use.

Older buildings present many problems for the appraiser. The market clearly demonstrates that upper-floor space is generally obsolete, and elevators often are too small and too slow. In many cases a low floor-load capacity limits the utility of the space. Bay sizes of 16 x 16 feet or less, and ceiling heights between 10 and 12 feet limit usability and indicate the existence of accrued depreciation due to functional obsolescence. Palletized operations generally require a minimum 16-foot clearance with a current trend to substantially higher clear heights, permitting the use of improved machinery and handling equipment as well as new storage techniques.

As trucks have become larger, enclosed docks and loading areas may be too small. The "spotting" and maneuvering of tractor-trailers usually requires 65 feet or more of clear area plus the depth of standing trailers in front of the unloading area.

In addition to its use for parking and loading, yard area is also needed for utility installations and storage. Experience has demonstrated that a site that provides some room for future expansion, a feature often lacking in older industrial properties, has greater demand than one that does not.

Among other important items to be noted are quantity and type of energy available, adequacy of sanitary facilities, lunchroom and locker-room area, lighting, water supply and waste disposal, sprinklers, fire hydrants, hose racks, power wiring, crane capacity, and compressed air or other piping.

Many existing industrial plants are a combination of older and modern industrial design, with plant or office space additions that reflect past expansion by a particular user or owner. Although such a complex may be adequately serving the needs of the existing occupant, it may have substantial obsolescence or functional inutility to typical users who are prospective purchasers. Even the more modern sections may suffer functional obsolescence from their combination with older buildings. In such a complex the principle of contribution (to the value of the whole) is a guide in measuring the value of any particular component. Balance (a viable relationship between the areas allocated to manufacturing, warehousing, employees' service areas, and office functions) is also an important principle here.

Gross areas should generally be used in referring to industrial buildings, and outside dimensions should be used in deriving the area of single buildings or a group of buildings taken as a whole. This applies to both single-story and multistory buildings, as well as entire floors used in multistory buildings. In cases where floors are subdivided among several tenants, inside measurements apply; space used in common, such as stairways, elevators, corridors, and toilet facilities, is excluded.

Warehouses

The history and development of warehouse facilities is similar to that of manufacturing plants. The single-story warehouse is often more efficient than the multistory warehouse. Docks and loading facilities are of major importance, with truck and rail docks frequently taking up an entire side of the building. Many warehouses are now arranged with the receiving function on one side of the building and shipping on the other. Load levelers, canopies, flexible accordion enclosures, and extensive heating and lighting are common at dock openings.

Extra land for expansion is important. However, parking facilities need not be so extensive as for the manufacturing building of similar size because there are fewer employees in a warehouse. The walls and frame may often be of lighter weight; the lighting, not so intensive; the office space, often less than 5% of the area; and heating and plumbing facilities, of simpler design and more limited quantity.

However, floors and truck driveways must be of heavy construction and capacity. Because warehouse buildings usually are less expensive to erect, they rent for lower rates per square foot of area than do manufacturing plants of similar size. Hence, in developing unit costs, rentals, or market sales data, the appraiser differentiates between the two types of facility.

Sales-and-Service Facilities

Another category of industrial improvement is the sales-and-service or wholesale-and-distribution facility. These facilities may be free-standing or in planned industrial parks; single-occupancy or (frequently) multiple-tenancy facilities with self-contained rental units having offices (often 10 to 35% of the area); finished display areas; storage or work space; separate loading docks and separate sanitary facilities.

The appraiser measures and balances the floor space devoted to each use. From the point of view of functional utility, such buildings are simple in appearance, usually one story in height, with an adequate amount of well-finished and air-conditioned office space, good receiving and shipping facilities, and adequate parking. They are in locations that are convenient for distribution and accessible for customers.

COMMERCIAL BUILDINGS

There are many types of commercial structures, frequently involving special purpose features. All present different challenges and areas of research to the appraiser. Drive-in businesses, such as restaurants, dairy stores, dry cleaners, and banks, represent one category. These have a common need for a good location on major thoroughfares, correct placement on the lot, ample parking, driveways of adequate size and number, with well-placed curb-cuts.

Freestanding "fast food" facilities are numerous in most communities. These typically involve substantial amounts of equipment, all of which is not real property; and their distinctive and changing designs generally imply a limited economic life.

Other types of structures for commercial or related uses include post offices, mortuaries, bowling alleys, greenhouses, automobile sales and service structures, nursing homes, research and development buildings. Each poses specific problems in appraisal analysis. Industry publications or appraisal literature[3] provide additional information concerning these and other categories of real estate.

Parking Garages

The older parking garage usually consisted of a multistory building with 22- to 24-foot bays with ramps and occasionally elevators. Changing car sizes over the years have combined with a lack of flexibility in structural design to create functional obsolescence in many existing parking garage structures. The current trend to smaller cars may tend to alleviate this problem in some older structures, but if continued, it may tend to introduce obsolescence due to superadequacy in others.

The typical parking ramp may be a series of open platforms, substituting "stub" wall barriers for exterior walls, and no longer an enclosed and heated building. A typical functional garage may be multilevel, frequently with separate entrances for alternate levels so that only half the levels must be traversed to reach the top level.

The pigeon-hole type of mechanical parking facility is a structure utilizing special car-moving equipment instead of ramps. Some parking decks with two to three levels, using a steel structural frame and precast prestressed floor slabs, have been designed to be taken down, moved, and reassembled. The unit term of reference for parking facilities is per car or per square foot of parking deck area.

Truck Terminals

The truck terminal is essentially an enclosed warehouse area with doors on each side of a heavy-duty floor at truck-bed height. There are usually offices, utilities, and washrooms at one end, and the roof may overhang to provide a protective dock canopy. Truck terminal rentals are frequently considered on a basis of dollars per door per month or dollars per square foot of gross area. Similarly, truck terminal sales may be expressed in relation to either door or square-foot

---

3. Listings of available readings may be found in *Real Estate Appraisal Bibliography (1945-1972)*, 2nd ed. (Chicago: American Institute of Real Estate Appraisers, 1973).

units. In some areas climatic conditions and type of operation may eliminate the need for installation of overhead doors along the truck dock.

Older terminals were as small as 30 feet deep (door to door), but this across-dock distance has gradually increased to 80 feet or more to accommodate storage space and mechanical equipment for handling and transhipment of cargo. Usually 100 feet or more of parking, turning, and backing area are needed on each side, plus trailer storage area, scales, pumps, or other facilities. Many larger modern terminals include a separate garage building for service of the tractor units.

Theatres

Theatres began to experience economic adversity as early as the 1930s following the advent of talking pictures, which required a change in the shape of the auditorium for optimum operation. The situation was later aggravated by the competition of television. With the decline in business, the cost of maintaining the larger theatres—especially the ornate, expensive "movie palaces" of the 1920s—became prohibitive. These older theatres were usually located downtown or in local business areas, where a further decline in attendance resulted from economic obsolescence, such as the lack of adequate parking and deteriorating environments.

At the same time, there has been an increase in drive-in theatres, art theatres, and theatres in shopping center locations. The new theatres are generally smaller, more functional, less lavish in design, furnished with good air-conditioning systems and simply but well-seated. Newer houses are frequently freestanding buildings with multiple-screen capability. They are often built in or near shopping centers, benefiting from the adequate convenient parking. The unit of sale or rental comparison for theatres is usually dollars per seat, but the square-foot unit is also used. Old abandoned theatres suffer substantial accrued functional depreciation because their special-purpose design limits their efficiency as theatres and makes them difficult to convert to alternate uses.

Service Stations

The size and design of gasoline service stations have changed over the years in response to economic and social forces affecting the industry. The original small station, with two to four pumps and a canopy, first expanded to include a service bay and more pump islands. This trend to larger sites and more service facilities continued, with ingress, egress, and locational factors of primary importance. Increasing labor costs have encouraged a trend to fewer stations which are designed to achieve high gallonage figures. A lower percentage of stations are company-owned, and self-service represents the latest competitive response to the higher costs of labor and the product.

For years major oil companies sought geographic coverage and made their own markets in an ever-expanding distribution system. With the recent necessity to balance production limitations and distribution facilities, some major distributors have withdrawn from selected marketing areas or disposed of stations that were uneconomic or on inadequate sites for modern use. This has created a secondary market in surplus locations and facilities. Conversions to alternate uses have salvaged value from many of these existing improvements. Remodeling programs have included conversion to freestanding offices or to commercial uses such as dry cleaners, laundry pickup stores, offices, equipment rental or specialty retail shops. When conversion is practical, the new use typically reflects the location and the character of surrounding improvements. The appraiser of such facilities recognizes the consistent use theory and includes a study of the contribution to value made by the improvements. It may be necessary to recognize use limitations prescribed by the former occupants or owners.

Independent or discount operations often utilize sites not acceptable to the major oil companies or combine operations with car-wash or auto-repair facilities, grocery stores, or other types of merchandising. These operations comprise a substantial segment of the market. Emphasis is on high gallonage volume with a relatively low investment in buildings.

The valuation of service stations or service station sites is related to the segment of the market represented and to current marketing goals and techniques. Application of the basic principles is reinforced by experience in the analysis of special purpose properties.

Hotels

Hotels have architectural style characteristics in common with apartments and office buildings. New hotel buildings usually have a steel or concrete frame with exterior curtain wall of masonry or metal or glass panels. With few exceptions, the rooms are larger, have lower ceilings, more windows, and better decorating than in older hotels. The bathrooms are smaller, on interior walls, adequately ventilated, and generally include counter tops or dressing rooms and other features. The building is air conditioned with individual room-temperature controls. Often the main lobby has been moved up one level to provide retail space at the street frontage. Assembly and meeting rooms, dining rooms, and ballrooms are arranged with folding walls to accommodate meetings of various sizes.

The success of the large hotel is usually tied to convention and meeting business. Commercial travelers and automobile tourists generally seem to prefer the convenience and free parking of motels, either urban or suburban. For this reason, the meeting facilities, restaurant capacity, and other services that relate to convention trade are important considerations in analyzing a hotel operation. The convention facilities of a city and of other hotels often are as important as the facilities within the hotel being appraised. Fundamentally, however, the hotel sells sleeping rooms, which may be booked by conventions far in advance. The physical facilities of the services and public rooms contribute to support the room rate and occupancy. Quality of management is a critical consideration. The appraiser notes whether a facility is owner- or lessee-operated, the chain or franchise relationships, and the potential for referral business. Familiarity with standard hotel accounting practice is essential for competent analysis of a hotel operation and for estimating the quality of existing management.

Motels

The facilities offered by the modern motel have changed since the days of the tourist court. Catering to smaller conventions and meetings, some motels are equal to full-scale hotels with restaurants, meeting and assembly rooms, swimming pools, telephones, TV, and room services. Some of the new, large, multistory motels or motor-hotels seem to be growing away from the original motel idea, which was to offer comfortable rooms with minimum service but maximum convenience of arrival and departure.

A location near a major highway or thoroughfare for convenient access to the community, the airport, or other centers of activity is desirable. Appearance of the exterior and attractive landscaping are other important considerations.

Because a small motel is less efficient to operate than a larger facility, most new motels have at least 100 units. The metropolitan motor-hotel of several hundred units is hardly distinguishable from the concept of any major hotel and is analyzed similarly in the appraisal process. Many motel owners find that membership in a chain with a referral and advance reservation service is important for maintaining a satisfactory occupancy level. This and the average rate per occupied room constitute the critical factors in any hotel or motel analysis.

The physical characteristics that are not functionally ideal in older motels are apparent when compared with newer ones. The term of reference for comparing one motel with another is generally the individual rental unit. Considered separately or included with this rental unit are the collateral facilities, such as those for dining, meetings, and recreation. Also acceptable is comparison on a square-foot basis.[4]

FARM BUILDINGS

The amount of utility farm buildings possess may have no fixed relation to their age or replacement cost. An old set of buildings could serve a farm as well as new buildings. The usefulness of the buildings is related to the type and size of the operation. This is so fundamental that the value of farm buildings is considered by buyer and seller in terms of how many dollars per acre the buildings add to the land.

The ratio of the value of farm buildings to all farm real estate has been declining since about 1940. Nationwide, the ratio dropped from 23.6% in 1960 to 21.0% in 1964, 19.7% in 1967, 17.5% in 1972, and 17.0% in 1977.

The average value of farmland and buildings per acre, the total value, and the total building value are shown in Table 10.1.

---

4. For further information on hotel-motel valuation, see Stephen Rushmore, *The Valuation of Hotels and Motels* (Chicago: American Institute of Real Estate Appraisers, 1978).

TABLE 10.1 Farm Property, 1977

Region	Value per Acre	Total Building Value (millions)	Total Value (millions)
Northeast	$1,178	$ 6,928	$ 23,952
Lake States	679	9,736	37,039
Corn Belt	1,101	24,965	134,592
Northern Plains	309	6,648	56,281
Appalachian	584	7,464	31,454
Southeast	571	4,499	26,071
Delta	509	3,091	19,306
Southern Plains	336	5,282	52,909
Mountain	188	4,715	41,578
Pacific	491	4,757	35,472
Average for 48 states	456		
Total		$78,085	$459,654

Source: *Farm Real Estate Market Developments,* Economic Research Service, U.S. Department of Agriculture, July 1977.

The economics of farming and more advanced mechanical methods increase the acreage one person can farm. This has resulted in larger land holdings.

When a contiguous farm is added to expand an operation, the new owner may have little need for the additional buildings. However, the vacant dwelling may be rented as a residence, and the expanded acreage creates a greater degree of utility for the primary set of farm buildings.

Since the average farm has been increasing in size, the farmer needs more and larger equipment. Therefore, the equipment sheds must be built to larger dimensions. Often structures built some years ago have no further use. In dairying, the need for more ensilage calls for more silos and less hay and straw storage. Baling permits more compact storage, so often the large barns that were once necessary are too big, except when more acreage is to be added. The stable, with horse stalls and stanchion space for cows, is being replaced by the loafing shed and milking parlor. A stable with a low ceiling prevents use of modern equipment, such as the front-end loader.

SUMMARY

To estimate functional inutility in a building, the appraiser compares it with a modern functional building. All variations of the problem of functional utility cannot be dealt with completely here, but certain broad observations are made.

Most enterprises now need more efficiently developed space in which to operate. With few exceptions, sites involve larger land-to-building area ratios to meet building-line restrictions and to provide parking, loading, yard storage, and room for expansion. This applies to most types of industrial, commercial, or income-producing properties.

Structures with more functional dimensions are the result of two developments: the use of modern lightweight materials (steel and prefabricated prestressed concrete building framing and roof structures) and more efficient construction methods. New materials and more functional dimensions have resulted from improvements in the design and efficiency of equipment (heating, air conditioning, lighting, plumbing, power, elevators, and built-in fixtures). New types of material requiring less maintenance and improved methods have rendered many older buildings obsolete and functionally inadequate.

Any study of the functional utility of a commercial or industrial building includes the energy efficiency and the flexibility of the heating and air conditioning equipment as well as the availability of the energy supply.

11
Building Material and Equipment

The appraisal of real property usually involves the valuation of building improvements in addition to the estimation of land value. An adequate and competent description of the improvements usually precedes the valuation analysis and comprises an important section in the appraisal report. A broad general knowledge of construction materials, methods, and equipment is desirable to prepare this description in a professional manner. Descriptions of proposed improvements, prepared from plans and specifications, require the ability to read and interpret blueprints and to understand the meaning of standard symbols found on blueprints for the architectural or mechanical aspects of design. In the appraisal of large properties or those with unusual characteristics, professional assistance may be desirable.

The character, quality, and appearance of the construction are reflected in each of the three appraisal approaches to a value estimate. They have a major influence on the cost estimate, the accrued depreciation estimate, the ability of the property to produce rental income, and comparability with other properties in the market data approach. An analysis of the quality of construction methods and materials is an important complement to the appraiser's consideration of the quality of structural design and architectural planning.

A structure may have good functional layout and attractive design, but be built with inferior materials and poor workmanship. These conditions increase maintenance and utility costs and adversely affect the marketability of a property. Conversely, a building can be built too well or at a cost beyond that justified by its utility. A purchaser will not pay for the excess cost. The loss may be recaptured only in part by the original owner through reduced future maintenance expense.

Economy of construction at a practical or reasonable level results in an improvement that during its economic life will produce a rental income commensurate with its cost. Maintenance and operation expenses may be slightly more than minimum, but the net result is more satisfactory than if the building were of superior construction, calling for a higher level of taxes, interest, and amortization charges.

To achieve this desired level of construction cost requires a proper choice and use of building materials and construction methods. Upon inspection, the appraiser recognizes the appropriate combination that results in a building adequate to serve its intended purpose.

CLIMATE

Since climatic conditions influence regional construction practices, they affect use of materials and architectural style. Neither the materials nor the styles typical of Florida and southern California would be functionally acceptable in New England. A house that is standard in the South would not be adequate shelter if built in Minnesota.

The same factors apply to commercial and industrial buildings. Climatic conditions affect the size and capacity of heating and air-conditioning equipment and the size and depth of foundations. Driveways require a deeper base and stronger design where subject to severe frost conditions.

AVAILABILITY OF MATERIALS

Availability of materials often is a more salient determinant than climate. Because of longer life and lower maintenance cost, a house built of brick might be assumed to have greater value than that of a house built of wood. But the question arises: how available is the material? Brick in Augusta, Maine, might cost twice as much as in

Chicago, while the cost of lumber in Augusta might be half the price in Chicago. In Augusta, a well-maintained house built of wood may have greater resale potential (at a price consistent with its cost) than a house built of brick that was brought from a distance at great expense.

Sometimes unusual building materials, which are native to the region, influence the construction and style of the local buildings. For example, in the suburban Philadelphia area, a particularly attractive stone is readily available and well adapted for use in the construction of homes of all sizes. For generations, its use has been popular in houses of colonial or Georgian design. Another example is Lannon stone, a hard and colorful limestone quarried near Lannon, Wisconsin. In that area its use is particularly popular for picturesque architectural types such as English, Norman, and French cottages. In California redwood has been widely used for exterior finish; similarly, cypress is popular in the South. Almost every section of the country uses native materials in building construction. In judging materials and construction, the appraiser considers local conditions as they relate to climate, source of materials, popularity of types, and any other special factors that influence local construction practice.

EQUIPMENT

The quality and extent of equipment are considerations in the analysis of a building. Central heating and air conditioning, ventilation, and electric lighting provide artificial climate and daylight. Plumbing and water supply lines, elevators, communication systems, and other items of building equipment provide essential services or comforts. As building equipment becomes more highly specialized, the structure tends to diminish in relative economic importance, and the equipment through which services and amenities are created becomes more important. For example, in a typical large office building, as much as 35 to 50% of the total cost of the building may be attributable to equipment. However, equipment is a primary source of depreciation in a property. Compared with the basic structural components, much of the equipment is short-lived. Thus income-producing properties lose appeal to tenants when competing properties offer newer and improved equipment and amenities. In the analysis of income-producing properties, operating and maintenance costs relate directly to the extent, quality, and design of the equipment. As equipment is properly or improperly selected and maintained, operating expenses may be higher or lower. Therefore, the appraiser also studies equipment in the analysis of an operating expense statement, in planning to remodel or modernize, and in arriving at the general estimate of accrued depreciation.

A house or other structure may be overequipped or underequipped for its size or location. Overequipment might consist of the installation of a combination hot-water heating and air-conditioning system with individual unit convectors in each room in a small ranch house in a neighborhood where forced warm-air furnaces and window air conditioners are typical. Another example might be the inclusion in a ranch house of an intercommunication system with AM-FM radio and with a microphone-speaker in each room as well as at the front and rear doors. Overequipment usually is the result of a whim of the owner or builder. It should not be confused with the installation of practical devices that are in general use. Underequipment is more common than overequipment. The loss in potential value is minor if installation of proper equipment is practical. The study of one aspect of functional obsolescence is directed toward the proper balance between the structure and its equipment.

Some years ago the fashion in houses was to install bracket and ceiling lighting with comparatively expensive light fixtures. Then came the trend to movable floor or table lamps, requiring many convenience outlets in strategic locations. Such small amenities that seem insignificant may be important to prospective purchasers and may provide important sales appeal in the single family home market.

BUILDING MATERIAL ANALYSIS

Many obvious structural details tend to indicate the quality of the construction and the materials used in a building. For example, a house built to provide maximum size and finish at a minimum cost may often be identified by items such as the following:

1. Poorly installed cement asbestos shingles, uneven horizontal edges, gaps in joints, corner boards instead of galvanized

metal corners. Drop siding with minimal overlap or defects similar to those above.

2. Rough concrete basement walls due to dirty forms, snap tie holds that are not pointed, rough form joints, uneven tops of walls, poorly waterproofed walls, honeycomb surface areas exposing gravel or stone.

3. Minimum number of posts under a beam, posts not plumb or lacking a properly supported bearing-plate, beam not leveled and not pointed in wall, rough, poorly troweled basement floor.

4. Low-grade of aluminum sliding sash, thin weak frames, low-quality glass and screens, frames not made to mount storm sash, sash loose and poorly weatherstripped.

5. Window frames badly set, poor caulking job, improperly designed lower frame members that are liable to cause sagging or stains on siding.

6. Poorly applied roofing, large surface exposure, uneven lines, variation in color from mixed lots, uneven ridge line.

7. Low-quality floor joists, excessive knots (particularly at bottom), insufficient bearing at ends, high and low spots in floor, substandard bridging, single joist under bearing partitions causing floors to squeak or to be uneven.

8. Use of ⅜-inch drywall, studs not properly trued, inadequate taping, poor nailing, badly sand-finished paint.

9. Low-grade wood trim, many knots, badly fitted, poor stain finish, inferior hardware, only one pair of hinges per door, defective oak flooring

10. Low-grade valves, galvanized water pipe, minimum-quality plumbing fixtures, lack of shut-off valves in fixture supply lines.

11. Furnace with minimum BTU[1] rating, small-sized heat ducts inadequate for central air conditioning.

12. Minimum-capacity electric service, inadequate number and no spare circuits, insufficient number of convenience outlets.

13. Ceiling insulation that is below standard thickness, minimal or no wall insulation except fibreboard sheathing.

---

1. One BTU (British thermal unit) is the amount of heat required to raise one pound of water one degree in temperature (Fahrenheit). The BTU requirement for heating-plant capacity relates to the cubic content, exposure, design, and insulation level of the structure to be heated.

14. Low-quality and limited size kitchen wall and base cabinets, minimum-size cabinet sink with porcelain top, minimum-quality and amount of kitchen equipment; wall-mounted bathroom lavatory without counter or vanity.

This is only a partial list for one type of building. National cost services typically describe several categories of construction graded by quality and reflect relative cost levels for each. The construction attributes of each category are described. The appraiser becomes familiar with similar characteristics for various types of buildings. The observation of these and similar details leads to a sound estimate of the quality of construction.

FOUNDATION

The foundation is the natural or prepared base supporting a structure. It may consist of wood posts, stone or concrete piers, a poured integral concrete slab with frost wall, or a reinforced concrete footing with concrete block, stone, or reinforced concrete basement wall. Wood posts are subject to deterioration, and piers may sink if not properly designed and installed.

The basement wall generally is made of poured concrete, often reinforced with steel bars. It gives a smooth wall which can be painted and waterproofed. Unreinforced concrete block is subject to cracking, provides less resistance to outside earth pressure, and is more difficult to waterproof. No foundation can be better than the footing on which the basement wall rests. A spread footing is all that is generally required for undisturbed, adequate load-bearing soil. Poor or filled soil may require poured concrete piers and grade beams. Adequate provision for drainage is essential for foundations to prevent collection of water which may lead to foundation problems involving settling or leaking. Buildings without basements in cold climates require frost walls and insulation with the poured concrete floor slab, usually reinforced with wire mesh. Unexcavated areas may be enclosed by foundation walls to create crawl space for access to utilities.

In commercial and industrial construction the walls, pilasters, and columns rest on reinforced concrete footings or on reinforced concrete grade beams resting on pilings or poured concrete piers or caissons. Interior columns may rest on spread footings or on piers or caissons. It may be necessary to consult building plans to ascertain foundation details.

FRAME AND FRAMING

The load-bearing skeleton members of the building constitute the structural frame. In wood residential construction,[2] the outside walls are framed by vertical members called studs, resting on plates bearing on the subfloor. Joists, in turn, rest on a plate that is placed on, and secured to, the foundation wall. Current requirements for depth of insulation frequently require 2 x 6 exterior wall studs in lieu of the 2 x 4 studs formerly in general use. When the studs are cut at ceiling height, horizontal plates laid on top, and more studs continued upward for the second story, the house is *platform framed*. When the studs are continuous, notched to receive a horizontal member at the second-floor line, it is *balloon framed*. Either solid masonry walls or a steel beam may carry the principal interior bearing partitions. Roof trusses have eliminated some need for interior bearing partitions, particularly in one-story structures, and made possible larger living spaces. Wall members and specially constructed panels are often assembled in component sections in plants, hauled to the site, and raised into position.

When a house has solid masonry walls, the exterior wall is load bearing and substitutes for the frame. Since many "brick" homes are actually of brick veneer construction, with the same wood-stud frame as the wood home, an important consideration is the number and quality of the wall ties securing the brick veneer to the structural frame behind it. Air circulation is necessary behind the brick work to prevent dry rot.

In apartment construction nonfireproof structures employ brick and other masonry bearing walls with interior steel beams and interior fire walls where required. Some of the smaller types are built in the same way as brick veneer homes. Most of the larger structures are of steel frame construction with masonry or panel curtain walls. Com-

---

2. Roof and wall framing diagram, in American Institute of Real Estate Appraisers and Society of Real Estate Appraisers, *Real Estate Appraisal Terminology*, ed., Byrl N. Boyce (Cambridge, Mass.: Ballinger Publishing Company, 1975), p. 259.

pletely fireproof apartment buildings usually have a poured reinforced concrete frame.

Hotels and office buildings generally are built in the same style as
large apartment buildings with either structural steel or reinforced
concrete frames. Store buildings are usually steel framed, but may be
concrete framed, particularly when multistory. Older store buildings
may have masonry bearing walls with wood roof and interior partition
framing.

Over the years the structural design of industrial buildings has
changed. Before the turn of the century, the multistory industrial or
loft building was timber framed, usually with 12 x 12-inch or larger
columns supporting wooden beams or joists. After 1900 steel began to
replace timber framing, and by 1910 many multistory industrial buildings were built of reinforced concrete with rectangular columns and
beams and heavy slab floors. Round mushroom-capped columns
under rectangular areas of heavier floor slab came into general use
about 1920. Several other types of integral beam and slab, such as the
tee-beam floor design with hollow tile between the tee-beams or the
use of pans to form beams or waffle patterns, became common,
particularly for buildings requiring lower live loads.

Precast units, frequently using prestressed reinforcing steel, are
widely employed. Tilt-up construction utilizes precast concrete
slabs, which may be lifted to a vertical position to become exterior
bearing or curtain walls. The interior frame may consist of precast
and prestressed concrete beams and columns with lighter precast
slabs constituting the structural roof.

With the trend to functional, single-story horizontal operation,
industrial plant framing usually is steel, with the bays becoming
progressively larger. Bays 30 to 50 feet are common, and some air-
craft plants have been built with over 100 feet clear span between
columns. When the frame also supports heavy cranes, the weight and
size of the structural steel members are increased.

Steel framing is usually less expensive and may be erected more
rapidly than poured concrete. Among the disadvantages are that it is
subject to bending and twisting in a fire, pulling adjacent members out
of position, and the necessity for painting, unless fireproofed. Reinforced concrete structures are slower to erect, but are relatively
undamaged by fire.

EXTERIOR WALLS

Load-bearing walls in residences are usually solid masonry or wood frame with siding or some type of veneer surface. Solid masonry walls may be of face brick with a less expensive block backing or a cavity wall (brick plus air space plus back-up block), or in some cases poured concrete. Exterior walls for wood frame houses usually have sheathing (fiberboard, plywood, or boards) on the studs covered by material such as wood siding, composition siding, stucco, cement asbestos shingles, wood shakes, plywood with battens, brick or stone veneer, or aluminum siding. Some homes have extensive areas of wall ornamentation.

Wood and similar materials require painting or other finish; brick and stone periodically need tuckpointing; cement asbestos shingles are relatively fragile; and aluminum siding may be dented by hail or vandals. Climatic conditions, availability, local customs, and personal preferences govern selection.

Three types of windows are in common use—double-hung, various types of casement or pivot, and sliding sash. The frames and sash are wood, aluminum, or steel. In addition to noting the type, the appraiser judges their quality, workability, and inclusion of screens or storm sash. There has been widespread use of aluminum windows, many with three or four tracks, in areas where there is seasonal variation in temperature. Picture windows, large areas of fixed glass in wood or metal frames, thermopane glass, weatherstripping, and aluminum storm doors are widely used.

Exterior doors may be wood or metal, panel or flush styles. Except in the most economical construction, exterior wood doors should be solid, although interior flush doors are generally hollow core.

Many commercial and industrial buildings use masonry walls, usually brick with back-up block or concrete block (which requires some type of waterproofing paint). Where the wall is load-bearing, usually masonry pilasters are integrated into the wall for structural strength. Most exterior walls are curtain walls (nonload-bearing), made of porcelain enamel, steel, aluminum, precast aggregate concrete slabs, or glass. For industrial buildings, less handsome but serviceable materials are available, such as corrugated iron, tilt-up precast concrete slabs, asbestos board, fiberglass, and metal sandwich panels.

Longer walls and large roof slabs require expansion joints at reasonable intervals.

Most sash in commercial or industrial buildings is of steel. There has been some trend to eliminate windows in many buildings that are air conditioned. Doors are usually metal or metal and glass. Truck doors may be electrically operated to rise vertically. Show windows, entries, and store fronts are glass, generally with aluminum or stainless steel construction. This kind of building is often very plain, except for the face exposed to traffic. In modern industry and commerce the public image is considered so important that the exposed side of a building may be made very attractive, with ornamentation, identification signs, lighting, and landscaping.

FLOORS

Value is also affected by the structural design of the floor and its covering. The floor structure in most residences consists of wood floor joists bearing on foundation walls and beams. Floor sheathing of plywood is typical, instead of the one-inch boards formerly used. In some residences steel bar joists support a thin concrete slab surface. In most rooms, except the kitchen and bath, floor finish is usually hardwood or carpeting over a plywood subfloor. Wood flooring may be traditional tongue-and-groove oak strips; parquet; or other kinds, such as hard maple, pecan, or ranch plank with pegs. The use of prefinished end-matched flooring eliminates on-the-job sanding and finishing.

Most kitchen floors are plywood covered with some type of linoleum, vinyl, or other resilient floor tile or sheet material. Many bathrooms may also have a resilient floor covering, but most have ceramic tile which is applied on a cement base over the sheathing. Some type of tile or resilient cover is common on entry hall floors.

The widespread use of wall-to-wall carpeting has eliminated much hardwood flooring. Panels of plywood or similar material are used as the underlayment for the carpeting. Many homes include a family room, which may be the only one with hardwood flooring. In homes with concrete slab floors, or in homes without basements when the concrete slab floor is on grade, the finish may be terrazzo or resilient tile.

Basement floors should be a concrete slab poured over a proper fill (tamped sand, crushed rock, or cinders) on a well-graded surface with sufficient slope for good drainage. More care is given to basement floors in modern homes because of the widespread use of basements for recreation rooms and workshops. The surface should be smooth, the joint between the floor and wall should be good, with adequate yard drainage away from the basement walls to minimize potential leakage or moisture. Portable electric dehumidifier units have also helped increase the use of basement areas.

The floors of porches, verandas, patios, and balconies should be pitched to drain away from the building. For appearance and serviceability, these floors are usually concrete, but stone, brick, or wood may also be used. Metal decking may be utilized for balconies. The indoor-outdoor living concept has increased the importance of these facilities in current residential design. An elevated deck with a patio area below may enhance residential marketability in moderate climates.

In modern commercial and industrial construction, floors are usually reinforced concrete. Floors on grade are usually concrete slabs on fill, with thickness and reinforcement depending on their intended use. Industrial floor surfaces are typically smooth and at one grade to allow easy movement of materials. Such surfaces may include a hardener. Commercial floors are troweled smooth to take resilient tile or carpet covering, or they may be finished in terrazzo.

For lightweight floors, the usual supporting structure consists of steel bar joists resting on beams or bearing walls with a corrugated metal slab form or deck material. Over this structure is poured a concrete slab 2 to 4 inches thick with wire mesh reinforcement and frequently using lightweight aggregate. Hollow concrete precast members may also be used as the floor structure. Such construction is common in motels and small commercial buildings. For medium floor loads, pan-type floor design may be used with integral reinforced ribs (tee-beams) which are part of the floor structure. For heavy floor loads and fire protection, floors may be heavy concrete slabs, reinforced with steel bars, poured integrally with beams and columns as part of the building frame.

Many older commercial and industrial buildings use wood joists, semi-mill and mill construction. Mill construction consists of timbers and planks placed in heavy, solid masses, to expose to fire the least number of corners or ignitable projections; and when fire occurs, to make it readily accessible to water from a fire hose. Accordingly, earlier joist and light floor construction was replaced by widely spaced, heavy wood beams supporting heavier floor designs. Beams might be 12 x 16 inches supporting 3-inch thick tongue-and-groove planking, sometimes with a maple or other finish floor added to provide the working surface.

INTERIORS

Residential partitions are usually constructed of 2 x 4 studs with wall and ceiling surfaces of drywall extensively replacing the former use of lath and plaster. With the increasing use of prefabricated components, 2 x 3 studs are frequently encountered. Drywall or smooth gypsumboard, of proper thickness and correctly installed on studs and roof trusses, makes an excellent interior surface, with most of the advantages of a plaster wall and few disadvantages. It is fire resistant, is relatively unaffected by cold weather, is much cleaner, introduces less moisture into a house during construction, and can be installed in less time than plaster.

Where plaster is required or desired, rock lath (gypsumboard) or expanded metal lath is generally used. The corners are usually reinforced with metal lath, and corner beads are used to protect edges.

Wallpaper and paint (including sand paint) are the customary finishes applied to drywall or plaster. There are endless varieties of each, and the materials are constantly being improved. Where hard wear, grease, moisture, or dirt are a problem, as in kitchens and bathrooms, tile may be used. Tile may be ceramic, plastic, or metal, and it may come in individual pieces or sheets with the tile affixed to backing that can be removed after installation. Other materials include prefinished panels, which require careful installation. There is a widespread use of wood paneling, selected according to taste, style, and expense. Attractive effects can be achieved at low cost through the use of prefinished plywood, masonite panels, or other suitable materials.

Interior trim in residences is usually wood. If stained, birch and mahogany are generally used. If painted or enameled, pine and gum are fairly standard. Door frames are often formed metal for use with drywall. Doors are paneled or flush hollow-core design. Folding and sliding doors of various types are becoming popular. Marble or formica sills are frequently used. Stairs in residences are usually wood construction and if exposed in an entrance hall or living room, may be of attractive hardwood for treads with decorative railings and posts. Increasing the slope in an effort to reduce the floor area occupied by the stairway is often indicative of inferior construction.

The metal appointments of a building (such as the doorknobs, hinges, latches, handles) are known as finish hardware. The type used is a good indication of the quality of a building. Neatly installed high-grade finish hardware usually indicates a well-built structure.

The insulation of outside walls, under roofs, and over ceilings has become increasingly important with the increasing cost of all forms of energy for heating or air conditioning. The type and extent of insulation is an important consideration in initial cost and in operating expense. The full extent and type of insulation is sometimes difficult to discern except from plans. Fiberboard sheathing (between studs and siding), which had been used for years instead of boards, has some insulating qualities.

A fireplace should be designed to have a good draft and a workable damper. It should have a hearth large enough to catch falling sparks. Masonry fireplaces require substantial foundations to carry the weight of the fireplace structure. Recent design has resulted in galvanized sheet metal fireplaces with lightweight masonry linings and brick surfacing for the mantel and hearth. They are light enough to be included without a special foundation or wall. Such fireplaces, which may be installed in modern garden apartments and townhouses with gas heating plants, obviate the need for brick chimneys. Lightweight, double-thick, galvanized steel chimneys may be used. Fireplaces and chimneys in older houses should be checked to make sure that they are well maintained in safe, usable condition.

In commercial buildings and in the finished areas of industrial buildings, nonbearing partitions may be constructed of wood studs, masonry, wood and glass, metal and glass, or steel studs with drywall or plaster. Modern construction frequently uses metal studs, with openings for pipes and conduits, to which drywall is fastened with sheet metal screws. This construction is widely used in remodeling. A variety of prefabricated modular partitions is available for use in office buildings, designed to be moved easily. Private offices may include any of a number of expensive finishes.

Ceilings are frequently suspended to allow space for utility pipes and ducts and for installation of flush or concealed lighting fixtures. Often the materials are acoustic and modular, so that panels can be easily removed for maintenance or remodeling.

The use of metal doors, trim, and door frames is common because of the reduced maintenance cost, desirable in commercial buildings. Finish materials, such as glazed tile, vinyl wall coverings, terrazzo, and other materials, are extensively used to reduce cleaning and maintenance expense. Hardware is usually simple and rugged for the same reason. Stairs in commercial and industrial buildings are usually steel or concrete, enclosed by masonry walls for fire protection. Most fire codes require two sets of stairs in public buildings.

ROOFS AND DRAINS

A roof—which includes its structure and cover—may be of various types, such as gable, hip, gambrel, mansard, shed or flat.[3] The usual residential construction uses rafters, joists, trusses, or glued wood beams, with sheathing of plywood or boards. The structure must be adequate to support the cover material and to conform to climatic requirements such as snow load and wind. The pitch of the roof should be appropriate for the roofing chosen.

Asphalt shingles are a common type of residential roofing in most regions of the United States. They are available in various weights and may have cemented tabs to protect against wind damage. Slate and tile are more expensive and require a heavier structure for support. Wood shake shingles may curl, and they carry a higher fire insurance rate. However, slate, tile, and heavy wood shakes often create a preferred architectural effect in better quality homes.

Flat roofs are pitched to drains or gutters. The built-up roof (tar and gravel, or composition) is rated by the number of plies or layers of felt paper. Gravel or other surfacing helps to keep the roof from drying out and cracking. In commercial and industrial construction, the roof

---

3. *Real Estate Appraisal Terminology, op. cit.,* p. 254.

structure may be steel or wood trusses, glued wood beams, or steel or concrete frame, with wood joists or purlins, or steel bar joists. Sheathing may be plywood, insulated sheathing in large sheets, steel roof deck, lightweight precast concrete slabs, or a reinforced concrete slab. Some type of insulation is used on most roofs. The usual roof cover is of the built-up type. The building design usually indicates the type of gutters or drains. Materials used for gutters and downspouts are galvanized iron, aluminum, and copper. The increasing cost of copper is reducing its use, particularly in residential construction where seamless installations using an acrylic finished aluminum are increasingly popular. In large structures storm water is collected by roof drains and conducted to the sewer by pipes within the building. Where there are gables or dormers, the valleys should have metal flashing of adequate width, properly installed. Openings through the roof, such as vents, pipes, monitors, and skylights, should also be correctly flashed and sealed to prevent collection of water and leakage. Where a flat roof meets a vertical wall, such as a perimeter firewall, counterflashing should extend from the wall back over the flashing.

HEATING

The common types of residential central heating systems are warm air (forced or gravity), hot water, steam, and various types of electric heat. The rated capacity of a heating plant is usually expressed in BTU's. Forced warm air heat is widely used at the present time. Air is heated in a furnace fired by coal, oil, gas, or electricity and is distributed through a single register or through ducts to the various rooms. Air circulation is maintained by means of a fan and a return duct system. Thermostats, filters, humidifiers, air cleaners, and air purification devices may be included. In many areas central air-conditioning equipment uses the same ducts as the heating system. Some earlier heating systems relied on gravity flow and involved the use of larger ducts with simpler distribution patterns for circulation. Warm air plants are also used in some apartment construction, especially in new garden apartment or townhouse developments. Where gas is available for fuel, the warm air system may be used in a number of variations, including unit heaters, radiant gas heaters, wall or floor furnaces, and individual gas furnaces. Gas-fired heating units require adequate ventilation. All open-flame heating sources must have a supply of air sufficient to support complete combustion.

The hot water system basically consists of a boiler, radiators, expansion tank, and interconnecting piping. The system is filled with water that is circulated through the pipes and radiators where its heat is liberated, with the water returning to the boiler. In general, the system is classified as gravity or forced circulation, with one or two pipes. Older installations were gravity circulation. Newer installations use motor-operated pumps to improve circulation.

Radiant heating is the warming of floors or other surfaces by means of hot water, hot air, or electric heating elements. Hot air or water is circulated by a pump through pipes embedded in the floor slab, side walls, or ceilings. Electric heating elements are similarly built into the structure. Lower temperatures are used in this system.

Steam heating uses radiators or other convectors in the rooms or space to be heated. Steam is delivered from the boiler by a system of piping. The one-pipe gravity system is used only for smaller installations, with the radiator served by a single riser from the main pipe through which the condensate returns to the main. The two-pipe system is used for all larger installations. The term *radiator* is accurately applied only to the type of exposed fixture that heats by a combination of radiation and convection effects. The common cast-iron radiator is the best example. Improvements in steam heating have been developed to increase the operating efficiency of the standard arrangements through greater flexibility and temperature control. In large installations, zone control is used to overcome the effects of varied exposures in different parts of a building. Each zone has individual piping and controls.

Older boilers were usually of the cast-iron, horizontal section design, which was originally coal fired and relatively low in efficiency. For larger installations, a vertical section cast-iron boiler was used. These units were more efficient and were covered with an insulated metal casing or jacket. Steel boilers were usually the low-pressure fire-tube type in which combustion gases passed through tubes inserted into a cylindrical drum that contained the water. There were several types, which were either two-pass or three-pass construction for higher efficiency. Small, efficient "package boilers" recently have become popular for heating and process-steam generating.

Finned heating elements, designed for installation in baseboards or concealed within walls or cabinets, are called convectors. The type that is combined with a fan is called a unit heater or room unit. In convector heating, air is heated in the enclosure and passed into the room through the chimney effect created by the enclosure. The design uses a pipe or passageway for the steam with many surrounding fins to increase the air heating surface and to compensate for the fact that radiation as a means of heating is eliminated by the enclosure. The more attractive convector, which replaced the radiator, does not project into the room. The temperature of the air discharged from the convector is lower than that heated by radiators and is more evenly diffused. This results in lower ceiling and wall temperatures and less heat loss through the walls.

In air-conditioned buildings, convectors may serve both as heating and cooling units with common piping switched from one system to the other at the change of seasons or in some installations with separate piping supply lines. Similar units may also be placed in duct systems heating or cooling corridors or interior spaces in stores or office buildings.

Unit heaters are widely encountered in commercial and industrial properties, such as stores, industrial buildings, warehouses, and garages where large spaces are to be heated. Whereas radiators and convectors are placed along the lower section of the outside walls of a room and under the windows, unit heaters, which deliver fan-driven hot air, are placed near the ceiling in the interior space to be heated.

Automatic regulation of a heating system is important because it permits a high degree of operating efficiency. In addition to the familiar single thermostat control or zone control of various parts of a building, systems include individual temperature control for each room. Apartment, commercial, and industrial buildings control systems may have the thermostat mounted outside the building to anticipate heating requirements more quickly. Office buildings may be heated on the shady side while being cooled on the sunny side. Some installations are augmented by the use of heat from air passed over lighting fixtures.

Electric heating equipment includes heat pumps, wall heaters or baseboard units with resistance elements, duct heating units, heat-cool units in which resistance elements are included with an air-conditioning unit, electric furnaces using forced warm air or hot water, radiant ceilings using panels or cable under the plaster, and infrared units that use radiant heat. The heat pump in various forms utilizes a liquid heating or cooling agent circulating in coils exposed to the air or buried in the earth. The use of electric heat depends on the availability of electrical energy in quantity at acceptable cost. This information is included in the feasibility studies that are generally prepared for large project installations. Extensive insulation, double glazing, and other conservation measures are becoming more important and receiving more general acceptance. The use of electricity for heating is increasing, and cost of all forms of energy for heating or air conditioning is rising.

The increasing cost and reduced availability of traditional energy sources for heating purposes is creating considerable interest in the development of solar heating systems. The initial expense, construction problems, and aesthetics have limited the use of these systems. However, development of a practical solar heating design, combined with the increasing acceptance necessary to achieve volume production and lower cost, is probably a reasonable anticipation. When this occurs, both construction and operating costs will be affected. The development and acceptance of solar heating may follow the pattern of the heat pump which was seldom encountered not too many years ago but is now quite common in new construction in many localities.

AIR CONDITIONING

Air conditioning of a building is merely one phase of the overall ventilation, which may include any or all of the following:

1. Simple removal of foul air with or without provision for entry of raw outside air
2. Bringing in outside air by mechanical means, preheating it in winter
3. Same as 2 above, with washing, filtering, and humidity correction
4. Summer air conditioning—cooling and dehumidification—separate from the heating system
5. Year-round air conditioning—complete conditioning as in 3 above, with summer cooling and dehumidification added

Ventilation alone may be accomplished with fresh air admitted through wall grills or through natural openings such as windows. The removal of foul air may be through outlets connected by metal ducts to roof ventilator heads with or without exhaust fans. Installation of the second and third types are forced warm air systems or indirect heating systems of the plenum type. The simpler system is found in many homes, and the more involved systems are found in older schools, theatres, and institutional buildings. A typical installation includes a fan, duct system, and heating coils or sections installed in the main duct. When conditioning is included, there is also a washer or filter to clean and condition the air. Package units for residential use are available. They incorporate heating, cooling, electrostatic air cleaning, and humidity control to provide year-round air conditioning in one installation.

The capacity of a central air-conditioning system is rated in tons or BTU's.[4] The two basic types are air cooled and liquid cooled. A gaseous refrigerant is compressed or condensed into liquid form by a compressor. This is circulated to a coil or evaporator where the liquid refrigerant is vaporized, lowering the surface temperature of the coil. Outside or recirculated air is fan-driven and cooled by passing over the finned coils. This may be in one large fan room or in many individual room units, depending on the system. The vaporous refrigerant is then returned for recompression, after which it is ready to start another cycle. Heat generated in compression is dissipated by either an air stream or a liquid coolant such as water.

As in heating systems, there are many variations of ductwork and controls providing for zone control, the mixing in of outside air, removal of foul air, disinfection and freshening of recirculated air. Complete air conditioning can be incorporated with heating in a duct system. However, additional perimeter or spot radiation may be required to assure uniform, comfortable heating.

The ordinary window, or sleeve through-the-wall, air conditioner is air cooled. Package air conditioners for larger spaces not needing duct work are usually air cooled. Larger package conditioners with duct work and zone control systems are air or water cooled. Except where water is too expensive, the water-cooled system is preferred

---

4. Twelve thousand BTU's equal one ton of air-conditioning capacity rating.

because it is quieter and uses less electricity. Water-cooling towers, often used for economy, recirculate rather than discharge the condensing water to a drain. Large installations may be extensive with compressors in the basement and cooling coils scattered throughout the building. For some installations—for example, in motels or apartments—small individual units in each room or space are preferable for ease of maintenance and continuity of service. Most installations utilize electrically driven compressors, but gas also may be used.

PLUMBING

Plumbing systems consist of fixtures or equipment, which are visible, and piping (supply and drainage), which is often covered or hidden. The piping comprises a large part of the cost of the system. The durability of the pipe, the way in which it is installed, and its accessibility for servicing are significant factors with a very important bearing on an income-producing enterprise. Depending on type, the greater part of the pipe installation may last through the economic life of the structure. Galvanized steel or copper pipe is generally used for water service; cast-iron, copper, or plastic pipe is used for drainage and venting above grade; and cast-iron, below grade. Copper has become almost universally used in modern construction for supply piping. Worn galvanized piping systems often are replaced with flexible copper pipe.

The value of appearance is evident in plumbing fixtures and equipment in bathrooms and kitchens. Prospective purchasers or tenants are particularly critical of these rooms. New designs, developments, and types of use of bathroom and kitchen fixtures also merit careful consideration. Plumbing fixtures and buildings have relatively long lives, sometimes lasting through a number of fashion changes. Design changes are important because a fixture may be replaced before it is physically worn out. Modernization of kitchens and bathrooms is frequently justified for income-producing properties on the basis of improved economic value. Newer plumbing installations include more kitchen equipment, such as dishwashers, garbage disposers, and multi-compartment sinks built into base cabinets. Bathrooms utilize shower stalls and lavatories in countertops, in addition to the standard fixtures.

Hot water in a newer building may be supplied by a direct heater with or without storage tank, or in some cases by an indirect transfer heater connected to the steam-heating boiler. The usual residential water heater is an insulated glass-lined, gas-fired or electric heater with large storage tank. The proper selection for any situation is an installation with sufficient capacity to supply the peak daily demand as well as the peak hourly demand. Temperature requirements may also be a critical factor in commercial installations such as restaurants.

Commercial and industrial buildings include drinking fountains, janitor's sinks, handwashing fountains, floor drains, urinals, and other special-purpose fixtures.

ELECTRIC SERVICE

In well-designed structures, ample electric service is provided for light and power through an adequate-sized service capacity augmented by a sufficient quantity of properly located outlets. These facilities in older structures may be inadequate and in violation of existing building codes. A history of continually increasing demand has demonstrated the desirability of service adequate for some future expansion. In residential construction heavy capacity 3-wire, single-phase service of adequate amperage and voltage to the main panel allows for a requisite number of circuits to prevent dimming, low voltage, or overloads. Radios, television sets, clocks, floor lamps, light fixtures, heaters, furnaces, air conditioners, washers and dryers, and bath and kitchen appliances need sufficient outlets properly spaced and located.

Wiring is generally enclosed in nonmetallic cable (Romex), thin-wall, or rigid conduit. BX (armored cable) was widely used for many years, and exposed knob and tube wiring may still be found in some older homes. A recent development in wiring is the use of aluminum wire in place of higher priced copper. Where this use is permitted by building codes, a larger sized wire is generally required to achieve the same capacity. Other problems involved in the use of aluminum wire may preclude general acceptance. Circuit breakers are replacing fuses in panel boxes. Silent switches and low-voltage switching may be found in more recent wiring. Lighting fixtures are the parts of a lighting system most subject to obsolescence and replacement.

Fluorescent lighting (suspended, surface-mounted, or recessed) is extensively used in commercial and industrial buildings. Often the design calls for continuous rows in large spaces. Incandescent fixtures may be used for smaller rooms, accent, or other special purposes. In newer lighting design, the intensity and quality of light at working and display surfaces are important considerations. Suitable degrees of intensity vary with the type of use. Some installations are designed for movement of air past the lighting fixtures to augment the heating system. Sound planning usually calls for extensive use of floor outlets or floor duct systems in commercial and office buildings. These systems provide electric convenience outlets for office machines and telephone outlets at desk locations with a minimum use of cords.

Power wiring is used in commercial and industrial buildings to operate utility systems, appliances, and machinery. The electric power is generally carried at higher voltages (240, 480, 600, or more volts) and is usually 3-phase or 3-phase-4-wire (which allows both lighting and 3-phase power loads to be delivered by the same supply). This wiring is carried in conduit or by means of plug-in bus ducts. Overhead bus ducts are frequently encountered in manufacturing plants where flexibility of service is desirable. Large capacity power wiring may contribute to the value of an industrial improvement but if not required by a current or typical user, it may contribute to functional obsolescence.

MISCELLANEOUS EQUIPMENT

Fire protection equipment includes fire escapes, stand pipes and hose cabinets, some form of alarm service, and automatic sprinklers. A wet sprinkler system requires adequate water pressure to ensure that the pipes are always filled. A dry system contains air in the pipes under pressure. When a sprinkler head opens, the pressure is relieved and water enters. This dry system is used where there is danger of freezing—for example, on loading docks or in unheated buildings.

Elevators are usually classified as passenger or freight and are either electric or hydraulic in operation. Hydraulic elevators are suitable for low-speed, low-rise operations. Since attended passenger elevators require full-time operator control, the high cost of operation has made this type obsolescent. The type, speed, and capacity of the elevator, as well as the number of floors served, are all related to the type of property and its utility. Most modern elevators are high-speed, completely automatic, and have control systems to collect signals and distribute service among the elevators in the system. Some elevators have auxiliary controls for manual operation when required.

Signal, alarm, and call systems and similar devices should not be overlooked. Smoke detectors are increasingly common in residential and multifamily structures. Many types of security alarm systems are available for residential as well as for commercial or industrial use. These provide warnings of forced entry, fire, or both. Among other items to note are clocks, pneumatic tube systems, mail chutes, incinerators, screens, and storm sash. In smaller buildings the telephone company supplies the wiring and equipment. In larger buildings there may be extensive systems of cabinets, conduits, and floor ducts built into the building for telephone service.

Facilities for loading and unloading trucks and freight cars may be important in commercial and industrial buildings. Off-street loading docks are usually required by most zoning ordinances. These docks may be open or covered, and in many cases the floor of an efficient one-story industrial building may be above grade at freight car or truck-bed level. In some cases the docks may be enclosed within the building for both trucks and freight cars, and leveling devices may be provided to assist in loading or unloading. Proper industrial design provides adequate space in front of truck docks for maneuver of vehicles, as much as 70 to 75 feet to maneuver a 45-foot trailer, plus the length of trailers already standing at the dock.

LAND IMPROVEMENTS

Many properties include paved driveways, parking areas, garages, walks, landscaping, as well as fencing and exterior lighting. Commercial buildings include large parking lots, signs, and light standards in addition to exterior or decorative lighting on the building. Large suburban industrial building sites are often extensively landscaped. Additional requirements may include large parking lots for employees; loading areas for trucks; railroad spurs; underground improvements; and outbuildings for water supply, sewage treatment, utility services, or other purposes. The area is often fenced. Tanks and other structures may be included for heavy industries.

CONDITION SURVEY

To obtain a suitable basis for an estimated current reproduction (or replacement) cost, the appraiser writes a description of the building or buildings, other site improvements, and their condition. This description should enable the reader to visualize the existing buildings as well as the site, the condition of the improvements, and their conformance to existing zoning laws and building codes. The amount of detail may be governed by the requirements of the report. The fact that building codes—fire, plumbing, electrical—may have been passed after the construction of the property necessitates recognizing nonconforming conditions.

From a survey of the physical condition of a building, the appraiser estimates the penalties and notes and records the apparent accrued depreciation to be applied to the building or its components. This includes physical depreciation, items of deferred maintenance, and functional obsolescence.

Maintenance is considered with respect to age and utility. Buildings may be overmaintained or undermaintained. Repairs are made to maintain a state of usefulness—not necessarily to prolong the normal life of an item. In many undermaintained buildings there may be deferred repairs. In other instances buildings may be repaired to keep them in a suitable state of usefulness or may be improved to attain a higher and better use. There comes a time when ordinary maintenance will no longer cure the inutility of certain parts of the building. In this case improvements either may have been made or their advisability may be indicated. Generally, the distinction between a repair (maintenance) and an improvement is that the improvement was or will be warranted economically by the production of additional income, whereas maintenance maintains existing income (see the principle of contribution in Chapter 3).

CHECKLIST

The character, quality, and condition of many construction details discussed in this chapter may be checked against the following:

A. Foundation
1. Excavation. Quantity, type of soil, any special site preparation
2. Footings and foundation walls. Design, material, dimensions, drainage, construction; check plans if available
B. Structure
1. Frame. Type of construction; column or bay spacing; types of columns, beams, and floor joists
2. Exterior walls. Bearing or nonbearing; material, size, thickness, type of construction; window sash, doors, show windows, or panels; wall ornamentation
3. Floors. Floor structure: size and material of joists and sheathing, load capacity; floor cover; material; treatment of special purpose areas
4. Roof. Structure: size and material of joists, rafters, trusses and sheathing or deck; cover: type of construction, material and quality; drainage; design and material; flashing; insulation; monitors or skylights
5. Interior construction. Partitions: material and type of construction; finish materials: wall, ceiling, trim, doors, hardware; stairs: material and enclosure walls; special purpose areas
C. Principal equipment
1. Heating and air conditioning. Type of heating system: warm air, hot water, steam or other; type of radiation: wall, ceiling, floor, ducts, registers, radiators, fan units, convectors, unit heaters, etc.; kind of fuel and controls; air-conditioning systems: description and capacity; ventilation: method, fans, ducts, etc.
2. Plumbing. Material and size for supply and drainage piping; the number of toilet rooms and fixtures; water service; sewage disposal; water heater; special purpose fixtures, such as janitor's sinks, drinking fountains, wash basins, floor drains, standpipes
3. Gas supply and piping
4. Electric service. Type of wiring and service capacity, amperage and voltage; adequacy of outlets; type of fixtures; floor ducts or outlets; power wiring
D. Miscellaneous
1. Residential. Built-in kitchen equipment: range, oven, exhaust fan, garbage disposer, dishwasher, bathroom

heater, vacuum cleaner system, intercommunication system

2. General. Fire escapes, standpipes, hose racks, screens, storm sash, shades and blinds, dumb waiter, wall beds, incinerators

3. Elevator. Type, capacity, speed, number of doors, floors served, control system, design for construction of enclosure

4. Sprinkler. Type (wet or dry), area covered, spacing of heads, reserve tanks

5. Commercial and industrial devices. Clocks, alarm and call systems, pneumatic tube systems, mail chutes, loading docks and doors

6. Land improvements. Parking areas: surface, base drainage; walks, patios, other paved areas; fences and gates; landscaping; lawn, shrubs, trees; signs, light standards, other exterior lighting; outbuildings, garages, sheds; pump houses, gas valve houses, canopies; water system, wells, sewage disposal system, sewers and manholes, septic tanks, treatment facilities, lagoons, etc.; railroad spurs; tanks; other structures

12
Building Cost Estimates

In most applications of the valuation process, the appraiser has some choice of applicable methods or procedures. In the cost approach method, value is the depreciated cost of all improvements to which is added the land value (as though vacant). The former figure is based on an estimate, arrived at by some acceptable procedure, of reproduction cost new as of the date of appraisal.

There is an important distinction between reproduction cost new and replacement cost new, which is shown by the following definitions:

REPRODUCTION COST—The cost of creating a replica building or improvement, on the basis of current prices, using the same or closely similar materials.

REPLACEMENT COST—The cost of creating a building or improvement having the same or equivalent utility, on the basis of current prices and using current standards of material and design.

Although it represents the basic concept, reproduction cost is sometimes difficult to estimate, because identical materials are not available or construction methods have changed. The use of replacement cost provides a practical alternative. It represents the cost to erect an equally desirable substitute property, not necessarily constructed with similar materials or to the same specifications.

For example, reproduction cost for an older structure erected with 21-inch brick bearing walls and unnecessary belt courses, coignes, corbeling, or cornices would be computed on the basis of identical design erected today. An estimate of replacement cost would not necessarily imply a structure of identical appearance. The nonessential or obsolete features would be omitted; probably a reinforced concrete or structural steel frame with 13-inch block and brick or 9-inch curtain walls would be substituted for the 21-inch brick bearing wall at a lower construction cost.

Accordingly, by use of replacement cost rather than reproduction cost, some of the obsolescence or inutility present in the building would be streamlined out of the replacement cost estimate before deduction for accrued depreciation. An accrued depreciation penalty for this functional obsolescence owing to the thick walls would represent a correct deduction from reproduction cost new; if charged against replacement cost, the effect would be to double this component of depreciation, since the additional cost of the 21-inch wall is not part of the initial estimate. To deduct depreciation on anything not included in the cost estimate is not logical. Therefore, the use of replacement cost rather than reproduction cost may represent a shortcut, for it eliminates functional lack of utility due to excessive cost (of an obsolete building). Since reproduction cost and replacement cost are not synonymous, the terms should not be used interchangeably.

IMPORTANCE OF REPRODUCTION COST

Separate valuation of improvements is needed for many of the same reasons a separate land valuation is required—for tax purposes (where ad valorem tax laws dictate this separation in value), for accounting (where it is desired to reflect depreciation of buildings), to estimate the most profitable use of land, to ascertain the amount of return attributable to the improvements when using the land residual technique, and in feasibility studies for conversion or renovation programs.

Further, a basic reason for the estimation of building cost, apart from land value, is the broad subjective principle that buyers will not pay more for something than it would cost to duplicate it. This is one application of the principle of substitution.

The cost of reproduction is not necessarily equivalent to value even when a building is new. It may not represent the highest and best use of the site, or it may involve built-in obsolescence owing to defects in design, or there may be a loss in value due to other adverse factors. Any of these may cause a deviation between the cost to create and value as defined in terms of the relationship between a thing desired and a potential purchaser. However, combined with a proper estimate of accrued depreciation, reproduction cost new is the foundation for the cost approach to a value estimate.

METHODS OF ESTIMATING REPRODUCTION COST

Comprehensive reproduction cost estimation requires preparation of a detailed inventory of the materials and equipment that comprise the improvements, followed by application of the current prices of similar materials, equipment, labor, overhead, and fees necessary to duplicate the property as of the appraisal date. Reproduction cost may be obtained in this way; but in actual practice it is more frequently derived by shortcut methods that are adequate, since the most competently prepared building-cost estimates are still subject to reasonable variation.

Although prices of materials and wage scales for labor usually can be determined for any date, the resultant cost of combining them in a completed building cannot be predicted with certainty. The profit incentive (or lack of it) is a strong influence that can raise or lower the cost estimate. This is illustrated when contractors are invited to submit bids. Frequently, cost estimates on the same set of specifications vary substantially. A contractor who is working at capacity is inclined to make a high bid, but one who is not so busy may submit a lower figure.

QUANTITY SURVEY METHOD

The most comprehensive method of cost estimating is the quantity survey method. In its strictest application, it is a repetition of the contractor's original process of developing a bid figure. *A quantity survey is computation of the quantity and quality of all materials used and of all categories of labor hours required, to which unit cost figures are applied to arrive at a total cost estimate for materials and labor. To this are added estimates for other contractor costs such as permits, insurance, equipment rental, field office, supervision, and other overhead, plus a margin for profit.*

Although still an estimate, the quantity survey is the most accurate and provable method of cost estimating. It produces a reproduction cost estimate in detail sufficient for any possible analysis.

The quantity survey and other cost estimation methods are demonstrated using the office and warehouse structure shown in Figure 12.1.

Figure 12.1. Plan of Warehouse Property

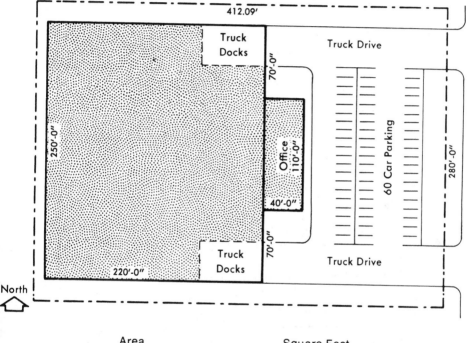

Area	Square Feet
Office	4,400
Warehouse	55,000
Total building	59,400

Office area. Heated, with air-conditioning equipment rated at 15 tons; ceiling height, 9 feet; flooring, asphalt tile over concrete slab; illumination, 60-footcandle-intensity fluorescent lighting; ceiling, acoustic tile; partitions; stud and drywall. Two washrooms, containing six fixtures.

Warehouse area: Heating to 65° at − 10°; clear ceiling height, 18 feet; bays, 41½ x 36½ feet; structural steel framing; insulated roof deck and slab over steel bar joists; 6-inch concrete floor slab at grade, waterproofed; electric service, 600 amperes, 120/240 volt. Four overhead wood truck doors. One washroom, containing three fixtures.

Exterior walls are block with brick facade; structural steel columns, steel deck; rigid insulation, built-up tar and gravel roofing. Structure has full sprinkler system. Other details are typical.

A summary of a contractor's cost breakdown for this improvement follows (based on a breakdown of labor and material which is not included here):

General conditions of contract	$ 4,415
Excavating and grading	13,930
Concrete	102,335
Carpentry	14,320
Masonry	109,180
Structural steel	157,585
Joists, deck, and deck slab	185,400
Roofing	32,320
Insulation	18,200
Sash	2,955
Glazing	6,368
Painting	4,278
Acoustical material	3,262
Flooring	1,875
Electric	42,346
Heating, ventilating, air conditioning	36,290
Piping	3,630
Plumbing and sprinkler system	43,542
Overhead and profit	59,030
Total	$841,261
Rounded	$841,000

Based on the preceding summary, an appraiser may estimate reproduction cost new at $841,000. This example is not in itself a complete quantity survey breakdown, but represents a recapitulation of the contractor's and subcontractor's quantity survey analyses. Items above, not subcontracted, are computed by the contractor on the basis of estimated labor hours at prevailing wage levels plus material quantities at current delivered cost to the contractor.

Figure 12.2 is an illustration of part of an actual contractor's cost breakdown (for an unrelated building).

Figure 12.2. Concrete Summary

CONC.		EST	CHECK	USE	UNIT	COST	LABOR
CAISSONS	3	206	206	206	3⁵⁰	721	721
% WASTE	3	20	21	21	3⁵⁰	74	74
WALLS	3	282	291	282	6⁴⁰	1485	928
ROUND WALL	3	2		12	4⁰⁰	48	48
COLUMNS	4	26	21	21	10⁻	210	218
ONE SIDE WALL	3	2		30	6⁰⁰	180	180
SLAB ON GR.	3	242	241	242	4⁰⁰	968	968
STRUCT SLABS	4	1556	1504	1600	4⁰⁰	6400	6400
THICK SLAB ST SLAB	4	13	STAIR LAND	15	4⁰⁰	60	60
STRUCT STAIRS	4	14	16	16	10⁻	160	160
BEAMS	4	84	81		—	—	—
PLANTER INTERIOR	2	21	29	29	3⁶⁰	104	104
SITE WALLS + FOOTS	3	58	52	52	6⁴⁰	333	208
CURBS	3	35	37	36	4⁰⁰	144	144
WALK + DRIVE	3	161	160	161	4⁰⁰	644	644
MISC	2	3	10	10	20⁻	200	200
TOTAL 3000		1049	989	1049	32⁻	33568	—
WASTE .03		31		31	32⁻	992	—
TOTAL 4000		1652	1602	1652	33⁻	54516	—
WASTE .03		50		55	33⁻	1089	—
PAN TREADS	3			.5	50⁻	25	25
FORMS	WALL BLK HEADS				1⁵⁰	95	63
WALLS 18750		18420	19010	6170	.90	5553	4514
ROUND WALL		132	126	130	3⁰⁰	390	364
COLUMNS		2315	1885	1890	2⁵⁰	4725	3780
ONE SIDE WALL		81		80	1⁰⁰	80	70
STRUCT SLABS		77410	76000	76000	.75	57000	41800
BALCONY EDGE		1857	1263	1300	1⁰⁰	1300	1040
STAIR SOFFIT		504	515	515	2⁰⁰	1150	1007
" LFR		494	510	510	2⁰⁰	1020	867
BEAM SIDES & BOTTOM		6287	5765	6000	3⁰⁰	18000	15000
PENTHOUSE CURB				51	1⁰⁰	51	41
WALK EDGE		1792	1785	1780	1⁰⁰	1780	1424
SITE STEPS		36		73	2⁰⁰	146	110
CURB W/GONG/F/FORM		42		42	2⁰⁰	84	63
EDGE STRUCT SLABS		5310	4200	4200	1⁰⁰	4200	3360
FINISH BULKHEADS				650	1⁰⁰	650	520
SLAB ON GRADE		18440	17793	18000	.12	2160	2160
STRUCT SLAB		77409		76400	.12	9168	9168
STRUCT STAIRS		494		510	1⁵⁰	765	765
TOP FOOT		849	891	890	in POUR	—	—
CURBS		1536	1874	1870	.50	935	935
WALK & DRIVE		11926	11404	11600	.12	1392	1392
EXPOSED WALK ADD		1220	1195	1200	.50	600	144
STEPS		36		73	1⁵⁰	110	110
PAN TREADS		108	108	108	.25	27	27
BLOCKS IN WALL + BM		EXP JT		150	1⁸⁰	120	15
EXCAVATION EXT.		24 EA				90	60

In recent years the percentage of a general contract that consists of subcontract work has been increasing. Subcontractors have become more efficient in their specialties, and subcontract unit-in-place cost compares favorably with the cost at which the work could be accomplished with the general contractor's own employees. Each contractor and subcontractor has a breakdown of material, labor, indirect costs, overhead, and profit items, which are part of the total estimated cost.

Overhead and profit are variables depending, among other things, on the volume of work the contractor may have in prospect. Contingencies represent another category, particularly if renovation is involved. A contractor may also allocate the anticipated profit among the various components of cost, rather than as a separate item, in a cost breakdown available to an appraiser.

The quantity survey procedure leading to a complete cost breakdown is time-consuming and costly for a specific appraisal, and its preparation requires the services of an experienced cost estimator. The individual appraiser, however, may accumulate available quantity survey cost summaries for various types of improvements. With suitable adjustment for physical differences or for time, these summaries provide a sound basis for estimating the reproduction cost of reasonably similar improvements, through the process of direct comparison.

The cost estimate for the warehouse given in the example above constitutes the basis for a general contract bid. Land improvements—for example, parking facilities, landscaping, signs—may not be included in the general contract. The costs for items not included are estimated separately and added to the general contract figure to derive a direct cost estimate for all improvements.

Additional costs are normally incurred by an owner in the process of improving the property, and the appraiser estimates these indirect costs on the basis that they typically add to the total direct cost of construction. Indirect cost may include architectural and engineering fees, soil borings, taxes and insurance during construction, construction loan fees, interest during construction, permanent financing costs, legal fees, appraisal fees, title costs, and similar necessary expenditures (see Chapter 14).

UNIT-IN-PLACE METHOD

Because the use of detailed quantity cost surveys may not be necessary except for special assignments, the appraiser may take advantage of less detailed methods of estimating cost. One of these is the unit-in-place method, also known as the segregated cost method. *The unit-in-place method employs unit costs for the various building components, using workable units such as the square foot or linear foot or other appropriate basic unit of measurement.*

On the basis of the actual quantity of brick and other materials plus the labor of assembly required per square foot of wall, a unit cost may be computed. This may be applied on the basis of square feet of wall or linear feet of wall of a certain height. The same procedure is followed for other components of the structure.

Unit cost estimates are made, in terms of standardized costs installed, for the various components of the structure. Excavating is typically in terms of dollars per cubic yard. Foundations may be in units of linear feet or cubic yards of concrete. Floor construction may be reduced to dollars per square foot. The basic unit for roofing is a square (100 square feet). Interior partitions may be reduced to dollars per linear foot. The unit in place on which the cost is based may be one used in a particular trade, such as cost per ton of air conditioning, or it may be any selected basic unit of measurement. The assembled total of all constituent unit costs provides an estimated direct cost for the entire improvement. Contractor's overhead and profit may be included in unit cost figures (as in some cost services) or may be computed separately. In using any unit price it is important to ascertain exactly what is included. Indirect costs are typically computed separately in the same manner as in the quantity survey method.

An illustration of this method is a cost estimate for a brick veneer wall. Assume the exterior walls above the foundation are 4-inch face brick tied to impregnated 4 × 8 foot ½-inch sheathing on 2 × 4-inch studs, 16 inches on center, with insulation between. The stud wall has ½-inch drywall on the inside, with two coats of paint. This wall is 17 feet high to the cornice line; for each square foot of wall surface, 7½ bricks are required. The following unit prices are developed for this wall (such figures vary according to time and location):

Face brick, installed; common bond, ½ in. struck joints, mortar, scaffolding, and cleaning included	$460.00 per 1,000 bricks
Dimension lumber in 2 × 4 in. wood stud framing, erected	360.00 per 1,000 board ft.
Sheathing, erected	.42 per sq. ft.
Insulation, installed, 2½ in. foil backing, one side	.22 per sq. ft.
½ in. drywall with finished joints	.30 per sq. ft.
Painting, primer and one coat flat paint	.25 per sq. ft.

On this basis an estimate of the cost per square foot of wall might be:

7.5 bricks	$3.45
⅔ foot board measure wood studding	.24
1 sq. ft. sheathing	.42
1 sq. ft. insulation	.22
1 sq. ft. drywall	.30
1 sq. ft. painting	.25
Total per sq. ft.	$4.88

Therefore, the estimate for a wall 17 feet high would be $83 per linear foot. The cost is estimated, without detailed quantities, for an above-ground exterior wall, including the interior finish. The base unit figure covers the greater percentage of the cost of the total wall.

In actual practice the estimator may refine this procedure, adding for waste and extra framing, and recognizing the existence of windows and doors (requiring wall openings, lintels, facing corners, etc.) with a resulting increase or decrease in the basic unit cost. Once basic unit figures are established, the cost of an entire building can be estimated expeditiously.

The unit-in-place method breaks down the cost of a building into figures for component parts. The cost estimate in this form is adapted to the appraiser's needs for various purposes, such as recording condition of components or computing the cost of replacement. However, the process of assembling basic costs of equipment, material, and labor and their combination into the final unit cost in place

Table 12.1. Warehouse Property, Unit-in-Place Application

Excavation	
59,400 cu. ft. @ $.11	$ 6,535[a]
Site	
115,385 sq. ft. @ $.07	8,075
Foundation	
59,400 sq. ft. @ (70% × $.69) = $.48	28,510
Framing	
59,400 sq. ft. @ ($2.42 × 1.2) = 2.90	172,260
Floor-concrete	
59,400 sq. ft. @ ($1.22 + $.20) = $1.42	84,350
Floor—asphalt tile	
4,400 sq. ft. @ $.54	2,375
Ceiling—acoustical tile, suspended	
4,400 sq. ft. @ $1.45	6,380
Plumbing (3 washrooms)	
9 fixtures @ $1,050	9,450
Drains @ $155 × 2	310
Sprinklers	
59,400 sq. ft. @ $.71	42,175
Heating, cooling, and ventilating	
55,000 sq. ft. @ ($.49 × 1.12) = $.55	30,250
4,400 sq. ft. @ $2.19	9,635
Electricity and lighting	
59,400 sq. ft. @ $.83	49,300
Exterior wall — 8″ concrete block, brick facade	
15,180 sq. ft. @ $5.36	81,365
5,060 sq. ft. @ $6.77	34,255
Partitions— 2 x 4 wood studs, 16 in. o.c., drywall, painted	
8,650 sq. ft. @ $1.45	12,540
10 doors @ $61.50	615
Overhead doors (4)	
10 ft. x 12 ft. x 4 = 480 sq. ft. @ $8	3,840
Roof joists and deck	
59,400 sq. ft. @ $3.44	204,335
Roof cover and insulation	
59,400 sq. ft. @ $.93	55,240
Miscellaneous specified items	17,840
Total[b]	$859,635

Source: *Marshall Valuation Service* (Los Angeles: Marshall and Swift Publication Co.) Segregated Cost Method, sections 44, 52, and 99, January, 1978.

[a]Figures are rounded.
[b]Contractor's overhead and profit, insurance, taxes, and permits are included. Architect's fees and indirect costs are not included.

may require specialized knowledge. Completely developed, this procedure is a useful substitute for a complete quantity survey. It should produce an accurate reproduction cost estimate, but with considerably less effort.

Application of the unit-in-place method is not limited to cubic, linear, or area units and may be applied using the cost in place of complete components such as the cost of a roof truss fabricated off-site, delivered, and erected.

Unit-in-place cost estimates may be based on the appraiser's compiled data and are also available through certain cost estimating sources that provide updated monthly figures.

An estimated reproduction cost of the warehouse illustrated in Figure 12.1, using the unit-in-place method, might be calculated as in Table 12.1. The estimated cost of $859,635 must be adjusted to bring the figure to current cost from the date as of which the unit-in-place costs were estimated, and must also be adjusted for the effect of location (city, community, or area) on the estimated unit prices. Such adjustments[1] would be calculated or derived from the cost service being used. Assume factors of 1.00 and 0.96 respectively in the following illustration.

Total (from estimated costs)	$859,635
Current cost multiplier	× 1.00
	$859,635
Local cost multiplier	× 0.96
Indicated reproduction cost	$825,250
Rounded	$825,000

This indicated reproduction cost of the building in its location and as of the current date, rounded to $825,000, when compared with the contractor's estimate of $841,000 shows a difference no greater than might be anticipated between contractors' bids.

---

1. These adjustment factors are published bimonthly by Marshall Valuation Service, Los Angeles, California.

COMPARATIVE METHODS: SQUARE FOOT AND CUBIC FOOT

The comparative methods derive a reproduction cost estimate in terms of dollars per square foot or per cubic foot based on known costs of similar structures, adjusted for time and physical differences. Indirect costs may be included in the unit cost or computed separately. If the benchmark property and the property being appraised are in different construction markets, an adjustment for location may also be in order.

These methods represent a relatively simple, practical approach to a cost estimate and are widely used for appraisal purposes. The unit-cost figures are in terms of gross building dimensions. Each is a method of estimating total cost by comparison with that of similar buildings, recently constructed, for which cost data is available in the appraiser's files or through current construction market research. This data is reduced to a cost per square foot or per cubic foot of building content. Alternately, a unit-cost figure may be developed by using a recognized cost service. A unit cost computed in this manner provides confirmation of figures developed by the appraiser from specific examples in the local market.

Measurement

Outside measurement is used to compute the number of square feet a building contains. It is customary to state the dimensions as width *times* depth, the first figure being the width or frontage. Projections are added, and insets subtracted. The gross area of a building is normally the sum of the gross areas of all floor levels. However, in some localities dwellings are figured in terms of square footage of ground floor coverage. In others the area is the gross square feet of living space; e.g., a two-story house, 24 × 24 feet, with unfinished basement and attic, has an area of 1,152 square feet (24 × 24 × 2).

To estimate the cubic feet of space in a building, width is multiplied by depth and by mean height (outside measurements). The mean height is measured from 6 inches below the basement floor surface to the mean height of the roof. The concept for measurement is a cube. Thus the mean height of a gable roof is one-half the distance from the top of the ceiling joists to the ridge; the mean height of a hip roof, one-third the distance. If the building does not have a basement, the method of cubing is the same, except that the height is figured from 1 foot below the top of the first floor or from grade, whichever is lower.

The advantages or disadvantages of the square-foot versus cubic-foot method must be judged in terms of local tradition, custom, and individual choice. The square-foot unit is sometimes preferred, particularly for single-story structures. Generally, the square-foot unit is less flexible, although not necessarily less accurate, because costs are affected substantially by ceiling heights, roof pitches, and similar elements. Although these factors are difficult to incorporate in the square-foot method, it is widely used and is ideally applicable to warehouses, loft buildings, store buildings, and similar structures. The cubic-foot method may be applied to apartments and office buildings—structures with a considerable degree of interior finish and partitioning.

Comparative Unit Cost Estimate

This is the simplest means to estimate reproduction (or replacement) cost. In the comparative methods, the actual costs of similar buildings are divided by the number of cubic feet or number of square feet of floor or ground area, resulting in a unit cost per cubic foot or per square foot.

The comparative unit cost varies materially with size. It reflects the fact that plumbing, heating units, doors, windows and similar items do not necessarily cost proportionately more in a large building than in a smaller one. If a similar cost is spread over a larger area or cubic content, the unit cost obviously is less.

Unit costs for benchmark buildings found in cost estimating manuals usually start with a base building of a certain size (that is, a base area or volume), with additions or deductions according to the actual number of square or cubic feet involved. As a building becomes larger in relation to the benchmark building, the unit cost decreases. Conversely, a building smaller than the reference building tends to cost more on a unit basis.

Because few buildings are exactly the same in size, design, and grade of construction, the benchmark building rarely is identical to the one being estimated. Variations of roof design and irregularity of perimeter and of building shape affect the comparative unit cost, sometimes to a substantial degree. As an example, the cost of walls alone, per square foot of ground area enclosed, may vary substantially from a building 100 × 100 feet to one that is 40 × 250 feet, although each encloses the same area. This is shown in Table 12.2.

Table 12.2. Effect of Shape (wall ratio) on Cost

	Building A	Building B
Building size	100 × 100 ft.	40 × 250 ft.
Area enclosed	10,000 sq. ft.	10,000 sq. ft.
Linear feet of wall	400	580
Wall ratio[a]	25/1	17.24/1
Cost of wall		
Per linear foot[b]	$50	$50
Total cost	$20,000	$29,000
Per square foot of enclosed area	$2	$2.90

[a]Ratio of the number of square feet of area enclosed to each linear foot of enclosing wall.
[b]Assumed.

To develop a reliable conclusion through application of the comparative methods, the unit cost must be properly adjusted to reflect variables such as size, shape, finish, equipment, and other attributes of the building and also to reflect cost level changes occurring between the date of the benchmark unit cost and the date of valuation.

The apparent simplicity of the square-foot or cubic-foot comparison method can be misleading. Dependable unit cost figures require the exercise of care and judgment in the process of comparison with similar or standard structures for which actual cost is known. Inaccuracies may result from selection of a unit cost that has not been properly related to the property being appraised. However, correct application of this procedure will provide estimates of reproduction or replacement cost that are reasonably accurate and entirely acceptable in appraisal practice. The use of square-foot or cubic-foot cost estimates involves a program of assembling, analyzing, and cataloging data on actual building costs. These detailed costs should be classified in general construction categories, such as warehouses or office buildings, with separate figures for special finish or equipment—for example, sprinkler systems. An overall square-foot or cubic-foot unit cost can then be broken down into its component elements. This, in turn, is helpful in adjusting a known cost for presence or absence of items in later comparisons. Several publications are available that provide square-foot and cubic-foot cost pricing units, some with periodic updating for different types of construction.

The same building that was used as an example in the preceding sections on the quantity survey method and the unit-in-place method is shown in Table 12.3 to illustrate application of the comparative unit-cost procedure using an established cost service.[2]

Table 12.3. Warehouse Property, Comparative Unit-Cost Method

Estimated Costs

Comparative cost per sq. ft.	$ 12.98
Add for sprinkler system	+ .71
	$ 13.69
Adjustment for 18′ ceiling height	× 1.086
	$ 14.87
Adjustment for area/perimeter relationship	× .895
	$ 13.31
Current cost multiplier (adjust benchmark cost to date of valuation)	× 1.11
	$ 14.77
Local cost multiplier (adjusts standard manual cost to specific city)	× 0.96
	$ 14.18
Cost per sq. ft.	
Total cost, 59,400 sq. ft. @ $14.18	$842,292
Rounded	$842,000

Source: *Marshall Valuation Service* (Los Angeles: Marshall and Swift Publication Co.), section 14, August 1976, p. 13; section 44, p. 3, January 1978; section 99, p. 2, January 1978. Contractor's overhead and profit are included in these base costs.

This figure is close to the $841,000 derived from application of the quantity survey method and provides additional confirmation of the $824,000 figure of the unit-in-place method. The estimated costs

2. The specifications and general description of this building are given in the section, Quantity Survey Method, and the structure is estimated to be Class C, with space heaters, midway between average and good, steel framed.

under all three methods are well within the anticipated range of contractors' estimates. The accuracy of these methods varies with the complexity of the building and skill with which the estimator adjusts for differences.

This example illustrates application of the comparative method on a square-foot basis, using a published cost service. The procedure may be used to confirm a cost indication derived from available data in the same construction market as the property being appraised. It may also be used independently when no local cost data is available.

Actual cost data for similar structures secured from local market constitutes a desirable base from which adjustments may be made to derive a comparative cost indication for the property being appraised. These adjustments are made for observed physical differences, using unit-in-place costs applied to the differences. In the illustration above adjustment was made for a complete sprinkler system using a square-foot unit cost. Similar adjustments may be in order for differing ceiling heights, extent of office areas, construction features, or equipment.

In using or comparing building reproduction costs on a unit basis— for example, dollars per square foot of gross area—it is helpful to eliminate land improvements. These vary widely between projects, and inclusion introduces a variable that distorts the overall unit cost and makes comparison difficult.

Cost data file.   A comprehensive current cost data file is part of an appraisal plant. It includes cost information for classes and types of buildings that meet the appraiser's need. It may also include data on current costs for material and labor and cost information on structures such as residences, apartments, hotels, office buildings, commercial and industrial buildings that are frame, steel, brick, or concrete construction, or combinations of these. A system of grading quality of construction may also be used to refine the data further. In accordance with existing building codes, cost of materials, and the wages and practice of labor, construction costs vary in different localities.

A file of this kind provides the basis for comparative unit cost computations to derive the probable cost of reproducing or replacing an existing building or for proposed buildings of varying types and classes. It also provides a check against the probable cost of different components of a building.

For example, a two-story brick residence cost $46,320 to build three years ago, exclusive of detached garage or other site improvements. The quality of construction is roughly comparable to that of an average mass-produced home with asphalt shingle roofing, ½-inch drywall, good average finish and equipment, with combination forced-air heat and air conditioning, plus a dishwasher, disposal, and fireplace. Included are three bedrooms, two-and-a-half baths, and full basement. Ground-floor measurements are 22 × 34 feet. This residence contains 22,440 cubic feet and 1,496 square feet, costing approximately $2.06 per cubic foot or $30.96 per square foot of gross area.[3]

The appraiser is preparing a cost estimate for a house roughly comparable to the benchmark house above. The house being appraised contains 24,700 cubic feet and 1,648 square feet of gross area. It has a concrete block foundation in lieu of poured concrete, no fireplace, and a good grade of wood siding instead of brick exterior walls. The appraiser makes downward adjustments for these differences: $300 for the block foundation, $1,800 for no fireplace, and $2,800 for wood siding. Unit costs are now $1.85 per cubic foot and $27.69 per square foot. If contractor's overhead and profit are not included in these unit cost adjustments, the totals may be increased by an additional 15 to 20%.

Assume that the cost of construction has risen 12% in the past three years. This is reflected by increasing the $1.85 unit cost by 12% to $2.07 per cubic foot, and the $27.69 per square foot becomes $31.01.

Application of the derived current cubic- or square-foot unit costs to the house being appraised results in current cost estimates of $51,129 and $51,104 respectively. These estimates are likely to be called $51,100. The minor difference is probably due to a small variation in size, ceiling height, roof pitch or roof design, which slightly altered the average height. This differential, however, does point up the fact that cubic-foot and square-foot methods do not always produce identical estimates. Table 12.4 summarizes this procedure.

---

3. The appraiser may elect to compute the basement area separately at an appropriate square-foot unit cost.

Table 12.4. Comparison and Time Adjustment

	Cost of Benchmark House 3 years ago	Estimated Current Cost of Comparable House Being Appraised
Cost	$46,320	$46,320
Adjustments		
Wood siding		− 2,800
Block foundation		− 300
Fireplace		− 1,800
Estimated reproduction cost		$41,420
(as of 3 years ago)		
Area, sq. ft.	1,496	1,648
Volume, cu. ft.	22,440	24,700
Per sq. ft.	$30.96	$27.69[a]
Per cu. ft.	$ 2.06	$ 1.85
Time adjustment to present		+ 12%
Estimated present reproduction cost		
Per sq. ft.		$31.01
Per cu. ft.		$ 2.07
Total		$51,104[b]
Rounded		$51,100

[a]$41,420 ÷ 1,496 sq. ft.
[b]24,700 × $2.07 = $51,129; 1,648 × $31.01 = $51,104.

Application of the comparative unit cost method to a residence in the example above is no different in principle than its application to any other type of improvement.

The discrepancy may be substantial between a one-story warehouse with a 14-foot ceiling height and one with a 20-foot ceiling height. Thus, in the use of cubic-foot or square-foot unit costs, it is essential that their application be to very similar structures.

Composition of unit-cost figures. Building cost estimates should include all costs. The cost of materials delivered on the job plus the cost of labor to assemble materials into a finished structure is basic, but indirect costs also must be considered. There may be two kinds of indirect costs pertinent to cost estimating: (1) the contractor's overhead and profit (which is normally included in the contract and may then be considered part of direct cost), architect's fees and other outside professional services, taxes, insurance, administrative expenses, and interest on borrowed funds during the period of construction; (2) for income-producing properties, additional costs incurred after completion of construction, while tenants are being secured and until average occupancy is attained. Indirect costs vary according to the circumstances prevailing at the time of construction.

The ratio of equipment to the basic building shell cost has been consistently increasing over the years. Equipment tends to increase unit building costs, and it also tends to depreciate more rapidly. Consequently, knowledge of the composition of the cubic- or square foot cost unit not only assures better cost estimates, but also assists in estimating depreciation. The condition of structural and mechanical components can be estimated or inferred from observable evidence. With good maintenance, the structural shell may last indefinitely; items of equipment require replacement in a foreseeable number of years. Unit costs for building components may be combined with estimates of existing depreciation applicable to each, to develop an appropriate estimate of accrued depreciation for a total structure.

In addition to estimating the cost of main buildings, other individual estimates are needed for improvements, such as garages and various outbuildings, or for land improvements, such as drives and paving, pools, underground drainage, rail sidings, fences, or landscaping. These may be individually estimated from applicable unit prices, on a square-foot, square-yard, or linear-foot basis. Such comparative unit costs may be developed, applicable to any situation.

COST INDEX TRENDING

Recognized cost reporting services are available. Some include illustrations of typical structures and provide adjustments to tailor the standard example to differently shaped or equipped buildings, as previously illustrated. Some provide adjustment for individual cities or areas. Some show cubic-foot costs, some square-foot, and some are designed for unit-in-place information. Extensive use may be made of these services to confirm estimates developed from local cost data.

Also useful is a cost index service that reflects the relative cost of construction over a period of years. When the actual cost of a building constructed some years ago is known, application of the index will indicate the present construction cost, provided the actual cost was a typical figure. *Cost index trending is the use of cost indexes to translate a known cost as of some past date to a current cost estimate.* For example, an apartment house cost $318,600 to build in early 1973 and a March/April cost index for that year is considered appropriate. In February 1978 a current reproduction cost estimate is desired. A national service cost modifier for the city in which the property is located is 599.0 for March/April 1973 and 867.4 for January/February 1978.[4] Based on this data, the 1978 cost is 1.45 times the original cost (867.4 ÷ 599.0 = 1.45) indicating a February 1978 cost estimate of $462,000.[5] Tables of cost indexes may be used to relate costs between different geographical locations as well as between periods in time. There is a practical limitation in the application of this procedure because increasing the time span tends to reduce the reliability of the current cost indication.

The difficulty inherent in this procedure is that the reported original cost may not represent a typical cost; and it may also be difficult to ascertain what components are included and what may be omitted in the reported original figure. Updating an historical cost provides a useful method of confirming a cost estimate, but it is not necessarily a substitute for other methods. Capital expenditures for improvements, subsequent to original construction, must also be taken into consideration insofar as they represent additional construction. They may also affect the separate estimate of accrued depreciation.

SUMMARY

Separate valuation of the improvements and the land, in the cost approach procedure, is needed for many reasons, including ad valorem taxation, accounting, highest and most profitable use estimates, feasibility studies, and application of certain residual techniques in appraisal.

The cost approach is based on the depreciated cost of all improvements to which is added an estimate of land value (as if vacant).

---

4. Such index figures can be found in publications such as those published bimonthly by Boeckh Publications, a Division of American Appraisal Associates, Milwaukee, Wisconsin.
5. Rounded.

Basic to the former figure is an estimate of reproduction cost new or replacement cost new.

Reproduction cost is the sum of money needed to construct a new replica of the improvement. Replacement cost is the cost of reproducing a substitute improvement that has equivalent utility. Since reproduction cost and replacement cost are not synonymous, the terms should not be used interchangeably.

The cost of reproduction may not be equivalent to value even when a building is new, for it may not be the highest and best use of the site, or it may have built-in functional obsolescence owing to defects in design. The alternate use of the replacement cost to reproduce a substitute improvement of equal utility may streamline out of the cost estimate some functional lack of utility in the existing building. Therefore, the use of replacement cost rather than reproduction cost may be a shortcut in eliminating the cost of over-adequate construction. When physical depreciation is estimated using a replacement cost base, care must be taken not to apply an additional accrued depreciation penalty for such functional excess, because it is illogical to deduct depreciation for anything not included in the cost estimate.

Of the methods available for estimating cost, the most comprehensive is the quantity survey method, which shows the quantity and quality of each type of material used and estimated labor hours required. Although still an estimate, the quantity survey is the most accurate and provable method of cost estimating.

Also available for the estimation of replacement cost is the unit-in-place (segregated cost) method, which is based on the use of installed prices for various building components, in terms of square-foot, linear-foot, or some other unit basis. This method is simple in application, and if the units are accurately developed, it provides a reliable substitute for the quantity survey method.

In the comparative square-foot or cubic-foot method, which is widely used in appraisal practice, unit costs of reproduction for a comparable or benchmark building are ascertained. Adjustments are made for variations between this standard and the property being appraised to arrive at a reliable unit reproduction cost estimate.

Reference to a cost index service enables the appraiser to bring known costs of a structure up to date. This is also a useful check against estimated current cost. A record of actual building costs, properly classified and broken down to a square- or cubic-foot basis for use in the comparative method, enables the appraiser to achieve reasonably accurate cost estimates in minimum time. In comparing and applying unit figures, it is necessary to recognize cost differentials caused by factors such as perimeter of the buildings, number of exterior corners, total linear feet of interior partitions, and extent and quality of mechanical equipment. Because these items can raise or lower the unit cost, appropriate adjustments are required. The accuracy of the comparative method depends primarily on the skill of the estimator in understanding and adjusting for these differences.

Building cost estimates should include both direct construction costs and indirect costs. Direct costs are those for material and labor, generally including the contractor's or subcontractors' overhead and profit; indirect costs include professional services, developer's overhead, and carrying costs during construction and until normal occupancy.

13
Accrued Depreciation

The estimation of accrued depreciation is an essential step in the cost approach because without a complete analysis of loss in value from all causes, the cost approach may not lead to a meaningful value conclusion. The reasoning and the sometimes extensive computations of this analysis may be only summarized in a report, but their preparation requires an understanding of the theory and of the components of depreciation and a knowledge of acceptable procedures for estimating their effect on market value.

> DEPRECIATION—An effect caused by deterioration and/or obsolescence. Deterioration . . . is evidenced by wear and tear, decay, dry rot, cracks, encrustations, or structural defects. Obsolescence is divisible into two parts, functional and economic. Functional obsolescence may be due to poor plan, mechanical inadequacy or overadequacy, functional inadequacy or overadequacy due to size, style, age, etc. It is evidenced by conditions within the property. Economic obsolescence is caused by factors external to the property.[1]

Depreciation includes loss in value from all causes; deterioration and functional obsolescence relate to deficiencies within the property itself; and economic obsolescence is due to environmental factors.

---

1. American Institute of Real Estate Appraisers and Society of Real Estate Appraisers, *Real Estate Appraisal Terminology,* ed. Byrl N. Boyce (Cambridge, Mass.: Ballinger Publishing Co., 1975), p. 63.

Depreciation represents a deviation from an initial standard of value. The basis of the cost approach is the current value of the land under its highest and best use, plus the current reproduction cost of the improvements. Depreciation is measured from this standard. Hence, only the improvements are subject to accrued depreciation as of the date of appraisal, and its measure is the difference between the current reproduction cost and the current value of the improvements.

On the assumption that improvements represent highest and best use with no initial obsolescence,[2] they generally have full value in terms of cost only at the moment of their completion. Depreciation begins at this point, although not usually at a constant rate, owing to physical deterioration and obsolescence. At the point when an improvement cannot be profitably utilized, or when it no longer contributes to the value of the property, it is at the end of its economic life, and depreciation is 100%. At this point it is a penalty on the land value equivalent to the cost of removal. *The economic life of an improvement* may be defined as *the period over which it contributes to the value of the property of which it is a part.*

In the cost approach to a value estimate, the appraiser is concerned with the extent of currently existing loss in value, which is accrued depreciation. Such accrued depreciation is a fact. It differs from provision for anticipated future loss in value—that is, recapture of investment.

Accrued depreciation (past depreciation) is the loss in value that has already taken place up to the date of appraisal. It is loss in value from any cause, estimated from inspection of the property and analysis of the neighborhood (environment). It constitutes a deduction from reproduction (or replacement) cost new to derive an estimate of the depreciated cost of the improvements as of the date of appraisal. Accordingly, *accrued depreciation* may be defined as:

1. The actual depreciation existing in the improvements at a given date, or
2. The difference between the cost of reproduction new of the improvements, as of the date of appraisal, and their present value

The distinction between the terms *reproduction cost* and *replace-*

---

2. Obsolescence may be built into the design of the structure.

ment cost should be clearly understood because the use of replacement cost in lieu of reproduction cost as a basis for the cost approach may affect the estimate of accrued depreciation.

Replacement cost is the cost of creating a replica building or improvement on the basis of current prices, using the same or closely similar materials.[3] In certain cases, materials may no longer be available to reproduce an existing structure, or new construction techniques and materials may make it possible to build a structure of equal utility at a lesser cost than that to reproduce the identical design with the same construction materials used in the property being appraised. In such a case the appraiser may begin with replacement cost new (cost for a building of equal utility) and depreciate from this base.

The use of replacement cost in lieu of reproduction cost does not change the principle of estimating physical deterioration. However, some calculations may be eliminated in estimating certain types of functional obsolescence frequently encountered in outdated structures (such as overadequacy of construction). Consequently, it is frequently desirable to estimate accrued depreciation for an outdated building in relation to estimated replacement cost of a more modern structure rather than in relation to the reproduction cost of a building identical in all respects to the original (see discussion of functional obsolescence). In eminent domain appraising, when a reproduction cost estimate is practical, use of this estimate with applicable deductions for all items of accrued depreciation may be easier to explain than the replacement cost concept. The latter may be preferable in other circumstances in order to simplify the estimates of accrued depreciation from all causes.

METHODS OF ESTIMATING ACCRUED DEPRECIATION

Accrued depreciation may be estimated indirectly through application of the market or income approaches to the value of the property being appraised. It may be estimated directly through use of an age-life relationship (based either on a remaining life estimate or on a rate extracted from the market) or through observation and analysis of the components of depreciation affecting the property.

---

3. Defined in Chapter 12.

These indirect and direct methods for estimating accrued depreciation may be outlined as follows:

A. Indirect methods
   1. Market data
   2. Income capitalization
B. Direct methods
   1. Straight line (age/life)
     a. Physical life basis
       i Overall application
       ii Component part (engineering) application
     b. Economic life basis
       i   Overall application
       ii Adjusted overall application
       iii Rate abstraction from market
   2. Breakdown

In the application of the breakdown method the components that make up accrued depreciation are individually analyzed. The effect of each on value is reduced to an estimated dollar amount, and the total of these represents estimated loss in value from all causes. Analysis by the components or categories of depreciation involves the following sequence:

A. Physical
   1. Curable
   2. Incurable
B. Functional
   1. Curable, due to
     a. Deficiency
     b. Excess
   2. Incurable, due to
     a. Deficiency
     b. Excess
C. Economic (environmental)

INDIRECT METHODS OF ANALYSIS

In using the indirect approaches, the difference between a value estimate based on reproduction cost new and the value estimate indicated by a market data or income capitalization approach to value is a measure of loss in value from all causes, or accrued depreciation as of the date of analysis. This is illustrated as follows:

		Indicated Property Value	
		Market Data Analysis	Income Capitalization Analysis
Estimated repro- duction cost as of date of appraisal	$400,000		
Land value	80,000		
Total	$480,000	$400,000	$390,000
Difference or in- dicated accrued depreciation		$80,000(20%)	$90,000(22.5%)

The last two figures indicate an amount of accrued depreciation as derived by the market data and income capitalization approaches respectively, and the indicated percentages relate these figures to the current estimate of reproduction cost new of the improvements.

Figures so derived may be used in support of an estimate of accrued depreciation. However, exclusive use of these indirect methods of analysis effectively reduces the appraisal process from three approaches to two. Despite recognition of interdependence among all three approaches, the development of each as independently as possible is considered desirable. Accordingly, some direct method of analysis is preferred for derivation of an estimate of accrued depreciation. A direct method is also essential for developing an estimate of accrued depreciation in the cost approach when the property being appraised involves a type of improvement not normally bought, sold, or rented in the market, and for which there is a lack of market and rental data.

DIRECT METHODS OF ANALYSIS

These direct methods are based primarily on observation combined with a straight-line or age-life formula or with an analysis of the components of depreciation.

Straight-Line Method

The straight-line concept may be applied on the basis of a physical life or an economic life projection.

Physical life—overall application. The straight-line basis for estimating accrued depreciation is based on the assumption that physical deterioration occurs at a constant average annual rate over the estimated life of the improvements. If, for example, the assumption is made that a building has depreciated on a 100-year basis, physical depreciation has accrued at the rate of 1% per year ($^1/_{100}$ = .01), and estimated depreciation at the end of 30 years is 30%. This percentage is then deducted from current reproduction cost new to arrive at a physically depreciated cost estimate. The assumption that depreciation accrues at a constant annual rate may not be generally valid because of variables in use patterns, maintenance standards, and renovation programs that vary from one building to another and from one period to another in the life of a structure.

Depreciation due to physical factors alone may accrue at a rate substantially below the 1% of the above example, if a structure is well maintained. If it experiences no destructive forces, such as tornadoes, earthquakes, floods, or wind storms, and if it is protected against fire or other major casualty loss, physical life may be considerably prolonged.

Physical life—component part application. A refinement of the above concept involves the application of individually estimated levels of accrued depreciation to the separate components of the structure, such as foundations; walls; floors; plumbing; electric, heating, and air-conditioning systems; elevators and other mechanical equipment. Also known as the *engineering* concept, it necessitates a more detailed inspection of the improvements and must be predicated on a reasonably comprehensive cost analysis such as a quantity survey or unit-in-place cost breakdown. These are frequently difficult to secure, particularly for older improvements. Accrued depreciation is estimated for each component based on observation.

A condensed example, applied to a 10-year-old structure with an estimated basic physical life of 100 years, is shown in Table 13.1. The deterioration estimates may reflect the appraiser's observation that there has been recent repainting, the parking lot has been resurfaced, and maintenance is generally good, but that the truck dock has received rough treatment. Individual judgments applied to each item based on observed condition are more reflective of

Table 13.1.   Component Physical Life (Engineering)

Building Component	Reproduction Cost New	Estimated % Deterioration	Accrued Deterioration[a]
Excavating	$ 17,250	10[b]	$ 1,720
Concrete	74,410	10	7,440
Carpentry/interior finish	11,480	20	2,300
Masonry	68,080	12.5	8,510
Structural steel/joists	42,180	11	4,640
Roof deck	15,470	11	1,700
Roofing[c]	20,830	50	10,420
Sash and glazing	5,030	20	1,000
Truck dock	3,930	50	1,970
Painting	2,040	10	200
Flooring	760	50	380
Electrical	18,120	20	3,620
Heating, ventilating, and air conditioning	24,190	45	10,890
Plumbing/sprinkler system	39,960	20	7,990
Parking area	6,460	20	1,290
Subtotal	$350,190		$64,070
Weighted average $64,070 ÷ $350,190 =		18.3	
General conditions/ overhead/profit[d]	$ 31,860 ×	18.3 =	$ 5,830
Indirect cost estimate	47,500 ×	18.3 =	8,690
Total	$429,550		$78,590
	$430,000	and	$79,000[e]

[a]Rounded.
[b]This figure is not a direct measure of physical depreciation, but reflects the fact that components of the physical improvement are assumed to be 100% depreciated over the 100-year projection.
[c]For this and other items there may be several replacements in a 100-year period.
[d]If this expense were included in, or prorated among, the individual breakdown figures above, this computation would not be necessary.
[e]This figure could be rounded to $79,000 or called $78,500 for subtraction from a $429,500 total. The 18.3% estimate of accrued depreciation could also be called 18.5% or 18%, either of which is within the reasonable range of the judgment decisions leading to the final estimate.

actual deterioration in a specific property than an overall straight-line average for an entire building; but since many items are not visible, their condition must be postulated from an understanding of typical situations.

Despite a 100-year basic physical life for the structure, accrued physical depreciation after 10 years is estimated at 18.3%. This reflects the increasing percentage of total construction cost which is accounted for by building equipment and other relatively short-lived components. An average physical life estimate applicable to the entire reproduction cost is difficult to establish, although the straight-line pattern, applied either to the entire structure or by component parts, represents a reasonable procedure that, combined with experience and judgment, should produce an acceptable estimate of accrued physical depreciation. The use of depreciation estimates so derived falls within the objective concept or cost-to-create philosophy which is basic to the cost approach.

However, the common statement "More buildings are torn down than fall down" implies that the estimation of physical deterioration may be insufficient as a measure of the loss in value from all causes. Deficiencies inherent in the improvements (functional obsolescence) or external factors that offset the desirability of the property in the marketplace (economic obsolescence) must also be considered by the appraiser if the indication of value derived from the cost approach is to have significance for reconciliation with the indications of value derived from the market data and income approaches. Lacking such consideration, the cost approach estimate is incomplete, reflecting only a physical concept of value.

To provide for these subjective elements of accrued depreciation, the appraiser either augments the estimate of physical depreciation with an analysis of functional and economic obsolescence or uses an economic life estimate in lieu of a physical life projection.

Economic life—overall application. The use of an economic life estimate in lieu of a physical life estimate is common practice. It is shown in Figure 13.1.

In this graph, since total economic life is estimated at 50 years, depreciation has accrued at an annual rate of 2% ($^1/_{50} = .02$). When the structure is 20 years old, depreciation has theoretically accrued to

Figure 13.1. Theoretical Straight-Line Depreciation

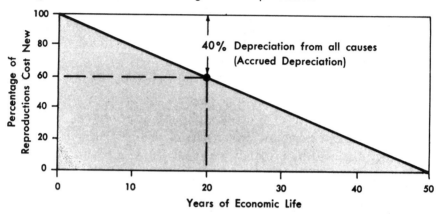

the extent of 40% of cost new. If *physical life* is estimated at 100 years for this specific type of property, physical deterioration represents 1% per year or half of the 40% total, and *obsolescence* factors comprise the remaining 20%. It is thus apparent that a percentage estimate based on economic life includes *all components* of accrued depreciation (physical, functional, and economic) but includes them on the basis of their *average* effect as indicated by experience surveys for specific types of property. Various tables of experience data have been developed from these surveys to indicate reasonable economic life expectancy or the characteristic rates of depreciation according to the type of construction (e.g., frame, brick, steel, reinforced concrete) and the type of property (e.g., apartment, industrial, commercial, office building, or service station).[4]

The utility of any empirical depreciation table depends on its basis and applicability to a particular property. Some tables represent physical deterioration only. Other tables are based on economic life and reflect the average effect of economic and functional obsolescence as well as physical deterioration.[5] Some depreciation tables add refinements by including separate percentages to reflect the poor,

---

4. An example of such tables appears in *Marshall Valuation Service* (Los Angeles: Marshall and Swift Publication Co., looseleaf service).
5. U.S. Treasury Department, Internal Revenue Service, "Depreciation Guidelines and Rules" (Washington, D.C.: Government Printing Office, 1964).

fair, or good condition of a building. Nevertheless, no table, however carefully derived from average experience, can effectively replace the appraiser's justification of accrued depreciation in a particular property, based on observation of the existing condition of the property and analysis of its functional and economic attributes. Using these factors, the appraiser can develop a judgment adjustment to a straight-line depreciation assumption (see discussion of Economic Life—Adjusted Overall Basis, p. 248) or a conclusion concerning an effective age for the property being appraised. The use of an effective age deviating from chronological age reflects the estimated effect of accrued depreciation that deviates from the typical on which the table or the straight-line relationship was based.

Effective age of a given structure is the age of a similar structure of equivalent usefulness, condition, and remaining life expectancy. Effective age may be more or less than chronological age. For example, in a 20-year-old neighborhood, a 30-year-old house designed and maintained in a manner similar to that of neighboring properties or modernized to conform, may sell for approximately the same price as adjacent homes and therefore may have an effective age closer to 20 years. A 40-year-old house that has been modernized so that it has the same utility and market appeal as houses built 25 years ago may have an effective age close to 25 years.

Modernization, remodeling, or superior maintenance tend to cure or reduce accrued depreciation and extend remaining economic life. Impaired utility, poor condition, adverse environmental influences, or obsolescence in style or design contribute to effective age and tend to reduce economic life. In adjusting from a chronological age to an effective age, the appraiser is recognizing the effect of these circumstances on the remaining economic life of the improvements.

Selection of an effective age that is different from chronological age is an opinion based on close observation; for the purpose of a valuation analysis, effective age may be more significant than chronological age, but a slight deviation can seldom be justified.

Because a remaining economic life estimate assumes only normal maintenance, a justifiable renovation program involving additional capital investment in a structure usually extends remaining economic life. In terms of utility and value, the resulting effective age is more valid than is chronological age.

In the application of effective age in an age-life relationship to derive an estimate of accrued depreciation from all causes, the ratio of effective age to the sum of the effective age plus estimated remaining economic life may be used.[6] This application of the age-life concept recognizes that valuation is concerned with future benefits rather than actual age. Illustrations of the computation of depreciation utilizing various age/life relationships follow:

$$\frac{\text{Actual age}}{\text{Actual age} + \text{remaining economic life}}$$

Assumption: A typical improvement is considered to be in average physical condition, and the obsolescence to date is proportional to the age/life ratio.

Typical economic life: 40 years
Chronological age: 10 years
Estimated effective age: 10 years
Estimated remaining economic life expectancy: 30 years
Computation of depreciation: $^{10}/_{40} = 25\%$

$$\frac{\text{Effective age}}{\text{Effective age} + \text{remaining economic life}}$$

Assumption: The improvements are considered to be in better than average physical condition, and obsolescence to date is less than proportional to the age/life ratio.

Typical economic life: 40 years
Chronological age: 10 years
Estimated effective age (from inspection): 6 years
Estimated remaining economic life expectancy: 34 years
Computation of depreciation: $^{6}/_{40} = 15\%$

Superior maintenance or capital improvements that reduce effective age tend to extend remaining economic life. In this situation a

---

6. Some appraisers prefer to use effective age divided by typical economic life new.

chronological expectancy of 30 years remaining becomes 34 years based upon effective age.

$$\frac{\text{Effective age}}{\text{Effective age + remaining economic life}}$$

Assumption: The improvements are considered to be in worse than average physical condition, and obsolescence to date is greater than usual for the age/life ratio.

Typical economic life: 40 years
Chronological age: 10 years
Estimated effective age (from inspection): 14 years
Estimated remaining economic life expectancy: 26 years
Computation of depreciation: $^{14}/_{40} = 35\%$

In this situation remaining economic life expectancy may be reduced by the factors that cause effective age to exceed chronological age; therefore, a 30-year expectancy becomes 26 years based on effective age.

Effective age plus remaining economic life estimates are not necessarily equivalent to typical economic life, but they tend to be so in early to middle years. Particularly in later years, inspection may reveal that a property is deviating from the typical due to environmental factors or to nontypical design or maintenance. A property with a typical economic life anticipation of 50 years may have reached or exceeded this age with some years of economic life apparently remaining.

In such cases chronological age plus a remaining economic life estimate may be an appropriate basis for estimating accrued depreciation.

$$\frac{\text{Actual age}}{\text{Actual age + remaining economic life}}$$

Assumption: The location has remained desirable, the improvements are subject to superior maintenance, and the design involves negligible obsolescence in utility or in market acceptance.

Typical economic life: 50 years
Chronological age: 53 years
Estimated remaining economic life expectancy: 10 years
Computation of depreciation: $^{53}/_{63} = 84\%$

Any computation based on a straight-line pattern is subject to confirmation, and the appraiser exercises judgment in estimating an age/life relationship that is logical and is considered to approximate market action most closely.

Economic life—adjusted overall basis. In a refinement of the economic-life, straight-line pattern, the appraiser analyzes existing accrued depreciation in the property being appraised for deviation from straight-line averages and endeavors to adjust the estimate from the straight line to the point on a curve that reflects the actual depreciation pattern for the property being appraised. Adjustments reflect judgment decisions based on experience, augmented, as appropriate, by computations within the concept of the breakdown method.

Experience indicates that the portion of depreciation due to functional and economic causes, rather than purely physical causes, tends to occur in steps corresponding to building cycles and changing demands affecting functional utility and style. With the beginning of a new building cycle, existing apartments may become obsolescent because of the competition of new styles. Industrial improvements may require new dimensions of bay size or clear ceiling height to accommodate contemporary requirements for warehousing, manufacturing processes, and modern machinery.

The procedure for making adjustments from an empirical straight-line assumption may vary. For example, if the appraiser has predicated depreciation analysis on a 40-year estimate of economic life, total depreciation has accrued at a rate of 2.5% per year. Based on judgment and experience, the appraiser may postulate that this is made up of 1.25% for deterioration, 0.75% for functional obsolescence, and 0.50% for economic obsolescence for a structure of the type being appraised.

For example, a 20-year-old warehouse improvement is being appraised. The appraiser inspects the property and gives consideration to the level of existing physical deterioration, as well as functional and economic deficiencies disclosed by study and analysis. The existing depreciation pattern of this building, in the appraiser's judgment, is as follows:

Reproduction cost	$400,000
Deterioration: No significant replacements but consider-ably above-average maintenance. 20 years @ 1% instead of 1.25%	20% or $80,000
Functional obsolescence: Ceiling height below current standards adversely affecting rental and sales market beyond level of normal obsolescence. 20 years @ 1.5% instead of 0.75%	30% or $120,000
Economic obsolescence: Normal decline of area due to age. No unusual influences. 20 years @ 0.5%	<u>10% or $40,000</u>
Total accrued depreciation	60% <u>−240,000</u>
Presently indicated depreciated cost	$160,000

In this case accrued depreciation has been estimated at 60%, or 10% above the straight-line indication of 50% (20 years at 2.5% per year). The appraiser has adjusted from the straight line of a typical improvement of the type under appraisal to arrive at a current esti-mate for the specific property. This situation is shown in Figure 13.2.

Figure 13.2 Theoretical Straight-Line Versus Actual Accrued Deprecia-tion

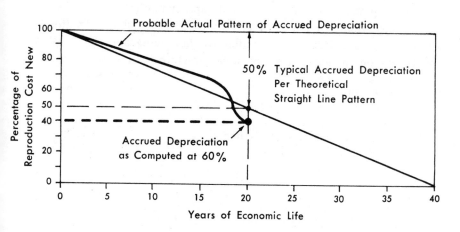

In this case a superior maintenance program reduced physical accrued depreciation in the early years, which would presumably have been reflected in improved market value during that period. At the point in years when palletizing became the accepted pattern for warehousing, the low ceiling restricted normal stacking height, adversely affecting the rental and market value of the property, causing the indicated sudden decrease in value. This pattern is not unusual for functional obsolescence, which frequently occurs in steps, rather than along a theoretical straight line.

An alternate or confirming procedure to the above direct method of estimating the functional obsolescence component might involve application of a breakdown analysis technique for incurable functional obsolescence. Assume that from a rental market analysis, the appraiser estimates that the net rent loss due to the ceiling height deficiency is $13,200 per year. If an 11% building capitalization rate[7] is used, the rental loss (due to functional obsolescence) capitalized at 11% reflects a loss in value of $120,000 (see p. 249).

The computations leading to the conclusion may not be made part of the report, but they do represent part of the analysis. Because accrued depreciation is subjective as well as objective, it does not necessarily lend itself to mathematical analysis. Judgment and sufficient experience may enable an appraiser to recognize deviation from the norm to a satisfactory degree of accuracy without reducing the mental process to arithmetic.

Rate abstraction from the market.   This is an effective procedure for developing an estimate of accrued depreciation from all causes, applicable when adequate sales information is available. In this method sales of properties similar to that being appraised are analyzed. The analysis of a typical sale might be as follows:

Sale price of property	$50,000
Less land value	− 10,000
Indicated improvements value	$40,000
Computation of depreciation	
Reproduction cost of improvements	$60,000
Less indicated improvements value	− 40,000
Indicated depreciation	$20,000

---

7. Rate includes interest on, and recapture of, building investment. If the income approach value estimate is based on use of an overall rate, the rent loss is capitalized at the overall rate to ascertain its effect on the economic value estimate.

The amount of the depreciation in this example is 33.3% of the reproduction cost. Assuming the improvements were 10 years old, the average annual depreciation would be 3.33%. Similar analysis of other sale properties might indicate a range in average annual depreciation of 3 to 3.5% and could provide a basis for estimating the depreciation applicable to the improvement being appraised.

Application of this method of analysis is limited when there are no sales of comparable properties, as in the appraisal of special-purpose or other unusual improvements and in periods of market inactivity. Despite this limitation, the method provides a valid approach to a depreciation estimate and is frequently utilized in residential appraising. Since the appraiser is usually seeking market value, an analysis based on market factors may be significant. The study of depreciation as reflected in actual market situations is also valuable in developing a background for the use of more subjective methods of analysis when market data is not available.

BREAKDOWN METHOD

The breakdown concept of estimating accrued depreciation involves an analysis of loss in value considered by the three categories of depreciation. Although the complete presentation of a breakdown analysis may not be appropriate in all reports, a grasp of this procedure's underlying principles is essential to an understanding of depreciation.

The terminology used reflects an effort to apply descriptive nomenclature to the three basic categories of depreciation—physical deterioration, functional obsolescence, and economic or environmental obsolescence.

Physical depreciation is the adverse effect on value caused by deterioration or impairment of condition as a result of wear and tear and disintegration. It may be curable or incurable.[8]

Functional obsolescence is the adverse effect on value resulting from defects in design that impair utility. It can also be caused by

---

8. The word *curable* as used here, relates to the principle of contribution (see Chapter 3) and implies that the defect can be corrected at a cost not in excess of the value of the contribution of the correction or addition to the property. *Incurable* implies that to repair or otherwise cure the condition is not economically feasible or profitable as of the date of valuation.

changes over the years that have made some aspect of the structure, material, or design obsolete by current standards. Functional obsolescence may be less obvious to the casual observer than physical deterioration, but its effect on value is no less real. The defect may be curable or incurable, and either classification may be caused by a deficiency or an excess (overadequacy).

Economic or environmental obsolescence is the adverse effect on value resulting from influences outside the property itself. This includes changing property or land use, shifting retail districts, and adverse economic climate. In an appraisal analysis of the property economic obsolescence is not considered curable since the source is not inherent in the property.

To estimate the extent of accrued depreciation attributable to each of these components of the breakdown procedure, the appraiser examines the physical property and analyzes existing elements of functional obsolescence from within, as well as factors creating economic obsolescence from without. The problem of translating observed deficiencies into a mathematical estimate of accrued depreciation requires judgment and the application of techniques that vary with the cause of the loss in value.

Physical Deterioration

This may be divided into two categories: curable and incurable.

Curable.   This involves an estimate of deferred maintenance and is applicable to items subject to current repair. *The measure of depreciation is the cost of restoring to new or reasonably new condition (i.e., the cost to cure)*—for example, the cost of exterior painting, roof repair, or tuckpointing.

Curable deterioration may also exist in some component of the structure that is not due for replacement or repair until some future point in time—for example, a nine-year-old heating plant with a normal useful life of 15 years may be considered 60% depreciated. If its present replacement cost new is $1,000, physical curable depreciation postponed may be estimated at $600 today. Some appraisers prefer to include such items under the physical incurable category since they are not considered to be curable on the date of the appraisal. Either procedure is acceptable if properly developed and explained.

A nominal amount of physical curable deterioration may be typical of similar properties in the market. An accumulation of such deficiencies constitutes deferred maintenance. If the accumulation is typical and sufficient to affect the market value of the property significantly, this adverse effect on value may be recognized by a similar deduction from the market data or income approach value estimates unless these were derived from comparison with properties having similar deficiencies.

Incurable. This involves an estimate of deterioration that is not practical or currently feasible to correct, and it pertains to all elements of the structure that were not listed in the physically curable category. It applies to the present reproduction cost new of the entire structure *less* the components treated as curable.

The overall *estimate of physically incurable depreciation may be based on an age/life concept adjusted for observed condition insofar as observation is possible and on an estimated remaining physical life.* For example, a 20-year-old structure with an estimated 100-year physical life has presumably suffered 20% normal depreciation and, if observation at the end of 20 years indicates a probable additional 5% extraordinary depreciation due to hard use or lack of maintenance, the total estimate becomes 25%. Accrued physical depreciation on this basis may be summarized as follows:

Reproduction cost new of existing structure	$60,000
Less reproduction cost of components renewed (depreciation cured under physical curable)[9]	−10,600
Reproduction cost new of remainder (bone structure and other components)	$49,400
Less accrued depreciation based on age/life basis plus observation: 25%	12,350
Depreciated cost after deduction for physical depreciation	$37,050

---

9. If there is functional curable depreciation attributable to an existing component of reproduction cost, the cost to cure presumably will restore it to new condition. Accordingly, the reproduction cost new of such an item is deducted prior to computing physical incurable depreciation. This does not apply to a functional curable item that is not included in current reproduction cost and for which the cure involves a new capital addition.

Functional Obsolescence

This may be divided into curable and incurable categories, each of which may be caused by a deficiency or an excess.

Curable caused by a deficiency.   This relates to some deficiency in the structure that is economically feasible to cure through a modernization program. Obsolescence can be due to age and style—for example, an out-of-date store front—or a lack of some item normally expected by the current market—air conditioning or a second bath or powder room in a residence.In the first example the measure of accrued depreciation is the cost to cure—that is, the current cost of replacing the obsolete storefront with one meeting modern standards. In the second example the deficiency is complete lack of a currently necessary component of the structure. Consequently, the lacking component is not included in the appraiser's estimate of reproduction cost. Only the excess cost of adding the item to the existing structure over the cost of incorporating the item in reproduction cost new, today, represents the measure of accrued depreciation.

In other words, it is neither proper nor logical to deduct from reproduction cost accrued depreciation on an item that has not been included in the reproduction cost estimate for the existing building. When such modernization is actually performed, the cost up to this excess amount represents a capital improvement and an addition to reproduction cost new. To illustrate, assume that in the light of current market expectation, a residence being appraised lacks a first-floor half-bath, but the existing plan will permit one to be added. The appraiser estimates that if this half-bath were included in reproduction cost new today, it would represent $1,200 of additional cost, but to add this additional facility to the existing structure would involve a current expenditure of $1,500. If this expenditure is actually incurred, it adds only $1,200 to reproduction cost new. The additional $300 of excess cost adds nothing to value and represents the economic penalty involved in correcting this item of curable functional obsolescence. It is the measure of accrued functional obsolescence due to this deficiency and constitutes the proper deduction from reproduction cost new of the existing improvement. This may be summarized as follows:

Depreciated cost after deducting accrued physical depreciation		$37,050
Cost to add a half-bath	$1,500	
Cost of half-bath if included in reproduction cost new	−1,200	
Accrued depreciation due to this deficiency		− 300
Depreciated cost after deduction for functional curable deficiency		$36,750

Curable caused by an excess.   An example of curable excess would be unnecessary partitioning in a retail or industrial structure. *The measure of accrued depreciation in such a situation is the reproduction cost new of the excess or overadequacy, less physical deterioration already charged (in order not to deduct this portion twice), plus the cost to cure.*

A warehouse is being appraised. It has interior partitions required by a former user but considered undesirable by prospective users or purchasers in the market. The cost of these partitions represents $10,000 in a total $200,000 estimate of reproduction cost new. The partitions can be removed and necessary repairs made at a cost of $1,200.

The appraiser has estimated physical accrued depreciation at 20% and hence has deducted $40,000 from the $200,000 cost. Since the partitioning represented $10,000 of the $200,000, it was also depreciated 20%, or $2,000, and now represents $8,000 of the depreciated cost. Accordingly, the measure of depreciation due to this functional obsolescence is now $8,000 ($10,000 less the $2,000 already deducted as accrued physical depreciation) plus the $1,200 cost of curing the situation, or $9,200. This may be summarized as follows:

Reproduction cost new of existing structure	$200,000
Less physical depreciation estimated at 20%	− 40,000
Depreciated cost after deducting accrued physical depreciation	$160,000

Reproduction cost new of the functional curable excess	$10,000
Less portion included in the deduction for physical depreciation (20%)	− 2,000
Plus cost to cure	+ 1,200
Accrued depreciation due to the excess	− 9,200
Depreciated cost after deduction for functional curable excess	$150,800

If the cost approach is based on a replacement cost estimate instead of a reproduction cost estimate, cost of items of excess construction or overadequacy are not included, and hence no deduction to eliminate them is necessary. However, the cost to cure—in this case to remove the existing unwanted partition—would still constitute an expense, and $1,200 then represents the extent of accrued curable functional depreciation due to the excess.

Incurable caused by a deficiency.   A lack of functional utility that is not economically curable *may be measured by the capitalized value of the net rent loss due to the condition.*

A small multi-tenancy office building has public halls that are wider than current standards or circumstances require. This defect of design decreases the efficiency of the building by reducing the ratio of rentable area to gross area without any corresponding increase in net income due to offsetting favorable considerations. The appraiser estimates the extent of rentable area thus lost at 1,000 square feet and has estimated a $6 per square foot per year rental value with a vacancy allowance of 10% and operating expenses of 40% which include management at 5% of effective gross income. The loss in gross income is $6,000 per year. The loss in net income may be estimated:

	$6,000
Less 10% vacancy	− 600
	$5,400
Less 5% management	− 270
	$5,130

This computation is based on the assumption that elimination of the deficiency would not affect other expenses in the operating statement. If other items of expense might also be affected, the appraiser considers the probable effect of the deficiency on the various items of expense to derive an appropriate estimate of the loss in net income. Capitalization of this net loss at the building capitalization rate (or at the overall rate if capitalization in the income approach is at that rate) will produce an estimate of the loss in value due to this element of incurable functional obsolescence.

On the assumption of a $5,130 loss in net income and an 11% building capitalization rate, the loss in value approximates $46,600. Alternately, the gross rent loss of $6,000 could be processed into an estimated loss in value through use of a gross rent multiplier derived from a market data analysis. For example, assuming a 7.5 gross rent multiplier, the loss in value from this cause would be $45,000 ($6,000 × 7.5). This procedure, which uses a gross rent multiplier, may be appropriate if there is sufficient rental data to establish a clearly discernible pattern for comparable improvements with and without the specific deficiency.

Incurable caused by an excess.   This pertains to components of a structure that exceed the usual requirements, such as excessive or overadequate foundations in original construction or a formerly useful component of the original structure, now obsolete and no longer contributing to the economic whole. *The measure of accrued depreciation is the reproduction cost new of the item, less physical depreciation already charged, to which is added the present worth of the added cost of ownership, if any, due to the condition.* This added cost might include taxes, insurance, or maintenance that are attributable to the excess.

An example is a building with structural members designed to support additional stories but with no foreseeable prospect of utilizing this extra strength. Using reproduction cost new, the additional cost due to this overadequate design at $10,000 may be the measure of accrued depreciation. (If 20% of this amount has already been deducted under physical deterioration, only the difference—$8,000— remains to be deducted as functional incurable depreciation.) If the physical excess results in any additional operating expense, the capitalized value of this added cost of ownership represents additional loss in value to the property. For example (assuming a building capitalization rate of 10%):

Depreciated cost after deduction of prior accrued depreciation estimates which included 20% physical loss in value		$150,800
Reproduction cost new of functional incurable excess	$10,000	
Less portion included in the deduction for physical depreciation (20%)	− 2,000	
Plus capitalized value of $180/year additional taxes due to the excess (180 ÷ .10)	+ 1,800	
Accrued depreciation due to the excess		9,800
Depreciated cost after deduction for functional incurable excess		$141,000

When replacement cost is used in lieu of reproduction cost, the estimated cost new for a modern building of equivalent utility does not include the cost of the overadequate design, and hence no deduction to eliminate it is necessary. However, the burden of ownership, in this case the capitalized value of the taxes due to the excess, would still exist, and $1,800 then represents the extent of accrued incurable functional depreciation due to the excess.

Economic Obsolescence

Economic obsolescence, caused by adverse environmental factors, results in some degree of market rejection, and the extent of this item of depreciation is the extent of the loss in market value. *This may be measured by capitalization of the estimated net rental loss due to the condition.*

Since economic obsolescence is not inherent in the improvements, its adverse effect on value may affect the land value, the improvement value, or both.

A residence close to a value-depreciating nuisance might still constitute the highest and best use of the land. If there is a loss in value of $1,000, this may be allocated entirely to land on the assumption that a prudent investor would recognize the potential loss due to the nearby nuisance and would not purchase the site except at $1,000 less than a similar site in the neighborhood that is not so affected.

Conversely, a well-designed and maintained house may be located on a corner lot that has been rezoned for other than single family residential use. Since the land is now valued for its more intensive highest and best use, the improvements are subject to economic loss in value. Similarly, an overimprovement loses value, in effect, to its environment and the extent of this loss or economic obsolescence due to location is attributable to the improvement.

A neighborhood may decline in market acceptance, owing to factors such as excessive taxes, special assessments or other governmental actions, conversions to industrial or commercial uses in a residential area, changes in the highest and best use of the land, and economic trends. Both the value of land and improvements may be adversely affected in the entire neighborhood. At one time it was considered appropriate to attribute economic obsolescence to changes in the ethnic character of the population in an area. However, with the evolution of social norms and standards, the reactions of the market to such changes are no longer so readily predictable. Accordingly, attribution of economic obsolescence to changes or anticipated changes in the racial or ethnic composition of a neighborhood is considered an unreliable procedure (see Chapter 6 and Chapter 3, Principle of Conformity).

A residence may be subject to economic obsolescence owing to factors that affect the neighborhood as a whole or to a specific nearby depreciating factor such as undesirable development of a nearby site. In either case the adverse effect on rental value may be estimated. Ideally, this estimate should be derived from a comparison of the rental for property so affected with one not so affected. In actual practice, if a lack of residential rental comparisons makes it difficult to select a specific figure for the estimated rent loss, the appraiser exercises judgment based on experience and knowledge of the rental market.

Where rental comparisons are available, application of a gross rent multiplier may be used to translate the estimated rental loss into its effect on market value, as follows: A figure of $10 per month (estimated rental loss) × 116 = $1,160 loss in value.[10] As in the previous example, there may be a logical basis for allocation of the loss to land or

---

10. 116 is the assumed gross monthly rent multiplier.

improvements, or the loss may be divided on the basis of a judgment decision. If land represents 25% of property value, and improvements 75%, $870 (75% of $1,160) may be ascribed to the improvements. The adverse effect of the depreciating factor on land value (25% of $1,160, or $290) may have been accounted for in the valuation of the site by comparison with other sites similarly affected. Assuming the land valued by comparison with sites not similarly affected, the $290 represents a deduction from the land value estimate.

In an analysis of income-producing property the same procedure involving use of a multiplier is appropriate. Alternately, the loss in rental value may be reduced to a net rental loss and capitalized into a loss in market value using the building capitalization rate.

ECONOMIC FACTORS OFFSETTING DEPRECIATION

Depreciation of a wasting asset constitutes a fact, although market experience may not always appear to reflect this. A property that has a current value of $100,000 may consist of 20% land value plus 80% building value with an estimated 40-year remaining economic life. On the assumption of a straight-line depreciation rate at 2.5% per year for the building, the total property value may anticipate an average decline at a rate of 2% per year, or 20% over a 10-year period. This is loss in terms of the ability to command other commodities in exchange.

If during this 10-year period the dollar as a unit of measurement has also declined in value, due to inflationary pressures in the economy, at a rate perhaps exceeding 2% per year, resale at the end of the period in terms of cheaper dollars may create the illusion that no loss of value has occurred or even that the property value has appreciated. However, this is true only in terms of different units of measurement and does not affect the validity of a declining real value concept or accrued depreciation in terms of value in exchange.

There has been recognition that prospective purchasers may look at value over an extended period of time in terms of numbers of dollars, regardless of their changing value in exchange. This has created a new dimension in appraisal methodology, the proper application of which is not inconsistent with the validity of an empirical declining value concept.

DEPRECIATED COST AND VALUE

The estimate of accrued depreciation in the cost approach represents a deduction from reproduction cost new. Since cost is not necessarily equal to market value, the resulting figure has been referred to herein as depreciated cost. However, the objective in each of the three approaches is an estimate of value. Application of the indirect methods of estimating accrued depreciation as described here provides a depreciated cost figure that corresponds to market value. Direct methods that rely on market evidence (e.g., use of rates of depreciation extracted from the market) also produce estimates of accrued depreciation leading to a depreciated cost figure in terms of value.

Other direct methods of estimating accrued depreciation based on an economic life estimate similarly translate a cost-related figure to a value-related estimate. In the application of the breakdown method, the analysis of accrued depreciation due to functional and economic factors goes beyond basic physical deterioration to introduce intangible considerations in the minds of potential purchasers. Again the result is transformation of an initial cost-related figure to a depreciated cost that is market related and represents a present depreciated value estimate.

Valid estimates of accrued depreciation go beyond purely physical considerations, and a comprehensive analysis of depreciation from all causes leads to a cost approach value estimate that is meaningful in reconciliation with other approach value estimates to derive a conclusion of market value.

SUMMARY

A measure of accrued depreciation in the cost approach is the difference between the value of a building (or other improvement) at a certain date and its cost of reproduction as of the same date. Depreciation is caused by physical deterioration, functional obsolescence, and economic obsolescence.

Indirect and direct methods are available for estimating the effect of accrued depreciation on value of the components. When accrued depreciation in the cost approach is measured indirectly by the market data or income methods, the derived value estimates are dependent on the market data or income approaches. However, these methods result in a valid single-figure estimate of depreciation from all causes.

Direct methods of estimating accrued depreciation, used in the cost approach, maintain the relative independence of the three approaches to value and are generally applicable to the appraisal of single-use improvements. A straight-line or age/life pattern may be applied on a physical or economic life basis. In the latter the effect of all types of accrued depreciation is reflected in accordance with average experience studies. When applied on a physical life basis, the effect of functional and economic obsolescence must be considered separately.

In report presentation, a straight-line pattern based on an economic life estimate is extensively used to rationalize the appraiser's estimate of accrued depreciation. This presentation is easily explained and widely understood. However, if a breakdown analysis for the property being appraised reveals deviation from average experience for any component of depreciation, the average effect being inherent in the straight line, a judgment adjustment from that line is in order.

A rate of depreciation from all causes may be extracted from market sales when adquate data is available to support a reasonably definitive conclusion.

In the breakdown method the extent of accrued depreciation owing to each individual component of depreciation is separately analyzed and its effect is estimated.

The fact that accrued depreciation may be offset in whole or in part, due to inflationary pressure, is not necessarily inconsistent with the validity of an empirical declining value concept.

The theory of accrued depreciation and methods of estimating need not always be presented in similar detail in reports for clients who may not be interested in documentation or in the step-by-step processes of reasoning followed by the appraiser.

There are various procedures leading to a correct estimate of accrued depreciation "from all causes." The selection of an applicable procedure in any instance requires an understanding of the nature, causes, and components of depreciation.

14
The Cost Approach

The cost, market, and income approaches are the three approaches in the valuation process. Essentially, the cost approach provides for an estimate of the depreciated reproduction or replacement cost (new) of the improvements to which is added an estimate of land value.[1] The basic steps in the procedure of the cost approach are:

1. Estimate the cost to reproduce (or replace) the basic improvements, new.
2. Estimate the dollar amount of accrued depreciation due to
    a. Physical deterioration
    b. Functional obsolescence
    c. Adverse economic influences
3. Deduct the total amount of accrued depreciation from cost new to derive the present depreciated cost of the basic improvements.
4. By the same or similar procedure, estimate the present depreciated cost of other improvements (minor structures or land improvements) excepting any that were included in the land value estimate.
5. Add the land estimate to the depreciated cost of basic and other improvements to arrive at a value indication by the cost approach.

UNDERLYING PRINCIPLES

Basic to the cost approach is the principle of substitution: no prudent person will pay more for a property than the amount for which he or

---

1. For definitions of reproduction and replacement, see Chapter 12.

she can obtain by purchase of a site and construction of a building without undue delay, a property of equal desirability and utility. Consequently, reproduction cost new, *prior to any deduction for accrued depreciation,* plus land value, tends to set the upper limit of value. Developer's profit in a typical development also becomes part of cost new in the context of this statement.

Reproduction cost is related to an objective value concept. However, cost to create is not necessarily value, as demonstrated by the classic example of an office building erected at great cost in a remote location where income would be insufficient to offset even the basic essentials of operating expense much less to produce a net income stream.

For the cost approach to produce a meaningful reflection of a market value in relation to the value estimates obtained through use of the other two approaches, it is necessary to analyze accrued depreciation, recognizing the effect of functional inutility or obsolescence and of economic or environmental factors, as explained in the preceding chapter. With the introduction of these considerations, the cost approach moves beyond a basically cost-related concept, and physical cost is modified by the effect of these factors in the minds of prospective purchasers in the marketplace. Thus depreciated cost becomes a present market value indication. This is an important transition, and it means that if depreciation from all causes is properly estimated, the resultant value indication should reflect market value and lend itself to reconciliation with value indications by the market data and income approaches in an appraisal of market value.

A significant use of the cost approach is in the valuation of public buildings or certain types of special-use properties for which rental or sales market data is limited. The principal difficulties in the approach arise in estimating viable construction cost figures and in reducing accrued depreciation from physical, functional, and economic causes to a dollar estimate, particularly for older properties.

ESTIMATING LAND VALUE

The characteristics of sites and the principles of site valuation have been discussed fully in previous chapters. However, it should be emphasized that land value is not the historic cost of the land or the acquisition price plus the expense of making it usable through the addition of underground or other improvements. The land value component of the cost approach does not reflect an original cost-to-create or cost-to-acquire concept, but is estimated whenever possible on the basis of current selling prices of comparable sites and other pertinent market data. It is this estimated market value of the land that is added to the depreciated cost of the improvements in this approach. When sufficient comparative data is not available, or if the market data indication is inconclusive, land value may be estimated by other methods.[2]

DIRECT AND INDIRECT BUILDING COSTS

The principles of building cost estimating, the various elements involved in the cost of improvements, and the possible confusion about what is or is not included in the unit costs available from different sources were discussed in Chapter 12. As pointed out, many tabulations that show the comparative costs of different types of buildings are published, but not all these sources specify the basis of the data. Therefore, before using published or locally obtained cubic-foot or square-foot cost data, the appraiser ascertains just what components are included in the unit cost figure.

Preliminary construction costs, special conditions (extra costs owing to traffic congestion; protection of adjacent streets, traffic, or properties; etc.), carrying charges during construction, and other indirect costs may vary, owing to many factors including job characteristics and location. Therefore, it is good practice to apply unit reproduction cost figures that exclude indirect costs. These may then be considered separately.

Landscaping, parking facilities, walks, drives, or other yard improvements apart from the basic structure should also be estimated separately, unless the amount is so minor it may be included with either the land estimate or the building estimate. More often, these elements involve substantial expenditures which, if included with the structure cost, would distort unit costs and reduce their usefulness for comparison purposes.

---

2. See Chapter 8.

Indirect costs frequently are figured as a lump sum percentage which is added to the direct costs of material, labor, and subcontracts. However, some indirect costs are not related to the size and direct cost of the improvements—for example:

1.   Expenses for title examinations, recording fees, legal fees, etc.
2.   Expenses preliminary to a construction program, such as consultations, surveys, soil borings, building permits (unless the last are included in the general contract for construction)
3.   Professional services of architects, engineers, and others
4.   Taxes paid during construction
5.   Casualty insurance during construction
6.   Administrative expense of the owner
7.   Cost of interim or long-term financing including necessary feasibility or appraisal reports.

Contractor's overhead and profit, unless the developer is also the contractor, are generally treated as direct costs, since the building contractor usually includes them in the construction contract. Leasing fees may be included in indirect cost when payable at the time of leasing and treated as a capital cost. When payable over the lease term, they may be treated as an operating expense.

The estimate of indirect costs cannot always be made with the same precision as direct costs because there may be no exact basis for some of them. In the actual construction of two similar properties, indirect costs may differ materially, although the direct costs are practically identical. This is to be expected because not all indirect costs are directly attributable to the physical property. They may be affected by conditions of delay, judgment, and circumstances which are rarely identical in the development of two similar properties.

The process of making an indirect cost estimate may be shown by this example. An apartment building involving a direct cost of $300,000 is to be built on a site valued at $80,000. The tax rate is 5%, and assessments are on a 40% basis, resulting in an effective tax of 2% per annum. Insurance rates for construction are $0.75 per $100. Cost of adequate supervision for the owner is $200 per month.

Under these conditions, the indirect cost estimate may thus be projected:

Taxes during construction (construction
    period estimated at 10 months plus
    4 months for plans and contracts)

Land: 14 months at 2% per yr. × $80,000	$1,865[a]	
Building: 10 months at 2% per yr. on		
50% of $300,000	2,500[b]	
Total taxes		$ 4,365
Insurance		
Building: average of $150,000 investment		
for 10 months at .75% per annum		940
Supervision		
Building: 10 months at $200		2,000
Legal fees, etc.		
Land and building: examination of title		
and contracts; services during construction		695
Financing: construction loan interest plus		
permanent loan fees based upon current		
mortgage market requirements		11,000
Architectural and engineering fees: 5% of		
$300,000 contract costs of construction		15,000
Total indirect costs		$34,000

---

[a]Figures are rounded.
[b]Assessment policies on partial completion of construction vary in different
jurisdictions.

The indirect costs in this case amount to about 11.3% of the total
of $300,000 for direct building cost. This estimate will be affected by
factors such as construction time, availability and terms of financing,
and extent of architectural and legal services. Factors that would
materially affect the above indirect-cost percentage are changes in
the money market and in the extent of professional design or supervision service.

This list of indirect costs omits some potential additional charges.
The equity portion of the money presumably was segregated and is
entitled to earn a return. Assuming that the rent schedule is to be
$4,000 per month, a lag in occupancy might represent a 50% vacancy
loss for six months, or $12,000. Such indirect costs are not actually
paid out, but are reflected in reduced income to the owner or developer. Other contingencies may contribute to the total. Sales commissions are not normally considered part of the indirect cost.

Items included in contractor's overhead on commercial construction are field supervision, allocation of main office expense, tools and minor equipment, rental of other equipment, employers' liability insurance, field office, photos, public liability insurance, and permits. All these expenses are normally included in the general contractor's bid figure, either under one heading or allocated and included under other headings. Direct building costs for material, labor, and subcontracts are only part of the overall costs. In valuation of a structure to be built from plans and specifications, the appraiser may include in the appraisal report under "qualifying and limiting conditions" a statement to this general effect:

> The estimated value is subject to satisfactory completion in accordance with plans and specifications as described herein, assuming that the building is occupied and in operation.

DEVELOPER'S PROFIT

Another factor that sometimes enters into the cost approach to an indication of value is entrepreneurial or developer's profit. This profit potential offers the incentive for much new construction, which may be for speculation or sale rather than for the owner's direct use.

For new properties that are well designed and represent the highest and best use of the site, a measure of developer's profit may be derived from a comparison of the value indicated by the cost approach with the value indications derived from the market data and income approaches.[3] For the example on p. 267, a cost approach value indication might be summarized:

Improvements		
Direct cost	$300,000	
Indirect cost	34,000	
		$334,000
Land value		80,000
Total		$414,000

Assume now that the market data and income approaches indicate a probable market value after completion of $460,000; the difference, which amounts to $46,000, represents developer's profit. A substan-

---

3. See Chapter 4.

tial operator with some purchasing advantages may augment this profit margin to the extent that the improvements can be erected at less-than-typical unit costs. If the developer is also the contractor, the margin is increased by the extent of contractor's overhead and profit.

Because the extent of developer's profit varies with economic conditions and personal circumstances, a typical relationship to other costs is difficult to establish as a basis for inclusion in the cost approach. It may be preferable to omit this estimate entirely, recognizing that its true measure is reflected by the extent that the other approaches exceed the cost approach value estimate, as illustrated above.

BUILDING INSPECTION

To develop the cost approach in any valuation the appraiser makes a complete building inspection and analysis. The logical point to begin the inspection of a building is to establish its general type and to note specific items to be inspected. These and any preliminary facts concerning the particular building are tabulated (see Chapter 11). From these items and facts, the appraiser constructs a skeleton arrangement or grouping of related parts for inspection.

The checklist for a building inspection may be more or less detailed, depending on the type of property. It may have enough space for all estimates and supporting comments on observed condition or space for only the observed condition at the site, leaving all or most of the estimating to be done as a desk operation. It also may be used as an outline and reminder sheet which may include:

1. Description of the structural and mechanical components of the improvements in outline form.
2. A list of building items or equipment installed in the building but owned by a third party who collects rent for their use. A sprinkler system or other such installation may be in this category.
3. Data of recent major repairs or capital expenditures.
4. An estimate of general deterioration, expressed either as a percentage of reproduction cost or as a dollar amount
5. A similar estimate for rehabilitation expressed in dollars
6. Estimated remaining useful life for items periodically replace-

able during the life of the main structure.
7. Description of functionally obsolete items and the estimated cost to cure, if curable
8. Pertinent comments on physical appearance and condition as observed.

The difference between reproduction cost and replacement cost may automatically reflect some of the functional obsolescence in the building. Care must be taken not to include a deduction for such functional inutility when replacement cost is used in preference to reproduction cost.

DEVELOPING THE ESTIMATE

After the estimates of the respective cost elements are made, the indicated value by the cost approach is found by deducting accrued depreciation. This analysis and recognition of loss in value from all causes constitutes the differential between a cost estimate and an estimate of market value. The value of the land is added to this depreciated cost of the improvements.[4] The computation is shown on p. 271.

Later, comparison with the value indications found by the market data and income approaches should confirm the estimate of accrued depreciation.

Cost Basis, Public Utility Valuations

In public utility valuations one of two value bases is used for rate-making purposes—that is, fair value, which is defined as replacement cost less actual existing depreciation, or historical original cost less

---

4. In preparing the appraisal report, the appraiser may elect to show the estimate of accrued depreciation from all causes as a single total figure, instead of breaking down accrued depreciation into the various categories and to reserve the details of the analysis in the working papers. The type of presentation made by the appraiser concerning accrued depreciation depends on the circumstances, the requirements and purpose of the report, and other considerations.
It is difficult in the cost approach to make a direct estimate of the exact amount of loss due to physical deterioration in hidden parts of the structure. It is equally difficult to estimate incurable functional obsolescence and loss in value due to adverse economic influences, without recourse to support by the market data and income approaches.

Reproduction cost new		
Direct cost	$300,000	
Indirect cost	34,000	
Total cost		$334,000
Accrued depreciation		
Physical deterioration		
Curable rehabilitation	$ 2,600	
Incurable	45,900	
Total		$ 48,500
Functional obsolescence		
Curable	none	
Incurable	$ 27,100	
Total		27,100
Economic obsolescence	none	none
Total accrued depreciation		$ 75,600
Reproduction cost depreciated		$258,400
Other improvements, depreciated[a]		23,600
Total depreciated cost		
of improvements		$282,000
Land value		80,000
Value indicated by cost approach		$362,000

---

[a]Alternately, other improvements may be listed on the basis of reproduction cost above, and appropriate accrued depreciation may be charged under the depreciation headings.

book depreciation that has been accrued for accounting purposes. The choice of which one to use depends on the rules of the state regulatory commissions. In the case of the federal regulatory commissions the latter has been used.

Major Considerations

All estimating requires a sense of balance and proportion, attention to detail, and exercise of a degree of judgment gained from experience. Although completed appraisal reports may vary in the extent of the inclusion of all of the various steps and details inherent in the appraiser's application of a comprehensive cost approach analysis, they usually set forth the essential basis for estimates of cost and accrued depreciation.

SUMMARY

The cost approach is one of the three approaches in the valuation process. Underlying the theory of the cost approach is the principle of substitution, which suggests that no prudent person will pay more for a property than the amount for which he or she can obtain, by purchase of a site and construction of a building without undue delay, a property of equal desirability and utility. Consequently, reproduction cost new, prior to any deduction for accrued depreciation, plus land value, tends to set the upper limit of value. For the cost approach to produce a valid indication of market value that may be reconciled with the value indications obtained by the other two approaches, it is necessary to consider accrued depreciation due to all causes—functional and economic, as well as physical.

The cost approach is particularly valuable when used as an analysis technique, to recognize the effect of the components of depreciation on a property, and to provide a basis for proceeding with the other two approaches to value.

15

The Market Data
Approach: Principles

The market data approach involves direct comparisons of the property being appraised to similar properties that have sold in the same or in a similar market in order to derive a market value indication for the property being appraised. This approach is also called the direct sales comparison approach.

Carefully verified and analyzed, market data is good evidence of value when it represents typical actions and reactions of buyers, sellers, users, and investors. The market value estimate has been categorized as an interpretation of the reactions of typical users and investors in the market. The market data approach, like the cost approach, is based on the principle of substitution. In this approach it implies that a prudent person will not pay more to buy a property than it will cost to buy a comparable substitute property. The price a typical purchaser pays is usually the result of an extensive shopping process in which available alternates are compared. The property purchased typically represents the best available balance between the buyer's specifications and the purchase price. Asking price may be more than a seller expects to realize because there is the possibility that a nontypical purchaser may be found willing to pay more than market value. After testing the market for a reasonable time without success, the seller may reduce the price or accept an offer that is less than the asking price. Although individual sales may deviate from a market norm, a sufficient number tend to produce a pattern indicating the action of typical buyers and sellers in the market. When information about a sufficient number of similar property sales made in the current market is available, the resulting pattern provides a good indication of market value.

STEPS IN THE MARKET DATA APPROACH

The market data approach may be applied in five steps:

1.   Research the market to identify similar properties for which pertinent sales, listings, offerings, and/or rental data is available.
2.   Qualify the prices as to terms, motivating forces, and bona fide nature.
3.   Compare each of the comparable properties' important attributes to the corresponding ones of the property being appraised, under the general categories of time, location, physical characteristics, and conditions of sale.
4.   Consider all dissimilarities and their probable effect on the price of each sale property to derive individual market value indications for the property being appraised.
5.   From the pattern developed, formulate an opinion of market value for the property being appraised.

MARKET DATA RESEARCH

Market data is assembled for many purposes. It may provide a basis for the analysis leading to a conclusion of probable market value for the property being appraised. It may involve specific studies of supply and demand relationships, absorption rates, land use types, and other evaluation goals.

To ensure valid market value conclusions, the process of comparison and adjustment must be based on sales that constitute acceptable evidence of typical market action within the market in which the property would be offered and sold. Reference to a real estate market implies no specific geographical location. The market for single family homes in a subdivision may be limited to a specific segment, economic or other, of the population within the community. Large investment properties may be offered in a national market. The market for any parcel of real estate consists of the potential purchasers, wherever they may be and whatever category they comprise within the population.

The research involved in the assemblage of market data reflects the scope of the potential market for the property being appraised. The appraiser develops and analyzes both primary and secondary data, which requires special training and experience. Primary data is original "raw" data generated through market surveys, interviews, field inspections, and the like. Secondary data is previously assembled or published data such as listing service sales, U.S. Bureau of the Census reports, purchasing power or demographic information, cost data, and similar material.

The proper mixture and artful application of research processes is the hallmark of the professional appraiser. The nature and extent of the research appropriate to a specific assignment reflects the type of property and the character of the problem. For market value assignments, the appraiser researches market perceptions, opinions, and attitudes. For other types of assignments, the appraiser may conduct primary research to develop data unrelated or only partly related to sales.

Because the market data approach is close to the market, it provides excellent evidence in support of a market value estimate when it is based on reliable data competently processed. However, available data may include transactions that reflect temporary shifts in supply and demand, improper improvements that do not approach highest and best use of a site, or conditions of sale that are not typical or do not conform to the requirements of the definition of market value. Since no conclusion is better than the quality of the data on which it is predicated, the appraiser screens and analyzes all data to establish its reliability and applicability before using it as the basis for a value indication in the market data approach.

DATA PROGRAM

The sources and methods by which pertinent data is collected in the valuation process have been presented in previous chapters. Customarily, the major areas of comparison between one property and another require data concerning time, location, physical characteristics, and conditions of sale. The latter term involves a comparison of all circumstances of the transaction with the criteria set forth in the definition of the value being sought.

Since systematic and orderly procedure for the process of comparison is important, the scope and organization of the data program are considered before the categories of comparative data.

Scope of Pertinent Data

The following outline is a guide to the character and scope of the data processed in this approach.

A.   Sales, offers, and listings of other properties
   1.   Description of properties
      a.   Physical information: terrain, construction, architecture, size, plan, number of rooms, condition, etc.
      b.   Desirability of location
      c.   Income data and leases
   2.   Price paid, offered, or asked, and the terms
   3.   Other conditions
      a.   Date of sale
      b.   Relative position, competence, and bargaining ability of each party
      c.   General economic conditions prevailing
      d.   Any special need for purchase or special desire for disposal
      e.   Any unusual financing
   4.   Identification of the property rights involved
B.   Supply and demand considerations
   1.   Number of similar properties available for purchase and rate of turnover
   2.   Number of similar properties or rental units vacant and the trend of demand
   3.   Number of similar properties or rental units under construction or in prospect
   4.   Extent of market activity pertaining to the property being appraised
C.   Informed opinions regarding purchase and rental of comparable properties
   1.   Asking price and price obtainable
   2.   Market conditions

Sources of Information

The appraiser learns where such information may be found and how it should be maintained for maximum usefulness. There are many sources of data: the appraiser's own files; public records; atlases and survey maps; lease records; published news; classified ads and listings; other Realtors, lenders, and appraisers; direct interviews, published listings; reported sales; and other local sources.

Office files. Appraisers who are also brokers may maintain office files relating to certain transactions. In addition, the facts obtained for one assignment may be of considerable help on another. Data the appraiser accumulates is called the appraisal plant, or data bank.

Public records. Many counties have maps, published publicly or privately, that show the ownership of land. Statutes in some states require a fee that reflects the consideration to be paid upon transfer of title. The amount of the fee is a public record and presumably indicates the consideration, but it is not necessarily dependable as a reflection of the sale price because some purchasers deduct the estimated value of personal property (e.g., in motels or apartments) from the true consideration in order to reduce transfer taxes. These personal property values are frequently inflated, making the recorded consideration for the real property less than the true consideration. In some localities legal or private publishing services issue information on revenue stamps and other pertinent facts about current transfers.

Atlases and survey maps. These give data on lot size, relate legal descriptions to street numbers, and frequently show building locations and dimensions to scale.

Lease records. There may be a county index of leases listing the parties to recorded leases and referring to the volume and page in which the lease is recorded. In some cities abstracts of recorded leases are printed by a private publishing service.

Published news. Real estate news is featured in the newspapers of cities of any size. Sometimes the news is inaccurate, but the names of the negotiating brokers and the parties involved generally are published, which enables the appraiser to confirm details.

Classified ads and listings.   The appraiser's name may be placed on the mailing list of banks, brokers, and others offering properties for sale. Classified ads are also a source of information on properties currently being offered for sale.

Realtors, appraisers, and bankers.   Such professionals are usually a prime source of information. Though unsupported hearsay may not be dependable, it may provide valuable leads to vital facts.

Direct interview.   Confirmation of statements of fact by one or both of the principals in a transaction is the ideal situation. Alternatively, confirmation may be sought through the brokers, closing agencies, and lenders in the transactions. Sometimes the owners and tenants of neighboring properties are a source of leads to factual information.

Multiple listing books.   In some communities books of multiple listings that have sold during a calendar year are published. Complete information, including a picture, a complete description of the property, the broker's name, and the authentic sale price, is given. In some areas such multiple listing books are offered for sale.

The Appraisal Plant

Through a sound data program, a large bank of market data can be accumulated. Only some of it is immediately pertinent. The problem is to organize the data in a way to serve the appraiser's needs most effectively. It may be accumulated as needed, or in the case of a research organization, a large staff may collect, index, and cross-index market data for use at some future time. Some appraisers may adopt a middle course—that is, accumulate the data themselves, which they index and file to suit their needs. The index may carry the address, a file number, and additional salient information. Ordinarily, sufficient information is included to indicate whether a property is related to the working assignment and whether the detailed file should be studied. Figure 15.1 shows a workable data card.

In addition to files recording address and property, detailed information may be entered on a master sheet for each comparative property. Figure 15.2 shows a typical entry, but more data may be included.

Figure 15.1. Property Data Card

```
┌─────────────────────────────────────────────────────────┐
│                                                           │
│  Address_____ Index No._____  │
│  Sold by _____ │
│  Purchaser_____ │
│  Date of sale_____ │
│  Price_____ │
│  Financing_____ │
│  Rent_____ │
│  Land description_____ │
│  Zoning at time of sale_____ │
│  Building description_____ Age_____   │
│  Verified by_____On_____(Date)  │
│  Comments and comparison_____ │
│                                                           │
└─────────────────────────────────────────────────────────┘
```

Figure 15.2 Market Data Approach—Residential Property

```
┌─────────────────────────────────────────────────────────┐
│  City: Any town, Illinois                                 │
│  Address: 20231 Wilmore Avenue      Property: Dwelling    │
│  Court House Identification: Book 642, pg. 22, item 22    │
│  Grantor: Joseph E. Smith                                 │
│  Grantee: E. W. and E. M. Reeve      Date: 3/20/78        │
│  Recording: Volume 9095-706                               │
│  Consideration: $10              Illinois Rev. Stamps: $40.00 │
│  Indicated Price: $40,000                                 │
│  Land: 40 × 120, 4,800 sq. ft.                            │
│  Improvements:                                            │
│    Typical 5-room frame, 1½ story and basement, 1-car garage, full │
│    concrete drive, combination storm sash. Good condition. About │
│    25 years old. 30 × 24 ft. on foundation.               │
│  Comment:                                                 │
│    Confirmed price as $40,000 per E. W. Reeve, 6/15/78. No special │
│    circumstances. Has not considered it necessary to redecorate │
│    since purchase. Has installed new water heater.        │
│                                                           │
└─────────────────────────────────────────────────────────┘
```

A data record system may be classified by property categories, such as the following:

Residential	Industrial
Acreage	Acreage
Vacant lots	Vacant sites
Residences	Factories and plants
Apartments	Warehouses
	Loft buildings
Commercial	Special purpose
Acreage	Gasoline service stations
Vacant sites	Hospitals and nursing homes
Retail stores	Theatres
Office buildings	Miscellaneous
Hotels and motels	Large housing projects
Service buildings	Institutional structures

Maintaining separate files and cross-indexing from the alphabetical address and area files to class-of-property files keeps the market data on location and type of property readily available. Such a system is functional and is well suited to the continuous weeding-out process necessary to keep the material current.

The market data master sheet may be supplemented by an attached photograph or, for larger properties, a copy of the printed brochure that was prepared in offering the property for sale.

Market data may be stored in a simple, indexed filing system or may be part of an elaborate computer storage system that is used for instant recall by categories such as type of property, location, age, or price range. In the collection and use of sales data, computers serve two purposes: calculation and storage. Computer techniques provide facilities for the storage and classification of sales data concerning different types of property and different locations, with instant access to the desired information. Whether the use of such computers is advisable in a given situation depends on the size of the appraiser's operation, the amount of information to be stored, and the practicalities of keeping it updated. The choice of a system to use depends largely on which most effectively meets the appraiser's requirements according to its cost, convenience, and the types of property usually appraised.

FACTORS IN DIRECT SALES COMPARISON

The factors to be considered in direct sales comparison are some-times referred to as elements of comparison. The appraiser's objective is to interpret, from sales of similar properties, the probable market value of the property being appraised. A comprehensive market file, augmented by current research, provides a variety of market information as a basis for the comparison process. Since no two properties are identical in all respects, the attributes of the potentially comparable sale (or rental) properties are reconciled with those of the property being appraised.

In making comparisons, the appraiser identifies similarities and dissimilarities. The most dependable conclusions are based on comparisons of the most similar factors and conditions. The appraiser considers the extent of the dissimilarities and estimates the amount these add to, or subtract from, the known price of the sale property in order to obtain an adjusted figure reflecting the probable sale price of the property being appraised.

Time

The length of time for which specific sale comparisons may be useful varies with the character of the market, the rate and extent of market change, and the type of property. For example, sales of farmland in a slowly changing market with a limited number of transactions annually may contrast sharply with the activity of the market for modern warehouse properties in an expanding industrial area. The appraiser may be justified in extending the time-range of sale comparison data for the farmlands beyond that appropriate for the warehouse properties.

In making adjustments for time the effect of general economic conditions and price levels is noted. To use sales data from a previous period as an indication of an anticipated sale price for a property, figures at which the comparable properties were sold are adjusted to reflect the current price level. If this level is approximately 10% higher than three years ago, an upward adjustment is applied to a three-year-old property sale.

Location

Because similar properties might sell for more in one neighborhood than in another, the sales data used for comparison is most meaningful when confined to the neighborhood of the property being appraised. The use of sales data from other neighborhoods may be misleading or invalid, particularly in the case of residential properties. A lack of sales data within a particular area may justify the consideration of data from another area, but in such cases a rational and objective basis for comparison is developed. Adjustments for differences in location, if any, should be consistent with market evidence. When selecting comparables and making adjustments for location, appraisers avoid reliance on factors related to the racial, religious, or ethnic composition of the residents of an area because of the unreliability of this type of data in predicting price variance.

Physical Characteristics

There are two kinds of physical characteristics, and they are treated in the same manner as the characteristics of neighborhood and location.

Site and land improvements.   Similar properties may differ regarding site qualities—that is, in frontage, size, land improvement (landscaping), or terrain. For example, the property being appraised has a 50-foot lot; a comparable property has a 60-foot lot. An adjustment may be required for any difference in the value of the two lots.

The difference in plantings, lawn, drives, fences, parking areas, barbecues, or perhaps even swimming pools may be handled on a direct dollar-adjustment basis, since the appraiser deals with net values rather than cost. Common denominators in the form of units of sale value may be used for effective comparison.

In the valuation of properties with *excess land,* the surplus land may be segregated and valued separately. This situation exists when the land area exceeds that necessary to serve existing improvements on the site. The excess land is available for future development, or it may have potential resale value. The portion of the land area that provides a typical land-to-building ratio, with the existing improvements, may be considered an economic entity. The market value of this portion of the whole may be estimated by sale comparisons. Assuming the excess land is marketable or that it does have value for future use, its market value as vacant land constitutes an addition to the estimated value of the economic entity.

Building improvements. For single family homes, the ultimate unit of comparison is the house; but the unit could be a room, with a standard room count, or a square foot, using dimensions of living area or of gross area.

For apartment houses, the unit of comparison may be the apartment, the room, or dollars per square foot of rentable area. If the last measure is used, the number of square feet of living area is logically a better measure than gross area. However, the number of square feet of gross area can be more accurately established and is more frequently used in the cost approach. The apartment as a unit is a rough measure of comparison unless there is considerable uniformity in the number, size, and character of rooms per apartment. Generally, the room or a square foot of apartment area is the unit used. The market price per room for two- or three-room units may be greater than that for five or six rooms, other things being equal.

In industrial properties the unit of comparison is usually the square foot of gross usable floor space, and in office buildings, a square foot of rentable area. Parking, service, and public areas usually are considered in relation to their effect on sale prices. Observed quality of construction, age, and other major variations in the building as well as functional inutilities also are taken into account.

At the time of sale the purchaser is acutely aware of the condition of the property. By the time the appraiser considers a property as a comparative sale, the buyer may have rehabilitated or modernized it. A personal interview may be necessary to ascertain the extent of such work so that the sale may be adjusted to a truly comparable basis.

Conditions of Sale

Market price may be affected by factors such as the relative negotiating position of the parties to the sale, by terms that deviate from typical terms available in the market, or by including other real estate at some arbitrary amount as part of a purchase price.

A sale that was not an arms-length transaction—for example, a sale between related parties—does not comply with the conditions for market value and cannot be adapted to the adjustment process.

A similar problem is presented by a sale in which one party was under pressure to consummate the transaction—for example, the real estate involved is adjacent to existing holdings and the buyer needed the specific parcel for expansion. Again, the sale data is eliminated from consideration in the adjustment process. This type of situation is discussed on p. 290.

Appropriate adjustment is possible in other situations where the sale price may be affected by conditions of sale. These include unusual terms such as assumption of existing financing which does not conform to the existing mortgage market or execution of a purchase money mortgage at terms or in an amount not typically available. Under these circumstances, the appraiser may adjust the sale price to an equivalent price assuming typical financing available at the time of sale.[1]

The sale of a property being used in the comparison process may have involved the acceptance of another parcel of real property as part of the sale price. The amount at which this other parcel is included in the transaction is frequently inflated with consequent effect on the comparable sale price. In such cases the appraiser may adjust the price of the property sold by the estimated amount of the deviation from market value of the property traded. The extent of this deviation may be revealed by a resale of the traded property or through a market value estimate by the appraiser.

The appraiser also ascertains whether a reported sale price represents the purchase of all the usual rights of ownership or whether the sale was subject to liens, leases, or other encumbrances that may have affected the purchase price. The reported sale of a similar property may be found to involve a leased fee subject to an unexpired lease which deviates from market rental, thus detracting from or enhancing market value free of lease.

---

1. The procedure for accomplishing this involves the use of present worth factors to establish the present value of the future mortgage payments on the basis of the market interest rate at the date of sale.

UNITS OF COMPARISON

Comparison of sale prices (or rentals) in terms of whole properties is difficult unless the properties are essentially identical. To reduce the process of comparison to a practical level, reduction of sale prices to some common denominator or unit of comparison is desirable. For example, knowledge that Warehouse A sold in the current market for $300,000 and Warehouse B sold for $400,000 does not provide the basis for a meaningful comparison with a property being appraised. However, if Warehouse A provides 20,000 square feet and Warehouse B provides 32,000 square feet, it becomes apparent that Warehouse A sold for $15 per square foot and Warehouse B sold for $12.50 per square foot. Reduction of these sales to a unit of comparison in terms of dollars per square foot of gross area enables the appraiser to compare the qualities of each with the attributes of a similar warehouse being appraised. Thus the probable sale price of the property being appraised can be derived.

Units of comparison include dollars per square foot of gross or rentable area, per room or per unit, per theatre seat, per truck door, per car space, or other common denominators.

METHODS OF ADJUSTMENT

There are many techniques for comparing or adjusting market data. The appraiser chooses one that is applicable to the specific market in which the property is located and is consistent with the quantity of data and the experience of the appraiser. Material presented in Appendix C, Mathematics in Appraising, covers basic concepts in arithmetic, algebra, statistics, and regression analysis. The concepts presented are the tools used by appraisers in implementing the appraisal process.

The procedures for market data adjustment presented in this chapter are the most commonly used. They are:

1. Whole property comparison
2. Dollar adjustments
3. Percentage adjustments

In the adjustment process sales may be paired in an effort to identify the effect of specific differences on probable price in the market. If two sale properties are closely comparable except in one respect, the relative sale prices may indicate reasonable adjustment for the specific difference. If a property sold and was resold at a later date with no significant changes in the property or the environment during the interim, the two sales may indicate the rate of change applicable in the market for a time of sale adjustment.

Application of this technique is complicated by the fact that more than one difference that has a significant impact on market value usually exists between sale properties. When the impact of one or more differences can be identified from market evidence, they may be used to reduce the unadjusted differences between other matched pairs. When successive pairings can thus be reduced to single unadjusted factors, a series of estimates for individual differences can be developed.

Whole property comparison involves a single lump sum adjustment based on a narration indicating why and to what extent the property being appraised is considered better or poorer than a comparable sale property. The estimated effect on value is presented as a single figure with no allocation in terms of the specific effect of particular factors contributing to the total.

Methods that include an analysis in terms of specific items and their individual effect on value are generally preferred. Adjustments may be in terms of dollars or in terms of a percentage effect on value. The use of dollars is easily adapted to detailed analysis and is more widely used.

A typical application of the dollar adjustment method involves a table or grid of multiple adjustments to a number of sales of comparable properties. Each sale is successively adjusted, leading to an indication of value for the property being appraised. Such a tabulation may properly be limited to factors that have measurable or significant effect on value and may include adjustments for time, location, physical characteristics, and conditions of sale. These adjustment tables may be included in an appraisal report or retained as worksheets in the appraiser's file, with a narrative summary presented in the report.

In any multiple-adjustment analysis, the appraiser is alert to recognize colinearity in the adjustment process, the potentially overlapping effects of two or more adjustments—for example, an adjustment for gross area and an adjustment for number of bedrooms. The proper extent of a specific adjustment is not always easily derived. Reproduction cost may provide an indication in some instances, but the appraiser also recognizes that a proper adjustment is in terms of the effect on market value, which may differ from the cost factor involved.

GROSS RENT MULTIPLIERS

The comparison process also concerns economic comparability. Income properties are sometimes compared on a gross multiple basis. For example, in appraising a standard apartment building, analysis of comparable sales may show that such sales have been made at a fairly uniform multiple of the gross income. This could be carried through and applied to net income. But at that point the process is more properly considered as part of the income approach, whereas comparisons of gross income may sometimes be used as a part of the market data approach.

A gross income or gross rent multiplier (GRM) is a factor reflecting the relationship between its sale price or value and the gross annual income of real estate. For a residence, it is computed on the basis of monthly income, but for all other types of property it is on the basis of annual gross income; for example, properties selling for $100,000, with an annual gross of $20,000, are selling at five times the gross, indicating that a GRM of 5 may be applied to the gross annual income of a closely comparable property to convert that gross to a value estimate. Similarly, a residence selling at $30,000 with a rental value of $200 per month reflects a GRM of 150 computed on the basis of the gross monthly rental.

Since the GRM relates value to gross income rather than net income, its use is valid only for types of properties that are:

1. Reasonably consistent in net-to-gross-income operating ratio, and
2. Sell with sufficient frequency in the market to produce a discernible GRM pattern.

Types of properties that frequently conform to these requirements include certain classes of apartment properties, retail properties, industrial properties, and others where a reasonable similarity of age, size, location, remaining economic life, land-to-building ratio, and operating experience exists.

A multiplier may be applied either to gross income or to effective gross income, if the method of application is consistent. The circumstances and available data indicate the appropriate procedure in a specific situation.

The GRM is closely related to market action and it is easy to explain. However, the principal advantage of the technique is that the reflection of rental income is direct. Therefore, differences between properties, which could involve adjustments based on judgment estimates, have been resolved by the free action of the rental market. If Property A has some advantage over Property B in age, condition, accessibility, location, or physical characteristics, the difference in actual rental presumably reflects the extent of this advantage as viewed in the market. Because some adjustments for relative desirability are thus inherent in the factor, a GRM may not be subject to adjustment after having been computed. An exception might be where tenant credit is a factor affecting the rental level or the rate of return necessary to attract investment capital. Another exception would be the sale of an improperly utilized or managed property that was not producing its potential income at the time of sale.

In the appraisal of single family residential property, where application of a typical income capitalization approach is not practical, the use of a GRM is accepted in some areas as an income approach to a value estimate.

ANALYSIS OF MARKET DATA

The sale prices of comparable properties (adjusted to the property being appraised) are convincing evidence of the appraiser's market value estimate. Considerations in the analysis of market data are:

1. Number of sales
2. Period of time covered
3. Terms on which properties were sold
4. Rate of turnover
5. Motivating force (objectives of sellers and buyers)
6. Degree of comparability

Listings or offers to sell and offers to purchase can also be used as market data.

Number of Sales

The number of comparative sales to be accumulated and analyzed depends somewhat on their comparability and the nature of the market. If there is a block of similar homes and several of them were sold in recent months, it seems unnecessary to look further. If, however, comparable sales must be sought in a wider area and over a longer time span, it may be necessary to find and analyze a greater number to indicate the market value by reflecting the actions of typical purchasers in the market. The numbers of sales to be analyzed is the number necessary to provide adequate support for a conclusion of value.

Period of Time Covered

In a less active market it may become necessary to check back for several years to find sales data. In a dynamic market the number of recent sales may be adequate. If establishing a market trend for a particular type of property is desirable, sales data may be obtained covering a reasonable period prior to the time of investigation. Such data may produce indicated percentages of increases or decreases for time that may be used to adjust prior-year sales of comparable properties to an indication of a current market price. Such adjusted prior-year sale prices may then be used as present-date comparables in the market approach.

Terms

In an arm's length transaction (unless there are some special considerations), the seller receives cash. The purchaser may not have all the cash, but may be able to borrow enough from a lending institution with the consequence that the seller receives cash for the property.

When real estate is sold on terms, the selling price is frequently higher than it would have been on a cash basis. For example, where a property is sold on contract with a small downpayment, the sale price is usually higher than a cash price. Frequently there are transactions that involve a purchase-money mortgage given to the sellers. If this was necessary because no other lenders were interested, the terms of financing by the seller are probably reflected in a higher sale price. Under these circumstances, if the seller desires to realize cash for the purchase contract or the purchase-money mortgage, it may be necessary to accept less than its face value to dispose of it in the market.

The details of the sales transactions used as comparable data are important in market value appraisals. Transactions that involve special financing by the seller must be described accordingly and either rejected or the considerations adjusted to reflect market value as defined in this text.

Rate of Turnover

When a large number of property sales occur in a neighborhood that has been relatively dormant for many years, the appraiser tries to identify the reason. There may have been a change in zoning that makes the property available for a higher use; or there may have been a change in the character of the neighborhood. If comparisons are made with properties in other neighborhoods in either of these situations, adjustments are in order.

The law of supply and demand exerts strong influence on the real estate market. Sales activity tends to fluctuate with economic conditions and oversupply or shortages of particular types of properties and space.

Motivating Force

Sometimes the concept of a sale made by "a willing buyer and a willing seller . . . neither being under abnormal pressure," seems to be realized infrequently. One person wants to buy and another wants to sell, and in the nature of things the motivation of one party is likely to be stronger than that of the other (see the section on buyer-seller subjective value concepts in Chapter 2). A wide variety of motivating forces can occur in real estate transactions that can affect market price in relation to market value. The most common are:

1. Desire to liquidate for inheritance tax or other pressing reasons
2. Desire and need to own a particular property for expansion, parking, or other purposes
3. Immediate possession, or lack of it
4. Low or high rentals under an existing lease
5. Sales between related or affiliated parties
6. Sentimental interest
7. Any factor that results in a negotiating advantage for either buyer or seller

Many situations could be cited to illustrate each of these motivating forces. For example, a man dies and when his estate is probated, cash is needed to pay the inheritance tax. This may necessitate selling one or more of the real estate holdings. Perhaps all the property must be sold because some of the heirs want immediate cash. Generally under these conditions, real estate appraisals of liquidation value tend to fall in the lower part of the range. If the holdings are comprised of single-use properties, which are usually hard to sell, the need to meet the time schedule may work against finding a buyer willing to pay the highest price.

A case history of a three-story walk-up apartment property with 36 units illustrates why a buyer may pay more than market value for a parcel of real estate. The apartment building occupied almost the whole site (except the U-shaped front court). The city passed an ordinance prohibiting overnight parking on any city street. It was, therefore, necessary to purchase land for parking. The land to the north was improved with two old residences on lots of 40 x 125 feet each. All other adjacent property was improved with good apartment buildings. The apartment owners offered $3 per square foot of land for the residences, which was the market value of the land. The homeowners would not sell for this price but would accept $5 per square foot. Instead of paying $30,000, the apartment owners paid $50,000. In this instance the apartment owners were "captive" purchasers.

Under abnormal conditions, such as during a shortage of any type of property, a purchaser usually pays a premium to obtain immediate possession. However, a property subject to lease may sell for less than its market value when possession is not available until a later date. Such motivating forces may affect the validity of a sale as evidence of market value.

All recognized definitions of market value include the following basic assumptions: Buyers and seller are willing and competent; neither is forced to act; each has freedom of choice; the seller receives all cash. Whenever these conditions are not present, the price may not represent the reactions of typical purchasers and sellers in the market. Examples include property that is being assembled and purchases made under threat of condemnation. When property is being assembled, the purchaser is captive because there is no choice. When property is purchased under threat of condemnation, the owner may not be a willing seller. Since many transactions do not reflect market value, they should be explained, adjusted, or excluded.

Degree of Comparability

Exact similarity is seldom found between comparable properties used as market data and the property being appraised. Occasionally in the case of residential property, and particularly when the property being appraised is one of many built at the same time by the same builder, close and recent comparisons are found. However, market data evidence usually is obtained on properties that, although similar in major respects, are sufficiently dissimilar to require adjustment to bring them into line with the property being appraised. Also, only some may have been recent sales. For example, in a rising market the market data pattern might be similar to that given in Table 15.1.

Table 15.1.   Analysis of Five Sales Compared to Subject Property

Comparable Sale	Price	Date of Sale	Comparison
1	$25,000	5 years ago	Equal
2	22,000	4 years ago	Inferior
3	31,000	2 years ago	Superior
4	37,000	1 year ago	Superior
5	36,000	1 year ago	Equal

A study of this pattern indicates that the sale price of the "equal" properties (1 and 5) increased from $25,000 to $36,000 in four years. Therefore, Sale 2 tends to support Sale 1 as a fair price for that year. Sale 4 increased $6,000 over Sale 3 in one year. However, Sale 4 is rated a better house than the property being appraised and may be better than Sale 3.

Indications are that the property being appraised is worth as much currently ($37,000) as the superior property (Sale 4) was worth a year ago. There is much to be said for bracketing the subject property between two recent sales, one a superior property and the other an inferior property.

In dealing with sales comparisons of vacant land, the procedure is similar. The general rule is that closely comparable properties are sought first, but the less comparable or older examples are utilized to build a pattern into which the probable market price of the property being appraised may be fitted.

A number of other factors should be noted in establishing the relationship of the comparative property to the one being appraised, in addition to qualifying the sale as bona fide. The factors of time, neighborhood and location, site and land improvement, the building itself, and the income from the property are all highly significant considerations in an analysis of comparability.

Listings or Offers to Sell

Listings are potential market prices, but they usually reflect the top of the range, and therefore, unless adjusted, are not acceptable as sound evidence of market value. Listings are analyzed in much the same way as are actual sales. The same qualifications are made: number of listings, period of time covered, terms (cash or contract), rate of turnover, motivating force, and degree of comparability. The number of listings frequently is a good indicator of a changing trend in use. If many people want to sell, the reason should be determined. Numerous listings in a limited area may mean competition between owners to sell, so that listing prices tend to approximate market prices more closely than they would otherwise. For example, there was a period following the depression of the 1930s when liquidating bank listings coincided with bottom selling prices, given a 20% downpayment. A buyer could purchase these listings for 10% less with cash, but nothing lower would be considered. At that time listing prices were almost as good as actual sales for comparative purposes. After World War II, however, listings frequently had little meaning. Owners were optimistic, anticipating a market much higher than appeared reasonable. In a modified way this condition, with only a few brief interruptions, has continued as a long-term trend.

The period of time for which a property is listed before it is sold affords an interesting study. The time factor varies with property types and market conditions. A very old frame residence, on land zoned for low-rise multiple-family building, was listed for $3 per square foot of land and declined in successive years to $2.50, $2, $1.75, and finally sold for $1.50 per square foot. Most of the owners nearby might have thought their land worth more than $1.50 per square foot, but the history of this listing suggests less optimism.

Offers to Purchase

Offers to sell tend to indicate a ceiling on market prices; offers to purchase tend to indicate a floor. The offer to purchase is more likely to approximate the market price than is an offer to sell. A valid offer to purchase usually is made seriously, but an offer to sell might be merely to test the market. When the offer to purchase is motivated by a special need, the price offered may exceed market value. Terms and motivating forces are key factors in qualifying a known offer to purchase.

Unlike listings or offers to sell, most offers to purchase are not common knowledge. The appraiser may not make any special effort to obtain such information, although if it becomes available and adequate market data is lacking, the information may be useful. Nevertheless, offers to purchase and sell become more credible when they remain under an option and still more credible when the offers to purchase and sell are supported by the signatures of both parties.

SUMMARY

The market data approach is based on the principle of substitution and involves the process of comparing the property being appraised to similar properties that have been sold in the market. Similarities and dissimilarities between the subject and comparable properties are noted. Such differences may be in time; location;

physical characteristics, including condition and functional utility; and conditions of sale. For investment property, income is also a factor. The information required by the market data approach calls for knowledge of the comparable properties in order to establish the character and extent of the specific differences.

Pertinent data is obtained by identification and inspection of comparable properties that have been sold and from deed transfer records, atlases, lease records, published news, advertisements, informed sources, and direct interviews. The facts are assembled and filed according to location and type. Sales data is processed to the convenient units of measurement, such as per dwelling, per apartment, per room, per square foot, and gross monthly or annual multiplier.

In addition to the physical items, the appraiser considers the number of comparable sale properties and geographical coverage of data, period of time covered, financing terms, rate of turnover, motivating forces behind transactions, and in general the degree of comparability of the sale properties with the one being appraised. Listings for sale and offers to purchase may be considered and accorded weight on their merits.

The actual comparison process, as set forth in the appraisal report, may require some type of statistical presentation showing adjustments that may be made by dollar amounts or percentages from the comparative properties to the property being appraised. The degree of similarity existing between the properties establishes the differences for which there must be adjustment.

The market value for the property being appraised is developed by adjusting the sale prices of the comparable properties (up or down) by a dollar amount that is an indication of the effect of the differences on its market value. The implication is that the adjusted price of each comparable sale indicates the amount at which the property being appraised would sell if offered in the market.

This procedure tends to produce an indication of value within a bracket, rather than a precise figure. When there is a sufficient amount of comparable data, such an indication is realistic. With more data obtained from additional comparable sales, the range of the indicated price at which the subject property would sell, if offered, narrows. With fewer and smaller adjustments to achieve comparability, the range within which the indicated value may be found becomes more reliable. In some circumstances — when, for example, a specific figure is difficult to establish — the appraiser may express the market data approach indication as a range.

A summary of comparison and adjustment procedures in the market data approach follows:

Factors in direct sales comparison
  1. Time
  2. Location
  3. Physical characteristics
  4. Conditions of sale[2]
Methods of adjustment
  1. Whole property comparison
  2. Dollar adjustments
  3. Percentage adjustments (converted to a dollar conclusion)

In addition to direct adjustment of sale prices to derive a market value indication for a property being appraised, comparable sales data may be used to develop gross rent multipliers or units of comparison, such as dollars per square feet of gross or rentable area. Units of comparison are subject to adjustment and a derived GRM or unit of comparison may be applied to the property being appraised to produce an estimate of market value, as illustrated in the next chapter.

The market data approach to a value estimate is direct and easily explained and understood. Its application is difficult only for types of property for which comparable sales data is not available or where excessive adjustments are necessary. It is ideal for types of property that sell frequently. It may be the only usable approach for properties that, because of age, excessive depreciation, and a lack of dependable income and expense data, are not suitable for application of the cost or income approaches.

---

2. Conditions of sale are a primary consideration in the initial screening process to eliminate sales that do not meet basic criteria for a meaningful comparison. Conditions of sale for which adjustment is practical, such as nontypical financing, receive consideration within the adjustment process.

16

The Market Data
Approach: Application

The general principles and procedures of the market data approach are applicable to all types of property commonly bought and sold in the market. In all cases the assumption is made that sales have been screened for motivation factors that would invalidate the sale as a reasonable indication of market value.

DWELLING

A valuation is to be made of a single family dwelling for an owner who is planning to put it on the market. The house is 35 years old and located in a fairly well-preserved neighborhood. It is brick with four rooms (living room, dining room, kitchen, and single-story attached sunroom) and lavatory on the first floor, four bedrooms and two baths on the second floor, and one bedroom and bath on the third floor. Its condition is average, but piping and kitchen are original equipment.

There are five sales of nearby properties of about the same age that are generally comparable. The following data is developed:

Sale No. 1. A dwelling of brick construction. Four rooms and lavatory on the first floor; four bedrooms and one bath on the second. Maid's room and bath on third. Has a remodeled kitchen, but original piping. Condition is superior. Sold this year for $55,000.

Sale No. 2. Frame construction, four rooms and lavatory on first floor, four bedrooms and two baths on second; one room and bath on third. Has original kitchen and piping. Average condition. Sold one year ago for $55,000.

Sale No. 3. Frame house, three rooms and lavatory on first floor; four bedrooms and two baths on second; no third floor. Has remodeled kitchen and piping replaced with copper. Average condition. Sold three years ago for $48,000.

Sale No. 4. Frame house, four rooms and lavatory on first floor; four bedrooms and one bath on second. Maid's room and bath on third. Has original kitchen, but water piping replaced. Condition is considered to be inferior. Lot is pie-shaped and inferior to the typical lot. Sold one year ago for $50,000

Sale No. 5. Brick house, four rooms on first floor: three bedrooms and two baths on second; no third. Has original kitchen, and piping has been replaced. Average condition. Sold two years ago for $48,000.

To obtain indications of market value of the property appraised, such generally comparable sales may be analyzed and adjusted as follows:

TABLE 16.1.   Analysis and Adjustment—Sale No. 1

Price	$55,000
Time adjustment	0
Location and neighborhood adjustment	0
Physical characteristics	
Lot value	0
Construction quality	0
Condition	−1,500
First floor rooms	0
Second floor rooms	0
Third floor	0
Second floor bath	+3,000
Lavatory	0
Remodeled kitchen	−3,000
Piping	0
Net adjustment for differences in characteristics	minus $ 1,500
Indicated market value of property being appraised by comparison	$53,500

After similar analysis and adjustment of the other comparable sales, the appraiser may conclude that a market value range from $50,000 to $54,000 is indicated. Experience and judgment in this case may suggest something slightly more than an average; for example, $53,000 as a reasonable indicated value of the property being appraised by the market data approach. In assessing dollar adjustments, the cost involved in a physical difference may be a factor in the appraiser's analysis, but the actual adjustment is in terms of the probable effect on market value.

Predicated on study of the data and application of experience and judgment to interpret, weigh, and rationalize the implications of each individual sale, a pattern should emerge that leads the appraiser to a logical market value conclusion about the property being appraised.

The adjustments shown in this example are based on market study and market reflection of the weights of observed differences. The adjustments should not be based on cost estimates in a market value assignment.

APARTMENT BUILDING

The appraiser has obtained data concerning an apartment house and nearby similar properties that have been sold recently. All seem to be in good condition. A study of neighborhood data shows that the locations are of equivalent desirability, so that neighborhood adjustments are insignificant.

Two principal units of sales comparison that may be applied effectively are dollars per room and dollars per apartment unit (see comparable sales analysis in Table 16.2). Dollars per square foot is also a valid unit of comparison, particularly when a substantial variation in room sizes results in a different utility for a similar gross area. A gross rent multiplier may also be an appropriate basis for a comparison.

The subject is most comparable in apartment size to Property B and in rental value per room to B and C. The lower rental per room for D combined with the higher GRM might suggest that the appraiser check to ascertain whether this means the rooms are less desirable or whether management has not been alert to maintain a rental schedule close to the market. If so, the purchaser may anticipate increasing rentals, thus reducing the GRM.

Table 16.2. Garden Apartment Properties—Comparable Sales Analysis

	Properties				Property Being Appraised
	A	B	C	D	
Stories	2	2	2	2	2
Years since sale	5	4	2	8	6
Units	400	90	114	384	177
Rooms	1,724	455	678	1,536	880
Baths	535	135	171	384	247
Rooms per unit	4.3	5	6	4	5
Rental (time of sale)	$1,070,650	$305,900	$435,625	$800,000	$574,000
Rental per room per month	$51.75	$56.03	$53.54	$43.40	$54.36
Sale price	$7,000,000	$2,050,000	$2,590,000	$5,600,000	$3,700,000 [a]
Sale price per room	$4,060	$4,505	$3,820	$3,646	$4,200 [a]
Sale price per unit	$17,500	$22,780	$22,719	$14,585	$21,000 [a]
GRM [b]	6.54	6.70	5.95	7.00	6.45 [a]

[a] Conclusions developed from market data.
[b] Gross rent multiplier equals sale price, or value, divided by gross income.

Since a difference in average number of rooms per apartment causes wide variation in the price per unit, the appraiser may decide to discard C and D for meaningful comparison.

From such an analysis, the indicated value for the property being appraised could be rationalized as follows:

880 rooms @ $4,200[a]		$3,696,000
$574,000 income × 6.45 (GRM)		3,702,000
177 units @ $21,000[b]		3,717,000
Indicated by market data approach	(say)	$3,700,000

[a]Indicated market value per room. If the properties being compared involve dissimilar room sizes, comparison should also be made on the basis of dollars per square foot of rentable area.
[b]Indicated market value per apartment unit.

Inspection of the properties and recognition of factors beyond those included in any summary such as the above all enter into judgment decisions leading to conclusions appropriate to the property being appraised.

RETAIL PROPERTY

In the absence of net lease information, the gross (annual) rent multiplier (GRM) may be useful as a comparison unit in the market data approach as applied to retail business property. However, if there is not a reasonable degree of consistency between the operating ratios of the property being appraised and the sale properties, an indication of value by the gross rent multiplier may not be reliable or definitive.

Units of comparison include dollars per square foot of gross or net rentable area, and adjustment for locational or physical differences may be necessary. Use of an overall capitalization rate[1] derived from an analysis of similar property sales in the market may also constitute a desirable basis for comparison, but is usually considered to belong in the income approach to a value indication. However, since the overall capitalization rate may be directly derived from market evidence, it can be appropriately considered in relation to the market data approach.

---

1. Net income before deduction for recapture, divided by sale price (not to be confused with GRM, which is sale price, or value, divided by gross, or more often effective gross, income).

Table 16.3. Retail Store Properties—Comparable Sales Analysis

	Properties				Property Being Appraised
	A	B	C	D	
Stories	1	1	1	1	1
Construction	Brick/steel	Brick/steel	Brick/steel	Brick/steel	Brick/steel
Age in years	5	3	12	8	10
Number of stores	3	5	5	3	4
Rental area in sq. ft.	6,000	8,000	6,000	5,400	6,000
On-site parking in sq. ft.	3,000	5,000	1,000	6,000	3,500
Gross rental at time of sale	$12,000	$17,600	$9,000	$12,200	$12,000
Tenant credit	A	C	C	A	B
Average rent per sq. ft.	$2	$2.20	$1.50	$2.25	$2
Years since sale	6 months	1 year	2 years	1 year	—
Sale price	$110,000	$140,000	$75,000	$110,000	$105,000[a]
GRM	9.2	8.0	8.3	9.0	8.5[a]
$ per square foot of gross building area	$18.30	$17.50	$12.50	$20.40	$17.75[a]

[a]Conclusion developed from market data.

Table 16.3 illustrates the application of the GRM and the dollars-per-square foot units of comparison obtained by an analysis of sales of comparable retail properties.

A GRM is not usually subject to adjustment, since relative desirability in the marketplace is presumably reflected in the rental the properties can command. An exception may occur when there is a substantial difference in the quality of the rental streams. This is based on recognition that an income supported by a superior credit is entitled to a lower risk rate and therefore may command a higher purchase price.

Properties B and C are of construction similar to the property being appraised, but other factors indicate C to be less desirable and D to be more desirable. After inspection and analysis, B seems most comparable, but there is also substantial similarity between A and the subject.

The indicated value of the property being appraised could be rationalized as follows:

$12,000 income × 8.5 GRM	$102,000
6,000 square feet @ $17.75 per sq. ft.	$106,500
Value conclusion	$105,000

This explanation is presented to illustrate an orderly process that may be followed. It includes only a limited number of the many factors entering into a comparative analysis. Such analysis need not be included in the appraisal report to a client; if included, it may be in either narrative or summarized form.

LIGHT INDUSTRIAL PROPERTY

The term *light industrial* is used here to apply to garage-type structures, typical warehouse, distribution facilities, and the like. In many localities this type of property is leased on a basis of the tenant paying all expenses except taxes, insurance, and exterior maintenance. Under these conditions, operating ratios are reasonably consistent; use of the GRM may produce a dependable value indication.

A unit expressed in dollars per gross square foot is also a valuable tool in the comparison process for different types and ages of one-story and multistory industrial properties. Comparisons may be made by assigning square-foot units separately to the land area and to the building area, or the square-foot unit price may be assigned to the building area only, considering the land and its improvements as merged. When the latter is used, the land-to-building area ratio should be reasonably typical. When this is not the case and excess land is included in the sale price, the unit of comparison is distorted. An acceptable procedure for handling excess land is discussed in Chapter 15.

Type of space represents another distinction. Construction cost for office area in any commercial-type building usually is considerably greater than for shop space and ordinarily is assigned a proportionately higher unit value.

As an example of an analysis of comparable sales in the market approach to value, assume a small, light-industrial building situated a mile from downtown on a major thoroughfare, built five years ago for owner occupancy. The building is 56 x 90 feet, on land 70 x 198 feet. The office space is 56 x 25 feet. It is modern in all respects, with paneled walls, asphalt tile floor, acoustical ceiling, and air conditioning. Office space of this type is judged at a premium of $5 per square foot more than the rate for warehouse space in the same building. The value of the site is estimated at $1.50 per square foot. The data search has disclosed two sales of properties comparable to the property being appraised (see Table 16.4).

Assuming close comparability of the open floor area, the indicated value of the property being appraised could be estimated as follows:

Building gross area:		
56 x 90 ft., 5,040 sq. ft. @ $10/sq. ft.		$50,400
Office premium:		
56 x 25 ft., 1,400 sq. ft. @ $5/sq. ft.		7,000
Land:		
70 x 198 ft., 13,860 sq. ft.		
@ $1.50 = $20,790	Rounded	20,800
Total		$78,200

SINGLE-STORY INDUSTRIAL PROPERTY

With industrial property, as for store property, parking and yard space are extremely important. There are also many other factors, as discussed in Chapter 10.

Table 16.4. Commercial—Light Industrial Properties: Comparable Sales Analysis

	Properties		Property Being Appraised
	A	B	
Sale price	$65,000	$112,500	$78,200[a]
Terms of sale	Typical	Typical	
Date of sale	2 yrs. ago	Current	
Adjustment for time	+10%	None	
Sale price adjusted for time	$71,500	$112,500	
Location	Inferior	Inferior	
Land rating, per sq. ft.	$1.25	$1	$1.50
Land area (sq. ft.)	11,600	18,000	13,860
Land allocation	$14,500	$17,500	$20,800
Net building allocation	$57,000	$95,000	$57,400
Office space premium, per sq. ft.	$8	$5	$5
Office space area (sq. ft.)	1,250	2,500	1,400
Office space premium	$10,000	$7,500	$7,000
Net to basic building	$47,000	$87,500	$50,400
Building area (sq. ft.)	4,800	8,500	5,040
Indicated basic building value per square foot	$9.80	$10.30	$10

[a]Conclusion developed from market data.

A case-study appraisal of a well-located medium-sized industrial plant, built 20 years ago, shows some of these considerations. The building measures 100 x 220 feet, including offices (70 x 40 feet). Ceiling height in the clear is 14 feet. Lighting is good; column spacing is 20 x 20 feet. There are two truck docks, 30 x 60 feet, built into the building along the front. A depressed rail siding runs along one side, with doors spotted for unloading two cars at floor level. The land is 115 x 300 feet. The building is set back from the street. The only parking is for visitors and office personnel. The appraiser believes that if it had ample parking, the property would be worth 20% more. A search discloses two similar and equally well-located properties that were recently sold.

Property A is 10 years old, comprises 20,000 square feet, and is a branch plant with only a foreman's office. Ceiling height is 18 feet. There are two truck docks, but no rail. Land is slightly over an acre. Parking for 50 cars is considered adequate. Good light. Column spacing, 20 x 40 feet. Sold within six months for $200,000.

Property B is 25 years old, comprises 25,000 square feet. Offices of 3,200 square feet. Ceiling height is 14 feet. One truck dock; rail siding on property at floor level. Land is approximately two acres, affording ample parking. Fair light. Column spacing, 20 x 20 feet. Currently being offered for $200,000.

Adjustment factors are time; location; physical characteristics which include land area for expansion, parking, age of building, shipping and receiving, column spacing, ceiling height, office facility and utilities, size and shape of building, type of construction, and land-to-building ratio. The rating of these two properties is shown in Table 16.5.

Table 16.5.   Single-Story Industrial Property—Comparative Sales Analysis

	Properties		Property Being Appraised
	A	B	
Price per sq. ft. (including land)	$12.60	$10.00	$ 9.50[a]
Time	Equal	Equal	
Location	Equal	Equal	
Land value (total)	Equal	Equal	
Expansion	Limited	Ample	
Parking	− 15% (better)	− 15% (better)	
Age of building	− 10% (newer)	Equal	
Shipping and receiving	+ 5%, (no rail)	+ 2.5% (poorer rail)	
Shipping and receiving	Equal truck	+ 7.5% (poorer truck)	
Column spacing	− 5% (better)	Equal	
Ceiling height	− 5% (better)	Equal	
Office facility	+ 5% (poorer)	Equal	
Net result[b]	− 25%	− 5%	

[a]Conclusion developed from market data.
[b]Net downward adjustment is indicated since A and B are superior to the property being appraised.

A rating of "better" for a sale property implies that in this respect the sale price should be adjusted downward to provide an equivalent price indication for the property being appraised. In this illustration Property A is better in many respects, but lacks rail and suitable office facility. Property B is poorer in two respects, but has better parking and expansion possibility. After comparing the various features of Properties A and B to the property being appraised, the appraiser might conclude that the sale price of Property A should be adjusted downward 25% and the sale price of Property B 5%, to derive an indication of the most probable sale price or market value for the property being appraised. The indication of value therefore is

$$\$12.60 - 25\% = \$9.45$$
$$\$10.00 - 5\% = \$9.50$$

The appraiser concludes that the value of the property being appraised is $9.50 per square foot, or

$$20,000 \text{ sq. ft. @ } \$9.50 \text{ per sq. ft.} = \$190,000$$

The gross square-foot sale prices are obtained by dividing the sale price of each comparable property, including both land and building, by the number of gross square feet in the building. The resulting prices per square foot are a merged unit because they include both the land and the building. When land area and value are relatively comparable, such a unit is a practical measure of comparison between the property being appraised and the comparable sale properties.

MULTISTORY INDUSTRIAL PROPERTY

Multistory (loft) space has been obsolete to many users because of lack of suitability for modern machinery, adding to the cost of manufacturing and of moving materials vertically rather than horizontally.

As an example of a comparative market analysis of such a property, assume a five-story factory building situated in an established industrial area. Data has been obtained regarding two comparable buildings. A comparable sales analysis is shown in Table 16.6.

Table 16.6. Multistory Industrial Warehouse—Comparable Sales
Analysis

	Properties			Property Being Appraised
	A	Resale A	B	
Date	3 yrs. ago	1 yr. ago	3 yrs. ago	Now
Price	$600,000	$675,000	$710,000	$560,000[a]
Purpose	Storage	Mfg.	Mfg.	Mfg.
Land area	1.7 acres	1.7 acres	7.6 acres	2.6 acres
Stories	4	4	1 to 4	5
Construction	Concrete	Concrete	Concrete and wood	Concrete
Age	30 yrs.	32 yrs.	40 yrs.	31 yrs.
Gross area	173,600	173,600	225,800	169,070
Sale price per sq. ft., gross building area	$3.46	$3.89	$3.14	$3.31
Percent first floor	27%	27%	36%	20%
Condition	Good	Good	Poor	Fair
Offices	Good	Good	Poor	Fair
Parking	Some	Some	Ample	Adequate
Expansion	None	None	Ample	None
Loading	Fair	Fair	Good	Fair
Elevators	Good	Good	Fair	Good

[a]Conclusion developed from market data.

The comparative properties that were sold are analyzed on a square-foot basis of gross building area, including all the land:

3 years ago at $3.46 per square foot for Property A
1 year ago at $3.89 per square foot for resale of A
3 years ago at $3.14 per square foot for Property B

The $675,000 resale of Property A two years after purchase for $600,000, with little or no capital improvements, reflects a 12% increase in the two-year period, or 6% linear per year. Other market evidence leads the appraiser to conclude that this trend has continued. It is good practice to make time adjustments first to derive an indicated current unit price for the sale property. This may then be adjusted for estimated locational or physical differences.

After an analysis of property differences, the appraiser concludes that the property being appraised is 20% inferior to Property A and 10% inferior to Property B. The Property A resale price of $3.89 per square foot plus a 6% time adjustment becomes $4.12, and adjusting this for a 20% quality difference indicates $3.30 per square foot of gross building area for the property being appraised ($4.12 × 80%).

As applied to Property B, an 18% time adjustment to the $3.14 sale price three years ago indicates a $3.71 price today which, adjusted for a 10% quality difference, produces an indication for the property being appraised of $3.34 per square foot of gross building area ($3.71 × 90%).

In both comparisons reasonable adjustment was necessary, and the conclusions at $3.30 per square foot and $3.34 per square foot are unusually close, leading to a probable value conclusion of $560,000 ($3.31 per sq. ft.). Additional comparisons, if available, might either confirm this value conclusion or establish a reasonable range bracketing this figure.

APPLICATION OF UNITS OF COMPARISON

The adjustment procedures illustrated in the examples above are typical, and with appropriate units of comparison, the procedures are adaptable to other types of improved properties. The appraiser identifies the unit of comparison appropriate to the type of improvement and to the locale of the property being appraised. Land and building components of value are normally merged in sales comparisons, but comparison may be made separately if data is available or if excess land is included.

As an appraisal plant increases in size and usability, the appraiser finds that there are few properties for which meaningful unit comparisons cannot be made with similar properties that have been sold— theatres at so much per seat or per square foot, truck terminals at so much per door or per square foot, mobile home parks at so much per pad, and golf courses at so much per hole.

Hotels and motels may be compared on a room or rental unit basis or by use of a gross income multiplier.[2] Office buildings may be

---

2. Stephen Rushmore, *The Valuation of Hotels and Motels* (Chicago: American Institute of Real Estate Appraisers, 1978).

compared using a gross rent multiplier or on a square-foot basis. A square foot of net rentable area may be preferable to a square foot of gross area as a unit of comparison when computed in accordance with established standards.

Retail properties may be compared on the basis of sales dollars per square foot of rentable area. Industrial properties are typically compared using a square foot of gross or rentable area as the unit of comparison. In either case further comparison may be made using the GRM.

Appropriate units of comparison for apartment properties include per unit, per room, and per square foot of gross or rentable area as well as the GRM. Apartment land values may be related on the basis of dollars per apartment unit.

Farm buildings are essentially related to the land they serve. The comparative value of farms is usually rated at so much per acre, buildings included. The percentage of the whole accounted for by land varies according to the type of farm operation. The small or part-time farm is likely to be as much a residence as an income producer. The price, therefore, is higher, partly because there are more purchasers for smaller properties, and partly because the buildings constitute a greater percentage than those on a primarily income-producing farm. Therefore, the sale price of a 15-acre rural plot does not indicate the average value of a 300-acre farm.

NUMBER OF SALES

The process of market data comparison is demonstrated in this chapter with a limited number of sales. Increasing the number of comparisons—assuming that they are valid and applicable—tends to improve the quality of the conclusion and correspondingly increases the significance of the value indication.

The number of sales appropriate to a specific appraisal problem varies with the type of property, the defined value sought, and the importance of the market data approach to a solution of the appraisal problem. In a subdivision of almost identical residential improvements of similar age, a few recent sales may produce a definite pattern and a narrow range of value, thus providing a well-supported value indication for the property being appraised. Conversely, types of property that sell less frequently and vary widely in design and size make comparison more difficult. For such types, comparable sales analysis may produce a wider initial range of value indications, requiring more sales and study to develop a pattern leading to a supported conclusion.

The appraiser should recognize that whenever two or more adjustment factors are used, there is a possibility of colinearity. Because this results in a "doubling up" of the adjustment process, care should be exercised in selection and application of adjustment factors. Computers and/or statistical analysis may often assist in locating and handling areas of concern in a given appraisal.

STATISTICAL ANALYSIS IN DIRECT SALES COMPARISON

Increasing use of computers with statistical analysis techniques permits more sophisticated mathematical applications of the comparison process in the market data approach.[3] The adjustment of a unit of comparison for physical differences between properties may involve a number of such differences, each of which may influence the unit of comparison independently of others. Quality of construction, for example, is a variable that is normally independent of gross area. There may be a number of independent variables in a specific appraisal analysis that interact with, or influence, other variables. When two or more variables produce the same pattern of influence on value, this colinearity complicates identification of their individual effects.

When sufficient data is available, the use of regression analysis permits development of more precise relationships in the comparision process. The quantities of residential sales in many markets has encouraged applications of regression analysis in the residential field, and the technique is particularly useful in mass appraisal work.

The use of a single basic unit of comparison implies that the value of a property equals the number of units times the unit value. For example, if the unit of comparison is $12 per square foot of gross area, the value of a 40,000-square-foot warehouse is 40,000 × $12 = $480,000. Arithmetically, this use of a single unit of comparison represents a simple linear regression that, in graph form, extends in a

---

3.   For additional material, see Appendix C.

straight line down to 0 square feet × $12 = 0 value. Obviously, such a unit of comparison loses validity with the extent of deviation from the arithmetical mean at which it was developed. Appraisers recognize this, and for structures with substantially different attributes, including size, a new unit value is derived, again based on reasonably comparable structures.

As above, simple linear regression may be expanded through recognition that the straight-line relationship need not pass through a zero origin but instead may be represented by a base unit cost, applicable to a benchmark size structure, which varies in relation to reasonable deviations from this benchmark size (see Figure 16.1).

Figure 16.1.   Comparison of Single Unit of Comparison with Simple Linear Regression Concept

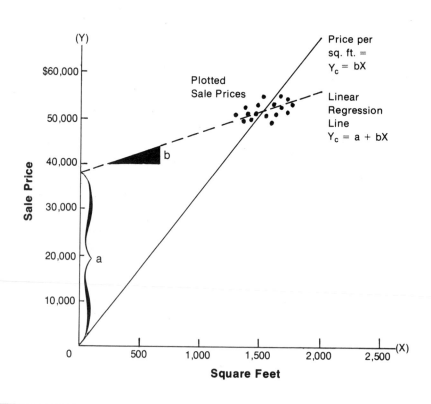

For example, assume a $12 per square foot unit of comparison derived for a 50,000-square-foot structure with a deviation of $0.15 in unit value for each 5,000 square feet of deviation from the 50,000-square-foot benchmark size. With unit value increasing for smaller size, the 40,000-square-foot warehouse value might then become

$$\$12.00 + (.15)(2) = \$12.30 \times 40,000 \text{ sq. ft.} = \$492,000$$

Thus a variation in unit value depending on one variable (size) has been introduced as a refinement to a simple linear regression relationship.

When sufficient data is available, multiple regression analysis may be expanded to include plus or minus adjustments for additional attributes that affect unit value. As in any comparison involving adjustments, minimizing the number or extent of adjustments usually improves reliability.

SUMMARY

The key to the market data approach is the use of *units of comparison.* Many are available. Generally, there are such units applicable to single family residences, retail stores, some types of commercial or light industrial property, hotels, motels, and office buildings.

Sale prices of comparable properties may be reduced to a multiple of gross income, sale price per square foot of gross or net rentable area, or per room, or per unit. The units of comparison used for dollars of sale price in the market data approach are the same as or similar to those used for rental dollar comparison in the income approach. Additional discussion of these units of comparison is presented in Chapter 18.

The emphasis placed on elements inherent in the comparison process changes according to the type of property. Major elements to be considered in all cases are gross-to-net income relationships as well as time, location, physical characteristics, and conditions of sale. The physical considerations include many special components, such as parking, room for expansion, bay spacing, elevator service, all types of functional utility, as well as the usual items of age, contemporary standards of construction, quality, and condition. In the process of adjusting for differences affecting value, the appraiser is alert to recognize situations where the colinearity of factors could result in duplication of an adjustment.

To be used as a valid indication of market value, any comparable sale must qualify as bona fide and have characteristics similar or adjustable to the property being appraised. When there is a sufficient amount of comparable data, the market data approach indication is usually persuasive. When applicable, it should be supported by value indications resulting from application of the income and cost approaches.

17

The Income Approach

Income-producing property is typically purchased for investment purposes, and the projected net income stream is the critical factor affecting its market value. An investor purchasing income-producing real estate is in effect trading a sum of present dollars for the right to a stream of future dollars. There is a relationship between the two, and the connecting link is the process of capitalization. Because future dollars are worth less than present dollars, the anticipated future dollars are discounted to a present worth on some basis that reflects the risk and the waiting time involved. Available capitalization methods, techniques, and rate selection procedures are discussed in following chapters.

The income approach, which is related to investor thinking and motivation, is a basic tool for the valuation of income-producing real estate. It is based on the principle of anticipation reflected in the definition of value as the present worth of all the rights to future benefits accruing to ownership. These future benefits consist of some pattern of annual net income for a projected period of years plus a capital sum at the end of this period. This capital sum consists of land value or of land value plus some remaining improvement value. The projection period may represent an economic life estimate for the improvements, the term of a lease, or a projected investment holding period to resale of the property.

The income approach is practical only when an income stream attributable to the real estate can be estimated. This income estimate may be developed and supported by comparisons in the local market or, alternately, by an allocation to the real estate of some portion of the total income derived from operation of a going business in which the real estate is a contributing component.

HISTORICAL DEVELOPMENT OF THE INCOME APPROACH

The concept of an economic value for types of real estate that have commercial utility or income-producing potential has long been recognized. In 1685 William Leybourne produced *A Platform for Purchasers* intended as a guide for valuing types of land estates and of calculating rates of return on purchase money. The estimation of potential annual income and expenses (yearly outgoings), the first two steps in the income approach, were described by John Richards in *The Gentlemen's Steward and Tenants of Manors Instructed* in 1730. The concept of economic rent was appreciated by this time and Richards recognized that an interest or discount rate could be rationalized by a comparative analysis of alternative investment opportunities. The development of urban investment real estate appraising in its present form in this country has largely developed since the second decade of this century, strongly influenced by members of the American Institute of Real Estate Appraisers.

The initial concept of capitalization involved division of estimated income by a rate to derive a capital value. This is expressed

$$\text{Value} = \frac{\text{Income}}{\text{Rate}}$$

The use of present worth factors for discounting future income was similarly recognized and typically applied to level annuity-type income projections using the present worth of 1 per period factors. These are the sum of individual annual reversion factors for the projection period. They are frequently referred to as Inwood factors because one of the first widely used tables of such factors was published by William Inwood in 1811. This method of capitalization is known as *annuity capitalization,* and the formula for value is expressed

$$\text{Value} = \text{Income} \times \text{Factor}$$

The factors are reciprocals of corresponding rates and are available in currently published tables.

To distinguish capitalization using a rate from annuity capitalization using a factor, the term *straight capitalization* was applied to the former. Application of straight capitalization using only an interest rate involved no limitation of time and constituted *capitalization in perpetuity*. Application using an overall rate derived directly from market sales constituted *direct capitalization*. Neither of these involved selection of a specific time period or a specific provision for recapture of invested capital.

A third application of straight capitalization recognized a finite life for the wasting asset component of value, the building. This recognition of a specific time period introduced provision for return of capital invested in the wasting asset at a rate that came to be called the *recapture rate*. This rate constituted an increment to the property return (risk) rate to make up the total rate applicable to the building investment, the building capitalization rate.

When this recapture was allocated in equal annual amounts over the estimated remaining economic life of the building, the procedure was described as *straight capitalization with straight-line recapture*. Inherent in this procedure is the assumption of a straight-line declining income stream because each year's recapture reduces the investment, with consequent reduction in the annual income necessary to pay a constant rate of return on the investment (see Chapter 21). Recognition of a recapture rate applicable only to the building reflected a concept of the capital structure as land value plus building value.

In the depression years of the 1930s, prior to the inflation that began later, the concept of a declining net income as property aged was generally accepted. However, early expansion of this procedure involved substitution of sinking-fund recapture at a "safe" rate for the straight-line recapture rate. Described as *straight capitalization with sinking-fund recapture,* application of this procedure reflected an assumption of a level income for the projection period that normally continued to be remaining economic life. Because this sinking fund assumption was seldom a reality and because it presupposes a financial operation separate and distinct from the real estate, it was less widely accepted than straight-line recapture in appraisal practice.

Within the concept of annuity capitalization, using a factor instead of a rate to derive the building value estimate, the mathematical equivalent of this sinking-fund procedure involves the use of Hoskold factors (reciprocals of the building capitalization rate when based upon sinking-fund recapture) and is commonly referred to as *Hoskold annuity capitalization.* Tables of factors based on a "speculative" rate of return on the investment and a "safe" rate of 3% applicable to the sinking fund were first published by H. E. Hoskold in 1877; the name is still used, although the factors may be computed for currently applicable rates rather than extracted from prepared tables. This annuity capitalization with sinking-fund recapture at a "safe" rate is seldom encountered in urban appraisal practice today but may appropriately be used in connection with valuation of real estate that includes a wasting natural resource.

The land, building, and property residual techniques constituted variations in the application of straight and annuity capitalization, and within the past decade, the recapture concept has been broadened to include a rationalization of the recapture rate as a "loading" or surcharge based on market evidence rather than related to a specific estimate of remaining economic life.

In 1932 Frederick M. Babcock, MAI, published a variation of the ordinary annuity tables, which provided factors conforming to four different income-stream patterns, two of which reflected declining curves between the level income and the straight-line declining assumptions.

A major contribution to capitalization concepts came in 1959 when L.W. Ellwood, MAI, introduced an important expansion of the concept of mortgage and equity components of an overall capitalization rate combined with relatively short-term periods of projected ownership. Mortgage equity analysis constitutes an important contribution to capitalization concepts. The impact on value of available financing, investor motivation, and equity internal rates of return is recognized, and it provides flexible new techniques for analysis in the income approach.

A recent addition to capitalization thinking involves extending concepts of mortgage-equity rate derivation to expand the application of straight capitalization. Straight capitalization is adapted to reflect straight-line changes in land or building components of an income stream, and it is applicable to selected projection periods that are shorter than an assumed economic life. This provides a new flexibility in the application of straight capitalization to current appraisal problems.

The historical development of the income approach reflects a movement away from an initial emphasis on physical components of value toward a greater emphasis on investment components. The initial division of capitalization was between the concept of value as income divided by a rate (straight capitalization) and as income multiplied by a factor (annuity capitalization). Capitalization can also be categorized in relation to the important concept of the recapture of invested capital which must be achieved before any return on capital can be realized. On this basis there is:

1. Capitalization with separate allowance for recapture, such as straight capitalization with straight-line, sinking-fund, or surcharge recapture rates, and
2. Capitalization without separate allowance for recapture, such as direct capitalization or annuity capitalization

In direct or annuity capitalization any recapture provision compensating for anticipated change in the value of physical components is included in the rate or factor used for capitalization. No specific recapture pattern is implied by the use of an overall rate in direct capitalization, but the rate does include an identifiable increment over the applicable risk rate. In the use of an annuity present worth factor, recapture is built into the factor and reflects a specific recapture pattern. The recapture premises inherent in these and other capitalization methods are recognized by the appraiser in selecting an appropriate method and technique.

Early emphasis on an economic life estimate as a basis for accomplishing recapture from allocation of annual income has been followed by recognition that recapture may be accomplished through the proceeds of resale at the end of a period of ownership that is less than a remaining economic life estimate.

Some income stream projections are irregular and do not conform to patterns inherent in traditional capitalization methods. Some assignments involve an investment analysis of projected future cash flow expectancies on before- and after-tax bases. In these situations a discounted cash flow (DCF) analysis provides the appraiser with a practical procedure for translating the irregular projection into a present worth estimate. In this procedure the diverse effects of various factors on future income are resolved into an effect on each periodic installment of income. This analysis may be applied to equity or other cash flows, either before or after tax considerations, and for annual or other selected periods. Each periodic installment of income is discounted individually at an appropriate rate, and the total of these discounted present worth figures represents the present investment value of the right to receive the anticipated incomes.

All methods of capitalization have some place in the income approach to an economic concept of market value, and a wide variety of applications are possible within the available capitalization concepts. The use of any particular method requires attention of the appraiser to any implicit assumptions that may be inherent in the method. New concepts and new or expanded applications of old concepts are evidence of the continuing dynamic character of appraisal thought in relation to investment and market values.

INCOME APPROACH PROCEDURE

The capitalization process begins with an estimate of net income before any provision for the investor's recapture of invested capital. Provision for this recapture (return *of* capital) is provided for within the capitalization procedures, which also provide for return *on* the invested capital. This estimate of net income before recapture, or net operating income (NOI), is basic to the income approach, and the derived value indication can be no better than the reliability of this net income projection. Accepted procedures for developing income and expense projections leading to this estimate are discussed in Chapters 18 and 19.

The steps involved in translating the net income projection into a value indication were described in Chapter 4. They are summarized:

1. Estimate potential gross income.
2. Estimate and deduct a vacancy and collection loss allowance to derive effect gross income.
3. Estimate and deduct expenses of operation to derive net operating income (net income before recapture).

4. Estimate remaining economic life or the duration and pattern of the projected income stream.
5. Select an applicable capitalization method and technique.
6. Develop the appropriate rate or rates.
7. Complete the necessary computations to derive an economic value indication by the income approach.

The analysis leading to a market value estimate by the income approach involves the appraiser in research into market attitudes and perceptions prior to critical judgment decisions concerning projected income patterns and amounts, capitalization methods and techniques, the selection of appropriate rates, and considerations of the capital structure of a value estimate (e.g., land plus building components, mortgage plus equity interests, or leased fee plus leasehold estates).

MARKET VALUE AND INVESTMENT VALUE

The income approach to the valuation of income-producing properties reflects probable market value to a typical investor. As such, it may also be described as the "investment value" to the typical investor. However, more specifically the term *investment value* designates a value to a specific investor whose objectives or investment requirements may deviate from the typical. In such cases the investment value conclusion reflects these atypical requirements and does not necessarily coincide with market value.

INCOME APPROACH ASSUMPTIONS

In the valuation of fee simple interests, traditional appraisal practice was based on the assumption that at the time of appraisal the real property was free of liens or encumbrances on the title. This did not preclude recognition of the effect of leases, easements, or other such factors on the income stream, or value or valuation of partial interests. Market value, expressed in terms of dollars as of the date of appraisal, was based on future projections of the same dollars. In these terms depreciation in value accrued over the years as improvements aged, and declined in desirability and rental value, when compared with similar newly constructed improvements. The assumption of a declining net income stream, measured in these dollars, reflected an economic life pattern for typical multi-occupancy real estate.

However, real estate competes with other forms of investment for available capital in the market. The investor in stocks or bonds has traditionally measured gains or losses in dollars as of the date the investment is liquidated. Appraisal procedures and techniques have expanded to provide for this type of market thinking and to recognize typical investment holding periods of less than an economic life projection. Procedures that are accepted now lend themselves to sophisticated analyses of the effect of potential gains or losses in terms of either changing or constant dollars, in terms of limited holding periods, and in terms of less than 100% equity positions. Valuation is still based on unencumbered title, but there is recognition that a typical purchaser will take advantage of available financing. It is also practical to develop an equity valuation assuming purchase subject to existing financing.

APPLICABILITY OF CAPITALIZATION METHODS

Traditional capitalization methods are applicable today; applied in the context of the inherent assumptions, a valid conclusion of current market value results. Properly applied, any *applicable* capitalization method develops essentially the same valid conclusion of value. However, all capitalization methods are not applicable to every appraisal problem because each involves certain inherent assumptions concerning the income stream pattern. These differences are explained in discussions of the various methods in later chapters. The appraiser selects the capitalization method and technique in which the inherent assumptions correspond to the indicated future income pattern, life expectancy, or other specific facts pertaining to the property being appraised.

In the income approach market value is revealed through analysis of market action and may be interpreted in terms of capitalization methods. Use of a specific method does not imply duplication of investor thinking. The investors whose actions make a specific market may all think differently, with one investor basing a purchase decision on use of a simple gross income multiplier, another considering only a requirement for annual cash flow to equity after debt service, a third analyzing prospects for equity yield including capital gain or loss, and others using traditional procedures or rules of thumb. The appraiser need not attempt the impossible task of reproducing any specific investor's thought processes. The appraiser's challenge is to analyze the collective action of these investors in the marketplace, identify a typical pattern, and interpret the pattern in terms of an appropriate capitalization method. Application of the derived rate or rates to the net income projection for the property being appraised, within the same capitalization concept, produces an indication of market value that is a valid reflection of market evidence.

SUMMARY

The income approach to value is applicable to income-producing property and not practical in the appraisal of properties for which a rental market or a rental value cannot be identified. The approach is based on the principle of anticipation and uses a process of capitalization to translate an income projection into a present capital value indication. There are various methods of capitalization that are based on various inherent assumptions concerning the quality, durability, and pattern of the income projection. The appraiser selects the capitalization method that best conforms to the future income pattern of the property being appraised.

18
Gross Income Estimates

The primary purpose of making gross income estimates is to project probable net income benefits from ownership. These benefits may be realized through use and occupancy or through a lessor-lessee relationship which produces a flow of income dollars. The first step in the development of a reasonable net income projection is an estimate of potential gross income expectancy. This is a critical estimate, and an error at this point may be compounded in the process of valuation. For example, if the gross income were $60,000 and the expenses were $30,000, the net income would be $30,000. A 10% increase in gross income to $66,000 with identical expenses, however, would return a net income of $36,000 which, when capitalized, would produce a 20% greater value estimate.

In some situations, such as the appraisal of hotels and motels or furnished apartment buildings, the income estimate may include income attributable to furnishings or fixtures which are not an integral part of the real estate but perhaps are necessary to its operation. If such chattels are minimal, income attributable to them may be omitted from the estimate of gross, their maintenance included in operating expense, and only a real estate value developed. In other situations the appraiser, at some point in the analysis, allocates gross or net income between chattels and real estate, in order to ascribe separate valuations to the real estate and personal property.[1]

---

1. In situations where it is impractical to separate the operation of the real estate from the operation of the business, a net income projection is further allocated between profit attributable to the business operation and a rental component attributable to the real estate.

The normal basis for a gross income projection in appraisal practice is economic rent. *Economic (market) rent is that which a tenant, using the premises for their highest and best use, is warranted in paying, and which the owner is warranted in accepting.* The extent of a reasonably foreseeable future varies with the circumstances of projection and reflects the probable attitudes of experienced investors in the market.

From this projected gross income, the appraiser deducts estimated future expenses to arrive at a prospective net income estimate. This net income is then converted by the capitalization process into an estimate of value. In appraising a property by the income approach, the appraiser translates an anticipated future net income to a present value figure.

Past and present incomes, either gross or net, are significant only as indications of prospective future income. To conclude otherwise would be as illogical as to value the stock of a business concern on the basis of its past earnings paying a dividend of $1.50 per share for 10 years, when the concern is now approaching bankruptcy.

A gross income estimate is basic to the income approach to a value indication, but since this estimate involves future projections, adequate and dependable current market research is basic to the gross income estimate. The future cannot be forecast with certainty, but trends can be analyzed and current market actions can be identified which affect future income expectancies. Appraisal practice requires that appraisers study and identify important supply and demand relationships. Such analyses are critical to income forecasting and evaluation of risks.

The starting point in a gross income projection is the record of actual gross income from the property in past years and the current income schedule. This historic and current factual data provides a basis from which a projection of estimated future gross income may be developed. However, this projected gross income estimate for appraisal purposes may be quite different from actual past or current figures. In the review and analysis of the factual data, comparison is made with known rentals for similar space in the same or comparable locations. This analysis leads to an informed estimate of the probable prospective income from the property and the degree of risk involved in its realization.

Competent property management is assumed. Comparison with

income levels achieved in similar properties in the same or comparable locations may provide the basis for a judgment decision concerning management. When supported by market evidence, past or current rental levels may be adjusted to conform to an assumption of competent future management for the property being appraised. This assumption is also reflected in the appraiser's operating expense projections.

The appraiser is concerned with income quantity, quality, and durability. This is because the prudent investor considers these factors in comparing the relative desirability of similar investment properties. The appraiser's evaluation of these three aspects of the income projection influences the selection of an appropriate method of processing the gross or net income.[2]

Rental data on comparable properties includes actual rents, listings to rent, or offers to rent. The last two classifications are related to actual rent in the same way that listings to sell or offers to purchase are related to actual sales. The lease term and provisions of the lease are also considered. Actual rentals may be classified as recorded leases, leases not recorded, and month-to-month rentals. Recorded leases provide desirable data because they are readily verified and can be cited without the limitations of confidential information. Unrecorded lease data can be equally helpful, but may be confidential or not available. Month-to-month rentals also may provide pertinent evidence, depending on their circumstances.

As with qualification of sales data, considerations of time and motivation are investigated. An existing rental, established under the terms of a lease made some years previously, is reviewed to ascertain its conformity with current market levels. Similarly, the relationship of the parties to a lease is a pertinent consideration. A non-negotiated or non-arms-length lease may not be relied on as an indication of a market rental.

QUANTITY OF PROSPECTIVE GROSS INCOME

In terms of rent, quantity refers to the amount earned in a year. The projection of this quantity reflects the appraiser's consideration of:

---

2. These factors also affect the selection of the capitalization rate, which is explained in Chapter 20.

1. Past and present tenant occupancy and rental terms
2. Rentals being paid for comparable space and services
3. Analysis of the rental level that is economically warranted for the premises
4. Ability to pay

The current environmental, economic, social, and governmental trends (both general and local) as well as conditions peculiar to the property and its location exert an influence on the probable trend of the future income it will produce. An understanding of these factors is essential in estimating the amount of income an informed investor is justified in expecting. This figure may differ from past or actual current earnings.

A current contract rental may be high or low in relation to the appraiser's opinion of the economic rent. If the actual rental is abnormally high, the tenant may seek the first opportunity to cancel the lease and in any case probably will renew only at a lower figure upon lease expiration. If the actual current rental seems abnormally low, the owner of the property probably will seek an increase at the first opportunity. The existence of an apparently abnormally high or low lease or rental agreement currently in force may create either an excess over the estimated economic rent or a deficiency from it. Such excess or deficiencies, where substantial, are usually isolated for special valuation treatment.[3]

The amount of rent stipulated in a lease may be affected by the cost of preparing the space for specific occupancy and by whether this cost is assumed by the lessor or the lessee. The rent may be lower than is typical because the tenant repaired, renovated, and perhaps altered the space at his or her own expense. The opposite may be true if the landlord installed special partitions or made other expensive alterations for the use of the tenant. In the latter situation the tenant may be paying a typical rental rate plus an amount necessary to amortize over the lease period all or part of the alteration costs.

The time element is important in all rental comparisons. General economic conditions that exist at one time may be quite different at another date even if not far removed, and leases that reflected market

---

3. See section on Contract, Economic, and Percentage Rents in Chapter 21.

conditions when negotiated may no longer indicate an economic rental level. The relative stability of the environment of the rental property for the reasonably foreseeable future also may be a factor in a rental projection.

Concessions or the occupancy of a rent-free suite by the manager or custodian of an apartment building may not appear in the actual income statement. However, an estimated market rent may be assigned to space on which rental concessions have been granted, with the amount of the concessions deducted later as an expense of operation.

Regardless of what procedures are used to develop the economic income projection, the objective is a reasonable estimate of the rent that the property would command, for the foreseeable future, if the space were currently available for rent in the open market. This prospective gross income estimate (before provision for vacancy and possible rental collection loss) is also referred to as gross rental or potential annual gross income.

Translating this income estimate to a value indication is an appraisal procedure, but this procedure cannot produce a satisfactory conclusion unless the starting point is a logical estimate of the probable quantity of future income.

QUALITY AND DURABILITY OF INCOME

There is a fundamental difference between the tenant with strong financial responsibility and the tenant whose financial responsibility is uncertain or transitory. The property owner anticipates little risk in collecting the rent if the tenant is a major, financially responsible corporation. Such a tenant—or one guaranteed by it—frequently trades on its desirability as a tenant to obtain a rent below the prevailing economic level. A building under lease to a corporation with strong credit is usually more attractive to investors, and thus a lower risk rate may compensate, in full or in part, for the lower rental. However, if an existing lease is thought to have a favorable effect on the value of the property being appraised, the appraiser examines the lease for provisions under which the tenant may be permitted to terminate the lease prior to its expiration (escape clauses).

Durability is an important consideration in the analysis of an income projection. Durability refers to the probable period over which the property can be expected to produce the estimated income. Location is also a consideration. Because a prime location may also contribute to minimum vacancy, it enhances both quality and durability.

In office building properties, leases to tenants without financial strength may involve greater risk of collection and increase vacancy. In retail store properties or single-occupancy properties, the financial stability of the lessee may be the principal or even the sole security for the rental.

In the process of estimating potential gross income, the appraiser not only analyzes the quantity of income, actual or economic, but also formulates an opinion of the quality and probable duration of the income projection. The latter two considerations are important because they affect risk. The factor of quality or reliability is used later when deciding on an applicable investment risk rate in the capitalization process of the income approach to value.

RENTAL DEFINITIONS

A logical and intelligent estimate of the gross income requires an understanding, among other things, of the terms *contract, economic, percentage, excess, and overage rent.*

CONTRACT RENT—Payment for the use of property, as designated in a lease. The term is used to establish the fact that the actual rent paid, or contract rent, may differ from economic rent.

ECONOMIC (MARKET) RENT—The probable rental expectancy if the property were available for renting at the time of its estimation; the rental warranted to be paid in the open real estate market based on current rentals being paid for comparable space, as distinguished from contract rent under an existing lease.

PERCENTAGE RENT—Rental income received in accordance with the terms of a percentage clause in a lease and related to the tenant's gross or net sales, as defined by the lease. A minimum rent is usually included, although a straight percentage lease is occasionally encountered. A maximum rental may be specified. In effect, the percentage lease makes the landlord a partner in the tenant's business and provides the lessor some protection against inflation.

EXCESS RENT—The part of contract rental income that is in excess of the economic rent at the time of the appraisal. This might be temporarily due to a factor such as favorable location; or it might be more permanent because of a fortuitous lease or unusual management. In the income approach it is usually treated separately from the economic rental and may require capitalization at a higher rate and possibly a shorter income projection term. Synonym: surplus income.

OVERAGE RENT—Any rental received under a percentage clause in a lease which is above a guaranteed minimum rental.

Percentage rent may be within the limit of economic rent or at a level that includes excess rent. Similarly, the relation between economic rent and a guaranteed minimum rental determines whether overage rent is all, or in part, excess rent.

TYPES OF LEASE AGREEMENTS

An understanding of the factors affecting prospective income begins with a knowledge of the various types of tenancy. This chapter deals with gross income. Although some lease agreements may be on a gross basis, with the lessor paying all expenses, others may provide for the lessee to pay part or all of the expenses. To compare one rental to another, certain provisions in the lease agreements should be analyzed, including the lessors' and lessees' respective responsibilities for the operating expenses, such as heat, power, and other utilities; exterior and interior building maintenance; taxes and insurance including special coverage for boiler, plate glass, and elevators. An understanding of the effect of such lease provisions is necessary to estimate rental value in relation to a known lease of comparable space.

Another clause in a lease that affects net income flow is the escalation clause, whereby the lessee agrees to pay increased taxes or operating costs, or even to pay increased rentals based on some agreed-on economic index or based on actual increases above a specified level.

The length or term of the lease has a direct bearing on the rent level. In static periods the middle- to long-term lease (5 to 15 years) assures the lessor of continued occupancy without loss of rent. In a fluctuating rental market, a one-year lease may indicate that the owner anticipates a rise in rents; that the tenant anticipates a decline; or that for some other reason, one or the other is unwilling to be committed for a longer period.

Month to Month

This type of tenancy may or may not involve a written lease. The tenant may be compelled to vacate, or may decide to vacate, on short notice. A corresponding advantage to the lessor is that he or she, too, may cause the property to be vacated, thereby making it available for owner occupancy or for leasing on more favorable terms.

Short-Term Leases

Agreements of this type usually are entered into for five years or less. The terms and provisions may be set forth in short form or in detail, and frequently standard lease forms are used. Any type of short-term lease rental should be considered with due attention to re-rental costs, such as lease commissions or necessary expenditures by the owner to prepare the space for new occupancy.

Long-Term Leases

Such leases are usually considered to be those extending for at least 10 years. The details of terms and provisions customarily are set forth in correct legal form. Often under this type of lease, the tenant desires, or is required, to spend considerable money for remodeling. If the property leased is land, the tenant may undertake the construction of a building or other improvements.

Percentage Leases

These may be short term or long term and are most frequently encountered in retail properties, where they may provide for the lessee to pay a percentage of sales volume in addition to a basic guaranteed rent. The appraiser weighs the effect of such clauses on the future rent expectancy and estimates whether the basic minimum or some higher figure represents a reasonable rental projection when the tenant actually is paying percentage income over a specified minimum. Because the basic minimum may be either too high or too low, the appraiser gauges a rental projection on the basis of past experience with other leases of similar character, for comparable locations, and in the light of specific factors pertaining to the property being appraised. The potential sales volume is one such factor.

Tables are available that detail, by categories of retail businesses, the current percentage rentals being paid by various merchants, related to sales volumes.[4] The general pattern varies, depending on the line of business, how successful the location proves to be, and whether the tenant is a member of a chain or is an independent outlet. Low profit and staple goods operations tend to be at the lower end of the percentage scale, with luxury goods in the higher percentage bracket. Where a fixed or flat rental is paid, with no percentage clause, the rental usually reflects a similar ratio to prospective or actual sales volume.

Graduated Leases

These may be short-term or long-term leases, with or without percentages. The flat rent or minimum rent is adjusted up or down after an initial period. A step-up lease is designed to favor the tenant during the early years, with the landlord benefiting later as the tenant's business becomes better established or as initial tenant expenditures for improving the real estate are amortized. Graduated leases also are employed to protect the landlord against a rental deficiency as the property increases in value. There are several forms of graduated leases, including those with predetermined changes at specified intervals and those with changes related to some agreed-on index or to periodic revaluation of the real estate.

Renewal or Revaluation Leases

At the time of negotiation, these provide for one or more options for the extension of the lease term. Under this type of agreement, the tenant is permitted to continue occupancy at a specified rent or at a rent to be determined by appraisal or arbitration. The cost-of-living index sometimes is specified as a basis for negotiating the rental at the time of renewal.

---

4. *Percentage Leases,* 13th ed., (Chicago: Realtors National Marketing Institute, 1973).

RENTAL UNIT FACTORS

The amount of data required to make a considered estimate of prospective gross rental frequently depends on the complexity of the problem. The present rental schedule is the starting point for its solution. Audits, leases, and interviews with tenants during the course of the property inspection may be used to verify the schedule. Spot-checks or complete verification may be advisable in some instances.

The sum of the current rent schedule figures may be compared with the totals for previous accounting periods. Profit-and-loss statements for the past several years facilitate this procedure. Individual statements of the rentals paid, including that under a percentage lease or escalation clause, should be examined for each classification of tenant, such as for stores or offices, wherever various types of tenants occupy the premises.

A useful procedure in estimating gross rental value is the collection and analysis of statements or rentals currently in force in comparable rental space. Such rental data is reduced to standard units of comparison. Lump-sum or total rental figures are usually difficult to compare; but reduction to some common denominator or unit figure such as dollars per room or per square foot of net rentable area makes comparison practical. These units vary according to the type of property and are similar to sales dollar units of comparison.

Apartment Property

The customary rental comparison units for apartment property are dollars per room per month or dollars per square foot of rentable area per month or per year. Confusion might exist on the rent per room due to differences in definition and in standards. Use of the half-room tends to improve the accuracy but does not necessarily compensate for differences in room sizes, a factor that should be noted and reflected in the rate. The rental per room also varies between larger apartments and one- or two-room efficiency units. Corner apartments or those with a view customarily rent for more per room than do inside apartments. Data on current rates per square foot of rentable apartment area tends to establish a significant comparison of rental value within each class of apartments. Division into rooms establishes the utility of the total space, but the quantity of space is better reflected in the square-foot figure. Thus both are meaningful.

Retail Property

Two units of comparison frequently used in the appraisal of retail property are dollars per (store) front foot and dollars per square foot of rentable area. For urban street frontages, with fairly consistent lot depth, the former provides a practical basis for comparison. With the increasing trend to shopping-center and freestanding retail improvements, the latter unit is generally more practical. Therefore, per square foot of net rentable area per year has become the usual unit of comparison. The important consideration in any rental comparison is that comparisons be made on the basis of like compared to like. In addition to using the same method of computing areas, consideration is given to services included in rentals or to extra charges added to a basic rental such as common area maintenance in shopping centers.

Industrial Property

Dollars per square foot per year is the unit generally employed in the valuation of industrial property, with due consideration to parking, loading, and yard service areas, together with any special services included. Excess land areas should be valued separately. Gross area is used for single-occupancy property or for independently served space. Rentable net area may be used for industrial properties housing multiple tenants where service space is shared. Rental rates are affected by the services included and the character of the parking facilities.

Office Buildings

The rent per square foot of net rentable area is also the unit of primary importance in office building appraisal. Net rentable area excludes exterior and corridor walls, public or common washrooms, corridors, stairwells, elevator and mechanical shafts.[5] When an entire floor is

5. *Downtown and Suburban Office Building Experience Exchange Report* Washington, D.C.: Building Owners and Managers Association International (BOMA), annual.

leased to a single tenant, the method of measurement changes, usually including as rentable area all space within exterior walls except that which also serves other floors, such as elevator, stairway, or duct space. Thus the stated total rentable area of an office building may vary, within a range, with the extent of whole-floor or multiple occupancy and with the method of area calculation.

There is an increasing tendency to compute office building rentable area on a full-floor basis with a percentage allocation of common areas to each tenant on multi-occupancy floors. Under this procedure, all floors are computed on the same basis, total rentable area is subject to minimal variation, unit rental rates are lower, and a higher ratio of rentable to gross area produces an apparent higher efficiency for the structure. Space may be classified to show premium rentals for the more desirable locations in the building, as well as special services and parking for tenants and outsiders.

Other Types of Property

For hotel and motel properties, the average rate per occupied room or per unit is the usual basis for comparison. This may be derived from the single occupancy rate to which is added an increment for double or family occupancy at an anticipated percentage. Parking lots and parking garages commonly are rated in terms of rental per square foot of area or per car space. Truck terminals may be rated in terms of dollars per square foot per year, or dollars per door per month. Theatres may be rated at so much per seat per year, although a rental per gross square foot is also applicable.

Rental values of other properties may generally be compared on the basis of per square foot per year. This square-foot unit is not applicable to some improvements—grain elevators, for example.

Having studied the existing rent schedule, the appraiser reduces the figures to a unit basis to ascertain whether the actual income is economic or one that requires adjustment before it can be effectively used to project prospective future income.

COMPARABLE RENTS

A major consideration in estimating a gross income projection involves rental comparisons. Actual (or projected) rental for the property being appraised is reduced to a unit for comparison to similar rentals that have been reduced to the same unit. Judgment adjustments may be made for differences in time, location, physical characteristics, and conditions of lease to decide whether the current or projected rent represents a reliable rental expectancy.

This analysis is expandable. If comparable rental data reduces to unit rentals different from those of the subject property, it is logical to consider whether the latter is superior, equal, or inferior physically, functionally, or in location and whether the tenants are equally responsible. The comparable unit rentals are considered in the light of these positive or negative factors. The rental projection for the property being appraised may then be adjusted to reflect the level of rental income indicated by this analysis.

In addition to the character and quality of the space, its condition, location, and other pertinent factors, attention is given to the relative functional efficiency of the space. Assume one lease at the rate of $0.70 per gross square foot per year and another at the rate of $0.80 per gross square foot per year. If, in the first case, the ratio of net usable area to gross square footage were 80%, the rent would be $0.88 per square foot of net usable space. If, in the second case, the ratio of usable space to total space were 90%, the rate per square foot of usable area would be $0.89.[6]

The development of comparative rents requires their reconciliation with the current actual and historical rents of the subject property—but not necessarily their conformance. Once having analyzed comparative rentals and the differences between the comparable properties and the subject property, the appraiser is in a position to project for the latter a supportable estimate of gross rental for the reasonably foreseeable future.

LEASE ANALYSIS

A property that is leased at a rental that deviates from the economic rental level indicated by a market analysis is not unusual. Unless the property is to be valued on a free-of-lease basis, it is necessary to consider the probable effect of the existing lease on rental value as defined in the appraisal. If the lease is above an economic rental level,

---

6. $0.70 ÷ 80% = $0.88, and $0.80 ÷ 90% = $0.88.

the tenant may be expected to take advantage of any opportunity to cancel the lease. The appraiser examines the lease terms for possible escape clauses and considers whether the lease may be a burden to the tenant and, if so, the ability of the tenant to meet the lease obligation. If the lease is below an economic rental level, the tenant may be expected to continue in possession as long as possible with a consequent adverse effect on the market value of the property subject to the lease.

The relationship of contract and economic rental levels is important because of the effect on the risk rate applicable to the resultant income stream and because of the potential effect on the value of the fee estate. Contract rent below economic rent potentially creates a leasehold estate at the expense of the value of the fee interest. Contract rent in excess of economic rent creates a lease benefit which is an intangible property concept enhancing the value of the fee ownership. When a property is sold encumbered by such a lease, any additional value is usually reflected in the sale price but should be separated in a report of estimated realty value by the appraiser.

When leases represent a market level, necessary lease information may be provided by the owner, but in most cases the appraiser secures copies of all leases for careful study. Many leases are long and complicated, and significant conditions may be included in the fine print. In some cases legal interpretation may be necessary.

Data to be obtained from existing leases when making a gross income estimate includes:

1. Date of the lease
2. Volume and page number for reference if the lease is recorded
3. Legal description or other identification of the premises leased
4. Name of the lessor (owner or landlord)
5. Name of the lessee (tenant)
6. Lease term: the date of occupancy and the period of years over which it extends
7. Amount of rental; percentage clause, if any; graduation, if any; how payable
8. Landlord's covenants: responsibility for taxes, insurance, maintenance, and any other items for which the owner or landlord is responsible

9. Tenant's covenants: responsibility for taxes, insurance, maintenance, utilities, and escalation clauses covering increases in the cost of these items
10. Right of assignment: whether the leasehold (the tenant's interest) may be assigned and, if so, under what conditions, and whether assignment relieves the initial tenant from future liability under the lease
11. Option to renew: date of notice, term of years, rent, and any other provisions specified in the lease
12. Security: advance rent, bond, cost of improvements by the lessee or other party
13. Disaster: whether the lease continues; if so, on what basis in the event of fire or other disaster
14. Lessee's improvements: whether these can be removed at the expiration of the lease or to whom they then belong
15. Condemnation: the respective rights of the lessor and the lessee in the event that all or any part of the property is appropriated by a public agency
16. Revaluation clauses
17. Special provisions

EFFECTIVE GROSS INCOME

Effective gross income is the anticipated income from all operations of the real estate after allowance for vacancy and collection loss. The purpose of the gross income estimate is to indicate the full potential quantity of an anticipated future rental income from the property and the degree of risk (quality) involved in its realization. Having arrived at this estimate of full potential rent expectancy, the appraiser estimates the probable actual rent to be received or the anticipated future effective gross income.

In practice, a building is not expected to be fully occupied throughout its useful life or any major portion of it, except under a blanket lease. Frequently a new tenant is not found until after the old tenant vacates. Rental income may also be lost during remodeling or rehabilitation projects. Rent losses from a tenant's inability or unwillingness to pay may accumulate before the owner can resort to remedial measures. With occasional exceptions, the appraiser recognizes an allowance for potential vacancy or other causes of rent loss. This allowance, which is usually estimated as a percentage of potential gross, varies according to the type of property, the tenancy, and general conditions. During periods of economic decline, allowance for prospective vacancy should be made in the light of these circumstances. In an era of depression and unemployment or when overbuilding results in oversupply, the amount of particular types of space may exceed the demand, producing a general increase in vacancy. Rapid expansion of demand, coupled with an undersupply due to a period of underbuilding may create a situation where the prospective future loss due to vacancy is negligible. Obsolete types of property may anticipate some vacancy even when economic conditions are favorable.

The selection of an appropriate vacancy factor is influenced by the appraiser's estimate of the quality and durability of the projected rental and by typical vacancy levels revealed by market surveys of similar properties under similar conditions. The vacancy allowance should be increased as the prospect of sustaining the estimated rent appears to be less assured. However, an annual allowance for vacancy could be unrealistic if a property were rented on a long-term basis to responsible tenants.

When the property being appraised is a new multi-occupancy improvement of substantial size, there may be an abnormally high vacancy in the early years while initial leasing is in progress. This may be of sufficient consequence to be reflected in the stabilized vacancy and loss allowance, particularly if the income is to be processed on the basis of a short-term projection period, as under the mortgage-equity method of capitalization. However, the effect of this consideration may be compensated for, in whole or in part, by a lower estimate for repairs, maintenance, and replacements during this limited projection period.

Income from services has been mentioned as part of the gross income estimate and, consequently, as part of the effective gross income estimate. This is not income directly attributable to the use of real property, but may be derived from the use of personal property or profit from services supplied to the tenant. It requires analysis of its probable durability and may prove to be irregular or short-lived. Such income may include, for example, a profit derived from electricity purchased wholesale from the utility company and billed to tenants at retail, billing to tenants for special alterations, or other types of income paid by the tenants in addition to rental. Other examples commonly encountered consist of income attributable to special equipment, such as coin-operated washers and dryers in apartment buildings.

There are no set rules for the treatment of other income, but it is fundamentally generated by the operation of the real property and may be basically attributed to it. Gross income from services may be included in the gross income estimate and the cost of services included in expenses. It is also possible to put only net profit from services in the gross income estimate or to show only a net loss in the expense estimate. This extraneous income should be specifically identified so that it may be eliminated or separately treated if necessary. Income that is attributable to hotel or apartment furnishings (chattels) requires special treatment separate from the real estate in the income approach.

Gross Income Analysis

Historical income and expense statements, a current rent roll, and documentation in support of a vacancy and collection loss estimate are usually set forth in a report. For multi-occupancy properties, separate schedules may be used. These provide the basis for projections leading to an effective gross income estimate. This, combined with a projection of expenses, constitutes the reconstructed operating statement for the property. Pertinent lease terms also are included in appropriate detail. Sales figures, if available, may be included in appraisals of retail properties, because this data substantiates the tenant's ability to pay the estimated rent. The report also includes an analysis of existing unit rentals in the property being appraised and a reconciliation with unit rentals in comparable properties.

In appraising apartment property the appraiser studies the rentals on a dollars per room per month basis, or per square foot of rentable area in buildings with comparable facilities—such as pools, recreation rooms, security provisions—before arriving at the estimate of economic rental. The actual current rent roll is studied for hidden concessions, disparities between units, and vacancies. The rate of tenant turnover is considered. A high rate tends to increase the vacancy allowance and the cost of maintenance.

Store properties require that the appraiser review the basic types of retail development. There is the neighborhood location in which food, service, and convenience goods stores predominate, forming a small retail community. These may be independent freestanding stores or neighborhood centers in which the satellite stores frequently are not chain outlets. They seldom are on percentage leases, and lease terms customarily are short. The appraiser may arrive at a supported estimate of economic rent by comparisons and by investigation of the tenant's sales volumes.

Some retail types are freestanding. Discount houses, service stations, and restaurants sometimes prefer locations apart from even small community centers.

Shopping centers involve a delineation and analysis of the supporting area and a consideration of existing and proposed competition. The appraiser may discover that key tenants—supermarkets, variety stores, and department stores—are paying below average rent—that is, less than the median front-foot or square-foot rentals being paid by other tenants for comparable space. Additional rents, to be paid by key tenants as percentage clauses in the leases become operative, are important. These rents may be components of economic rent. Excess or overage rental may be segregated for separate analysis in the valuation process.

Stores in central business districts comprise another category. Consideration should be given to decentralization and competition from suburban shopping centers, public transportation, parking facilities for customers, and the tendency toward elimination of the independent merchant in central business districts. Customarily, the key tenants are department stores which often own the property they occupy or rent it under a long-term lease. In such cases gross rental value may be estimated through application of appropriate percentage rental rates to retail sales volume.

Economic rental for theatres may be estimated on a comparative seat basis which varies with size, plan, attendance, location, and type of operation. Percentage clauses may be involved, and rental analysis on a square-foot basis is also appropriate.

Gross rental values of parking lots and garages may be analyzed on a comparative unit basis or as a percentage of income. Garages with ramps or elevators (open or with pigeon-holes) are special-purpose buildings. Here the unit of comparison is the parking space. Although parking facilities may be compared on a square-foot-of-area rental basis, they also are analyzed in terms of car capacity. Even if similarly located, not all specialized parking facilities command the same rent because varying lot or building shapes and dimensions cause differences in capacity. Type of operation (self-park or other) is also a factor in parking garage analysis.

An understanding of office buildings income involves a knowledge of their standards of operation. Guides for the analysis of their income and expense data are available.[7] It also requires an understanding of the local practice in renting office space. The rate to the tenant actually could be more than currently quoted square-foot rates because of requirements that the tenant pay for remodeling or other items. Leases may contain escalation clauses requiring the tenant to participate in increased operating expenses.

Industrial buildings, manufacturing plants or warehouses may be multiple-tenancy, single-tenancy, or owner-occupied structures. Economic rental values of the multiple-tenancy buildings are usually estimated on a comparative square-foot basis. Rental rates vary according to factors such as type of property, ceiling height, transportation facilities, and labor market. Vacancy rates often are influenced more by the district identity than some physical attributes of a more or less standardized industrial property.

Hotels and motels are both income-producing properties and complicated business enterprises. Completely separating the business operation from the real property is difficult. The principal income is derived from room sales and food and beverage sales. Extra income may be provided by minor concessions or departments such as telephone service, cigar stand, and valet service. The income from rooms, customarily the basic comparative item, is the product of the number of available rooms multiplied by the average rate per occupied room and by the occupancy percentage. Direct hotel operating expense is then deducted to arrive at a gross departmental room profit. The gross profit or loss from other departments is then added or deducted, after which nondepartmental general and fixed expenses are deducted to arrive at a net income projection imputable to the real

---

7. See, for example, BOMA, *op. cit.*

estate, the chattels, and the business. Studies and monthly reports, unit room rental and occupancy rates, and departmental profits by cities and by other classifications are available.[8]

SUMMARY

The gross income estimate is the first step in the income approach of the appraisal process. The appraiser attempts to assume the point of view of the fully informed investor with respect to anticipated gross income. Existing lease agreements and the present and past income history of the property and of comparable space are reviewed in estimating the level of economic rental, the amount the space should be expected to produce in the current rental market. Establishing the property's economic rental value by comparison to contemporary rentals involves reducing comparative rental data to units of comparison. Information about personal income levels, business activity, retail sales volume, and the percentage of sales a business can afford to pay are also valuable checks on the prospective quantity of economic rent obtainable in the market for a particular property, type of space, or location.

The rental to be received under a lease may be greater or less than current economic rent. Accordingly, in the projection of effective gross income, the terms of existing leases are a controlling factor. Contract rent below the market represents a more secure income stream than economic (market) rent, but has the effect of creating leasehold value at the expense of the leased fee estate. Contract rent in excess of economic rent creates an intangible economic estate which accrues the ownership of the leased fee. Income in excess of economic rent is usually segregated for separate consideration (see Chapter 21).

In addition to the prospective quantity of income, quality and durability are also important characteristics of a gross income projection. They are affected by tenant financial responsibility, the term and provisions of the lease, the age of the property, and strength of the location. These factors contribute to an estimate of the length of time

8. *Trends in the Hotel-Motel Business* (New York: Harris, Kerr, Forster, annual); Stephen Rushmore, *The Valuation of Hotels and Motels* (Chicago: American Institute of Real Estate Appraisers, 1978).

the prospective income is likely to be sustained.

Except in unusual situations, an allowance is made for anticipated vacancy and loss of rent. Effective gross income is that which remains after deducting a reserve for vacancy and rent loss from gross potential economic rent and service income. From the effective gross income, expenses are deducted to arrive at the net operating income estimate, the second step in the income approach.

19
Analysis of Expense

The derivation of the prospective net income estimate from a real property begins with an estimate of the potential gross income. This consists of economic rent plus income from associated real estate services. A provision for anticipated vacancy and collection loss is deducted to arrive at an effective gross income estimate. From this figure, prospective annual expense for operation of the property is deducted. This expense is necessary to maintain the projected income and is estimated after review of operating experience data for the subject property and comparison with operating experience for similar properties. The income remaining represents the net operating income projection for capitalization into a value estimate. This procedure may be summarized.

Gross potential income		$xxxx
Vacancy and collection loss		− xx
Effective gross income		$xxxx
Expenses		
Fixed	$xx	
Variable (frequently called operating expense)	xx	
Reserves for replacement	xx	
Total operating expense		−$ xxx
Net operating income projection		$ xxx

This net operating income projection is referred to as net operating income (NOI) or as net income before recapture (NIBR).

The expense statement for any one year can seldom be accepted as typical. Most expenses vary from year to year. Others, which are periodical rather than annual, may not occur at all in a specific year. Accordingly, in projecting the probable future expenses, it is necessary to analyze more than one year's experience and to confirm the indicated conclusions by comparison with known figures for similar properties.

PERIODIC FLUCTUATION IN EXPENSES

The principle of change implies that neither income nor expenses remain static. They may fluctuate in terms of the purchasing power of the dollar and in terms of commodities in exchange.

In projecting incomes and expenses in valuation assignments, the appraiser endeavors to reflect the typical attitude of informed investors concerning observable trends. The risk inherent in the projection is weighed and reflected in the capitalization rate applied to the net income in the income approach. The appraiser's judgment is not subject to criticism by the single fact that the income or expenses prove to be higher or lower than an estimate that was made in previous years. To be realistic in the light of all factual data at the time of valuation, whatever projections are made need only reflect the opinion of informed investors at that time. In evaluation assignments, however, the appraiser often forecasts future income and expenses based on judgments drawn from more specialized market research.

The appraiser endeavors to reflect typical market patterns leading to a conclusion of market value. When an assignment involves an investment value conclusion based on a specific management program, income and expense projections that reflect this type of assignment are developed.

In situations where the pattern of a fluctuating net income projection can be reasonably identified and specific annual figures derived, the appraiser may choose to develop separate income and expense projections for each year of a selected projection period. A discounted cash flow analysis may then be made to derive a present worth estimate for the fluctuating net income stream.

A market value objective based on reconstruction of factual data in terms of apparent market expectancy for the reasonably foreseeable future is assumed in the discussion in this chapter, unless otherwise noted. The foreseeable future is not a fixed period. It does not purport to reflect a long-term economic life projection in terms of dollars. The aim of a reconstructed operating statement (sometimes referred to as a stabilized statement) is to reflect a typical pattern for the reasonably foreseeable future as viewed by informed investors comprising the market.

CLASSIFICATION OF EXPENSE

The deductions from gross income shown on profit-and-loss or operating statements fall into four general categories. Only three are recognized for the purpose of appraisal analysis. They are:

1. Fixed expense
2. Variable expense
3. Reserves for replacements

Other charges may be properly part of an owner's statement for tax or other accounting purposes but are not appropriate in the appraisal process.

Fixed expense, which may be shown on an actual or accrual basis, includes primarily real estate taxes and building insurance. These two items of expense apply to all properties except those leased on a net basis. Although they do not remain constant from year to year, they are not subject to the wide fluctuation of many other expenses, they do not vary in response to changing levels of occupancy, and they are expenses over which management has little control.

Variable expense includes all out-of-pocket costs involved in providing services for tenants and maintaining the income stream — for example, administration, utilities, payroll, supplies, and contract work such as cleaning. These expenses vary widely. Services provided to the tenants are usually minor in a store or a factory building, but may consume a large percentage of the income dollar in apartment buildings, office structures, and hotels. Maintenance charges include everything necessary to maintain the property in rentable condition and in good repair.

Reserves for replacements provide adequate allowances for the replacement of short-lived equipment items, such as stoves, refrigerators, washers, dryers, compressors, and for portions of the building, such as the roof, that require replacement during the life of the building. When the remaining useful life of the structure no longer exceeds the life expectancy of the item, a replacement reserve need not be provided.

In addition to fixed and variable expenses and reserves for re-placements, accounting statements received by an appraiser fre-quently include items not constituting a proper deduction from effec-tive gross income in appraisal analysis. These are deleted in the process of developing the appraiser's reconstructed operating state-ment. Such items include book depreciation, additions to capital investment, mortgage interest and amortization, income tax, special corporation costs, or other expenditures which may be proper in an accounting statement but are not essential to the operation of the property.

FIXED EXPENSE

The current amount of the local real estate taxes is an item that may be specified with some certainty because tax records are usually public. The basis and method of their determination varies from place to place. The appraiser is acquainted with the local system and the amount of the recent annual tax assessments, rates, and amounts paid. The amount of real estate tax indicated in an operating state-ment is not necessarily a reliable guide. The assessor's office may have information concerning the trend of tax and assessment rates, with some indication of possible increases or decreases. The actual operating statement may show only a partial payment or include tax payments for a previous year; in this case proper adjustments should be made to project taxes and assessments on a realistic annual basis. Depending on findings, the appraiser may use the stated taxes or may adjust the allowance for taxes in the reconstructed statement. Where an increasing trend is indicated, some time may elapse before an additional increase becomes effective; then a moderate upward rounding of the figures is sufficient to provide for the reasonably foreseeable future.

If the property is found to be unfairly assessed, an adjustment is in order. In cases of high or low assessments or apparent exceptions to the standard pattern of the jurisdiction, thorough analysis of the most probable amount and trend of taxes should be made. Records of changes that have been made in the assessment of the subject property should be studied. If the assessment is low, the assessor may raise it sooner or later; but if the figure is too high, relief may not be easily obtainable. Costly legal action may be required. In a real estate tax projection the appraiser endeavors to reflect the reasonable anticipation of an informed investor.

A cash operating statement may show insurance charges either at the actual annual cost or on the basis of premiums paid in one year which cover several years. For example, three-year policies may be more economical and are frequently used. Since the insurance carried may not be the proper amount, the term and cost should be checked and an adjustment made if appropriate. Fire, extended coverage, and owner's liability insurance are the principal items. Other types of coverage, which depend on the character of the property, include elevator, boiler, and plate glass insurance. Rent insurance, intended to reimburse the owner for losses such as those incurred during repairs caused by casualty loss, is another type of special coverage. Insurance on inventory and contents—special liability—is usually a tenant's obligation and is not included. When there is doubt about the complexities of co-insurance, extended coverage, liability, or other types, it is advisable to seek expert counsel from professional insurance agents or brokers.

VARIABLE EXPENSE

Although there may be more sophisticated subdivisions, this classification of expense frequently includes the following broad categories.[1]

1. Management
2. Electricity
3. Heat
4. Water

---

1. A record of operating expenses for any particular building may be kept under a unified system of categories of expense designed by an association to which the owner may belong. Two such systems are shown later in this chapter. In other instances the record of operating expenses may be kept according to categories selected by the owner.

5. Gas
6. Air conditioning
7. General payroll
8. Cleaning
9. Maintenance and repair
   a. Decorating
   b. Alterations
   c. Grounds maintenance
   d. Elevators
10. Miscellaneous
    a. Security
    b. Supplies
    c. Rubbish removal and exterminating

Management fees (and rental commissions) are considered proper expense deductions, whether the property is managed by a professional manager or the owner. A considerable expenditure of time for accounting, supervision, and other managerial duties is required for multi-tenancy properties; additional costs for on-site management facilities and personnel may be required for larger properties. The amount of management fees, usually established in terms of a percentage of effective gross income, may be influenced by local custom.

Legal, accounting, advertising, or other fees; items such as owner's or manager's telephone charges; bookkeeping and office rent should not be overlooked when they are necessary to the operation of the property. Because certain book charges, such as salaries of corporate officers who actually perform no service, are not proper charges against the operation of the property, they are not usually included as expenses in the appraiser's reconstructed operating statement.

Retail chain-store tenants usually assume most of the operating expenses. For these properties, leasing commissions may account for a major portion of management cost. Day-to-day management details are less burdensome when a property is leased to a single tenant.

The cost of *electricity* has been reasonably projected from experience data. The increasing cost of all forms of energy has introduced a new problem in making these projections, particularly in locations where the cost of electricity has increased more than is typical. The appraiser combines an experience trend analysis with a consideration of anticipated local cost changes in an effort to develop a valid projection of this cost for a reasonably foreseeable future. If the resale of purchased electricity at a net profit is permitted under existing agreement with the local utility company, any net income so derived may be included as service income without entry on the expense side of the statement. However, the cost of electricity for lighting public areas, such as halls, corridors, and parking lots, and power for elevators or other owner-operated equipment constitutes an owner's expense, even when tenant areas are metered. When the owner provides electric service under the terms of the rental arrangement (as in some apartments, hotels, and office buildings), the owner's electrical cost may become substantial.[2]

Heat is another basic cost carried to the reconstructed statement. The fuel may be coal, oil, gas, electricity, or public steam. Supplies, maintenance, and applicable wages are included in this category under some methods of accounting. Public steam suppliers and gas companies keep records of the degree days from year to year. Reference to these records and fuel costs makes it practical to compare the most recent year or years with the average. Prospective changes in the cost of the fuel used are reflected in the appraiser's projection. Local anti-pollution ordinances may be responsible for increasing fuel costs. The opportunity to change to a more economical type of fuel may result in a decrease in projected heating expense, but this may involve an analysis of the feasibility of a capital expenditure for new equipment.

Water cost customarily is incurred in the ownership of apartments, hotels, and other residential types of property. Comparative figures per family unit per year provide a basis for analysis. Usually domestic water needs are light in commercial properties; but exceptions are laundries, restaurants, taverns, and buildings that use water for air conditioning where there are no cooling towers.

Gas is a major expense only when used for heating or air conditioning. Tenants' gas is usually metered to individual units.

Air-conditioning cost is not always separated from the costs of electricity and water. For heating and air conditioning, there may be central systems, as in some large office buildings, or individual units in each tenant's space, as in store buildings and some apartment

---

2. State laws differ as to the legality of reselling electricity.

houses. When paid by the owner, the cost of inspection and maintenance is included in the operating expense. Air-conditioning costs vary widely, but local standards provide a valid basis for operating cost comparisons.

General payroll includes all employees not specifically assigned to other categories. The cost of custodial or janitorial service is based on union schedules in some areas and is a bargaining matter governed by local custom and practice in others. If a custodian or manager occupies an apartment as partial payment for services, its rental value may be included as income with an identical amount deducted as expense. For some properties there is the additional cost of employing watchmen, doormen, porters, or elevator starters. Unemployment and social security taxes may be carried in a separate classification or may be included in general payroll.

Cleaning is a major item of cost in office-building operation. This expense is usually estimated in terms of cents per square foot of the net rentable area whether the work is done by payroll personnel or by a contract cleaning firm. Its equivalent in hotels and apartments is maid service or housekeeping. For hotel or motel operations, these expenses, attributable to the rooms department, may be based on a percentage of departmental gross that reflects previous experience and industry standards.

Maintenance and repair includes roof repair, window caulking, tuckpointing, exterior painting, and structural work and may include repair of heating, lighting, and plumbing equipment, depending on lease provisions. The extent of this item in an expense projection is affected by the extent to which building component and equipment replacements are covered in the reserves for replacements allowance.

Decorating costs may include interior maintenance and minor repairs. Necessary provision for this category of expense varies according to local custom and may also vary from year to year depending on supply and demand factors for the type of space.

Alterations are another phase of maintenance. If sufficiently extensive, they may be charged to capital addition, instead of to annual expense. The lessor may perform some alterations in the space rented, the expense of which may or may not be amortized by additional rental, or which, alternately, may be paid for by the tenant.

Grounds maintenance may be a major or minor item. Expense is entailed in the development of extensive grounds and parking areas serving properties such as garden apartment developments and shopping centers. Maintenance of a hard-surfaced public parking area with drains, lights, and marked car spaces, subject to intensive use and wear, may be substantial. This expense may be compensated for, entirely or in part, by an increment added to the rent of tenants served by the facility. Both income and expense are included in the appraiser's projection.

Operation and maintenance of elevators, a major item of cost in high-rise buildings, may be carried in the same account. Frequently, the existence of a maintenance contract facilitates analysis. However, such contracts vary, and it is important to ascertain the probable extent of additional operating cost not covered by the maintenance contract.

Miscellaneous costs and items vary from property to property. However, if this category includes more than a minor percentage of the effective income, it should be analyzed, reallocated, or clearly explained.

Certain types of buildings in some areas require security provisions, which vary in cost according to the number of employees needed to control entries and exits and to circulate within the property. Further expense is incurred when provisions for security include electric alarm sytems, closed circuit television, and flood lighting.

Supplies include the cost of cleaning materials and miscellaneous small items not carried elsewhere.

Rubbish removal and exterminating costs are usually contracted services.

RESERVES FOR REPLACEMENTS

Where essential to protection of real estate operating income, items customarily provided for within this category for apartment properties include:

1. Stoves, refrigerators, dishwashers, garbage disposals, or laundry equipment
2. Furniture or lobby accessories

3.   Carpet, linens, dishes, and other chattels

4.   Specific building components

The provision for appliances is made by estimating the total cost of replacement and dividing it by the average useful life of the appliance. In recent years there has been a growing tendency for more kitchen equipment to be built in and for provision of coin-operated laundry units.

Furniture replacement is a major consideration in furnished apartments, hotels, and motels where the furniture is a principal factor in producing income. The annual allowance normally amounts to the cost of replacement divided by its useful life, depending on the type and quality of the different categories of furniture. Provision for a fair interest return on, and a recapture of, the investment in such chattels represents a separate consideration in the income approach to value. Replacement of carpet customarily is treated by spreading the cost of replacement over a long enough period to arrive at a reasonable annual allowance. Linens, dishes, and silverware are short-lived chattels customarily figured for replacement in a comparatively brief time.

Reserves for replacement of building parts are for components of the structure that wear out more rapidly than the structure itself and *are not covered by other repair and maintenance charges in the expense statement.* These may include the roof, boilers, elevators, store fronts in retail properties, or other items. The annual allowance in the reserve account customarily is the total cost of replacement divided by an anticipated useful life. A sinking-fund reserve may be used in unusual circumstances if the appraiser feels that this pattern is appropriate. Because elaborate modern store fronts are subject to rapid obsolescence, an allowance for their replacement may be accrued annually over their estimated economic life. New elevators may be expected to serve during the structure's remaining economic life. Items that are expected to have a life equal to, or exceeding, that of the structure do not require a reserve for replacement.[3] The scope

---

3.   Reserves for replacements provide for periodic expenditures during the economic life of the structure which leave no funds remaining in the reserve account. No reserves are accrued for replacement of items that will depreciate coincident with the economic life of the structure. The recapture provision of the capitalization process includes provision for this one-time recapture of the item's cost. Thus a proper use of the reserves for replacement does not duplicate recapture in the capitalization process.

of items covered by reserves is a matter of appraisal judgment in each case.

A total expense estimate, including provision for all the items of repair and replacement, may exceed the actual expenditures shown on the owner's operating statements for the most recent or prior years. This applies when the building is reasonably new and when (often in actual practice) the owner sets up no reserves for replacements.

The extent of a replacement reserve should be related to the annual repair and maintenance charge in order to avoid duplication. Historical operating statements on a cash basis may include periodic replacement charges under repair and maintenance. Extensive provision for replacement reserves in a reconstructed statement may have the effect of reducing the annual maintenance expense projection.

Understanding what is included in an operating statement may also be important in deriving a capitalization rate from the market for use in the income approach. A rate derived from a comparative sale property is valid only when applied on the same basis to the subject property. Consequently, a rate derived from a market sale with an expense estimate that ignores reserves for replacements may not be applicable to a net income projection that includes reserves for replacements unless the rate or the net operating income is correspondingly adjusted.

It is important to ascertain owners' and tenants' respective responsibilities for items of operating expense and to develop a reasonable program for operation of the property consistent with the character and terms of the lease or leases. Some types of leases contain escalation clauses that may include provision that all or part of any increase in operating costs and taxes above a specified level are passed on to the tenant.

COMPARATIVE UNIT COSTS AND RATIOS

After individual items of expense have been estimated, based on a computation of requirements or a review of past operating experience, it is helpful to reduce these estimates to some unit basis for comparison to experience standards of similar properties. Such standards are frequently expressed as a percentage of the effective gross income estimate or as a dollar cost per room or per square foot.

Management or leasing fees are typically related to a percentage of effective gross income. Other items, such as real estate taxes, may be confirmed but not derived on this basis. Elevator maintenance may be related to dollars per door opening per year or per month. Parking lot maintenance is frequently considered on a cents per square foot of lot area per year. The typical unit of comparison for most expenses is dollars per square foot of rentable area per year or per month.

Expense ratios or unit costs are usually established from operating experience data in the appraiser's files and often may be confirmed by published experience for various types of properties.

The tendency toward a consistent pattern for many individual items of expense for similar types of properties generally extends to the total expense ratio for such properties within a community. Total expense ratio refers to the relationship of the total expense estimate to the effective gross income estimate. All these ratios tend to fall within limited ranges for different categories of property. The appraiser recognizes approximately correct ratios of total expense to income or, conversely, the ratio of net operating income (before provision for recapture) to effective gross income. This recognition provides immediate identification of statements that deviate from typical patterns and hence require further analysis.

USE OF INCOME AND EXPENSE STATEMENTS

A basic step in preparing future expense projections is a review of the property's present and historical operation. The historical expense record, adjusted for known changes in prices or wages, provides an indication of possible future expense. These figures may then be compared to those of similar properties. A thorough application of this procedure leads to a proper reconstruction of the expense statement. Comparison is on a unit basis for specific items and on an overall basis in terms of the ratio of total expense to effective gross income. This ratio is referred to as the operating expense ratio. The complement of this figure is the net income ratio (net operating income to effective gross income).

The appraisal of real property is predicated on the assumption of competent management. This assumption may not be reflected by historical operating statements. This fact, plus additional complications due to atypical entries or the omission of specific items, may pose perplexing problems in the effort to reconstruct a typical expense projection. Nevertheless, operating statements for prior years are helpful to the appraiser even when they cannot be used exactly as presented. By combining the operating statements for three or more years with observations of the property and comparisons with the records of similar properties, the appraiser is able to reconstruct a realistic prospective or stabilized expense estimate.

The necessity for the appraiser's reconstruction of an actual operating statement may reflect any or all of the following deficiencies inherent in the statement:

1. It may not reflect competent management.
2. It may include improper charges.
3. It may omit essential items of expense.
4. It may be on a cash flow accounting basis unadjusted to a typical year.

Table 19.1. Reconstructed Operating Expense Estimate

	Preceding years			Projected
	3	2	1	Stabilized
Administrative/management	$ 17,200	$ 22,100	$ 21,600	$ 22,000
Cleaning	40,800	46,400	50,100	50,000
Electricity	3,100	4,000	4,800	6,000
Heating	6,300	6,600	7,000	7,500
Air conditioning	18,700	25,600	25,400	26,500
Plumbing	2,000	2,900	4,100	3,800
Elevators	8,900	10,100	9,900	10,000
Alterations—space revisions	21,900	24,900	26,000	20,000
Decorating	7,000	10,900	9,500	9,000
General repairs and maintenance	2,400	3,000	1,800	2,200
Carpentry	1,100	1,000	3,100	2,000
General building	11,000	13,300	14,500	14,000
Insurance	—	—	12,000	4,000
Real estate and personal property tax	73,000	78,800	85,400	90,000
Franchise tax	1,000	1,000	1,000	—
Total	$215,200	$250,600	$276,200	$267,000

Table 19.1. illustrates a reconstructed estimate of projected operating expenses for an office building, compared with the actual record of the three previous years.

Typically, accounting statements of past operation will be in precise amounts. A projection from such data is an estimate, based on application of experience and judgment to available data. The precision with which this estimate is expressed should reflect the practical limitations of the estimating process and the reliability of historical and comparative data.

Experience data of similar properties provides a basis for judging the probable validity of the various items of historical expense as shown on audits and periodic financial statements. Operating cost experience is published by various sources, including trade associations. The Institute of Real Estate Management (IREM) publishes an analysis of income and expense for apartment buildings. The Building Owners and Managers Association International (BOMA) has been compiling unit expenses for office buildings for many years. Laventhol & Horwath, and Harris, Kerr, Forster & Company publish studies in the hotel and motel fields. Cornell University, New York State College of Agriculture analyzes (rental) costs for variety stores and food chains. Costs for department and specialty stores are analyzed by the National Retail Merchants Association. The Urban Land Institute provides income and expense data for neighborhood, community, and regional shopping centers.[3]

---

3. *Income/Expense Analysis: Apartments, Condominiums, & Cooperatives* (Chicago: Institute of Real Estate Management, annually). Figures are analyzed according to region and selected metropolitan areas.
Downtown and Suburban Office Building Exchange Report (Washington: Building Owners and Managers Association International, annually).
Lodging Industry (Philadelphia: Laventhol & Horwath, annually).
Trends in the Hotel-Motel Business (New York: Harris, Kerr, Forster & Company, annually).
Operating Results of Food Chains (Ithaca, N.Y.: Cornell University, New York State College of Agriculture, annually). Originally published by Harvard University Graduate School of Business.
Financial and Operating Results of Department and Specialty Stores (New York: National Retail Association, Controllers Congress, annually). Originally published by Harvard University Graduate School of Business.
Dollars and Cents of Shopping Centers (Washington, D.C.: Urban Land Institute, 1978).

Table 19.2. Low-Rise Apartment Buildings 25 Units and Over—Average Income and Operating Costs—Selected City Averages—Dollars per Square Foot Rentable Area per Annum

1976	Atlanta	Chicago	Los Angeles	Philadelphia
Number of buildings	4	66	52	3
Number of apartments	246	3,292	4,123	436
Number of rentable rooms	1,065	13,022	17,134	1,963
Gross square feet	225,900	3,182,937	4,268,379	599,244
Rentable square feet	211,840	3,339,746	4,398,716	506,034
Income [a]				
Rents—apartments	2.03	2.52	2.55	4.62
Rents—garages and parking	.07	.15	.03	3.51
Rents—stores	—	.21	—	—
Rents—offices	—	.14	—	—
Gross possible rental income	2.06	2.55	2.56	4.62
Miscellaneous other income	—	.04	.07	.11
Gross possible total income	2.06	2.58	2.63	4.73
Less vacancies and delinquent rents	.11	.11	.09	.02
Total actual collections	1.95	2.49	2.55	4.71
Expenses				
Total payroll expenses	.12	.23	.13	.23
Supplies	.02	.02	.02	.06
Painting and decorating (interior only)	.08	.08	.07	.15
Maintenance repairs (interior and exterior)	.07	.12	.15	.24
Services	.02	.03	.04	.04
Miscellaneous operating	.01	.02	.04	.04
Subtotal—maintenance and operating	.32	.50	.45	.76
Electricity	.09	.04	.08	.35
Water	.04	.05	.03	.09
Gas (excluding heating fuel)	.03	.05	.04	.07
Heating fuel	—	.22	.03	.25
Subtotal—utilities	.16	.36	.18	.76
Management fees	.11	.12	.13	.20
Other administrative expense	.03	.05	.03	.10
Subtotal—administrative	.14	.17	.16	.30
Insurance	.05	.06	.03	.05
Real estate taxes	.18	.40	.39	.60
Other taxes	—	.01	.01	.05
Subtotal—taxes and insurance	.23	.47	.43	.70
Total all expenses	.80	1.40	1.15	2.50
Net operating income	1.15	1.09	1.40	2.21

Source: *Income/Expense Analysis: Apartments, Condominiums, & Cooperatives* (Chicago: Institute of Real Estate Management, 1977) 1976 data.
[a]Figures may not total 100%.

Table 19.3.   Office Building Operating Costs
Selected City Averages—Costs per Square Foota

1976	Atlanta	Chicago	Los Angeles	Philadelphia
Number of buildings	16	46	27	30
Square feet in analysis	3,429,786	2,864,904	11,199,326	8,746,463
Account	Building Total			
A1 Cleaning	47.9 (16)	105.5 (45)	68.0 (27)	96.4 (30)
A2 Electrical systems	3.3 (15)	12.3 (42)	8.5 (21)	11.7 (28)
A3A Heating	.8 (2)	17.6 (15)	7.7 (5)	9.8 (17)
A3B Air conditioning-ventilating	4.8 (2)	18.6 (15)	15.9 (5)	19.4 (19)
A3C Combined HVAC	20.7 (14)	37.5 (32)	23.2 (22)	45.5 (10)
A5 Elevators	10.8 (15)	26.8 (45)	17.6 (27)	21.8 (30)
A6A General building costs	43.6 (16)	38.5 (46)	51.3 (27)	38.3 (30)
A6B Administrative costs	23.9 (15)	34.7 (46)	24.0 (27)	18.4 (30)
A7 Energy	77.3 (15)	77.4 (46)	76.4 (27)	114.9 (30)
Total operating, A	222.8 (15)	332.4 (46)	267.8 (27)	334.5 (30)
B1 Alterations—tenant area	4.0 (7)	29.9 (25)	10.4 (15)	12.5 (7)
B3 Decorating—tenant area	7.4 (11)	8.6 (37)	1.9 (9)	6.3 (10)
Total Construction B	7.8 (14)	28.6 (37)	7.6 (17)	13.4 (11)
Total Operating expenses, A and B	212.0 (14)	351.1 (37)	236.8 (17)	385.8 (11)
C1 Insurance	4.5 (15)	8.4 (37)	6.2 (27)	7.0 (15)
C2A Real estate tax				
Land	15.4 (11)	39.1 (35)	22.6 (27)	15.0 (17)
Building	63.3 (11)	128.7 (37)	123.4 (27)	69.7 (17)
C2B Personal property tax, etc.	61.6 (3)	8.0 (8)	9.5 (14)	11.7 (7)
Total fixed charges C[b]	72.1 (15)	155.1 (40)	158.9 (27)	96.4 (17)
Total operating expenses A+B+C[b]	294.7 (13)	518.0 (33)	377.5 (17)	482.1 (11)
Net income				
Gain	262.0 (13)	248.1 (35)	274.6 (21)	259.9 (14)
Loss	116.4 (1)	370.8 (7)	236.6 (1)	— (2)
Lease expense	13.0 (5)	7.8 (14)	13.2 (11)	10.5 (6)
Amortized tenant alterations	9.3 (6)	32.3 (18)	15.4 (11)	24.4 (4)
C3 Depreciation	70.5 (12)	97.4 (20)	100.0 (21)	91.6 (10)
Net income				
Gain	198.1 (11)	147.2 (23)	182.0 (15)	252.2 (6)
Loss	239.3 (1)	235.4 (12)	42.7 (3)	38.8 (6)
Rental income				
Store area	703.8 (7)	952.4 (34)	701.3 (11)	591.2 (9)
Storage area	288.7 (6)	284.0 (28)	358.8 (10)	157.8 (1)

Special area	794.7 (2)	514.9 (13)	209.9 (8)	645.6 (4)
Total rental income	564.9 (16)	661.1 (42)	680.4 (19)	654.9 (12)
Electrical income	8.6 (2)	25.8 (26)	20.9 (2)	9.2 (3)
Miscellaneous income	12.2 (9)	15.6 (35)	22.0 (11)	44.1 (7)
Total operating income	576.2 (16)	688.7 (44)	693.2 (22)	682.9 (14)
Operating ratio	67.4 (13)	95.2 (30)	76.4 (17)	76.0 (11)
Management ratio	39.7 (16)	53.4 (44)	38.0 (22)	47.7 (14)
Average office vacancy	7.3 (16)	6.3 (46)	13.6 (27)	8.5 (30)
Average office occupancy	92.7 (16)	93.7 (46)	86.4 (27)	91.5 (30)
Labor cost	43.9 (14)	124.4 (37)	65.2 (16)	118.0 (6)
Average office tenant (sq. ft.)	5,206 (16)	5,465 (42)	9,908 (19)	5,196 (24)
Average store tenant (sq. ft.)	2,879 (7)	2,404 (28)	6,393 (12)	7,353 (11)
Average sq. ft. per employee	12,589 (14)	9,828 (37)	16,911 (16)	7,354 (6)
Average sq. ft. per person	207.5 (16)	194.9 (39)	264.9 (25)	201.1 (20)

Source: *Downtown and Suburban Office Building Exchange Report* (Washington, D.C.: Building Owners and Managers Association International, 1977). 1976 data.

[a]The figures presented here represent an extract from the original page which also presents the data in terms of office area and office rented area.

[b]Does not include expense for depreciation.

[c]Includes expenses for depreciation.

() Indicates number of buildings giving this information.

The pattern of items of expense as shown by the various trade organizations and their accountants usually follows an order that the particular group deems most suitable for its own needs. Accordingly, the items of expense may follow a different grouping for various types of property, as shown by the IREM and BOMA studies. Such published statistical material is frequently useful as comparison checks against expenses for a specific property.

Tables 19.2 and 19.3, taken from such periodic reports, illustrate, in part, expense breakdowns in which the statistics may be presented.

Net Operating Income

The appraiser is concerned with developing reasonable estimates of potential gross income, vacancy allowance, effective gross income, expenses, and the prospective net operating income (before provision for projected recapture and mortgage debt service). This net income stream is referred to as net operating income, net income before recapture, or net income before debt service.

Not included in the estimate of expenses leading to this figure are book depreciation, mortgage interest and amortization, income tax, special corporation costs, and additions to capital.

Book depreciation. The actual reserve shown on the profit-and-loss statement is usually based on historical cost. However, the appraiser looks at the property as if it were on the market today, then processes operating income separately from any allowance or reserve for projected depreciation, which may be shown, if required for financial purposes. Provision for recapture (future depreciation) is inherent in the capitalization method selected.

Mortgage interest and amortization. Interest is a charge for borrowing. Amortization is a return of a loan by installments. These items do enter into the mortgage-equity method of capitalization. They are not properly included as expense items in the appraiser's operating statement.

Income tax. The amount of this item varies with the character of the ownership. The owner may be a corporation, a public utility, a wealthy individual, or perhaps an individual in moderate or average circumstances. The income tax costs of the owner, like mortgage interest and amortization, are not proper inclusions in the operating statement.

Special corporation costs. Items such as franchise taxes and directors' fees are charges against the type of ownership, not charges against the property.

Additions to capital. These are not items of annual expense. They are capital additions that usually tend to increase or prolong the income and to extend the useful life of the property.

NET INCOME TO BE CAPITALIZED

Regardless of the capitalization method employed, the basis for an income approach to a value indication is the estimate of net operating income. It is a critical figure that merits careful analysis to assure that it reasonably reflects a typical purchaser's anticipations as assumed in the selected capitalization process.

A purchaser buying for use may look at income and expense projections differently than an investor projecting a short-term period of ownership. The latter, particularly when purchasing a new property, may give minimal consideration to repairs or reserves for replacements. The appraiser considers the probable composition of the market in which the property may be expected to sell and endeavors to develop risk rates and net income projections that reflect this market. The objective of the report may be indicative. A lender, contemplating long-term financing, is making a commitment to the real property which may imply a different motive than a short-term investor with some speculative motivation.

SUMMARY

The forecast of annual expense is as essential to the income approach as is the gross annual income estimate. Current and historical expenses constitute only a guide to estimating future expense. Subject to actual lease provisions, the fixed expense, variable expense, and reserves for replacements typically comprise the expense estimate for deduction from effective gross income leading to net operating income. Not usually included among the projected annual expense estimates for appraisal purposes are book or accounting depreciation, mortgage payments, income tax, corporation tax, and capital additions.

Units of comparison and overall percentages are helpful in analyzing the record of actual expense and for developing and refining the expense estimate. The end product of the carefully devised reconstructed income and expense statement is net operating income before provision for recapture of invested capital and before debt service. The following chapters demonstrate the processing of this net income before recapture into an estimate of indicated value by use of various methods and techniques of capitalization available to the appraiser.

20
Rates in Capitalization

Capitalization is a process that translates an income projection into an indication of value. The connecting link is a rate that reflects the return necessary to attract investment capital. Hence the selection of an appropriate rate represents a critical factor in the capitalization process.

Before discussing rates or rate selection, a study of terminology is in order. Because certain terms used in accounting or financial fields may involve a more limited concept than in the context of appraisal practice, the following definitions apply particularly to appraising.[1]

RATE—A term expressing a fixed relationship between two magnitudes, and used as a means of measurement or to derive one magnitude from the other. A ratio of income to capital (value).

CAPITALIZATION RATE—Any rate used for the conversion of income into value. An adjective, such as recapture, building, overall, is usually applied to the rate indicating the income and value relationship involved.

INTEREST RATE—A rate of return on capital. Interest rate frequently implies a contract rate—for example, a mortgage interest rate. Synonymous terms in appraisal practice are *risk rate* or *discount rate*.

RISK RATE—Rate of return necessary to attract investment capital.

---

1. Additional information may be found in American Institute of Real Estate Appraisers and Society of Real Estate Appraisers, *Real Estate Appraisal Terminology*, ed. Byrl N. Boyce (Cambridge, Mass.: Ballinger Publishing Co., 1975).

DISCOUNT RATE—An interest or risk rate that is used as the basis for present worth factors to discount future benefits. *Discount* identifies the use made of the rate.

YIELD—A return on capital.

YIELD RATE—A rate of return on capital. In appraisal practice, commonly used to imply a realized rate of return—for example, a mortgage with a 7% contract "interest" rate may be sold at less than face value to realize a "yield" of 9%. With reference to equity capital, *equity yield rate* implies a realized rate of return that includes recognition of the effect of capital gain or loss on an annual earnings rate.

RECAPTURE RATE—The rate at which a capital investment is assumed to be returned to the investor. In appraisal practice, usually related to return of investment in a wasting asset.

STRAIGHT-LINE RECAPTURE—Return of investment in equal periodic amounts, usually related to an estimate of remaining economic life.

SINKING-FUND RECAPTURE—Return of investment through equal periodic payments into a sinking fund that accumulates to provide recapture at the end of a project period.

SURCHARGE RECAPTURE—Return of investment in equal periodic amounts as derived from market analysis with no implication of a specific projection period or a specific income stream pattern.

BUILDING CAPITALIZATION RATE—The sum of the risk rate and the recapture rate, applicable to income imputable to improvements.

OVERALL RATE—The direct relationship between net income before recapture and value/price. Return on the investment plus applicable recapture are not identified but are inherent in the overall rate.

EQUITY DIVIDEND RATE—The annual cash flow to equity (net income after deduction of debt service) as a percentage of equity investment.

CASH FLOW RATE—Synonymous with equity dividend rate. May also be modified to reflect the cash flow after payment of income taxes.

INCOME—Money or other benefits, generally assumed to be received periodically.

CAPITALIZATION—The process of converting into present value (or obtaining the present worth of) a series of anticipated future periodic installments of net income. Also defined as the process of estimating the value of a capital good—for example, real estate—through the use of a rate that represents the proper relationship between that capital good and the net income it produces.

REVERSION—(1) The return of an item of real estate, such as the return of all rights of possession at the termination of a lease, or (2) the net proceeds of resale of the real estate at the end of a period of ownership.

VALUE—The quantity of one thing that can be obtained in exchange for another. In real estate valuation it is the amount of money equal in worth to the property being appraised.

A basic principle of real property value is anticipation, which affirms that value is created by the expectation of future benefits to be derived from ownership. The past is relevant only to the extent that it furnishes a basis for future expectations. Real estate value, consequently, is the present worth of the benefits of ownership as anticipated by typical prospective purchasers who constitute the market.

Capitalization is the procedure of expressing such anticipated future benefits of ownership in dollars and processing them into a present worth at a rate that is attracting purchase capital to similar investments. In its simplest form this procedure uses a projection of periodic income as the numerator and a capitalization rate as the denominator in an equation for value. The process is most directly applicable to the appraisal of the value of income-producing property because a primary benefit of such ownership is income in the form of net rent. An expectation of income is a primary motivation for the purchase of income-producing real estate. Return on an investment is usually measured on an annual basis and is expressed as an annual rate. For example, an investment returning 10% is one on which the return equals $0.10 each year on each $1.00 of capital remaining in the investment from year to year.

The phrase "remaining in the investment from year to year" is of special significance because a net return cannot exist until provision has been made to recover all purchase capital and all other costs attributable to the investment. Part of the net periodic income is normally allocated to the recapture or amortization of purchase capital, and the balance, plus any appreciation in capital value, is profit that is discounted to present worth.

Profit from the purchase of income-producing real estate generally is the excess of two collections over cost. (This is developed further under Annuity Capitalization in Chapter 21.) The first collection is the periodic net income produced by the property during the term of ownership. The second collection is the net proceeds of resale at the end of the term of ownership. This is called the reversion. Thus the capitalization process may be accomplished by estimating the present worth of an income stream for a certain term of years and the present worth of a lump sum reversion at the end of the term. Any estimate of value, regardless of the process used, reflects a combination of these two value components.

RATES OF RETURN

Generally, the applicable rate of return to use in an appraisal problem is the rate that investors in that type or class of property require as a condition for purchase. The rate such investors require varies from time to time, depending on economic and other conditions. Accordingly, in estimating rates for capitalization, the appraiser carefully considers competitive market conditions since they influence or reflect opinions and actions of investors.

All investments—real estate or other—are in competition. The investor has the choice of bank rate securities such as government bonds, industrial or municipal bonds, debentures; stocks and other securities; selected enterprises; and real estate investments at varying rates of return.

Consideration of risk, burden of management, degree of liquidity, and other factors (including personal preference) affect the rate of return acceptable to a given investor in a specific real estate investment. An adjustment for risk is an increment added to a base, or safe, rate to compensate for the extent of risk believed to be involved in the use of the capital sum. Additional upward adjustment of the rate because of a need for management is the increment added to compensate for the cost, in time or dollars, involved in managing the investment. This is not to be confused with a fee for managing the real estate itself, which is an operating expense unrelated to the investment return rate.

The upward adjustment above a safe rate, to compensate for lack of liquidity, results in an increment applying generally to real property because of the time often required to realize cash from resale of the property. This may vary with the general marketability of the type of property and the amount of the cash investment required.

In recognition of the above, a rate of return appropriate to real property investments may be rationalized in the following terms:

	%
Safe rate (minimum risk)	x
Add for additional risk	I_1
Add for burden of management	I_2
Add for lack of liquidity	I_3
Rate applicable to the investment	Total

This summation provides a theoretical presentation to explain why a rate used in the valuation of real property is in excess of the safe rate. Nevertheless, because of the intangible character of the components, it is not currently considered a valid procedure through which a specific rate may actually be derived, but consideration is appropriate to identify points of balance and so on. Procedures applicable in the selection of specific rates are presented in this chapter, and familiarity with current rates obtainable in competitive investment markets offers the appraiser a frame of reference within which real estate equity rates of return may be related and compared. Identification of trends in money market rates also permits current rate estimation from recent historical rate levels for similar risks.

INFLUENCE OF INCOME QUALITY ON RATES OF RETURN

The nature of income is discussed in Chapter 18 where the income from real property is analyzed in terms of quantity, quality, and durability. After analysis of gross income and deduction for vacancy and operating expense, a quantity of prospective net income before recapture is derived. The quality element of net income is interpreted in terms of risk, and the capitalization of net income from income-producing real estate is at a rate commensurate with the risk of realizing the anticipated benefits. In this respect it is no different from any other investment. The yield expected from an investment reflects the risk involved, as viewed by the investor.

The term *risk,* as here used, connotes not only relative safety, but also the degree to which all the requisites of a good investment are met. An investment may be quite safe as far as principal is concerned, but may have other qualities that make it less desirable. Among the investment considerations are:

1. Safety. The degree of certainty of return of capital is a prime consideration.
2. Reliability of yield. Important because many investors are primarily concerned with income.
3. Marketability. Essential prerequisite to liquidity, which may be important at some point in the anticipated life of the investment.
4. Denominations. Amounts that can be handled by typical prospective investors in the market. Smaller denominations improve liquidity.
5. Acceptability as collateral. Enables an investor to achieve a measure of liquidity without losing title to the investment.
6. Duration. Some people prefer a long-term investment for their funds; others prefer a short period only.
7. Freedom from care. Important because many of the investors managing their own portfolios do not want an investment requiring a great deal of attention.
8. Potential appreciation. Provides a hedge against a decline in the purchasing power of money.
9. Tax advantage. Tax savings or shelter may be an important consideration.

Any investment risk rate reflects the extent to which these or other factors modify the basic safe rate found in the money market.

THE OVERALL RATE

The overall rate reflects the relationship between the projection of periodic net income and a sale price or an estimate of capital value. For example:

$$\text{Overall rate} = \frac{\text{Net operating income}}{\text{Sale price or value}}$$

$$\text{OAR} = \frac{\$44,000}{\$400,000} = .11 \text{ or } 11\%$$

This overall rate may be analyzed in terms of probable amount and duration of the future income stream, reasonable provision for anticipated depreciation,[2] and the resulting probable rate of return on the investment. Because the numerator in the equation is income only, it is apparent that the overall rate of the denominator must be a combination of several ingredients, which will not only reflect a satisfactory return on the investment, but also adjust for any effect on the value of the investment due to potential depreciation (or appreciation) of the asset.

Recapture of the investment may be accomplished by several means. If the value of the property at reversion (the net proceeds of resale) is the same as the initial investment, the entire recapture is in the reversion. If the value of the property at reversion is less than the original investment, the recapture is only partially in the reversion, and the balance must be provided from income produced during ownership. If the reversion is greater than the investment, it provides all the recapture and part of the profit.

In the example above the overall rate of 11% would be the rate of return on the total property investment if the value of the unmortgaged property would not increase or decrease. If there is a decrease, part of the income must be allocated to a commensurate amount of recapture, which reduces the rate of return to less than 11%. Conversely, if there is an increase in value, a gain would be realized in the reversion, and the rate of return would be greater than 11%. However, regardless of any potential value change, if the rate of

---

2. Depreciation of the wasting asset component of value (the building) in terms of dollars as of the date of appraisal normally is anticipated. Appreciation may occur, particularly in terms of future dollars.

11% reflects the action of typical buyers of that particular type of real estate, it is a valid overall capitalization rate applicable to like property.

The critical factors in any capitalization method—amount, time, yield, and provision for recapture—are inherent in the overall rate, but they are not separately analyzed or quantified in the process by which an overall rate is extracted from market sales and used in direct capitalization. An overall rate thus derived is independent of any prescribed income pattern. There are alternate capitalization methods in which the components of an overall rate are separately identified.

After appropriate research in the execution of an appraisal assignment, the appraiser forms certain basic assumptions as to the critical factors of amount, time, and yield as they relate to anticipated income for the property being appraised. When these basic assumptions, reflecting judgment decisions of the appraiser, conform to the inherent assumptions of a specific capitalization method and technique, these procedures are appropriately selected for use in the income approach. A properly selected capitalization procedure should not be changed without a corresponding change in some basic assumption unless the alternate procedure is also consistent with available data and projected income patterns.

In its most persuasive form, the capitalization process comprises an analysis of the property being appraised as an investment opportunity. To one investor, the most important question may be: What are the prospects for yield on the cash (or equity) investment? Clearly, the potential reward, in amount, time, and yield, must be attractive in the light of management burden and the risk of error in projecting the benefits of ownership, and it must compare favorably in yield and benefits with alternative investment opportunities available. Other investors may favor certainty, security, regularity, or other factors.

The overall rate at which comparable properties have been bought or sold is factual support of a market capitalization rate acceptable to typical prospective purchasers, even though rates of return to specific components of the investment—that is, land and building or mortgage and equity—are not identified.

Rationalization of this overall rate, in terms of amount, time, and yield of the anticipated net income, makes possible selection of a capitalization method suitable to the property being appraised, as demonstrated in this and succeeding chapters.

INFLUENCE OF INCOME TAX BENEFITS

Certain types of property may attract purchasers in high income-tax brackets who, because of tax benefits of ownership or prospect of capital gain, buy on the basis of what appears to be a low overall rate and a low return on their equity purchase funds. Such rates may not be an indication of capitalization rates currently applicable to such properties. However, they are valid if there are sufficient potential buyers in this category to constitute a market.

In the extraction of rates from market sales, the appraiser seeks to identify sales that reflect the impact of tax considerations, recognizing that the effect of such considerations is inherent in the derived rates. The possibility of changes in tax laws is of interest to the appraiser to the extent that impending changes may affect investor attitudes and rate requirements and hence the investment value of income-producing real estate.

RISK AND RECAPTURE RATES

The result of subtracting expense from income is net operating income (NOI or NIBR). This net income projection provides for return on, and provision for recapture of, invested capital.

Land, which generally is not subject to depreciation, usually can be leased and sold on the basis of an appropriate rate of return, reflecting the risk of ownership. Land improved with a building often sells on the basis of a higher rate than for land alone. Because there is no reason to believe that the building itself should command a higher rate of return than the land, the difference between the land rate and the combined land and building rate must represent an addition, or a surcharge, providing an annual margin to compensate for the anticipated risk of depreciation inherent in the building. This margin provides for recovery of capital invested in the building; it has traditionally been referred to as recapture. The amount of this annual capital recovery is related to the building value by the recapture rate.

An investor in income-producing property anticipates receiving a return *on* invested capital and eventual recovery *of* the invested capital. When the investment includes improvements that may depreciate with the passage of time, recovery of this portion of the investment may be projected from annual net income over the remaining productive life of the improvements. With proper maintenance, well-constructed buildings are not subject to rapid physical deterioration. A building ceases to be productive more frequently due to a combination of functional or economic obsolescence than due to physical deterioration. Consequently, an anticipated recapture period may be referred to as estimated remaining economic life. This remaining economic life concept, converted to an annual percentage, has traditionally been used to provide the basis for computation of recapture in terms of dollars per year.

Remaining economic life, like remaining physical life, is difficult to estimate. Consequently, investors and appraisers have gradually come to look on *remaining economic life as the period over which an investor would expect to recapture the investment.* This still poses a problem because prudent investors do not agree on the length of time in which a particular building investment should be recaptured. Accordingly, the annual recapture rate is less frequently related to a specific remaining economic life estimate and more often considered simply as an annual loading rate[3] providing an additional return to compensate for the relative risk of future depreciation. Conversely, prospects of future appreciation might be considered by the investor as a favorable factor reducing the risk rate.

This annual loading rate is derived from an analysis of market sales and is referred to as surcharge recapture. This surcharge may be converted to reflect a specific period over which the prudent investor presumably expects to recapture the investment; or it may be recognized simply as a market indicated loading, added to the risk rate, without conversion to any implied period of time.

EXTRACTING RATES FROM MARKET DATA

The appropriate rates to employ in an appraisal of market value are rates that reflect market action. Investors may rationalize investment

---

3. An annual addition or surcharge added to the risk rate.

decisions in diverse ways, but their collective action creates the market. Accordingly, the appraiser makes use of market data to extract current rates and to identify trends that may be reflected in future market changes.

Sales may be analyzed to indicate the current rate of return necessary to attract investment capital to a particular class of real estate. Such analysis is made within the concept of a capitalization method that involves assumptions that fit the property. The extracted rate may then be used to derive a value indication for a similar property being appraised, provided the capitalization method employed is the same as that within which the rate was extracted.

Available procedures for extracting or analyzing rates include direct sale comparisons in terms of dollar components of the income stream and use of the band of investment procedure in terms of rates. The band of investment procedure develops, or breaks down, a weighted average of the rates applicable to components of the capital structure of an investment. Components that make up the capital structure of a real estate investment may consist of land and building, mortgage(s) and equity, leased fee and leasehold estates.

EXTRACTION OF RECAPTURE RATE FROM A SALE

These facts apply to a 10-year-old building:

Sale price	$400,000
Net income	$ 44,000

In the judgment of the appraiser, after a market analysis of vacant land sales, the price may be allocated:

Land	$ 80,000
Building	320,000
Sale price	$400,000

The overall capitalization rate reflected by this sale is 11%.

$$\frac{\$ 44,000}{\$400,000} = .11$$

If the annual rate of return *on* investments in similar properties is believed to be 9%, the 11% overall rate at which the property was sold may be analyzed, within the concept of straight capitalization with straight-line or surcharge recapture.

Net income before provision for recapture		$44,000 per year
Sale price (investment in land and building)	$400,000	
Rate of return *on* land and building	× .09	
Less dollar return *on* land and building		−36,000 per year
Available for recapture		$ 8,000 per year
Ratio of recapture installment to building value:		

$8,000 ÷ $320,000 = .025

Recapture rate demonstrated is
2.5% per year.

In accordance with this recapture rate, the $44,000 net income before provision for recapture is allocated:

	Rate	Value	Income
Return *on* land investment	9.0% ×	$ 80,000 =	$ 7,200
Return *on* building investment	9.0% ×	320,000 =	28,800
Recapture *of* building investment	2.5% ×	320,000 =	8,000
Total		$400,000	$44,000

This method of sale analysis, based on a straight capitalization concept, assumes that the typical buyer is one who would purchase this type of property for cash on the basis of a 9% return on invested capital after a provision for recapture of the building investment at the rate of 2.5% per year.

A recapture rate thus obtained does not in itself reveal the remaining life expectancy of the building. If future net income is expected to decline as a result of building depreciation, the net income of $44,000 may be viewed as the first-year income level, and the annual building recapture of $8,000 might be interpreted as a provision for gradual recovery of the $320,000 building value over a 40-year life. Alternately, if market research indicates that net operating income is not expected to decline, the $44,000 figure could be viewed as a stabilized annuity. According to annuity tables, the recapture rate of 2.5% in company with a 9% interest rate would then suggest a recapture period of approximately 18 years.[4] Thus the recapture rate may be related to a remaining economic life estimate and a pattern of projected income, or it may be considered simply as a market indicated surcharge without rationalization in terms of years or income pattern.

In a strict sense remaining economic life means the period over which a property earns interest on the land plus a return attributable to the improvements. Use of a surcharge recapture rate implies a distinction between remaining economic life and the investor's concept of an acceptable capital recapture period. An investor may be influenced to accept a shortened or extended investment recapture period because of governmental or economic factors, contemporary investment standards, or inflationary or deflationary prospects.

Appraisers who follow their past work and test market reactions may find that a building to which a remaining economic life of 40 years was assigned 20 years ago still has a remaining economic life in excess of 20 years, as tested in the market today. This is not difficult to explain when the recapture rate is recognized as a surcharge added to the risk rate to reflect market evidence rather than considered to be a direct reflection of a specific economic life projection. The economic life of the building in question could also have been extended by renovation, by capital expenditures, or by other environmental or economic changes since the original projection.

RISK RATE SELECTION USING BAND OF INVESTMENT

Another method of analysis, or rationalization of the overall rate of 11% indicated by the sale ($44,000 income ÷ $400,000 sale price), is use of the band of investment.

The risk rate developed by application of the band of investment is a synthesis of equity and mortgage interest rates that market data

---

4. $44,000 net income, present value of ordinary annual annuity for 18 years, 9% interest; factor 8.7556 (Appendix B, 9% Table, Column 5): $44,000 × 8.7556 = $385,246; plus reversion of land value at $80,000 in 18 years, 9% interest, factor .2120 (Appendix B, 9% Table, Column 4): $80,000 × .2120 = $16,960.

disclose as applicable to comparable properties. The rate developed is a weighted average, the weighting being for the respective portions of the value represented by the mortgage and equity positions; or bands of investment.

Assume that the currently available market interest rate is 8.5% for a 75% mortgage on the type of property being appraised, and equity investors may be attracted by a 10.25% return *exclusive* of provision for recapture. The composite property rate of return is:

	Portion of Value		Interest Rate		Weighted Contribution
Mortgage	.75	×	.085	=	.0638
Equity	.25	×	.1025[a]	=	.0256
Property	1.00	×	risk rate	=	.0894 (say) 8.9%

[a]Since equity investment is typically related to a dividend or cash flow rate after debt service or to a projected equity yield rate (internal rate of return), the *equity interest rate,* as a component of the equity return, is seldom quantified, although it may be derived from a sale analysis when the mortgage interest rate and the property risk rate are known or assumed. The procedure is demonstrated later in this chapter under the heading Equity Interest Rate Extraction from Market Sales.

The above 8.9% rate includes no provision for recapture of invested capital and is applicable to a net income projection from a property *after* provision for recapture. It may be applied to the estimated net income (after deducting provision for recapture) from a similar property being appraised to translate that income into a value estimate for the property.

The 2.1% differential between the 8.9% interest derived in the foregoing example and the 11% overall rate reflected by the sale is imputable to recapture and/or any anticipated increase or decrease in the value of the total property during the mortgage term. This change in property value may result from changes in the land or building components or in both. The traditional concept of a stable land value and a depreciating building value may be reflected in a recapture rate applicable only to the building investment. A change in property value, caused by changes in one or more components of that value, may be expressed as a percentage of the property value or in terms of separate percentages applicable to, and reflecting changes in, the value of the separate components that make up the property value.

EQUITY DIVIDEND RATE SELECTION
USING BAND OF INVESTMENT

Overall rates may be extracted from market sales and combined with actual or typical mortgage terms to derive the equity dividend rate necessary to attract investment capital. This procedure represents another application of the band of investment technique which is used extensively. The mortgage debt service rate includes both interest and recapture (amortization) of the mortgage. The portion of NOI allocated to debt service constitutes an annual cash flow to the mortgage component of the capital structure. The equity dividend rate pertains to the remainder of the net income, which is the anticipated cash flow to the equity investment. The 11% overall rate (reflected by the sale property) may be analyzed in conjunction with known or assumed mortgage financing (25-year monthly payment loan at 8.5%) to develop the equity dividend, or cash flow, rate of the sale.

	Portion of Value		Rate		Weighted Contribution
Overall property return	1.00	×	.1100	=	.1100
Less mortgage debt service	−0.75	×	.0966[a]	=	.0725
Equity return	0.25	×	equity rate	=	.0375
Equity dividend rate		=	$\frac{.0375}{.25}$ = .1500[b] or 15%		

---

[a]Annual mortgage payment, 8.5% per annum interest and complete amortization of mortgage in 25 years. The above annual rate, .0966, is based on monthly payments and is commonly referred to as the mortgage constant. Charles B. Akerson, *Study Guide: Course 1/b, Capitalization Theory & Techniques* (Chicago: American Institute of Real Estate Appraisers, 1977), p. T-20, col. 7.
[b]Anticipated cash flow (or dividend) to the equity after mortgage payments

$$\frac{\$44,000 - \$28,980}{\$100,000 \text{ equity}} = .1502$$

This calculation is based on the following factual data:

Value	$400,000
Mortgage	−300,000
Equity	$100,000

Mortgage debt service: $300,000 × .0966 = $28,980
Net income before debt service: $44,000

This is the annual rate of return to equity reflected by the amount and terms of sale. When sufficient market evidence is available to lead to a conclusion concerning the equity dividend rate necessary to attract equity capital, this information may be combined with amount and terms of available financing to derive the probable market value of a property being appraised. This procedure is demonstrated in Chapter 21 under Investors' Approach to Capitalization.

OVERALL RATE SELECTION USING BAND OF INVESTMENT

If the available mortgage terms are known, the debt service or mortgage constant can be calculated, and if the equity dividend rate required to attract equity capital is known or can be estimated, the overall rate applicable in direct capitalization may be computed, using the following relationship:

Mortgage	× mortgage constant	= debt service
Equity	× equity dividend rate	= cash flow
Property	× overall rate	= net operating income

By definition, the overall rate expresses the relationship between the net operating income and the property value. Assuming available financing for 75% of value with a mortgage constant of .0966 and an equity dividend rate requirement of 15% derived from market analysis, the overall rate may be developed:

	Portion of Value		Rate		Weighted Contribution
Mortgage	0.75	×	.0966	=	.0725
Equity	0.25	×	.1500	=	.0375
	1.00	×	overall rate	=	.1100
			OAR	=	11%

This overall rate provides for recapture of 75% of the investment in 25 years, plus a cash flow of 15% per annum on the equity investment. The eventual equity yield rate will be greater than 15% if the value of the property declines less than 75% in 25 years. If the property value declines more than 75% in 25 years, the equity yield rate will be less than 15%.

Thus the 11% overall rate has been synthesized from the currently obtainable market debt service rate and current cash flow requirements of equity investors. The validity of this analysis, or any analysis, depends on whether the built-in assumptions of the method and the rates used fit the time and amount factors inherent in the property being analyzed or appraised.

Different methods of capitalization or of capitalization rate analysis may be inappropriate for a specific property if varying values or rates result. If answers vary in one or more of the methods applied, assumptions were made that do not fit the property.

RISK RATE SELECTION BY DIRECT COMPARISON

With sufficient market sales data, closely comparable with respect to quality attributes and anticipated declining income pattern, the appraiser may develop rates that are applicable in straight capitalization with straight-line recapture. Each analysis involves the sale price, the net operating income, and estimation of a reasonable recapture period for the sale property. The risk rate reflected by each sale is extracted.

Net income before recapture		$44,000[a]
Sale price	$400,000	
Land allocation (usually by comparison)	− 80,000	
Building component of purchase price	$320,000	
Estimated remaining life (*n*)	40 years	
Indicated recapture rate (1 ÷ *n*)	2.5%	
Less recapture ($320,000 × 2.5%)		−8,000
Return on land and building		$36,000
Risk rate ($36,000 ÷ $400,000)		9%

[a]First-year income. See Chapter 21 for explanation of straight capitalization with straight-line recapture.

Thus a combination of 9% return *on* and 2.5% recapture *of* is developed from a market sale at an 11% overall rate. The sum of these two rates constitutes the building capitalization rate (9% +2.5% = 11.5%) and exceeds the overall rate because the overall rate is a weighted average of the risk rate applied to the land investment and the building capitalization rate applied to the building investment.

Land	20%	×	.090	=	.0180
Building	80%	×	.115	=	.0920
Property	100%	×	OAR	=	.1100 (11%)

The appraiser may accumulate a sufficient number of open-market property sales to establish the contemporary rates acceptable to typical investors for various types of property.

When such data is available and research is conducted effectively, the development of rates for capitalization is given factual support. Further, when the objective of the appraisal is a market value conclusion for the property being appraised, rate selection from the market is generally considered the best evidence in support of an applicable rate.

In the above development of the 9% risk rate, the overall rate of 11% is known and the building component of the sale price is \$320,000 ÷ \$400,000 = .80, or 80%. The band of investment technique, using percentages and rates in lieu of dollar amounts, may also be used to derive this 9% risk rate:

Overall rate	$1.00 \times .11$	$= .1100$
Less the recapture component		
of this OAR	$- 0.80 \times .025$	$= .0200$
Equals the risk rate	$1.00 \times$ risk rate	$= .0900\ (9\%)$

In this analysis the 2.5% recapture rate applicable to the building component of value is translated into a percentage of property value and subtracted from the overall rate applicable to the property. The remainder is the risk rate applicable to the property.

In both analyses above the risk rate was extracted within the context of straight capitalization and is applicable only when applied within this capitalization method.

Implied assumptions concerning remaining economic life or future declining income stream pattern may or may not be realized in future years. However, *if the property being appraised is similar to the sale properties, application of the extracted rates using the concept within which they were derived will reflect a valid indication of the market value of the property being appraised as indicated by the collective action of investors in the current market.*

EQUITY INTEREST RATE EXTRACTION FROM MARKET SALES

Within the concept of straight capitalization, the net income provides for return of the building investment plus return on the property value.

This return on the property value is at the risk rate, which may be related to mortgage and equity components of the property value in the form of the mortgage interest rate and what has been called the equity interest rate. Because investors think in terms of an equity dividend (cash flow) rate or an equity yield rate, this equity interest rate is seldom identified. However, it may be derived from an analysis of sales and then used in a band of investment with the mortgage interest rate to derive a property interest (risk) rate. This application of the band of investment technique has historically been presented in support of a rate to be used in straight capitalization. Although seldom used today, this extraction of an equity interest rate is presented here to help clarify the distinction between the historical use of this procedure and current applications of the band of investment technique based on equity dividend or yield rates.

Assume a property selling at $400,000 with the previous allocation to land and improvements and the same $44,000 net income, plus assumption by the purchaser of a $279,820 loan balance on an original 25-year, 9% mortgage with 20 years remaining. The building is a well-maintained five-year-old improvement, with an estimated straight-line annual recapture rate of 2.22% (45-year estimated remaining life). The rate of return on the $120,180 equity may be derived:

Net income before recapture	$44,000
Less recapture estimate (2.22% × $320,000)	−7,104
Return *on* total investment	$36,896
Less interest on $279,820 mortgage balance @ 9%	−25,184
Return *on* $120,180 equity	$11,712

Equity interest rate applicable in

$$\text{straight capitalization}\quad \frac{\$11,712}{\$120,180} = .0975 \text{ (say) } 9.8\%$$

A current equity interest rate thus extracted from market evidence could be used to derive a property risk rate in combination with typical financing.

Mortgage	75% ×	.09	(mortgage interest rate)	= .0675
Equity	25% ×	.098	(equity interest rate)	= .0245
Property	100% ×		(risk rate)	= .0920 (say) 9.2%

A lower mortgage interest rate would increase the extracted rate of return on the equity investment by increasing the dollars available for equity. Similarly, a higher ratio of mortgage value would reduce the amount of the equity and increase the equity interest rate. This demonstrates leverage in real property investment. Positive leverage is the advantage accruing to the equity position through use of purchase capital available at an interest rate below the rate of return available from, or applicable to, the property as a whole. An increase in the cost of purchase capital to a level above that produced by the investment creates negative equity leverage.

RATE SELECTION BY COMPARISON OF QUALITY ATTRIBUTES

For application of this procedure the appraiser will have developed a probable range of applicable risk rates by direct comparison from several comparable market sales. To resolve these indications to a single conclusion, the appraiser may consider each in relation to the requisites of a good investment.

This has the merit of involving the appraiser in a detailed consideration of factors affecting the relative desirability of the property being appraised as an investment opportunity. Although the procedure is seldom mathematically implemented, the concept is reflected in any analysis through which the appraiser resolves several rate indications to a selected conclusion. Reduction of this mental process to a mathematical computation may be accomplished by allocation of numerical values to selected quality attributes and using these to assign a quality rating to the property being appraised and to each derived rate indication. Among the attributes that may be considered are:

1. Reliability of the gross income prediction. How certain is it that the income will be forthcoming? Income is more dependable when the property is leased on a long-term basis to financially responsible tenants than when rented on a month-to-month basis to less reliable tenants.
2. Likelihood of competitive construction. Certain types of properties are subject to severe competition. If a property is located on a site adjacent to vacant land, there will probably be additional construction. This will result in competition that may tend to depress the net income from all the properties, unless

consumer demand correspondingly increases. But if the property is in a completely utilized, seasoned business location with strong demand, the possibility of competitive construction may be more remote.

3. Reliability of the expense prediction. Is there great danger of having expenses increased materially, or is there a fair chance that they will remain about the same or even decrease?

4. Expense ratio. If the expenses are low in relation to gross income, the quality of the net income may be better, because a moderate reduction in gross income or a moderate increase in expenses does not affect the net income substantially.

5. Burden of management. Even when real estate management is employed, a property that requires constant attention, because of either maintenance or rent collection problems, is less desirable than one that needs minimal management. A long-term lease that requires a tenant to take care of all repairs and to pay taxes and insurance presents a situation that is relatively free from this burden of management.

6. Marketability of the property. An investment that has marketability and liquidity appeals to a wider group of investors than one lacking these attributes.

7. Stability of value. The value or market price of a piece of real property tends to remain within a narrower range for longer periods of time than do most other commodities, such as a carload of hogs or wheat.

Ideally, the numerical values assigned to each of these seven qualities would total 100%, and an ideal property would receive a 100% rating. Consider four sales of comparable properties from which rate indications were derived:

Property	Sale Price	Net Income After Recapture (NIAR)	Actual Interest Rate (%)
A	$450,000	$38,250	8.5
B	405,000	37,660	9.3
C	430,000	38,700	9.0
D	360,000	36,000	10.0

These properties are now put to the test of quality attributes. On the basis of 100% for an ideal property, Property A rated 90%; Property B, 80%; Property C, 85%; Property D, 75%. To reflect relative quality, the actual interest rate is multiplied by the rating assigned.

Property	Actual Rate (%)	Quality Rating (%)	Indicated Rate (%) for Ideal Income
A	8.5	90	7.65
B	9.3	80	7.45
C	9.0	85	7.65
D	10.0	75	7.50

Within the above range, the selected rate for an ideal property might be 7.6%.[5]

The property being appraised is next rated on the basis of the same quality attributes. Assume the developed quality rating is 85%; then the applicable interest rate will be higher than 7.6% and may be ascertained by dividing 7.6% by .85, thus developing for this property a rate of 8.94, say 8.9%.

There is no uniform rate of return applicable to all income streams. Each property justifies its own rate, depending on its inherent elements of risk. Rates also may differ for similar properties in various sections of a city or in other parts of the country and vary from time to time even for the same property. This variation reflects basic principles at work in the economy and affecting the specific property, including the principles of change, supply and demand, substitution, use-density, and highest and best use.

As can be seen in the analysis above, quality attributes tend to overlap. The reliability of income and expense predictions may be covered in the income and expense analysis. Competitive construction and stability of value tend to overlap into the durability of income. The quality analysis by comparison of attributes helps the appraiser to consider and to justify selected rates.

RATE SELECTION FROM GROSS RENT MULTIPLIER

In the absence of expense figures, the market risk rate can be abstracted from annual gross rent multipliers if reasonable estimates

---

5. Selection is not necessarily precise, but a figure (perhaps the nearest one-tenth or the nearest one-quarter of a percent) that in the judgment of the appraiser reflects a typical rate indicated by the analysis.

can be made of long-term operating ratios, land and building ratios, and capital recapture periods for the comparable sales. The operating ratio (ratio of all expenses to income) may be based on the gross rent schedule or on the effective gross income if all computations are on a uniform basis.

Table 20.1 demonstrates that rates of return extracted by this procedure tend to follow a pattern confirming a current market rate requirement even when the gross rent multiplier, operating ratios, and land and building ratios may differ.

Table 20.1. Effect of Operating Expense Ratio on Gross Rent Multiplier

	Property		
	A	B	C
Sale price	$400,000	$480,000	$300,000
Effective gross income	64,000	88,000	65,000
Operating ratio, % of effective gross	35%	45%	55%
Capital recapture rate (40 years)	2.5%	2.5%	2.5%
Land ratio	25%	35%	50%
Building ratio	75%	65%	50%
Gross rent multiplier (sale price ÷ effective gross income)	6.25	5.45	4.61
Gross capitalization rate	16.00%	18.33%	21.69%
All expenses as percent of sale price[a]	5.60%	8.25%	11.93%
Overall capitalization rate	10.40%	10.08%	9.76%
Straight-line recapture provision, 2.5% times building ratio	− 1.88%	− 1.62%	− 1.25%
Resulting return on investment (risk rate)	8.52%	8.46%	8.51%
	(say) 8.5%	(say) 8.5%	(say) 8.5%

[a]35% × 16%; 45% × 18.33%; 55% × 21.69%.

A similar analysis applied in situations where sinking-fund or surcharge recapture rates are appropriate would support a similar conclusion.

Any selection of a rate by comparison recognizes the reaction of people in the marketplace. For instance, if a number of properties of essentially the same quality are selling for approximately $400,000 and have a net income around $44,000 before a reasonable provision for recapture, it is readily understandable that the desired overall rate of return for this type of property is 11%.

In any capitalization method sufficient sales should be analyzed to obtain a reliable indication for a derived rate. Sales of properties considered comparable should be those that reflect net income characteristics reasonably similar to those pertaining to the property being appraised. These characteristics should be consistent with the assumptions made for the appraised property as to income and recapture patterns, and extracted capitalization rates are then applicable to the appraised property within the framework of a capitalization method appropriate to these assumptions.

SPLIT RATES

The term *split rates* refers to the application of different interest (risk) rates to land and to improvements and is not to be confused with the application of a capitalization rate for improvements which differs from a land capitalization rate only because of the addition to the risk rate of a recapture component. The use of split rates was defended at one time on the basis that improvements are subject to more hazards than is land. It is now generally accepted that the land and the improvements are wedded in a single use which presumably will endure well into the future. Since the resultant whole property is bought and sold in the marketplace as a single entity, ascribing different risk to the two components is generally not significant. The loading or recapture rate applied only to the improvements provides the adjustment for any estimated risk differential.

Where a property involves two or more separate estates, such as a leased fee and one or more leasehold positions, the separate interests may properly be capitalized at different rates to reflect the different risks inherent in the separate ownership estates. These estates constitute separate marketable entities. Similarly, large projects such as planned unit developments may involve different rates attributable to components of the project. Again, such components would probably be marketable as separate estates. It is also proper to capitalize excess income that constitutes a lease benefit (an intangible property concept) at a rate reflecting the greater risk inherent in the excess income stream. In situations such as these, applicable rates may differ, but their use is not considered in the category of split rates as defined above.

SUMMARY

Interest and capitalization rates are fundamentally influenced by the quantity, quality, and durability or timing of prospective income and reversionary gain or loss. The quantity is the amount to be capitalized, which is the annual net income before deduction for recapture. The quality relates to the relative dependability of the income. The third consideration involves the estimated period during which the income is anticipated to continue.

Interest rates can be derived by the band of investment technique, direct comparison (extraction from market sales) or from gross income multipliers. A selection of rates thus derived may be resolved to a single conclusion through a comparison of quality attributes.

The appraiser researches comparable sales for market evidence of rates appropriate to the property being appraised, extracting gross income multipliers or overall rates. These may be allocated, on the basis of facts and judgment, into a risk rate and recapture rate acceptable to typical purchasers in the market.[6] The rates demonstrated by these sale properties may be analyzed for all categories of risk, and from such analysis a rate may be derived for the property being appraised reflecting its relative attractiveness as an investment.

In relation to capitalization rates and theory, rates necessary to attract investment capital to any specific type of real property are indicated by the collective action of investors in the marketplace. Their individual philosophies concerning return and recapture may vary widely, but if their collective action creates a discernible pattern in the market, the appraiser may identify and interpret this pattern in terms of rates that are applicable within any appropriate capitalization method. Using this same capitalization method, the rates may then be applied to the property being appraised to produce a market value estimate that is a valid reflection of market evidence.

It is now generally accepted that land and improvement are wedded

---

6. An overall rate may also be analyzed in terms of mortgage and equity rate components (see Chapter 22).

in a single use and usually share the same interest rate. However, for a property involving two or more separate estates, the estates may properly be valued at different rates of return to reflect the different risks inherent in the separate ownerships.

21

Straight and Annuity Capitalization

Capitalization is a procedure in the appraisal process by which the value of a property can be estimated from the quantity, quality, and durability (probable duration) of its net income expectancy. To convert net income estimates into an indication of value, an understanding of the available capitalization methods and techniques is essential.

The preceding chapter presented procedures for developing or selecting rates for use in capitalization. This chapter deals with the basic principles and assumptions inherent in developing a capital value through application of the selected rates to an income projection within an appropriate straight or annuity capitalization method. In straight capitalization, rates are applied directly to income projections to derive a value estimate; in annuity capitalization, factors (reciprocals of rates) are used to discount estimated future benefits to a present worth or current capital value.

STRAIGHT CAPITALIZATION

Straight capitalization in any form implies use of the basic relationship between income, rate, and value, expressed as

$$\text{Value} = \frac{\text{Income}}{\text{Rate}}$$

Within this concept are included capitalization in perpetuity, which assumes an unchanging capital value; direct capitalization, in which no specific provision for return of capital is identified; and straight capitalization, with one of three residual techniques, in which a finite life is recognized for the improvements and provision is made for a proportionate recapture of invested capital. Expanded straight capitalization provides flexibility in terms of the income projection period and in anticipated rates of change in the value of the land or improvements during this period.

Capitalization in Perpetuity

A capital sum deposited in a fixed interest account produces a consistent flow of dollars. Assuming the account is not terminated, this rate of dollar return continues indefinitely. For example, $5,000 deposited at 5% returns interest each year in the amount of

$$\$5,000 \times 5\% = \$250$$
$$\text{Capital value} \times \text{Rate} = \text{Income}$$

This may be expressed as $V \times R = I$; it is equally true that $V = I \div R$ and $R = I \div V$. Thus with any two quantities known, the third quantity may be computed. In the above example, if the income and rate are known, the capital value may be computed

$$V = \frac{I}{R} = \frac{\$250}{5\%} = \$5,000$$

This is the process of capitalization in its simplest form, utilizing an income and a rate to ascertain a capital value. In this situation the rate is the interest or risk rate and there is no time limitation on the investment return. Accordingly, an unchanging capital value is implied and the concept represents capitalization in perpetuity.

This concept has traditionally been considered applicable in the valuation of land because land is imperishable. When existing improvements reach the end of their economic life, the assumption is that a new structure or use will perpetuate income or amenities to the land in whatever amount is needed to support its value at that time. The capitalization rate, developed through market research, has traditionally been considered to represent only a return on investment, thus constituting an interest or risk rate. Capitalization of net income attributable to the land at this rate represents a capitalization in perpetuity concept. The risk of future value changes may be inherent in the rate at which the market sales were consummated, but in relation to other capitalization methods, the mathematics has been construed under the assumption that the rate represents return on an unchanging capital investment. In a relatively stable economy with a relatively constant purchasing power for the dollar, the inherent assumption of a continuing land value over a reasonable projection period was long considered to have acceptable validity.

Within this concept, a leased site producing an annual net income of $8,000, purchased for $100,000, reflects a rate of return of

$$\frac{\$\ 8,000}{\$100,000} = .08, \text{ or } 8\%$$

This rate may be used in the valuation of similar parcels of land in the same or a similar market. When there is reason to anticipate a change in the land value during a specific projection period, this basic risk rate may be adjusted to reflect the potential change, as is demonstrated later in the discussion of expanded straight capitalization.

Direct Capitalization

Direct capitalization is based on use of the basic relationship between net income and capital value interpreted in terms of an overall rate. As the name implies, the overall rate is extracted directly from market sales and applied to a net income projection for the property being appraised. The process includes no consideration of a time limitation for the income projection, and there is no attempt to analyze the overall rate in terms of its components. The procedure is:

1. Research the market for sale prices of similar properties for which the net income is known or can be closely estimated.
2. Using the relationship that $I \div V = R$, develop the overall rate for each sale.
3. From the pattern of rates thus derived, select the overall rate considered applicable to the property being appraised.

4. Using the relationship that $V = I \div R$, capitalize the net income projection for the property being appraised at the derived overall rate to arrive at a value indication through direct capitalization.

Direct capitalization is closely related to the market and is easy to explain and understand. When market evidence is definitive in support of an overall rate applicable to a property being appraised, direct capitalization provides an acceptable approach to a market value conclusion. Conclusions reached through other methods of capitalization may be reduced to an overall rate basis for comparison with competing investment opportunities in the market. Apparent discrepancies should be explained and justified. The extraction of overall rates from market sales is also the first step in extracting risk and recapture rates or equity return rates on a comparative basis from market evidence.

The percentage of property value represented by land plays an important part in analyzing capitalization rates. To review the example used in Chapter 20, a property (Property A) with a net income before recapture of $44,000 per year sold for $400,000, of which $80,000 was imputable to land and $320,000 to building. The risk rate was 9%, and the demonstrated recapture rate was 2.5% per year. Contrast this with a property (Property B) of the same quality and same durability of income, where the land is worth $200,000 and the building $200,000.

	Properties	
	A	B
Sale price	$400,000	$400,000
Less land value (by comparison)	80,000	200,000
Land value ratio	20%	50%
Balance to building value	$320,000	$200,000
Building recapture		
40 yrs. @ 2.5% per year	$ 8,000	$ 5,000
Return on land and		
building value @ 9%	36,000	36,000
Total net income required to		
meet the above conditions	$ 44,000	$ 41,000
Overall capitalization rate		
reflected by this net income		
projection and the sale price	11%	10.25%

Imputing the same quality and pattern to each income stream and assuming the consistent 9% rate of return and $400,000 sale price, Property B, with half the value in land, sold on a 10.25% overall rate; Property A, with one-fifth the value in land, sold on an 11% overall rate. This illustrates that despite the same sale price and risk rate, a difference in the ratio of land to building may result in different overall capitalization rates and reflect a different net income.

If these two sales are assumed to be at the same overall rate, the risk rates differ. For example, if each property involved the same $44,000 net income projection, analysis will disclose that Property B, with $200,000 in land value, sold on the basis of a 9.75%[1] rate of return instead of the 9% of Property A.

It may also be demonstrated that wide variations in age or in expense ratios may cause changes in the relationship between the rate of return and the overall rate. For these reasons, the direct capitalization method should be used only when the overall rate can be extracted from sales that are similar in investor motivation and financing and when the properties are reasonably comparable in age, operating expense ratio, and land-to-building ratio.

When these conditions are met, direct capitalization is applicable. Since it is easily explained and understood, it is a convincing method of capitalization.

Investor's Approach to Capitalization

Through sales and purchases, investors in real estate establish the market value of property. These actions create patterns in the market which the appraiser researches to extract current rates necessary to attract capital.

Many rules of thumb, from gross income multipliers to more sophisticated concepts, are used by investors. A cash flow (equity dividend) requirement is a frequent basis for attracting investment capital. As in previous examples, assume that annual net income before recapture is $44,000 and that typical equity investors are willing to purchase property of this type and in this location on the basis of a 13% cash flow to the equity investment. Maximum financing is $314,000, available at 8.5% on a 25-year monthly payment

---

1. $44,000 income − $5,000 recapture = $39,000; ÷ $400,000 investment = 9.75%.

amortization schedule. Under these circumstances, the probable market value of the property may be derived.

Maximum available mortgage loan	$314,000	
Annual net income projection		$44,000
Less annual debt service on $314,000 mortgage at available terms (factor .0966)[a]		−30,332
Available cash flow (dividend) to equity		$13,668
Capitalized at 13% to derive amount of equity capital attracted by this potential income stream ($13,668 ÷ .13)	105,138	
Total value of property to satisfy investor requirement	$419,138	
(say)	$419,000	

[a]Annual mortgage constant based on 25-year, 8.5% monthly payment loan, .0966. Charles B. Akerson, MAI, *Study Guide: Course 1-B, Capitalization Theory & Techniques* (Chicago: American Institute of Real Estate Appraisers, 1977), Page T-20, Column 7.

In this same situation the appraiser's investigation of available financing might not reveal a specific dollar amount but might reveal that a mortgage would be available at 75% of the purchase price. Using a band of investment technique, the same conclusion of probable market value may be derived:

Mortgage	.75 ×	.0966	=	.0725
Equity	.25 ×	.13	=	.0325
Property	1.00 ×	overall rate	=	.1050

$$\text{Probable market value} = \frac{44,000}{.1050} = \$419,047$$

(say) $419,000 (as before)

In the event of purchase at the indicated market value, the investor receives an annual dividend to equity consisting of the cash flow after payment of mortgage debt service. Some investors plan an investment holding period of not more than 10 years. In the above example such an investor would have the benefit of the dividend or cash flow for 10 years plus the proceeds of a resale of the property at the end of the period.

Investment (initial capital structure)	
Mortgage	$314,000
Equity	105,000
Total capital investment	$419,000
Mortgage balance in 10 years $310,000 × .8163[a]	256,303
Equity investment (unchanged)	105,000
Total unamortized investment in 10 years	$253,053

[a] Principal balance, 8.5%, 25-year monthly payment loan at the end of 10 years. L.W. Ellwood, *Ellwood Tables for Real Estate Appraising and Financing,* 4th ed. (Cambridge, Mass.: Ballinger Publishing Co., 1977).

Any amount for which the property could be sold after 10 years that is less than, or in excess of, $358,053 would represent, respectively, a decrease or increase in the realized equity yield to the investor from the 13% cash flow level. This is more fully explored in Chapter 22.

STRAIGHT CAPITALIZATION WITH STRAIGHT-LINE RECAPTURE

Straight-Line Recapture Concept

The building component of a real property investment constitutes a wasting asset. For this reason, an accounting principle is to recover, in some manner, its cost prior to the expiration of its productive life. The traditional solution has been to account for expiration of a fraction of historical cost with each passing year. The current year's revenues are charged for depreciation. Logically, the amount of such charge each year should follow some prearranged consistent pattern, rather than be varied to achieve a manipulated profit.

From an accounting point of view, when the building cost is incurred, management is forced to declare a plan of cost recovery. The practice is to make an estimate of the number of years the building will be serviceable. Each future year during that estimate of life will bear a predetermined fraction of cost which, in combination with other expenses, will be deducted from that year's revenue. A general assumption is that land has an infinite life and is not destroyed or consumed. Accordingly, it is not usual practice to ''recover'' its cost periodically.

Depreciation accounting is not a valuation process; it is a process of historical cost allocation. Appraisers recognize that regardless of the selected accounting method, as buildings grow older and deteriorate physically and functionally, the typical investor requires some addition to the rate of return to cover the increased risk of probable loss in the value of the wasting asset. However, although this has a relation to an anticipated future life of the building or other improvement, possible decline in value is frequently offset by fluctuations in land value, construction costs, and economic conditions. Any change in value frequently is different from that currently acceptable to investors as part of the overall market capitalization rate. This fact does not invalidate current value estimates based on rates derived from current market evidence.

In selecting a rate of recapture, the appraiser is not predicting that a property will have a specific remaining economic life. The rate selection reflects that research has revealed a market behavior pattern that, interpreted within the concept of the capitalization method selected, implies this pattern of remaining life.

The following is a simple example of straight-line recapture based on remaining economic life concepts.

Estimated remaining economic life	25 years	30 years	40 years	50 years
Annual recapture rate $(1 \div n)$	4%	3.3%	2.5%	2.0%

In the application of the straight capitalization method in the income approach to a value estimate, recapture is projected at this same rate to compensate for the possible annual loss in capital value. Thus the projected annual depreciation rate is added to the risk rate to arrive at the capitalization rate applicable to the net income imputable to the building. In the tabulation on p. 398 the building is assumed to represent 80% of total value, and the land, 20%. These computations demonstrate that the overall rate is affected by changes in the recapture rate applicable to the improvements.

	25 years	30 years	40 years	50 years
Estimated remaining economic life	25 years	30 years	40 years	50 years
Risk rate (return *on* investment)	9.0%	9.0%	9.0%	9.0%
Annual recapture rate (return *of* investment)	4.0	3.3	2.5	2.0
Building capitalization rate	13.0%	12.3%	11.5%	11.0%
Building component of overall rate (80% of total value at building capitalization rate)	10.4%	9.8%	9.2%	8.8%
Land component of overall rate (20% of total value at risk rate)	1.8	1.8	1.8	1.8
Overall rate	12.2%	11.6%	11.0%	10.6%

Under the straight-line recapture assumption, each annual recapture payment reduces the amount of the investment remaining in the property from year to year, with a consequent annual reduction in the number of dollars needed to pay the selected rate of return on the investment outstanding. Thus use of a straight-line recapture provision implies a future annual decline in net income equal to the number of dollars recaptured each year times the risk rate. This declining pattern is demonstrated later in this chapter.

Straight capitalization with straight-line recapture differs from direct capitalization. In straight capitalization with straight-line recapture:

1. The capital structure of the property (total investment) is recognized to consist of two components, land and improvements.
2. A finite life is recognized for the wasting asset (the improvements).
3. The overall rate is analyzed in terms of return *on* land and return *on* and *of* the improvements.

Application of Straight Capitalization with Straight-Line Recapture

The assumptions implicit in traditional straight capitalization with straight-line recapture are:

1. The portion of income imputable to land remains constant and that imputable to improvements declines in a fixed annual amount due to reduction of the investment through annual recapture.
2. Recapture is a constant annual amount over the remaining economic life of the improvements.
3. Return on the amount of investment remaining after recapture is received each year and hence follows a straight-line declining pattern.

To illustrate, assume a land value of $80,000, a building value of $320,000, a remaining useful building life estimate of 40 years, a 40-year income stream starting at $44,000 the first year, and a risk rate of 9%.

Assumptions essential to the validity of the arithmetic of straight capitalization with straight-line recapture are that the market value of this improvement will decline 2.5% of $320,000, or $8,000 each year for 40 years, and that $8,000 will be extracted from income each year to recapture this prospective loss in value. Because each $8,000 extraction will reduce the capital investment by that amount, return on the investment will decline 9% of $8,000, or $720 annually. Thus the building return component of the income stream will be $28,800 the first year and will decline $720 each year thereafter to the end of the 40th year, as shown in the following tabulation.

Return on land value	$ 80,000	×	9% =	$ 7,200
Return on building value	320,000	×	9% =	28,800
Recapture of building value	320,000	×	2.5% =	8,000
Total first-year net income				$44,000

Table 21.1. Analysis of Declining Income Stream [a]

Year	Building Value	Land Value	Return of Building	Return on Building	Return on Land	Total Income
0	$320,000	$80,000				
1	312,000	80,000	$8,000	$28,800	$7,200	$44,000
2	304,000	80,000	8,000	28,080	7,200	43,280
3	296,000	80,000	8,000	27,360	7,200	42,560
4	288,000	80,000	8,000	26,640	7,200	41,840
5	280,000	80,000	8,000	25,920	7,200	41,120
		6th through 35th year omitted				
36	32,000	80,000	8,000	3,600	7,200	18,800
37	24,000	80,000	8,000	2,880	7,200	18,080
38	16,000	80,000	8,000	2,160	7,200	17,360
39	8,000	80,000	8,000	1,440	7,200	16,640
40	0	80,000	8,000	720	7,200	15,920

Total recaptured $320,000
Remaining value $ 80,000 (land)

[a]With end-of-year payments. Assumptions: Land value, $80,000; building value, $320,000; building life, 40 years; risk rate, 9%.

This automatic assumption that income declines $720 per year is equivalent to saying that from its $36,800-per-year starting point, the total net income imputable to the building drops 1.957% per year.[2] The rate of decline varies with different combinations of interest and recapture rates. Using i as the interest rate and d as the recapture rate, the formula for computing the rate of decline in the net income imputable to building investment is:

$$\frac{i \times d}{i + d} = \text{rate of decline}$$

As applied to the example, the computation is

$$\frac{.09 \times .025}{.09 + .025} = \frac{.00225}{.115} = .01957 \text{ or } 1.957\%$$

Accordingly, in the above application of the straight capitalization

2. $28,800 return on building plus $8,000 recapture = $36,800.
   $720 ÷ $36,800 = 1.957%.

method, the appraiser has assumed that the net income imputable to the building will decline at a rate of 1.957% per year.

To apply the straight-line recapture procedure correctly, the appraiser must believe that the net income will decline as the building gets older, and/or that the typical investor will require a return in excess of the interest rate on the investment imputable to the building to compensate for possible future depreciation. In other words, the building should be of a type that suffers future depreciation as assumed in the calculation, and a prudent investor would therefore expect an addition to the risk rate to compensate for this anticipated future loss in building value.

A pattern of a declining net income (particularly in terms of dollars as of the date of appraisal) is frequently typical of aging multi-occupancy real estate faced with increasing expenses of operation and declining desirability in the rental market. Figure 21.1 represents this situation.

Figure 21-1. Pattern of Declining Net Income Stream

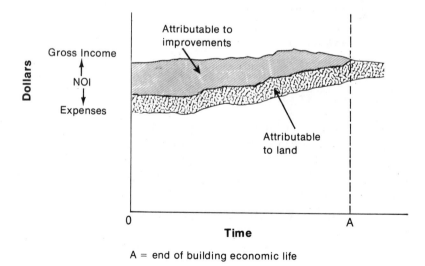

A = end of building economic life

If interest rates or land value increases, the annual return to land increases, narrowing the margin of return attributable to the improvements. Thus a decline in net income may precede a decline in gross, particularly if operating costs follow a typical increasing pattern as the structure ages. Expenses are also subject to the same economic pressures that may produce a dollar increase in gross income. As age and obsolescence reduce desirability in the market, increasing vacancy combines with an adverse effect on rental levels to squeeze the margin of net income produced by the property. Straight capitalization with straight-line recapture may appropriately reflect an anticipated future pattern of net income under these circumstances.

Straight Capitalization with Sinking-Fund Recapture

Straight capitalization is generally applied in appraisal practice with straight-line recapture. However, it may also be applied in combination with a sinking-fund recapture rate. When so applied, the recapture rate for a given period is lower than under the straight-line recapture concept, and a level income stream is assumed. The procedure corresponds mathematically to use of a Hoskold-concept annuity factor as illustrated under Annuity Capitalization.

THE RESIDUAL TECHNIQUES

The valuation of an income-producing property involves processing its projected net income potential by an applicable method of capitalization, in combination with an appropriate residual technique. There are three such techniques: land residual, building residual, and property residual. All of them may be used in straight capitalization, in annuity capitalization, or in mortgage-equity capitalization, as demonstrated in this chapter and in Chapter 22.

The term *residual* is used to indicate that in the last steps of these techniques the portion of the net income to be capitalized consists only of the remainder or residual portion attributable to return on the land value, the building value, or both.

In the *land residual technique* the building is valued separately, and the fair annual net return to the building value (return *on* plus provision for recapture) is deducted from the estimated net income attributable to the whole property. The residual amount is attributable to the land and is capitalized at the risk rate to arrive at an estimate of land value.

The value ascribed to the building, if it is a new and proper structure, is the recently completed cost, provided this cost is considered typical and all inclusive. If relatively new, it may be the depreciated cost as of the date of the appraisal. This estimate is subject to error if applied to older buildings because of the difficulty involved in estimating the extent of accrued depreciation. The greater the depreciation, the greater the possible error. It may be preferable to estimate the construction cost of, and the potential net rental income from, a hypothetical new and proper structure as the basis on which to derive a residual allocation of net income that will reasonably reflect the current value of the land. This use of the land residual technique, presented in Chapter 8, represents one approach to the valuation of vacant land.

In the *building residual technique* the land is valued separately, and the fair annual net return on the land value is deducted from the estimated net income before recapture attributable to the whole property. The residual amount is attributable to the building and is capitalized at the building capitalization rate to indicate the building value. The value assigned to the land may be based on recent sales of similar but vacant lots or computed by the land residual technique, assuming a hypothetical new and proper structure. This building residual technique was employed in illustrating straight-line recapture.

In the *property residual technique* the estimated allocation of the net income to recapture of the building investment is deducted from the total estimated net income before recapture and the remainder, which constitutes net income after recapture, is capitalized at the risk rate to derive a value indication for the property. This capitalization of net after recapture is generally acceptable when the improvements represent only a nominal part of value, as in some rural appraisals. However, when improvements constitute a major component of value, there may be some problem introduced in resolving the allocation of a resulting economic value for the improvements with the estimated value for which the recapture was computed. For this reason, straight capitalization with the property residual technique was frequently avoided in urban appraisal, and eventually direct capitalization replaced this technique in urban appraisal work.

Residual techniques are in fact mathematical procedures that enable the appraiser to use certain known or reliably estimated factors to find an unknown.

1.   In the land residual technique the known or assumed factors are net income before recapture, building value, risk rate, and the remaining useful life of the building. The unknown or residual factor is the land value.
2.   In the building residual technique the known or assumed factors are net income before recapture, land value, risk rate, and the remaining useful life of the building. The unknown factor is the building value.
3.   In the property residual technique the known or assumed factors are net income before recapture, risk rate, and the recapture amounts (typically based on an estimated building value and remaining economic life). The unknown or residual factor is the property value.

The general purpose of the residual techniques is to estimate the economic value of the property when a reliable estimate is available for only one component of the capital structure (land or building).

Application of Residual Techniques

Mathematics is a valuable tool in the appraisal process. However, no one has ever been able to devise an automatic, mechanical procedure for measuring the likes and dislikes of people. What people do depends on the many conscious and subconscious influences to which they are exposed. The various mathematical processes for capitalizing income help the appraiser to translate reactions of people into terms of value reactions as evidenced by the market. Appraising is an observational process. Observation indicates that people tend to act rationally. Under comparable conditions, their reaction and thinking tend to follow predictable patterns. However, this does not mean that in the appraisal process the appraiser follows the thought processes of specific investors or reproduces the resulting cause and effect relationships. The appraisal process does attempt to simulate market behavior in a pattern related to market decision processes and to reflect the collective action of investors in the market, thus producing a supportable conclusion of probable market action. Mathematical methods and techniques provide tools for implementing the appraisal process, but in the final analysis the validity of the answer depends on the appraiser's judgment and ability to use these tools effectively. Proper use of the residual techniques assists in the development of valid conclusions and provides rational support for their presentation.

Following are examples of the building, land, and property residual techniques. Each is illustrated, using straight capitalization with straight-line recapture. However, the residual techniques also are applicable with sinking-fund recapture and in other capitalization methods. This is demonstrated as each is presented and explained.

When applied to the same net income figure, different methods of capitalization may produce different answers unless the different inherent assumptions about recapture, income pattern, and allocation of net income to return on, and of, the investment are recognized by the appraiser and reflected in each analysis. However, use of different residual techniques within one capitalization method should produce the same value estimate. The only reason for choosing one of these residual techniques over another is to enable the appraiser to predicate the appraisal process on the assumptions that can be best supported.

Building Residual Technique

The land value first must be estimated from sales of comparable parcels, offers, asking prices, or from the capitalized value under a hypothetically proper improvement. The building value is then computed by capitalizing the residual net income after deducting return on the land value. The computations in obtaining an indication of value by straight capitalization, using straight-line recapture, follow.

In the building residual technique the value of the building is predicated on the quantity of its contribution to the net income, rather

Building Residual Technique
Straight Capitalization Method—Straight-Line Recapture

Estimated land value	$ 80,000
Net annual income projection (before recapture)[a]	$ 44,000
Less return to land, $80,000 @ 9%	− 7,200
Net income imputable to building	$ 36,800
Estimated annual depreciation or recapture rate, based on a 40-year remaining economic life estimate, $1/40 = .025$	
Capitalization rate for building income Risk rate (.09) plus recapture rate (.025) = .115	
Building valuation: $36,800 ÷ .115	$320,000
Land value	+80,000
Indicated property value estimate	$400,000

[a]First year.

than on the appraiser's estimate of its currently depreciated reproduction cost. This technique is particularly applicable where substantial accrued depreciation exists, the extent of which is difficult to estimate in the cost approach. This technique is also appropriate when the property being appraised includes improvements that are improper for the site.

Beginning with a $400,000 sale under the circumstances of the above example, the risk rate reflected by the sale may be extracted.

Annual net income before recapture	$44,000
Recapture (based upon a 40-year remaining life estimate) 2.5% × ($400,000 − $80,000), or 2.5% × $320,000	−8,000
Net income after provision for recapture	$36,000

$$\text{Risk rate} = \frac{\$36,000}{\$400,000} = 9\%$$

Such computations, based on market research (as noted in Chapter 20), provide the appraiser with supporting documentaion for the 9% rate of return as used in the example above.

Land Residual Technique

In the land residual technique the positions of land and building are reversed. This technique is applicable when the building represents a

Land Residual Technique
Straight Capitalization Method—Straight-Line Recapture

Estimated building value		$320,000
Estimated annual net income before recapture[a]		44,000
Return on and recapture of building value		
Risk rate	9 %	
Recapture rate (40-year life estimate)	2.5%	
Building capitalization rate	11.5%	
$320,000 × .115		−36,800
Net income imputable to the land		$ 7,200
Risk rate: 9%		
Land value ($7,200 ÷ .09)		$ 80,000
Building value		+320,000
Indicated property value estimate		$400,000

[a]First year.

proper use of the site and the building value has been reliably estimated. This usually implies minimal accrued depreciation with highest and best use. The anticipated annual net income attributable to this building value is deducted from the estimated net operating income produced by the property.

The residual earnings are considered attributable to the land and are capitalized to indicate the land value. The value assigned to the building is customarily based on an estimate of its current cost new, less any existing accrued depreciation, which should generally be minimal to validate this technique. The building should also represent the highest and best use of the land, and the value of either the existing building or a hypothetical building is assumed equal to its present reproduction cost including all carrying charges and profits.

The land residual technique must be used with care because errors can seriously distort the land value estimate. The residual income after return on, and recapture of, building value may include income that is imputable to components other than the land. These include items such as developer's profit or excess income resulting from an advantageous lease. A portion of the residual income, after interest and recapture of the building value, is imputable to a fair rate of return on the land. The balance may be attributable to the entrepreneurial contribution.

The four agents involved in the production of income—labor, capital, coordination (entrepreneur), and land—are all essential to the production of gross income, The land provides location and support. The structure furnishes the rentable space. The entrepreneur coordinates land and improvements into an income-producing property. Labor and utilities are necessary to build and operate the property. However, these four productive agents do not enjoy the same degree of preference in the distribution of the gross income. Labor (the salaries and wages of those rendering personal services) must be paid first. Capital must be considered next. This includes the interest on, and the eventual return of, the capital invested in the improvements. Third is the cost of organization and promotion. Finally, the residue of the gross income, constituting the earnings of the land, is capitalized to reflect the value of the land.

Because in economic theory land's share of the gross income is considered residual, some people maintain that land should always be made residual in the capitalization process. This belief is not valid. The use of the land residual technique may or may not be advisable, depending on the age and the character of the improvement and its suitability to the site. The appraisal of many improved properties by the land residual technique would result in a residual land value of less than the value of the land if it were vacant. This situation exists where the structure is not considered a proper improvement of the site.

Many buildings that at one time might have been the proper improvement (the highest and best use) for the land, with the passage of time become over- or underimprovements. Since use of the land residual technique in such cases produces a distorted land value, the building residual technique is indicated. This recognizes land value on the basis of its highest and best use, and the resulting residual building value estimate will reflect any loss in value due to the unsuitable improvement or accrued depreciation.

Application of the previously demonstrated building residual technique may be used to illustrate this situation. A new building may be erected at a cost of $280,000 on a vacant site purchased at its market value of $120,000; the net income projection is $32,400 per year; 3% represents a reasonable addition to the capitalization rate on the building as a provision for recapture of the investment in the building; and market research indicates 9% as an appropriate rate of return to attract capital. Accordingly,

Investment cost	
Land	$120,000
Building	280,000
Total	$400,000
Annual net income[a]	$ 39,600
Return to $120,000 land value @ 9%	− 10,800
Return to building	$ 28,800
Capitalized at 12% (9% + 3% recapture)	
indicates a building value of	$240,000
Add land	120,000
Indicated economic value of property	$360,000

[a]First year.

Through application of the building residual technique to a new property, this example illustrates that this building would not be the highest and best use of this site; and the $400,000 investment cost, minus the $360,000 economic value of the property, reflects a loss in value of $40,000 due to the improper improvement. If the $280,000 figure represented an estimate of reproduction cost new for an existing structure on the site, the $40,000 would represent accrued depreciation from all causes.

Property Residual Technique

In the property residual technique the provision for recapture is deducted from the net income projection, and the net income after recapture is capitalized at the appropriate risk rate to derive a property value.

Property Residual Technique
Straight Capitalization Method—Straight-Line Recapture

Estimated building value	$320,000
Estimated annual net income before recapture	$ 44,000
Less recapture on building value	
$320,000 @ 2.5% (40-year life estimate)	− 8,000
Annual net income imputable to the property (land and building)	$ 36,000
Property value ($36,000 capitalized at 9%)	$400,000

This technique is useful when the estimated value of the improvements to be depreciated and the recapture rate can be substantiated or when the value of the improvements is nominal in relation to the value of the land. The latter is frequently true in rural property valuation. When improvements comprise the major component of property value, as is typical for urban investment real estate, and when the economic value of the improvements may differ from that estimated in the cost approach, the basis for the recapture deduction may be difficult to identify, and successive recomputation may be necessary to achieve balance within the approach.[3] Because of this, the property residual technique is seldom used in urban appraising.

Expanded Concepts Within Straight Capitalization

The traditional application of straight capitalization with straight-line recapture involves identification of the components of an overall rate in terms of rates of return on, and of, the land and building components of property value. This may be demonstrated using band of investment to build up the overall rate.[4]

	Value	Ratio		Rate		Weighted
Land	$ 80,000	0.20	×	.09	=	.018
Building	+320,000	0.80	×	(.09 + .025)	=	.092
Property	$400,000	1.00	×	overall rate	=	.110, or 11%

Thus the overall rate of 11% constitutes a weighted average of the rates applicable to the land and building components of value. It reflects the previously developed property value estimate of $400,000.

In straight capitalization with straight-line recapture, the annual

---

3. For example, if the income approach value indication differs from the cost approach value indication, allocation of the income approach value between land and building components might reveal that the recapture dollars had been computed on the basis of a building value that differed from the income approach allocation. A recomputation would be necessary to ensure that recapture is correctly related to the income approach building value.

4. Land value, $80,000; building value, $320,000; remaining economic life, 40 years; risk rate, 9%.

rate of return on the building value has traditionally been increased by the rate of annual recapture to derive a building capitalization rate as shown above. The annual recapture implies a projected annual decline in net operating income and in building value. This concept may be expanded to reflect either a projected annual decline or a projected annual increase, and the concept may be extended to the land component of value as well as the building component.

Thus, within this concept of a land rate and a building rate applicable to these two components of value, the rate of return on either or both can be adjusted to reflect projected straight-line changes in value. These changes may be for the traditional economic life projection or for specific lesser projection periods. In either case, annual changes in value are reflected in an annual effect on the net income.

Assume that the property in the above example is in an aging area of declining values and the risk rate of 9% is derived from market sales of similar properties involving locations that are not experiencing a similar trend. A decline of 28% in property value (without allocation to land and improvements) is anticipated over an eight-year ownership projection period. The applicable overall rate for use in direct capitalization may be developed:

$$\text{OAR} = \text{Risk rate} + \text{average annual rate of change in property value}$$

$$\text{OAR} = .09 + \frac{.28}{8} = .125, \text{ or } 12.5\%$$

The annual net income of $44,000 capitalized at 12.5% results in a value estimate for the property of $352,000. This is substantially below the earlier $400,000 value estimate, reflecting the accelerated decline in value during an eight-year period of ownership. The value estimate derived here is equivalent to the discounted present worth of the eight-year declining income stream and the reversion of the depreciated property value at the end of the eight-year ownership period.

In an inflationary period of increasing property values, a rate may be similarly adjusted downward to reflect an increase in current market value due to anticipated appreciation over a short-term projected holding period. The effect on present market value due to any projected change is inherent in the adjusted rates which are then applicable to *current value estimates.*

Assume now that current land value has been reliably estimated at $80,000 and that land values are increasing as the area experiences strong growth. An increases of 50% in land value is anticipated at the end of a 10-year projection period while the improvements are expected to decline in value at the rate of 1% per year. Use of straight capitalization is indicated, and rates for land and building components of value may be developed and applied.

$$\text{Land capitalization rate} = .09 - \frac{.50}{10} = .04, \text{ or } 4\%$$

$$\text{Building capitalization rate} = .09 + .01 = .10, \text{ or } 10\%$$

Straight Capitalization—Building Residual Technique	
Estimated land value	$ 80,000
Annual net income before recapture	$ 44,000
Less return on $80,000 land value @ 4%	– 3,200
Net income imputable to building	$ 40,800
Capitalized at 10% building capitalization rate	
indicates a building value estimate of	$408,000
Land value	+ 80,000
Indicated property value estimate	$488,000

This $488,000 value estimate is substantially above the earlier $400,000 value estimate, reflecting the combination of increasing land value with a lower rate of building depreciation. The overall rate reflected by these assumptions may be computed:

	Ratio			Weighted
	$	Decimal	Rate	Contribution
Land	$\frac{80,000}{488,000}$	.1639 ×	.04 =	.0066
Building	$\frac{408,000}{488,000}$	.8361 ×	.10 =	.0836
Overall rate			=	.0902

$$\frac{\$\ 44,000}{.0902}$$ $487,805 (say) $488,000, as above

A projected decline in value acts to increase the applicable capitalization rate, and a projected increase in value acts to lower the rate. Thus in the above examples, anticipated depreciation is reflected by "loading" the building rate, and anticipated appreciation acts to "unload" the rate applicable to land. The absence of any loading or unloading of the risk rate applied to land in traditional straight capitalization reflects the concept of an unchanging land value.

The straight capitalization method provides flexibility in application within the concept of straight-line value change patterns for land or building components of the capital structure. Application may be over a remaining economic life estimate or for any specific period within this estimate.

Excess Land

In the valuation of properties with undeveloped land areas, the surplus land may be segregated and valued separately in the market data approach (see Chapter 15). The same concept and treatment of excess land extends to the income approach. If the burden of ownership for the currently nonincome-producing land constitutes an expense (e.g., taxes) in the operating statement of the property as currently developed, the net income projection is adversely affected. As a result, the surplus land, instead of adding its value to the value of the developed economic entity, reduces and distorts the indication of value by the income approach.

This may be avoided if taxes or other expenses attributable to the excess land are omitted in the computation of net income leading to a value estimate for the economic entity. The market value of the excess land constitutes an addition to the value of the developed parcel to derive a market value estimate for the entire property.

Contract, Economic, and Percentage Rents

Straight capitalization is normally applied with a net income projection based on an economic rent level. Appraisers frequently encounter contract rents that deviate from estimated economic rent. Percentage rentals are also commonly encountered in the appraisal of retail properties. Since a property must generally be sold in the market subject to the provisions of an existing lease or rental contract, the appraiser is obliged to consider any effect of these leases on the market value of the property appraised free of lease. It may be judicious to clarify with a client whether the objective of the appraisal is a value estimate of the leased fee or a value estimate as in fee simple. Any enhancement of value due to a favorable lease constitutes an intangible property concept and is separately identified in the appraisal analysis.

The contract rent may be more or less than economic rent. If the discrepancy is minimal, it may not exceed the accuracy involved in the estimation of the economic rental level, and hence the contract rent may be considered to represent economic rent. However, a substantial excess or deficiency in relation to the economic level is recognized by the appraiser for the remaining life of the lease or leases creating it and may be capitalized (discounted) to a present worth. This figure represents an addition or a deduction from a value estimate based on economic rent.

A tenant whose contract rent is less than economic rent will probably take advantage of this favorable position to lease maturity. In reducing the income difference to a present-worth figure, the discount rate usually coincides with that used in processing the economic rental into a value estimate. Theoretically, a higher risk rate is appropriate because the dollars involved represent the top portion of the total income. This is a matter of appraisal judgment in a specific case, but since the lower contract income level represents a lower risk than the higher economic income level, use of the discount rate reflects a practical balance.

Where contract rent exceeds economic rent, the dependability of the excess income must be considered. The credit of the lessee is an important factor. In the absence of top credit or other assurance that the excess income stream will continue to lease expiration, the risk inherent in this excess income is higher than for economic rent. The extent of this increase in risk (as estimated by the appraiser in the light of market research) is reflected in a higher capitalization or discount rate for this excess income. The value increment resulting from an excess rental is referred to as a lease benefit.

Percentage rental represents a special category of income, not fixed but sensitive to changes in business volume, due to general economic conditions, varying levels of competition, or other factors. Inherently less dependable than a fixed rental, the appraiser's percentage income projection is normally discounted to a present-worth

Figure 21.2. Applicable Rate Level Indications for Three Possible Lease Situations

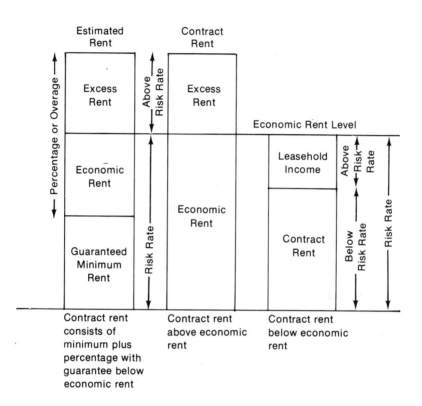

figure at a rate reflecting the increased risk. In situations where the guaranteed contract rental is very low or where there is no fixed rental stipulated in the lease, all or part of percentage rent may be included in the estimate of economic rent and may be treated as such.

Where percentage leases are encountered, the total net income projection may involve three components with three levels of risk. A guaranteed minimum fixed rental is normally below the economic rental level and represents a well-secured contract rental with minimum risk. The percentage income up to the economic rent level involves a little more risk because the tenant is entitled to continue occupancy even if, for some reason, this income ceases. Estimated percentage rental in excess of economic rent represents an even more vulnerable income stream, the level of which may fall rapidly with any decline in business volume (e.g., if percentage rental is being paid on the top 20% of business volume, a 10% decline in volume results in a 50% decline in percentage rental).

In such a situation in the appraisal of income-producing real estate, the appraiser analyzes the income projection and considers the relative risks applicable to each component. The rate selected for application to the guaranteed rental reflects a judgment decision. Percentage income above economic rent is capitalized at a higher rate which reflects the appraiser's estimate of the level of risk involved in the projection (see Figure 21.2).

ANNUITY CAPITALIZATION

Straight capitalization methods employ rates to develop an estimate of capital value; annuity capitalization uses present worth factors. Application of these factors to projections of future benefits, in terms of dollars at specific points in time, produces a discounted present worth or current capital value estimate. The compound interest tables consist of six functions of a dollar as explained in the introduction to Appendix B. The two tables essential to the discounting process are the present worth of 1[5] and the present worth of 1 per period.[6] Factors from the latter table may be applied to a periodic payment of income to derive the present worth of this income stream for a specific period at a selected discount rate that reflects the risk inherent in receipt of the projected payments. Factors from the present worth of one table are used to derive the present worth of future benefits to be received in single sums such as a reversion.

In the use of these factors a separate recapture rate need not be estimated because each factor includes provision for return of principal or recapture of the capital investment. The amount recaptured is the investment in the right to receive the income, only indirectly related to depreciation of the physical structure that is responsible for production of the income.

---

5. Column 4 Table, Appendix B.
6. Column 5 Table, Appendix B.

It is helpful in understanding annuity capitalization to understand the implications of the above statements. The annuity factor (present worth of 1 per period) and the partial payment factor (mortgage constant or payment that will amortize and pay interest on an investment of one over a specific payment period) are reciprocals. That is, the numeral 1 divided by either factor will equal the other factor. Using I to represent the interest rate, this may be expressed

Partial payment factor[7] $\quad = \quad 1 +$ Sinking-fund factor at I

Annuity present worth factor[8] $\quad = \quad \dfrac{1}{1 + \text{Sinking-fund factor at } I}$

Thus the mortgage constant consists of the interest rate plus the sinking fund factor at the same rate. Accordingly, payments made on a constant payment amortizing mortgage provide recapture of the capital amount in a sinking-fund pattern at the mortgage interest rate and, at the same time, include interest on the declining mortgage balance. Reference to any such mortgage repayment schedule confirms that early payments are principally mortgage interest but that the portion of each payment representing repayment of the mortgage (amortization) increases at an increasing rate until the final payment consists almost entirely of amortization.

A lender making a mortgage is, in effect, buying an annuity income stream consisting of the mortgage payments. The amount of the mortgage represents the present worth of the right to receive this annuity income. This is equivalent to an investor's purchase of the right to receive an income stream such as a projected net lease rental. The mortgage lender's recapture of invested capital through the mortgage payments is inherent in the partial payment factor. Recapture is also inherent in the annuity present worth factor so that an investor paying the discounted present worth for the right to receive a future income stream recaptures this investment and receives interest on the declining balance. In each case the recapture pattern is that of a sinking-fund accumulating at the interest rate.

---

7. Column 6 Table, Appendix B.
8. Column 5 Table, Appendix B.

Application of Hoskold Annuity (Sinking-Fund) Capitalization

Annuity capitalization using Hoskold annuity factors corresponds to straight capitalization with sinking-fund recapture and thus provides a transition from straight to annuity capitalization concepts. Straight capitalization with sinking-fund recapture differs from the same method using straight-line recapture only in that the sinking-fund factor (expressed as a rate) is substituted for the straight-line recapture rate to derive the building rate. Because of this procedural identity, these two applications of the straight capitalization method are presented below in a parallel pattern. The essential identity of the second procedure with Hoskold annuity capitalization is then demonstrated.

Assume a property with a net income projection of $44,000 per year, a selected risk rate of 9% per year, a land value estimate of $80,000, and an estimated remaining economic life or projection period of 40 years.

Straight Capitalization

With Straight-Line Recapture		With Sinking-Fund Recapture	
Net income	$ 44,000		$ 44,000
Return on land value at 9%	− 7,200		− 7,200
Net return imputable to building	$ 36,800		$ 36,800
Risk rate	.090	Risk rate	.0900
Recapture rate, 40 years	.025	Recapture rate using a sinking-fund factor for 40 years at an assumed safe rate of 5%[a]	.0083
Building capitalization rate	.115	Building capitalization rate	.0983
Building return capitalized at 11.5%	$320.000	Building return capitalized at 9.83%	$374,364
Add back land value	+80,000		+80,000
Indicated property value	$400,000		$454,364
			(say) $454,000

[a]Factors for annual compounding at selected "safe" rates from sinking fund tables. See Appendix B, 5% Table, Column 3. "Safe" rates, such as those for United States Government bonds, vary with the times and the money market.

The resulting value indication exceeds that derived by straight capitalization with straight-line recapture because of a change in the basic assumption of a declining income stream to the assumption of a level income stream and sinking-fund recapture. The assumption that recapture installments will be deposited to accumulate at interest is not generally considered typical of investor behavior. Since recapture is deferred, net income remains constant and drops to zero at the end of the economic life estimate. This pattern is frequently inconsistent with typical experience. Consequently, the procedure outlined here is seldom encountered in current appraisal practice. Where such a net income pattern is apparent, as in the case of a long-term lease, use of annuity capitalization with the property residual technique is usually considered appropriate. As previously noted, annuity (present worth of one per period) factors include mathematical provision for recapture in a sinking-fund pattern; but this recapture is received periodically, and the concept does not envision the actual creation of a separate recapture fund as assumed above.

Although annuity capitalization using Hoskold factors is equivalent to straight capitalization with sinking-fund recapture, the application differs in that instead, of applying a risk rate plus a sinking-fund[9] rate to the net income attributable to the building, the reciprocal of the resultant rate is applied as a factor. This is the Hoskold annuity factor, and it may be derived by the formula

$$\frac{1}{\text{Interest rate + sinking-fund factor @ a selected ''safe rate''}}$$

To illustrate, assume a 9% per year interest (risk) rate and a 40-year sinking-fund factor at a 5% ''safe'' rate per year and substitute in the formula

$$\frac{1}{.09 + .00828^a} = \frac{1}{.09828} = 10.17501$$

[a]This is the sinking-fund factor (Appendix B, 5% Table, Column 3, 40 years).

This 10.17501 figure is the Hoskold factor for the circumstances of the preceding example.

---

9. Usually at a ''safe'' interest rate that is lower than the interest (risk) rate.

The similarity between Hoskold annuity capitalization and straight capitalization with sinking-fund recapture is demonstrated. Assume a net income of $44,000 per year for 40 years with a land value of $80,000, an interest rate of 9%, and a sinking-fund "safe" interest rate of 5%.[10] The two methods may now be compared.

Annual income	$44,000
Income imputable to land ($80,000 at 9%)	− 7,200
Income imputable to building	$36,800

Within the concept of straight capitalization with sinking-fund recapture, the "safe" reinvestment sinking-fund recapture rate (at 5% interest) is .00828,[11] which, added to the interest rate of .0900, results in a building capitalization rate of .09828.

Capitalized building value ($36,800 ÷ .09828) =	$374,440
Plus land value	+ 80,000
Indicated value estimate by straight capitalization with sinking-fund recapture	$454,440

Within the concept of Hoskold annuity capitalization, the net income of $36,800 imputable to the building is multiplied by the Hoskold factor of 10.17501 to achieve the same value estimate as above.

$36,800 × factor 10.17501	$374,440
Plus land value	+ 80,000
Indicated value estimate using Hoskold annuity factor	$454,440

The allocation of the $36,800 annual net building income to interest on, and recapture of, the building investment of $374,440, as indicated in the first computation above, is:

Annual interest ($374,440 × 9%)	$ 33,700
Annual recapture sinking-fund installment ($374,400 × .00828)	3,100
Total annual net income	$ 36,800

10. "Safe" rate fluctuates with economic conditions and may be disclosed by historical yields, such as those produced by United States government bonds.
11. .008278 is shown in Appendix B, 5% Table, Column 3, 40 years. Factor is rounded.

The $374,440 building investment figure cannot be justified mathematically unless a constant annual net income of $36,800 for 40 years is achieved. This income is necessary to provide interest at 9% per year on the building investment over the 40-year term and to deposit $3,100 each year in a sinking fund, which accumulates interest at a rate of 5% per annum, compounded annually.

In summary, the use of a sinking-fund procedure is based on the assumption that an investor is willing to place the level annual recapture payments in a safe, lower-rate, interest-bearing account that will grow to an amount equaling the original building investment at the end of the 40-year projection period. Thus in theory, at the end of 40 years, the investor has the land, a completely depreciated building, and the amount of the original building investment from the sinking fund. This is demonstrated in Table 21.2.

Table 21.2. Recapture of the Building Investment under the Sinking Fund Concept

Year	Building Investment	9% Return on Investment	.00828[a] Deposit	Sinking Fund 5% Interest on Balance	Sinking Fund Accumulation for Recapture[b]
0 (Begin)					$ 0
1	$374,440	$33,700	$3,100	$ 0	3,100
2	374,440	33,700	3,100	155	6,355
3	374,440	33,700	3,100	318	9,773
4	374,440	33,700	3,100	489	13,362
5	374,440	33,700	3,100	668	17,130
. . .					
40 (end)	0	33,700	3,100	$17,645	374,440

[a].008278 is shown in Appendix B, 5% Table, Column 3, 40 years. Factor is rounded.
[b]May be calculated directly from Appendix B, 5% Table, Column 2, amount of one per period (paid at end of year).

5 years $3,100 × 5.5256   = $ 17,129
40 years $3,100 × 120.7998   = $374,479 (Difference is due to rounding.)

The accumulated growth of the sinking-fund for any period can be ascertained by use of the factors from the table giving the accumulation of one per period.[12] The following tabulation is based on the

12. Column 2, any table, Appendix B.

assumption of deposits made at the end of the year. At the end of 10-year intervals, the accumulation is

Year	Percentage of Total Accumulated during 10-Year Periods	Percentage of Total Accumulated to End of Each Period[a]
10	10.4	10.4
20	17.0	27.4
30	27.6	55.0
40	45.0	100.0

[a]Example calculated from Appendix B, 5% Table, Column 2

$$\frac{\text{(10-year factor)}}{\text{(40-year factor)}} \quad \frac{12.5779}{120.7998} = 10.4\%$$

The annual allocation of $3,100 per year (.00828 × $374,440) from net income to sinking-fund recapture is constant over the 40-year period. Similarly straight-line recapture allocation is constant over the 40-year period but in the larger amount of $8,000 per year (2.5% × $320,000 building value).

This differential reflects the difference in income-stream patterns and contributes to the higher value produced by the sinking-fund procedure. This sinking-fund procedure is based on a constant income of $44,000 per year for 40 years, rather than an income that starts at $44,000 and declines $720 annually in accordance with the assumption of straight-line depreciation as illustrated earlier in this chapter.

In summary, the following assumptions are inherent in the Hoskold annuity method of capitalization, as well as in straight capitalization with sinking-fund recapture.

1. Net income over the projection period is assumed to be in equal amounts.
2. Recapture installments are in a fixed annual amount which is less than in straight-line recapture because the annual amounts are segregated to accumulate at a safe rate of interest over the term of the projection.
3. Interest is received each year in a constant amount based on the initial investment. (This reflects the fact that recapture is not received periodically, but is accumulating in a sinking fund to be received in a single payment at the end of the term of the projection.)

As for actually funding recapture installments, this procedure is seldom encountered except perhaps in the case of public buildings. Another view of the use of the sinking-fund factor is that, similar to the straight-line (age-life) recapture rate, it is simply a premium added to the risk rate to allow for future market fluctuations, and the funding of recapture may or may not be a physical act. This sinking-fund concept reduces the annual recapture allocation from income to a level below that of the straight-line concept and may be acceptable under circumstances where the latter concept is considered inapplicable.

Application of Ordinary Annuity Capitalization

Annuity capitalization may be combined with the residual techniques and applied in a manner similar to that demonstrated for straight capitalization in Chapter 20.

Annuity Capitalization Method—Building Residual Technique	
Estimated land value	$200,000
Annual net income projection before recapture of building investment	$ 42,000
Return on estimated land value (9% per year on $200,000)	– 18,000
Annual net income imputable to building	$ 24,000
Assumed remaining economic life, 20 years; interest rate, 9% per year. The present value of 1 per annum discounted for 20 years at 9% is 9.128.[a]	$219,000[b]
Residual building value, $24,000 × 9.1285	
Estimated land value as above	200,000
Indicated property value estimate	$419,000[b]

[a]Appendix B, 9% Table, Column 5.
[b]Rounded.

This technique might be applicable where the land value is a substantial portion of the total value of the property and the building is not new or is not the highest and best use of the land.

The land residual technique reverses the building residual procedure.

Annuity Capitalization Method—Land Residual Technique

Estimated building value	$400,000
Annual net income projection before recapture	$44,000

Interest and recapture on estimated building value:
Assumed remaining economic life: 40 years
Annual interest rate: 9%
Level annual amount necessary to amortize the
building value in 40 years and pay 9% interest
on the outstanding investment is the income
attributable to the building.

$$\text{Income} = \frac{\text{Value}}{\text{Factor}} = \frac{\$400,000}{10.7574^a} = \underline{37,184}$$

Residual annual net income imputable to return	
on the value of the land	$ 6,816
Residual land value: $6,815 capitalized at 9%	$ 75,700[b]
Estimated building value (as above)	400,000
Indicated property value estimate	$475,700

[a]Appendix B, 9% Table, Column 5, present value of one per annum.
[b]Rounded.

This technique is primarily applicable when the building is the highest and best use of the land, is new, or is being planned, and represents a substantial portion of the total value of the property, as assumed in the above example.

A third technique is the property residual technique in which the present value of the income stream for a selected period is added to the present value of the anticipated reversion of the property at the conclusion of the selected income stream (or selected investment life).

Annuity Capitalization—Property Residual Technique

Estimated land value (for purpose of reversion)	$100,000
Annual net income to property before recapture	$ 44,000
Assumed remaining economic life	20 years
Discount rate	9%
Present worth of 20-year income stream discounted	
@ 9%, $44,000 × 9.1285[a]	$401,654
Land reversion, $100,000 × .1784[b]	17,840
Indicated property value estimate	$419,494
(say)	$419,000

[a]Factor for the present worth of one per annum for 20 years, discounted @ 9%. Appendix B, 9% Table, Column 5.
[b]Factor for the present worth of one, 20 years deferred, discounted @ 9%. Appendix B, 9% Table, Column 4.

This application of the property residual technique is different from the application shown in Chapter 20 where the property residual technique consisted of capitalization of net income, after deduction of recapture, at the risk rate. Under this annuity capitalization, property residual technique, the land (or land and depreciated improvements) is assumed to revert to the owner at the termination of the income stream. This reversion is valued by discounting its then anticipated value to a present worth. The total value of the property is the sum of the present worth of the right to receive the projected net income plus the present worth of the reversionary interest. This technique is applicable where the property as improved develops its highest value, or where land and building values cannot be readily separated, or where the estimated remaining economic life of the property is relatively short. This technique is also basic in the mortgage equity method of valuation, in the valuation of leased fees, and for properties under long-term lease. It is the usual application of annuity capitalization.

This property residual technique may be used when property is subject to a relatively long-term lease that tends to support an income-stream projection for a specific period at an identifiable level or levels. In such a case, the projection period is usually the term of the lease or of the assumed income stream, and the reversionary interest consists of the value of the land together with the depreciated value of the improvements at lease expiration. The building component may be a substantial part of the reversionary value.

Assume, as above, a new improvement costing $420,000 erected on an $86,000 site, under a 15-year net lease at $44,000 per year, to a lessee with excellent credit rating. Since the risk inherent in this income stream is minimal, assume an 8% rate is considered appropriate in the existing investment market. On the assumption of a 40-year life and straight-line recapture, the building reversion at the end of the lease (25 years) would be

$$\$420,000 \quad \times \quad \frac{25 \text{ (years)}}{40 \text{ (years)}} \quad = \quad \$262,500$$

The total reversion of $348,500 ($86,000 land plus $262,500 building) may be discounted to a present worth at an 8% rate. However, if the 8% rate reflected market recognition of a lesser risk due to strong lease credit supporting the income projection, the reversion of a 15-year-older property without benefit of lease may justify a rate applicable to vacant properties of the same type generally, perhaps 1% higher. On this basis, if the appraiser considers 9% an appropriate risk rate applicable to the reversion, the indicated property residual calculation would be as follows.

Annuity Capitalization—Property Residual Technique
(Long-term Lease)

Estimated land value (at time of reversion)	$ 86,000
Estimated building value (at time of reversion)	262,500
Total value (at time of reversion)	$348,500
Annual net income projection for term of 15-year lease	$ 44,000
Annual discount rate on income stream	8%
Annual discount rate on reversion	9%
Present value of the net income for 15 years discounted at 8% is $44,000 × 8.5595[a]	$376,600[b]
Present value of the anticipated worth of both land and depreciated building at reversion (15 years hence) discounted at 9%, factor .2745[c]	
$348,500 × .2745	95,700[b]
Indicated value of property, as leased	$472,300[b]
(say)	$472,000

[a]Appendix B, 8% Table, Column 5.
[b]Rounded.
[c]Appendix B, 9% Table, Column 4.

The reversion at the end of 15 years may not actually conform to the figures projected, and the risk rate may change due to a different money market in 15 years. However, buyers and sellers today must reach decisions in the light of existing circumstances, and the appraiser endeavors to reflect the market created by their contemporary actions in the current value estimate. In this example, the economic value indication as leased ($472,000) is below the current estimated value of the land plus the building cost ($506,000). It would appear that the building does not develop the highest and best use of the site or it is leased below economic rent.

Features of the annuity capitalization method are:

1. Annual net income over the projection period is assumed to be

in periodic payments of stipulated amounts. These may be level, increasing, decreasing, or graduated, provided they occur at regular time intervals.
2. Recapture installments are relatively low initially, but increase each year.
3. Interest received each year on the amount of investment remaining after recapture follows a declining curve.

In the valuation of real property, it is customary to think in terms of annual statements of income and expense. Annuity capitalization typically conforms to this concept with annual discounting, using factors for ordinary annuities (payable in arrears). Rental incomes are usually payable monthly and in advance. However, there may be collection delays, owners typically compute profit and loss statements on an annual basis, and generally the potential error introduced through use of annual discount factors is within the accuracy of the judgment decisions involved in the total appraisal process. However, when considered desirable, monthly discount factors may be used, and these may be further refined through adjustment to represent annuities in advance.[13] These monthly factors are commonly converted to an annual basis for use with annual real property operating figures.

Selection of Methods and Techniques

No effort has been made in the preceding material to contrast the dollar results obtained by one capitalization method or technique with those obtained by another. Appropriate techniques, capitalization methods, and interest rates should be selected according to the type of property and the projected income stream and risk assumptions for the particular property being appraised. The appraiser decides which procedure may be the most suitable and the circumstances under which a particular capitalization technique should be employed.

For the appropriate use of the residual techniques, general

---

13. An ordinary annuity factor may be adjusted to become an annuity-in-advance factor through multiplication by the base. The base is 1 plus the effective interest rate $(1 + i)$.

guidelines are discussed in this chapter and in Chapter 20. The guidelines also apply to annuity capitalization.

1.   The land residual technique may be appropriate if the land value is not readily estimated from market data or if the result obtained from market data requires confirmation. Under these circumstances, the technique is applicable in connection with the existing building, providing it is essentially new, involves little or no accrued depreciation, and represents the highest and best use of the land. If the site is vacant, the land residual technique may be used in connection with a hypothetical building that is the highest and best use of the site to derive a land value estimate.

2.   The building residual technique may be appropriate whenever the land value estimate is considered dependable. The technique is applicable whether the improvements are new or old, whether they are or are not subject to accrued depreciation, and whether they do or do not represent highest and best use of the site.

3.   The property residual technique may be appropriate if the property being appraised is subject to a long-term lease, if the improvements are no longer new, or if a limited remaining economic life is projected for the improvements. The property residual technique probably represents the most typical application of annuity capitalization.

The variations among the capitalization methods—straight capitalization with straight-line or sinking-fund recapture, annuity capitalization with Inwood or Hoskold factors—may seem perplexing. However, each is predicated on basic assumptions about the property's characteristics, such as its age, highest and best use, and the durability and pattern of its prospective income stream. Therefore, the basis for the appraiser's choice of method is a belief that the property being appraised has characteristics that conform to those inherent in the method selected.

Indicated values that may be obtained by the various methods do not conflict when the methods are applicable to the property being appraised. The land and building residual techniques produce the same result if the method of capitalization is the same and there is consistent application of data. The building residual technique of annuity capitalization can be employed to produce the same result as the property residual technique. The result does not differ if the interest on the land is first deducted and the balance is capitalized, or if all the income is capitalized and the present value of the land reversion is added. Straight capitalization with sinking-fund recapture alternatively may be employed to produce an answer identical to the Hoskold annuity method because the two methods are the same in concept. Contrasting results from different capitalization methods using the same residual technique arise from their different inherent assumptions concerning income, how recapture is obtained, and on what amount of investment interest is being received. If the inherent assumptions in the technique used contradict those of the appraiser about the property being appraised and the projected income stream, the result is an erroneous indication of value.

In order, these are the considerations leading to the selection of a suitable method and technique, applicable in any appraisal situation:

1. The data available
2. The rate of return that is appropriate to attract investment capital
3. The capitalization method that conforms to the character and prospective behavior of income and the assumptions concerning recapture
4. The residual technique that is most applicable to the circumstances of the property being appraised

SUMMARY

Direct capitalization and straight capitalization using straight-line or sinking-fund recapture are methods that may be applied to the net income of properties in the income approach to value. These methods may be used either in processing net income into indicated value estimates or in extracting interest rates and recapture rates from sales of similar properties. The overall rate may be rationalized on the basis of a division into a rate of return on land and building, and a recapture rate to provide for anticipated depreciation of the investment imputable to the building.

The investor's approach to an economic value estimate may also be used to reflect investor attitudes. Under this concept, market value is equivalent to the sum of the maximum mortgage financing plus the equity attracted by the cash flow after debt service.

Straight capitalization, using a recapture rate to provide for anticipated depreciation, may be applied by use of the following residual techniques:

1. Building residual technique. This technique involves an allocation of net income to the land. The remainder is considered attributable to return on, and recapture of, the building investment and is capitalized into an indicated value of the building through use of the building capitalization rate. In most cases where land value can be adequately estimated by comparison or other means, the building residual technique is used. The value estimate produced by this technique reflects any under- or overimprovement of the site.

2. Land residual technique. This technique reverses the procedure used in the building residual techniqe. The net income is allocated first to the building, providing a return on, and recapture of, the estimated building value. The remainder is considered attributable to the land and is capitalized into an indicated land value. The land residual technique is used when land value cannot be supported adequately by other means or to provide confirmation of a land value estimate. It is generally most reliable when building value is known, usually when the building is new or nearly new and represents the highest and best use of the site. In conjunction with a hypothetical structure, the technique may be a basis for indicating land value. In applying this technique, the residual income to the land may, in fact, be imputable not only to the land, but also to entrepreneurial increment or developer's profit. Care must be taken that the portion of the net income assigned to these items is not capitalized into an indication of added residual land value.

3. Property residual technique. The net income after recapture of building investment is capitalized at the risk (interest) rate. This technique is applicable when the value of the improvements is nominal in relation to land value or when the improvement value estimate is reliable or conforms to the economic value indication by this approach.

Except where leases support contract rent for the period of projection, capitalization is usually based on economic rent. Where contract rent indicates a future income expectancy deviating from an economic rental level, the anticipated contract rental level is recognized for the period of the lease creating it. Excess rent develops a lease benefit, an intangible property concept with economic value that accrues to ownership.

Capitalization normally reflects a net income projection based on an economic rent level. However, since a property must generally be sold in the market subject to the provisions of an existing lease or rental contract, the appraiser is obliged to consider the effect of any leases on the defined value of the interest being valued.

Annuity capitalization in real estate valuation is a procedure for estimating the present worth of future benefits accruing to the ownership of real property. These benefits typically take the form of a projected income stream and reversion of a capital value at the conclusion of the projection period.

The projection period may reflect an estimate of the remaining economic life of improvements or the remaining term of a lease. Value is derived through the use of compound interest tables to discount the estimated future benefits to a present worth at the rate of return necessary to attract investment capital.

Annuity capitalization may be applied under any of the three residual techniques. Discounting is typically on an annual basis through use of ordinary annuity factors. When desired, discounting may be on the basis of a shorter time interval and on the basis of payment in advance rather than in arrears.

Recapture in ordinary annuity capitalization is included in the factor on the basis of a sinking fund at the discount rate and is realized in increasing proportions of each annuity payment. A variation of annuity capitalization involves the use of Hoskold annuity factors, which differ from ordinary annuity factors in the use of a different rate for the sinking-fund recapture and in the assumption that a sinking fund actually exists with recapture deferred to the end of the projection period.

22

Mortgage Equity and
Discounted Cash Flow

In this chapter the fundamentals of mortgage-equity analysis and the application of discounted cash flow procedures are presented and related to previously introduced capitalization concepts. Examples are provided to illustrate basic concepts and provide an introduction to their application in capitalization and investment analysis. The potential for additional applications of mortgage-equity analysis is extensive, and no attempt is made to duplicate the explanatory text in *Ellwood Tables* where mortgage-equity application in various facets of investment analysis is treated in greater depth.[1]

Discounted cash flow analysis comes within the concept of annuity capitalization applied to an income stream that does not conform to a set pattern and therefore does not easily lend itself to traditional ordinary annuity capitalization. Each of a series of projected periodic income estimates is treated as an individual reversion and separately discounted to derive the amount of its contribution to present value. The procedure is applicable to income projections attributable to the property or to any interest in the property on either a before- or after-tax basis.

---

1. L. W. Ellwood, *Ellwood Tables for Real Estate Appraising and Financing,* 4th ed. (Cambridge, Mass: Ballinger Publishing Co., 1977).

MORTGAGE EQUITY

The development of mortgage-equity analysis was intended primarily to provide a method of testing or analyzing value conclusions, and it provides an extremely useful technique for real property investment counseling. Overall rates are analyzed and related to mortgage and venture capital money markets. When these are properly researched and understood, a valid overall rate may be derived that is applicable in the capitalization process to develop an economic value estimate.

Reference to overall rate analysis in the above terms reflects recognition that changes in the cost of money affect real property market values. The impact of such changes spreads through all facets of real estate development and operation. A rapid increase in the prime rate for commercial funds may cause a withdrawal of funds from thrift institutions that supply mortgage money, thus decreasing the supply and increasing the cost of available mortgage capital. This increases the mortgage constant, which is a major component of the overall rate in market sales. At the same time, the cost of construction funds escalates, and the cost of such funds is a major indirect cost in real estate development. Increasing costs in all areas, including energy and operating expenses, increases the rent levels necessary for economic feasibility and may seriously affect market price levels and market activity. Accordingly, a method of market value analysis that reflects the requirements of mortgage and equity capital in terms of the overall rate offers the appraiser an effective analytical tool when the implications of its use are clearly understood and the concept is properly applied.

Basic Concept and Relation to Traditional Capitalization

In direct capitalization an overall rate derived from market sales is applied to a net income estimate to derive an indication of market value for the property being appraised. There is no division of this value in terms of a capital structure.

In straight capitalization the capital structure of property value consists of land plus improvements. Thus the overall rate is a weighted average of the risk rate, which is applicable to land, and the building capitalization rate, which is applicable to the improvements. The same overall rate, analyzed on the basis of a capital structure consisting of mortgage and equity components, becomes a weighted average of the mortgage constant and the equity dividend rate.

In straight capitalization a band of investment procedure may be used to synthesize the overall rate in terms of the risk rate and the recapture rate or in terms of the rate applicable to land and the building capitalization rate. In mortgage equity a band of investment may be similarly used to synthesize the same overall rate in terms of mortgage and equity components. Assume a property on which a 25-year, 8.5% monthly payment mortgage is available for 75% of value, and typical equity investors are willing to purchase on the basis of a 13% equity dividend (cash flow) rate. The overall rate at which the property may be expected to sell in this market is

	Value Ratio		Applicable Rate		Weighted Average
Mortgage component	.75	×	.0966[a]	=	.0725
Equity component	.25	×	.13	=	.0325
Property	1.00	×	overall rate	=	.1050
			R	=	10.5%

[a]The mortgage constant for a 25-year, 8.5% monthly payment mortgage. Charles B. Akerson, MAI, *Study Guide: Course 1-B, Capitalization Theory & Techniques* (Chicago: American Institute of Real Estate Appraisers), p. T-20, col. 7.

This analysis shows that any change in the mortgage money market or in typical investor expectations will act to change the overall rate. Since a change in the overall rate reflects a change in the probable price at which a property will sell, the market value of investment real estate is affected by the availability and terms of mortgage money as well as by changes in the rate of return necessary to attract equity capital.

A mortgage is normally the major component of the capital structure; typically, available mortgage terms can usually be identified. Estimation of the applicable equity dividend rate involves market research leading to a judgment decision; but since the equity represents only a fraction of the total investment, the effect on the overall rate is correspondingly reduced.

Recognition of the impact of available financing on market value is fundamental to understanding mortgage equity, but the concept extends beyond this basic synthesis of an overall rate. Recognition of the impact of potential gain or loss in the value of the equity investor's position represents an added consideration and permits a more sophisticated analysis of potential investment return over typically anticipated periods of ownership.

Equity Yield Rate

In all capitalization methods the appraiser discounts anticipated future benefits to derive a present value estimate. The benefits available to an equity investor may be viewed as:

1. A series of periodic cash dividends extending throughout the period of ownership and consisting of the net income remaining after payment of debt service.
2. Any reversion of the proceeds of sale in excess of the balance due on the mortgage at the end of the period of ownership.

The amount of the second benefit is affected by mortgage amortization and by any change in the market value of the property during the period of ownership. Mortgage amortization enhances equity through reduction in mortgage indebtedness. For example, a property was acquired for $400,000, subject to a $300,000 fully amortizing 25-year mortgage at an 8% per year interest rate. The property was held for 10 years and then sold. The mortgage terms provide amortization over the 10 years of $57,810. If the property were resold at the original acquisition price, the equity position would have grown to the extent of this $57,810.

If resale is at a price greater than the $400,000 acquisition cost, the equity growth is further enhanced. If the property were sold at a price $40,000 less than the cost of acquisition, the equity would still have grown in the net amount of $17,810. Any variety of situations can occur. However, when the rate of mortgage amortization exceeds the rate of property depreciation, equity growth results, and vice versa.

The rate of return actually realized on the equity investment is thus a combination of the equity dividend rate and the discounted effect of the capital gain or loss. This rate of return is referred to as the equity yield rate.[2] It may be defined:

---

2. Also referred to as the *internal rate of return*. For additional information, see Charles B. Akerson, *Internal Rate of Return on Real Estate Investment* (Chicago: American Society of Real Estate Counselors and American Institute of Real Estate Appraisers, 1976).

1. The rate at which the present worth of the equity dividends for
    the investment period, plus the present worth of the equity
    reversion at the end of the period, equals the original equity
    investment; or
2. The annual equity dividend rate adjusted for the effect of capital
    gain or loss in the equity position over the investment period.

When income taxes on earned income are high, equity growth may
well be the most attractive component of yield. Although investors
are typically interested in cash dividends, these dividends may be rendered less attractive by prevailing high income tax rates. The equity
enhancement realized by sale at the end of an investment period may
be more attractive as a capital gain if it receives somewhat more favorable income tax treatment. Such equity growth may also be realized
without any immediate income tax consequences by refinancing the
property. The difference between the old mortgage balance and the
new increased mortgage is capital received in a lump sum without
current tax liability.

Mortgage-equity application typically involves relatively short-
term investment projection periods in relation to remaining economic
life estimates. Shorter periods improve the quality of income projections and recognize that ownership of investment property is frequently terminated when income tax deduction for depreciation of
building improvements ceases to shelter the mortgage amortization
payments. Shorter projection periods also have the effect of increasing the impact of the reversionary gain or loss on equity yield and
reducing the importance of the annual cash flow rate.

In all investments the element of recapture is important. Clearly an
investor deserves a return on invested capital and eventual return of
the capital. Recapture of the mortgage investment is accomplished
through amortization during the investment term with repayment of
any remaining balance made from the proceeds of sale when the
investment is liquidated. Recapture of the equity investment may be
accomplished through allocation from annual income and/or from the
proceeds of sale at the end of the investment period. The impact of
equity growth on the annual equity dividend rate to produce the
equity yield rate is based on use of the sinking-fund factor to discount
and annualize the equity growth. This may be expressed

$$Y = \text{equity dividend rate} + \left(\frac{\text{equity growth}}{\text{original equity}} \times \frac{\text{SFF for investment}}{\text{period at } Y \text{ rate}}\right)$$

In the event of a decline in the value of the equity position, the plus sign changes to a minus sign and the equity yield rate is correspondingly reduced.

The Basic Rate and the Overall Rate in Mortgage Equity

When an overall rate is clearly indicated from market sales within the concept of direct capitalization, additional analysis is not necessary. However, sales data for closely comparable properties may not be available in the quantity needed to establish a convincing overall rate pattern. In such circumstances, it may still be possible to research the mortgage market and investor requirements to develop an applicable overall rate. A rate, or rates, derived from market data can also be adjusted for changed circumstances to develop an adjusted rate considered applicable to current circumstances and to the property being appraised. To do this, an understanding of the overall rate *(R)* and how it may be dissected or synthesized is necessary.

Assume a 75% mortgage at 8% interest only (no amortization) and a 25% equity investor attracted by a 12% return. No change in property value over a projected period of ownership is anticipated. A band of investment based on this data develops.

	Value Ratio		Interest Rate		Weighted Average
Mortgage	.75	×	.08	=	.06
Equity	.25	×	.12	=	.03
Property	1.00	×	basic rate	=	.09

With no mortgage amortization and no equity buildup, the mortgage balance remains constant. With no change in property value, the equity also remains constant. The resultant property rate reflects the concept of capitalization in perpetuity, and in mortgage-equity terminology this rate is referred to as *the basic rate (r)* to distinguish it from the overall rate *(R)*.

The 12% equity interest rate above reflects the cash flow to equity and hence it is also the equity dividend rate.[3] However, in this era of constant payment amortizing mortgages, the introduction of amortization creates equity buildup which accrues to the equity investor as a capital gain when the investment is terminated. Under these circumstances, the yield realized by the equity investor is increased above the level of the annual equity dividend rate. The band of investment may be restructured to reflect this situation.

For example, assume the 75% mortgage is a 25-year, 8% interest, monthly payment mortgage with an annual debt service constant of .0926.[4] (The symbol f is used to indicate a mortgage constant.) Use of this mortgage constant in the band of investment introduces equity buildup and the realized equity return is the equity yield rate (Y). Assuming investor expectations involve an equity yield rate of 12%, the band of investment becomes

	Value Ratio		Rate		Weighted Average
Mortgage	.75	×	.0926 *(f)*	=	.0695
Equity	.25	×	.12 *(Y)*	=	.0300
Weighted average	1.00				.0995

The above rates are not interest rates so the weighted average is no longer the basic rate (r). Use of the equity yield rate in place of the equity dividend rate also means that the weighted average is no longer the overall rate (R). This figure is the basic rate plus the effect of equity buildup due to the amortization which is inherent in the mortgage constant and reflected in the yield rate. An additional line is necessary to remove this effect and develop the basic rate (r).

The amortization inherent in the mortgage constant is on the basis of a sinking fund at the 8% mortgage interest rate. The investor requirement is on the basis of a 12% equity yield, and a lesser annual amount accumulating in a sinking fund at 12% would achieve the same total buildup. This buildup with full mortgage amortization amounts

---

3. In this unusual situation in which there is no change in the value of the equity, the equity dividend rate also corresponds to the total realized annual rate of return to the equity investment which is the equity yield rate (Y).

4. Charles B. Akerson, *Study Guide: Course 1-B. Capitalization Theory & Techniques* (Chicago: American Institute of Real Estate Appraisers, 1977), p. T-18, col. 7.

to 75% of the property value, realized by the equity investor in the reversion at the end of 25 years. Since we are dealing with the equity component of value, this buildup is removed from the weighted average above on the basis of the equity investor's anticipated yield rate. Multiplication by the 25-year, 12% sinking fund factor discounts this buildup and reduces it to an annual percentage for adjustment to the band of investment above.

Weighted average (as above)		.0995
Less credit for equity buildup due to		
amortization of the mortgage	.75 × .0075[a]	−.0056
Property basic rate *(r)*		.0939
		or 9.39%

[a]Appendix B, 12% Table, Column 3, sinking-fund factor, 25 years.

This basic rate reflects complete mortgage amortization and implies a 25-year investment holding period. As previously noted, typical periods of ownership for investment real estate approach, but usually do not exceed, about 10 years. The above credit for equity buildup due to mortgage amortization may be adjusted to reflect any projection period by adjusting the amount of the mortgage amortization to reflect the amount of the principal paid off in the selected period. Assume a projection period of 10 years instead of the 25 years above. The credit for equity buildup line in the computation becomes:

Weighted average (as above)	.0995
Less .1924[a] × .75 × .0570[b]	−.0082
Property basic rate *(r)* for 10-year	
projection period.	.0913
	or 9.13%

[a]19.24% of the described 25-year mortgage is amortized during the first 10 years.
[b]Appendix B, 12% Table, Column 3, sinking-fund factor, 10 years.

Within the concept of mortgage equity capitalization, the basic rate *(r)* may be adjusted to derive the overall rate *(R)* necessary to develop a property value estimate. The basic rate also may be adjusted to derive a capitalization rate applicable to the land or to the building component of value for use within the land or building residual techniques. In each case the desired rate consists of the basic rate adjusted for anticipated change in the value of the property or of the land or building component during the projection period.

Assume a 10-year projection period and the basic rate of 9.13% derived above. If the property value is expected to decline 10% over the projected 10-year period of ownership, this loss in value will be realized in the reversion at the time of resale or liquidation of the investment. This loss may be reduced to an annual basis for addition to the basic rate using the same procedure as for the buildup due to mortgage amortization which is similarly realized in the reversion. The extent of the change (expressed as a percentage of value) is multiplied by the sinking-fund factor for the projection period at the investor's yield rate.

Basic rate	.0913
Adjustment for anticipated 10% depreciation	
in property value, .10 × .0570[a]	+ .0057
Property overall rate (R)	.0970
	or 9.70%

[a]Appendix B, 12% Table, Column 3, sinking-fund factor, 10 years.

A projected decline in value acts to increase the capitalization rate.

Under the frequent assumption of an unchanging land value during a projected period of ownership, the basic rate represents the applicable capitalization rate for income attributable to land. However, if land value is expected to increase 30% over a 10-year projection period, the capitalization rate applicable to land value may be computed to reflect this expectation.

Basic rate, as derived	.0913
Adjusted for anticipated 30% increase	
in land value, .30 × .0570[a]	− .0171
Land capitalization rate	.0742
	or 7.42%

[a]Appendix B, 12% Table, Column 3, sinking fund factor, 10 years.

A building capitalization rate may be similarly derived, based on an anticipated change in building value. For example, assuming the building will depreciate at the rate of 2% per year for 10 years for a 20% total loss in value, the building capitalization rate is

Basic rate, as derived	.0913
Adjusted for anticipated 20% decline	
in building value, .20 × .0570[a]	+ .0114
Building capitalization rate	.1027
	or 10.27%

[a]Appendix B, 12% Table, Column 3, sinking fund factor, 10 years.

Thus the capitalization rate applicable to land, building, or total property may be derived from the basic rate through adjustment for anticipated change in the respective value of the land, building, or total property over the projection period. The formula for this adjustment is

$$+ \text{ depreciation}$$
$$\text{or} \quad \times \ (SFF \text{ at } Y \text{ rate for the projection period})$$
$$- \text{ appreciation}$$

Mortgage equity without algebra uses the band of investment formulation to present the concept of mortgage-equity rate analysis in familiar terms. Because of the step-by-step procedure, the analysis leading to a land, building, or overall capitalization rate is easily understood.

The same series of steps may be condensed into a single line and reduced to an algebraic formula with a portion of the equation represented by a single coefficient C. This is the formulation as developed and used with the Ellwood Tables of precalculated factors which are designed to simplify practical applications of the mortgage-equity concept.

Mortgage Equity with Ellwood Formulation

L. W. Ellwood, MAI, author of *Ellwood Tables*,[5] was the first to organize, develop to a practical conclusion, and promulgate the concepts of mortgage-equity analysis within the area of real property valuation. The mathematical addition of the band of invest-

5. Ellwood, *op. cit.*

ment to develop an overall rate was reduced to a single equation for the overall rate (R) as follows:

$$R = Y - MC \quad {+\text{dep} \atop -\text{app}} \quad (SFF)$$

In this equation

Y = Equity yield rate

M = Ratio of mortgage to value

P = Percent of mortgage amortized within the projection period[6]

SFF = Sinking-fund factor at Y rate for the ownership projection period

r = Basic rate

$r = Y - MC$

dep = Depreciation in property value for the projection period

app = Appreciation in property value for the projection period

f = Mortgage constant

C = Mortgage coefficient[7]

The mortgage coefficient (C) is a factor that reflects the effect of mortgage terms on equity yield. The Ellwood Tables include precalculated mortgage coefficients for a wide range of mortgage terms and equity yields and precalculated basic rates (r) on the basis of 75% or 66⅔% financing for a similar range of mortgage terms and equity yields. The above formula for R may be used in combination with the Ellwood Tables (Figure 22.1 a and b) to expedite the computation of an overall rate.

Assume the same circumstances as in the example illustrating mortgage-equity: 75% financing at 8% with monthly payments to amortize over 25 years, a 10-year projection period during which the property value is expected to depreciate 10%, and typical investors attracted by prospects of a 12% equity yield rate. Using the Ellwood Tables, the rate for this property may be developed.

The Ellwood Capitalization Rate Tables include a 10-year projection table for 75% financing with a 25-year amortizing mortgage in

---

6. $P = \dfrac{f_n - I}{f_p - I}$

7. The mortgage coefficient C may be computed using the formula: $C = Y + P(SFF) - f$.

Figure 22.1a

TABLE C	Mortgage Coefficients for Computing Capitalization Rates. 20 YEARS AMORTIZATION: 7¾% TO 9%						TABLE C
Interest Rate **Annual Requirement (f)** **Installment f/12**	7¾% .098520 .008210	8% .100440 .008370	8¼% .102360 .008530	8½% .104160 .008680	8¾% .106080 .008840	9% .108000 .009000	$\frac{1}{s\,\overline{n}\rceil}$

Projection	Balance (b)	.872128	.874844	.877600	.881140	.883981	.886863	+ Dep.
	Equity Yield		Mortgage Coefficients					– App.
	4 % .04	.034911–	.037332–	.039761–	.042215–	.044659–	.047111–	.184627
	5 % .05	.025378–	.027789–	.030208–	.032649–	.035083–	.037525–	.180974
	6 % .06	.015836–	.018237–	.020646–	.023074–	.025498–	.027930–	.177396
	7 % .07	.006284–	.008676–	.011075–	.013491–	.015905–	.018326–	.173090
	8 % .08	.003276	.000893	.001496–	.003899–	.006303–	.008715–	.170456
	9 % .09	.012846	.010472	.008092	.005700	.003305	.000904	.167092
	10 % .10	.022425	.020060	.017688	.015308	.012923	.010531	.163797
	11 % .11	.032012	.029656	.027293	.024925	.022549	.020166	.160570
	12 % .12	.041608	.039260	.036906	.034549	.032182	.029808	.157409
	13 % .13	.051212	.048873	.046528	.044181	.041823	.039458	.154314
	14 % .14	.060824	.058493	.056157	.053821	.051471	.049115	.151283
5 Years n = 5	15 % .15	.070445	.068122	.065793	.063468	.061127	.058779	.148315
	16 % .16	.080073	.077758	.075438	.073123	.070790	.068451	.145409
	17 % .17	.089709	.087402	.085089	.082785	.080460	.078129	.142563
	18 % .18	.099353	.097053	.094748	.092453	.090136	.087813	.139777
	19 % .19	.109004	.106712	.104414	.102129	.099820	.097505	.137050
	20 % .20	.118663	.116378	.114088	.111812	.109510	.107203	.134379
	21 % .21	.128329	.126051	.123768	.121501	.119207	.116907	.131765
	22 % .22	.138001	.135730	.133454	.131197	.128910	.126617	.129205
	23 % .23	.147681	.145417	.143148	.140899	.138619	.136334	.126700
	24 % .24	.157367	.155110	.152847	.150608	.148335	.146056	.124247
	25 % .25	.167060	.164809	.162554	.160322	.158056	.155785	.121846
	26 % .26	.176760	.174515	.172266	.170043	.167783	.165519	.119496
	27 % .27	.186466	.184227	.181984	.179769	.177516	.175259	.117195
	28 % .28	.196178	.193945	.191709	.189502	.187255	.185004	.114943
	29 % .29	.205896	.203669	.201439	.199240	.196999	.194754	.112739
	30 % .30	.215620	.213399	.211175	.208983	.206749	.204510	.110581

	Balance (b)	.683970	.688381	.692964	.699605	.704573	.709728	+ Dep.
	Equity Yield		Mortgage Coefficients					– App.
	4 % .04	.032197–	.034485–	.036786–	.039139–	.041473–	.043823–	.083290
	5 % .05	.023394–	.025664–	.027949–	.030277–	.032592–	.034922–	.079504
	6 % .06	.014543–	.016798–	.019065–	.021369–	.023666–	.025977–	.075867
	7 % .07	.005646–	.007885–	.010137–	.012418–	.014697–	.016990–	.072377
	8 % .08	.003295	.001070	.001165–	.003423–	.005686–	.007962–	.069020
	9 % .09	.012281	.010070	.007849	.005611	.003365	.001105	.065820
	10 % .10	.021309	.019112	.016905	.014688	.012456	.010213	.062745
	11 % .11	.030379	.028195	.026001	.023804	.021586	.019358	.059801
	12 % .12	.039488	.037317	.035136	.032957	.030754	.028540	.056984
	13 % .13	.048637	.046477	.044308	.042148	.039958	.037758	.054289
	14 % .14	.057823	.055674	.053517	.051374	.049197	.047010	.051713
10 Years n = 10	15 % .15	.067045	.064907	.062762	.060635	.058470	.056296	.049252
	16 % .16	.076302	.074175	.072040	.069928	.067775	.065614	.046901
	17 % .17	.085592	.083475	.081351	.079254	.077112	.074962	.044656
	18 % .18	.094915	.092808	.090693	.088611	.086479	.084340	.042514
	19 % .19	.104270	.102171	.100066	.097997	.095876	.093747	.040471
	20 % .20	.113654	.111564	.109467	.107412	.105300	.103182	.038522
	21 % .21	.123067	.120985	.118897	.116854	.114751	.112642	.036665
	22 % .22	.132507	.130433	.128353	.126322	.124229	.122129	.034894
	23 % .23	.141974	.139908	.137836	.135815	.133730	.131639	.033208
	24 % .24	.151467	.149407	.147342	.145333	.143256	.141173	.031602
	25 % .25	.160983	.158931	.156873	.154873	.152804	.150729	.030072
	26 % .26	.170523	.168477	.166426	.164436	.162374	.160306	.028616
	27 % .27	.180085	.178045	.176000	.174019	.171964	.169904	.027230
	28 % .28	.189668	.187634	.185595	.183623	.181575	.179521	.025911
	29 % .29	.199272	.197243	.195210	.193246	.191204	.189157	.024657
	30 % .30	.208895	.206871	.204844	.202888	.200851	.198810	.023463

Source: L.W. Ellwood, *Ellwood Tables for Real Estate Appraising and Financing* 4th ed. (Cambridge, Mass.: Ballinger Publishing Co., 1977), pp. 345 and 484.

Figure 22.1b

CAP. RATES			CAPITALIZATION RATES					
75% Mtg.			Assuming 75% of Purchase Price Financed by Mortgage					
25 Years			25 YEARS AMORTIZATION: 7¼% TO 9%					

Interest Rate		7¼%	8%	8¼%	8½%	8¾%	9%	$\frac{1}{s\overline{\frac{}{n}}}$
Annual Requirement (f)		.090720	.092640	.094680	.096720	.098760	.100800	
Coverage Min. Rate		.068040	.069480	.071010	.072540	.074070	.075600	

Projection	Balance (b)	.919578	.922604	.924932	.927294	.929689	.932118	+ Dep
								– App
	Equity Yield	Basic Rate before Depreciation or Appreciation						
	6 % .06	.072340	.074182	.076022	.077866	.079715	.081568	.177396
	7 % .07	.075051	.076886	.078719	.080557	.082400	.084247	.173890
	8 % .08	.077758	.079585	.081413	.083245	.085081	.086921	.170456
	9 % .09	.080461	.082280	.084102	.085928	.087758	.089593	.167092
	10 % .10	.083160	.084972	.086788	.088608	.090432	.092260	.163797
	11 % .11	.085854	.087659	.089469	.091284	.093102	.094925	.160570
	12 % .12	.088545	.090342	.092147	.093956	.095769	.097586	.157409
	13 % .13	.091232	.093022	.094822	.096625	.098432	.100243	.154314
	14 % .14	.093915	.095698	.097492	.099290	.101092	.102897	.151283
	15 % .15	.096594	.098370	.100159	.101952	.103748	.105549	.148315
5 Years	16 % .16	.099269	.101039	.102823	.104610	.106402	.108197	.145409
n = 5	17 % .17	.101941	.103704	.105483	.107266	.109052	.110841	.142563
	18 % .18	.104609	.106366	.108140	.109918	.111699	.113483	.139777
	19 % .19	.107273	.109024	.110794	.112566	.114342	.116122	.137050
	20 % .20	.109934	.111679	.113444	.115212	.116983	.118758	.134379
	21 % .21	.112592	.114331	.116091	.117854	.119621	.121391	.131765
	22 % .22	.115246	.116980	.118735	.120494	.122256	.124021	.129205
	23 % .23	.117897	.119625	.121376	.123131	.124888	.126649	.126700
	24 % .24	.120545	.122267	.124014	.125764	.127518	.129274	.124247
	25 % .25	.123190	.124907	.126649	.128395	.130144	.131896	.121846
	26 % .26	.125832	.127543	.129282	.131023	.132768	.134516	.119496
	27 % .27	.128471	.130177	.131911	.133649	.135389	.137133	.117195
	28 % .28	.131107	.132807	.134538	.136272	.138008	.139748	.114943
	29 % .29	.133739	.135435	.137162	.138892	.140624	.142360	.112739
	30 % .30	.136370	.138061	.139784	.141510	.143238	.144970	.110581

	Balance (b)	.801241	.807296	.811697	.816251	.820963	.825837	+ Dep
								– App
	Equity Yield	Basic Rate before Depreciation or Appreciation						
	6 % .06	.071730	.073515	.075295	.077084	.078882	.080689	.075867
	7 % .07	.074750	.076519	.078288	.080065	.081851	.083645	.072377
	8 % .08	.077749	.079503	.081261	.083026	.084800	.086583	.069029
	9 % .09	.080728	.082467	.084214	.085969	.087731	.089502	.065820
	10 % .10	.083686	.085411	.087148	.088892	.090644	.092404	.062745
	11 % .11	.086625	.088337	.090064	.091798	.093540	.095288	.059801
	12 % .12	.089545	.091244	.092962	.094686	.096418	.098156	.056984
	13 % .13	.092447	.094133	.095842	.097558	.099280	.101008	.054289
	14 % .14	.095331	.097005	.098706	.100413	.102126	.103845	.051713
	15 % .15	.098198	.099861	.101554	.103252	.104956	.106666	.049252
10 Years	16 % .16	.101048	.102701	.104386	.106076	.107772	.109473	.046901
n = 10	17 % .17	.103883	.105525	.107203	.108885	.110573	.112266	.044656
	18 % .18	.106702	.108335	.110005	.111680	.113361	.115046	.042514
	19 % .19	.109506	.111130	.112794	.114462	.116135	.117813	.040471
	20 % .20	.112297	.113912	.115569	.117231	.118897	.120568	.038522
	21 % .21	.115074	.116680	.118331	.119987	.121646	.123310	.036665
	22 % .22	.117838	.119436	.121081	.122731	.124384	.126041	.034894
	23 % .23	.120589	.122180	.123820	.125463	.127110	.128762	.033208
	24 % .24	.123329	.124912	.126546	.128184	.129826	.131472	.031602
	25 % .25	.126057	.127633	.129262	.130895	.132531	.134171	.030072
	26 % .26	.128774	.130344	.131968	.133596	.135227	.136862	.028616
	27 % .27	.131480	.133044	.134664	.136287	.137913	.139543	.027230
	28 % .28	.134177	.135735	.137350	.138969	.140590	.142215	.025911
	29 % .29	.136864	.138416	.140027	.141641	.143259	.144879	.024657
	30 % .30	.139542	.141088	.142696	.144306	.145919	.147535	.023463

which, on the 12% yield line in the 8% mortgage interest rate column, a basic rate of 0.091244 is given. On the same line at the right of the page, the 12%, 10-year sinking-fund factor is given as .056984. Substitution in the formula is as follows:

$R = r + \text{dep } (SFF)$
$R = .091244 + (.10)(.056984)$
$R = .096942 \text{ (say) } 9.69\%$

This is the same overall rate computed previously (p. 440).

Assume the same circumstances as above except that the mortgage involves a 20-year amortization plan and is for 80% of property value. When mortgage financing does not involve a loan ratio of 66-2/3% or 75%, the basic rate cannot be derived directly from the tables. It may be computed using the "C" tables which include a 10-year projection table for 20-year financing in which, on the 12% yield line in the 8% mortgage interest rate column, a mortgage coefficient of .037317 is given, together with the 12% sinking-fund factor at the right side of the page. Substitution in the formula is now

$R = Y - MC + \text{dep } (SFF)$
$R = .12 - (.80)(.037317) + (.10)(.056984)$
$R = .095844 \text{ (say) } 9.58\%$

This change to 9.58% from an overall rate of 9.69% reflects the effect of the above change in mortgage ratio and term.

When circumstances permit—that is, for 75% or 66-2/3% financing—the basic rate may be extracted directly from the tables and adjusted for anticipated change in land, building, or total property value to derive a land or building capitalization rate or an overall rate applicable to the property. For other mortgage terms, the basic rate may be computed using the formula: $r = Y - MC$. When C is not available in the tables, it may be computed.

Graphic Analysis of an Overall Rate

Since growth or decline in the value of the equity position contributes to the equity yield rate, the actual yield realized by the equity investor cannot be confirmed until the investment has been liquidated. Market decisions made by the equity investor prior to the investment can be rationalized only in terms of *prospects* for yield. The mortgage component of value represents a current commitment and can be projected from current mortgage market research. Assuming a supportable net income projection, the probable sale at the end of a period of ownership is the major variable affecting the prospects for equity yield.

Application of mortgage-equity concepts provides the appraiser and the investor with an effective tool for gauging the prospects for yield within a range of probable resale prices. Assume that the appraiser has derived capitalization rates from the best available market data and developed a market value estimate for the property being appraised through an appropriate capitalization method. Assuming purchase on this basis, with currently available financing, a reasonable range of equity yields can be related to the property value changes that must occur to produce these yields. If resale of the property being appraised within this range appears to represent a reasonable expectation, this is supportive evidence of probable investment appeal at the appraised value. Acceptability of an appraisal of market value hinges on whether prospects for equity yield are sufficient to attract a typical purchaser.

The formula for change in value is based on the previously developed equation

$$R = r - \text{appreciation } (SFF)$$

This may be expressed as

$$\text{appreciation} = \frac{r - R}{SFF}$$

If the overall rate is not part of the capitalization process used, it can be computed for use in this formula from the net income projection and the market value estimate. Assume a property with a $42,000 per year net income projection, appraised at $400,000. The overall rate is 10.5%. Assume typical financing is available at 70% of value at 9% on a 25-year monthly payment amortization plan. Tables 22.1 and 22.2 show the computations to derive the changes in property value corresponding to some selected range of equity yield rates, assuming resale after a five-year or 10-year period of ownership.

Table 22.1. Five-Year Projections

Y	R	C	MC (.70×C)	Y−MC (r)	r−R	SFF	$\frac{r-R}{SFF}$	Change in Value
.11	.105	.020099	.014069	.095931	−.009069	.160570	−.0565	5.7% dep.
.13	.105	.039675	.027773	.102227	−.002773	.157314	−.0176	1.8% dep.
.15	.105	.059267	.041487	.108513	+.003513	.148315	+.0237	2.4% app.

Table 22.2 10-Year Projections

Y	R	C	MC (.70×C)	Y−MC (r)	r−R	SFF	$\frac{r-R}{SFF}$	Change in Value
.11	.105	.019615	.013731	.096269	−.008731	.059801	−.1460	14.6% dep.
.13	.105	.038655	.027059	.102941	−.002059	.054289	−.0379	3.8% dep.
.15	.105	.057777	.040444	.109556	+.004556	.049252	+.0925	9.3% app.

The changes in property value corresponding to each yield rate may then be plotted on a graph as shown in Figure 22.2. Computation is simplified when the mortgage ratio *(M)* is 75% or 66-2/3% because the basic rate *(r)* then is found in the Ellwood capitalization rate tables, thus eliminating reference to the mortgage coefficient *(C)* and the computation of *Y−MC*.

The appraisal at $400,000 is presumably based on contemporary attitudes of buyers and sellers in the current market. However, even the most probable objectives are not always achieved. Accordingly, it is helpful to have a pictorial representation of the relationship between possible changes in market value during a probable period of ownership and the corresponding effect on equity yield prospects.

Figure 22.2 indicates that even if the property declines 14.6% in value over the next 10 years, equity yield will not fall below 11%. However, inflationary trends in dollar values and construction costs may result in resale at essentially the present price (equity yield would be 13 to 14%), or if the price is 10% higher, the equity yield would approximate 15%.

Such considerations, indicated trends, and the character of the property itself are studied by the informed investor in income prop-

Figure 22.2.   Graphic Analysis of 10.5% Overall Capitalization Rate

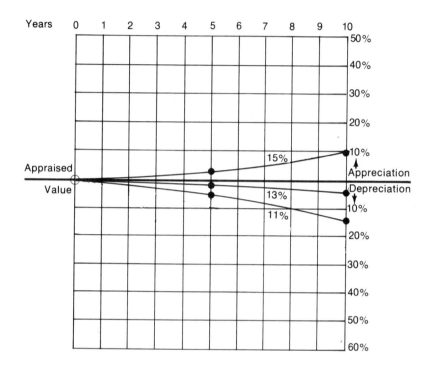

erty equities. In providing consultation services or confirming a market value estimate, the appraiser is similarly thorough in developing a comprehensive analysis.

COMPUTATION OF THE EQUITY YIELD RATE

The equity yield rate (internal rate of return) includes both components of equity return, expressed in terms of an annual rate. Since the amount of the reversionary component cannot be identified until the investment is liquidated, only prospects for an equity yield rate can be estimated at the moment of investment.

Understanding equity yield may be improved through a computation based on the history of an actual investment. A parcel of investment real estate with an annual net income of $61,200 was purchased for $600,000 subject to a $450,000, 8.5%, 22-year monthly payment mortgage, held for 10 years, and sold for $550,000. This situation can be set out as follows:

Purchase		Holding Period		Liquidation	
Purchase	$600,000	NIBR	$ 61,200	Sale	$550,000
Mortgage	450,000	Debt service	45,273[a]	Mortgage balance[b]	−339,878
Equity	$150,000	Equity dividend	$15,926	Equity reversion	$210,122
				Original equity	−150,000
				Equity growth	$ 60,122

$$\text{Equity dividend rate} = \frac{\$15,926}{\$150,000} = \underline{.1062}$$

$$\text{Equity \% growth} = \frac{\$60,122}{\$150,000} = \underline{.4008}$$

---

[a]$450,000 × .1006087 mortgage constant. Akerson, *op cit.*, p. T-20, col. 7.
[b]Unamortized portion of $450,000 mortgage at end of 10-year holding period.

The equity yield rate may now be computed through iteration (successive approximations) or by formula and interpolation. In iteration the definition of Y is:

$$Y = \text{Equity dividend rate} + \left(\text{Equity \% growth} \times SFF \text{ at } Y \text{ rate for holding period} \right)$$

Since the sinking-fund factor for 10 years at the Y rate cannot be identified without knowing Y, a trial-and-error procedure may be used to develop Y. Without discounting, the 40.08% equity growth during the 10-year holding period would add 4.01% annually to the equity dividend rate of 10.62%. Consequently, Y will exceed 10.62% and be less than 14.63% (10.62% + 4.01%).

An initial computation may be made, assuming $Y = 12.5\%$. If this assumption is correct, the equation will balance.

$$.125 = .1062 + (.4008)(.0556)^a$$
$$.125 \neq .1285 \text{ (higher than the .125 trial } Y)$$

---

[a]SFF from Appendix B, 12½% Table, 10-year period, Column 3.

The 12.85% figure implies that Y is slightly above the 12.5% trial Y, but less than 13% and could approximate the computed figure. A second computation may be made assuming $Y = 13\%$ as follows:

$$.13 = .1062 + (.4008)(.0543)^a$$
$$.13 \neq .1280 \text{ (lower than the .13 trial } Y\text{)}$$

[a]SFF from Appendix B, 13% Table, 10-year period, Column 3.

With the previous 12.85%, this confirms a conclusion at, say, 12.8%.

An alternate method of computing Y is based on the definition that Y is the rate that makes the present worth of the future equity benefits equal the original equity. The future benefits in this situation are $15,926 per year for 10 years plus a reversion of $210,122 at the end of the 10-year period.

Assuming a trial Y of 12.5%, the present worth of the two benefits may be computed as follows:

$ 15,926	×	5.5364[a]	=	$ 88,173
$210,122	×	.3079[b]	=	64,697
				$152,870

[a]Appendix B, 12½%, 10-year factor, Column 5.
[b]Appendix B, 12½%, 10-year factor, Column 4.

This is above the original equity of $150,000, implying that the discount rate used was below the true yield rate. The true yield rate may be bracketed between 12.5 and 13% so a recomputation may be made using a trial Y of 13% as follows:

$ 15,926	×	5.4262[a]	=	$ 86,418
$210,122	×	.2946[b]	=	61,902
				$148,320

[a]Appendix B, 13%, 10-year factor, Column 5.
[b]Appendix B, 13%, 10-year factor, Column 4.

A more precise indication now may be developed through interpolation between 12.5% and 13% as follows:

	Rate		
	.125	$152,870	$152,870
	(target Y)		150,000
	.130	148,320	
Difference	= .005	$ 4,550	$ 2,870

$$Y = .125 + \frac{\$2,870}{\$4,550} \times .005 = .1282, \text{ or } 12.8\%$$

Thus the equity yield rate has been confirmed at 12.8%. Precision to the nearest one-tenth of 1 percent represents a level of accuracy within the normal requirements of the computation and current practice.

An investor client may have completed negotiations for the purchase of investment real estate, including the terms of financing. The income-stream projection may be reliable, perhaps based on a long-term net lease, and the investor may want to know what equity yield can be anticipated, assuming some specific range of changes in market value over a projected period of ownership. Use of the above procedures enables an appraiser to provide the requested information.

The potential uses of mortgage-equity concepts and techniques in valuation analysis and investment counseling are extensive. The appraiser is able to analyze the relative impacts of cash flow rates and the potential for capital gain or loss. Rates derived from market evidence may be analyzed and explained in terms of equity investor motivation, and the impact of financing is identified. Since market value is a reflection of the mortgage market and equity investor thinking, the mortgage-equity concept is closely related to reality and provides the appraiser with a valuable analytical tool.

DISCOUNTED CASH FLOW

Discounted cash flow analysis (DCF) is a method for estimating the present worth (value) of future cash flow expectancies, before or after taxes, by individually discounting each anticipated collection at an appropriate discount rate. The analysis is typically applied to annual equity cash flow projections, but the procedure is equally applicable to other income projections and on other than an annual basis.

The discounting technique employs the present worth of 1 (reversion) factors (as illustrated in Chapter 21 under Annuity Capitalization), and the discounted cash flow concept is the same as the last step of the anticipated use or development approach to undeveloped land value (see Chapter 8).

Many income-stream patterns are encountered in the analysis of income-producing real properties. When the periodic income fluctuations are within a reasonable range or fluctuate around a reasonably definable trend line, appraisers have traditionally tended to "stabilize" the net income pattern within the assumptions of an appropriate capitalization method. A combination of adequate market research with experience and judgment may, in such cases, produce a valid reflection of market value. However, the majority of income-producing properties probably do not actually produce periodic incomes following a level or consistent change pattern. Except for long-term net leases, the net income may be subject to variation despite a fixed level of gross rent established by a lease. When specific figures for a periodic income stream can be projected with a reasonable degree of dependability, a discounted cash flow analysis is appropriate. It provides the most precise handling of estimated future amounts of income projected at specific future intervals of time.

A major advantage of discounted cash flow techniques is that any income-stream pattern, however irregular, may be processed without the necessity for what may be unwarranted assumptions in regard to the income pattern. Figure 22.3 illustrates several income streams as they might be anticipated in an income approach projection. When income streams B, C, or D fluctuate in a consistent pattern, they may be convertible to some straight-line assumption, either increasing, decreasing, or level. When this is not the case, a discounted cash flow technique may provide the only acceptable alternative method of converting the projected installments to a present value estimate. Discounted cash flow is the only procedure applicable in all cases without the necessity for some assumption that adjusts the income-stream pattern to reflect a consistent rate of change or to a level, or series of level, projections.

DISCOUNTED CASH FLOW IN VALUATION

Mathematical precision within computations should not be mistaken as assuring the accuracy of derived answers. The final conclusion can

Figure 22.3. Income Patterns

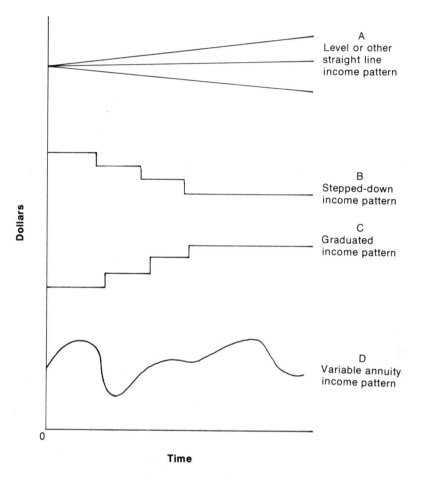

be no better than the accuracy of the estimates and judgment decisions throughout the valuation process. However, increasing mathematical precision may permit avoidance of some factors that can reduce accuracy in a conclusion. For example, the five income streams illustrated in Table 22.3 all "average" $50,000 per year. However, an inspection of these income stream patterns show that averaging these to a "typical" $50,000 per year level would fail to

Table 22.3.   Cash Flows Averaging $50,000

Year	Income Streams				
	1	2	3	4	5
1	$100,000	$ 10,000	$230,000	$ 75,000	$ 50,000
2	0	15,000	50,000	25,000	50,000
3	0	20,000	45,000	10,000	50,000
4	0	25,000	40,000	90,000	50,000
5	0	30,000	35,000	30,000	50,000
6	0	35,000	30,000	70,000	50,000
7	0	40,000	25,000	40,000	50,000
8	0	45,000	20,000	15,000	50,000
9	0	50,000	15,000	85,000	50,000
10	400,000	230,000	10,000	60,000	50,000
Total	$500,000	$500,000	$500,000	$500,000	$500,000

recognize the impact on present worth of time in relation to the value of money.

A discounted cash flow procedure permits a more precise treatment of the five income streams as illustrated in Table 22.4, using a 10% discount rate.

Table 24.4.   Present Worth of Cash Flows Discounted @ 10%

Year	Factor[a] @ 10%	Present Worth of Income				
		1	2	3	4	5
1	.90919	$ 90,909	$ 9,091	$209,091	$ 68,182	$ 45,455
2	.82645	0	12,397	41,322	20,661	41,322
3	.75131	0	15,026	33,809	7,513	37,565
4	.68301	0	17,075	27,321	61,471	34,151
5	.62092	0	18,628	21,732	18,628	31,046
6	.56447	0	19,757	16,934	39,513	28,224
7	.51316	0	20,526	12,829	20,526	25,658
8	.46651	0	20,993	9,330	6,998	23,325
9	.42410	0	21,205	6,361	36,048	21,205
10	.38554	154,217	88,675	3,855	23,133	19,277
Total		$245,126	$243,373	$382,584	$302,673	$307,228

Present worth $50,000 per year discounted @ 10%	307,228	307,228	307,228	307,228	307,228
Difference	$ 62,102	$ 63,855	$ 75,356	$ 4,455	$ 0

[a]Appendix B, 10% Table, Column 4.

This discounted cash flow analysis reveals that, on the basis of 10% discounting, Cash Flow Streams 1 and 2 involve similar present worths, but each is more than $60,000 below the present worth of the level "average" Income Stream 5. Income Stream Pattern 3, which also "averages" $50,000 per year, has a present worth more than $75,000 in excess of 5, and there is over $139,000 separating the present worth of Income Stream Patterns 2 and 3. These differences would be lost if the incomes had been stabilized at a $50,000 per year level income pattern. The use of an ordinary annuity factor at 10% for 10 years represents a mathematical substitute for the discounted cash flow process when the income is expected to remain level or essentially level over a projection period.

Developing Cash Flow Projections

Increasing use of the discounted cash flow technique has led to increased efforts to refine periodic cash flow projections. In this process emphasis has moved from interpretation of a projected income stream in terms of an identifiable pattern to recognition of individual amounts without regard to any prescribed pattern limitation. Market research frequently indicates patterns of change that differ between components of income or categories of expense. Generalizations may reasonably reflect a future net operating income pattern, but a more precise handling of research data may permit specific estimates of future annual income and expense figures prior to application of the discounting process.

Assume, for example, that market research has developed the following income and expense indications.

Item	Current Monthly Income/Expense	Annual Change (%)
Income		
50 Units	$175	+5
75 Units	200	+3
25 Units	225	+2
Vacancies	Now 10%; decline to 4% over 10 years	
Expenses		
Real estate tax	$3,250	+6
Insurance	300	+1
Management	1,850	+3.5

Utilities	6,300	+5
Maintenance	1,650	+4
Supplies	500	+4
Miscellaneous	900	+4

Stabilization for appraisal use might be aimed to adjust from current levels to reflect a reasonably typical figure for a foreseeable future projection. Use of the discounted cash flow technique permits a more precise projection based on the research data applicable to individual income and expense components. Such a projection need not be interpreted within the limitations of a prescribed pattern, and the result is an irregular but increasing net operating income pattern as shown in Table 22.5. These annual projections provide the basis for a 10-year discounted cash flow analysis as previously described.

The discounted cash flow procedure is adaptable to either a before- or an after-tax analysis, as illustrated in Table 22.6 (see pp. 458-459).

In this example a level annual net lease income is projected for 10 years at $100,000, and a $750,000 mortgage is assumed with terms as

Table 22.5. Income and Expense Projections

	Year 1	Year 2	Year 3	Year 4
Gross scheduled income (annualized)				
Apartments				
50 units @ $175	$105,000	$110,250	$115,762	$121,550
75 units @ $200	180,000	185,400	190,962	196,690
25 units @ $225	67,500	68,850	70,227	71,631
Total	$352,500	$364,500	$376,951	$389,873
Less vacancy and collection losses	28,200	29,160	26,386	27,291
Total	$324,300	$335,340	$350,564	$362,581
Deduct expenses				
Real estate taxes	39,000	41,430	43,820	46,449
Insurance	3,600	3,636	3,672	3,709
Management	22,200	22,977	23,781	24,613
Utilities	75,600	79,380	83,349	87,516
Maintenance	19,800	20,592	21,415	22,272
Supplies	6,000	6,240	6,489	6,749
Miscellaneous	10,800	11,232	11,681	12,148
Total	$177,000	$185,397	$194,209	$203,458
Net operating income	$147,300	$149,943	$156,355	$159,123

shown. The analysis leads to a projection of annual cash flows to equity before income taxes, and after an income tax burden at a 50% level. With level annual debt service as in this case, the before-tax cash flow constitutes a level annuity, because net operating income is also projected at a constant figure. However, after-tax flow declines at an increasing rate. Deductions from net income consist of mortgage interest and a book depreciation figure, which in this case is unchanging. There is no limit to the variations that may be reflected in the cash flow patterns, particularly if the net operating income were to vary as in the example of Table 22.5.

Cash flow patterns, thus projected, lend themselves to a discounted cash flow analysis and permit a fuller understanding of the impact of changes in basic data. A conclusion of value based on such an analysis may constitute a more precise reflection of market value than other capitalization concepts, if all assumptions and projections are well-founded and conform to market action. Nevertheless, the precision of the analysis does not necessarily imply the same degree

Year 5	Year 6	Year 7	Year 8	Year 9	Year 10
$127,628	$134,009	$140,710	$147,745	$155,132	$162,889
202,591	208,669	214,929	221,377	228,018	0234,859
73,064	74,525	76,015	77,536	79,087	80,668
$403,283	$417,204	$431,655	$446,659	$462,238	$478,417
24,197	25,032	21,582	22,332	18,489	19,136
$379,086	$392,172	$410,072	$424,326	$443,748	$459,280
49,236	52,190	55,322	58,641	62,160	65,889
3,746	3,783	3,821	3,859	3,898	3,937
25,475	26,366	27,289	28,244	29,233	30,256
91,892	96,486	101,311	106,376	111,695	117,280
23,163	24,089	25,053	26,055	27,097	28,181
7,019	7,299	7,591	7,895	8,211	8,539
12,634	13,139	13,665	14,212	14,780	15,371
$213,166	$223,357	$234,055	$245,285	$257,076	$269,456
$165,919	$168,814	$176,017	$179,040	$186,672	$189,823

Table 22.6   Cash Flow Projection

Mortgage number: 1   Interest rate: 9.250%   Payments per year: 12
Status: new   Beginning period: Yr. 0, Mo. 0   Debt service per
Type: amortizing   Original term: 35 yrs., 0 mos.   year: $77,074.32
Amount:$750,000   Period to maturity:
                   25 yrs., 0 mos.

Year	Net or Income	Interest Expense	Principal Amortized	Mortgage Balance	Cash Flow
1	$ 100,000	$ 69,040	$ 8,034	$741,965	$ 22,925
2	100,000	68,264	8,809	733,155	22,925
3	100,000	67,414	9,660	723,495	22,925
4	100,000	66,481	10,952	712,903	22,925
5	100,000	65,459	11,615	701,288	22,925
6	100,000	64,338	12,736	688,552	22,925
7	100,000	63,108	13,965	674,586	22,295
8	100,000	61,760	15,313	659,273	22,925
9	100,000	60,282	16,791	642,481	22,925
10	100,000	58,661	18,412	624,069	22,295
Total	$1,000,000	$644,812	$125,930		$229,256

Total cash and benefits = $310,927

of precision in the final conclusion because the accuracy of basic estimates and judgment decisions are still critical factors.

SUMMARY

Within the mortgage-equity concept the capital structure of value is mortgage plus equity. The mortgage component is typically the major component of value, and mortgage amounts and terms are subject to research in the current mortgage market. The value of the equity component is two-fold and includes the present worth of the annual equity cash flow during a projected period of ownership plus the present worth of the equity reversion when the investment is liquidated. This equity reversion may include capital gain or loss in the equity position resulting from a combination of mortgage amortization and a changing market value for the property. The resultant return to equity in annual terms is referred to as the equity yield rate or internal rate of return.

In addition to building up or adjusting an overall rate, the

Tax bracket: 50%

Depreciation:		Base:	Life:	Method:
Building		$800,000	30	Straight-line
Personal		0	0	N/A

Total Depreciation	Total Deduction	Taxable Income (loss)	Tax Liability (savings)	Tax-Free Cash Flow
$ 26,666	$ 95,706	$ 4,293	$ 2,146	$ 20,779
26,666	94,931	5,068	2,534	20,391
26,666	94,080	5,919	2,959	19,966
26,666	93,148	6,851	3,425	19,499
26,666	92,125	7,874	3,937	18,988
26,666	91,004	8,995	4,497	18,428
26,666	89,775	10,224	5,112	17,813
26,666	88,427	11,572	5,786	17,139
26,666	86,949	13,050	6,525	16,400
26,666	85,328	14,671	7,335	15,589
$266,666	$911,479	$88,520	$44,260	$184,996

mortgage-equity concept offers the appraiser a valuable tool for confirming the market appeal of a value estimate derived by other methods of capitalization. It provides a prospective investor with a projection of potential equity yields within a range of probable circumstances. Application of mortgage-equity concepts may be simplified through use of the techniques and mathematical concepts developed by L. W. Ellwood.

Discounted cash flow involves use of the present worth of 1 factors to discount an irregular series of periodic installments of net income. The appraiser does not attempt to fit a cash flow projection into the income-stream assumption of a specific capitalization method.

Projections of net operating income may reflect the differing impact of numerous factors affecting individual components of the income or expense statement. The resulting cash flow pattern may be highly irregular, and installments are discounted individually and then totaled to derive a present worth estimate.

The periodic projections are usually made on an annual basis but may be made at other intervals. The technique is applicable to any net income stream but is typically applied to equity cash flows on either a before-tax or after-tax basis, or both may be included in the analysis of a specific property.

23
Valuation of Partial Interests

Partial interests in real estate may include fractional interests, ownership in land trusts, partnerships, cooperatives, condominiums, air and subsurface rights, easements, leased fees, and leasehold interests. Ownership of real property consists of a number of advantages or rights. Each right may be sold, given away, or otherwise disposed of. The result is a corresponding reduction in the value of the other rights.[1]

The material in this chapter is divided into two sections: (1) lease interests, including valuation of leased fees, leaseholds, and possessory interests, and (2) other legal and physical fractional interests, including public rights and private rights.

LEASE INTERESTS

Leased Fees

An owner who leases real estate transfers a right—the right of use or occupancy—to a tenant in accordance with the provisions of the lease contract. Retained are (1) the right to receive the income and other items called for in the lease, and (2) the right to regain the use of the property at the end of the lease term.

The value of a leased fee or a leasehold interest can be estimated only after ascertaining the duration and terms of the lease. The terms

---

1. See Chapter 2.

of the lease may cover a wide range of provisions agreed to by the parties. The quantity, quality, and durability of the income attributable to the different interests as well as the value of the property at the end of the lease term are affected by the provisions of the lease. A sample outline of some typical provisions for long-term net leases follows.

Introduction

  Date

  Lessor

  Lessee

  Legal description

  Matters to which lease is made subject, such as taxes, special assessments, leases, agreements, restrictions on use, and party-wall agreements

  Use of space under or on streets, alleys, and sidewalks; agreement for joint signature of lessor and lessee to petitions and consents involving use of such space; obligation of lessee to pay city compensation

  Assignment of existing leases to lessee

Term of lease

Rental

  Amount, period, and amount of periodic payment, place of payment, and kind of funds

  Nonabatement of rent or conditions under which rent shall abate

Taxes and assessments payable by lessee

  General real estate taxes; general and special assessments; water rates or taxes; taxes in lieu of, or in substitution, in whole or in part, for general real estate taxes, license fees, and other governmental impositions

Time when taxes must be paid

  Proration of taxes and other assessments during first and last years of term

  Filing of receipts with lessor

  Deposits by lessee to cover accruing taxes and use of such deposits

  Right of lessee to protest taxes and conditions precedent thereto

Use of premises

Limited or specific uses

Illegal use; obligation to comply with all federal, state, and city laws and ordinances; liquor clause; prohibiting sale or giving away, or conditions required prior to such use

Maintenance and care

To keep in good order and repair (perhaps including a statement that premises were so received by lessee, if such is fact)

Obligation to rebuild in case of loss or damage by fire or other casualty

Alterations and improvements

Lessor's consent required

Deposit of funds and use of such funds

Waivers of lien

To become property of lessor at lease termination without compensation to lessee

Lessee not to permit overloading of building

To surrender and deliver up possession of premises at lease termination; building to be in good order and repair, ordinary wear and tear excepted

Insurance

Coverage

Personal injuries, or death, in amounts satisfactory to lessor or in stated amounts for one person and one accident; form to include contractual liability

Rent losses in amount of rent and taxes paid by lessee and in a stated form (such a $1/9$, $1/12$, or $1/24$)

Dramshop bond (if lessee is given right to sell or permit sale of liquor on or from premises) in amounts satisfactory to lessor or in stated dollar amount for injuries, death, loss of support, and property damage

Fire and extended coverage for the full insurable value

Fire and rent insurance policy to be written in name of lessor

Other policies to be written in name of lessor in its individual capacity and as trustee

All policies to be in companies satisfactory to lessor, and deposited with lessor (or deposited with insurance trustee, in which case loss under fire policies shall be made payable to insurance trustee)

Right (or no right) to make loss payable to leasehold mortgagee or trustee in whole or in part

Lessee to furnish an appraisal of value of building for insurance purpose upon request of lessor, not more often than annually

Lessee to maintain in compliance with rules of board of underwriters

Renewal policies to be deposited with lessor (or insurance trustee) five days prior to expiration date of policies being renewed

Loss prior to commencement of lease term

Loss after commencement of lease term; use of funds to rebuild; excess, if any, to belong to lessee if lessee rebuilds

Insurance trustee

Trustee not responsible except for fire loss proceeds it receives

Use of fire loss proceeds for rebuilding in same manner as in Article_____ relating to new construction

Compensation, costs, and expenses of trustee to be paid by lessee

Right of trustee to resign; method of appointing successor and powers of successor

Further convenants by lessee

Against liens

Against waste

Indemnity of lessor against costs, expenses, damages, fines, and attorneys' fees

Against assignment of lessee's interest directly or by operation of law (except under conditions specified)

Against subletting (except under conditions specified)

Against erecting signs on building without written consent of lessor

Certain rights of lessor

To make advances upon default of lessee
Advances to be payable as additional rent
Interest to be paid on advances

Excused from inquiring into such things as validity of taxes and insurance premiums before paying

To enter premises at any reasonable time to inspect; and to maintain "For Rent" signs and to show premises to prospective tenants during a specified period at end of lease

To have lien for rent

To mortgage lessor's interest subject to lease

To transfer to assignee deposits made by lessee, without further liability to lessee

Upon default by lessee

Period of notice, if any, as to rent, payment of taxes, and maintenance of insurance; and as to other covenants of lessee

Lessor may distrain for rent or other moneys due

Lessor may reenter and either terminate lease or rent for account of lessee

Receipt of rent after default not a waiver of notice of default

No waiver of a breach to constitute waiver of succeeding breaches

Lessor's remedies to be cumulative

Liquidated damages for holding over after termination

Interest on defaults of rent and advances by lessor

Attorneys' fees incurred by reason of lease and in enforcing lease

Receiver to be obtained under certain conditions

Rights and obligations of mortgagee of lessee's interest

Eminent domain—entire or part of premises

Taking for use

Taking of fee title

Rights of lessee in event of ouster, limited to rent reserved during period lessee is deprived of possession

Covenants to run with land

Notices

Registered mail or delivered in person

Addressed to lessor at _____

Addressed to lessee at _____

Proof of service

Limitation of lessor's liability, in capacity as trustee, to property or trust estate

Signature clause

Clauses for special uses

Percentage rental

Restrictions with respect to conducting business

Manner of computing percentage rental

Form of statement or audits, when they are due, lessor's right to examine books, and manner of preserving claim

Due date for payment of percentage rental during term and for last period of term

No relation of partnership created—only that of lessor and lessee

Sale of present improvement to lessee

Construction of new building

Obligation to build and date for completion

Kind of improvement and restrictions with respect thereto

Approval of plans and specifications

Deposit of funds prior to wrecking present building

Application of deposited funds

Right of lessee to enter into party-wall agreements and restrictions and limitations thereon

Deposit of security for lessee's performance or for special purposes, together with disposition of such funds

Variation in types of long-term leases.   Leases vary in term and type of rental agreements. Such variations, however, do not change the basic principle that the leased fee interest is limited by the contract rent, and the leasehold value is limited by the amount of the economic rent the lessee can keep after paying the contract rental to the lessor.

In general, long-term leases may be classified as those extending more than 10 years. The probable life of the existing building or of a proposed new building frequently is a determining factor when the lessor and lessee agree on the lease term. There are several types of long-term leases, which are distinguished by their rental provisions.

The *flat rental lease* provides that the lessee pay a fixed rental (annually, quarterly, or monthly) for the entire term of the lease. This type of lease resembles a sale, in that any subsequent increase in dollar earnings of the property during the lease are not participated in by the lessor.

The *graduated* or *step-up lease* provides that the rental shall be increased at various stipulated times in the future. The purpose of this lease may be to provide a lower rental in the earlier years, to enable a new improvement to become established in its earning power. Sometimes it may be an attempt by the fee owner to participate in anticipated increase in earning power due to projected growth of the area or due to a changing value of the dollar as a medium of exchange. The problem with this form of lease has been that when it is made at the top of a real estate cycle, the step-up provisions at a later date may prove difficult for the lessee to meet.

The *step-down lease* usually is an attempt by lessor and lessee to take advantage of the lessee's ability to pay a high rent in the immediate future or to amortize the cost of special improvements made by the lessor for the benefit of the lessee. Often a tax situation favors the employment of this device.

The *revaluation lease* is another effort by the lessor to participate in any future increase in economic rent. Such leases often provide that every 10 years the property shall be revalued and the rental shall be revised to provide an agreed-on rate of return on the new value. These leases usually provide for the appointment of appraisers or arbitrators by the lessor and lessee, if they cannot agree on a value, and for the selection of a third party acceptable to both in the event that the appointed appraisers cannot agree.

The *index lease* is another attempt to protect against possible future loss on the part of the lessor. This form of lease ideally gives the parties protection against variation in dollar productivity brought about by a change in purchasing power. A recognized national index of the value of the dollar is used, and the rental under the lease is adjusted in accordance with this index.

In an inflationary situation such a lease might prove to be unfair. If the economic rent of the land and building does not keep pace with building costs, high building prices might adversely affect residual land value. It does not always follow that the value of land will decrease or increase in the same measure as economic rentals or the purchasing power of the dollar.

The *percentage lease* is perhaps the most effective attempt on the part of the lessor to benefit from the rent produced by a property used for a retail business. The percentage lease provides that the lessee pay to the lessor a fixed percentage of gross of retail sales transacted on the premises. Different types of retail business pay different percentages of their sales as rental. If the amount for rent in a percentage lease is in accordance with rental usually paid by businesses similar to the lessee's, such leases tend to produce the economic rent of the property. However, even these percentages often change because of changes in operating costs or net retail (profit) margins over a long period of time. The rental obtained at the percentage prescribed in the lease eventually may produce either more or less than the current economic rental value.

Another arrangement is the *lease-purchase or sale-and-leaseback agreement,* whereby the real estate owner transfers the title to the property to another party—usually an insurance company, foundation, or other institution—and takes back a long-term lease. The properties are usually single-occupancy properties used by the lessees in their own businesses. There are certain advantages in being a lessee rather than an owner. The two principal advantages are that the lessee can use his or her capital in the business instead of tying it up in real estate and can realize certain tax advantages, such as charging off rent (instead of depreciation) as an operating expense. The purchase price in such sales is often not evidence of value. It is characteristically based on the rental the lessee agrees to pay. If the purchaser depends primarily on the credit standing of the lessee, the value of the real estate becomes a secondary consideration. Therefore, the amount of the lease rent is largely a matter of satisfying the needs and convenience of the lessee. Under such distinguishable conditions either a positive or negative leasehold value could exist at the time the transaction is concluded.

All these types of long-term leases create a division of rights between leased fee and leasehold interests.

Nature of lease interests. When a lease has been executed, the bundle of rights in the real property becomes divided into two separate interests, commonly referred to as the leased fee estate and the leasehold estate.

LEASED FEE ESTATE—The right to receive the contract rent provided by the lease, the reversion of the real estate at the end of the lease, plus any other benefits but minus any penalties according to the provisions of the lease

LEASEHOLD ESTATE—The use and occupancy of the real estate, the value of which arises from the margin of the economic productivity of the property, subject to meeting the terms and provisions of the lease

When a fee, subject to a long-term lease, has been sold, published news articles often quote the sale price, which may then be expressed as the price per front foot or per square foot. This unit figure reflects a leased fee value and would not be an indication of the value of the total bundle of rights or other leased fees without documentation of comparability of lease payments, lease terms, and so on.

Basically, the valuation of a leased fee or leasehold is a matter of dividing the value of the real property, free of the lease, into separate values imputable to the leased fee and leasehold interests. The sum of the values of the fee, subject to the lease, and leasehold interests tends to be the same as the value of the property free and clear. However, under certain circumstances, the total value of the property as a unit can be more or less than the sum of the fee and leasehold values. It can be more if a financially capable lessee were liable for contract rent in excess of the present fair economic rent. If these circumstances exist and the leased fee interest exceeds the value of the property on an unleased basis, the property is composed of both tangible and intangible components. The definition of real property embraces the idea that property rights may attach to tangibles, such as real estate, and to intangibles, such as a lease favorable to the property owner.

Contract and economic rent. If the real estate currently is leased at its fair rental value, contract rent and economic rent are the same. However, in time, with changing conditions affecting the physical real estate and its earning power, or with changes in the purchasing power of the dollar, contract rent and economic rent tend to separate. Accordingly, analysis of leases that have been in effect for some time discloses that if the factors influencing the value have been favorable since the lease was executed, the current economic rent exceeds the contract rent with resulting enhancement in value of the lessee's leasehold interest in the property. Conversely, in instances where economic factors affecting value have been unfavorable since a lease was made, or where contract rent was established on too high a basis, contract rent may exceed current economic rent. In this situation the value of the leasehold interest is adversely affected. A negative leasehold interest, which reflects the extent to which the capitalized value of the excess rental liability detracts from the value of the leasehold estate, is created. If this negative interest is substantial, reaching a level where it becomes too burdensome, the tenant may default, and legal proceedings or rental adjustment may result. A financially sound lessee may be obliged to meet the contract rental payments. There are instances where lessees have paid to be relieved of this liability, in effect purchasing the negative leasehold interest. In other cases where only the land is leased and the lessee has constructed the building, the currently excessive contract rent may cause the fee interest to encroach on the value of the building.

For example, assume that a property on a retail business street consists of a parcel of land subject to an existing ground lease with a contract rent of $25,000 per year. The lessee built a two-story commercial building and operates the real estate which produces a net income of $50,000 per year. The present value of the land free and clear, for its highest and best use, is $200,000, and 9% is a fair rate of interest on the current land value. Under these circumstances, if the real estate were free and clear of lease, the return on the building investment over and above the fair economic rental value of the land would be:

Present annual net income to lessee	$50,000
Economic annual rental value of land	
$200,000 × .09	−18,000
Balance imputable to the building	$32,000

However, the owner of the building does not own the land, but has possession under a long-term net lease at $25,000 per annum ground rent, which results in a balance imputable to the lessee's interest as follows:

Present annual net income to lessee	$50,000
Contract rent under terms of ground lease	−25,000
Balance imputable to lessee's equity in building	$25,000

Therefore, the lessee must pay to the owner of the fee $7,000 of the $32,000 that should be received as building income. In effect, the lessor's interest has come to include not only the value of the land, but part of the economic value of the lessee's building as well.

Conversely, where economic rent exceeds contract rent, a positive leasehold interest in land is created. For instance, if in the previous example the contract ground rental were $15,000, the lessee's position would be:

Present annual net income to lessee	$50,000
Contract rent under terms of ground lease	−15,000
Balance imputable to leasehold estate, which now includes an interest in the land as well as the building	$35,000

In this situation the lessee's interest consists not only of the building, but also includes a leasehold interest in the land because the contract rental for the land is $3,000 less per annum than its current economic rental value.

Similarity between leasehold and equity interest.   There is a similarity between a leasehold interest and an equity interest. In a leasehold interest the lessee enjoys possession of the real estate, subject to paying the rental reserved in the lease. Remaining net income accrues to the lessee. In an equity interest the equity owner owns the real estate, subject to the rights of the owner of the mortgage to receive interest and principal payments as provided. In appraising a leasehold interest, the appraiser recognizes this similarity in giving consideration to the selection of a capitalization rate that reflects the risk in the lessee's interest. At the same time he or she recognizes that the lessor's interest—the ownership of the leased fee—bears the characteristics of a first mortgage in many respects, such as risk of collection and right of possession in the event of a default in payments. It follows that if the original lessee has subleased to a third party, the sublessor's interest has risk characteristics similar to those of a second mortgage. The sublessee has the equivalent of an equity position.

Valuation of leased fee interest—land reversion.   In the valuation of leased fees, the amount of the rental income is set by contract and need not be estimated by the appraiser. However, the appraiser estimates the net rental value of the real estate free and clear, in order to ascertain the margin of security between the economic rental value of the real estate and the contract rent reserved in the lease. This allows the appraiser to judge the element of risk that the owner of the leased fee interest is assuming in anticipating the payment of the contract rent. The estimate of this risk is the appraiser's principal problem in arriving at the value of the leased fee. A greater margin of security reduces risk and is one of the factors influencing the rate of return acceptable in the market.

The fixed contract rent for the term of the lease is income with the characteristics of an annuity. This calls for the application of factors from the present-value tables[2] at an appropriate discount rate for the remaining term of the lease. This computation produces the capitalized value of the rentals, which may be the greater part of the value of the leased fee.

The next step is to value the present worth of the property that reverts to the lessor at the expiration of the lease. The reversion may be either the land only or land and building together. The reasonable view is that the reversion is of land only where the lease extends to or beyond the remaining economic life of the building. Here the value of the land at the time of reversion is usually assumed to be the same as at the present time. Any error in this assumption is minimized because the compound interest table for the present worth of 1 substantially discounts the future reversion. A 9% per annum discount rate applied for a 20-year period produces a present value of only 18 cents on the dollar of the face amount; and for a 50-year period, less than 1.5 cents on the dollar.[3]

For example, a parcel of land with a present value of $200,000 is, or may be, leased for 20 years on a basis of 9% yield per annum or a net ground rental of $18,000 per year. The following calculation of value is applicable.

---

2. Appendix B.
3. Appendix B, 9% Table, Column 4.

Annual net rental for 20 years	$ 18,000
Present value of contract rent for 20 years discounted at an interest rate of 9% per annum $18,000 × 9.128546[a]	$164,314
Present value of the anticipated reversion of the land at the expiration of the lease discounted at the rate of 9% per annum $200,000 × .178431[b]	35,686
Total value of leased fee	$200,000[c]

[a]Appendix B, 9% Table, Column 5.
[b]Appendix B, 9% Table, Column 4.
[c]Note that this achieves the same result as $18,000 ÷ .09 = $200,000.

Valuation of leased fee interest—property (land and building) reversion. When the reversion involves both land and building at the end of the contract term, the appraiser is faced with the problem of supporting a value for the reversion before applying the discount factor. Again, the usual concept is to consider the land to have the same value at the time of reversion as it has at the present time. If the appraiser believes otherwise and supports the opinion, the land reversion figure may be adjusted. The improvements will be older at the expiration of the lease and may be depreciated accordingly. The present worth of the reversion may be calculated:

Lease term: 20 years		
Land: by comparison		$ 80,000
Building: (assume new) value today	$400,000	
Assumed depreciation in 20 years	50%	
Building value, at the end of 20 years		200,000
Total reversion		$280,000
Present value factor for 20 years, at assumed 9% rate		× .178431[a]
Present value of property (land and building) reversion	(say)	$ 50,000

[a]Appendix B, 9% Table, Column 4.

Essentially this computation applies a cost approach to the reversion component of value. The appraiser could support this conclusion by applying the market data approach to the reversion substantiating the estimate of value in the future by comparison with similar existing

20-year-old buildings. An income approach could also be developed, although projecting an estimate of economic rental 20 years from now borders on the theoretical to a degree that might detract from the acceptability of the conclusion.

Valuation of leased fee and leasehold interests.   The following three examples demonstrate a procedure in processing contract and excess rental in estimating the value of the leased fee and the leasehold interests where the site has a value of $80,000 and is improved with a new building having a (cost) value of $426,000.

EXAMPLE 1. Annual contract rent and economic rent are the same. 20-year lease. Building reversion at end of lease assumed at 50% of present value. (9% interest rate is assumed as applicable.)

Annual contract rent	$ 50,000
Annual economic rental value	$ 50,000
Present value of contract rent for	
20 years discounted at 9%	
$50,000 × 9.128546[a]	$456,000[b]
Present value of property reversion	
as above	50,000[b]
Total value of lessor's interest	$506,000[b]

[a]Appendix B, 9% Table, Column 5, 20 years.
[b]Rounded.

In Example 1 the contract rental equals the economic rent. In theory, the leasehold has no value, because there is no margin of net income attributable to the leasehold interest and the value of the lessor's interest is the value of the property. However, possession of the premises under the lease may in certain circumstances have some value to the lessee.

EXAMPLE 2. Annual contract rent is less than economic rent. 20-year lease. Same economic rent and property reversion assumed as in Example 1.

Annual economic rental value	$ 50,000
Annual contract rent	39,000
Lessee's annual advantage	$ 11,000

Lessor's leased fee interest

Present value of contract rent for 20 years discounted at 8.25%	
$39,000 × 9.638148[a]	$376,000[b]
Present value of property reversion in 20 years discounted at 9%	
$280,000 × .178431[c]	50,000[b]
Total present value of lessor's leased fee interest	$426,000[b]

Lessee's leasehold interest

Present value of lessee's $11,000 annual rental advantage for 20 years, discounted at 12.5%	
$11,000 × 7.241353[d] =	80,000[b]
Total value leased fee and leasehold interests	$506,000[c]

[a]Appendix B, 8.25% Table, Column 5, 20 years.
[b]Figure is rounded.
[c]Appendix B, 9% Table, Column 4, 20 years.
[d]Appendix B, 12.5% Table, Column 5, 20 years. The factor to produce $80,000 would be $80,000 ÷ $11,000 = 7.272727, which by interpolation reflects an interest rate of approximately 12.4%.

In Example 2 an 8.25% interest rate is used in discounting income to derive the leased fee interest. This rate is selected to illustrate the reduced risk of collecting the contract rent because it is below economic rent. The interest rate applicable to the reversion is unchanged at the 9% rate selected above as appropriate for the type of property. However, an interest rate of 12.5% is used in discounting the lessee's rental advantage to derive the value of the leasehold interest. In this case the total of the two interests is the same as the value of the entire property as shown in Example 1. Although the total of the two interests may differ, there is a tendency for the total of the separate values of the divided interests to equal the value of the whole property as a single unit of ownership. Thus the value of a leasehold estate may be indicated by the difference between the value of the property and the value of the lessor's interest. It is common practice to check leasehold value on this premise. The risk rate appropriate to the lessor's estate can usually be estimated from data on current interest rates, within a reasonably narrow range. Thus Example 2 might be developed as follows.

Estimated property value as in fee (Example 1)	$506,000
Less estimated value of lessor's interest (Example 2)	426,000
Estimated value of leasehold estate	$ 80,000

The approximate risk rate applicable to the leasehold estate may then be computed through interpolation using annuity factors. The 20-year present-worth factor applicable to the leasehold is:

$$\frac{\text{Value}}{\text{Income}} = \frac{\$80,000}{\$11,000} = 7.272727$$

This is equal to a compound interest factor for the present discounted worth of 1 per annum for 20 years at an interest rate between 12.25% and 12.50% per annum.

	Rate	Factor	Factor	
	12.25%	7.353914	7.353914	
	(target)		7.272727	(factor applicable to the leasehold)
	12.50%	7.241353		
Difference	.25%	.112661	.081187	

The leasehold rate is 12.25% plus a fractional part of the distance to 12.50% represented by .081187 ÷ .112661 × .25% = .1802%. Hence by interpolation the developed interest rate applicable to the leasehold estate is 12.43% (12.25% + .18%).

EXAMPLE 3. Annual contract rent is in excess of economic rent. 20-year lease. Reversion, same as Example 2.

Annual contract rent	$ 55,000
Annual economic rental value	50,000
Lessor's excess rent	$ 5,000
Present value of economic rent as in Example 1	$456,000
Present value of reversion as in Example 1	50,000
Value of leased fee	$506,000

Present value of lessor's $5,000 annual excess
rental advantage for 20 years, discounted at 15%
$5,000 × 6.259331[a]   (say) $ 31,000

[a]Appendix B, 15% Table, Column 5, 20 years.

The value of these two lessors' interests may be summarized:

Value of leased fee	$506,000
Excess value due to favorable lease	31,000
Total value of lessors' interests	$537,000

The excess value due to the favorable lease in this example is not imputable either to land or building. It is a third element. If these circumstances exist and the combined interests of all parties total more than the value of the property on an unleased basis, the property is composed of both tangible and intangible components. This concept has been referred to as the two-property concept which affirms that property rights may attach to tangible things, such as real estate, and to intangible conditions, such as the existence of a lease favorable to the property owner.[4]

The $31,000 excess value due to a favorable lease is secured by the credit of the lessee, rather than by the intrinsic value of the property leased. Therefore, it takes the characteristics of an obligation of the lessee, secured only by the lessee's credit. Its capitalization into value should therefore be at a risk rate consistent with the contractual obligation and credit standing of the lessee. Such excess value due to a favorable lease is therefore an asset to the lessor and an obligation of the lessee.

In Example 3 a 15% interest rate is used in discounting the excess rent. However, this risk rate varies with the obligation of the lessee and his or her credit standing. Payment of the excess rent may be additionally secured by any investment of the lessee in improvements to the property. Some leases provide that the lessee may be relieved of all obligation by transferring the lease.

These three examples are presented for the purpose of illustrating a

4. George L. Schmutz, *The Appraisal Process* (North Hollywood, Calif.: Author, 1951), pp. 14-16.

logical procedure in estimating the value of leased fees, leasehold interests, and excess value due to a favorable lease. Also illustrated is the tendency of risk to decrease or increase the appropriate interest rate used in capitalizing net rent into a value estimate.

Another element of risk is the risk of a change in money value (inflation or deflation). Many leases made prior to 1930 included clauses that the rental was to be paid in gold. When the United States discontinued its gold standard, these clauses became inoperative. As a result, rental obligations carry the risk of future payments in money of a changed purchasing power. This has the effect of increasing the risk factor acceptable to purchasers of leased fees for long terms. Therefore, the acceptable interest rate on long-term leased fees increases as the assurance of receiving the income dollars of unchanged purchasing power decreases.

Sandwich leases.   If a property is leased and then subleased, the original lessee becomes the owner of a sandwich leasehold. The sandwich position is between the original lessor and the sublessee. In complex situations there can be more than one sandwich position. There is no particular difficulty in valuing an intermediate position in a parcel of real property, if all the facts are known. The owner of a sandwich lease has the right to retain the margin of contract income between that which is received from the sublessee and that which is paid to the owner of the leased fee. A sandwich leasehold is an intangible in that there is no right to use and occupy or ultimately to repossess the physical real estate. The rights of this leaseholder terminate at the end of the original lease.

Occasionally, the sandwich lessee is faced with default by the sublessee and is obliged to step in to operate the property. This circumstance and any other potential hazards are reflected in the capitalization rate applicable to the income retained by the sandwich lessee.

Assume a leased fee with 30 years remaining on a net lease at $6,400 per year. The lessee has subleased at $36,400 per year to expiration of the 30-year term. The economic rental value of the property is $42,000 per year.

Assume the property, unencumbered by the leases, has a market value of $400,000 and market research reveals that the rate applicable to the leased fee is 8% and the reversion value in 30 years is estimated at $100,000 to which a 9% discount rate is considered applicable.

The value of the leased fee interest consists of

Present value of contract rent	
$6,400 × 11.257783[a] =	$ 72,000[c]
Present value of reversion	
$100,000 × 0.75371[b] =	7,500[c]
Total present value, leased fee interest	$ 79,500

[a]Appendix B, 8% Table, Column 5, 30 years.
[b]Appendix B, 9% Table, Column 4, 30 years.
[c]Rounded.

The value of the combined leasehold interests may be assumed to approximate

Present value of property as in fee simple	$400,000
Present value of leased fee interest	− 79,500
Present value of combined leasehold interests	$320,500

Income to the combined leasehold interests is $42,000 − $6,400 = $35,600. The 30-year annuity factor applicable to the combined interest is

$$\frac{\$320,000}{\$ 35,600} = 9.002809$$

The interest rate applicable to the combined leasehold interests is the rate represented by this 30-year annuity factor. Reference to the tables in Appendix B reveals that this factor is between the 30-year factors for 10.50% and 10.75%. Interpolation reveals a rate of, say, 10.6% applicable to the combined leasehold interests.

This rate represents a weighted average of the rates applicable to the sandwich and sublessee interests. At this point the appraiser considers the relative risk position of the two positions. If the leased fee were land only and the owner of the sandwich position invested the funds necessary to erect a building, his risk may be close to that of the sublessee and hence only slightly under this weighted average rate for both interests. However, if the sublessee erected the improvements, the risk inherent in the sandwich position may be closer to the

8% applicable to the leased fee. In this example the leased fee rental represents only a return on land value. The owner of the sandwich interest erected the improvements and his risk is closer to the 10.6% rate applicable to the combined leasehold interests than to the 8% applicable to the leased fee. A judgment decision, based on this and any other pertinent considerations, may reflect a 10.25% rate considered applicable to the sandwich interest.

On this basis the value of the sandwich interest is easily computed

$36,400 − $6,400 = $30,000 per year for 30 years	
Present value $30,000 × 9.233800[a]	$277,000
The value of the sublessee's estate may be estimated at	
$400,000 − ($79,500 + $277,000)	$ 43,500

[a]Appendix B, 10¼% Table, Column 5, 30 years.

The rate applicable to the sublessee's estate may be computed in the same manner as for the combined estates. In this case the 30-year factor is $43,500 ÷ $5,600 = 7.767857, and by inspection of the tables, the interest rate is 12.5%±.

The interests and the applicable rates are summarized.

		Percent of Total Value	Risk Rate (%)
Leased fee	$ 79,500	20	8.00
Sandwich interest	277,000	69	10.25
Sublessee interest	43,500	11	12.50
Total	$400,000	100	

The leased fee position is well secured, not only by the lease obligations of the lessee and sublessee but also by the substantial leasehold improvements erected on the site. The sandwich position, which consists of the right to retain a $30,000 per year economic margin between the rent received from the sublessee and the rent paid to the owner of the fee, is secured by the obligation of the sublessee and any investment by the sublessee in additional leasehold improvements. The sublessee has the burden of management and the 12.50% rate reflects the greater risk inherent in this position where changes in the level of economic rent may be magnified in their effect on the $5,600 economic margin currently accruing to the subleasehold position. The rates developed for these three interests reasonably reflect the risk relationships as viewed by investors in the market.

It is not always practical to develop rates applicable to several interests in a property through an analysis of market transactions involving similar interests and similar circumstances. However, the rate applicable to the leased fee position is normally available through market research. In such cases the procedure presented here permits a logical development of rates applicable to the leasehold positions and provides support for judgment decisions involved in the process. When a rate applicable to either leasehold position can be supported by market evidence, the rate applicable to the other may be computed as that rate necessary to maintain the level attributable to the combined leasehold interests.

The sum of the leased fee and leasehold interests may be worth more or less than the real estate free and clear. To appraise a leased fee or a leasehold, the appraiser reviews the terms of the lease or leases that create a division of the property rights. The lease terms may adversely affect the lessor's interest, or they may restrict the lessee in utilizing the full present or potential productivity of the real estate.

For example, there have been instances of long-term leases in which the lessee does not have the unrestricted right to raze the existing building and build a new one. This could occur when the structure is obsolete and ready for razing and the lessee desires to build a new modern improvement, but the lessor withholds consent. The lessor may hope to obtain a favorable revision of the lease terms, thereby recapturing part of the leasehold interest. This prevents the lessee from improving the real estate to its highest and best use and from realizing its full potential return. Another example is the situation of a lease nearing its expiration, and the remaining term may not warrant the lessee's constructing improvements representing the highest and best use. Here again, the sum of the fee and the leasehold interests may be worth less than the value of the whole.

To an extent, leasehold values may also be restricted by lenders' prejudice against leaseholds as security for loans or by existing state laws. Some insurance companies have been prohibited by law from lending on leaseholds. Others will not lend on leaseholds because of the similarity of a leasehold loan to a second mortgage. Any lack of available financing tends to limit the number of potential purchasers and to depress the price. Under all the above circumstances, the sum of the prices obtainable for the sale of each separately at a given time may be less than the amount that a single purchaser would pay for the two together—that is, the value of the unencumbered fee.

Graduated rentals.   The tables giving the present value of an ordinary annuity of 1 per period permit calculation of the value of segments of income to reflect the mathematical consequences of variations in an income stream.[5] Assume two identical plots of land, A and B, each under a 50-year ground lease with a lessee of the same quality. The leased parcels are valued at $80,000 each, although the amount and time of rental payments stipulated in the leases vary. The lease on Plot A provides a level annual rental of $6,400 per year for the entire term of the lease. The lease on Plot B provides for an annual rental at $5,500 per year for the first five years of the lease, $6,000 per year for the second five years, $6,500 per year for the third five years, and $7,623 per year for the remaining 35 years.

Assuming the same 8% risk rate, both income streams reflect the same value of $80,000 for the leased fee, using present value tables[6]— property residual technique—as shown by the following:

Plot A—Level Annual Lease Rental

Present value of $6,400 per year		
$6,400 divided by .08		$80,000
Or, using present value tables—property		
residual technique, 50-year term		
$6,400 × 12.233485[a]	$78,294	
Plus reversion		
$80,000 × .021321[b]	$ 1,706	
		$80,000

---

5. Appendix B Tables, Column 5.
6. Appendix B Tables, Columns 4 and 5.

Plots A and B—Annual Lease Rental by Graduated Steps

	Present Value	
	Plot A level annual rental	Plot B graduated annual rental
Step 1 Present value of first five years' income 8% factor 3.9927[a] A: level income $6,400 × 3.992710 B: graduated income $5,500 × 3.992710	$25,553	$21,960
Step 2 Present value of second five years' income 8% factor 6.710081[a] − 3.9927a = 2.717371 A: level income $6,400 × 2.717371 B: graduated income $6,000 × 2.717371	17,391	16,304
Step 3 Present value of third five years' income 8% factor: 8.559479[a] − 6.710081 = 1.849398 A: level income $6,400 × 1.849398 B: graduated income $6,500 × 1.849398	11,836	12,021
Step 4 Present value of last 35 years' income 8% factor: 12.233485[a] − 8.559479 = 3.674006 A: level income $6,400 × 3.674006 B: graduated income $7,623 × 3.674006	23,514	28,007
Total present value 50 years' income	$78,294	$78,292
Add reversion as before	1,706	1,706
Total value, leased fee interest	$80,000	$79,998

[a]See Appendix B, 8% Table, Column 5.
[b]See Appendix B, 8% Table, Column 4.

In summary, capitalization in perpetuity at the selected risk rate, or application of annuity factors to net rent, produces the same mathematical result if the same interest rate and reversion assumptions are applied. The use of annuity tables, however, provides a flexibility that permits capitalization of varying income and reversion situations. In the above example the level income and graduated income capitalize to the same value. In actual practice they vary in accordance with the amount and timing of the rental payments. For example, consider the same 50-year lease with the same average annual rent of $6,400 per annum, but with the first half of the period at a lower annual rental and the second half at a correspondingly higher rental level.

Present worth of 50 years' rental
First 25 years @ $5,200 per year × 10.674776[a]	$55,500[b]
Second 25 years @ $7,600 per year × 1.558709	11,800[b]
(12.233485[a] − 10.6748776[a] = 1.558709)	
Add reversion as above	1,700
Value of leased fee interest	$69,000[b]

[a]Appendix B, 8% Table, Column 5.
[b]Rounded.

Despite the same average annual rental over the term of the lease, a lower valuation reflects the fact that the level of rentals in the early years has a greater impact on discounted present worth than do the rental levels of later years.

Advance rentals.   The annuity table assumes equal amounts, payable at the end of the year. The following computation demonstrates application of the annuity table when the payments are to be made in advance on January 1 instead of December 31 of the same year. With payment in advance, the lessor can immediately reinvest the money, at least theoretically, and realize the benefit of such reinvestment during the year.

A lessor is to receive a rental of $6,400 per year, for 20 years at 8% interest, with a reversion of $80,000. Rents are payable in advance.

		Present Worth
Step 1		
Receipt of $6,400 at beginning of first year		$ 6,400
Step 2		
Receipt of 19 more payments, corresponding in time to a 19-year annuity at 8%, factor 9.603559[a] × $6,400		61,463
Present value of the 20-year annuity, payable in advance		$67,863
Step 3		
Reversion $80,000 to be received in 20 years, discounted at 8%, factor .214548[b]		17,163
Total, based on rentals to be received in advance		$85,026
	(say)	$85,000

[a]Appendix B, 8% Table, Column 5, 19 years.
[b]Appendix B, 8% Table, Column 4, 20 years.

In effect, what was accomplished in Steps 1 and 2 was a computation of the present worth for payment in advance through multiplication by 1 plus the factor for one less year. The 19-year factor + 1 = 10.603599 which, multiplied by $6,400, produces the same present value as Steps 1 and 2 ($67,863).

Alternately, the present worth of an annuity in arrears may be converted to the present worth of the same annuity payable in advance through multiplication by the "base," which is 1 plus the effective interest rate $(1 + i)$ or, in the above example, 1.08.

$$\$6,400 \times 9.818147^a \times 1.08 = \$67,863$$

[a]Appendix B, 8% Table, Column 5, 20 years.

There is no change in calculation of present worth of the reversion. Lease payments in advance cannot advance the end of the lease when the reversion is received.

In actual practice, long-term rentals are paid monthly or quarterly, seldom at the end of the year. Technically, rentals paid semi-annually, quarterly, or monthly should be processed by using semi-annual, quarterly, or monthly tables.[7] Practically, income is ac-

7. Such semi-annual, quarterly, and monthly tables are shown for 8% in Appendix B, Column 5.

counted for at the end of the year. Therefore, even if the rental were received monthly or quarterly, the tendency is to consider the income as if received once a year, at the end of the year.

Possessory Interests

Possessory interest is the right to the occupancy and use of any benefit in the transferred property, granted under any lease, permit, license, concession, or other type of contract. To avoid confusion regarding the values of possessory interests, as commonly used, it is necessary to clarify whose interest is being appraised.

The value of a possessory interest usually refers to the value of the interest leased—that is, the value of the use and occupancy of the property for the lease term. This cannot be confused with the value of the lessee's leasehold interest in the right of possession under the terms of the occupancy contract, which is subject to the obligation to pay the rent and to comply with the other terms of the lease.

The usual measure of value of a lessee's interest in a lease, recognized by the courts, is the present worth of the difference between the actual rental value of the property leased and the amount of the contract rental the lessee must pay under the terms of the lease, plus the value of any leasehold improvements owned by the lessee.

The commonly recognized measure of value of the lessor's interest in a leased property is the present worth of the remaining rental payments set forth in the lease until the lease expiration, plus the present worth of the value of the real estate reverting to the lessor.

Although the lessee has both a possessory interest and a leasehold interest under any particular lease, the value to the lessee of these two interests may not be the same.

For example, assume a value of $100,000 for land leased for 20 years at its full present rental value of $8,000 per year (which rests in the lessor). The values of the lessor's interest, the leasehold interests, and possessory interest are shown in Example 4. In this case the lessee's interest has no calculable value. However, the possessory interest of the lessee is defined as the value of the interest which he leases, or $78,545, excluding the reversion in which he has no possessory interest. Discount rate is 8%.

Now assume the same property is leased at a rental of $100 per year, as shown in Example 5. Under this situation the value of the possessory interest remains the same as in Example 4, but the value of the lessor's interest is greatly decreased, and a valuable leasehold has resulted for the lessee.

EXAMPLE 4

Present value to lessor of reversion of the property in 20 years	
$100,000 × .214548[a]	$ 21,455[b]
Present value to lessor of 20 years' rental to be paid	
$8,000 × 9.818147[c]	78,545[d]
Total property value	$100,000

EXAMPLE 5

Present value to lessor of reversion of the property in 20 years, as above	$ 21,455[b]
Present value of 20 years' rental to be paid to lessor under lease	
$100 × 9.818147[c]	980[d]
Present value of difference between economic rent and contract rent ($8.000 − $100 = $7,900 per year × 9.818147[c]) is the value of the lessee's interest	77,565[d]
Total property value	$100,000

[a]Appendix B, 8% Table, Column 4.
[b]Retained by lessor and not under control of lessee.
[c]Appendix B, 8% Table, Column 5.
[d]Also value of possessory interest.

In Example 4, $78,545 is the value of the possessory interest *leased* to the lessee. Although under *possession* by the lessee, it is a value asset only to the lessor and not to the lessee; and in no way can the value of the possessory interest be construed as a value of the lessee's interest.

Example 5 shows the reverse situation, where the lessee is paying such a low rental that practically the entire value of the leased interest is vested in the lessee.

In Example 4 the value of the lessee's interest is zero, but in Example 5 it is actually $77,565. Nevertheless, in both 4 and 5,

Figure 23.1. Valuation of Leasehold Compared to Possessory Interest

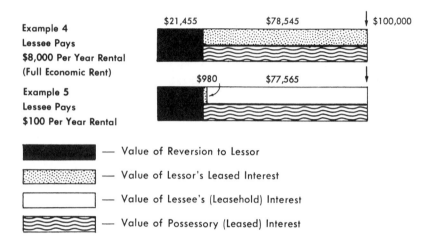

according to the accepted concept of the value of possessory interests (meaning the value of the *leased* interest belonging to the lessor), its value could be calculated at $78,545. Therefore, in accordance with this concept, value of this possessory interest inures to the *lessor* and does not reflect the value of the *lessee's leasehold interest* (see Figure 23.1).

In consequence, an appraisal of the value of the interest of the *lessee* in the property—be it called leasehold interest or possessory interest—can only be obtained by the procedures for valuing leasehold interest and can arise only when the economic rent exceeds the contract rent.

RIGHTS AND INTERESTS

The rights and interests in real estate may be considered under legal or physical divisions of ownership. The bundle of rights may include a number of types of separate interests, including rights or estates other than those created by leases for use and occupancy of the physical real estate.

Public Rights

Included in public rights are certain rights that belong to the sovereign government and not to the private owner. All private ownership of real estate is subject to the power of the sovereign government acting in the public interest. Real estate ownership is always subject to taxation, escheat, eminent domain (condemnation), and the police power of the state.

The effect on value of the right of taxation needs little commentary here. The power to tax is the power to reduce property value or to destroy it.

Escheat pertains to the reversion to the state of property if there are no legal heirs. Police power pertains specifically to regulation in the areas of health, safety, morals, and general welfare; it includes regulation of land use and of air and noise pollution by zoning, other laws, and ordinances, plus alteration of direction and arrangement of traffic patterns in streets adjacent to properties.

Under eminent domain the taking of a property or a property interest requires that the owner be justly compensated (for its market value). However, taking of abutter's rights under the police power in the form of street changes, such as the installation of median strips, or initiation of one-way traffic, may not be compensable, even though an owner may suffer damage from forced circuitry of travel.

Private Rights

The rights in any real estate in private ownership may be divided. The valuation of these rights begins with the value of the whole (subject to the public rights). Division of the whole may decrease or, under some circumstances, increase the value of the parts. Like the value of the whole, the value of any partial interest may be reflected in the market.

Division of privately owned real estate may be due to the existence of undivided fractional interests or to a physical separation.

Undivided fractional interests. Division of earnings or productivity occurs when ownership rests in undivided fractional interests such as tenancy in common or joint tenancy. A discussion of the nature of such interests can be found in other books on real estate and real estate law. For the purposes of this text it is sufficient to state that such an interest is usually an undivided fractional interest. The value of such fractional interests is usually less than the fraction that ownership bears to the value of the entire property, particularly where the ownership is less than a 50% interest in the property. Such ownership may be subject to a suit for a partition with the possibility of sale of the property to the highest bidder. Unless the fractional owner is prepared to bid and to buy the entire property, the resulting forced sale price may be below market value, and in any event the costs of the partition action will be subtracted from the price.

Land trusts.   Fractional interests may be established under a land trust where title is held for the benefit of the fractional owners. The trustee is usually a bank or a trust company that performs no duties other than to hold title for the beneficiaries. Such an arrangement usually includes an agreement between the respective interests, stating the rights and the duties of the parties with respect to the operation of the property and, in the event of certain contingencies, including sale of the entire property or one of the interests. Although these written agreements remove some of the risks of the bare undivided fractional interest, some risks remain—for example, a forced sale if death of one of the parties introduces conflicting interests through inheritance.

General and limited partnerships.   Similar to land trusts, this type of fractional ownership usually includes a multiplicity of "limited" partners who share pro rata in the net earnings and other benefits (including depreciation), but have no voice in the management decisions or responsibility. The general partners are often the persons who developed the partnership and retained special benefits, including the right of management decisions. The value of such fractional interests usually depends on the property itself, the terms of the agreement, and the competency of the general partners.

Cooperative apartments.   Although the public sometimes confuses them, cooperatives are essentially different from condominiums. Ownership in a cooperative is usually in the form of stock in a corporation owning the entire property. Each stockholding "owner" is given a proprietary lease on one apartment or unit, subject to certain conditions and obligations as to its use, lease, and sale. Usually lease or sale is subject to the approval of the board of directors.

Cooperative apartments eventually reach the stage where the mortgage has been paid to so low a sum that a great amount of cash is required by a purchaser. Since the balance of the ownership may be satisfied with the existing mortgage balance, an owner obliged to sell may be required to finance the purchase or find the market restricted to prospective purchasers who can pay almost the entire price in cash.

Corporate ownership. Some large projects are incorporated, and ownership is in the form of stock. One of the disadvantages of fractional-interest ownership in this form of real estate is that depreciation for income tax purposes cannot be passed through directly to the owner of the fractional interest. Ownership through corporate stock usually implies a broader ownership base involving far more people than in a partnership. One advantage of the former, however, is liquidity, since most large real estate stock issues have a proven market, with daily stock price quotations.

The value of undivided fractional interests reflects the present worth of future benefits accruing to ownership and varies in accordance with the agreement, if any, by which they were created, and the degree of risk in ownership. Usually the market value of a fractional interest is less than the same fraction of the market value of the entire property.

Physical division. Another category of fractional ownership is a division in the physical use of the property. Such divisions include:

1. Horizontal subdivision
2. Vertical subdivision (air and subsurface rights)
3. Easement (horizontal or vertical)
4. Condominium
5. Leased fee (creating lessee's and lessor's interests) (see pp. 474-478).

Horizontal and vertical subdivision. The division of air rights and subsurface rights is a less familiar subject than horizontal subdivision, by which the boundaries of surface areas of the earth are delineated. Subsurface rights in the form of oil or mineral rights are commonly leased and sold. Their exclusion may have little effect on surface land values if the terms of the conveyance protect it from interference. Subsurface rights may also involve underground pipe and cable lines.

Air rights.   Early common law stated, "To whomsoever the soil belongs, he owns the sky and the depths." On this basis, delineation of ownership is represented by a pyramid-like shape, its apex at the center of the earth with sides extending outward through the boundaries of the site on the earth's surface. However, within the distances normally encompassed above or below this surface, real estate ownership may be considered to be between vertical boundaries above and below the site. Practically, this means that ownership of a 100 x 100-foot parcel of land is not of a square surface but of a cube. Accordingly, this cube may be divided, not only vertically, similar to a slice of a layer cake, but also horizontally, as in individual layers of the slice of cake. The useful height or depth of this cube (number of stories) is limited only by the practicalities of engineering, economics (highest and best use), and zoning.

The railroads acquired extensive areas of centrally located land when it was of comparatively little value. Now that some of it has become valuable, the railroads are endeavoring to dispose of surplus land, retaining only what they need for right of way. Where it is practical and legal for highway authorities to acquire valuable centrally located land in excess of the need for improvement, such excess condemnation may be followed by disposition of the valuable air rights.

The schematic drawings in Figures 23.2 and 23.3 show descriptive identification of (1) a vertical air-rights subdivision into air lot, column lots, caisson lots, tunnel areas; and (2) air rights or easement for an electric transmission right-of-way. Horizontal and vertical dimensions with reference to city data may, of course, be substituted for the letters and numbers in the diagrams.

Like many complicated problems, the principle involved in air rights and access is simple. It may be expressed in terms of the value of the land before and after the taking of the vertical access layer. It is based on a consideration of the added cost of, and/or savings in, construction as well as the reduction in the economic value of an improvement erected on air rights compared with that of the same improvement if erected on unencumbered land.

Figure 23.2. Three-Dimensional Subdivision for Air and Tunnel Rights (schematic drawing)

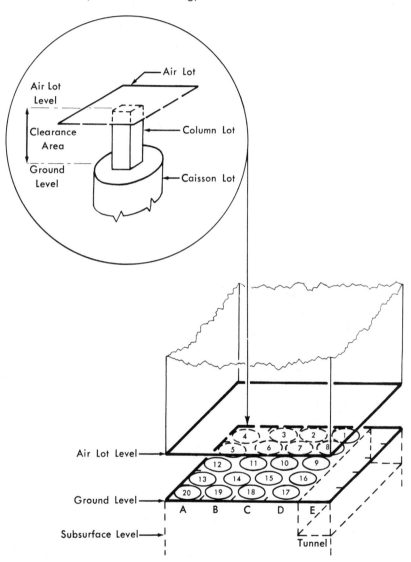

Air rights:
As an example, these may be identified as air rights above air lot level
  column lots between air lot level and ground, 1–20
  caisson lots below ground level, 1–20
  tunnel rights between ground level and subsurface level, space E

Figure 23.3.   Three-Dimensional Subdivision for Air or Tunnel Rights (electrical transmission lines right of way). Electrical transmission rights: 3, above and/or below ground level.

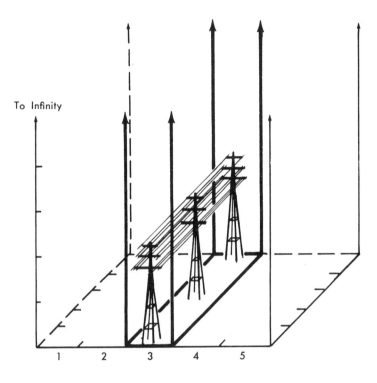

Easements.   Easements are usually on the surface and created for access to a property from a public thoroughfare or between properties, over another private ownership. However, they may be vertical as well as horizontal, as in the case of underground or overhead utility lines, tunnels for railroads, subways, overhead streets, and bridges.

Interesting value questions are raised in the creation of such easements or subsurface fee title rights. A publicized explosion involving a gas main may raise questions of loss in value of the property through which the right of way is sought for gas mains (damage to remainder as the result of the use of the part taken). Overhead transmission towers are being designed for greater attractiveness to counteract both the claims of unsightliness and the adverse influence on the remainder property through which a right of way is taken. Where an existing right of way is sought for a new use, an approach to its value may be the principle of substitution—that is, the cost of acquisition of equivalent right of way through adjacent areas.

Condominiums. As a form of ownership, a condominium interest differs substantially from a cooperative interest. Ownership of a condominium unit is basically ownership of the cubical area within the confines of its outer walls, floor, and ceiling, plus joint ownership rights in all public space that, together with the condominium units, comprises the entire property. The condominium unit is a separate ownership, with title in the owner. It may be leased, sold, mortgaged, or refinanced separately. There is much more flexibility in the condominium unit ownership than in the cooperative unit ownership in regard to resale, leasing, or financing. The appraisal of condominiums includes a study of the rights and restrictions that are part of the declaration or legal document agreed to by all parties, which creates and defines the condominium interests and obligation.

SUMMARY

The value of various types of partial interests in real property requires appraisal.

The private ownership of any parcel of real estate is comprised of a bundle of rights which may be individually transferred to different ownerships. Such rights or partial interests may involve undivided fractional interests or the transfer of certain rights of use of the physical property by lease, permit, easement, or other device. Partial interests in property may also be established through land trusts and various forms of partnership.

The physical property may be divided not only horizontally (lots, blocks), but also vertically (air or subsurface rights). Easements for use and access may also be established both horizontally and vertically. Condominium agreements divide a single property into a number of individual ownerships by means of three-dimensional subdivisions.

Leased fees, leaseholds and possessory interests, and easements are divisions of use, possession, or rental of a single property between a fee owner and a lessee or licensee. The value of these ownerships varies with the contract rental and the economic rental value of the property as well as with the agreements creating them.

The purpose of this chapter is not to convey the idea that the appraisal of the value of partial interests in real estate is purely a mathematical process or to deal with the legal aspects of partial interests. The objective is to emphasize the need for familiarity with the terms of the documents and the programs by which the partial interests are created and to present orderly processes, involving simple mathematics, as useful tools for the appraisal of such interests. As shown in the examples, the appraiser may begin the appraisal of a partial interest in a particular property with the value of the entire property free and clear. The appraiser may then divide this value between the various interests. The assumption is that the total of these various interests tends to be neither greater nor less than the value of the property free and clear. However, special conditions brought about by the division of a real property into various interests may increase or reduce its earning power for as long as these various separate interests exist. The procedures presented are to assist the appraiser in making—after analysis—appropriate valuations of the affected interests.

24

Rehabilitation, Modernization,

and Remodeling

The terms *rehabilitation, modernization,* and *remodeling* often are used as if they were synonymous, although each term has a specific meaning. The following definitions state the distinctions between these terms:

REHABILITATION—The restoration of a property to satisfactory condition without changing the plan, form, or style of a structure. In urban renewal, the restoration to good condition of deteriorated structures, neighborhoods and public facilities. . . . [1]

MODERNIZATION—taking corrective measures to bring a property into conformity with changes in style, whether exterior or interior, or additions to meet standards of current demand. It normally involves replacing parts of the structure or mechanical equipment with modern replacements of the same kind.[2]

REMODELING—Changing the plan, form, or style of a structure to correct functional or economic deficiencies.[3] Remodeling may also be to change the use or utility of the structure.

---

1. American Institute of Real Estate Appraisers and Society of Real Estate Appraisers, *Real Estate Appraisal Terminology* (Cambridge, Mass.: Ballinger Publishing Co., 1975), p. 174.
2. *Ibid.*, p. 142.
3. *Ibid.*, p. 175.

The collective changes arising from rehabilitation, modernization, and remodeling may be grouped under the general heading of renovation.

REHABILITATION

Appraisers often find that expenditures are necessary to bring properties up to a competitive level. When inspecting improvements, the appraiser examines the need for painting, tuckpointing, carpentry repairs, roof repairs, decoration of rentable or public space; the condition of fixtures, piping, and other equipment; and similar items. Then, in analyzing accrued depreciation, allowance is made for the cost of rehabilitating the property to satisfactory condition. This competitive standard of condition could be at a lower level for an old building than that required for a new building. All curable deterioration is not necessarily rehabilitation, since all defects included in the curable physical depreciation category do not require immediate attention. Items that properly come under the heading of rehabilitation are commonly referred to as items of deferred maintenance.

MODERNIZATION

Modernization implies replacements or remodeling specifically designed to offset the effect of obsolescence or additions necessary to meet standards of current demand. The replacement of old radiators, lighting, or plumbing fixtures with new items of fundamentally the same type is nothing more than improving the *condition* of the old installation. However, the substitution of convectors for cast-iron radiators, of built-in bathtubs for tubs on legs, or of modern lighting fixtures for old-fashioned types would not necessarily have any relation to the physical condition of the replaced items, and therefore it constitutes an improvement of the property. These expenditures offset obsolescence and may be classified as modernization. Modernization may cost more than simple renewal, but can be economically justified where it offsets the obsolescence inherent in the older type of equipment.

Modernization and simple renewals differ in their effects on the value estimate. Although rehabilitation through renewals may result in sustaining or increasing tenancy and income and reducing operating costs, these effects may be temporary. In contrast, modernization usually has the additional basic effect of extending economic life. This could raise the property to a competitive level closer to that which it held when nearly new.

This need for modernization is recognized when items are discovered that are subject to curable functional obsolescence. The corrective action may involve additions to the structure or to the equipment, or it may take the form of changes to the existing structure or equipment.

Changes in layout made to obtain or satisfy tenants may be temporary or permanent. Temporary changes are usually referred to as alterations; more lasting changes, which involve a revised program of use and added value, constitute remodeling.

Alterations, in this context, add to value only indirectly through extending and preserving lease rents. In major properties such changes are frequent, and office space that is subdivided one year may be changed again in two or three years. Such changes are not considered to have a permanent effect on the structure.

To be justified, a modernization program must be economically feasible. It should be initiated only after a feasibility study, with the modernization program related to a soundly conceived plan of operation for the property as a whole.

REMODELING

Remodeling becomes a practical consideration when the present use of a structure is not its highest and best use, and it is necessary to embark on a program involving extensive changes in the property to achieve the desired usage. Functional and economic obsolescence usually are underlying motives for a remodeling program. Examples of the effects of these two causes are found in all cities where large, old buildings no longer physically or economically serve the purpose for which they were built; but through remodeling programs they have retained their original or attained a new highest and best use.

As in modernization, considerable remodeling that is not necessary or practical may be undertaken. Any program for remodeling must be analyzed carefully to ascertain whether the results achieved can be economically justified. For example, remodeling the attic space in a residence to provide an apartment may not increase the value of the property by as much as the cost of the remodeling. If done without complying with building codes, remodeling may result in health or safety ordinance violations. Expenditures for such remodeling in any type of structure may not be proportionately reflected in increased value.

COSTS

General standards of cost data for rehabilitation or renovation are developed through experience and research. Current reproduction cost new, frequently estimated by the unit-in-place procedure, represents basic cost, and to this is added any additional cost for performing the work in an existing structure. Rehabilitation estimates may frequently be based on actual recent costs for the same or equivalent work performed in the property or in similar properties. Management records may even include bids for specific rehabilitation items that have not been performed, such as exterior painting, roof repair, or interior decorating.

The cost of some rehabilitation work may approximate that for similar work in new construction. However, the cost of modernization or remodeling work is usually higher than for new construction, for several reasons. Although the quantity of material may be the same as for new work, more labor is involved, and the conditions are different. The alteration of a structure generally involves tearing out old work and performing small quantities of new work under conditions not conducive to the degree of efficiency attainable on new construction. If the estimate made by the contractor is on a flat-fee basis, he may charge substantially more than the cost of identical work in new construction in order to protect himself against complications, such as the unforeseen placement of existing conduits, pipes, and structural load-bearing members, that may develop as the remodeling progresses.

Other costs to be considered are those that may be incurred by the owner rather than the contractor. These include items such as architect's fee, owner's cost of supervision, and loss of rents due to vacancies while the work is being done. These costs are in addition to the direct cost estimate.

CONTROLLING PRINCIPLES

Renovation surveys and estimates are controlled primarily by the following principles:[4]

1. Contribution
2. Increasing and decreasing returns
3. Conformity

According to the principle of contribution, each component of a building should contribute to the production of income or to the value of the whole. For example, if elevators or air-conditioning systems are to be installed in an existing building, their installation should improve (preserve or increase) the net income before recapture to an extent sufficient to amortize and pay a proper return on the additional investment.

Beyond some point the net revenue probably cannot be increased, making it uneconomic to invest more money in the property. Computations involving a number of alternatives may be necessary to ascertain this turning point between increasing and decreasing return.

The principle of conformity implies a consideration of the neighborhood. A building may be an improper improvement for the land and the location, and although the design might lend itself well to modernization or remodeling, the rental level that can be achieved and maintained in the location may not justify the expenditure involved.

PROCEDURES

Whether rehabilitation, modernization, or remodeling is involved, the justification for any renovation program depends on the answer to the basic questions of what constitutes the property's highest and best use. The study that the appraiser gives to this question produces the cost estimates necessary for a program to achieve this use; they provide the basis for a decision on its economic justification. If the property is old but in sufficiently sound condition for remodeling, if the district standards and trends are materially higher than the proper-

---

4. See Chapter 2.

ty's present status, and if the prospective income improvement is substantial, a comprehensive program may be feasible. A wide range of potential programs may justify consideration, but there is only one satisfactory way to select a final plan. This is to explore the alternatives, to estimate the cost and potential income (value) benefits, and then be guided by the results of a comparison of the data thus developed.

A four-story, 40-year-old apartment building is located in a neighborhood that is still in reasonable demand. There are two apartments per floor, seven rooms each, renting for $96 per month. The building has been allowed to deteriorate but is structurally sound. Remodeling will double the number of units. Indicated values, before and after remodeling, as derived by the income approach using the straight capitalization method with straight-line recapture and the building residual technique, may be developed as follows.

Estimated Value Before and After Proposed Remodeling of 40-Year-Old 4-story Apartment Building

A. Indicated Value "As Is"

Prospective gross annual income		
8 units @ $96 × 12		$ 9,216
Allow for vacancy and loss, 10%		− 921
Effective gross annual income		$8,295
Expense		
Fixed	$1,200	
Variable	1,450	
Repairs and replacements	900	− 3,550
Net operating income		$ 4,745
Imputable to land, 8% × $12,000		− 960
		$ 3,785
Capitalized at 13% to include interest and (5%) recapture		$29,115
Add land value		+12,000
Total indicated value		$41,115
Less allowance for deferred maintenace (considered necessary to maintain present net income level)		− 2,215
Total indicated value		$38,900

Remodeled three-room suites will each bring $85 per month. Taxes will be increased by $650, insurance $150. Operating cost will be reduced by the new boilers, but administration, water, and other maintenance (i.e., decorating, repairs, and replacements) will result in a net increase of $1,345 to produce $4,895 of total expense.

B. Indicated Value after Remodeling

Prospective gross annual income,		
16 units @ $85 × 12		$16,320
Allow for vacancy and loss, 7.5%		− 1,225
Effective gross annual income		$15,095
Expense		
Fixed	$1,975	
Variable	1,800	
Repairs and replacements	1,120	− 4,895
Net operating income		$10,200
Imputable to land, 8% × $12,000		− 960
Net to building value		$ 9,240
Capitalized at 11% to include interest and		
(3%) recapture		$84,000
Add land value		+12,000
Total indicated value		$96,000

The following costs are estimated for the remodeling.

Rehabilitation		$ 2,215[a]
Capital Improvements		
Modernization		
Two gas-fired heating boilers	$1,875	
Electric fixtures and wiring	1,730	
8 baths at $320 (existing rooms)	2,560	
8 kitchens at $400 (existing rooms)	3,200	
		9,365
Remodeling		
Partition rearrangement	$9,800	
8 baths at $600 (new rooms)	4,800	
8 kitchens at $840	6,720	
		21,320
Estimated total cost		$32,900

[a] In both the before and after remodeling situations, it is assumed that deferred maintenance, curable for $2,215, must be cared for to maintain net incomes as projected.

CONCLUSION AS TO FEASIBILITY

The above computation indicates whether the proposed program is feasible. For the remodeling to be feasible, there should be a profit after all costs including allowance for vacancy during construction, allowance for contingencies, and perhaps even a sale commission. In this case the conclusion might be that 20 to 25% of the total investment would represent a sufficient incentive. From the before-and-after values and estimated costs, this incentive would appear to be

Indication of "after" value		$96,000
Indication of "as is" value		38,900
Projected value increment		$57,100
Cost of renovation program	$32,900	
Estimated loss of rent during implementation of program	3,100	
Allowance for contingencies	750	
		36,750
Net incentive		$20,350
Net incentive as a percentage of $75,650 investment		26.9%

Part of the enhancement in value can be accounted for by the lower building capitalization rate, reflecting an extended economic life projection. To support this projection, a reexamination of neighborhood conditions and trends may be in order.

This project would appear to be profitable to an investor prepared to invest a potential $75,650 ($38,900 "as is" value plus $36,750 in renovation) to achieve a $96,000 investment. The net incentive represents 26.9% of total cost.

An owner's existing commitment to the property may involve a change in this incentive analysis. A $57,100 enhancement in value produced by a $36,750 investment represents a profit margin of over 55% ($36,750 × 1.5537 = $57,100). In this case a decision concerning feasibility appears less questionable. However, the valuation, cost, and before-and-after values should be developed on the basis of a typical prospective purchaser.

In some cases, where the profit potential due to a renovation program is substantial, the "as is" value estimate for the property being appraised may be modified upward. In many cities old office and commercial buildings have been purchased at relatively low prices by imaginative investors who have undertaken a program of selective modernization, sometimes involving new exterior ("skin") treatment and other major expenditures. Modernized and attractive properties thus created have resulted in higher occupancy and increased rentals, becoming marketable at levels substantially above the investments involved.

Whether this is practical in any specific situation can be ascertained only after completion of a before-and-after feasibility analysis. This includes, as above, the potential increase in income, the concurrent possible increase in expense, the difference (if any) in capitalization, and the fair share of the "after" value imputable to entrepreneurial increment.

SUMMARY

In any appraisal of mid-life or older buildings, the possibility of additional value that might be created by a well-advised renovation program should be considered. Rehabilitation costs are normally a simple deduction from the value indicated by the usual approaches to the value estimate, if the final valuation is predicated on the building being in satisfactory rentable condition. However, modernization and remodeling may create additional net income, prolong economic life, and produce an economic margin of value over and above the cost of the work. An owner should anticipate a profit incentive sufficient to justify undertaking such a renovation program. Certain broad appraisal principles apply. The method for deciding whether a property is suited to a renovation program includes estimating value as is, cost of the work, and value after completion. The appraiser then considers whether there is sufficient profit incentive to warrant the indicated cost.

In the final analysis, the appraiser's estimate of a feasible rehabilitation, modernization, or remodeling program is part of the process leading to a value estimate for the property. Whether or not the owner actually carries out this program, the value of the property in its existing state may be influenced by its potential for increased income production or utility under a feasible remodeling program.

25

Reconciliation of

Value Indications

The process of analysis, interpretation, and reconciliation is continuous throughout an appraisal: the definition of the problem, the preliminary survey, the data assemblage, and the three approaches to a value indication. In each of these steps data is analyzed, interpreted, and reconciled to develop supportable conclusions. Each of the three approaches, if applicable, should conform in general to the indicated conclusion of value for the property. In this ideal situation there is no problem involved in reconciling the value estimates from the three approaches.

In actual practice, the assembly, analysis, and interpretation of data within the approaches seldom lead to this ideal situation. Consequently, a critical step in the appraisal process is a reconciliation of all value indications. This step brings together the facts and fits them into cause-and-effect relationships leading to a final conclusion of the defined value.

Consideration of the relative merit of each value indication involves the appraiser in a review of each approach in respect to

1. The reliability of data used
2. The applicability of the approach to the type of property being appraised
3. The applicability of the approach in the light of the definition of value sought

Assuming the value sought is market value, this process of reconciliation would involve weighing each estimate in the light of its dependability as a reflection of the probable actions of users and investors in the market. The appraiser's final conclusion of value may coincide with one of the approach estimates, or it may reflect a weighting of the relative merits of each leading to a final conclusion at some adjusted figure. Use of an average would imply that all value indications are equally valid. Since this is seldom true, the use of an average fails to reflect a proper application of the appraiser's experience and judgment in reconciliation of the value indications.

REVIEW OF LAND VALUE

The estimated value of the land is reliable when

1. The amount of available market data is adequate
2. The relative advantages and deficiencies of the land being appraised and the comparative land sales are not too extensive and have been correctly weighed

REVIEW OF THE COST APPROACH

The cost approach involves several critical judgment decisions and produces a significant indication of value when

1. The reproduction or replacement cost new has been correctly estimated
2. The building is new or nearly new and is the highest and best use of the site
3. Physical and functional depreciation are measurable
4. The physical deterioration and functional and economic obsolescence have all been correctly estimated

In reviewing this approach the appraiser considers the relative reliability of all the above in the light of the objective of the appraisal and the applicability of the cost approach to the client's problem. Under certain conditions, the cost approach may influence a typical user or investor because the land value is well supported, and a new building represents a justifiable economic use. However, the value indication from the cost approach by itself may not be so conclusive when accrued depreciation is substantial or when reproduction cost is difficult to establish.

REVIEW OF THE MARKET DATA APPROACH

It is axiomatic that the purpose of analyzing comparable sales is to attain an indication of the probable price at which the property being appraised would sell, if offered in the market.

The market data approach provides a meaningful indication of value when

1.   The amount of available market data is adequate
2.   The relative advantages and deficiencies of the property being appraised and the comparative sale properties are not too extensive and have been correctly weighed

The market data approach is most reliable when the data is closely comparable and in sufficient quantity to establish a pattern. The sales of comparable properties within a narrow price range should indicate a pattern that represents the reactions of typical purchasers in the market. Under these conditions the market data approach usually provides the most significant indication of value. However, the market data approach may require support from the income approach, especially if comparable sales reflecting the reaction of typical users and investors in the market are limited in number.

The market data approach may provide a critical value indication in the appraisal of older properties for which accrued depreciation is extensive and for which there is no clearly identifiable rental market.

REVIEW OF THE INCOME APPROACH

The income approach produces a meaningful indication of value when

1.   Gross income and operating costs have been properly forecast
2.   The capitalization rate reflects the market
3.   Appropriate methods and techniques have been used

Income-producing real estate is typically purchased for use or for investment. In either case the income-producing potential is the key to the value of the property, and the income approach provides a valid indication of the most probable selling price. For example, the value of an office building for which sound operating experience is available may be strongly indicated by the income approach and can be given the major share of the weight because experience discloses that investment considerations (present value of anticipated future income) typically provide the principal motivation for purchase.

CONCLUSION

Having analyzed the data and obtained indications of the value by the appropriate approach or approaches, the appraiser reconciles the value indications into a final conclusion of the defined value. Approach value indications may have been resolved to single figures or within reasonably narrow ranges. However, the final conclusion is normally reduced to a specific figure. In its precision this final figure reflects appraisal judgment and the applicability of the factual data on which it is based. It also depends on the knowledge and experience of the appraiser in interpreting the data. All pertinent data is analyzed in forming the basis for a final conclusion.

26
The Appraisal Report

The form, length, and content of a report may vary in different appraisals, depending on the requirements of the client, the type of property, and the nature of the assignment. An appraisal report may be written or oral. There are two kinds of written appraisal reports: standard form reports and narrative reports. Regardless of the type or length of these, the appraiser conforms to accepted standards of appraisal procedure and reporting.[1]

ORAL REPORT

An oral report may be made when circumstances do not permit or warrant the preparation of a written report. Such a report should include a statement of facts, assumptions, and conditions as well as the reasoning on which the conclusion is based. When an oral report is made, the appraiser preserves all notes and data, together with a complete memorandum of the analysis, conclusion, or opinion contained in the oral report.

Members of the American Institute of Real Estate Appraisers are obligated to comply with the provisions of Canon 5 of Regulation 10, Code of Professional Ethics and Standards of Professional Conduct, as they pertain to oral and written reports.

---

1. See *Regulation No. 10–Code of Professional Ethics and Standards of Professional Conduct* (Chicago: American Institute of Real Estate Appraisers, 1974).

CERTIFICATE OR LETTER

A certificate or letter giving the appraiser's opinion of value does not constitute a written appraisal report. These usually state only the appraiser's opinion of value, without inclusion of the supporting data or the analysis and interpretation leading to the conclusion. The instances in which the use of the appraisal letter is acceptable are limited. There may be circumstances when the client desires and specifically requests the appraiser to present an opinion in letter form without including detailed documentation. Usually the appraiser presents the report in the form the client requests. However, the simplicity of the final form can never preclude the necessity for the appraiser to meet the detailed requirements of a complete appraisal. Although only the opinion may be reported, all the material and data and all the working papers that would be assembled and processed in a complete analysis, interpretation, and conclusion for a narrative report are kept in a permanent file. Although the appraiser may not be asked to submit a written substantiation of the opinion that is remitted in abbreviated form, it may be necessary at a later date to explain or defend the opinion.

FORM REPORT

Institutions and governmental agencies frequently find that form appraisal reports best meet their purposes. Because such clients use many appraisals during a year, a standardized report form may be more efficient and convenient for their purposes. It enables those responsible for reviewing the appraisals to know exactly where in the report to find any particular category or item of data, and completion of the form ensures that no item required by the reviewer is overlooked.

If the report form seems to be too rigid, with no provision for certain data the appraiser believes to be pertinent, the relevant information and comments are added as a supplement.

NARRATIVE REPORT

The narrative appraisal report affords the appraiser the opportunity to support and explain opinions and conclusions and to convince the reader of the soundness of the estimate. Accordingly, the discussion in this chapter concerning the appraisal report is directed primarily to the narrative form.

Every appraisal report is intended to answer a particular value-related question and generally is intended to constitute the basis for a decision by the client. Questions may be: What is the market value? In condemnation, what is the value of the part taken as part of the whole? What is the damage to the remainder of the property as the result of the taking? The objective of the appraisal report is (1) to set forth in writing the answers to the questions asked by the client, and (2) to substantiate those answers. To achieve this objective and to be of maximum service to the client, the report must present the appraiser's conclusions and guide a reader to similar conclusions through the adequacy and pertinence of the supporting data, the logic of interpretation and analysis, and the soundness of the appraiser's reasoning.

In a sense, the report is a summary of the appraisal methods and techniques the appraiser has applied to factual material, within the framework of the valuation process, to arrive at a value conclusion. Such a report reflects the appraiser's understanding of basic economic and appraisal principles, ability to interpret pertinent data, and judgment in selecting appropriate methods and techniques, as well as skill in applying them to derive an estimate of a specifically defined value.

Regulation No. 10 of the American Institute of Real Estate Appraisers sets forth its Code of Professional Ethics and Standards of Professional Conduct and includes specific and general reporting requirements for narrative appraisals. The essential canons of the regulation are included in Appendix A of this book. The interpretation and specific provisions of these canons as presented in the regulation constitute recommended supplementary reading in relation to the preparation of a professional report.

FORMAT

Every report made with the expectation that its conclusions will be accepted should be aimed at maximum communication with a reader who may be the client or other person to whom the report may be submitted. Since readers tend to scan rather than to study the report, it should be presented in a manner that readily discloses the description of the property, the essential analysis of the problem, and the value conclusion.

A well-prepared report goes beyond thorough research, logic of organization, and soundness of reasoning. These basic attributes are enhanced by good composition, excellence of style, and clarity of expression. Overly technical jargon is avoided, and the report is written in terms that will be understood by the reader. The material is set forth as succinctly as possible, in order to achieve effective, efficient communication with the reader. Important to format and appearance are the quality and the assembly of the materials used, coherence in organization of the facts, arrangement of the supporting data, and the physical presentation.[2]

Because the appraiser may not be present when the report is reviewed or examined, it becomes the appraiser's representative— creating a favorable impression of professional competence. Considerations that tend to improve the impression created by a report include the following:

1. A good grade of paper, cover, and binding should be used. The paper may bear the appraiser's mark or imprint.
2. The report may be typed or printed. In either case, type should be attractive, and the size and style should be chosen for easy readability. Graphic aids always should be well drawn.[3] Style of main and subheadings should be consistent with subject matter.
3. Exhibits that are lengthy or might interrupt continuity in the body of the report may be relegated to the addenda. They are usually most effective when they fit the size of the report.
4. The content of the report should be presented in appropriate separate sections, clearly identified.

A detailed outline for an appraisal report and discussion of each section are provided in the remainder of this chapter.

---

2. A great deal of published material on how to write good reports may be found in other sources. For example, see William C. Himstreet, *Writing Appraisal Reports* (Chicago: American Institute of Real Estate Appraisers, 1971).
3. *Ibid,* Chapter VI.

OUTLINE OF REPORT

Although appraisal reports vary in content and arrangement, certain elements are common to all. Essentially, the report follows the outline of the valuation process.

Whether carried through in a flowing manner or arranged by formal sections, there are normally three major divisions to a report: (1) introduction, (2) description, analyses, and conclusions, and (3) the addenda. Within these divisions, the organization of the report may be varied. The following is typical of good organization.

Part One—Introduction
    Title page. Frontispiece, if any, may face or follow the title page[4]
    Letter of transmittal. May include certification of value
    Table of contents
    Summary of important conclusions
Part Two—Description, analyses, and conclusions
    Identification of the property
    Objective of the appraisal
    Definition of value
    Property rights appraised and date valuation applies
    City, neighborhood, and location data
    Zoning and taxes
    Site data
    History
    Description of improvements
    Highest and best use analysis
    Land value
    The cost approach
    The market data approach
    The income approach
    Reconciliation of the value indications
    Qualifying and limiting conditions, including general underlying assumptions. This may be followed by a certificate of value, signature, and seal.
    Certification of value if not combined with letter of transmittal
    Qualifications of the appraiser

---

4. A single photograph of the property or other exhibit may be used as a frontispiece or appear instead in the addenda.

Part Three—Addenda
 Maps, plats, photographs
 Detailed statistical data
 Detailed property data, if too lengthy to be included in Part Two
 Detailed market data, if too lengthy to be included in Part Two
 Leases or lease summaries

This general outline is illustrative, and the arrangement set forth is flexible and adaptable to almost all appraisal assignments and all classifications of real property. In practice, the appraiser adapts it to the particular requirements of the assignment and personal preference. Specific types of property may suggest unique treatment within, or in addition to, the above outline.

INTRODUCTION

Letter of Transmittal

The letter of transmittal formally presents the appraisal report to the person for whom the appraisal was made and should be drafted in compliance with approved practices of business correspondence. It should be as brief as the character and nature of the assignment permit. A suitable letter of transmittal may include the following:

1. Date of letter and salutation
2. Street address of the property involved and a brief description, if necessary
3. Statement as to the interest in the property being appraised
4. Statement that inspection of the property and necessary investigation and analysis were made by the appraiser
5. Reference that the letter is accompanied by a complete appraisal report
6. Date as of which the value estimate applies
7. The value estimate
8. The appraiser's signature

Some appraisers prefer to include their certification of value in the letter of transmittal. It may be a separate page in Part Two of the report.

Table of Contents

The identification and sequence of components in the report customarily are listed in the table of contents. A well-prepared table of contents indicates the scope and adequacy of the appraiser's investigations and analyses.

Summary of Important Conclusions

If the appraisal report is long and complicated, a statement of the major points and important conclusions in the report may be desirable. This provides the reader with a convenient summary and affords the appraiser an opportunity to stress points that have been considered in reaching the final estimate. Among the items that may be presented in this section are:

1. Estimate of land value and highest and best use
2. Total reproduction and/or replacement cost new of improvements (per square foot and/or cubic foot)
3. Age of improvements and their net depreciated value
4. Gross economic rental value and rental as leased
5. Net income expectancy
6. Capitalized value estimate
7. Estimated market price obtainable and unit basis
8. The final estimate of defined value

All these items do not apply to all appraisal assignments. This list is illustrative of the character of material frequently included.

The appraiser may use a summary for longer or more complex reports. However, in many appraisal assignments the summary is omitted, particularly if the letter of transmittal contains some brief discusssion of conclusions concerning the more important items.

DESCRIPTION, ANALYSES, AND CONCLUSIONS

Identification of the Property

The appraised property must be so identified that it cannot be confused with any other parcel of real estate. This can be achieved by giving the full legal description. If a copy of the official plat is used, it should be referred to at this point and included in the addenda. In the absence of a plat, the property should be described by locating it by name and side of street on which it fronts as well as by street number and the distance from the nearest cross street. Such a description might read:

> The site, commonly known as 205 North Miami Avenue, consists of the southwest corner of North Miami Avenue and N.W. Second Street. It is rectangular with 150 feet frontage on North Miami Avenue and 100 feet frontage on N.W. Second Street. The two-story stucco hotel and store building with which the site is improved is 90 feet by 150 feet. The west 10 feet of the site is a private concrete paved alley.

> The legal description of the above-described property is:

> Lots One (1) and Two (2), Block 160N., City of Miami, a subdivision of Dade County, State of Florida, as recorded in the public records of Dade County, State of Florida, in Plat Book B at page 41.

Objective of the Appraisal

This section states the objective of the report. In short or medium-length reports, it could easily be combined with the property identification. The appraiser may simply state:

> The objective (or purpose) of this report is to estimate market value as of (a given date).

Definition of Value

An acceptable definition of the value sought is related to the objective of the report and eliminates confusion in the mind of the client or any reader of the report. Market value is the usual value concept and acceptable definitions are included in Chapter 2 of this book, in *Real Estate Appraisal Terminology,* and in other sources.

Property Rights Appraised and Date of Value

Clearly defining particular rights or interests may be as important as identifying the actual property being appraised. Examples where this is the case are an assignment involving a partial interest in a property, or limited rights such as surface or mineral rights, or the value of the fee subject to a long-term lease, or a leasehold interest.[5] Any other encumbrances—for example, easement, mortgage, special occupancy or use—are also identified and explained in relation to the defined value to be estimated.

The principle of change implies a transient nature to any present value estimate. An appraisal assignment may involve a value estimate as of some past point in time. In either situation the date as of which a reported conclusion of value is applicable becomes an important part of the report.

City, Neighborhood, and Location Data

All the important facts about the city and its surrounding territory that the appraiser has judged pertinent to the specific appraisal problem may be included under city data. The types of data, their appropriate use in relation to the various classifications of property and to specific types of problems, and their degree of influence have been discussed in Chapter 6. In making the appraisal, all pertinent factors are considered and weighed, but discussion in the report should be confined to data found significant to the problem under consideration. If the data to be used is statistical, the type and importance to the discussion indicate whether it should be included in the body of the report or placed in the addenda. Usually, where the appraisal problem involves a considerable amount of supporting data—such as population figures, cost-of-living indexes, or payroll figures—these are placed in the addenda and referred to in the report in connection with the conclusions drawn from them. In many reports no separate section is needed for city data; it may be combined with the neighborhood data.

The character of the data to be included in any appraisal report should be related to the objective of the report and the appraiser's conclusion of value. Under this heading, items such as the following may be included:

1. Distance and direction from employment centers
2. Public transportation

---

5. See Chapter 23.

3. Road pattern, layout, and width of streets
4. Proximity to good shopping
5. Proximity to grade and other schools
6. Proximity to parks and recreation
7. Proximity to nuisances
8. Police and fire protection, rubbish collection
9. Life stage of neighborhood
10. Population trend
11. Percentage of homeownership
12. Vocations, wage levels, rent levels
13. Conformity of development
14. Vacancy in living or commercial facilities
15. Restrictions and zoning
16. New construction activity
17. Percentage of vacant land
18. Changing land use
19. Level of taxes
20. Adequacy of utilities and street improvements
21. Adequacy of parking, street and off-street
22. Concentration of advertising by retail merchants
23. Street traffic, type and amount
24. Pedestrian traffic, type and amount
25. Proximity to expressways, tollroads, and airports
26. Rail connections and service for freight
27. Labor supply, quantity, and type

As in other sections of the report, the extent of neighborhood and location data depends on circumstances. For example, if the appraisal were being made for an out-of-town client who is unfamiliar with the property or even the community, including more community and neighborhood data than necessary for a local client may be desirable. In the case of an important business property where the income is derived from the purchasing power of the entire supporting area, it is important to have a detailed description of the neighborhood and the influence of the population and its purchasing power on the value of the property being appraised.

The presence of special amenities or detrimental conditions should be noted and described with particularity. Accordingly, the report of neighborhood trends should be accompanied by reasons or data that support the conclusion. If it is reported that an area is growing, reference is appropriate to actual growth figures or building projects. Similarly, if the report is of neighborhood decline, specific data or reasons should be included. For example, if there is abnormal deterioration or poor maintenance in an area, reference is appropriate to specific properties that exhibit these detrimental conditions.

City and neighborhood data represents the background against which the property being appraised is considered, and it acquires significance in proportion to the extent that it affects the value of this property. Hence these sections in an appraisal are incomplete without some analysis of trends indicated by the data and some conclusion reached by the appraiser. This conclusion reflects application of the appraiser's professional experience and judgment to an interpretation of the data presented in terms of its meaning to the future marketability or economic life expectancy of the property being appraised. Without this, city and neighborhood data loses significance in a report; proper use of this data may be critical in establishing the future potential of the property being appraised.

Zoning and Taxes

The inclusion of zoning data is optional in the neighborhood section. Where important, the zoning and private restrictions should be discussed in detail. If the ordinance itself is included, the text may be reproduced in the addenda. When not included, sufficient data should be provided for a reader to identify the limitations zoning places on the use or development of the site and, when pertinent, the possibility of zoning changes. The appraiser also points out existing public, deed, and private restrictions and their effect on the utility and the value of the property.

Current assessed values and ad valorem tax rates, together with an analysis of existing trends or prospective changes in tax rates or assessments, are reported.

Site Data

In this section of the report belong those factors the appraiser judges pertinent, all of which have been discussed in detail in earlier chapters. Among these items are:

1. Description of the site area, shape, contour, soil and subsoil; utilities
2. Highest and best use

Site description and pertinent data are included at this point in the report. An analysis of highest and best use may be included here or under an independent heading. The number of separate divisions and the precise organization of a report reflect the scope and extent of the appraisal problem and the appraiser's concept of a clear and logical presentation of the facts and the reasoning involved.

If the appraiser's estimate of the value of the property is being based on a suggested program to achieve a particular highest and best use, the report should clearly state this fact and that the estimate of value does not apply unless the future use of the property will be in accordance with the program proposed. If for some reason the property cannot be thus adapted and used, the report should so indicate and state what utilization does underlie the appraiser's value estimate. The character and amount of data presented and analyzed depend on the objective of the appraisal.

History

Under this heading may be included original assemblage, acquisition or construction cost information, capital additions or modernization expenditures that affect accrued depreciation, effective age, remaining economic life; financial data or transfers of ownership; casualty loss experience; history and type of occupancy; reputation or prestige; and any other information that may pertain to or affect computations, estimates, or conclusions in the report.

Description of Improvements

In this section the appraiser includes and discusses all building and improvement data relevant to the appraisal problem. Although during the appraisal process a large amount of data is considered and processed, only the significant factors and elements that influence conclusions need be set forth. These include:

1. Age and size of building
2. Number and size of units
3. Structural and construction detail
4. Mechanical equipment
5. Physical condition
6. Discussion of functional utility

Presentation of this information may be supplemented through the use of drawings, photographs, floor plans, and elevations. If not highly pertinent, this illustrative material should be placed in the addenda with other supplementary matter. If descriptions of the structural and mechanical details are lengthy, only an outline with emphasis on the important items need be presented in the body of the report.

Land Value

This section includes the presentation of market data or other information pertaining to land value together with the appraiser's analysis of this data and the reasoning leading to a value conclusion. Available methods for developing this land value conclusion are presented in Chapter 8.

Approaches to Value

The applicable approaches are developed in this section to achieve indications of value. In each approach the factual data and the analysis and reasoning leading to each conclusion are presented.

Because many clients may not be familiar with the mechanics of the three approaches, the appraiser may explain the procedures in the development of the data, as may appear advisable in the circumstances of the case. Simple statements such as the following of what is included in each of the three approaches help the reader to understand what is to follow.

In the cost approach an estimated reproduction or replacement cost new of the building and land improvements is developed, together with an estimate of loss in value due to wear and tear, design and plan, or neighborhood influences. To this depreciated building cost estimate is added the estimated value of the land. The total represents the value indicated by the cost approach.

In the market data approach the subject property is compared to similar properties that have been sold recently or for which listing prices or offering figures are known. Data for generally comparable properties is used, and comparisons are made to demonstrate a probable price at which the property being appraised would sell if offered on the market.

In the income approach the present rental value is shown with a deduction for vacancy and other expense, and a conclusion about the prospective net operating income of the property is developed. In support of this net operating income estimate, operating statements for previous years may be reviewed together with available experience operating-cost estimates. An applicable capitalization method and appropriate rates are developed for use in computations that lead to an indication of value by the income approach.

The three approaches rarely are completely independent. The entire appraisal process is comprised of integrated, interrelated, and inseparable procedures with the common objective of arriving at a convincing and reliable estimate of value. At times the three approaches are so intertwined that some appraisers prefer a "one approach" concept and do not subscribe to the custom of separate presentations of the cost approach, the market data approach, and the income approach. The semantics of "three approaches" versus "one approach" are less important than the requirement to utilize all the recognized appraisal methods and techniques and available data that materially contribute to a proper valuation of the property or to a solution of the problem.

Reconciliation of Value Indications

A sound principle to follow in the preparation of an appraisal report generally is to keep description separate from analysis and interpretation. This implies that factual and descriptive data are limited to the sections of the report where they may logically be presented as such.

Analysis and interpretation then include references to, and the evaluation of, the facts in terms of their influence on the final value estimate. Repetition or unnecessary duplication is also undesirable in a report, and application of the above principle may be dependent on the character and length of a specific report.

Reconciliation of the value indications should lead logically to the appraiser's statement of the final estimate of value. The concluding statement of the final estimate of value may be presented in many ways. The following is a simple example:

As a result of my investigation and my general experience, it is my opinion that the market value of this property, as of July 20, 19__[6] was

FOUR HUNDRED THOUSAND DOLLARS

When the value conclusion is divided, the appraiser may add after the amount:

. . . which may be allocated as follows:

Land	$ 80,000
Improvements	320,000
Total	$400,000

Qualifying and Limiting Conditions

Qualifying and limiting conditions, which may be stated in the letter of transmittal, are usually included as a separate page in the report. They are statements used for the appraiser's protection and for the information and protection of the client and others using the report. Appropriate standard conditions are an important part of the report and should be set forth clearly. Included may be items such as the following:

This Appraisal is Subject to the Following Underlying Assumptions and Qualifying and Limiting Conditions:

This appraisal covers the property as described in this report, and the areas and dimensions as shown herein are assumed to be correct.

---

6. Date as of which the value opinion applies may differ from that of the letter of transmittal.

The appraiser has made no survey of the property and assumes no responsibility in connection with such matters. Any sketch or identified survey of the property included in this report is only for the purpose of assisting the reader to visualize the property.

Responsible ownership and competent management are assumed.

No responsibility is assumed for matters involving legal or title considerations.

The information identified in this report as being furnished by others is believed to be reliable, but no responsibility for its accuracy is assumed.

Possession of this report, or a copy thereof, does not carry with it the right of publication, nor may it be used for any purpose by any but the client for whom it was made without the consent of the appraiser or the client.[7]

The appraiser is not required to give testimony or attendance in court by reason of this appraisal unless arrangements have been previously made.

The allocation of total value to land or to buildings, as shown in this report, is invalidated if used separately in conjunction with any other appraisal.

Certification of Value

A certification of value may follow, or be combined with, the final conclusion of value. The signature of the appraiser, the date, and (when appropriate) a seal are then added. This certification states that the appraiser personally conducted the appraisal in an objective manner. It may include statements that the appraiser:

1. Personally inspected the property
2. Considered all available factors affecting value in forming an opinion of value
3. Has no present or contemplated interest in the property
4. Conducted the appraisal in conformity with the ethics of the

---

7. A Standard Form Restriction Upon Disclosure and Use for reports prepared by members of the American Institute of Real Estate Appraisers is included in Standard Form Statements published with *Regulation No. 10, op. cit.*

appraisal profession, with reference to membership (if any) in the American Institute of Real Estate Appraisers[8]

5.   Did not base the fee on the value reported
6.   Attests that the data included in the report is correct to the best of the appraiser's knowledge[9]

Whether included in the transmittal letter or a separate signed page, the certification is a highly important part of the appraisal report because it permits a statement of the appraiser's position, protecting both the appraiser's integrity and the validity of the appraisal.

A frequently used form of certification is the following:

I certify that I have personally inspected the property described herein, located at 5525 Wilshire Boulevard, Los Angeles, California; that I have no past, present, or prospective direct or indirect interest in the property or use of this appraisal; that employment for this appraisal is not in any manner contingent on returning appraisal findings in any specified or implied amount or otherwise contingent on anything else other than the delivery of this report; that, to the best of my knowledge and belief, all the statements and opinions contained in this report are correct; and that this appraisal has been made in conformity with [here are cited standards of professional conduct and their source].[10]

> Respectfully submitted,[11]
>
> [signature]

[date]

Qualifications of the Appraiser

A statement of the qualifications of the appraiser usually is included in the appraisal report as evidence of competence to make such an appraisal. These qualifications should be classified in some orderly form that includes facts concerning:

---

8. Standards are defined in *Regulation No. 10, op. cit.*
9. William C. Himstreet, *op. cit.,* pp. 20-21
10. The appropriate phrase for MAIs, RMs, and candidates for membership in the American Institute of Real Estate Appraisers is " . . . in conformity with the Code of Professional Ethics and Standards of Professional Conduct of the American Institute of Real Estate Appraisers." The canons of this code are in Appendix A.
11. Himstreet, *loc. cit.*

1. Professional experience
2. Educational background and training
3. Business, professional, and academic affiliations and activities
4. Clients for whom the appraiser has rendered professional services, the types of properties appraised, and the nature of the appraisal assignments

The use of such statements has become so general that many appraisers have found it expedient to prepare a printed statement of their qualifications for insertion in each appraisal report.

ADDENDA

Depending on the size and complexity of an appraisal assignment, addenda may be used to avoid interrupting the narrative portions of the report. Data such as the following may be included:

Plot plan
Plans and elevations of buildings
Photographs of properties referred to in the report
City, neighborhood, and other maps, with data
Charts and graphs
Abstracts of leases
Historical income and expense data
Specifications of buildings
Detailed estimates of reproduction costs of buildings
Sales and listing data
Tax and assessment data

SUMMARY

The form, length and content of an appraisal report may vary. An appraisal report is written to portray the property, the facts concerning that property, and the reasoning by which the estimate of defined value was developed. This estimate is an opinion, reflecting consideration of all the data in the light of the appraiser's experience and judgment. It is an estimate, not a determination of value; only courts and legally constituted authorities *determine* value.

Because it is an answer to a question by a client, every report should state the problem or a definition of the value sought and set forth the facts considered, clearly outlining the reasoning employed by the appraiser in developing the reported conclusions.

Whether the report is brief or voluminous, the same steps appear, and the extent of consideration given to each depends on the character and complexity of the problem. These steps include stating that the appraiser made an appraisal, defining the objective of the assignment, setting forth what was done, describing the property, presenting the reasoning leading to the conclusion and underlying assumptions and qualifying or limiting conditions. The report should be a systematic and orderly presentation that, with its physical appearance, is a reflection of the appraiser's professional stature.

The best report is the one that enables the reader to understand the problem and the factual data and to follow the appraiser's reasoning from these facts to the final conclusion.

Appendix A

Code of Ethics

American Institute of Real Estate Appraisers of the National Association of Realtors

Canon 1

A Member of the Institute must refrain from conduct that is detrimental to the real estate appraisal profession.

Canon 2

A Member of the Institute must assist the Institute in carrying out its responsibilities to the public and to the other Members of the Institute.

Canon 3

When performing a real estate appraisal assignment, a Member of the Institute must render his professional services without advocacy for his client's interests or the accommodation of his own interests.

The full text is published in *Regulation No. 10, Code of Professional Ethics and Standards of Professional Conduct*. Chicago: American Institute of Real Estate Appraisers. The essence of Regulation No. 10 appears in the seven Canons.

Canon 4

In rendering professional real estate appraisal services, a Member of the Institute must perform competently at all times.

Canon 5

In making written and oral real estate appraisal reports, a Member of the Institute must comply with the rules of the Institute relating to the contents of such reports.

Canon 6

A Member of the Institute must not violate the confidential nature of the appraiser-client relationship by improperly disclosing the confidential portions of a real estate appraisal report.

Canon 7

A Member of the Institute must refrain from unprofessional conduct in securing real estate appraisal assignments and in using advertising media in connection with his real estate appraisal practice.

Appendix B

Compound Interest Tables

CONSTRUCTION OF BASIC INTEREST TABLES

Problems involving capital investment for profit in the form of periodic interest or yield generally belong to one or two broad classifications:

1. The future worth of money at interest—the amount to which money will grow in a given length of time when invested or deposited at a given rate of interest
2. The present value of future collections—the present value of money to be collected at a specific future time when discounted from that time to the present date at a given rate of interest

The amount involved may be a single lump sum or a series of periodic installments, such as rent. Often it is a combination of both. Each of these two general categories entails three types of problems. Hence, there are six basic formulas for problem solution.

Because applying the formulas directly to each problem would consume a great deal of time, standard tables have been compiled. Each table presents one of six precomputed functions of one dollar, or any other unit, at selected rates of interest for various periods of time. When the desired function for one unit is known, it can be applied to any number of units by multiplication.

When compounding or discounting periods are less than one year, the fraction of the annual or *nominal interest rate (I)* that is applicable to the lesser period is the *effective interest rate (i)*. For example, a nominal rate of 12% becomes a 6% effective rate for semi-annual conversion periods or 1% for monthly installments. The user of compound interest tables is cautioned to select the appropriate conversion frequency (monthly, quarterly, or annually). The compound interest tables presented here are for nominal interest rates of 3 to 30%, on the basis of annual collections or conversions; and monthly, quarterly, and semi-annual factors are also presented in the 8% and 10% tables.

The tables for the selected interest rates have six columns showing the factors for the six standard functions of one (dollar or any other unit), with the formula and standard actuarial symbol for each:

Column 1 AMOUNT OF ONE $S^n = (1 + i)^n$	The amount to which an investment or deposit of one dollar will grow in a given number of time periods including the accumulation of interest at the effective rate per period. This factor is commonly known as the *future worth of one dollar with interest*.
Column 2 AMOUNT of ONE PER PERIOD $S\,\overline{\underset{n}{\vert}} = \dfrac{S^n - 1}{i}$	The total accumulation of principal and interest of a series of deposits or installments of one per period for a given number of periods with interest at the effective rate per period. This factor is also known as the *future worth of one per period with interest*.
Column 3 SINKING-FUND FACTOR $1/S\,\overline{\underset{n}{\vert}} = \dfrac{i}{S^n - 1}$	The level periodic investment or deposit required to accumulate one in a given number of periods including the accumulation of interest at the effective rate. This is commonly known as the *amortization rate*.

Column 4
PRESENT WORTH
of ONE

$$V^n = \frac{1}{S^n}$$

The present value of one to be collected at a given future time when discounted at the effective interest rate for the number of periods from now to the date of collection. This is called the *reversion factor*.

Column 5
PRESENT WORTH
ONE PER PERIOD

$$A\overline{n|} = \frac{1 - V^n}{i}$$

The present value of a series of future installments or payments of one per period for a given number of periods when discounted at the effective interest rate. The factors in this table are ordinary annuity factors, also referred to as *Inwood coefficients*.

Column 6
PARTIAL
PAYMENT

$$1/A\overline{n|} = \frac{i}{1 - V^n}$$

The level periodic installment[1] that will pay interest and provide full amortization or recapture of an investment of one in a given number of periods with interest at a given rate per period. A common application is as the periodic mortgage installment per dollar and is, in fact, the *ordinary annuity that has a present value of one* where n is the number of periods, and i is the effective rate.

The tables provide a means of solving many arithmetic problems that are fundamental in the process of valuation, thus aiding the appraiser in applications of the capitalization process. However, in the final analysis a value estimate is a matter of appraisal judgment based on appropriate research and developed data. Mathematical tables and formulas provide the appraiser with tools to assist in developing and explaining judgment decisions leading to a sound value estimate. Good tools and the ability to use them efficiently enhance the effectiveness of the most experienced practitioner.

---

1. This factor may be found in Column 6 or by taking the reciprocal of Column 5—that is, 1 divided by the factor in Column 5.

Implicit in each precomputed factor and capitalization method are specific built-in assumptions that are automatically effected when the table is employed. It is therefore essential for the appraiser to identify assumptions applicable to the circumstances of the property being appraised and then to use the table or capitalization method that corresponds to these assumptions. There is nothing particularly complex or difficult about this. The only essential requisite is understanding the arithmetic of money at interest. Thus the point of beginning is an understanding of the basic formulas, how the various functions relate to each other, and how they may be used or combined to simplify the appraisal process.

Except for the numeral 1, which may represent one dollar, and i, the effective interest rate, there are only two quantities in all the formulas. And since V^n is the reciprocal of S^n, the only quantity involving more than rudimentary arithmetic is S^n. It is important to grasp the nature of this function.

AMOUNT TO WHICH ONE WILL GROW

When money is invested or deposited in an account bearing interest at a fixed rate, it grows according to the interest rate and to the number of compounding (conversion) periods it remains in the account. To illustrate how and why this growth occurs, assume an investment of $1.00, a nominal interest rate of 10% with annual conversion, and an investment term of five years.

Original investment	$1.00
Interest, first year at 10%	.10
Accumulation, end of 1 year	$1.10
Interest, second year at 10%	.11
Accumulation, end of 2 years	$1.21
Interest, third year at 10%	.121
Accumulation, end of 3 years	$1.331
Interest, fourth year at 10%	.1331
Accumulation, end of 4 years	$1.4641
Interest, fifth year at 10%	.14641
Accumulation, end of 5 years	$1.61051

One dollar grows to $1.61051 in five years with interest at 10% (see 10% Table, Column 1), and $1,000 would grow 1,000 times this amount to $1,610.51, in the same time at the same rate. When interest is not collected or withdrawn as earned but is added to the capital account on which additional interest accumulates, the result is called compounding.

The same results are obtained by the formula $(1 + i)^n$ where n is the number of compounding periods, as follows:

Year (n)			
1	$1.10 \times 1 = 1.10^1$	$=$	1.10
2	$1.10 \times 1.10 = 1.10^2$	$=$	1.21
3	$1.10 \times 1.10 \times 1.10 = 1.10^3$	$=$	1.331
4	$1.10 \times 1.10 \times 1.10 \times 1.10 = 1.10^4$	$=$	1.4641
5	$1.10 \times 1.10 \times 1.10 \times 1.10 \times 1.10 = 1.10^5$	$=$	1.61051

Thus the factors in Column 1, the amount of one, or the future worth of one, reflect the growth of $1.00 accumulating at interest for the number of compounding periods shown in the column at the left of each page of tables. Reference to the 10% Table, Column 1, reveals a factor 2.593742 for 10 periods. This means that $1.00 deposited at 10% interest compounded annually for 10 years will grow to $1.00 × 2.593742 or just over $2.59. Reference to the factors for seven years and eight years indicate $1.00 (or any investment earning 10% per year) would double in value in approximately 7.5 years. Similarly, an investment of $10,000 made 10 years ago, earning no return during the 10-year holding period, must be liquidated in the current market at $10,000 × 2.593742, or $25,937.42, to realize a 10% return on the original cost.

The factors in this column reflect the growth of the original deposit at the end of each compounding period measured from the moment of the initial deposit. Thus at the end of the first period at 10% the original $1.00 has grown to $1.10, and the factor is 1.100000.

AMOUNT OF ONE PER PERIOD or THE FUTURE WORTH OF ONE PER PERIOD

The factors in Column 2 are similar to Column 1 except that deposits are assumed to be made at the end of the first compounding period and periodically thereafter at the end of each period. Thus the initial deposit, made at the end of the first period, has earned no interest and the factor is 1.00000.

If compounding is annually at 10% for 10 years, the factor of 15.937425 (10% Table, Column 2) reveals that a series of 10 deposits of $1.00 made at the end of each of the 10 years, will have accumulated to $1 × 15.937425, or almost $15.94.

SINKING-FUND FACTOR

Assuming deposits made at the end of each compounding period, as in Column 2, the factors in Column 3 reflect the fractional portion of $1.00, which must be deposited periodically at interest to accumulate to $1.00 at the end of the series of deposits.

Assuming that $10,000 is to be accumulated over a 10-year period and that annual deposits will be compounded at 10% interest, the factor on the 10-year line in the sinking-fund column of the 10% table reveals that each annual deposit must be in the amount of $10,000 × .062745 or $627.45.

Factors in this column are the reciprocals of corresponding factors in Column 2.

PRESENT WORTH OF ONE

The factors in Column 4 are also known as reversion factors. They reflect the discounted present worth of $1.00 to be received at some future point in time.

As demonstrated in the discussion of Column 1, $1.00 compounded annually at 10% would grow to $1.61051 in five years. Accordingly, the amount that would grow to $1.00 in five years is $1.00 divided by 1.61051 or $0.62092 (10% Table, Column 4 shows this factor precomputed). In other words, $1.00 to be collected five years from today would have a present value of $0.620921 when discounted at 10% per annum. And $10,000 to be collected five years from today, when discounted at the same rate, would have a present value of $10,000× .620921= $6,209.21. The $10,000 sum to be received in five years is called a reversion.

The present value of each dollar of any future reversion is based on the formula

$$\frac{1}{(1 + i)^n}$$

and may be quickly ascertained by use of the precomputed factors in Column 4 of the tables for the applicable discount (interest) rate.

PRESENT WORTH OF ONE PER PERIOD

The factors in Column 5 are also known as ordinary annuity factors. They reflect the present worth of a series of future collections such as periodic payments of rent.

Money presently in hand commands a premium over future money. Finding the present value of a future income stream is a discounting process in which future payments may be treated as a series of reversions. The present value of a series of future amounts may be quickly ascertained through use of the precomputed factors in Column 5 for the selected discount rate.

For example, if the amount to be received one year from today is $1.00 and if 10% per year is a fair rate of interest, it would be justifiable to pay $0.909091 (10% Table, Column 4) for the right to receive $1.00 one year from today. Assuming the cost of this right is $0.909091, the $1.00 received at the end of the year would be divided between principal and interest as follows:

Return of principal	$0.90909
Interest on above for one year @ 10%	0.09091
Total received	$1.00000

If approximately $0.91 is the present value of the right to receive $1.00 of income which is to be paid one year from today, coupled with 10% interest, then the present value of the right to receive $1.00 two years from today is less. By reference to the same column, the present value of that $1.00 that would be paid two years from today is shown as the factor .826446. The present value of $1.00 payable at the end of two years may be confirmed as follows:

Return of principal	$0.82645[a]
Interest for first year at 10% on 0.82645	0.08264
	$0.90909
Interest for second year at 10% on 0.90909	0.09091
Total principal repayment and interest received	$1.00000

[a]Present worth factor, 0.826446 × $1.00 = $0.82645 (rounded).

Similarly, the present value of the right to receive $1.00 at the end of three years is $0.751315, at the end of four years is $0.683013, and the present value of the right to receive $1.00 at the end of the fifth year is $0.620921. The present value of these rights to receive income at one-year intervals for five years is accumulated as the present value of $1.00 per annum. This is known as the compound interest valuation premise, sometimes referred to as the annuity table. Therefore, the sum of the five individual rights to receive $1.00 each year, payable at the end of the year, for five years is $3.790787 (10% Table, Column 5).

Sum of Individual Present Values of $1.00
Payable at the End of the Period

Present value of $1.00 due in 1 year	$0.909091[a]
Present value of $1.00 due in 2 years	.826446[a]
Present value of $1.00 due in 3 years	.751315[a]
Present value of $1.00 due in 4 years	.683013[a]
Present value of $1.00 due in 5 years	.620921[a]
Total (present value of $1.00 per year for 5 years)	$3.790786[b]

[a]10% Table, Column 4.
[b]10% Table, Column 5, 3.790787 (difference is due to rounding).

Reference to Column 5 for five conversion periods ($n = 5$) gives a factor representing the total of the present values of a series of periodic amounts of $1.00, payable at the end of each period. Thus the need for the above addition is eliminated since multiplying $1.00 by the factor for the present value of one per year for five years develops the same present value ($1.00 × 3.790787 = $3.790787). Restated for appraisal practice, this column gives single factors that may be used to multiply periodic income to derive a present worth (investment value) of the right to receive the income stream. The future payments of income provide for recapture of, and interest on, this present worth. These present value factors are multipliers and perform the same function as the building capitalization rate (not risk rate) used as a divisor in straight capitalization. Use of annuity present worth factors to reduce a future net income stream expectancy to a present value estimate is a direct application of the principle of anticipation, which affirms that value is the present worth of the rights to expected future benefits accruing to ownership (see Chapter

3). This principle is basic to the income approach to a value estimate.

The 10% annuity factor above (3.790787) for five discounting periods represents the present worth of each $1.00 of annual end-of-year collection on the basis of a nominal (annual) discount rate of 10%. Tables for semi-annual, quarterly, and monthly payments are also available. The ordinary annuity factor for semi-annual payments in the 10% nominal annual rate table is 7.721735. If payment continues for five years, each $1.00 of semi-annual payment represents $10.00 received, but reflects only $7.72 of discounted present worth. The factor for the present worth of monthly payments for five years in the monthly table at a 10% nominal rate is 47.065369, indicating that the present worth of an income stream of 60 monthly payments of $1.00 each, discounted at a nominal rate of 10%, is 47.065369 × $1.00 or about $47.065.

On the basis of five years at a 10% nominal rate, the semi-annual payments involve an effective rate of 5%. In the 5% annuity table, the factor for 10 periods is 7.721735, the same factor as in the 10% semi-annual table for a five-year period. Thus when tables are available at the effective rate, annuity factors for less than annual payment periods can be derived using only nominal annual rate tables.

In computing the present worth of an income stream in appraisal practice, it may be desirable to assume periodic payments at the beginning instead of the end of each payment period. This is known as an annuity in advance, and the present worth of such an annuity is equal to the present worth of an ordinary annuity (in arrears) multiplied by the base (1 plus the effective interest rate for the discounting period). Thus the present worth of semi-annual payments in advance over a five-year period discounted at a nominal rate of 10% becomes $1.00 × 7.721735 × 1.05 = $8.107822 or $8.11 (rounded) instead of $7.72 as computed above.

PARTIAL PAYMENT or AMORTIZATION FACTORS

The factors in Column 6 reflect the amount of annuity payment that $1.00 will purchase. Also known as mortgage constants, they reflect the periodic payment that will extinguish a debt and include interest on the declining balance of the debt over the life of the payments. The mortgage constant may be expressed on a basis related to the periodic payments. Thus a mortgage constant related to a monthly payment is the ratio of the monthly payment amount to the original amount of the loan. Whether payments are monthly or less frequent, the mortgage constant is usually expressed in terms of the total payments in one year as a percentage of the original loan amount. This is called the annual constant, represented in formulas by the symbol f. In appraisal computations pertaining to some point in the life of a constant payment loan, the annual mortgage constant may be the ratio of total annual payments to the unpaid balance of the loan at that time.

A mortgage of $10,000 to be amortized in 10 annual end-of-year payments at a mortgage interest rate of 10% would require level annual payments of $10,000 × .162745 (10% Table, Column 6) = $1,627.45. Column 6 factors consist of the interest rate plus the sinking-fund factor (Column 3) at the same rate. Column 6 factors are also reciprocals of corresponding Column 5 factors.

All the factors in the tables reflect some function of a single unit. If this unit is $1.00, any number of dollars can be multiplied by the applicable figure shown in the table to obtain a total result. The basic construction of each table is repeated in the formulas at the base of each of the six columns.

The following tables are for the purpose of illustration and include only tables for nominal rates of 3% through 12% at quarter percent intervals and 13% through 30% at 1% intervals, plus monthly, quarterly, and semi-annual tables at a nominal rate of 8% and 10%.

More comprehensive tables, showing a greater range of rates, periods, and compounding frequencies, may be found in books of tables such as two books by Charles B. Akerson, MAI, *Introduction to Mortgage Equity Capitalization* (Chicago: American Institute of Real Estate Appraisers) and *Study Guide: Course 1-B, Capitalization Theory and Techniques* (Chicago: American Institute of Real Estate Appraisers); L.W. Ellwood, MAI, *Ellwood Tables for Real Estate Appraising and Financing* (Cambridge, Mass.: Ballinger Publishing Co.); *Financial Compound Interest and Annuity Tables* (Boston: Financial Publishing Company).

The following tables were prepared for this text by Financial Publishing Company of Boston.

	1	2	3	4	5	6
YEARS	AMOUNT OF ONE	AMOUNT OF ONE PER PERIOD	SINKING FUND FACTOR	PRESENT WORTH OF ONE	PRESENT WORTH ONE PER PERIOD	PARTIAL PAYMENT
1	1.030 000	1.000 000	1.000 000	.970 874	.970 874	1.030 000
2	1.060 900	2.030 000	.492 611	.942 596	1.913 470	.522 611
3	1.092 727	3.090 900	.323 530	.915 142	2.828 611	.353 530
4	1.125 509	4.183 627	.239 027	.888 487	3.717 098	.269 027
5	1.159 274	5.309 136	.188 355	.862 609	4.579 707	.218 355
6	1.194 052	6.468 410	.154 598	.837 484	5.417 191	.184 598
7	1.229 874	7.662 462	.130 506	.813 092	6.230 283	.160 506
8	1.266 770	8.892 336	.112 456	.789 409	7.019 692	.142 456
9	1.304 773	10.159 106	.098 434	.766 417	7.786 109	.128 434
10	1.343 916	11.463 879	.087 231	.744 094	8.530 203	.117 231
11	1.384 234	12.807 796	.078 077	.722 421	9.252 624	.108 077
12	1.425 761	14.192 030	.070 462	.701 380	9.954 004	.100 462
13	1.468 534	15.617 790	.064 030	.680 951	10.634 955	.094 030
14	1.512 590	17.086 324	.058 526	.661 118	11.296 073	.088 526
15	1.557 967	18.598 914	.053 767	.641 862	11.937 935	.083 767
16	1.604 706	20.156 881	.049 611	.623 167	12.561 102	.079 611
17	1.652 848	21.761 588	.045 953	.605 016	13.166 118	.075 953
18	1.702 433	23.414 435	.042 709	.587 395	13.753 513	.072 709
19	1.753 506	25.116 868	.039 814	.570 286	14.323 799	.069 814
20	1.806 111	26.870 374	.037 216	.553 676	14.877 475	.067 216
21	1.860 295	28.676 486	.034 872	.537 549	15.415 024	.064 872
22	1.916 103	30.536 780	.032 747	.521 893	15.936 917	.062 747
23	1.973 587	32.452 884	.030 814	.506 692	16.443 608	.060 814
24	2.032 794	34.426 470	.029 047	.491 934	16.935 542	.059 047
25	2.093 778	36.459 264	.027 428	.477 606	17.413 148	.057 428
26	2.156 591	38.553 042	.025 938	.463 695	17.876 842	.055 938
27	2.221 289	40.709 634	.024 564	.450 189	18.327 031	.054 564
28	2.287 928	42.930 923	.023 293	.437 077	18.764 108	.053 293
29	2.356 566	45.218 850	.022 115	.424 346	19.188 455	.052 115
30	2.427 262	47.575 416	.021 019	.411 987	19.600 441	.051 019
31	2.500 080	50.002 678	.019 999	.399 987	20.000 428	.049 999
32	2.575 083	52.502 759	.019 047	.388 337	20.388 766	.049 047
33	2.652 335	55.077 841	.018 156	.377 026	20.765 792	.048 156
34	2.731 905	57.730 177	.017 322	.366 045	21.131 837	.047 322
35	2.813 862	60.462 082	.016 539	.355 383	21.487 220	.046 539
36	2.898 278	63.275 944	.015 804	.345 032	21.832 252	.045 804
37	2.985 227	66.174 223	.015 112	.334 983	22.167 235	.045 112
38	3.074 783	69.159 449	.014 459	.325 226	22.492 462	.044 459
39	3.167 027	72.234 233	.013 844	.315 754	22.808 215	.043 844
40	3.262 038	75.401 260	.013 262	.306 557	23.114 772	.043 262
41	3.359 899	78.663 298	.012 712	.297 628	23.412 400	.042 712
42	3.460 696	82.023 196	.012 192	.288 959	23.701 359	.042 192
43	3.564 517	85.483 892	.011 698	.280 543	23.981 902	.041 698
44	3.671 452	89.048 409	.011 230	.272 372	24.254 274	.041 230
45	3.781 596	92.719 861	.010 785	.264 439	24.518 713	.040 785
46	3.895 044	96.501 457	.010 363	.256 737	24.775 449	.040 363
47	4.011 895	100.396 501	.009 961	.249 259	25.024 708	.039 961
48	4.132 252	104.408 396	.009 578	.241 999	25.266 707	.039 578
49	4.256 219	108.540 648	.009 213	.234 950	25.501 657	.039 213
50	4.383 906	112.796 867	.008 865	.228 107	25.729 764	.038 865
51	4.515 423	117.180 773	.008 534	.221 463	25.951 227	.038 534
52	4.650 886	121.696 197	.008 217	.215 013	26.166 240	.038 217
53	4.790 412	126.347 082	.007 915	.208 750	26.374 990	.037 915
54	4.934 125	131.137 495	.007 626	.202 670	26.577 660	.037 626
55	5.082 149	136.071 620	.007 349	.196 767	26.774 428	.037 349
56	5.234 613	141.153 768	.007 084	.191 036	26.965 464	.037 084
57	5.391 651	146.388 381	.006 831	.185 472	27.150 936	.036 831
58	5.553 401	151.780 033	.006 588	.180 070	27.331 005	.036 588
59	5.720 003	157.333 434	.006 356	.174 825	27.505 831	.036 356
60	5.891 603	163.053 437	.006 133	.169 733	27.675 564	.036 133

$$S^n = (1 + i)^n \qquad S_{\overline{n}|} = \frac{S^n - 1}{i} \qquad 1/S_{\overline{n}|} = \frac{i}{S^n - 1} \qquad V^n = \frac{1}{S^n} \qquad A_{\overline{n}|} = \frac{1 - 1/S^n}{i} \qquad \frac{1}{A_{\overline{n}|}} = \frac{i}{1 - 1/S^n}$$

	1	2	3	4	5	6
YEARS	AMOUNT OF ONE	AMOUNT OF ONE PER PERIOD	SINKING FUND FACTOR	PRESENT WORTH OF ONE	PRESENT WORTH ONE PER PERIOD	PARTIAL PAYMENT
1	1.032 500	1.000 000	1.000 000	.968 523	.968 523	1.032 500
2	1.066 056	2.032 500	.492 005	.938 037	1.906 560	.524 505
3	1.100 703	3.098 556	.322 731	.908 510	2.815 070	.355 231
4	1.136 476	4.199 259	.238 137	.879 913	3.694 983	.270 637
5	1.173 411	5.335 735	.187 416	.852 216	4.547 199	.219 916
6	1.211 547	6.509 147	.153 630	.825 391	5.372 590	.186 130
7	1.250 923	7.720 694	.129 522	.799 410	6.172 000	.162 022
8	1.291 578	8.971 616	.111 463	.774 247	6.946 247	.143 963
9	1.333 554	10.263 194	.097 436	.749 876	7.696 123	.129 936
10	1.376 894	11.596 748	.086 231	.726 272	8.422 395	.118 731
11	1.421 643	12.973 642	.077 079	.703 411	9.125 806	.109 579
12	1.467 847	14.395 285	.069 467	.681 270	9.807 076	.101 967
13	1.515 552	15.863 132	.063 039	.659 826	10.466 902	.095 539
14	1.564 807	17.378 684	.057 542	.639 056	11.105 958	.090 042
15	1.615 663	18.943 491	.052 789	.618 941	11.724 899	.085 289
16	1.668 173	20.559 155	.048 640	.599 458	12.324 358	.081 140
17	1.722 388	22.227 327	.044 990	.580 589	12.904 947	.077 490
18	1.778 366	23.949 715	.041 754	.562 314	13.467 261	.074 254
19	1.836 163	25.728 081	.038 868	.544 614	14.011 875	.071 368
20	1.895 838	27.564 244	.036 279	.527 471	14.539 346	.068 779
21	1.957 453	29.460 082	.033 944	.510 868	15.050 214	.066 444
22	2.021 070	31.417 534	.031 829	.494 787	15.545 002	.064 329
23	2.086 755	33.438 604	.029 906	.479 213	16.024 215	.062 406
24	2.154 574	35.525 359	.028 149	.464 129	16.488 343	.060 649
25	2.224 598	37.679 933	.026 539	.449 519	16.937 863	.059 039
26	2.296 897	39.904 531	.025 060	.435 370	17.373 233	.057 560
27	2.371 546	42.201 428	.023 696	.421 666	17.794 899	.056 196
28	2.448 622	44.572 975	.022 435	.408 393	18.203 292	.054 935
29	2.528 202	47.021 596	.021 267	.395 538	18.598 830	.053 767
30	2.610 368	49.549 798	.020 182	.383 088	18.981 917	.052 682
31	2.695 205	52.160 167	.019 172	.371 029	19.352 947	.051 672
32	2.782 800	54.855 372	.018 230	.359 350	19.712 297	.050 730
33	2.873 241	57.638 172	.017 350	.348 039	20.060 336	.049 850
34	2.966 621	60.511 412	.016 526	.337 084	20.397 420	.049 026
35	3.063 036	63.478 033	.015 753	.326 473	20.723 893	.048 253
36	3.162 585	66.541 069	.015 028	.316 197	21.040 090	.047 528
37	3.265 369	69.703 654	.014 346	.306 244	21.346 335	.046 846
38	3.371 493	72.969 023	.013 704	.296 604	21.642 939	.046 204
39	3.481 067	76.340 516	.013 099	.287 268	21.930 207	.045 599
40	3.594 201	79.821 583	.012 528	.278 226	22.208 433	.045 028
41	3.711 013	83.415 784	.011 988	.269 468	22.477 901	.044 488
42	3.831 621	87.126 797	.011 478	.260 986	22.738 888	.043 978
43	3.956 149	90.958 418	.010 994	.252 771	22.991 659	.043 494
44	4.084 723	94.914 566	.010 536	.244 815	23.236 473	.043 036
45	4.217 477	98.999 290	.010 101	.237 109	23.473 582	.042 601
46	4.354 545	103.216 767	.009 688	.229 645	23.703 227	.042 188
47	4.496 068	107.571 312	.009 296	.222 417	23.925 644	.041 796
48	4.642 190	112.067 379	.008 923	.215 416	24.141 059	.041 423
49	4.793 061	116.709 569	.008 568	.208 635	24.349 694	.041 068
50	4.948 835	121.502 630	.008 230	.202 068	24.551 762	.040 730
51	5.109 673	126.451 466	.007 908	.195 707	24.747 469	.040 408
52	5.275 737	131.561 138	.007 601	.189 547	24.937 016	.040 101
53	5.447 198	136.836 875	.007 308	.183 581	25.120 597	.039 808
54	5.624 232	142.284 074	.007 028	.177 802	25.298 399	.039 528
55	5.807 020	147.908 306	.006 761	.172 205	25.470 604	.039 261
56	5.995 748	153.715 326	.006 506	.166 785	25.637 389	.039 006
57	6.190 610	159.711 074	.006 261	.161 535	25.798 924	.038 761
58	6.391 805	165.901 684	.006 028	.156 450	25.955 374	.038 528
59	6.599 538	172.293 489	.005 804	.151 526	26.106 900	.038 304
60	6.814 023	178.893 027	.005 590	.146 756	26.253 656	.038 090

$$S^n = (1+i)^n \qquad S_{\overline{n}|} = \frac{S^n - 1}{i} \qquad 1/S_{\overline{n}|} = \frac{i}{S^n - 1} \qquad V^n = \frac{1}{S^n} \qquad A_{\overline{n}|} = \frac{1 - 1/S^n}{i} \qquad \frac{1}{A_{\overline{n}|}} = \frac{i}{1 - 1/S^n}$$

	1	2	3	4	5	6
YEARS	AMOUNT OF ONE	AMOUNT OF ONE PER PERIOD	SINKING FUND FACTOR	PRESENT WORTH OF ONE	PRESENT WORTH ONE PER PERIOD	PARTIAL PAYMENT
1	1.035 000	1.000 000	1.000 000	.966 184	.966 184	1.035 000
2	1.071 225	2.035 000	.491 400	.933 511	1.899 694	.526 400
3	1.108 718	3.106 225	.321 934	.901 943	2.801 637	.356 934
4	1.147 523	4.214 943	.237 251	.871 442	3.673 079	.272 251
5	1.187 686	5.362 466	.186 481	.841 973	4.515 052	.221 481
6	1.229 255	6.550 152	.152 668	.813 501	5.328 553	.187 668
7	1.272 279	7.779 408	.128 544	.785 991	6.114 544	.163 544
8	1.316 809	9.051 687	.110 477	.759 412	6.873 956	.145 477
9	1.362 897	10.368 496	.096 446	.733 731	7.607 687	.131 446
10	1.410 599	11.731 393	.085 241	.708 919	8.316 605	.120 241
11	1.459 970	13.141 992	.076 092	.684 946	9.001 551	.111 092
12	1.511 069	14.601 962	.068 484	.661 783	9.663 334	.103 484
13	1.563 956	16.113 030	.062 062	.639 404	10.302 738	.097 062
14	1.618 695	17.676 986	.056 571	.617 782	10.920 520	.091 571
15	1.675 349	19.295 681	.051 825	.596 891	11.517 411	.086 825
16	1.733 986	20.971 030	.047 685	.576 706	12.094 117	.082 685
17	1.794 676	22.705 016	.044 043	.557 204	12.651 321	.079 043
18	1.857 489	24.499 691	.040 817	.538 361	13.189 682	.075 817
19	1.922 501	26.357 180	.037 940	.520 156	13.709 837	.072 940
20	1.989 789	28.279 682	.035 361	.502 566	14.212 403	.070 361
21	2.059 431	30.269 471	.033 037	.485 571	14.697 974	.068 037
22	2.131 512	32.328 902	.030 932	.469 151	15.167 125	.065 932
23	2.206 114	34.460 414	.029 019	.453 286	15.620 410	.064 019
24	2.283 328	36.666 528	.027 273	.437 957	16.058 368	.062 273
25	2.363 245	38.949 857	.025 674	.423 147	16.481 515	.060 674
26	2.445 959	41.313 102	.024 205	.408 838	16.890 352	.059 205
27	2.531 567	43.759 060	.022 852	.395 012	17.285 365	.057 852
28	2.620 172	46.290 627	.021 603	.381 654	17.667 019	.056 603
29	2.711 878	48.910 799	.020 445	.368 748	18.035 767	.055 445
30	2.806 794	51.622 677	.019 371	.356 278	18.392 045	.054 371
31	2.905 031	54.429 471	.018 372	.344 230	18.736 276	.053 372
32	3.006 708	57.334 502	.017 442	.332 590	19.068 865	.052 442
33	3.111 942	60.341 210	.016 572	.321 343	19.390 208	.051 572
34	3.220 860	63.453 152	.015 760	.310 476	19.700 684	.050 760
35	3.333 590	66.674 013	.014 998	.299 977	20.000 661	.049 998
36	3.450 266	70.007 603	.014 284	.289 833	20.290 494	.049 284
37	3.571 025	73.457 869	.013 613	.280 032	20.570 525	.048 613
38	3.696 011	77.028 895	.012 982	.270 562	20.841 087	.047 982
39	3.825 372	80.724 906	.012 388	.261 413	21.102 500	.047 388
40	3.959 260	84.550 278	.011 827	.252 572	21.355 072	.046 827
41	4.097 834	88.509 537	.011 298	.244 031	21.599 104	.046 298
42	4.241 258	92.607 371	.010 798	.235 779	21.834 883	.045 798
43	4.389 702	96.848 629	.010 325	.227 806	22.062 689	.045 325
44	4.543 342	101.238 331	.009 878	.220 102	22.282 791	.044 878
45	4.702 359	105.781 673	.009 453	.212 659	22.495 450	.044 453
46	4.866 941	110.484 031	.009 051	.205 468	22.700 918	.044 051
47	5.037 284	115.350 973	.008 669	.198 520	22.899 438	.043 669
48	5.213 589	120.388 257	.008 306	.191 806	23.091 244	.043 306
49	5.396 065	125.601 846	.007 962	.185 320	23.276 564	.042 962
50	5.584 927	130.997 910	.007 634	.179 053	23.455 618	.042 634
51	5.780 399	136.582 837	.007 322	.172 998	23.628 616	.042 322
52	5.982 713	142.363 236	.007 024	.167 148	23.795 765	.042 024
53	6.192 108	148.345 950	.006 741	.161 496	23.957 260	.041 741
54	6.408 832	154.538 058	.006 471	.156 035	24.113 295	.041 471
55	6.633 141	160.946 890	.006 213	.150 758	24.264 053	.041 213
56	6.865 301	167.580 031	.005 967	.145 660	24.409 713	.040 967
57	7.105 587	174.445 332	.005 732	.140 734	24.550 448	.040 732
58	7.354 282	181.550 919	.005 508	.135 975	24.686 423	.040 508
59	7.611 682	188.905 201	.005 294	.131 377	24.817 800	.040 294
60	7.878 091	196.516 883	.005 089	.126 934	24.944 734	.040 089

$S^n = (1+i)^n$	$S_{\overline{n}|} = \dfrac{S^n - 1}{i}$	$1/S_{\overline{n}|} = \dfrac{i}{S^n - 1}$	$V^n = \dfrac{1}{S^n}$	$A_{\overline{n}|} = \dfrac{1 - 1/S^n}{i}$	$\dfrac{1}{A_{\overline{n}|}} = \dfrac{i}{1 - 1/S^n}$

YEARS	1 AMOUNT OF ONE	2 AMOUNT OF ONE PER PERIOD	3 SINKING FUND FACTOR	4 PRESENT WORTH OF ONE	5 PRESENT WORTH ONE PER PERIOD	6 PARTIAL PAYMENT
1	1.037 500	1.000 000	1.000 000	.963 855	.963 855	1.037 500
2	1.076 406	2.037 500	.490 798	.929 017	1.892 873	.528 298
3	1.116 771	3.113 906	.321 140	.895 438	2.788 311	.358 640
4	1.158 650	4.230 678	.236 369	.863 073	3.651 384	.273 869
5	1.202 100	5.389 328	.185 552	.831 878	4.483 262	.223 052
6	1.247 179	6.591 428	.151 712	.801 810	5.285 072	.189 212
7	1.293 948	7.838 607	.127 574	.772 829	6.057 900	.165 074
8	1.342 471	9.132 554	.109 498	.744 895	6.802 796	.146 998
9	1.392 813	10.475 025	.095 465	.717 971	7.520 767	.132 965
10	1.445 044	11.867 838	.084 261	.692 020	8.212 787	.121 761
11	1.499 233	13.312 882	.075 115	.667 008	8.879 795	.112 615
12	1.555 454	14.812 116	.067 512	.642 899	9.522 694	.105 012
13	1.613 784	16.367 570	.061 096	.619 662	10.142 356	.098 596
14	1.674 301	17.981 354	.055 613	.597 264	10.739 620	.093 113
15	1.737 087	19.655 654	.050 876	.575 676	11.315 296	.088 376
16	1.802 228	21.392 742	.046 745	.554 869	11.870 165	.084 245
17	1.869 811	23.194 969	.043 113	.534 813	12.404 978	.080 613
18	1.939 929	25.064 781	.039 897	.515 483	12.920 461	.077 397
19	2.012 677	27.004 710	.037 031	.496 851	13.417 312	.074 531
20	2.088 152	29.017 387	.034 462	.478 892	13.896 204	.071 962
21	2.166 458	31.105 539	.032 149	.461 583	14.357 787	.069 649
22	2.247 700	33.271 996	.030 055	.444 899	14.802 686	.067 555
23	2.331 989	35.519 696	.028 153	.428 819	15.231 505	.065 653
24	2.419 438	37.851 685	.026 419	.413 319	15.644 824	.063 919
25	2.510 167	40.271 123	.024 832	.398 380	16.043 204	.062 332
26	2.604 298	42.781 290	.023 375	.383 981	16.427 185	.060 875
27	2.701 960	45.385 588	.022 033	.370 102	16.797 286	.059 533
28	2.803 283	48.087 548	.020 795	.356 725	17.154 011	.058 295
29	2.908 406	50.890 831	.019 650	.343 831	17.497 842	.057 150
30	3.017 471	53.799 237	.018 588	.331 403	17.829 245	.056 088
31	3.130 627	56.816 709	.017 600	.319 425	18.148 670	.055 100
32	3.248 025	59.947 335	.016 681	.307 879	18.456 549	.054 181
33	3.369 826	63.195 360	.015 824	.296 751	18.753 301	.053 324
34	3.496 194	66.565 186	.015 023	.286 025	19.039 326	.052 523
35	3.627 302	70.061 381	.014 273	.275 687	19.315 013	.051 773
36	3.763 326	73.688 682	.013 571	.265 722	19.580 735	.051 071
37	3.904 450	77.452 008	.012 911	.256 118	19.836 853	.050 411
38	4.050 867	81.356 458	.012 292	.246 861	20.083 714	.049 792
39	4.202 775	85.407 326	.011 709	.237 938	20.321 652	.049 209
40	4.360 379	89.610 100	.011 159	.229 338	20.550 990	.048 659
41	4.523 893	93.970 479	.010 642	.221 049	20.772 039	.048 142
42	4.693 539	98.494 372	.010 153	.213 059	20.985 097	.047 653
43	4.869 547	103.187 911	.009 691	.205 358	21.190 455	.047 191
44	5.052 155	108.057 458	.009 254	.197 935	21.388 391	.046 754
45	5.241 610	113.109 612	.008 841	.190 781	21.579 172	.046 341
46	5.438 171	118.351 223	.008 449	.183 885	21.763 057	.045 949
47	5.642 102	123.789 394	.008 078	.177 239	21.940 296	.045 578
48	5.853 681	129.431 496	.007 726	.170 833	22.111 129	.045 226
49	6.073 194	135.285 177	.007 392	.164 658	22.275 787	.044 892
50	6.300 939	141.358 371	.007 074	.158 707	22.434 493	.044 574
51	6.537 224	147.659 310	.006 772	.152 970	22.587 463	.044 272
52	6.782 370	154.196 534	.006 485	.147 441	22.734 904	.043 985
53	7.036 709	160.978 904	.006 212	.142 112	22.877 016	.043 712
54	7.300 585	168.015 613	.005 952	.136 975	23.013 992	.043 452
55	7.574 357	175.316 198	.005 704	.132 024	23.146 016	.043 204
56	7.858 396	182.890 556	.005 468	.127 252	23.273 268	.042 968
57	8.153 086	190.748 952	.005 242	.122 653	23.395 921	.042 742
58	8.458 826	198.902 037	.005 028	.118 220	23.514 141	.042 528
59	8.776 032	207.360 864	.004 823	.113 947	23.628 088	.042 323
60	9.105 134	216.136 896	.004 627	.109 828	23.737 916	.042 127

$S^n = (1+i)^n$	$S_{\overline{n}} = \dfrac{S^n - 1}{i}$	$1/S_{\overline{n}} = \dfrac{i}{S^n - 1}$	$V^n = \dfrac{1}{S^n}$	$A_{\overline{n}} = \dfrac{1 - 1/S^n}{i}$	$\dfrac{1}{A_{\overline{n}}} = \dfrac{i}{1 - 1/S^n}$

	1	2	3	4	5	6
YEARS	AMOUNT OF ONE	AMOUNT OF ONE PER PERIOD	SINKING FUND FACTOR	PRESENT WORTH OF ONE	PRESENT WORTH ONE PER PERIOD	PARTIAL PAYMENT
1	1.040 000	1.000 000	1.000 000	.961 538	.961 538	1.040 000
2	1.081 600	2.040 000	.490 196	.924 556	1.886 095	.530 196
3	1.124 864	3.121 600	.320 349	.888 996	2.775 091	.360 349
4	1.169 859	4.246 464	.235 490	.854 804	3.629 895	.275 490
5	1.216 653	5.416 323	.184 627	.821 927	4.451 822	.224 627
6	1.265 319	6.632 975	.150 762	.790 315	5.242 137	.190 762
7	1.315 932	7.898 294	.126 610	.759 918	6.002 055	.166 610
8	1.368 569	9.214 226	.108 528	.730 690	6.732 745	.148 528
9	1.423 312	10.582 795	.094 493	.702 587	7.435 332	.134 493
10	1.480 244	12.006 107	.083 291	.675 564	8.110 896	.123 291
11	1.539 454	13.486 351	.074 149	.649 581	8.760 477	.114 149
12	1.601 032	15.025 805	.066 552	.624 597	9.385 074	.106 552
13	1.665 074	16.626 838	.060 144	.600 574	9.985 648	.100 144
14	1.731 676	18.291 911	.054 669	.577 475	10.563 123	.094 669
15	1.800 944	20.023 588	.049 941	.555 265	11.118 387	.089 941
16	1.872 981	21.824 531	.045 820	.533 908	11.652 296	.085 820
17	1.947 900	23.697 512	.042 199	.513 373	12.165 669	.082 199
18	2.025 817	25.645 413	.038 993	.493 628	12.659 297	.078 993
19	2.106 849	27.671 229	.036 139	.474 642	13.133 939	.076 139
20	2.191 123	29.778 079	.033 582	.456 387	13.590 326	.073 582
21	2.278 768	31.969 202	.031 280	.438 834	14.029 160	.071 280
22	2.369 919	34.247 970	.029 199	.421 955	14.451 115	.069 199
23	2.464 716	36.617 889	.027 309	.405 726	14.856 842	.067 309
24	2.563 304	39.082 604	.025 587	.390 121	15.246 963	.065 587
25	2.665 836	41.645 908	.024 012	.375 117	15.622 080	.064 012
26	2.772 470	44.311 745	.022 567	.360 689	15.982 769	.062 567
27	2.883 369	47.084 214	.021 239	.346 817	16.329 586	.061 239
28	2.998 703	49.967 583	.020 013	.333 477	16.663 063	.060 013
29	3.118 651	52.966 286	.018 880	.320 651	16.983 715	.058 880
30	3.243 398	56.084 938	.017 830	.308 319	17.292 033	.057 830
31	3.373 133	59.328 335	.016 855	.296 460	17.588 494	.056 855
32	3.508 059	62.701 469	.015 949	.285 058	17.873 551	.055 949
33	3.648 381	66.209 527	.015 104	.274 094	18.147 646	.055 104
34	3.794 316	69.857 909	.014 315	.263 552	18.411 198	.054 315
35	3.946 089	73.652 225	.013 577	.253 415	18.664 613	.053 577
36	4.103 933	77.598 314	.012 887	.243 669	18.908 282	.052 887
37	4.268 090	81.702 246	.012 240	.234 297	19.142 579	.052 240
38	4.438 813	85.970 336	.011 632	.225 285	19.367 864	.051 632
39	4.616 366	90.409 150	.011 061	.216 621	19.584 485	.051 061
40	4.801 021	95.025 516	.010 523	.208 289	19.792 774	.050 523
41	4.993 061	99.826 536	.010 017	.200 278	19.993 052	.050 017
42	5.192 784	104.819 598	.009 540	.192 575	20.185 627	.049 540
43	5.400 495	110.012 382	.009 090	.185 168	20.370 795	.049 090
44	5.616 515	115.412 877	.008 665	.178 046	20.548 841	.048 665
45	5.841 176	121.029 392	.008 262	.171 198	20.720 040	.048 262
46	6.074 823	126.870 568	.007 882	.164 614	20.884 654	.047 882
47	6.317 816	132.945 390	.007 522	.158 283	21.042 936	.047 522
48	6.570 528	139.263 206	.007 181	.152 195	21.195 131	.047 181
49	6.833 349	145.833 734	.006 857	.146 341	21.341 472	.046 857
50	7.106 683	152.667 084	.006 550	.140 713	21.482 185	.046 550
51	7.390 951	159.773 767	.006 259	.135 301	21.617 485	.046 259
52	7.686 589	167.164 718	.005 982	.130 097	21.747 582	.045 982
53	7.994 052	174.851 306	.005 719	.125 093	21.872 675	.045 719
54	8.313 814	182.845 359	.005 469	.120 282	21.992 957	.045 469
55	8.646 367	191.159 173	.005 231	.115 656	22.108 612	.045 231
56	8.992 222	199.805 540	.005 005	.111 207	22.219 819	.045 005
57	9.351 910	208.797 762	.004 789	.106 930	22.326 749	.044 789
58	9.725 987	218.149 672	.004 584	.102 817	22.429 567	.044 584
59	10.115 026	227.875 659	.004 388	.098 863	22.528 430	.044 388
60	10.519 627	237.990 685	.004 202	.095 060	22.623 490	.044 202

$S^n = (1+i)^n$	$S_{\overline{n}|} = \dfrac{S^n - 1}{i}$	$1/S_{\overline{n}|} = \dfrac{i}{S^n - 1}$	$V^n = \dfrac{1}{S^n}$	$A_{\overline{n}|} = \dfrac{1 - 1/S^n}{i}$	$\dfrac{1}{A_{\overline{n}|}} = \dfrac{i}{1 - 1/S^n}$

YEARS	1 AMOUNT OF ONE	2 AMOUNT OF ONE PER PERIOD	3 SINKING FUND FACTOR	4 PRESENT WORTH OF ONE	5 PRESENT WORTH ONE PER PERIOD	6 PARTIAL PAYMENT
1	1.042 500	1.000 000	1.000 000	.959 233	.959 233	1.042 500
2	1.086 806	2.042 500	.489 596	.920 127	1.879 360	.532 096
3	1.132 996	3.129 306	.319 560	.882 616	2.761 976	.362 060
4	1.181 148	4.262 302	.234 615	.846 634	3.608 610	.277 115
5	1.231 347	5.443 450	.183 707	.812 119	4.420 729	.226 207
6	1.283 679	6.674 796	.149 817	.779 011	5.199 740	.192 317
7	1.338 235	7.958 475	.125 652	.747 253	5.946 993	.168 152
8	1.395 110	9.296 710	.107 565	.716 789	6.663 782	.150 065
9	1.454 402	10.691 820	.093 529	.687 568	7.351 350	.136 029
10	1.516 214	12.146 223	.082 330	.659 537	8.010 887	.124 830
11	1.580 654	13.662 437	.073 193	.632 650	8.643 537	.115 693
12	1.647 831	15.243 091	.065 603	.606 858	9.250 395	.108 .103
13	1.717 864	16.890 922	.059 203	.582 118	9.832 513	.101 703
14	1.790 873	18.608 786	.053 738	.558 387	10.390 900	.096 238
15	1.866 986	20.399 660	.049 020	.535 623	10.926 523	.091 520
16	1.946 332	22.266 645	.044 910	.513 787	11.440 309	.087 410
17	2.029 052	24.212 978	.041 300	.492 841	11.933 151	.083 800
18	2.115 286	26.242 029	.038 107	.472 749	12.405 900	.080 607
19	2.205 186	28.357 316	.035 264	.453 477	12.859 376	.077 764
20	2.298 906	30.562 501	.032 720	.434 989	13.294 366	.075 220
21	2.396 610	32.861 408	.030 431	.417 256	13.711 622	.072 931
22	2.498 466	35.258 018	.028 362	.400 246	14.111 868	.070 862
23	2.604 651	37.756 483	.026 486	.383 929	14.495 796	.068 986
24	2.715 348	40.361 134	.024 776	.368 277	14.864 073	.067 276
25	2.830 750	43.076 482	.023 215	.353 263	15.217 336	.065 715
26	2.951 057	45.907 233	.021 783	.338 862	15.556 198	.064 283
27	3.076 477	48.858 290	.020 467	.325 047	15.881 245	.062 967
28	3.207 228	51.934 767	.019 255	.311 796	16.193 041	.061 755
29	3.343 535	55.141 995	.018 135	.299 085	16.492 125	.060 635
30	3.485 635	58.485 530	.017 098	.286 892	16.779 017	.059 598
31	3.633 775	61.971 165	.016 137	.275 196	17.054 213	.058 637
32	3.788 210	65.604 939	.015 243	.263 977	17.318 190	.057 743
33	3.949 209	69.393 149	.014 411	.253 215	17.571 405	.056 911
34	4.117 050	73.342 358	.013 635	.242 892	17.814 298	.056 135
35	4.292 025	77.459 408	.012 910	.232 990	18.047 288	.055 410
36	4.474 436	81.751 433	.012 232	.223 492	18.270 780	.054 732
37	4.664 599	86.225 869	.011 597	.214 381	18.485 160	.054 097
38	4.862 845	90.890 468	.011 002	.205 641	18.690 801	.053 502
39	5.069 516	95.753 313	.010 444	.197 257	18.888 059	.052 944
40	5.284 970	100.822 829	.009 918	.189 216	19.077 275	.052 418
41	5.509 581	106.107 799	.009 424	.181 502	19.258 777	.051 924
42	5.743 739	111.617 381	.008 959	.174 103	19.432 879	.051 459
43	5.987 848	117.361 119	.008 521	.167 005	19.599 884	.051 021
44	6.242 331	123.348 967	.008 107	.160 197	19.760 081	.050 607
45	6.507 630	129.591 298	.007 717	.153 666	19.913 747	.050 217
46	6.784 204	136.098 928	.007 348	.147 401	20.061 148	.049 848
47	7.072 533	142.883 133	.006 999	.141 392	20.202 540	.049 499
48	7.373 116	149.955 666	.006 669	.135 628	20.338 168	.049 169
49	7.686 473	157.328 782	.006 356	.130 099	20.468 266	.048 856
50	8.013 148	165.015 255	.006 060	.124 795	20.593 061	.048 560
51	8.353 707	173.028 403	.005 779	.119 707	20.712 769	.048 279
52	8.708 740	181.382 110	.005 513	.114 827	20.827 596	.048 013
53	9.078 861	190.090 850	.005 261	.110 146	20.937 742	.047 761
54	9.464 713	199.169 711	.005 021	.105 656	21.043 397	.047 521
55	9.866 963	208.634 424	.004 793	.101 348	21.144 746	.047 293
56	10.286 309	218.501 387	.004 577	.097 217	21.241 962	.047 077
57	10.723 477	228.787 696	.004 371	.093 253	21.335 216	.046 871
58	11.179 225	239.511 173	.004 175	.089 452	21.424 667	.046 675
59	11.654 342	250.690 398	.003 989	.085 805	21.510 472	.046 489
60	12.149 651	262.344 740	.003 812	.082 307	21.592 779	.046 312

$S^n = (1+i)^n$	$S_{\overline{n}} = \dfrac{S^n - 1}{i}$	$1/S_{\overline{n}} = \dfrac{i}{S^n - 1}$	$V^n = \dfrac{1}{S^n}$	$A_{\overline{n}} = \dfrac{1 - 1/S^n}{i}$	$\dfrac{1}{A_{\overline{n}}} = \dfrac{i}{1 - 1/S^n}$

	1	2	3	4	5	6
YEARS	AMOUNT OF ONE	AMOUNT OF ONE PER PERIOD	SINKING FUND FACTOR	PRESENT WORTH OF ONE	PRESENT WORTH ONE PER PERIOD	PARTIAL PAYMENT
1	1.045 000	1.000 000	1.000 000	.956 938	.956 938	1.045 000
2	1.092 025	2.045 000	.488 998	.915 730	1.872 668	.533 998
3	1.141 166	3.137 025	.318 773	.876 297	2.748 964	.363 773
4	1.192 519	4.278 191	.233 744	.838 561	3.587 526	.278 744
5	1.246 182	5.470 710	.182 792	.802 451	4.389 977	.227 792
6	1.302 260	6.716 892	.148 878	.767 896	5.157 872	.193 878
7	1.360 862	8.019 152	.124 701	.734 828	5.892 701	.169 701
8	1.422 101	9.380 014	.106 610	.703 185	6.595 886	.151 610
9	1.486 095	10.802 114	.092 574	.672 904	7.268 790	.137 574
10	1.552 969	12.288 209	.081 379	.643 928	7.912 718	.126 379
11	1.622 853	13.841 179	.072 248	.616 199	8.528 917	.117 248
12	1.695 881	15.464 032	.064 666	.589 664	9.118 581	.109 666
13	1.772 196	17.159 913	.058 275	.564 272	9.682 852	.103 275
14	1.851 945	18.932 109	.052 820	.539 973	10.222 825	.097 820
15	1.935 282	20.784 054	.048 114	.516 720	10.739 546	.093 114
16	2.022 370	22.719 337	.044 015	.494 469	11.234 015	.089 015
17	2.113 377	24.741 707	.040 418	.473 176	11.707 191	.085 418
18	2.208 479	26.855 084	.037 237	.452 800	12.159 992	.082 237
19	2.307 860	29.063 562	.034 407	.433 302	12.593 294	.079 407
20	2.411 714	31.371 423	.031 876	.414 643	13.007 936	.076 876
21	2.520 241	33.783 137	.029 601	.396 787	13.404 724	.074 601
22	2.633 652	36.303 378	.027 546	.379 701	13.784 425	.072 546
23	2.752 166	38.937 030	.025 682	.363 350	14.147 775	.070 682
24	2.876 014	41.689 196	.023 987	.347 703	14.495 478	.068 987
25	3.005 434	44.565 210	.022 439	.332 731	14.828 209	.067 439
26	3.140 679	47.570 645	.021 021	.318 402	15.146 611	.066 021
27	3.282 010	50.711 324	.019 719	.304 691	15.451 303	.064 719
28	3.429 700	53.993 333	.018 521	.291 571	15.742 874	.063 521
29	3.584 036	57.423 033	.017 415	.279 015	16.021 889	.062 415
30	3.745 318	61.007 070	.016 392	.267 000	16.288 889	.061 392
31	3.913 857	64.752 388	.015 443	.255 502	16.544 391	.060 443
32	4.089 981	68.666 245	.014 563	.244 500	16.788 891	.059 563
33	4.274 030	72.756 226	.013 745	.233 971	17.022 862	.058 745
34	4.466 362	77.030 256	.012 982	.223 896	17.246 758	.057 982
35	4.667 348	81.496 618	.012 270	.214 254	17.461 012	.057 270
36	4.877 378	86.163 966	.011 606	.205 028	17.666 041	.056 606
37	5.096 860	91.041 344	.010 984	.196 199	17.862 240	.055 984
38	5.326 219	96.138 205	.010 402	.187 750	18.049 990	.055 402
39	5.565 899	101.464 424	.009 856	.179 665	18.229 656	.054 856
40	5.816 365	107.030 323	.009 343	.171 929	18.401 584	.054 343
41	6.078 101	112.846 688	.008 862	.164 525	18.566 109	.053 862
42	6.351 615	118.924 789	.008 409	.157 440	18.723 550	.053 409
43	6.637 438	125.276 404	.007 982	.150 661	18.874 210	.052 982
44	6.936 123	131.913 842	.007 581	.144 173	19.018 383	.052 581
45	7.248 248	138.849 965	.007 202	.137 964	19.156 347	.052 202
46	7.574 420	146.098 214	.006 845	.132 023	19.288 371	.051 845
47	7.915 268	153.672 633	.006 507	.126 338	19.414 709	.051 507
48	8.271 456	161.587 902	.006 189	.120 898	19.535 607	.051 189
49	8.643 671	169.859 357	.005 887	.115 692	19.651 298	.050 887
50	9.032 636	178.503 028	.005 602	.110 710	19.762 008	.050 602
51	9.439 105	187.535 665	.005 332	.105 942	19.867 950	.050 332
52	9.863 865	196.974 769	.005 077	.101 380	19.969 330	.050 077
53	10.307 739	206.838 634	.004 835	.097 014	20.066 345	.049 835
54	10.771 587	217.146 373	.004 605	.092 837	20.159 181	.049 605
55	11.256 308	227.917 959	.004 388	.088 839	20.248 021	.049 388
56	11.762 842	239.174 268	.004 181	.085 013	20.333 034	.049 181
57	12.292 170	250.937 110	.003 985	.081 353	20.414 387	.048 985
58	12.845 318	263.229 280	.003 799	.077 849	20.492 236	.048 799
59	13.423 357	276.074 597	.003 622	.074 497	20.566 733	.048 622
60	14.027 408	289.497 954	.003 454	.071 289	20.638 022	.048 454

$S^n = (1+i)^n$	$S_{\overline{n}|} = \dfrac{S^n - 1}{i}$	$1/S_{\overline{n}|} = \dfrac{i}{S^n - 1}$	$V^n = \dfrac{1}{S^n}$	$A_{\overline{n}|} = \dfrac{1 - 1/S^n}{i}$	$\dfrac{1}{A_{\overline{n}|}} = \dfrac{i}{1 - 1/S^n}$

	1	2	3	4	5	6
YEARS	AMOUNT OF ONE	AMOUNT OF ONE PER PERIOD	SINKING FUND FACTOR	PRESENT WORTH OF ONE	PRESENT WORTH ONE PER PERIOD	PARTIAL PAYMENT
1	1.047 500	1.000 000	1.000 000	.954 654	.954 654	1.047 500
2	1.097 256	2.047 500	.488 400	.911 364	1.866 018	.535 900
3	1.149 376	3.144 756	.317 990	.870 037	2.736 055	.365 490
4	1.203 971	4.294 132	.232 876	.830 585	3.566 640	.280 376
5	1.261 160	5.498 103	.181 881	.792 921	4.359 561	.229 381
6	1.321 065	6.759 263	.147 945	.756 965	5.116 526	.195 445
7	1.383 816	8.080 328	.123 757	.722 640	5.839 166	.171 257
8	1.449 547	9.464 144	.105 662	.689 871	6.529 036	.153 162
9	1.518 400	10.913 691	.091 628	.658 588	7.187 624	.139 128
10	1.590 524	12.432 091	.080 437	.628 723	7.816 348	.127 937
11	1.666 074	14.022 615	.071 313	.600 213	8.416 561	.118 813
12	1.745 213	15.688 690	.063 740	.572 996	8.989 557	.111 240
13	1.828 110	17.433 902	.057 360	.547 013	9.536 570	.104 860
14	1.914 946	19.262 013	.051 916	.522 208	10.058 778	.099 416
15	2.005 906	21.176 958	.047 221	.498 528	10.557 306	.094 721
16	2.101 186	23.182 864	.043 135	.475 922	11.033 228	.090 635
17	2.200 992	25.284 050	.039 551	.454 341	11.487 568	.087 051
18	2.305 540	27.485 042	.036 383	.433 738	11.921 306	.083 883
19	2.415 053	29.790 582	.033 568	.414 070	12.335 376	.081 068
20	2.529 768	32.205 635	.031 050	.395 293	12.730 669	.078 550
21	2.649 932	34.735 402	.028 789	.377 368	13.108 037	.076 289
22	2.775 803	37.385 334	.026 748	.360 256	13.468 293	.074 248
23	2.907 654	40.161 137	.024 900	.343 920	13.812 213	.072 400
24	3.045 768	43.068 791	.023 219	.328 324	14.140 538	.070 719
25	3.190 442	46.114 559	.021 685	.313 436	14.453 974	.069 185
26	3.341 988	49.305 000	.020 282	.299 223	14.753 197	.067 782
27	3.500 732	52.646 988	.018 994	.285 655	15.038 852	.066 494
28	3.667 017	56.147 720	.017 810	.272 701	15.311 553	.065 310
29	3.841 200	59.814 736	.016 718	.260 335	15.571 888	.064 218
30	4.023 657	63.655 936	.015 709	.248 530	15.820 418	.063 209
31	4.214 781	67.679 593	.014 776	.237 260	16.057 679	.062 276
32	4.414 983	71.894 374	.013 909	.226 501	16.284 180	.061 409
33	4.624 694	76.309 357	.013 105	.216 231	16.500 410	.060 605
34	4.844 367	80.934 051	.012 356	.206 425	16.706 836	.059 856
35	5.074 475	85.778 419	.011 658	.197 065	16.903 901	.059 158
36	5.315 512	90.852 894	.011 007	.188 129	17.092 029	.058 507
37	5.567 999	96.168 406	.010 398	.179 598	17.271 627	.057 898
38	5.832 479	101.736 405	.009 829	.171 454	17.443 081	.057 329
39	6.109 522	107.568 884	.009 296	.163 679	17.606 759	.056 796
40	6.399 724	113.678 406	.008 797	.156 257	17.763 016	.056 297
41	6.703 711	120.078 131	.008 328	.149 171	17.912 187	.055 828
42	7.022 137	126.781 842	.007 888	.142 407	18.054 594	.055 388
43	7.355 689	133.803 980	.007 474	.135 949	18.190 543	.054 974
44	7.705 084	141.159 669	.007 084	.129 784	18.320 328	.054 584
45	8.071 076	148.864 753	.006 718	.123 899	18.444 227	.054 218
46	8.454 452	156.935 829	.006 372	.118 281	18.562 508	.053 872
47	8.856 038	165.390 280	.006 046	.112 917	18.675 425	.053 546
48	9.276 700	174.246 319	.005 739	.107 797	18.783 222	.053 239
49	9.717 343	183.523 019	.005 449	.102 909	18.886 131	.052 949
50	10.178 917	193.240 362	.005 175	.098 242	18.984 373	.052 675
51	10.662 416	203.419 279	.004 916	.093 787	19.078 160	.052 416
52	11.168 881	214.081 695	.004 671	.089 534	19.167 695	.052 171
53	11.699 402	225.250 576	.004 440	.085 474	19.253 169	.051 940
54	12.255 124	236.949 978	.004 220	.081 599	19.334 768	.051 720
55	12.837 242	249.205 102	.004 013	.077 898	19.412 666	.051 513
56	13.447 011	262.042 344	.003 816	.074 366	19.487 032	.051 316
57	14.085 744	275.489 356	.003 630	.070 994	19.558 026	.051 130
58	14.754 817	289.575 100	.003 453	.067 774	19.625 801	.050 953
59	15.455 671	304.329 917	.003 286	.064 701	19.690 502	.050 786
60	16.189 815	319.785 589	.003 127	.061 767	19.752 269	.050 627

$$S^n = (1+i)^n \qquad S_{\overline{n}|} = \frac{S^n - 1}{i} \qquad 1/S_{\overline{n}|} = \frac{i}{S^n - 1} \qquad V^n = \frac{1}{S^n} \qquad A_{\overline{n}|} = \frac{1 - 1/S^n}{i} \qquad \frac{1}{A_{\overline{n}|}} = \frac{i}{1 - 1/S^n}$$

	1	2	3	4	5	6
YEARS	AMOUNT OF ONE	AMOUNT OF ONE PER PERIOD	SINKING FUND FACTOR	PRESENT WORTH OF ONE	PRESENT WORTH ONE PER PERIOD	PARTIAL PAYMENT
1	1.050 000	1.000 000	1.000 000	.952 381	.952 381	1.050 000
2	1.102 500	2.050 000	.487 805	.907 029	1.859 410	.537 805
3	1.157 625	3.152 500	.317 209	.863 838	2.723 248	.367 209
4	1.215 506	4.310 125	.232 012	.822 702	3.545 951	.282 012
5	1.276 282	5.525 631	.180 975	.783 526	4.329 477	.230 975
6	1.340 096	6.801 913	.147 017	.746 215	5.075 692	.197 017
7	1.407 100	8.142 008	.122 820	.710 681	5.786 373	.172 820
8	1.477 455	9.549 109	.104 722	.676 839	6.463 213	.154 722
9	1.551 328	11.026 564	.090 690	.644 609	7.107 822	.140 690
10	1.628 895	12.577 893	.079 505	.613 913	7.721 735	.129 505
11	1.710 339	14.206 787	.070 389	.584 679	8.306 414	.120 389
12	1.795 856	15.917 127	.062 825	.556 837	8.863 252	.112 825
13	1.885 649	17.712 983	.056 456	.530 321	9.393 573	.106 456
14	1.979 932	19.598 632	.051 024	.505 068	9.898 641	.101 024
15	2.078 928	21.578 564	.046 342	.481 017	10.379 658	.096 342
16	2.182 875	23.657 492	.042 270	.458 112	10.837 770	.092 270
17	2.292 018	25.840 366	.038 699	.436 297	11.274 066	.088 699
18	2.406 619	28.132 385	.035 546	.415 521	11.689 587	.085 546
19	2.526 950	30.539 004	.032 745	.395 734	12.085 321	.082 745
20	2.653 298	33.065 954	.030 243	.376 889	12.462 210	.080 243
21	2.785 963	35.719 252	.027 996	.358 942	12.821 153	.077 996
22	2.925 261	38.505 214	.025 971	.341 850	13.163 003	.075 971
23	3.071 524	41.430 475	.024 137	.325 571	13.488 574	.074 137
24	3.225 100	44.501 999	.022 471	.310 068	13.798 642	.072 471
25	3.386 355	47.727 099	.020 952	.295 303	14.093 945	.070 952
26	3.555 673	51.113 454	.019 564	.281 241	14.375 185	.069 564
27	3.733 456	54.669 126	.018 292	.267 848	14.643 034	.068 292
28	3.920 129	58.402 583	.017 123	.255 094	14.898 127	.067 123
29	4.116 136	62.322 712	.016 046	.242 946	15.141 074	.066 046
30	4.321 942	66.438 848	.015 051	.231 377	15.372 451	.065 051
31	4.538 039	70.760 790	.014 132	.220 359	15.592 811	.064 132
32	4.764 941	75.298 829	.013 280	.209 866	15.802 677	.063 280
33	5.003 189	80.063 771	.012 490	.199 873	16.002 549	.062 490
34	5.253 348	85.066 959	.011 755	.190 355	16.192 904	.061 755
35	5.516 015	90.320 307	.011 072	.181 290	16.374 194	.061 072
36	5.791 816	95.836 323	.010 434	.172 657	16.546 852	.060 434
37	6.081 407	101.628 139	.009 840	.164 436	16.711 287	.059 840
38	6.385 477	107.709 546	.009 284	.156 605	16.867 893	.059 284
39	6.704 751	114.095 023	.008 765	.149 148	17.017 041	.058 765
40	7.039 989	120.799 774	.008 278	.142 046	17.159 086	.058 278
41	7.391 988	127.839 763	.007 822	.135 282	17.294 368	.057 822
42	7.761 588	135.231 751	.007 395	.128 840	17.423 208	.057 395
43	8.149 667	142.993 339	.006 993	.122 704	17.545 912	.056 993
44	8.557 150	151.143 006	.006 616	.116 861	17.662 773	.056 616
45	8.985 008	159.700 156	.006 262	.111 297	17.774 070	.056 262
46	9.434 258	168.685 164	.005 928	.105 997	17.880 066	.055 928
47	9.905 971	178.119 422	.005 614	.100 949	17.981 016	.055 614
48	10.401 270	188.025 393	.005 318	.096 142	18.077 158	.055 318
49	10.921 333	198.426 663	.005 040	.091 564	18.168 722	.055 040
50	11.467 400	209.347 996	.004 777	.087 204	18.255 925	.054 777
51	12.040 770	220.815 396	.004 529	.083 051	18.338 977	.054 529
52	12.642 808	232.856 165	.004 294	.079 096	18.418 073	.054 294
53	13.274 949	245.498 974	.004 073	.075 330	18.493 403	.054 073
54	13.938 696	258.773 922	.003 864	.071 743	18.565 146	.053 864
55	14.635 631	272.712 618	.003 667	.068 326	18.633 472	.053 667
56	15.367 412	287.348 249	.003 480	.065 073	18.698 545	.053 480
57	16.135 783	302.715 662	.003 303	.061 974	18.760 519	.053 303
58	16.942 572	318.851 445	.003 136	.059 023	18.819 542	.053 136
59	17.789 701	335.794 017	.002 978	.056 212	18.875 754	.052 978
60	18.679 186	353.583 718	.002 828	.053 536	18.929 290	.052 828
	$S^n = (1 + i)^n$	$S_{\overline{n}} = \dfrac{S^n - 1}{i}$	$1/S_{\overline{n}} = \dfrac{i}{S^n - 1}$	$V^n = \dfrac{1}{S^n}$	$A_{\overline{n}} = \dfrac{1 - 1/S^n}{i}$	$\dfrac{1}{A_{\overline{n}}} = \dfrac{i}{1 - 1/S^n}$

	1	2	3	4	5	6
YEARS	AMOUNT OF ONE	AMOUNT OF ONE PER PERIOD	SINKING FUND FACTOR	PRESENT WORTH OF ONE	PRESENT WORTH ONE PER PERIOD	PARTIAL PAYMENT
1	1.052 500	1.000 000	1.000 000	.950 119	.950 119	1.052 500
2	1.107 756	2.052 500	.487 211	.902 726	1.852 844	.539 711
3	1.165 913	3.160 256	.316 430	.857 697	2.710 541	.368 930
4	1.227 124	4.326 170	.231 151	.814 914	3.525 455	.283 651
5	1.291 548	5.553 294	.180 073	.774 265	4.299 719	.232 573
6	1.359 354	6.844 842	.146 095	.735 643	5.035 363	.198 595
7	1.430 720	8.204 196	.121 889	.698 949	5.734 311	.174 389
8	1.505 833	9.634 916	.103 789	.664 084	6.398 396	.156 289
9	1.584 889	11.140 749	.089 761	.630 959	7.029 355	.142 261
10	1.668 096	12.725 638	.078 582	.599 486	7.628 840	.131 082
11	1.755 671	14.393 734	.069 475	.569 583	8.198 423	.121 975
12	1.847 844	16.149 405	.061 922	.541 171	8.739 595	.114 422
13	1.944 856	17.997 249	.055 564	.514 177	9.253 772	.108 064
14	2.046 961	19.942 105	.050 145	.488 529	9.742 301	.102 645
15	2.154 426	21.989 065	.045 477	.464 161	10.206 462	.097 977
16	2.267 533	24.143 491	.041 419	.441 008	10.647 469	.093 919
17	2.386 579	26.411 025	.037 863	.419 010	11.066 479	.090 363
18	2.511 874	28.797 603	.034 725	.398 109	11.464 588	.087 225
19	2.643 748	31.309 478	.031 939	.378 251	11.842 839	.084 439
20	2.782 544	33.953 225	.029 452	.359 383	12.202 223	.081 952
21	2.928 628	36.735 769	.027 221	.341 457	12.543 679	.079 721
22	3.082 381	39.664 397	.025 212	.324 425	12.868 104	.077 712
23	3.244 206	42.746 778	.023 394	.308 242	13.176 346	.075 894
24	3.414 527	45.990 984	.021 743	.292 866	13.469 212	.074 243
25	3.593 789	49.405 511	.020 241	.278 258	13.747 470	.072 741
26	3.782 463	52.999 300	.018 868	.264 378	14.011 848	.071 368
27	3.981 043	56.781 763	.017 611	.251 190	14.263 038	.070 111
28	4.190 047	60.762 806	.016 457	.238 661	14.501 699	.068 957
29	4.410 025	64.952 853	.015 396	.226 756	14.728 455	.067 896
30	4.641 551	69.362 878	.014 417	.215 445	14.943 901	.066 917
31	4.885 233	74.004 429	.013 513	.204 699	15.148 599	.066 013
32	5.141 707	78.889 662	.012 676	.194 488	15.343 087	.065 176
33	5.411 647	84.031 369	.011 900	.184 787	15.527 874	.064 400
34	5.695 758	89.443 016	.011 180	.175 569	15.703 443	.063 680
35	5.994 786	95.138 774	.010 511	.166 812	15.870 255	.063 011
36	6.309 512	101.133 560	.009 888	.158 491	16.028 745	.062 388
37	6.640 761	107.443 071	.009 307	.150 585	16.179 331	.061 807
38	6.989 401	114.083 833	.008 765	.143 074	16.322 404	.061 265
39	7.356 345	121.073 234	.008 259	.135 937	16.458 341	.060 759
40	7.742 553	128.429 579	.007 786	.129 156	16.587 498	.060 286
41	8.149 037	136.172 132	.007 344	.122 714	16.710 212	.059 844
42	8.576 861	144.321 169	.006 929	.116 593	16.826 804	.059 429
43	9.027 147	152.898 030	.006 540	.110 777	16.937 581	.059 040
44	9.501 072	161.925 176	.006 176	.105 251	17.042 833	.058 676
45	9.999 878	171.426 248	.005 833	.100 001	17.142 834	.058 333
46	10.524 872	181.426 126	.005 512	.095 013	17.237 847	.058 012
47	11.077 427	191.950 998	.005 210	.090 274	17.328 121	.057 710
48	11.658 992	203.028 425	.004 925	.085 771	17.413 891	.057 425
49	12.271 089	214.687 418	.004 658	.081 492	17.495 384	.057 158
50	12.915 322	226.958 507	.004 406	.077 427	17.572 811	.056 906
51	13.593 376	239.873 829	.004 169	.073 565	17.646 376	.056 669
52	14.307 028	253.467 205	.003 945	.069 896	17.716 272	.056 445
53	15.058 147	267.774 233	.003 734	.066 409	17.782 681	.056 234
54	15.848 700	282.832 380	.003 536	.063 097	17.845 778	.056 036
55	16.680 757	298.681 080	.003 348	.059 949	17.905 727	.055 848
56	17.556 496	315.361 837	.003 171	.056 959	17.962 686	.055 671
57	18.478 212	332.918 333	.003 004	.054 118	18.016 804	.055 504
58	19.448 319	351.396 546	.002 846	.051 418	18.068 222	.055 346
59	20.469 355	370.844 864	.002 697	.048 854	18.117 076	.055 197
60	21.543 997	391.314 220	.002 555	.046 417	18.163 493	.055 055

$S^n = (1+i)^n$	$S_{\overline{n}|} = \dfrac{S^n - 1}{i}$	$1/S_{\overline{n}|} = \dfrac{i}{S^n - 1}$	$V^n = \dfrac{1}{S^n}$	$A_{\overline{n}|} = \dfrac{1 - 1/S^n}{i}$	$\dfrac{1}{A_{\overline{n}|}} = \dfrac{i}{1 - 1/S^n}$

	1	2	3	4	5	6
YEARS	AMOUNT OF ONE	AMOUNT OF ONE PER PERIOD	SINKING FUND FACTOR	PRESENT WORTH OF ONE	PRESENT WORTH ONE PER PERIOD	PARTIAL PAYMENT
1	1.055 000	1.000 000	1.000 000	.947 867	.947 867	1.055 000
2	1.113 025	2.055 000	.486 618	.898 452	1.846 320	.541 618
3	1.174 241	3.168 025	.315 654	.851 614	2.697 933	.370 654
4	1.238 825	4.342 266	.230 294	.807 217	3.505 150	.285 294
5	1.306 960	5.581 091	.179 176	.765 134	4.270 284	.234 176
6	1.378 843	6.888 051	.145 179	.725 246	4.995 530	.200 179
7	1.454 679	8.266 894	.120 964	.687 437	5.682 967	.175 964
8	1.534 687	9.721 573	.102 864	.651 599	6.334 566	.157 864
9	1.619 094	11.256 260	.088 839	.617 629	6.952 195	.143 839
10	1.708 144	12.875 354	.077 668	.585 431	7.537 626	.132 668
11	1.802 092	14.583 498	.068 571	.554 911	8.092 536	.123 571
12	1.901 207	16.385 591	.061 029	.525 982	8.618 518	.116 029
13	2.005 774	18.286 798	.054 684	.498 561	9.117 079	.109 684
14	2.116 091	20.292 572	.049 279	.472 569	9.589 648	.104 279
15	2.232 476	22.408 663	.044 626	.447 933	10.037 581	.099 626
16	2.355 263	24.641 140	.040 583	.424 581	10.462 162	.095 583
17	2.484 802	26.996 403	.037 042	.402 447	10.864 609	.092 042
18	2.621 466	29.481 205	.033 920	.381 466	11.246 074	.088 920
19	2.765 647	32.102 671	.031 150	.361 579	11.607 654	.086 150
20	2.917 757	34.868 318	.028 679	.342 729	11.950 382	.083 679
21	3.078 234	37.786 076	.026 465	.324 862	12.275 244	.081 465
22	3.247 537	40.864 310	.024 471	.307 926	12.583 170	.079 471
23	3.426 152	44.111 847	.022 670	.291 873	12.875 042	.077 670
24	3.614 590	47.537 998	.021 036	.276 657	13.151 699	.076 036
25	3.813 392	51.152 588	.019 549	.262 234	13.413 933	.074 549
26	4.023 129	54.965 981	.018 193	.248 563	13.662 495	.073 193
27	4.244 401	58.989 109	.016 952	.235 605	13.898 100	.071 952
28	4.477 843	63.233 510	.015 814	.223 322	14.121 422	.070 814
29	4.724 124	67.711 354	.014 769	.211 679	14.333 101	.069 769
30	4.983 951	72.435 478	.013 805	.200 644	14.533 745	.068 805
31	5.258 069	77.419 429	.012 917	.190 184	14.723 929	.067 917
32	5.547 262	82.677 498	.012 095	.180 269	14.904 198	.067 095
33	5.852 362	88.224 760	.011 335	.170 871	15.075 069	.066 335
34	6.174 242	94.077 122	.010 630	.161 963	15.237 033	.065 630
35	6.513 825	100.251 364	.009 975	.153 520	15.390 552	.064 975
36	6.872 085	106.765 189	.009 366	.145 516	15.536 068	.064 366
37	7.250 050	113.637 274	.008 800	.137 930	15.673 999	.063 800
38	7.648 803	120.887 324	.008 272	.130 739	15.804 738	.063 272
39	8.069 487	128.536 127	.007 780	.123 924	15.928 662	.062 780
40	8.513 309	136.605 614	.007 320	.117 463	16.046 125	.062 320
41	8.981 541	145.118 923	.006 891	.111 339	16.157 464	.061 891
42	9.475 525	154.100 464	.006 489	.105 535	16.262 999	.061 489
43	9.996 679	163.575 989	.006 113	.100 033	16.363 032	.061 113
44	10.546 497	173.572 669	.005 761	.094 818	16.457 851	.060 761
45	11.126 554	184.119 165	.005 431	.089 875	16.547 726	.060 431
46	11.738 515	195.245 719	.005 122	.085 190	16.632 915	.060 122
47	12.384 133	206.984 234	.004 831	.080 748	16.713 664	.059 831
48	13.065 260	219.368 367	.004 559	.076 539	16.790 203	.059 559
49	13.783 849	232.433 627	.004 302	.072 549	16.862 751	.059 302
50	14.541 961	246.217 476	.004 061	.068 767	16.931 518	.059 061
51	15.341 769	260.759 438	.003 835	.065 182	16.996 699	.058 835
52	16.185 566	276.101 207	.003 622	.061 783	17.058 483	.058 622
53	17.075 773	292.286 773	.003 421	.058 563	17.117 045	.058 421
54	18.014 940	309.362 546	.003 232	.055 509	17.172 555	.058 232
55	19.005 762	327.377 486	.003 055	.052 616	17.225 170	.058 055
56	20.051 079	346.383 247	.002 887	.049 873	17.275 043	.057 887
57	21.153 888	366.434 326	.002 729	.047 273	17.322 316	.057 729
58	22.317 352	387.588 214	.002 580	.044 808	17.367 124	.057 580
59	23.544 806	409.905 566	.002 440	.042 472	17.409 596	.057 440
60	24.839 770	433.450 372	.002 307	.040 258	17.449 854	.057 307
	$S^n = (1+i)^n$	$S_{\overline{n}|} = \dfrac{S^n - 1}{i}$	$1/S_{\overline{n}|} = \dfrac{i}{S^n - 1}$	$V^n = \dfrac{1}{S^n}$	$A_{\overline{n}|} = \dfrac{1 - 1/S^n}{i}$	$\dfrac{1}{A_{\overline{n}|}} = \dfrac{i}{1 - 1/S^n}$

	1	2	3	4	5	6
YEARS	AMOUNT OF ONE	AMOUNT OF ONE PER PERIOD	SINKING FUND FACTOR	PRESENT WORTH OF ONE	PRESENT WORTH ONE PER PERIOD	PARTIAL PAYMENT
1	1.057 500	1.000 000	1.000 000	.945 626	.945 626	1.057 500
2	1.118 306	2.057 500	.486 027	.894 209	1.839 836	.543 527
3	1.182 609	3.175 806	.314 881	.845 588	2.685 424	.372 381
4	1.250 609	4.358 415	.229 441	.799 611	3.485 035	.286 941
5	1.322 519	5.609 024	.178 284	.756 133	4.241 167	.235 784
6	1.398 564	6.931 543	.144 268	.715 019	4.956 187	.201 768
7	1.478 981	8.330 107	.120 046	.676 141	5.632 328	.177 546
8	1.564 023	9.809 088	.101 946	.639 377	6.271 705	.159 446
9	1.653 954	11.373 110	.087 927	.604 612	6.876 317	.145 427
10	1.749 056	13.027 064	.076 763	.571 737	7.448 054	.134 263
11	1.849 627	14.776 120	.067 677	.540 650	7.988 703	.125 177
12	1.955 980	16.625 747	.060 148	.511 253	8.499 956	.117 648
13	2.068 449	18.581 728	.053 816	.483 454	8.983 410	.111 316
14	2.187 385	20.650 177	.048 426	.457 167	9.440 576	.105 926
15	2.313 160	22.837 562	.043 788	.432 309	9.872 886	.101 288
16	2.446 167	25.150 722	.039 760	.408 803	10.281 688	.097 260
17	2.586 821	27.596 888	.036 236	.386 575	10.668 263	.093 736
18	2.735 563	30.183 710	.033 130	.365 555	11.033 819	.090 630
19	2.892 858	32.919 273	.030 377	.345 679	11.379 498	.087 877
20	3.059 198	35.812 131	.027 923	.326 883	11.706 381	.085 423
21	3.235 101	38.871 329	.025 726	.309 109	12.015 490	.083 226
22	3.421 120	42.106 430	.023 749	.292 302	12.307 792	.081 249
23	3.617 834	45.527 550	.021 965	.276 408	12.584 200	.079 465
24	3.825 860	49.145 384	.020 348	.261 379	12.845 580	.077 848
25	4.045 846	52.971 243	.018 878	.247 167	13.092 747	.076 378
26	4.278 483	57.017 090	.017 539	.233 728	13.326 474	.075 039
27	4.524 495	61.295 573	.016 314	.221 019	13.547 494	.073 814
28	4.784 654	65.820 068	.015 193	.209 002	13.756 495	.072 693
29	5.059 772	70.604 722	.014 163	.197 637	13.954 132	.071 663
30	5.350 708	75.664 493	.013 216	.186 891	14.141 024	.070 716
31	5.658 374	81.015 202	.012 343	.176 729	14.317 753	.069 843
32	5.983 731	86.673 576	.011 538	.167 120	14.484 873	.069 038
33	6.327 795	92.657 307	.010 792	.158 033	14.642 906	.068 292
34	6.691 643	98.985 102	.010 103	.149 440	14.792 346	.067 603
35	7.076 413	105.676 745	.009 463	.141 315	14.933 660	.066 963
36	7.483 307	112.753 158	.008 869	.133 631	15.067 291	.066 369
37	7.913 597	120.236 464	.008 317	.126 365	15.193 656	.065 817
38	8.368 629	128.150 061	.007 803	.119 494	15.313 150	.065 303
39	8.849 825	136.518 690	.007 325	.112 997	15.426 146	.064 825
40	9.358 690	145.368 514	.006 879	.106 853	15.532 999	.064 379
41	9.896 814	154.727 204	.006 463	.101 043	15.634 041	.063 963
42	10.465 881	164.624 018	.006 074	.095 549	15.729 590	.063 574
43	11.067 669	175.089 899	.005 711	.090 353	15.819 943	.063 211
44	11.704 060	186.157 568	.005 372	.085 440	15.905 384	.062 872
45	12.377 044	197.861 628	.005 054	.080 795	15.986 178	.062 554
46	13.088 724	210.238 672	.004 756	.076 402	16.062 580	.062 256
47	13.841 325	223.327 396	.004 478	.072 247	16.134 828	.061 978
48	14.637 201	237.168 721	.004 216	.068 319	16.203 147	.061 716
49	15.478 841	251.805 922	.003 971	.064 604	16.267 751	.061 471
50	16.368 874	267.284 763	.003 741	.061 092	16.328 842	.061 241
51	17.310 084	283.653 637	.003 525	.057 770	16.386 612	.061 025
52	18.305 414	300.963 721	.003 323	.054 629	16.441 241	.060 823
53	19.357 975	319.269 135	.003 132	.051 658	16.492 899	.060 632
54	20.471 059	338.627 110	.002 953	.048 849	16.541 749	.060 453
55	21.648 145	359.098 169	.002 785	.046 193	16.587 942	.060 285
56	22.892 913	380.746 314	.002 626	.043 682	16.631 624	.060 126
57	24.209 256	403.639 227	.002 477	.041 307	16.672 930	.059 977
58	25.601 288	427.848 482	.002 337	.039 061	16.711 991	.059 837
59	27.073 362	453.449 770	.002 205	.036 937	16.748 927	.059 705
60	28.630 080	480.523 132	.002 081	.034 928	16.783 856	.059 581

$$S^n = (1+i)^n \qquad S_{\overline{n}|} = \frac{S^n - 1}{i} \qquad 1/S_{\overline{n}|} = \frac{i}{S^n - 1} \qquad V^n = \frac{1}{S^n} \qquad A_{\overline{n}|} = \frac{1 - 1/S^n}{i} \qquad \frac{1}{A_{\overline{n}|}} = \frac{i}{1 - 1/S^n}$$

	1	2	3	4	5	6
YEARS	AMOUNT OF ONE	AMOUNT OF ONE PER PERIOD	SINKING FUND FACTOR	PRESENT WORTH OF ONE	PRESENT WORTH ONE PER PERIOD	PARTIAL PAYMENT
1	1.060 000	1.000 000	1.000 000	.943 396	.943 396	1.060 000
2	1.123 600	2.060 000	.485 437	.889 996	1.833 393	.545 437
3	1.191 016	3.183 600	.314 110	.839 619	2.673 012	.374 110
4	1.262 477	4.374 616	.228 591	.792 094	3.465 106	.288 591
5	1.338 226	5.637 093	.177 396	.747 258	4.212 364	.237 396
6	1.418 519	6.975 319	.143 363	.704 961	4.917 324	.203 363
7	1.503 630	8.393 838	.119 135	.665 057	5.582 381	.179 135
8	1.593 848	9.897 468	.101 036	.627 412	6.209 794	.161 036
9	1.689 479	11.491 316	.087 022	.591 898	6.801 692	.147 022
10	1.790 848	13.180 795	.075 868	.558 395	7.360 087	.135 868
11	1.898 299	14.971 643	.066 793	.526 788	7.886 875	.126 793
12	2.012 196	16.869 941	.059 277	.496 969	8.383 844	.119 277
13	2.132 928	18.882 138	.052 960	.468 839	8.852 683	.112 960
14	2.260 904	21.015 066	.047 585	.442 301	9.294 984	.107 585
15	2.396 558	23.275 970	.042 963	.417 265	9.712 249	.102 963
16	2.540 352	25.672 528	.038 952	.393 646	10.105 895	.098 952
17	2.692 773	28.212 880	.035 445	.371 364	10.477 260	.095 445
18	2.854 339	30.905 653	.032 357	.350 344	10.827 603	.092 357
19	3.025 600	33.759 992	.029 621	.330 513	11.158 116	.089 621
20	3.207 135	36.785 591	.027 185	.311 805	11.469 921	.087 185
21	3.399 564	39.992 727	.025 005	.294 155	11.764 077	.085 005
22	3.603 537	43.392 290	.023 046	.277 505	12.041 582	.083 046
23	3.819 750	46.995 828	.021 278	.261 797	12.303 379	.081 278
24	4.048 935	50.815 577	.019 679	.246 979	12.550 358	.079 679
25	4.291 871	54.864 512	.018 227	.232 999	12.783 356	.078 227
26	4.549 383	59.156 383	.016 904	.219 810	13.003 166	.076 904
27	4.822 346	63.705 766	.015 697	.207 368	13.210 534	.075 697
28	5.111 687	68.528 112	.014 593	.195 630	13.406 164	.074 593
29	5.418 388	73.639 798	.013 580	.184 557	13.590 721	.073 580
30	5.743 491	79.058 186	.012 649	.174 110	13.764 831	.072 649
31	6.088 101	84.801 677	.011 792	.164 255	13.929 086	.071 792
32	6.453 387	90.889 778	.011 002	.154 957	14.084 043	.071 002
33	6.840 590	97.343 165	.010 273	.146 186	14.230 230	.070 273
34	7.251 025	104.183 755	.009 598	.137 912	14.368 141	.069 598
35	7.686 087	111.434 780	.008 974	.130 105	14.498 246	.068 974
36	8.147 252	119.120 867	.008 395	.122 741	14.620 987	.068 395
37	8.636 087	127.268 119	.007 857	.115 793	14.736 780	.067 857
38	9.154 252	135.904 206	.007 358	.109 239	14.846 019	.067 358
39	9.703 507	145.058 458	.006 894	.103 056	14.949 075	.066 894
40	10.285 718	154.761 966	.006 462	.097 222	15.046 297	.066 462
41	10.902 861	165.047 684	.006 059	.091 719	15.138 016	.066 059
42	11.557 033	175.950 545	.005 683	.086 527	15.224 543	.065 683
43	12.250 455	187.507 577	.005 333	.081 630	15.306 173	.065 333
44	12.985 482	199.758 032	.005 006	.077 009	15.383 182	.065 006
45	13.764 611	212.743 514	.004 700	.072 650	15.455 832	.064 700
46	14.590 487	226.508 125	.004 415	.068 538	15.524 370	.064 415
47	15.465 917	241.098 612	.004 148	.064 658	15.589 028	.064 148
48	16.393 872	256.564 529	.003 898	.060 998	15.650 027	.063 898
49	17.377 504	272.958 401	.003 664	.057 546	15.707 572	.063 664
50	18.420 154	290.335 905	.003 444	.054 288	15.761 861	.063 444
51	19.525 364	308.756 059	.003 239	.051 215	15.813 076	.063 239
52	20.696 885	328.281 422	.003 046	.048 316	15.861 393	.063 046
53	21.938 698	348.978 308	.002 866	.045 582	15.906 974	.062 866
54	23.255 020	370.917 006	.002 696	.043 001	15.949 976	.062 696
55	24.650 322	394.172 027	.002 537	.040 567	15.990 543	.062 537
56	26.129 341	418.822 348	.002 388	.038 271	16.028 814	.062 388
57	27.697 101	444.951 689	.002 247	.036 105	16.064 919	.062 247
58	29.358 927	472.648 790	.002 116	.034 061	16.098 980	.062 116
59	31.120 463	502.007 718	.001 992	.032 133	16.131 113	.061 992
60	32.987 691	533.128 181	.001 876	.030 314	16.161 428	.061 876

$$S^n = (1+i)^n \qquad S_{\overline{n}|} = \frac{S^n - 1}{i} \qquad 1/S_{\overline{n}|} = \frac{i_j}{S^n - 1} \qquad V^n = \frac{1}{S^n} \qquad A_{\overline{n}|} = \frac{1 - 1/S^n}{i} \qquad \frac{1}{A_{\overline{n}|}} = \frac{i}{1 - 1/S^n}$$

	1	2	3	4	5	6
YEARS	AMOUNT OF ONE	AMOUNT OF ONE PER PERIOD	SINKING FUND FACTOR	PRESENT WORTH OF ONE	PRESENT WORTH ONE PER PERIOD	PARTIAL PAYMENT
1	1.062 500	1.000 000	1.000 000	.941 176	.941 176	1.062 500
2	1.128 906	2.062 500	.484 848	.885 813	1.826 990	.547 348
3	1.199 463	3.191 406	.313 341	.833 706	2.660 696	.375 841
4	1.274 429	4.390 869	.227 745	.784 665	3.445 361	.290 245
5	1.354 081	5.665 298	.176 513	.738 508	4.183 869	.239 013
6	1.438 711	7.019 380	.142 463	.695 067	4.878 936	.204 963
7	1.528 631	8.458 091	.118 230	.654 180	5.533 116	.180 730
8	1.624 170	9.986 722	.100 133	.615 699	6.148 815	.162 633
9	1.725 681	11.610 892	.086 126	.579 481	6.728 297	.148 626
10	1.833 536	13.336 572	.074 982	.545 394	7.273 691	.137 482
11	1.948 132	15.170 108	.065 919	.513 312	7.787 003	.128 419
12	2.069 890	17.118 240	.058 417	.483 117	8.270 121	.120 917
13	2.199 258	19.188 130	.052 116	.454 699	8.724 819	.114 616
14	2.336 712	21.387 388	.046 757	.427 952	9.152 771	.109 257
15	2.482 756	23.724 100	.042 151	.402 778	9.555 549	.104 651
16	2.637 928	26.206 856	.038 158	.379 085	9.934 635	.100 658
17	2.802 799	28.844 784	.034 668	.356 786	10.291 421	.097 168
18	2.977 974	31.647 583	.031 598	.335 799	10.627 220	.094 098
19	3.164 097	34.625 557	.028 880	.316 046	10.943 266	.091 380
20	3.361 853	37.789 655	.026 462	.297 455	11.240 721	.088 962
21	3.571 969	41.151 508	.024 300	.279 958	11.520 678	.086 800
22	3.795 217	44.723 477	.022 360	.263 490	11.784 168	.084 860
23	4.032 418	48.518 695	.020 611	.247 990	12.032 158	.083 111
24	4.284 445	52.551 113	.019 029	.233 402	12.265 560	.081 529
25	4.552 222	56.835 558	.017 595	.219 673	12.485 233	.080 095
26	4.836 736	61.387 780	.016 290	.206 751	12.691 984	.078 790
27	5.139 032	66.224 516	.015 100	.194 589	12.886 573	.077 600
28	5.460 222	71.363 549	.014 013	.183 143	13.069 716	.076 513
29	5.801 486	76.823 771	.013 017	.172 370	13.242 086	.075 517
30	6.164 079	82.625 256	.012 103	.162 230	13.404 316	.074 603
31	6.549 333	88.789 335	.011 263	.152 687	13.557 003	.073 763
32	6.958 667	95.338 668	.010 489	.143 706	13.700 709	.072 989
33	7.393 583	102.297 335	.009 775	.135 252	13.835 961	.072 275
34	7.855 682	109.690 918	.009 117	.127 296	13.963 258	.071 617
35	8.346 663	117.546 601	.008 507	.119 808	14.083 066	.071 007
36	8.868 329	125.893 263	.007 943	.112 761	14.195 827	.070 443
37	9.422 600	134.761 592	.007 421	.106 128	14.301 955	.069 921
38	10.011 512	144.184 192	.006 936	.099 885	14.401 840	.069 436
39	10.637 231	154.195 704	.006 485	.094 009	14.495 849	.068 985
40	11.302 058	164.832 935	.006 067	.088 479	14.584 329	.068 567
41	12.008 437	176.134 994	.005 677	.083 275	14.667 603	.068 177
42	12.758 964	188.143 431	.005 315	.078 376	14.745 980	.067 815
43	13.556 400	200.902 395	.004 978	.073 766	14.819 746	.067 478
44	14.403 675	214.458 795	.004 663	.069 427	14.889 172	.067 163
45	15.303 904	228.862 470	.004 369	.065 343	14.954 515	.066 869
46	16.260 398	244.166 374	.004 096	.061 499	15.016 014	.066 596
47	17.276 673	260.426 772	.003 840	.057 882	15.073 896	.066 340
48	18.356 465	277.703 445	.003 601	.054 477	15.128 372	.066 101
49	19.503 744	296.059 911	.003 378	.051 272	15.179 645	.065 878
50	20.722 728	315.563 655	.003 169	.048 256	15.227 901	.065 669
51	22.017 899	336.286 384	.002 974	.045 418	15.273 318	.065 474
52	23.394 018	358.304 283	.002 791	.042 746	15.316 064	.065 291
53	24.856 144	381.698 300	.002 620	.040 232	15.356 296	.065 120
54	26.409 653	406.554 444	.002 460	.037 865	15.394 161	.064 960
55	28.060 256	432.964 097	.002 310	.035 638	15.429 799	.064 810
56	29.814 022	461.024 353	.002 169	.033 541	15.463 340	.064 669
57	31.677 398	490.838 375	.002 037	.031 568	15.494 908	.064 537
58	33.657 236	522.515 773	.001 914	.029 711	15.524 619	.064 414
59	35.760 813	556.173 009	.001 798	.027 964	15.552 583	.064 298
60	37.995 864	591.933 822	.001 689	.026 319	15.578 902	.064 189

| $S^n = (1+i)^n$ | $S_{\overline{n}|} = \dfrac{S^n - 1}{i}$ | $1/S_{\overline{n}|} = \dfrac{i}{S^n - 1}$ | $V^n = \dfrac{1}{S^n}$ | $A_{\overline{n}|} = \dfrac{1 - 1/S^n}{i}$ | $\dfrac{1}{A_{\overline{n}|}} = \dfrac{i}{1 - 1/S^n}$ |

	1	2	3	4	5	6
YEARS	AMOUNT OF ONE	AMOUNT OF ONE PER PERIOD	SINKING FUND FACTOR	PRESENT WORTH OF ONE	PRESENT WORTH ONE PER PERIOD	PARTIAL PAYMENT
1	1.065 000	1.000 000	1.000 000	.938 967	.938 967	1.065 000
2	1.134 225	2.065 000	.484 262	.881 659	1.820 626	.549 262
3	1.207 950	3.199 225	.312 576	.827 849	2.648 476	.377 576
4	1.286 466	4.407 175	.226 903	.777 323	3.425 799	.291 903
5	1.370 087	5.693 641	.175 635	.729 881	4.155 679	.240 635
6	1.459 142	7.063 728	.141 568	.685 334	4.841 014	.206 568
7	1.553 987	8.522 870	.117 331	.643 506	5.484 520	.182 331
8	1.654 996	10.076 856	.099 237	.604 231	6.088 751	.164 237
9	1.762 570	11.731 852	.085 238	.567 353	6.656 104	.150 238
10	1.877 137	13.494 423	.074 105	.532 726	7.188 830	.139 105
11	1.999 151	15.371 560	.065 055	.500 212	7.689 042	.130 055
12	2.129 096	17.370 711	.057 568	.469 683	8.158 725	.122 568
13	2.267 487	19.499 808	.051 283	.441 017	8.599 742	.116 283
14	2.414 874	21.767 295	.045 940	.414 100	9.013 842	.110 940
15	2.571 841	24.182 169	.041 353	.388 827	9.402 669	.106 353
16	2.739 011	26.754 010	.037 378	.365 095	9.767 764	.102 378
17	2.917 046	29.493 021	.033 906	.342 813	10.110 577	.098 906
18	3.106 654	32.410 067	.030 855	.321 890	10.432 466	.095 855
19	3.308 587	35.516 722	.028 156	.302 244	10.734 710	.093 156
20	3.523 645	38.825 309	.025 756	.283 797	11.018 507	.090 756
21	3.752 682	42.348 954	.023 613	.266 476	11.284 983	.088 613
22	3.996 606	46.101 636	.021 691	.250 212	11.535 196	.086 691
23	4.256 386	50.098 242	.019 961	.234 941	11.770 137	.084 961
24	4.533 051	54.354 628	.018 398	.220 602	11.990 739	.083 398
25	4.827 699	58.887 679	.016 981	.207 138	12.197 877	.081 981
26	5.141 500	63.715 378	.015 695	.194 496	12.392 373	.080 695
27	5.475 697	68.856 877	.014 523	.182 625	12.574 998	.079 523
28	5.831 617	74.332 574	.013 453	.171 479	12.746 477	.078 453
29	6.210 672	80.164 192	.012 474	.161 013	12.907 490	.077 474
30	6.614 366	86.374 864	.011 577	.151 186	13.058 676	.076 577
31	7.044 300	92.989 230	.010 754	.141 959	13.200 635	.075 754
32	7.502 179	100.033 530	.009 997	.133 295	13.333 929	.074 997
33	7.989 821	107.535 710	.009 299	.125 159	13.459 088	.074 299
34	8.509 159	115.525 531	.008 656	.117 520	13.576 609	.073 656
35	9.062 255	124.034 690	.008 062	.110 348	13.686 957	.073 062
36	9.651 301	133.096 945	.007 513	.103 613	13.790 570	.072 513
37	10.278 636	142.748 247	.007 005	.097 289	13.887 859	.072 005
38	10.946 747	153.026 883	.006 535	.091 351	13.979 210	.071 535
39	11.658 286	163.973 630	.006 099	.085 776	14.064 986	.071 099
40	12.416 075	175.631 916	.005 694	.080 541	14.145 527	.070 694
41	13.223 119	188.047 990	.005 318	.075 625	14.221 152	.070 318
42	14.082 622	201.271 110	.004 968	.071 010	14.292 161	.069 968
43	14.997 993	215.353 732	.004 644	.066 676	14.358 837	.069 644
44	15.972 862	230.351 725	.004 341	.062 606	14.421 443	.069 341
45	17.011 098	246.324 587	.004 060	.058 785	14.480 228	.069 060
46	18.116 820	263.335 685	.003 797	.055 197	14.535 426	.068 797
47	19.294 413	281.452 504	.003 553	.051 828	14.587 254	.068 553
48	20.548 550	300.746 917	.003 325	.048 665	14.635 919	.068 325
49	21.884 205	321.295 467	.003 112	.045 695	14.681 615	.068 112
50	23.306 679	343.179 672	.002 914	.042 906	14.724 521	.067 914
51	24.821 613	366.486 351	.002 729	.040 287	14.764 808	.067 729
52	26.435 018	391.307 963	.002 556	.037 829	14.802 637	.067 556
53	28.153 294	417.742 981	.002 394	.035 520	14.838 157	.067 394
54	29.983 258	445.896 275	.002 243	.033 352	14.871 509	.067 243
55	31.932 170	475.879 533	.002 101	.031 316	14.902 825	.067 101
56	34.007 761	507.811 702	.001 969	.029 405	14.932 230	.066 969
57	36.218 265	541.819 463	.001 846	.027 610	14.959 840	.066 846
58	38.572 452	578.037 728	.001 730	.025 925	14.985 766	.066 730
59	41.079 662	616.610 180	.001 622	.024 343	15.010 109	.066 622
60	43.749 840	657.689 842	.001 520	.022 857	15.032 966	.066 520

	$S^n = (1+i)^n$	$S_{\overline{n}|} = \dfrac{S^n - 1}{i}$	$1/S_{\overline{n}|} = \dfrac{i}{S^n - 1}$	$V^n = \dfrac{1}{S^n}$	$A_{\overline{n}|} = \dfrac{1 - 1/S^n}{i}$	$\dfrac{1}{A_{\overline{n}|}} = \dfrac{i}{1 - 1/S^n}$

	1	2	3	4	5	6
YEARS	AMOUNT OF ONE	AMOUNT OF ONE PER PERIOD	SINKING FUND FACTOR	PRESENT WORTH OF ONE	PRESENT WORTH ONE PER PERIOD	PARTIAL PAYMENT
1	1.067 500	1.000 000	1.000 000	.936 768	.936 768	1.067 500
2	1.139 556	2.067 500	.483 676	.877 535	1.814 303	.551 176
3	1.216 476	3.207 056	.311 812	.822 046	2.636 349	.379 312
4	1.298 588	4.423 533	.226 064	.770 067	3.406 416	.293 564
5	1.386 243	5.722 121	.174 760	.721 374	4.127 790	.242 260
6	1.479 815	7.108 364	.140 679	.675 760	4.803 551	.208 179
7	1.579 702	8.588 179	.116 439	.633 031	5.436 581	.183 939
8	1.686 332	10.167 881	.098 349	.593 003	6.029 584	.165 849
9	1.800 159	11.854 213	.084 358	.555 506	6.585 091	.151 858
10	1.921 670	13.654 372	.073 237	.520 381	7.105 471	.140 737
11	2.051 383	15.576 042	.064 201	.487 476	7.592 947	.131 701
12	2.189 851	17.627 425	.056 730	.456 652	8.049 600	.124 230
13	2.337 666	19.817 276	.050 461	.427 777	8.477 377	.117 961
14	2.495 459	22.154 942	.045 137	.400 728	8.878 105	.112 637
15	2.663 902	24.650 401	.040 567	.375 389	9.253 494	.108 067
16	2.843 715	27.314 303	.036 611	.351 653	9.605 146	.104 111
17	3.035 666	30.158 019	.033 159	.329 417	9.934 563	.100 659
18	3.240 574	33.193 685	.030 126	.308 587	10.243 151	.097 626
19	3.459 312	36.434 259	.027 447	.289 075	10.532 225	.094 947
20	3.692 816	39.893 571	.025 067	.270 796	10.803 021	.092 567
21	3.942 081	43.586 387	.022 943	.253 673	11.056 695	.090 443
22	4.208 172	47.528 468	.021 040	.237 633	11.294 327	.088 540
23	4.492 223	51.736 640	.019 329	.222 607	11.516 934	.086 829
24	4.795 448	56.228 863	.017 784	.208 531	11.725 465	.085 284
25	5.119 141	61.024 311	.016 387	.195 345	11.920 811	.083 887
26	5.464 683	66.143 452	.015 119	.182 993	12.103 804	.082 619
27	5.833 549	71.608 135	.013 965	.171 422	12.275 226	.081 465
28	6.227 314	77.441 684	.012 913	.160 583	12.435 809	.080 413
29	6.647 657	83.668 998	.011 952	.150 429	12.586 238	.079 452
30	7.096 374	90.316 655	.011 072	.140 917	12.727 155	.078 572
31	7.575 380	97.413 030	.010 266	.132 007	12.859 162	.077 766
32	8.086 718	104.988 409	.009 525	.123 660	12.982 821	.077 025
33	8.632 571	113.075 127	.008 844	.115 840	13.098 662	.076 344
34	9.215 270	121.707 698	.008 216	.108 516	13.207 177	.075 716
35	9.837 300	130.922 967	.007 638	.101 654	13.308 831	.075 138
36	10.501 318	140.760 268	.007 104	.095 226	13.404 057	.074 604
37	11.210 157	151.261 586	.006 611	.089 205	13.493 262	.074 111
38	11.966 843	162.471 743	.006 155	.083 564	13.576 826	.073 655
39	12.774 605	174.438 586	.005 733	.078 280	13.655 107	.073 233
40	13.636 890	187.213 190	.005 342	.073 331	13.728 437	.072 842
41	14.557 380	200.850 080	.004 979	.068 694	13.797 131	.072 479
42	15.540 004	215.407 461	.004 642	.064 350	13.861 481	.072 142
43	16.588 954	230.947 464	.004 330	.060 281	13.921 762	.071 830
44	17.708 708	247.536 418	.004 040	.056 469	13.978 231	.071 540
45	18.904 046	265.245 127	.003 770	.052 899	14.031 130	.071 270
46	20.180 069	284.149 173	.003 519	.049 554	14.080 684	.071 019
47	21.542 224	304.329 242	.003 286	.046 420	14.127 104	.070 786
48	22.996 324	325.871 466	.003 069	.043 485	14.170 589	.070 569
49	24.548 576	348.867 789	.002 866	.040 736	14.211 325	.070 366
50	26.205 605	373.416 365	.002 678	.038 160	14.249 485	.070 178
51	27.974 483	399.621 970	.002 502	.035 747	14.285 232	.070 002
52	29.862 761	427.596 453	.002 339	.033 487	14.318 718	.069 839
53	31.878 497	457.459 213	.002 186	.031 369	14.350 087	.069 686
54	34.030 295	489.337 710	.002 044	.029 386	14.379 473	.069 544
55	36.327 340	523.368 006	.001 911	.027 527	14.407 000	.069 411
56	38.779 436	559.695 346	.001 787	.025 787	14.432 787	.069 287
57	41.397 048	598.474 782	.001 671	.024 156	14.456 944	.069 171
58	44.191 349	639.871 830	.001 563	.022 629	14.479 572	.069 063
59	47.174 265	684.063 178	.001 462	.021 198	14.500 770	.068 962
60	50.358 527	731.237 443	.001 368	.019 858	14.520 628	.068 868

$$S^n = (1+i)^n \qquad S_{\overline{n}} = \frac{S^n - 1}{i} \qquad 1/S_{\overline{n}} = \frac{i}{S^n - 1} \qquad V^n = \frac{1}{S^n} \qquad A_{\overline{n}} = \frac{1 - 1/S^n}{i} \qquad \frac{1}{A_{\overline{n}}} = \frac{i}{1 - 1/S^n}$$

	1	2	3	4	5	6
YEARS	AMOUNT OF ONE	AMOUNT OF ONE PER PERIOD	SINKING FUND FACTOR	PRESENT WORTH OF ONE	PRESENT WORTH ONE PER PERIOD	PARTIAL PAYMENT
1	1.070 000	1.000 000	1.000 000	.934 579	.934 579	1.070 000
2	1.144 900	2.070 000	.483 092	.873 439	1.808 018	.553 092
3	1.225 043	3.214 900	.311 052	.816 298	2.624 316	.381 052
4	1.310 796	4.439 943	.225 228	.762 895	3.387 211	.295 228
5	1.402 552	5.750 739	.173 891	.712 986	4.100 197	.243 891
6	1.500 730	7.153 291	.139 796	.666 342	4.766 540	.209 796
7	1.605 781	8.654 021	.115 553	.622 750	5.389 289	.185 553
8	1.718 186	10.259 803	.097 468	.582 009	5.971 299	.167 468
9	1.838 459	11.977 989	.083 486	.543 934	6.515 232	.153 486
10	1.967 151	13.816 448	.072 378	.508 349	7.023 582	.142 378
11	2.104 852	15.783 599	.063 357	.475 093	7.498 674	.133 357
12	2.252 192	17.888 451	.055 902	.444 012	7.942 686	.125 902
13	2.409 845	20.140 643	.049 651	.414 964	8.357 651	.119 651
14	2.578 534	22.550 488	.044 345	.387 817	8.745 468	.114 345
15	2.759 032	25.129 022	.039 795	.362 446	9.107 914	.109 795
16	2.952 164	27.888 054	.035 858	.338 735	9.446 649	.105 858
17	3.158 815	30.840 217	.032 425	.316 574	9.763 223	.102 425
18	3.379 932	33.999 033	.029 413	.295 864	10.059 087	.099 413
19	3.616 528	37.378 965	.026 753	.276 508	10.335 595	.096 753
20	3.869 684	40.995 492	.024 393	.258 419	10.594 014	.094 393
21	4.140 562	44.865 177	.022 289	.241 513	10.835 527	.092 289
22	4.430 402	49.005 739	.020 406	.225 713	11.061 240	.090 406
23	4.740 530	53.436 141	.018 714	.210 947	11.272 187	.088 714
24	5.072 367	58.176 671	.017 189	.197 147	11.469 334	.087 189
25	5.427 433	63.249 038	.015 811	.184 249	11.653 583	.085 811
26	5.807 353	68.676 470	.014 561	.172 195	11.825 779	.084 561
27	6.213 868	74.483 823	.013 426	.160 930	11.986 709	.083 426
28	6.648 838	80.697 691	.012 392	.150 402	12.137 111	.082 392
29	7.114 257	87.346 529	.011 449	.140 563	12.277 674	.081 449
30	7.612 255	94.460 786	.010 586	.131 367	12.409 041	.080 586
31	8.145 113	102.073 041	.009 797	.122 773	12.531 814	.079 797
32	8.715 271	110.218 154	.009 073	.114 741	12.646 555	.079 073
33	9.325 340	118.933 425	.008 408	.107 235	12.753 790	.078 408
34	9.978 114	128.258 765	.007 797	.100 219	12.854 009	.077 797
35	10.676 581	138.236 878	.007 234	.093 663	12.947 672	.077 234
36	11.423 942	148.913 460	.006 715	.087 535	13.035 208	.076 715
37	12.223 618	160.337 402	.006 237	.081 809	13.117 017	.076 237
38	13.079 271	172.561 020	.005 795	.076 457	13.193 473	.075 795
39	13.994 820	185.640 292	.005 387	.071 455	13.264 928	.075 387
40	14.974 458	199.635 112	.005 009	.066 780	13.331 709	.075 009
41	16.022 670	214.609 570	.004 660	.062 412	13.394 120	.074 660
42	17.144 257	230.632 240	.004 336	.058 329	13.452 449	.074 336
43	18.344 355	247.776 496	.004 036	.054 513	13.506 962	.074 036
44	19.628 460	266.120 851	.003 758	.050 946	13.557 908	.073 758
45	21.002 452	285.749 311	.003 500	.047 613	13.605 522	.073 500
46	22.472 623	306.751 763	.003 260	.044 499	13.650 020	.073 260
47	24.045 707	329.224 386	.003 037	.041 587	13.691 608	.073 037
48	25.728 907	353.270 093	.002 831	.038 867	13.730 474	.072 831
49	27.529 930	378.999 000	.002 639	.036 324	13.766 799	.072 639
50	29.457 025	406.528 929	.002 460	.033 948	13.800 746	.072 460
51	31.519 017	435.985 955	.002 294	.031 727	13.832 473	.072 294
52	33.725 348	467.504 971	.002 139	.029 651	13.862 124	.072 139
53	36.086 122	501.230 319	.001 995	.027 711	13.889 836	.071 995
54	38.612 151	537.316 442	.001 861	.025 899	13.915 735	.071 861
55	41.315 001	575.928 593	.001 736	.024 204	13.939 939	.071 736
56	44.207 052	617.243 594	.001 620	.022 621	13.962 560	.071 620
57	47.301 545	661.450 646	.001 512	.021 141	13.983 701	.071 512
58	50.612 653	708.752 191	.001 411	.019 758	14.003 458	.071 411
59	54.155 539	759.364 844	.001 317	.018 465	14.021 924	.071 317
60	57.946 427	813.520 383	.001 229	.017 257	14.039 181	.071 229

$S^n = (1+i)^n$	$S_{\overline{n}|} = \dfrac{S^n - 1}{i}$	$1/S_{\overline{n}|} = \dfrac{i}{S^n - 1}$	$V^n = \dfrac{1}{S^n}$	$A_{\overline{n}|} = \dfrac{1 - 1/S^n}{i}$	$\dfrac{1}{A_{\overline{n}|}} = \dfrac{i}{1 - 1/S^n}$

	1	2	3	4	5	6
YEARS	AMOUNT OF ONE	AMOUNT OF ONE PER PERIOD	SINKING FUND FACTOR	PRESENT WORTH OF ONE	PRESENT WORTH ONE PER PERIOD	PARTIAL PAYMENT
1	1.072 500	1.000 000	1.000 000	.932 401	.932 401	1.072 500
2	1.150 256	2.072 500	.482 509	.869 371	1.801 772	.555 009
3	1.233 650	3.222 756	.310 293	.810 603	2.612 375	.382 793
4	1.323 089	4.456 406	.224 396	.755 807	3.368 182	.296 896
5	1.419 013	5.779 496	.173 025	.704 715	4.072 897	.245 525
6	1.521 892	7.198 509	.138 918	.657 077	4.729 974	.211 418
7	1.632 229	8.720 401	.114 674	.612 659	5.342 633	.187 174
8	1.750 566	10.352 630	.096 594	.571 244	5.913 877	.169 094
9	1.877 482	12.103 196	.082 623	.532 628	6.446 505	.155 123
10	2.013 599	13.980 677	.071 527	.496 623	6.943 128	.144 027
11	2.159 585	15.994 276	.062 522	.463 052	7.406 180	.135 022
12	2.316 155	18.153 861	.055 085	.431 750	7.837 930	.127 585
13	2.484 076	20.470 016	.048 852	.402 564	8.240 495	.121 352
14	2.664 172	22.954 093	.043 565	.375 351	8.615 846	.116 065
15	2.857 324	25.618 264	.039 035	.349 978	8.965 824	.111 535
16	3.064 480	28.475 588	.035 118	.326 320	9.292 143	.107 618
17	3.286 655	31.540 069	.031 706	.304 261	9.596 404	.104 206
18	3.524 937	34.826 724	.028 714	.283 693	9.880 097	.101 214
19	3.780 495	38.351 661	.026 074	.264 516	10.144 612	.098 574
20	4.054 581	42.132 156	.023 735	.246 635	10.391 247	.096 235
21	4.348 538	46.186 738	.021 651	.229 962	10.621 209	.094 151
22	4.663 808	50.535 276	.019 788	.214 417	10.835 626	.092 288
23	5.001 934	55.199 084	.018 116	.199 923	11.035 549	.090 616
24	5.364 574	60.201 017	.016 611	.186 408	11.221 957	.089 111
25	5.753 505	65.565 591	.015 252	.173 807	11.395 764	.087 752
26	6.170 634	71.319 096	.014 021	.162 058	11.557 822	.086 521
27	6.618 005	77.489 731	.012 905	.151 103	11.708 925	.085 405
28	7.097 811	84.107 736	.011 890	.140 889	11.849 814	.084 390
29	7.612 402	91.205 547	.010 964	.131 365	11.981 178	.083 464
30	8.164 301	98.817 949	.010 120	.122 484	12.103 663	.082 620
31	8.756 213	106.982 251	.009 347	.114 205	12.217 867	.081 847
32	9.391 039	115.738 464	.008 640	.106 484	12.324 352	.081 140
33	10.071 889	125.129 503	.007 992	.099 286	12.423 638	.080 492
34	10.802 101	135.201 392	.007 396	.092 575	12.516 213	.079 896
35	11.585 253	146.003 492	.006 849	.086 317	12.602 529	.079 349
36	12.425 184	157.588 746	.006 346	.080 482	12.683 011	.078 846
37	13.326 010	170.013 930	.005 882	.075 041	12.758 052	.078 382
38	14.292 146	183.339 940	.005 454	.069 969	12.828 021	.077 954
39	15.328 326	197.632 085	.005 060	.065 239	12.893 259	.077 560
40	16.439 630	212.960 411	.004 696	.060 829	12.954 088	.077 196
41	17.631 503	229.400 041	.004 359	.056 717	13.010 805	.076 859
42	18.909 787	247.031 544	.004 048	.052 883	13.063 687	.076 548
43	20.280 747	265.941 331	.003 760	.049 308	13.112 995	.076 260
44	21.751 101	286.222 078	.003 494	.045 975	13.158 970	.075 994
45	23.328 055	307.973 178	.003 247	.042 867	13.201 837	.075 747
46	25.019 339	331.301 234	.003 018	.039 969	13.241 806	.075 518
47	26.833 242	356.320 573	.002 806	.037 267	13.279 073	.075 306
48	28.778 652	383.153 815	.002 610	.034 748	13.313 821	.075 110
49	30.865 104	411.932 466	.002 428	.032 399	13.346 220	.074 928
50	33.102 824	442.797 570	.002 258	.030 209	13.376 429	.074 758
51	35.502 779	475.900 394	.002 101	.028 167	13.404 596	.074 601
52	38.076 730	511.403 173	.001 955	.026 263	13.430 858	.074 455
53	40.837 293	549.479 903	.001 820	.024 487	13.455 346	.074 320
54	43.797 997	590.317 195	.001 694	.022 832	13.478 178	.074 194
55	46.973 351	634.115 192	.001 577	.021 289	13.499 467	.074 077
56	50.378 919	681.088 544	.001 468	.019 850	13.519 316	.073 968
57	54.031 391	731.467 463	.001 367	.018 508	13.537 824	.073 867
58	57.948 667	785.498 854	.001 273	.017 257	13.555 081	.073 773
59	62.149 945	843.447 521	.001 186	.016 090	13.571 171	.073 686
60	66.655 816	905.597 466	.001 104	.015 002	13.586 173	.073 604

$S^n = (1+i)^n$	$S_{\overline{n}|} = \dfrac{S^n - 1}{i}$	$1/S_{\overline{n}|} = \dfrac{i}{S^n - 1}$	$V^n = \dfrac{1}{S^n}$	$A_{\overline{n}|} = \dfrac{1 - 1/S^n}{i}$	$\dfrac{1}{A_{\overline{n}|}} = \dfrac{i}{1 - 1/S^n}$

7½% ANNUAL TABLE 7½%

	1	2	3	4	5	6
YEARS	AMOUNT OF ONE	AMOUNT OF ONE PER PERIOD	SINKING FUND FACTOR	PRESENT WORTH OF ONE	PRESENT WORTH ONE PER PERIOD	PARTIAL PAYMENT
1	1.075 000	1.000 000	1.000 000	.930 233	.930 233	1.075 000
2	1.155 625	2.075 000	.481 928	.865 333	1.795 565	.556 928
3	1.242 297	3.230 625	.309 538	.804 961	2.600 526	.384 538
4	1.335 469	4.472 922	.223 568	.748 801	3.349 326	.298 568
5	1.435 629	5.808 391	.172 165	.696 559	4.045 885	.247 165
6	1.543 302	7.244 020	.138 045	.647 962	4.693 846	.213 045
7	1.659 049	8.787 322	.113 800	.602 755	5.296 601	.188 800
8	1.783 478	10.446 371	.095 727	.560 702	5.857 304	.170 727
9	1.917 239	12.229 849	.081 767	.521 583	6.378 887	.156 767
10	2.061 032	14.147 087	.070 686	.485 194	6.864 081	.145 686
11	2.215 609	16.208 119	.061 697	.451 343	7.315 424	.136 697
12	2.381 780	18.423 728	.054 278	.419 854	7.735 278	.129 278
13	2.560 413	20.805 508	.048 064	.390 562	8.125 840	.123 064
14	2.752 444	23.365 921	.042 797	.363 313	8.489 154	.117 797
15	2.958 877	26.118 365	.038 287	.337 966	8.827 120	.113 287
16	3.180 793	29.077 242	.034 391	.314 387	9.141 507	.109 391
17	3.419 353	32.258 035	.031 000	.292 453	9.433 960	.106 000
18	3.675 804	35.677 388	.028 029	.272 049	9.706 009	.103 029
19	3.951 489	39.353 192	.025 411	.253 069	9.959 078	.100 411
20	4.247 851	43.304 681	.023 092	.235 413	10.194 491	.098 092
21	4.566 440	47.552 532	.021 029	.218 989	10.413 480	.096 029
22	4.908 923	52.118 972	.019 187	.203 711	10.617 191	.094 187
23	5.277 092	57.027 895	.017 535	.189 498	10.806 689	.092 535
24	5.672 874	62.304 987	.016 050	.176 277	10.982 967	.091 050
25	6.098 340	67.977 862	.014 711	.163 979	11.146 946	.089 711
26	6.555 715	74.076 201	.013 500	.152 539	11.299 485	.088 500
27	7.047 394	80.631 916	.012 402	.141 896	11.441 381	.087 402
28	7.575 948	87.679 310	.011 405	.131 997	11.573 378	.086 405
29	8.144 144	95.255 258	.010 498	.122 788	11.696 165	.085 498
30	8.754 955	103.399 403	.009 671	.114 221	11.810 386	.084 671
31	9.411 577	112.154 358	.008 916	.106 252	11.916 638	.083 916
32	10.117 445	121.565 935	.008 226	.098 839	12.015 478	.083 226
33	10.876 253	131.683 380	.007 594	.091 943	12.107 421	.082 594
34	11.691 972	142.559 633	.007 015	.085 529	12.192 950	.082 015
35	12.568 870	154.251 606	.006 483	.079 562	12.272 511	.081 483
36	13.511 536	166.820 476	.005 994	.074 011	12.346 522	.080 994
37	14.524 901	180.332 012	.005 545	.068 847	12.415 370	.080 545
38	15.614 268	194.856 913	.005 132	.064 044	12.479 414	.080 132
39	16.785 339	210.471 181	.004 751	.059 576	12.538 989	.079 751
40	18.044 239	227.256 520	.004 400	.055 419	12.594 409	.079 400
41	19.397 557	245.300 759	.004 077	.051 553	12.645 962	.079 077
42	20.852 374	264.698 315	.003 778	.047 956	12.693 918	.078 778
43	22.416 302	285.550 689	.003 502	.044 610	12.738 528	.078 502
44	24.097 524	307.966 991	.003 247	.041 498	12.780 026	.078 247
45	25.904 839	332.064 515	.003 011	.038 603	12.818 629	.078 011
46	27.847 702	357.969 354	.002 794	.035 910	12.854 539	.077 794
47	29.936 279	385.817 055	.002 592	.033 404	12.887 943	.077 592
48	32.181 500	415.753 334	.002 405	.031 074	12.919 017	.077 405
49	34.595 113	447.934 835	.002 232	.028 906	12.947 922	.077 232
50	37.189 746	482.529 947	.002 072	.026 889	12.974 812	.077 072
51	39.978 977	519.719 693	.001 924	.025 013	12.999 825	.076 924
52	42.977 400	559.698 670	.001 787	.023 268	13.023 093	.076 787
53	46.200 705	602.676 070	.001 659	.021 645	13.044 737	.076 659
54	49.665 758	648.876 776	.001 541	.020 135	13.064 872	.076 541
55	53.390 690	698.542 534	.001 432	.018 730	13.083 602	.076 432
56	57.394 992	751.933 224	.001 330	.017 423	13.101 025	.076 330
57	61.699 616	809.328 216	.001 236	.016 208	13.117 233	.076 236
58	66.327 087	871.027 832	.001 148	.015 077	13.132 309	.076 148
59	71.301 619	937.354 919	.001 067	.014 025	13.146 334	.076 067
60	76.649 240	1008.656 538	.000 991	.013 046	13.159 381	.075 991

$S^n = (1 + i)^n$	$S_{\overline{n}|} = \dfrac{S^n - 1}{i}$	$1/S_{\overline{n}|} = \dfrac{i}{S^n - 1}$	$V^n = \dfrac{1}{S^n}$	$A_{\overline{n}|} = \dfrac{1 - 1/S^n}{i}$	$\dfrac{1}{A_{\overline{n}|}} = \dfrac{i}{1 - 1/S^n}$

YEARS	1 AMOUNT OF ONE	2 AMOUNT OF ONE PER PERIOD	3 SINKING FUND FACTOR	4 PRESENT WORTH OF ONE	5 PRESENT WORTH ONE PER PERIOD	6 PARTIAL PAYMENT
1	1.077 500	1.000 000	1.000 000	.928 074	.928 074	1.077 500
2	1.161 006	2.077 500	.481 348	.861 322	1.789 396	.558 848
3	1.250 984	3.238 506	.308 784	.799 371	2.588 767	.386 284
4	1.347 936	4.489 490	.222 742	.741 875	3.330 642	.300 242
5	1.452 401	5.837 426	.171 308	.688 515	4.019 157	.248 808
6	1.564 962	7.289 827	.137 177	.638 993	4.658 151	.214 677
7	1.686 246	8.854 788	.112 933	.593 033	5.251 184	.190 433
8	1.816 930	10.541 034	.094 867	.550 379	5.801 563	.172 367
9	1.957 742	12.357 964	.080 919	.510 792	6.312 355	.158 419
10	2.109 467	14.315 707	.069 853	.474 053	6.786 409	.147 353
11	2.272 951	16.425 174	.060 882	.439 957	7.226 365	.138 382
12	2.449 105	18.698 125	.053 481	.408 312	7.634 678	.130 981
13	2.638 910	21.147 229	.047 288	.378 944	8.013 622	.124 788
14	2.843 426	23.786 140	.042 041	.351 688	8.365 310	.119 541
15	3.063 791	26.629 566	.037 552	.326 393	8.691 703	.115 052
16	3.301 235	29.693 357	.033 678	.302 917	8.994 620	.111 178
17	3.557 081	32.994 592	.030 308	.281 129	9.275 750	.107 808
18	3.832 755	36.551 673	.027 359	.260 909	9.536 659	.104 859
19	4.129 793	40.384 428	.024 762	.242 143	9.778 802	.102 262
20	4.449 852	44.514 221	.022 465	.224 727	10.003 528	.099 965
21	4.794 716	48.964 073	.020 423	.208 563	10.212 091	.097 923
22	5.166 306	53.758 788	.018 602	.193 562	10.405 653	.096 102
23	5.566 695	58.925 095	.016 971	.179 640	10.585 293	.094 471
24	5.998 114	64.491 789	.015 506	.166 719	10.752 012	.093 006
25	6.462 967	70.489 903	.014 186	.154 728	10.906 740	.091 686
26	6.963 847	76.952 870	.012 995	.143 599	11.050 338	.090 495
27	7.503 546	83.916 718	.011 917	.133 270	11.183 609	.089 417
28	8.085 070	91.420 264	.010 938	.123 685	11.307 293	.088 438
29	8.711 663	99.505 334	.010 050	.114 789	11.422 082	.087 550
30	9.386 817	108.216 997	.009 241	.106 532	11.528 614	.086 741
31	10.114 296	117.603 815	.008 503	.098 870	11.627 484	.086 003
32	10.898 154	127.718 110	.007 830	.091 759	11.719 243	.085 330
33	11.742 760	138.616 264	.007 214	.085 159	11.804 402	.084 714
34	12.652 824	150.359 024	.006 651	.079 034	11.883 436	.084 151
35	13.633 418	163.011 849	.006 135	.073 349	11.956 785	.083 635
36	14.690 008	176.645 267	.005 661	.068 073	12.024 858	.083 161
37	15.828 484	191.335 275	.005 226	.063 177	12.088 036	.082 726
38	17.055 191	207.163 759	.004 827	.058 633	12.146 669	.082 327
39	18.376 969	224.218 950	.004 460	.054 416	12.201 085	.081 960
40	19.801 184	242.595 919	.004 122	.050 502	12.251 587	.081 622
41	21.335 775	262.397 103	.003 811	.046 870	12.298 456	.081 311
42	22.989 298	283.732 878	.003 524	.043 499	12.341 955	.081 024
43	24.770 969	306.722 176	.003 260	.040 370	12.382 325	.080 760
44	26.690 719	331.493 145	.003 017	.037 466	12.419 791	.080 517
45	28.759 249	358.183 864	.002 792	.034 771	12.454 562	.080 292
46	30.988 091	386.943 113	.002 584	.032 270	12.486 833	.080 084
47	33.389 668	417.931 204	.002 393	.029 949	12.516 782	.079 893
48	35.977 368	451.320 873	.002 216	.027 795	12.544 577	.079 716
49	38.765 614	487.298 240	.002 052	.025 796	12.570 373	.079 552
50	41.769 949	526.063 854	.001 901	.023 941	12.594 314	.079 401
51	45.007 120	567.833 803	.001 761	.022 219	12.616 533	.079 261
52	48.495 171	612.840 922	.001 632	.020 621	12.637 153	.079 132
53	52.253 547	661.336 094	.001 512	.019 137	12.656 291	.079 012
54	56.303 197	713.589 641	.001 401	.017 761	12.674 052	.078 901
55	60.666 695	769.892 838	.001 299	.016 484	12.690 535	.078 799
56	65.368 364	830.559 533	.001 204	.015 298	12.705 833	.078 704
57	70.434 412	895.927 897	.001 116	.014 198	12.720 031	.078 616
58	75.893 079	966.362 309	.001 035	.013 176	12.733 207	.078 535
59	81.774 793	1042.255 388	.000 959	.012 229	12.745 436	.078 459
60	88.112 339	1124.030 180	.000 890	.011 349	12.756 785	.078 390

$S^n = (1+i)^n$	$S_{\overline{n}} = \dfrac{S^n - 1}{i}$	$1/S_{\overline{n}} = \dfrac{i}{S^n - 1}$	$V^n = \dfrac{1}{S^n}$	$A_{\overline{n}} = \dfrac{1 - 1/S^n}{i}$	$\dfrac{1}{A_{\overline{n}}} = \dfrac{i}{1 - 1/S^n}$

EFFECTIVE RATE 8%   BASE 1.08

	1	2	3	4	5	6
YEARS	AMOUNT OF ONE	AMOUNT OF ONE PER PERIOD	SINKING FUND FACTOR	PRESENT WORTH OF ONE	PRESENT WORTH ONE PER PERIOD	PARTIAL PAYMENT
1	1.080 000	1.000 000	1.000 000	.925 926	.925 926	1.080 000
2	1.166 400	2.080 000	.480 769	.857 339	1.783 265	.560 769
3	1.259 712	3.246 400	.308 034	.793 832	2.577 097	.388 034
4	1.360 489	4.506 112	.221 921	.735 030	3.312 127	.301 921
5	1.469 328	5.866 601	.170 456	.680 583	3.992 710	.250 456
6	1.586 874	7.335 929	.136 315	.630 170	4.622 880	.216 315
7	1.713 824	8.922 803	.112 072	.583 490	5.206 370	.192 072
8	1.850 930	10.636 628	.094 015	.540 269	5.746 639	.174 015
9	1.999 005	12.487 558	.080 080	.500 249	6.246 888	.160 080
10	2.158 925	14.486 562	.069 029	.463 193	6.710 081	.149 029
11	2.331 639	16.645 487	.060 076	.428 883	7.138 964	.140 076
12	2.518 170	18.977 126	.052 695	.397 114	7.536 078	.132 695
13	2.719 624	21.495 297	.046 522	.367 698	7.903 776	.126 522
14	2.937 194	24.214 920	.041 297	.340 461	8.244 237	.121 297
15	3.172 169	27.152 114	.036 830	.315 242	8.559 479	.116 830
16	3.425 943	30.324 283	.032 977	.291 890	8.851 369	.112 977
17	3.700 018	33.750 226	.029 629	.270 269	9.121 638	.109 629
18	3.996 019	37.450 244	.026 702	.250 249	9.371 887	.106 702
19	4.315 701	41.446 263	.024 128	.231 712	9.603 599	.104 128
20	4.660 957	45.761 964	.021 852	.214 548	9.818 147	.101 852
21	5.033 834	50.422 921	.019 832	.198 656	10.016 803	.099 832
22	5.436 540	55.456 755	.018 032	.183 941	10.200 744	.098 032
23	5.871 464	60.893 296	.016 422	.170 315	10.371 059	.096 422
24	6.341 181	66.764 759	.014 978	.157 699	10.528 758	.094 978
25	6.848 475	73.105 940	.013 679	.146 018	10.674 776	.093 679
26	7.396 353	79.954 415	.012 507	.135 202	10.809 978	.092 507
27	7.988 061	87.350 768	.011 448	.125 187	10.935 165	.091 448
28	8.627 106	95.338 830	.010 489	.115 914	11.051 078	.090 489
29	9.317 275	103.965 936	.009 619	.107 328	11.158 406	.089 619
30	10.062 657	113.283 211	.008 827	.099 377	11.257 783	.088 827
31	10.867 669	123.345 868	.008 107	.092 016	11.349 799	.088 107
32	11.737 083	134.213 537	.007 451	.085 200	11.434 999	.087 451
33	12.676 050	145.950 620	.006 852	.078 889	11.513 888	.086 852
34	13.690 134	158.626 670	.006 304	.073 045	11.586 934	.086 304
35	14.785 344	172.316 804	.005 803	.067 635	11.654 568	.085 803
36	15.968 172	187.102 148	.005 345	.062 625	11.717 193	.085 345
37	17.245 626	203.070 320	.004 924	.057 986	11.775 179	.084 924
38	18.625 276	220.315 945	.004 539	.053 690	11.828 869	.084 539
39	20.115 298	238.941 221	.004 185	.049 713	11.878 582	.084 185
40	21.724 521	259.056 519	.003 860	.046 031	11.924 613	.083 860
41	23.462 483	280.781 040	.003 561	.042 621	11.967 235	.083 561
42	25.339 482	304.243 523	.003 287	.039 464	12.006 699	.083 287
43	27.366 640	329.583 005	.003 034	.036 541	12.043 240	.083 034
44	29.555 972	356.949 646	.002 802	.033 834	12.077 074	.082 802
45	31.920 449	386.505 617	.002 587	.031 328	12.108 402	.082 587
46	34.474 085	418.426 067	.002 390	.029 007	12.137 409	.082 390
47	37.232 012	452.900 152	.002 208	.026 859	12.164 267	.082 208
48	40.210 573	490.132 164	.002 040	.024 869	12.189 136	.082 040
49	43.427 419	530.342 737	.001 886	.023 027	12.212 163	.081 886
50	46.901 613	573.770 156	.001 743	.021 321	12.233 485	.081 743
51	50.653 742	620.671 769	.001 611	.019 742	12.253 227	.081 611
52	54.706 041	671.325 510	.001 490	.018 280	12.271 506	.081 490
53	59.082 524	726.031 551	.001 377	.016 925	12.288 432	.081 377
54	63.809 126	785.114 075	.001 274	.015 672	12.304 103	.081 274
55	68.913 856	848.923 201	.001 178	.014 511	12.318 614	.081 178
56	74.426 965	917.837 058	.001 090	.013 436	12.332 050	.081 090
57	80.381 122	992.264 022	.001 008	.012 441	12.344 491	.081 008
58	86.811 612	1072.645 144	.000 932	.011 519	12.356 010	.080 932
59	93.756 540	1159.456 755	.000 862	.010 666	12.366 676	.080 862
60	101.257 064	1253.213 296	.000 798	.009 876	12.376 552	.080 798

$S^n = (1+i)^n$	$S_{\overline{n}\|} = \dfrac{S^n - 1}{i}$	$1/S_{\overline{n}\|} = \dfrac{i}{S^n - 1}$	$V^n = \dfrac{1}{S^n}$	$A_{\overline{n}\|} = \dfrac{1 - 1/S^n}{i}$	$\dfrac{1}{A_{\overline{n}\|}} = \dfrac{i}{1 - 1/S^n}$

EFFECTIVE RATE ⅔%   BASE 1.0066+

	1	2	3	4	5	6
MONTHS	AMOUNT OF ONE	AMOUNT OF ONE PER PERIOD	SINKING FUND FACTOR	PRESENT WORTH OF ONE	PRESENT WORTH ONE PER PERIOD	PARTIAL PAYMENT
1	1.006 667	1.000 000	1.000 000	.993 377	.993 377	1.006 667
2	1.013 378	2.006 667	.498 339	.986 799	1.980 176	.505 006
3	1.020 134	3.020 044	.331 121	.980 264	2.960 440	.337 788
4	1.026 935	4.040 178	.247 514	.973 772	3.934 212	.254 181
5	1.033 781	5.067 113	.197 351	.967 323	4.901 535	.204 018
6	1.040 673	6.100 893	.163 910	.960 917	5.862 452	.170 577
7	1.047 610	7.141 566	.140 025	.954 553	6.817 005	.146 692
8	1.054 595	8.189 176	.122 112	.948 232	7.765 237	.128 779
9	1.061 625	9.243 771	.108 181	.941 952	8.707 189	.114 848
10	1.068 703	10.305 396	.097 037	.935 714	9.642 903	.103 703
11	1.075 827	11.374 099	.087 919	.929 517	10.572 420	.094 586

YEARS

	1	2	3	4	5	6
1	1.083 000	12.449 926	.080 322	.923 361	11.495 782	.086 988
2	1.172 888	25.933 190	.038 561	.852 596	22.110 544	.045 227
3	1.270 237	40.535 558	.024 670	.787 255	31.911 806	.031 336
4	1.375 666	56.349 915	.017 746	.726 921	40.961 913	.024 413
5	1.489 846	73.476 856	.013 610	.671 210	49.318 433	.020 276
6	1.613 502	92.025 325	.010 867	.619 770	57.034 522	.017 533
7	1.747 422	112.113 308	.008 920	.572 272	64.159 261	.015 586
8	1.892 457	133.868 583	.007 470	.528 414	70.737 970	.014 137
9	2.049 530	157.429 535	.006 352	.487 917	76.812 497	.013 019
10	2.219 640	182.946 035	.005 466	.450 523	82.421 481	.012 133
11	2.403 869	210.580 392	.004 749	.415 996	87.600 600	.011 415
12	2.603 389	240.508 387	.004 158	.384 115	92.382 800	.010 825
13	2.819 469	272.920 390	.003 664	.354 677	96.798 498	.010 331
14	3.053 484	308.022 574	.003 247	.327 495	100.875 784	.009 913
15	3.306 921	346.038 222	.002 890	.302 396	104.640 592	.009 557
16	3.581 394	387.209 149	.002 583	.279 221	108.116 871	.009 249
17	3.878 648	431.797 244	.002 316	.257 822	111.326 733	.008 983
18	4.200 574	480.086 128	.002 083	.238 063	114.290 596	.008 750
19	4.549 220	532.382 966	.001 878	.219 818	117.027 313	.008 545
20	4.926 803	589.020 416	.001 698	.202 971	119.554 292	.008 364
21	5.335 725	650.358 746	.001 538	.187 416	121.887 606	.008 204
22	5.778 588	716.788 127	.001 395	.173 053	124.042 099	.008 062
23	6.258 207	788.731 114	.001 268	.159 790	126.031 475	.007 935
24	6.777 636	866.645 333	.001 154	.147 544	127.868 388	.007 821
25	7.340 176	951.026 395	.001 051	.136 237	129.564 523	.007 718
26	7.949 407	1042.411 042	.000 959	.125 796	131.130 668	.007 626
27	8.609 204	1141.380 571	.000 876	.116 155	132.576 786	.007 543
28	9.323 763	1248.564 521	.000 801	.107 253	133.912 076	.007 468
29	10.097 631	1364.644 687	.000 733	.099 033	135.145 031	.007 399
30	10.935 730	1490.359 449	.000 671	.091 443	136.283 494	.007 338
31	11.843 390	1626.508 474	.000 615	.084 435	137.334 707	.007 281
32	12.826 385	1773.957 801	.000 564	.077 964	138.305 357	.007 230
33	13.890 969	1933.645 350	.000 517	.071 989	139.201 617	.007 184
34	15.043 913	2106.586 886	.000 475	.066 472	140.029 190	.007 141
35	16.292 550	2293.882 485	.000 436	.061 378	140.793 338	.007 103
36	17.644 824	2496.723 526	.000 401	.056 674	141.498 923	.007 067
37	19.109 335	2716.400 273	.000 368	.052 330	142.150 433	.007 035
38	20.695 401	2954.310 082	.000 338	.048 320	142.752 013	.007 005
39	22.413 109	3211.966 288	.000 311	.044 617	143.307 488	.006 978
40	24.273 386	3491.007 831	.000 286	.041 197	143.820 392	.006 953
41	26.288 065	3793.209 686	.000 264	.038 040	144.293 988	.006 930
42	28.469 961	4120.494 145	.000 243	.035 125	144.731 289	.006 909
43	30.832 954	4474.943 053	.000 223	.032 433	145.135 075	.006 890
44	33.392 074	4858.811 045	.000 206	.029 947	145.507 916	.006 872
45	36.163 599	5274.539 891	.000 190	.027 652	145.852 183	.006 856
46	39.165 160	5724.774 027	.000 175	.025 533	146.170 065	.006 841
47	42.415 849	6212.377 374	.000 161	.023 576	146.463 586	.006 828
48	45.936 344	6740.451 558	.000 148	.021 769	146.734 612	.006 815
49	49.749 038	7312.355 639	.000 137	.020 101	146.984 866	.006 803
50	53.878 183	7931.727 477	.000 126	.018 560	147.215 942	.006 793

$S^n = (1+i)^n$	$S_{\overline{n}|} = \dfrac{S^n - 1}{i}$	$1/S_{\overline{n}|} = \dfrac{i}{S^n - 1}$	$V^n = \dfrac{1}{S^n}$	$A_{\overline{n}|} = \dfrac{1 - 1/S^n}{i}$	$\dfrac{1}{A_{\overline{n}|}} = \dfrac{i}{1 - 1/S^n}$

EFFECTIVE RATE 2%   BASE 1.02

	1	2	3	4	5	6
QUARTERS	AMOUNT OF ONE	AMOUNT OF ONE PER PERIOD	SINKING FUND FACTOR	PRESENT WORTH OF ONE	PRESENT WORTH ONE PER PERIOD	PARTIAL PAYMENT
1	1.020 000	1.000 000	1.000 000	.980 392	.980 392	1.020 000
2	1.040 400	2.020 000	.495 050	.961 169	1.941 561	.515 050
3	1.061 208	3.060 400	.326 755	.942 322	2.883 883	.346 755
YEARS						
1	1.082 432	4.121 608	.242 624	.923 845	3.807 729	.262 624
2	1.171 659	8.582 969	.116 510	.853 490	7.325 481	.136 510
3	1.268 242	13.412 090	.074 560	.788 493	10.575 341	.094 560
4	1.372 786	18.639 285	.053 650	.728 446	13.577 709	.073 650
5	1.485 947	24.297 370	.041 157	.672 971	16.351 433	.061 157
6	1.608 437	30.421 862	.032 871	.621 721	18.913 926	.052 871
7	1.741 024	37.051 210	.026 990	.574 375	21.281 292	.046 990
8	1.884 541	44.227 030	.022 611	.530 633	23.468 335	.042 611
9	2.039 887	51.994 367	.019 233	.490 223	25.488 842	.039 233
10	2.208 040	60.401 983	.016 556	.452 890	27.355 479	.036 556
11	2.390 053	69.502 657	.014 388	.418 401	29.079 963	.034 388
12	2.587 070	79.353 519	.012 602	.386 538	30.673 120	.032 602
13	2.800 328	90.016 409	.011 109	.357 101	32.144 950	.031 109
14	3.031 165	101.558 264	.009 847	.329 906	33.504 694	.029 847
15	3.281 031	114.051 539	.008 768	.304 782	34.760 887	.028 768
16	3.551 493	127.574 662	.007 839	.281 572	35.921 415	.027 839
17	3.844 251	142.212 525	.007 032	.260 129	36.993 564	.027 032
18	4.161 140	158.057 019	.006 327	.240 319	37.984 063	.026 327
19	4.504 152	175.207 608	.005 708	.222 017	38.899 132	.025 708
20	4.875 439	193.771 958	.005 161	.205 110	39.744 514	.025 161
21	5.277 332	213.866 607	.004 676	.189 490	40.525 516	.024 676
22	5.712 354	235.617 701	.004 244	.175 059	41.247 041	.024 244
23	6.183 236	259.161 785	.003 859	.161 728	41.913 619	.023 859
24	6.692 933	284.646 659	.003 513	.149 411	42.529 434	.023 513
25	7.244 646	312.232 306	.003 203	.138 033	43.098 352	.023 203
26	7.841 838	342.091 897	.002 923	.127 521	43.623 944	.022 923
27	8.488 258	374.412 879	.002 671	.117 810	44.109 510	.022 671
28	9.187 963	409.398 150	.002 443	.108 838	44.558 097	.022 443
29	9.945 347	447.267 331	.002 236	.100 550	44.972 523	.022 236
30	10.765 163	488.258 152	.002 048	.092 892	45.355 389	.022 048
31	11.652 559	532.627 934	.001 877	.085 818	45.709 097	.021 877
32	12.613 104	580.655 213	.001 722	.079 283	46.035 869	.021 722
33	13.652 830	632.641 484	.001 581	.073 245	46.337 756	.021 581
34	14.778 262	688.913 196	.001 452	.067 667	46.616 652	.021 452
35	15.996 466	749.823 299	.001 334	.062 514	46.874 310	.021 334
36	17.315 089	815.754 461	.001 226	.057 753	47.112 345	.021 226
37	18.742 409	887.120 471	.001 127	.053 355	47.332 253	.021 127
38	20.287 387	964.369 336	.001 037	.049 292	47.535 414	.021 037
39	21.959 720	1047.985 991	.000 954	.045 538	47.723 104	.020 954
40	23.769 907	1138.495 348	.000 878	.042 070	47.896 500	.020 878
41	25.729 312	1236.465 587	.000 809	.038 866	48.056 691	.020 809
42	27.850 234	1342.511 724	.000 745	.035 906	48.204 683	.020 745
43	30.145 989	1457.299 473	.000 686	.033 172	48.341 405	.020 686
44	32.630 988	1581.549 425	.000 632	.030 646	48.467 714	.020 632
45	35.320 831	1716.041 568	.000 583	.028 312	48.584 405	.020 583
46	38.232 404	1861.620 189	.000 537	.026 156	48.692 209	.020 537
47	41.383 983	2019.199 170	.000 495	.024 164	48.791 803	.020 495
48	44.795 355	2189.767 727	.000 457	.022 324	48.883 813	.020 457
49	48.487 932	2374.396 619	.000 421	.020 624	48.968 816	.020 421
50	52.484 897	2574.244 869	.000 388	.019 053	49.047 345	.020 388
	$S^n = (1+i)^n$	$S_{\overline{n}} = \dfrac{S^n - 1}{i}$	$1/S_{\overline{n}} = \dfrac{i}{S^n - 1}$	$V^n = \dfrac{1}{S^n}$	$A_{\overline{n}} = \dfrac{1 - 1/S^n}{i}$	$\dfrac{1}{A_{\overline{n}}} = \dfrac{i}{1 - 1/S^n}$

EFFECTIVE RATE 4%   **BASE 1.04**

	1	2	3	4	5	6
HALF YEARS	AMOUNT OF ONE	AMOUNT OF ONE PER PERIOD	SINKING FUND FACTOR	PRESENT WORTH OF ONE	PRESENT WORTH ONE PER PERIOD	PARTIAL PAYMENT
1	1.040 000	1.000 000	1.000 000	.961 538	.961 538	1.040 000
YEARS						
1	1.081 600	2.040 000	.490 196	.924 556	1.886 095	.530 196
2	1.169 859	4.246 464	.235 490	.854 804	3.629 895	.275 490
3	1.265 319	6.632 975	.150 762	.790 315	5.242 137	.190 762
4	1.368 569	9.214 226	.108 528	.730 690	6.732 745	.148 528
5	1.480 244	12.006 107	.083 291	.675 564	8.110 896	.123 291
6	1.601 032	15.025 805	.066 552	.624 597	9.385 074	.106 552
7	1.731 676	18.291 911	.054 669	.577 475	10.563 123	.094 669
8	1.872 981	21.824 531	.045 820	.533 908	11.652 296	.085 820
9	2.025 817	25.645 413	.038 993	.493 628	12.659 297	.078 993
10	2.191 123	29.778 079	.033 582	.456 387	13.590 326	.073 582
11	2.369 919	34.247 970	.029 199	.421 955	14.451 115	.069 199
12	2.563 304	39.082 604	.025 587	.390 121	15.246 963	.065 587
13	2.772 470	44.311 745	.022 567	.360 689	15.982 769	.062 567
14	2.998 703	49.967 583	.020 013	.333 477	16.663 063	.060 013
15	3.243 398	56.084 938	.017 830	.308 319	17.292 033	.057 830
16	3.508 059	62.701 469	.015 949	.285 058	17.873 551	.055 949
17	3.794 316	69.857 909	.014 315	.263 552	18.411 198	.054 315
18	4.103 933	77.598 314	.012 887	.243 669	18.908 282	.052 887
19	4.438 813	85.970 336	.011 632	.225 285	19.367 864	.051 632
20	4.801 021	95.025 516	.010 523	.208 289	19.792 774	.050 523
21	5.192 784	104.819 598	.009 540	.192 575	20.185 627	.049 540
22	5.616 515	115.412 877	.008 665	.178 046	20.548 841	.048 665
23	6.074 823	126.870 568	.007 882	.164 614	20.884 654	.047 882
24	6.570 528	139.263 206	.007 181	.152 195	21.195 131	.047 181
25	7.106 683	152.667 084	.006 550	.140 713	21.482 185	.046 550
26	7.686 589	167.164 718	.005 982	.130 097	21.747 582	.045 982
27	8.313 814	182.845 359	.005 469	.120 282	21.992 957	.045 469
28	8.992 222	199.805 540	.005 005	.111 207	22.219 819	.045 005
29	9.725 987	218.149 672	.004 584	.102 817	22.429 567	.044 584
30	10.519 627	237.990 685	.004 202	.095 060	22.623 490	.044 202
31	11.378 029	259.450 725	.003 854	.087 889	22.802 783	.043 854
32	12.306 476	282.661 904	.003 538	.081 258	22.968 549	.043 538
33	13.310 685	307.767 116	.003 249	.075 128	23.121 810	.043 249
34	14.396 836	334.920 912	.002 986	.069 460	23.263 507	.042 986
35	15.571 618	364.290 459	.002 745	.064 219	23.394 515	.042 745
36	16.842 262	396.056 560	.002 525	.059 374	23.515 639	.042 525
37	18.216 591	430.414 776	.002 323	.054 895	23.627 625	.042 323
38	19.703 065	467.576 621	.002 139	.050 754	23.731 162	.042 139
39	21.310 835	507.770 873	.001 969	.046 924	23.826 888	.041 969
40	23.049 799	551.244 977	.001 814	.043 384	23.915 392	.041 814
41	24.930 663	598.266 567	.001 671	.040 111	23.997 219	.041 671
42	26.965 005	649.125 119	.001 541	.037 085	24.072 872	.041 541
43	29.165 349	704.133 728	.001 420	.034 287	24.142 818	.041 420
44	31.545 242	763.631 041	.001 310	.031 701	24.207 487	.041 310
45	34.119 333	827.983 334	.001 208	.029 309	24.267 278	.041 208
46	36.903 471	897.586 774	.001 114	.027 098	24.322 557	.041 114
47	39.914 794	972.869 854	.001 028	.025 053	24.373 666	.041 028
48	43.171 841	1054.296 034	.000 949	.023 163	24.420 919	.040 949
49	46.694 664	1142.366 591	.000 875	.021 416	24.464 607	.040 875
50	50.504 948	1237.623 705	.000 808	.019 800	24.504 999	.040 808

$S^n = (1+i)^n$	$S_{\overline{n}|} = \dfrac{S^n - 1}{i}$	$1/S_{\overline{n}|} = \dfrac{i}{S^n - 1}$	$V^n = \dfrac{1}{S^n}$	$A_{\overline{n}|} = \dfrac{1 - 1/S^n}{i}$	$\dfrac{1}{A_{\overline{n}|}} = \dfrac{i}{1 - 1/S^n}$

	1	2	3	4	5	6
YEARS	AMOUNT OF ONE	AMOUNT OF ONE PER PERIOD	SINKING FUND FACTOR	PRESENT WORTH OF ONE	PRESENT WORTH ONE PER PERIOD	PARTIAL PAYMENT
1	1.082 500	1.000 000	1.000 000	.923 788	.923 788	1.082 500
2	1.171 806	2.082 500	.480 192	.853 383	1.777 171	.562 692
3	1.268 480	3.254 306	.307 285	.788 345	2.565 516	.389 785
4	1.373 130	4.522 787	.221 103	.728 263	3.293 779	.303 603
5	1.486 413	5.895 916	.169 609	.672 760	3.966 540	.252 109
6	1.609 042	7.382 330	.135 459	.621 488	4.588 027	.217 959
7	1.741 788	8.991 372	.111 218	.574 123	5.162 150	.193 718
8	1.885 486	10.733 160	.093 169	.530 367	5.692 517	.175 669
9	2.041 038	12.618 646	.079 248	.489 947	6.182 464	.161 748
10	2.209 424	14.659 684	.068 214	.452 607	6.635 071	.150 714
11	2.391 701	16.869 108	.059 280	.418 112	7.053 183	.141 780
12	2.589 017	19.260 809	.051 919	.386 247	7.439 430	.134 419
13	2.802 611	21.849 826	.045 767	.356 810	7.796 240	.128 267
14	3.033 826	24.652 436	.040 564	.329 617	8.125 857	.123 064
15	3.284 117	27.686 262	.036 119	.304 496	8.430 353	.118 619
16	3.555 056	30.970 379	.032 289	.281 289	8.711 642	.114 789
17	3.848 348	34.525 435	.028 964	.259 852	8.971 494	.111 464
18	4.165 837	38.373 784	.026 059	.240 048	9.211 542	.108 559
19	4.509 519	42.539 621	.023 507	.221 753	9.433 295	.106 007
20	4.881 554	47.049 140	.021 254	.204 853	9.638 148	.103 754
21	5.284 282	51.930 694	.019 256	.189 240	9.827 388	.101 756
22	5.720 236	57.214 976	.017 478	.174 818	10.002 206	.099 978
23	6.192 155	62.935 212	.015 889	.161 495	10.163 701	.098 389
24	6.703 008	69.127 366	.014 466	.149 187	10.312 888	.096 966
25	7.256 006	75.830 374	.013 187	.137 817	10.450 705	.095 687
26	7.854 626	83.086 380	.012 036	.127 314	10.578 018	.094 536
27	8.502 633	90.941 006	.010 996	.117 611	10.695 629	.093 496
28	9.204 100	99.443 639	.010 056	.108 647	10.804 276	.092 556
29	9.963 439	108.647 740	.009 204	.100 367	10.904 643	.091 704
30	10.785 422	118.611 178	.008 431	.092 718	10.997 361	.090 931
31	11.675 220	129.396 600	.007 728	.085 651	11.083 012	.090 228
32	12.638 425	141.071 820	.007 089	.079 124	11.162 136	.089 589
33	13.681 095	153.710 245	.006 506	.073 094	11.235 230	.089 006
34	14.809 786	167.391 340	.005 974	.067 523	11.302 752	.088 474
35	16.031 593	182.201 126	.005 488	.062 377	11.365 129	.087 988
36	17.354 199	198.232 719	.005 045	.057 623	11.422 752	.087 545
37	18.785 921	215.586 918	.004 639	.053 231	11.475 984	.087 139
38	20.335 759	234.372 839	.004 267	.049 174	11.525 158	.086 767
39	22.013 459	254.708 598	.003 926	.045 427	11.570 585	.086 426
40	23.829 570	276.722 058	.003 614	.041 965	11.612 549	.086 114
41	25.795 509	300.551 627	.003 327	.038 766	11.651 316	.085 827
42	27.923 639	326.347 137	.003 064	.035 812	11.687 128	.085 564
43	30.227 339	354.270 775	.002 823	.033 083	11.720 210	.085 323
44	32.721 094	384.498 114	.002 601	.030 561	11.750 772	.085 101
45	35.420 585	417.219 209	.002 397	.028 232	11.779 004	.084 897
46	38.342 783	452.639 793	.002 209	.026 081	11.805 085	.084 709
47	41.506 063	490.982 576	.002 037	.024 093	11.829 177	.084 537
48	44.930 313	532.488 639	.001 878	.022 257	11.851 434	.084 378
49	48.637 064	577.418 952	.001 732	.020 560	11.871 995	.084 232
50	52.649 621	626.056 015	.001 597	.018 993	11.890 988	.084 097
51	56.993 215	678.705 636	.001 473	.017 546	11.908 534	.083 973
52	61.695 155	735.698 851	.001 359	.016 209	11.924 743	.083 859
53	66.785 006	797.394 007	.001 254	.014 973	11.939 716	.083 754
54	72.294 768	864.179 012	.001 157	.013 832	11.953 548	.083 657
55	78.259 087	936.473 781	.001 068	.012 778	11.966 326	.083 568
56	84.715 462	1014.732 868	.000 985	.011 804	11.978 131	.083 485
57	91.704 487	1099.448 329	.000 910	.010 905	11.989 035	.083 410
58	99.270 107	1191.152 816	.000 840	.010 074	11.999 109	.083 340
59	107.459 891	1290.422 924	.000 775	.009 306	12.008 415	.083 275
60	116.325 332	1397.882 815	.000 715	.008 597	12.017 011	.083 215

$$S^n = (1+i)^n \qquad S_{\overline{n}|} = \frac{S^n - 1}{i} \qquad 1/S_{\overline{n}|} = \frac{i}{S^n - 1} \qquad V^n = \frac{1}{S^n} \qquad A_{\overline{n}|} = \frac{1 - 1/S^n}{i} \qquad \frac{1}{A_{\overline{n}|}} = \frac{i}{1 - 1/S^n}$$

569

	1	2	3	4	5	6
YEARS	AMOUNT OF ONE	AMOUNT OF ONE PER PERIOD	SINKING FUND FACTOR	PRESENT WORTH OF ONE	PRESENT WORTH ONE PER PERIOD	PARTIAL PAYMENT
1	1.085 000	1.000 000	1.000 000	.921 659	.921 659	1.085 000
2	1.177 225	2.085 000	.479 616	.849 455	1.771 114	.564 616
3	1.277 289	3.262 225	.306 539	.782 908	2.554 022	.391 539
4	1.385 859	4.539 514	.220 288	.721 574	3.275 597	.305 288
5	1.503 657	5.925 373	.168 766	.665 045	3.940 642	.253 766
6	1.631 468	7.429 030	.134 607	.612 945	4.553 587	.219 607
7	1.770 142	9.060 497	.110 369	.564 926	5.118 514	.195 369
8	1.920 604	10.830 639	.092 331	.520 669	5.639 183	.177 331
9	2.083 856	12.751 244	.078 424	.479 880	6.119 063	.163 424
10	2.260 983	14.835 099	.067 408	.442 285	6.561 348	.152 408
11	2.453 167	17.096 083	.058 493	.407 636	6.968 984	.143 493
12	2.661 686	19.549 250	.051 153	.375 702	7.344 686	.136 153
13	2.887 930	22.210 936	.045 023	.346 269	7.690 955	.130 023
14	3.133 404	25.098 866	.039 842	.319 142	8.010 097	.124 842
15	3.399 743	28.232 269	.035 420	.294 140	8.304 237	.120 420
16	3.688 721	31.632 012	.031 614	.271 097	8.575 333	.116 614
17	4.002 262	35.320 733	.028 312	.249 859	8.825 192	.113 312
18	4.342 455	39.322 995	.025 430	.230 285	9.055 476	.110 430
19	4.711 563	43.665 450	.022 901	.212 244	9.267 720	.107 901
20	5.112 046	48.377 013	.020 671	.195 616	9.463 337	.105 671
21	5.546 570	53.489 059	.018 695	.180 292	9.643 628	.103 695
22	6.018 028	59.035 629	.016 939	.166 167	9.809 796	.101 939
23	6.529 561	65.053 658	.015 372	.153 150	9.962 945	.100 372
24	7.084 574	71.583 219	.013 970	.141 152	10.104 097	.098 970
25	7.686 762	78.667 792	.012 712	.130 094	10.234 191	.097 712
26	8.340 137	86.354 555	.011 580	.119 902	10.354 093	.096 580
27	9.049 049	94.694 692	.010 560	.110 509	10.464 602	.095 560
28	9.818 218	103.743 741	.009 639	.101 851	10.566 453	.094 639
29	10.652 766	113.561 959	.008 806	.093 872	10.660 326	.093 806
30	11.558 252	124.214 725	.008 051	.086 518	10.746 844	.093 051
31	12.540 703	135.772 977	.007 365	.079 740	10.826 584	.092 365
32	13.606 663	148.313 680	.006 742	.073 493	10.900 078	.091 742
33	14.763 229	161.920 343	.006 176	.067 736	10.967 813	.091 176
34	16.018 104	176.683 572	.005 660	.062 429	11.030 243	.090 660
35	17.379 642	192.701 675	.005 189	.057 539	11.087 781	.090 189
36	18.856 912	210.081 318	.004 760	.053 031	11.140 812	.089 760
37	20.459 750	228.938 230	.004 368	.048 876	11.189 689	.089 368
38	22.198 828	249.397 979	.004 010	.045 047	11.234 736	.089 010
39	24.085 729	271.596 808	.003 682	.041 518	11.276 255	.088 682
40	26.133 016	295.682 536	.003 382	.038 266	11.314 520	.088 382
41	28.354 322	321.815 552	.003 107	.035 268	11.349 788	.088 107
42	30.764 439	350.169 874	.002 856	.032 505	11.382 293	.087 856
43	33.379 417	380.934 313	.002 625	.029 959	11.412 252	.087 625
44	36.216 667	414.313 730	.002 414	.027 612	11.439 864	.087 414
45	39.295 084	450.530 397	.002 220	.025 448	11.465 312	.087 220
46	42.635 166	489.825 480	.002 042	.023 455	11.488 767	.087 042
47	46.259 155	532.460 646	.001 878	.021 617	11.510 384	.086 878
48	50.191 183	578.719 801	.001 728	.019 924	11.530 308	.086 728
49	54.457 434	628.910 984	.001 590	.018 363	11.548 671	.086 590
50	59.086 316	683.368 418	.001 463	.016 924	11.565 595	.086 463
51	64.108 652	742.454 733	.001 347	.015 599	11.581 194	.086 347
52	69.557 888	806.563 386	.001 240	.014 377	11.595 570	.086 240
53	75.470 308	876.121 273	.001 141	.013 250	11.608 821	.086 141
54	81.885 284	951.591 582	.001 051	.012 212	11.621 033	.086 051
55	88.845 534	1033.476 866	.000 968	.011 255	11.632 288	.085 968
56	96.397 404	1122.322 400	.000 891	.010 374	11.642 662	.085 891
57	104.591 183	1218.719 804	.000 821	.009 561	11.652 223	.085 821
58	113.481 434	1323.310 987	.000 756	.008 812	11.661 035	.085 756
59	123.127 356	1436.792 421	.000 696	.008 122	11.669 157	.085 696
60	133.593 181	1559.919 777	.000 641	.007 485	11.676 642	.085 641
	$S^n = (1 + i)^n$	$S_{\overline{n}|} = \dfrac{S^n - 1}{i}$	$1/S_{\overline{n}|} = \dfrac{i}{S^n - 1}$	$V^n = \dfrac{1}{S^n}$	$A_{\overline{n}|} = \dfrac{1 - 1/S^n}{i}$	$\dfrac{1}{A_{\overline{n}|}} = \dfrac{i}{1 - 1/S^n}$

YEARS	1 AMOUNT OF ONE	2 AMOUNT OF ONE PER PERIOD	3 SINKING FUND FACTOR	4 PRESENT WORTH OF ONE	5 PRESENT WORTH ONE PER PERIOD	6 PARTIAL PAYMENT
1	1.087 500	1.000 000	1.000 000	.919 540	.919 540	1.087 500
2	1.182 656	2.087 500	.479 042	.845 554	1.765 094	.566 542
3	1.286 139	3.270 156	.305 796	.777 521	2.542 616	.393 296
4	1.398 676	4.556 295	.219 477	.714 962	3.257 578	.306 977
5	1.521 060	5.954 971	.167 927	.657 436	3.915 014	.255 427
6	1.654 153	7.476 031	.133 761	.604 539	4.519 553	.221 261
7	1.798 891	9.130 183	.109 527	.555 898	5.075 451	.197 027
8	1.956 294	10.929 074	.091 499	.511 171	5.586 622	.178 999
9	2.127 470	12.885 368	.077 607	.470 042	6.056 664	.165 107
10	2.313 623	15.012 838	.066 610	.432 222	6.488 886	.154 110
11	2.516 065	17.326 461	.057 715	.397 446	6.886 332	.145 215
12	2.736 221	19.842 527	.050 397	.365 468	7.251 800	.137 897
13	2.975 640	22.578 748	.044 289	.336 062	7.587 862	.131 789
14	3.236 009	25.554 388	.039 132	.309 023	7.896 884	.126 632
15	3.519 160	28.790 397	.034 734	.284 159	8.181 043	.122 234
16	3.827 086	32.309 557	.030 951	.261 295	8.442 338	.118 451
17	4.161 956	36.136 643	.027 673	.240 272	8.682 610	.115 173
18	4.526 127	40.298 600	.024 815	.220 939	8.903 549	.112 315
19	4.922 164	44.824 727	.022 309	.203 163	9.106 712	.109 809
20	5.352 853	49.746 891	.020 102	.186 816	9.293 528	.107 602
21	5.821 228	55.099 744	.018 149	.171 785	9.465 313	.105 649
22	6.330 585	60.920 971	.016 415	.157 963	9.623 277	.103 915
23	6.884 511	67.251 556	.014 870	.145 254	9.768 530	.102 370
24	7.486 906	74.136 067	.013 489	.133 567	9.902 097	.100 989
25	8.142 010	81.622 973	.012 251	.122 820	10.024 917	.099 751
26	8.854 436	89.764 984	.011 140	.112 938	10.137 854	.098 640
27	9.629 199	98.619 420	.010 140	.103 851	10.241 705	.097 640
28	10.471 754	108.248 619	.009 238	.095 495	10.337 200	.096 738
29	11.388 033	118.720 373	.008 423	.087 811	10.425 012	.095 923
30	12.384 485	130.108 406	.007 686	.080 746	10.505 758	.095 186
31	13.468 128	142.492 891	.007 018	.074 249	10.580 007	.094 518
32	14.646 589	155.961 019	.006 412	.068 275	10.648 282	.093 912
33	15.928 166	170.607 608	.005 861	.062 782	10.711 064	.093 361
34	17.321 880	186.535 774	.005 361	.057 730	10.768 795	.092 861
35	18.837 545	203.857 654	.004 905	.053 085	10.821 880	.092 405
36	20.485 830	222.695 199	.004 490	.048 814	10.870 695	.091 990
37	22.278 340	243.181 029	.004 112	.044 887	10.915 581	.091 612
38	24.227 695	265.459 369	.003 767	.041 275	10.956 856	.091 267
39	26.347 618	289.687 064	.003 452	.037 954	10.994 810	.090 952
40	28.653 035	316.034 682	.003 164	.034 900	11.029 711	.090 664
41	31.160 175	344.687 716	.002 901	.032 092	11.061 803	.090 401
42	33.886 691	375.847 892	.002 661	.029 510	11.091 313	.090 161
43	36.851 776	409.734 582	.002 441	.027 136	11.118 449	.089 941
44	40.076 306	446.586 358	.002 239	.024 952	11.143 401	.089 739
45	43.582 983	486.662 664	.002 055	.022 945	11.166 346	.089 555
46	47.396 494	530.245 648	.001 886	.021 099	11.187 444	.089 386
47	51.543 687	577.642 142	.001 731	.019 401	11.206 846	.089 231
48	56.053 760	629.185 829	.001 589	.017 840	11.224 686	.089 089
49	60.958 464	685.239 589	.001 459	.016 405	11.241 090	.088 959
50	66.292 330	746.198 053	.001 340	.015 085	11.256 175	.088 840
51	72.092 909	812.490 383	.001 231	.013 871	11.270 046	.088 731
52	78.401 038	884.583 291	.001 130	.012 755	11.282 801	.088 630
53	85.261 129	962.984 329	.001 038	.011 729	11.294 529	.088 538
54	92.721 478	1048.245 458	.000 954	.010 785	11.305 314	.088 454
55	100.834 607	1140.966 936	.000 876	.009 917	11.315 232	.088 376
56	109.657 635	1241.801 543	.000 805	.009 119	11.324 351	.088 305
57	119.252 678	1351.459 178	.000 740	.008 386	11.332 737	.088 240
58	129.687 287	1470.711 856	.000 680	.007 711	11.340 447	.088 180
59	141.034 925	1600.399 143	.000 625	.007 090	11.347 538	.088 125
60	153.375 481	1741.434 068	.000 574	.006 520	11.354 058	.088 074

$$S^n = (1 + i)^n \qquad S_{\overline{n}|} = \frac{S^n - 1}{i} \qquad 1/S_{\overline{n}|} = \frac{i}{S^n - 1} \qquad V^n = \frac{1}{S^n} \qquad A_{\overline{n}|} = \frac{1 - 1/S^n}{i} \qquad \frac{1}{A_{\overline{n}|}} = \frac{i}{1 - 1/S^n}$$

	1	2	3	4	5	6
YEARS	AMOUNT OF ONE	AMOUNT OF ONE PER PERIOD	SINKING FUND FACTOR	PRESENT WORTH OF ONE	PRESENT WORTH ONE PER PERIOD	PARTIAL PAYMENT
1	1.090 000	1.000 000	1.000 000	.917 431	.917 431	1.090 000
2	1.188 100	2.090 000	.478 469	.841 680	1.759 111	.568 469
3	1.295 029	3.278 100	.305 055	.772 183	2.531 295	.395 055
4	1.411 582	4.573 129	.218 669	.708 425	3.239 720	.308 669
5	1.538 624	5.984 711	.167 092	.649 931	3.889 651	.257 092
6	1.677 100	7.523 335	.132 920	.596 267	4.485 919	.222 920
7	1.828 039	9.200 435	.108 691	.547 034	5.032 953	.198 691
8	1.992 563	11.028 474	.090 674	.501 866	5.534 819	.180 674
9	2.171 893	13.021 036	.076 799	.460 428	5.995 247	.166 799
10	2.367 364	15.192 930	.065 820	.422 411	6.417 658	.155 820
11	2.580 426	17.560 293	.056 947	.387 533	6.805 191	.146 947
12	2.812 665	20.140 720	.049 651	.355 535	7.160 725	.139 651
13	3.065 805	22.953 385	.043 567	.326 179	7.486 904	.133 567
14	3.341 727	26.019 189	.038 433	.299 246	7.786 150	.128 433
15	3.642 482	29.360 916	.034 059	.274 538	8.060 688	.124 059
16	3.970 306	33.003 399	.030 300	.251 870	8.312 558	.120 300
17	4.327 633	36.973 705	.027 046	.231 073	8.543 631	.117 046
18	4.717 120	41.301 338	.024 212	.211 994	8.755 625	.114 212
19	5.141 661	46.018 458	.021 730	.194 490	8.950 115	.111 730
20	5.604 411	51.160 120	.019 546	.178 431	9.128 546	.109 546
21	6.108 808	56.764 530	.017 617	.163 698	9.292 244	.107 617
22	6.658 600	62.873 338	.015 905	.150 182	9.442 425	.105 905
23	7.257 874	69.531 939	.014 382	.137 781	9.580 207	.104 382
24	7.911 083	76.789 813	.013 023	.126 405	9.706 612	.103 023
25	8.623 081	84.700 896	.011 806	.115 968	9.822 580	.101 806
26	9.399 158	93.323 977	.010 715	.106 393	9.928 972	.100 715
27	10.245 082	102.723 135	.009 735	.097 608	10.026 580	.099 735
28	11.167 140	112.968 217	.008 852	.089 548	10.116 128	.098 852
29	12.172 182	124.135 356	.008 056	.082 155	10.198 283	.098 056
30	13.267 678	136.307 539	.007 336	.075 371	10.273 654	.097 336
31	14.461 770	149.575 217	.006 686	.069 148	10.342 802	.096 686
32	15.763 329	164.036 987	.006 096	.063 438	10.406 240	.096 096
33	17.182 028	179.800 315	.005 562	.058 200	10.464 441	.095 562
34	18.728 411	196.982 344	.005 077	.053 395	10.517 835	.095 077
35	20.413 968	215.710 755	.004 636	.048 986	10.566 821	.094 636
36	22.251 225	236.124 723	.004 235	.044 941	10.611 763	.094 235
37	24.253 835	258.375 948	.003 870	.041 231	10.652 993	.093 870
38	26.436 680	282.629 783	.003 538	.037 826	10.690 820	.093 538
39	28.815 982	309.066 463	.003 236	.034 703	1 .725 523	.093 236
40	31.409 420	337.882 445	.002 960	.031 838	1 .757 360	.092 960
41	34.236 268	369.291 865	.002 708	.029 209	1(.786 569	.092 708
42	37.317 532	403.528 133	.002 478	.026 797	1(.813 366	.092 478
43	40.676 110	440.845 665	.002 268	.024 584	1(.837 950	.092 268
44	44.336 960	481.521 775	.002 077	.022 555	1(.860 505	.092 077
45	48.327 286	525.858 734	.001 902	.020 692	10.881 197	.091 902
46	52.676 742	574.186 021	.001 742	.018 984	1(.900 181	.091 742
47	57.417 649	626.862 762	.001 595	.017 416	10.917 597	.091 595
48	62.585 237	684.280 411	.001 461	.015 978	10.933 575	.091 461
49	68.217 908	746.865 648	.001 339	.014 659	10.948 234	.091 339
50	74.357 520	815.083 556	.001 227	.013 449	10.961 683	.091 227
51	81.049 697	889.441 076	.001 124	.012 338	10.974 021	.091 124
52	88.344 170	970.490 773	.001 030	.011 319	10.985 340	.091 030
53	96.295 145	1058.834 943	.000 944	.010 385	10.995 725	.090 944
54	104.961 708	1155.130 088	.000 866	.009 527	11.005 252	.090 866
55	114.408 262	1260.091 796	.000 794	.008 741	11.013 993	.090 794
56	124.705 005	1374.500 057	.000 728	.008 019	11.022 012	.090 728
57	135.928 456	1499.205 063	.000 667	.007 357	11.029 369	.090 667
58	148.162 017	1635.133 518	.000 612	.006 749	11.036 118	.090 612
59	161.496 598	1783.295 535	.000 561	.006 192	11.042 310	.090 561
60	176.031 292	1944.792 133	.000 514	.005 681	11.047 991	.090 514

$$S^n = (1+i)^n \qquad S_{\overline{n}|} = \frac{S^n - 1}{i} \qquad 1/S_{\overline{n}|} = \frac{i}{S^n - 1} \qquad V^n = \frac{1}{S^n} \qquad A_{\overline{n}|} = \frac{1 - 1/S^n}{i} \qquad \frac{1}{A_{\overline{n}|}} = \frac{i}{1 - 1/S^n}$$

	1	2	3	4	5	6
YEARS	AMOUNT OF ONE	AMOUNT OF ONE PER PERIOD	SINKING FUND FACTOR	PRESENT WORTH OF ONE	PRESENT WORTH ONE PER PERIOD	PARTIAL PAYMENT
1	1.092 500	1.000 000	1.000 000	.915 332	.915 332	1.092 500
2	1.193 556	2.092 500	.477 897	.837 832	1.753 164	.570 397
3	1.303 960	3.286 056	.304 316	.766 895	2.520 059	.396 816
4	1.424 577	4.590 016	.217 864	.701 963	3.222 022	.310 364
5	1.556 350	6.014 593	.166 262	.642 529	3.864 551	.258 762
6	1.700 312	7.570 943	.132 084	.588 127	4.452 678	.224 584
7	1.857 591	9.271 255	.107 860	.538 332	4.991 010	.200 360
8	2.029 418	11.128 846	.089 857	.492 752	5.483 762	.182 357
9	2.217 139	13.158 264	.075 998	.451 032	5.934 793	.168 498
10	2.422 225	15.375 404	.065 039	.412 844	6.347 637	.157 539
11	2.646 281	17.797 629	.056 187	.377 889	6.725 526	.148 687
12	2.891 062	20.443 909	.048 914	.345 894	7.071 419	.141 414
13	3.158 485	23.334 971	.042 854	.316 608	7.388 027	.135 354
14	3.450 645	26.493 456	.037 745	.289 801	7.677 828	.130 245
15	3.769 829	29.944 100	.033 396	.265 264	7.943 092	.125 896
16	4.118 539	33.713 930	.029 661	.242 805	8.185 896	.122 161
17	4.499 503	37.832 468	.026 432	.222 247	8.408 143	.118 932
18	4.915 707	42.331 972	.023 623	.203 430	8.611 573	.116 123
19	5.370 410	47.247 679	.021 165	.186 206	8.797 778	.113 665
20	5.867 173	52.618 089	.019 005	.170 440	8.968 218	.111 505
21	6.409 887	58.485 262	.017 098	.156 009	9.124 227	.109 598
22	7.002 801	64.895 149	.015 409	.142 800	9.267 027	.107 909
23	7.650 560	71.897 951	.013 909	.130 709	9.397 736	.106 409
24	8.358 237	79.548 511	.012 571	.119 642	9.517 379	.105 071
25	9.131 374	87.906 748	.011 376	.109 513	9.626 891	.103 876
26	9.976 026	97.038 122	.010 305	.100 240	9.727 132	.102 805
27	10.898 809	107.014 149	.009 345	.091 753	9.818 885	.101 845
28	11.906 949	117.912 958	.008 481	.083 985	9.902 869	.100 981
29	13.008 341	129.819 906	.007 703	.076 874	9.979 743	.100 203
30	14.211 613	142.828 247	.007 001	.070 365	10.050 108	.099 501
31	15.526 187	157.039 860	.006 368	.064 407	10.114 516	.098 868
32	16.962 359	172.566 047	.005 795	.058 954	10.173 470	.098 295
33	18.531 378	189.528 407	.005 276	.053 963	10.227 432	.097 776
34	20.245 530	208.059 784	.004 806	.049 394	10.276 826	.097 306
35	22.118 242	228.305 315	.004 380	.045 212	10.322 037	.096 880
36	24.164 179	250.423 556	.003 993	.041 384	10.363 421	.096 493
37	26.399 365	274.587 735	.003 642	.037 880	10.401 301	.096 142
38	28.841 307	300.987 101	.003 322	.034 672	10.435 973	.095 822
39	31.509 128	329.828 407	.003 032	.031 737	10.467 710	.095 532
40	34.423 722	361.337 535	.002 767	.029 050	10.496 760	.095 267
41	37.607 916	395.761 257	.002 527	.026 590	10.523 350	.095 027
42	41.086 649	433.369 173	.002 308	.024 339	10.547 689	.094 808
43	44.887 164	474.455 822	.002 108	.022 278	10.569 967	.094 608
44	49.039 226	519.342 985	.001 926	.020 392	10.590 358	.094 426
45	53.575 355	568.382 212	.001 759	.018 665	10.609 024	.094 259
46	58.531 075	621.957 566	.001 608	.017 085	10.626 109	.094 108
47	63.945 199	680.488 641	.001 470	.015 638	10.641 747	.093 970
48	69.860 130	744.433 840	.001 343	.014 314	10.656 061	.093 843
49	76.322 192	814.293 970	.001 228	.013 102	10.669 164	.093 728
50	83.381 995	890.616 163	.001 123	.011 993	10.681 157	.093 623
51	91.094 830	973.998 158	.001 027	.010 978	10.692 134	.093 527
52	99.521 101	1065.092 987	.000 939	.010 048	10.702 182	.093 439
53	108.726 803	1164.614 089	.000 859	.009 197	10.711 380	.093 359
54	118.784 033	1273.340 892	.000 785	.008 419	10.719 798	.093 285
55	129.771 556	1392.124 924	.000 718	.007 706	10.727 504	.093 218
56	141.775 424	1521.896 480	.000 657	.007 053	10.734 558	.093 157
57	154.889 651	1663.671 904	.000 601	.006 456	10.741 014	.093 101
58	169.216 944	1818.561 555	.000 550	.005 910	10.746 924	.093 050
59	184.869 511	1987.778 499	.000 503	.005 409	10.752 333	.093 003
60	201.969 941	2172.648 011	.000 460	.004 951	10.757 284	.092 960

$S^n = (1 + i)^n$	$S_{\overline{n}|} = \dfrac{S^n - 1}{i}$	$1/S_{\overline{n}|} = \dfrac{i}{S^n - 1}$	$V^n = \dfrac{1}{S^n}$	$A_{\overline{n}|} = \dfrac{1 - 1/S^n}{i}$	$\dfrac{1}{A_{\overline{n}|}} = \dfrac{i}{1 - 1/S^n}$

	1	2	3	4	5	6
YEARS	AMOUNT OF ONE	AMOUNT OF ONE PER PERIOD	SINKING FUND FACTOR	PRESENT WORTH OF ONE	PRESENT WORTH ONE PER PERIOD	PARTIAL PAYMENT
1	1.095 000	1.000 000	1.000 000	.913 242	.913 242	1.095 000
2	1.199 025	2.095 000	.477 327	.834 011	1.747 253	.572 327
3	1.312 932	3.294 025	.303 580	.761 654	2.508 907	.398 580
4	1.437 661	4.606 957	.217 063	.695 574	3.204 481	.312 063
5	1.574 239	6.044 618	.165 436	.635 228	3.839 709	.260 436
6	1.723 791	7.618 857	.131 253	.580 117	4.419 825	.226 253
7	1.887 552	9.342 648	.107 036	.529 787	4.949 612	.202 036
8	2.066 869	11.230 200	.089 046	.483 824	5.433 436	.184 046
9	2.263 222	13.297 069	.075 205	.441 848	5.875 284	.170 205
10	2.478 228	15.560 291	.064 266	.403 514	6.278 798	.159 266
11	2.713 659	18.038 518	.055 437	.368 506	6.647 304	.150 437
12	2.971 457	20.752 178	.048 188	.336 535	6.983 839	.143 188
13	3.253 745	23.723 634	.042 152	.307 338	7.291 178	.137 152
14	3.562 851	26.977 380	.037 068	.280 674	7.571 852	.132 068
15	3.901 322	30.540 231	.032 744	.256 323	7.828 175	.127 744
16	4.271 948	34.441 553	.029 035	.234 085	8.062 260	.124 035
17	4.677 783	38.713 500	.025 831	.213 777	8.276 037	.120 831
18	5.122 172	43.391 283	.023 046	.195 230	8.471 266	.118 046
19	5.608 778	48.513 454	.020 613	.178 292	8.649 558	.115 613
20	6.141 612	54.122 233	.018 477	.162 824	8.812 382	.113 477
21	6.725 065	60.263 845	.016 594	.148 697	8.961 080	.111 594
22	7.363 946	66.988 910	.014 928	.135 797	9.096 876	.109 928
23	8.063 521	74.352 856	.013 449	.124 015	9.220 892	.108 449
24	8.829 556	82.416 378	.012 134	.113 256	9.334 148	.107 134
25	9.668 364	91.245 934	.010 959	.103 430	9.437 578	.105 959
26	10.586 858	100.914 297	.009 909	.094 457	9.532 034	.104 909
27	11.592 610	111.501 156	.008 969	.086 262	9.618 296	.103 969
28	12.693 908	123.093 766	.008 124	.078 778	9.697 074	.103 124
29	13.899 829	135.787 673	.007 364	.071 943	9.769 018	.102 364
30	15.220 313	149.687 502	.006 681	.065 702	9.834 719	.101 681
31	16.666 242	164.907 815	.006 064	.060 002	9.894 721	.101 064
32	18.249 535	181.574 057	.005 507	.054 796	9.949 517	.100 507
33	19.983 241	199.823 593	.005 004	.050 042	9.999 559	.100 004
34	21.881 649	219.806 834	.004 549	.045 700	10.045 259	.099 549
35	23.960 406	241.688 483	.004 138	.041 736	10.086 995	.099 138
36	26.236 644	265.648 889	.003 764	.038 115	10.125 109	.098 764
37	28.729 126	291.885 534	.003 426	.034 808	10.159 917	.098 426
38	31.458 393	320.614 659	.003 119	.031 788	10.191 705	.098 119
39	34.446 940	352.073 052	.002 840	.029 030	10.220 735	.097 840
40	37.719 399	386.519 992	.002 587	.026 512	10.247 247	.097 587
41	41.302 742	424.239 391	.002 357	.024 211	10.271 458	.097 357
42	45.226 503	465.542 133	.002 148	.022 111	10.293 569	.097 148
43	49.523 020	510.768 636	.001 958	.020 193	10.313 762	.096 958
44	54.227 707	560.291 656	.001 785	.018 441	10.332 203	.096 785
45	59.379 340	614.519 364	.001 627	.016 841	10.349 043	.096 627
46	65.020 377	673.898 703	.001 484	.015 380	10.364 423	.096 484
47	71.197 313	738.919 080	.001 353	.014 045	10.378 469	.096 353
48	77.961 057	810.116 393	.001 234	.012 827	10.391 296	.096 234
49	85.367 358	888.077 450	.001 126	.011 714	10.403 010	.096 126
50	93.477 257	973.444 808	.001 027	.010 698	10.413 707	.096 027
51	102.357 596	1066.922 065	.000 937	.009 770	10.423 477	.095 937
52	112.081 568	1169.279 661	.000 855	.008 922	10.432 399	.095 855
53	122.729 317	1281.361 229	.000 780	.008 148	10.440 547	.095 780
54	134.388 602	1404.090 545	.000 712	.007 441	10.447 988	.095 712
55	147.155 519	1538.479 147	.000 650	.006 796	10.454 784	.095 650
56	161.135 293	1685.634 666	.000 593	.006 206	10.460 990	.095 593
57	176.443 146	1846.769 959	.000 541	.005 668	10.466 657	.095 541
58	193.205 245	2023.213 106	.000 494	.005 176	10.471 833	.095 494
59	211.559 743	2216.418 351	.000 451	.004 727	10.476 560	.095 451
60	231.657 919	2427.978 094	.000 412	.004 317	10.480 877	.095 412

$S^n = (1+i)^n$	$S_{\overline{n}} = \dfrac{S^n - 1}{i}$	$1/S_{\overline{n}} = \dfrac{i}{S^n - 1}$	$V^n = \dfrac{1}{S^n}$	$A_{\overline{n}} = \dfrac{1 - 1/S^n}{i}$	$\dfrac{1}{A_{\overline{n}}} = \dfrac{i}{1 - 1/S^n}$

	1	2	3	4	5	6
YEARS	AMOUNT OF ONE	AMOUNT OF ONE PER PERIOD	SINKING FUND FACTOR	PRESENT WORTH OF ONE	PRESENT WORTH ONE PER PERIOD	PARTIAL PAYMENT
1	1.097 500	1.000 000	1.000 000	.911 162	.911 162	1.097 500
2	1.204 506	2.097 500	.476 758	.830 216	1.741 377	.574 258
3	1.321 946	3.302 006	.302 846	.756 461	2.497 838	.400 346
4	1.450 835	4.623 952	.216 265	.689 258	3.187 096	.313 765
5	1.592 292	6.074 787	.164 615	.628 026	3.815 122	.262 115
6	1.747 540	7.667 079	.130 428	.572 233	4.387 355	.227 928
7	1.917 925	9.414 619	.106 218	.521 397	4.908 752	.203 718
8	2.104 923	11.332 544	.088 241	.475 077	5.383 828	.185 741
9	2.310 153	13.437 468	.074 419	.432 872	5.816 700	.171 919
10	2.535 393	15.747 621	.063 502	.394 416	6.211 116	.161 002
11	2.782 594	18.283 014	.054 696	.359 377	6.570 493	.152 196
12	3.053 897	21.065 607	.047 471	.327 450	6.897 944	.144 971
13	3.351 652	24.119 504	.041 460	.298 360	7.196 304	.138 960
14	3.678 438	27.471 156	.036 402	.271 855	7.468 159	.133 902
15	4.037 085	31.149 594	.032 103	.247 703	7.715 862	.129 603
16	4.430 701	35.186 679	.028 420	.225 698	7.941 560	.125 920
17	4.862 695	39.617 380	.025 241	.205 647	8.147 207	.122 741
18	5.336 807	44.480 075	.022 482	.187 378	8.334 585	.119 982
19	5.857 146	49.816 882	.020 074	.170 732	8.505 317	.117 574
20	6.428 218	55.674 028	.017 962	.155 564	8.660 881	.115 462
21	7.054 969	62.102 246	.016 102	.141 744	8.802 625	.113 602
22	7.742 828	69.157 215	.014 460	.129 152	8.931 777	.111 960
23	8.497 754	76.900 043	.013 004	.117 678	9.049 455	.110 504
24	9.326 285	85.397 797	.011 710	.107 224	9.156 679	.109 210
25	10.235 598	94.724 083	.010 557	.097 698	9.254 377	.108 057
26	11.233 569	104.959 681	.009 527	.089 019	9.343 396	.107 027
27	12.328 842	116.193 249	.008 606	.081 111	9.424 506	.106 106
28	13.530 904	128.522 091	.007 781	.073 905	9.498 411	.105 281
29	14.850 167	142.052 995	.007 040	.067 339	9.565 751	.104 540
30	16.298 058	156.903 162	.006 373	.061 357	9.627 108	.103 873
31	17.887 119	173.201 221	.005 774	.055 906	9.683 014	.103 274
32	19.631 113	191.088 340	.005 233	.050 940	9.733 953	.102 733
33	21.545 147	210.719 453	.004 746	.046 414	9.780 368	.102 246
34	23.645 798	232.264 599	.004 305	.042 291	9.822 658	.101 805
35	25.951 264	255.910 398	.003 908	.038 534	9.861 192	.101 408
36	28.481 512	281.861 661	.003 548	.035 110	9.896 303	.101 048
37	31.258 459	310.343 173	.003 222	.031 991	9.928 294	.100 722
38	34.306 159	341.601 633	.002 927	.029 149	9.957 443	.100 427
39	37.651 010	375.907 792	.002 660	.026 560	9.984 003	.100 160
40	41.321 983	413.558 802	.002 418	.024 200	10.008 203	.099 918
41	45.350 877	454.880 785	.002 198	.022 050	10.030 253	.099 698
42	49.772 587	500.231 662	.001 999	.020 091	10.050 345	.099 499
43	54.625 414	550.004 249	.001 818	.018 306	10.068 651	.099 318
44	59.951 392	604.629 663	.001 654	.016 680	10.085 331	.099 154
45	65.796 653	664.581 055	.001 505	.015 198	10.100 530	.099 005
46	72.211 827	730.377 708	.001 369	.013 848	10.114 378	.098 869
47	79.252 480	802.589 534	.001 246	.012 618	10.126 996	.098 746
48	86.979 596	881.842 014	.001 134	.011 497	10.138 493	.098 634
49	95.460 107	968.821 610	.001 032	.010 476	10.148 968	.098 532
50	104.767 467	1064.281 717	.000 940	.009 545	10.158 513	.098 440
51	114.982 295	1169.049 185	.000 855	.008 697	10.167 210	.098 355
52	126.193 069	1284.031 480	.000 779	.007 924	10.175 135	.098 279
53	138.496 894	1410.224 549	.000 709	.007 220	10.182 355	.098 209
54	152.000 341	1548.721 443	.000 646	.006 579	10.188 934	.098 146
55	166.820 374	1700.721 784	.000 588	.005 994	10.194 928	.098 088
56	183.085 360	1867.542 158	.000 535	.005 462	10.200 390	.098 035
57	200.936 183	2050.627 518	.000 488	.004 977	10.205 367	.097 988
58	220.527 461	2251.563 701	.000 444	.004 535	10.209 902	.097 944
59	242.028 888	2472.091 162	.000 405	.004 132	10.214 033	.097 905
60	265.626 705	2714.120 050	.000 368	.003 765	10.217 798	.097 868

$$S^n = (1+i)^n \qquad S_{\overline{n}|} = \frac{S^n-1}{i} \qquad 1/S_{\overline{n}|} = \frac{i}{S^n-1} \qquad V^n = \frac{1}{S^n} \qquad A_{\overline{n}|} = \frac{1-1/S^n}{i} \qquad \frac{1}{A_{\overline{n}|}} = \frac{i}{1-1/S^n}$$

	1	2	3	4	5	6
YEARS	AMOUNT OF ONE	AMOUNT OF ONE PER PERIOD	SINKING FUND FACTOR	PRESENT WORTH OF ONE	PRESENT WORTH ONE PER PERIOD	PARTIAL PAYMENT
1	1.100 000	1.000 000	1.000 000	.909 091	.909 091	1.100 000
2	1.210 000	2.100 000	.476 190	.826 446	1.735 537	.576 190
3	1.331 000	3.310 000	.302 115	.751 315	2.486 852	.402 115
4	1.464 100	4.641 000	.215 471	.683 013	3.169 865	.315 471
5	1.610 510	6.105 100	.163 797	.620 921	3.790 787	.263 797
6	1.771 561	7.715 610	.129 607	.564 474	4.355 261	.229 607
7	1.948 717	9.487 171	.105 405	.513 158	4.868 419	.205 405
8	2.143 589	11.435 888	.087 444	.466 507	5.334 926	.187 444
9	2.357 948	13.579 477	.073 641	.424 098	5.759 024	.173 641
10	2.593 742	15.937 425	.062 745	.385 543	6.144 567	.162 745
11	2.853 117	18.531 167	.053 963	.350 494	6.495 061	.153 963
12	3.138 428	21.384 284	.046 763	.318 631	6.813 692	.146 763
13	3.452 271	24.522 712	.040 779	.289 664	7.103 356	.140 779
14	3.797 498	27.974 983	.035 746	.263 331	7.366 687	.135 746
15	4.177 248	31.772 482	.031 474	.239 392	7.606 080	.131 474
16	4.594 973	35.949 730	.027 817	.217 629	7.823 709	.127 817
17	5.054 470	40.544 703	.024 664	.197 845	8.021 553	.124 664
18	5.559 917	45.599 173	.021 930	.179 859	8.201 412	.121 930
19	6.115 909	51.159 090	.019 547	.163 508	8.364 920	.119 547
20	6.727 500	57.274 999	.017 460	.148 644	8.513 564	.117 460
21	7.400 250	64.002 499	.015 624	.135 131	8.648 694	.115 624
22	8.140 275	71.402 749	.014 005	.122 846	8.771 540	.114 005
23	8.954 302	79.543 024	.012 572	.111 678	8.883 218	.112 572
24	9.849 733	88.497 327	.011 300	.101 526	8.984 744	.111 300
25	10.834 706	98.347 059	.010 168	.092 296	9.077 040	.110 168
26	11.918 177	109.181 765	.009 159	.083 905	9.160 945	.109 159
27	13.109 994	121.099 942	.008 258	.076 278	9.237 223	.108 258
28	14.420 994	134.209 936	.007 451	.069 343	9.306 567	.107 451
29	15.863 093	148.630 930	.006 728	.063 039	9.369 606	.106 728
30	17.449 402	164.494 023	.006 079	.057 309	9.426 914	.106 079
31	19.194 342	181.943 425	.005 496	.052 099	9.479 013	.105 496
32	21.113 777	201.137 767	.004 972	.047 362	9.526 376	.104 972
33	23.225 154	222.251 544	.004 499	.043 057	9.569 432	.104 499
34	25.547 670	245.476 699	.004 074	.039 143	9.608 575	.104 074
35	28.102 437	271.024 368	.003 690	.035 584	9.644 159	.103 690
36	30.912 681	299.126 805	.003 343	.032 349	9.676 508	.103 343
37	34.003 949	330.039 486	.003 030	.029 408	9.705 917	.103 030
38	37.404 343	364.043 434	.002 747	.026 735	9.732 651	.102 747
39	41.144 778	401.447 778	.002 491	.024 304	9.756 956	.102 491
40	45.259 256	442.592 556	.002 259	.022 095	9.779 051	.102 259
41	49.785 181	487.851 811	.002 050	.020 086	9.799 137	.102 050
42	54.763 699	537.636 992	.001 860	.018 260	9.817 397	.101 860
43	60.240 069	592.400 692	.001 688	.016 600	9.833 998	.101 688
44	66.264 076	652.640 761	.001 532	.015 091	9.849 089	.101 532
45	72.890 484	718.904 837	.001 391	.013 719	9.862 808	.101 391
46	80.179 532	791.795 321	.001 263	.012 472	9.875 280	.101 263
47	88.197 485	871.974 853	.001 147	.011 338	9.886 618	.101 147
48	97.017 234	960.172 338	.001 041	.010 307	9.896 926	.101 041
49	106.718 957	1057.189 572	.000 946	.009 370	9.906 296	.100 946
50	117.390 853	1163.908 529	.000 859	.008 519	9.914 814	.100 859
51	129.129 938	1281.299 382	.000 780	.007 744	9.922 559	.100 780
52	142.042 932	1410.429 320	.000 709	.007 040	9.929 599	.100 709
53	156.247 225	1552.472 252	.000 644	.006 400	9.935 999	.100 644
54	171.871 948	1708.719 477	.000 585	.005 818	9.941 817	.100 585
55	189.059 142	1880.591 425	.000 532	.005 289	9.947 106	.100 532
56	207.965 057	2069.650 567	.000 483	.004 809	9.951 915	.100 483
57	228.761 562	2277.615 624	.000 439	.004 371	9.956 286	.100 439
58	251.637 719	2506.377 186	.000 399	.003 974	9.960 260	.100 399
59	276.801 490	2758.014 905	.000 363	.003 613	9.963 873	.100 363
60	304.481 640	3034.816 395	.000 330	.003 284	9.967 157	.100 330
	$S^n = (1 + i)^n$	$S_{\overline{n}|} = \dfrac{S^n - 1}{i}$	$1/S_{\overline{n}|} = \dfrac{i}{S^n - 1}$	$V^n = \dfrac{1}{S^n}$	$A_{\overline{n}|} = \dfrac{1 - 1/S^n}{i}$	$\dfrac{1}{A_{\overline{n}|}} = \dfrac{i}{1 - 1/S^n}$

	1	2	3	4	5	6
MONTHS	AMOUNT OF ONE	AMOUNT OF ONE PER PERIOD	SINKING FUND FACTOR	PRESENT WORTH OF ONE	PRESENT WORTH ONE PER PERIOD	PARTIAL PAYMENT
1	1.008 333	1.000 000	1.000 000	.991 736	.991 736	1.008 333
2	1.016 736	2.008 333	.497 925	.983 539	1.975 275	.506 259
3	1.025 209	3.025 069	.330 571	.975 411	2.950 686	.338 904
4	1.033 752	4.050 278	.246 897	.967 350	3.918 036	.255 230
5	1.042 367	5.084 031	.196 694	.959 355	4.877 391	.205 028
6	1.051 053	6.126 398	.163 228	.951 427	5.828 817	.171 561
7	1.059 812	7.177 451	.139 325	.943 563	6.772 381	.147 659
8	1.068 644	8.237 263	.121 400	.935 765	7.708 146	.129 733
9	1.077 549	9.305 907	.107 459	.928 032	8.636 178	.115 792
10	1.086 529	10.383 456	.096 307	.920 362	9.556 540	.104 640
11	1.095 583	11.469 985	.087 184	.912 756	10.469 296	.095 517

YEARS

	1	2	3	4	5	6
1	1.104 713	12.565 568	.079 583	.905 212	11.374 508	.087 916
2	1.220 391	26.446 915	.037 812	.819 410	21.670 855	.046 145
3	1.348 182	41.781 821	.023 934	.741 740	30.991 236	.032 267
4	1.489 354	58.722 492	.017 029	.671 432	39.428 160	.025 363
5	1.645 309	77.437 072	.012 914	.607 789	47.065 369	.021 247
6	1.817 594	98.111 314	.010 193	.550 178	53.978 665	.018 526
7	2.007 920	120.950 418	.008 268	.498 028	60.236 667	.016 601
8	2.218 176	146.181 076	.006 841	.450 821	65.901 488	.015 174
9	2.450 448	174.053 713	.005 745	.408 089	71.029 355	.014 079
10	2.707 041	204.844 979	.004 882	.369 407	75.671 163	.013 215
11	2.990 504	238.860 493	.004 187	.334 392	79.872 986	.012 520
12	3.303 649	276.437 876	.003 617	.302 696	83.676 528	.011 951
13	3.649 584	317.950 102	.003 145	.274 004	87.119 542	.011 478
14	4.031 743	363.809 201	.002 749	.248 032	90.236 201	.011 082
15	4.453 920	414.470 346	.002 413	.224 521	93.057 439	.010 746
16	4.920 303	470.436 376	.002 126	.203 240	95.611 259	.010 459
17	5.435 523	532.262 780	.001 879	.183 975	97.923 008	.010 212
18	6.004 693	600.563 216	.001 665	.166 536	100.015 633	.009 998
19	6.633 463	676.015 601	.001 479	.150 751	101.909 902	.009 813
20	7.328 074	759.368 836	.001 317	.136 462	103.624 619	.009 650
21	8.095 419	851.450 244	.001 174	.123 527	105.176 801	.009 508
22	8.943 115	953.173 779	.001 049	.111 818	106.581 856	.009 382
23	9.879 576	1065.549 097	.000 938	.101 219	107.853 730	.009 272
24	10.914 097	1189.691 580	.000 841	.091 625	109.005 045	.009 174
25	12.056 945	1326.833 403	.000 754	.082 940	110.047 230	.009 087
26	13.319 465	1478.335 767	.000 676	.075 078	110.990 629	.009 010
27	14.714 187	1645.702 407	.000 608	.067 962	111.844 605	.008 941
28	16.254 954	1830.594 523	.000 546	.061 520	112.617 635	.008 880
29	17.957 060	2034.847 258	.000 491	.055 688	113.317 392	.008 825
30	19.837 399	2260.487 925	.000 442	.050 410	113.950 820	.008 776
31	21.914 634	2509.756 117	.000 398	.045 632	114.524 207	.008 732
32	24.209 383	2785.125 947	.000 359	.041 306	115.043 244	.008 692
33	26.744 422	3089.330 596	.000 324	.037 391	115.513 083	.008 657
34	29.544 912	3425.389 447	.000 292	.033 847	115.938 387	.008 625
35	32.638 650	3796.638 052	.000 263	.030 639	116.323 377	.008 597
36	36.056 344	4206.761 236	.000 238	.027 734	116.671 876	.008 571
37	39.831 914	4659.829 677	.000 215	.025 105	116.987 340	.008 548
38	44.002 836	5160.340 305	.000 194	.022 726	117.272 903	.008 527
39	48.610 508	5713.260 935	.000 175	.020 572	117.531 398	.008 508
40	53.700 663	6324.079 581	.000 158	.018 622	117.765 391	.008 491
41	59.323 824	6998.858 921	.000 143	.016 857	117.977 204	.008 476
42	65.535 804	7744.296 475	.000 129	.015 259	118.168 940	.008 462
43	72.398 259	8567.791 082	.000 117	.013 812	118.342 502	.008 450
44	79.979 303	9477.516 336	.000 106	.012 503	118.499 612	.008 439
45	88.354 181	10482.501 711	.000 095	.011 318	118.641 830	.008 429
46	97.606 018	11592.722 188	.000 086	.010 245	118.770 568	.008 420
47	107.826 641	12819.197 256	.000 078	.009 274	118.887 103	.008 411
48	119.117 502	14174.100 291	.000 071	.008 395	118.992 591	.008 404
49	131.590 661	15670.879 379	.000 064	.007 599	119.088 081	.008 397
50	145.369 923	17324.390 796	.000 058	.006 879	119.174 520	.008 391

$$S^n = (1+i)^n \qquad S_{\overline{n}|} = \frac{S^n - 1}{i} \qquad 1/S_{\overline{n}|} = \frac{i}{S^n - 1} \qquad V^n = \frac{1}{S^n} \qquad A_{\overline{n}|} = \frac{1 - 1/S^n}{i} \qquad \frac{1}{A_{\overline{n}|}} = \frac{i}{1 - 1/S^n}$$

QUARTERS	1 AMOUNT OF ONE	2 AMOUNT OF ONE PER PERIOD	3 SINKING FUND FACTOR	4 PRESENT WORTH OF ONE	5 PRESENT WORTH ONE PER PERIOD	6 PARTIAL PAYMENT
1	1.025 000	1.000 000	1.000 000	.975 610	.975 610	1.025 000
2	1.050 625	2.025 000	.493 827	.951 814	1.927 424	.518 827
3	1.076 891	3.075 625	.325 137	.928 599	2.856 024	.350 137
YEARS						
1	1.103 813	4.152 516	.240 818	.905 951	3.761 974	.265 818
2	1.218 403	8.736 116	.114 467	.820 747	7.170 137	.139 467
3	1.344 889	13.795 553	.072 487	.743 556	10.257 765	.097 487
4	1.484 506	19.380 225	.051 599	.673 625	13.055 003	.076 599
5	1.638 616	25.544 658	.039 147	.610 271	15.589 162	.064 147
6	1.808 726	32.349 038	.030 913	.552 875	17.884 986	.055 913
7	1.996 495	39.859 801	.025 088	.500 878	19.964 889	.050 088
8	2.203 757	48.150 278	.020 768	.453 771	21.849 178	.045 768
9	2.432 535	57.301 413	.017 452	.411 094	23.556 251	.042 452
10	2.685 064	67.402 554	.014 836	.372 431	25.102 775	.039 836
11	2.963 808	78.552 323	.012 730	.337 404	26.503 849	.037 730
12	3.271 490	90.859 582	.011 006	.305 671	27.773 154	.036 006
13	3.611 112	104.444 494	.009 574	.276 923	28.923 081	.034 574
14	3.985 992	119.439 694	.008 372	.250 879	29.964 858	.033 372
15	4.399 790	135.991 590	.007 353	.227 284	30.908 656	.032 353
16	4.856 545	154.261 786	.006 482	.205 908	31.763 691	.031 482
17	5.360 717	174.428 663	.005 733	.186 542	32.538 311	.030 733
18	5.917 228	196.689 122	.005 084	.168 998	33.240 078	.030 084
19	6.531 513	221.260 504	.004 520	.153 104	33.875 844	.029 520
20	7.209 568	248.382 713	.004 026	.138 705	34.451 817	.029 026
21	7.958 014	278.320 556	.003 593	.125 659	34.973 620	.028 593
22	8.784 158	311.366 333	.003 212	.113 841	35.446 348	.028 212
23	9.696 067	347.842 687	.002 875	.103 135	35.874 616	.027 875
24	10.702 644	388.105 758	.002 577	.093 435	36.262 606	.027 577
25	11.813 716	432.548 654	.002 312	.084 647	36.614 105	.027 312
26	13.040 132	481.605 296	.002 076	.076 686	36.932 546	.027 076
27	14.393 866	535.754 649	.001 867	.069 474	37.221 039	.026 867
28	15.888 135	595.525 404	.001 679	.062 940	37.482 398	.026 679
29	17.537 528	661.501 133	.001 512	.057 021	37.719 177	.026 512
30	19.358 150	734.325 993	.001 362	.051 658	37.933 687	.026 362
31	21.367 775	814.711 013	.001 227	.046 799	38.128 022	.026 227
32	23.586 026	903.441 034	.001 107	.042 398	38.304 081	.026 107
33	26.034 559	1001.382 375	.000 999	.038 410	38.463 581	.025 999
34	28.737 282	1109.491 289	.000 901	.034 798	38.608 080	.025 901
35	31.720 583	1228.823 303	.000 814	.031 525	38.738 989	.025 814
36	35.013 588	1360.543 518	.000 735	.028 560	38.857 586	.025 735
37	38.648 450	1505.937 989	.000 664	.025 874	38.965 030	.025 664
38	42.660 657	1666.426 280	.000 600	.023 441	39.062 368	.025 600
39	47.089 383	1843.575 325	.000 542	.021 236	39.150 552	.025 542
40	51.977 868	2039.114 724	.000 490	.019 239	39.230 442	.025 490
41	57.373 841	2254.953 633	.000 443	.017 430	39.302 818	.025 443
42	63.329 985	2493.199 404	.000 401	.015 790	39.368 388	.025 401
43	69.904 454	2756.178 156	.000 363	.014 305	39.427 790	.025 363
44	77.161 437	3046.457 494	.000 328	.012 960	39.481 606	.025 328
45	85.171 789	3366.871 568	.000 297	.011 741	39.530 361	.025 297
46	94.013 719	3720.548 753	.000 269	.010 637	39.574 530	.025 269
47	103.773 555	4110.942 190	.000 243	.009 636	39.614 545	.025 243
48	114.546 587	4541.863 497	.000 220	.008 730	39.650 797	.025 220
49	126.438 000	5017.519 991	.000 199	.007 909	39.683 639	.025 199
50	139.563 894	5542.555 761	.000 180	.007 165	39.713 393	.025 180
	$S^n = (1+i)^n$	$S_{\overline{n}|} = \dfrac{S^n - 1}{i}$	$1/S_{\overline{n}|} = \dfrac{i}{S^n - 1}$	$V^n = \dfrac{1}{S^n}$	$A_{\overline{n}|} = \dfrac{1 - 1/S^n}{i}$	$\dfrac{1}{A_{\overline{n}|}} = \dfrac{i}{1 - 1/S^n}$

	1	2	3	4	5	6
HALF YEARS	AMOUNT OF ONE	AMOUNT OF ONE PER PERIOD	SINKING FUND FACTOR	PRESENT WORTH OF ONE	PRESENT WORTH ONE PER PERIOD	PARTIAL PAYMENT
1	1.050 000	1.000 000	1.000 000	.952 381	.952 381	1.050 000
YEARS						
1	1.102 500	2.050 000	.487 805	.907 029	1.859 410	.537 805
2	1.215 506	4.310 125	.232 012	.822 702	3.545 951	.282 012
3	1.340 096	6.801 913	.147 017	.746 215	5.075 692	.197 017
4	1.477 455	9.549 109	.104 722	.676 839	6.463 213	.154 722
5	1.628 895	12.577 893	.079 505	.613 913	7.721 735	.129 505
6	1.795 856	15.917 127	.062 825	.556 837	8.863 252	.112 825
7	1.979 932	19.598 632	.051 024	.505 068	9.898 641	.101 024
8	2.182 875	23.657 492	.042 270	.458 112	10.837 770	.092 270
9	2.406 619	28.132 385	.035 546	.415 521	11.689 587	.085 546
10	2.653 298	33.065 954	.030 243	.376 889	12.462 210	.080 243
11	2.925 261	38.505 214	.025 971	.341 850	13.163 003	.075 971
12	3.225 100	44.501 999	.022 471	.310 068	13.798 642	.072 471
13	3.555 673	51.113 454	.019 564	.281 241	14.375 185	.069 564
14	3.920 129	58.402 583	.017 123	.255 094	14.898 127	.067 123
15	4.321 942	66.438 848	.015 051	.231 377	15.372 451	.065 051
16	4.764 941	75.298 829	.013 280	.209 866	15.802 677	.063 280
17	5.253 348	85.066 959	.011 755	.190 355	16.192 904	.061 755
18	5.791 816	95.836 323	.010 434	.172 657	16.546 852	.060 434
19	6.385 477	107.709 546	.009 284	.156 605	16.867 893	.059 284
20	7.039 989	120.799 774	.008 278	.142 046	17.159 086	.058 278
21	7.761 588	135.231 751	.007 395	.128 840	17.423 208	.057 395
22	8.557 150	151.143 006	.006 616	.116 861	17.662 773	.056 616
23	9.434 258	168.685 164	.005 928	.105 997	17.880 066	.055 928
24	10.401 270	188.025 393	.005 318	.096 142	18.077 158	.055 318
25	11.467 400	209.347 996	.004 777	.087 204	18.255 925	.054 777
26	12.642 808	232.856 165	.004 294	.079 096	18.418 073	.054 294
27	13.938 696	258.773 922	.003 864	.071 743	18.565 146	.053 864
28	15.367 412	287.348 249	.003 480	.065 073	18.698 545	.053 480
29	16.942 572	318.851 445	.003 136	.059 023	18.819 542	.053 136
30	18.679 186	353.583 718	.002 828	.053 536	18.929 290	.052 828
31	20.593 802	391.876 049	.002 552	.048 558	19.028 834	.052 552
32	22.704 667	434.093 344	.002 304	.044 044	19.119 124	.052 304
33	25.031 896	480.637 912	.002 081	.039 949	19.201 019	.052 081
34	27.597 665	531.953 298	.001 880	.036 235	19.275 301	.051 880
35	30.426 426	588.528 511	.001 699	.032 866	19.342 677	.051 699
36	33.545 134	650.902 683	.001 536	.029 811	19.403 788	.051 536
37	36.983 510	719.670 208	.001 390	.027 039	19.459 218	.051 390
38	40.774 320	795.486 404	.001 257	.024 525	19.509 495	.051 257
39	44.953 688	879.073 761	.001 138	.022 245	19.555 098	.051 138
40	49.561 441	971.228 821	.001 030	.020 177	19.596 460	.051 030
41	54.641 489	1072.829 776	.000 932	.018 301	19.633 978	.050 932
42	60.242 241	1184.844 828	.000 844	.016 600	19.668 007	.050 844
43	66.417 071	1308.341 422	.000 764	.015 056	19.698 873	.050 764
44	73.224 821	1444.496 418	.000 692	.013 657	19.726 869	.050 692
45	80.730 365	1594.607 301	.000 627	.012 387	19.752 262	.050 627
46	89.005 227	1760.104 549	.000 568	.011 235	19.775 294	.050 568
47	98.128 263	1942.565 266	.000 515	.010 191	19.796 185	.050 515
48	108.186 410	2143.728 205	.000 466	.009 243	19.815 134	.050 466
49	119.275 517	2365.510 346	.000 423	.008 384	19.832 321	.050 423
50	131.501 258	2610.025 157	.000 383	.007 604	19.847 910	.050 383

$$S^n = (1+i)^n \qquad S_{\overline{n}|} = \frac{S^n - 1}{i} \qquad 1/S_{\overline{n}|} = \frac{i}{S^n - 1} \qquad V^n = \frac{1}{S^n} \qquad A_{\overline{n}|} = \frac{1 - 1/S^n}{i} \qquad \frac{1}{A_{\overline{n}|}} = \frac{i}{1 - 1/S^n}$$

	1	2	3	4	5	6
YEARS	AMOUNT OF ONE	AMOUNT OF ONE PER PERIOD	SINKING FUND FACTOR	PRESENT WORTH OF ONE	PRESENT WORTH ONE PER PERIOD	PARTIAL PAYMENT
1	1.102 500	1.000 000	1.000 000	.907 029	.907 029	1.102 500
2	1.215 506	2.102 500	.475 624	.822 702	1.729 732	.578 124
3	1.340 096	3.318 006	.301 386	.746 215	2.475 947	.403 886
4	1.477 455	4.658 102	.214 680	.676 839	3.152 787	.317 180
5	1.628 895	6.135 557	.162 984	.613 913	3.766 700	.265 484
6	1.795 856	7.764 452	.128 792	.556 837	4.323 537	.231 292
7	1.979 932	9.560 308	.104 599	.505 068	4.828 605	.207 099
8	2.182 875	11.540 240	.086 653	.458 112	5.286 717	.189 153
9	2.406 619	13.723 114	.072 870	.415 521	5.702 238	.175 370
10	2.653 298	16.129 734	.061 997	.376 889	6.079 127	.164 497
11	2.925 261	18.783 031	.053 240	.341 850	6.420 977	.155 740
12	3.225 100	21.708 292	.046 065	.310 068	6.731 045	.148 565
13	3.555 673	24.933 392	.040 107	.281 241	7.012 286	.142 607
14	3.920 129	28.489 065	.035 101	.255 094	7.267 379	.137 601
15	4.321 942	32.409 194	.030 855	.231 377	7.498 757	.133 355
16	4.764 941	36.731 136	.027 225	.209 866	7.708 623	.129 725
17	5.253 348	41.496 078	.024 099	.190 355	7.898 978	.126 599
18	5.791 816	46.749 426	.021 391	.172 657	8.071 635	.123 891
19	6.385 477	52.541 242	.019 033	.156 605	8.228 240	.121 533
20	7.039 989	58.926 719	.016 970	.142 046	8.370 286	.119 470
21	7.761 588	65.966 708	.015 159	.128 840	8.499 126	.117 659
22	8.557 150	73.728 295	.013 563	.116 861	8.615 987	.116 063
23	9.434 258	82.285 446	.012 153	.105 997	8.721 984	.114 653
24	10.401 270	91.719 704	.010 903	.096 142	8.818 126	.113 403
25	11.467 400	102.120 974	.009 792	.087 204	8.905 329	.112 292
26	12.642 808	113.588 373	.008 804	.079 096	8.984 426	.111 304
27	13.938 696	126.231 182	.007 922	.071 743	9.056 169	.110 422
28	15.367 412	140.169 878	.007 134	.065 073	9.121 241	.109 634
29	16.942 572	155.537 290	.006 429	.059 023	9.180 264	.108 929
30	18.679 186	172.479 862	.005 798	.053 536	9.233 800	.108 298
31	20.593 802	191.159 048	.005 231	.048 558	9.282 358	.107 731
32	22.704 667	211.752 851	.004 722	.044 044	9.326 402	.107 222
33	25.031 896	234.457 518	.004 265	.039 949	9.366 351	.106 765
34	27.597 665	259.489 414	.003 854	.036 235	9.402 586	.106 354
35	30.426 426	287.087 078	.003 483	.032 866	9.435 452	.105 983
36	33.545 134	317.513 504	.003 149	.029 811	9.465 263	.105 649
37	36.983 510	351.058 638	.002 849	.027 039	9.492 302	.105 349
38	40.774 320	388.042 148	.002 577	.024 525	9.516 827	.105 077
39	44.953 688	428.816 469	.002 332	.022 245	9.539 072	.104 832
40	49.561 441	473.770 157	.002 111	.020 177	9.559 249	.104 611
41	54.641 489	523.331 598	.001 911	.018 301	9.577 550	.104 411
42	60.242 241	577.973 087	.001 730	.016 600	9.594 150	.104 230
43	66.417 071	638.215 328	.001 567	.015 056	9.609 206	.104 067
44	73.224 821	704.632 399	.001 419	.013 657	9.622 863	.103 919
45	80.730 365	777.857 220	.001 286	.012 387	9.635 250	.103 786
46	89.005 227	858.587 585	.001 165	.011 235	9.646 485	.103 665
47	98.128 263	947.592 813	.001 055	.010 191	9.656 676	.103 555
48	108.186 410	1045.721 076	.000 956	.009 243	9.665 919	.103 456
49	119.275 517	1153.907 486	.000 867	.008 384	9.674 303	.103 367
50	131.501 258	1273.183 003	.000 785	.007 604	9.681 907	.103 285
51	144.980 137	1404.684 261	.000 712	.006 897	9.688 805	.103 212
52	159.840 601	1549.664 398	.000 645	.006 256	9.695 061	.103 145
53	176.224 262	1709.504 999	.000 585	.005 675	9.700 736	.103 085
54	194.287 249	1885.729 261	.000 530	.005 147	9.705 883	.103 030
55	214.201 692	2080.016 510	.000 481	.004 668	9.710 551	.102 981
56	236.157 366	2294.218 203	.000 436	.004 234	9.714 786	.102 936
57	260.363 496	2530.375 569	.000 395	.003 841	9.718 626	.102 895
58	287.050 754	2790.739 064	.000 358	.003 484	9.722 110	.102 858
59	316.473 456	3077.789 818	.000 325	.003 160	9.725 270	.102 825
60	348.911 986	3394.263 275	.000 295	.002 866	9.728 136	.102 795

$S^n = (1+i)^n$	$S_{\overline{n}|} = \dfrac{S^n - 1}{i}$	$1/S_{\overline{n}|} = \dfrac{i}{S^n - 1}$	$V^n = \dfrac{1}{S^n}$	$A_{\overline{n}|} = \dfrac{1 - 1/S^n}{i}$	$\dfrac{1}{A_{\overline{n}|}} = \dfrac{i}{1 - 1/S^n}$

	1	2	3	4	5	6
YEARS	AMOUNT OF ONE	AMOUNT OF ONE PER PERIOD	SINKING FUND FACTOR	PRESENT WORTH OF ONE	PRESENT WORTH ONE PER PERIOD	PARTIAL PAYMENT
1	1.105 000	1.000 000	1.000 000	.904 977	.904 977	1.105 000
2	1.221 025	2.105 000	.475 059	.818 984	1.723 961	.580 059
3	1.349 233	3.326 025	.300 659	.741 162	2.465 123	.405 659
4	1.490 902	4.675 258	.213 892	.670 735	3.135 858	.318 892
5	1.647 447	6.166 160	.162 175	.607 000	3.742 858	.267 175
6	1.820 429	7.813 606	.127 982	.549 321	4.292 179	.232 982
7	2.011 574	9.634 035	.103 799	.497 123	4.789 303	.208 799
8	2.222 789	11.645 609	.085 869	.449 885	5.239 188	.190 869
9	2.456 182	13.868 398	.072 106	.407 136	5.646 324	.177 106
10	2.714 081	16.324 579	.061 257	.368 449	6.014 773	.166 257
11	2.999 059	19.038 660	.052 525	.333 438	6.348 211	.157 525
12	3.313 961	22.037 720	.045 377	.301 754	6.649 964	.150 377
13	3.661 926	25.351 680	.039 445	.273 080	6.923 045	.144 445
14	4.046 429	29.013 607	.034 467	.247 132	7.170 176	.139 467
15	4.471 304	33.060 035	.030 248	.223 648	7.393 825	.135 248
16	4.940 791	37.531 339	.026 644	.202 397	7.596 221	.131 644
17	5.459 574	42.472 130	.023 545	.183 164	7.779 386	.128 545
18	6.032 829	47.931 703	.020 863	.165 760	7.945 146	.125 863
19	6.666 276	53.964 532	.018 531	.150 009	8.095 154	.123 531
20	7.366 235	60.630 808	.016 493	.135 755	8.230 909	.121 493
21	8.139 690	67.997 043	.014 707	.122 855	8.353 764	.119 707
22	8.994 357	76.136 732	.013 134	.111 181	8.464 945	.118 134
23	9.938 764	85.131 089	.011 747	.100 616	8.565 561	.116 747
24	10.982 335	95.069 854	.010 519	.091 055	8.656 616	.115 519
25	12.135 480	106.052 188	.009 429	.082 403	8.739 019	.114 429
26	13.409 705	118.187 668	.008 461	.074 573	8.813 592	.113 461
27	14.817 724	131.597 373	.007 599	.067 487	8.881 079	.112 599
28	16.373 585	146.415 097	.006 830	.061 074	8.942 153	.111 830
29	18.092 812	162.788 683	.006 143	.055 271	8.997 423	.111 143
30	19.992 557	180.881 494	.005 528	.050 019	9.047 442	.110 528
31	22.091 775	200.874 051	.004 978	.045 266	9.092 707	.109 978
32	24.411 412	222.965 827	.004 485	.040 964	9.133 672	.109 485
33	26.974 610	247.377 238	.004 042	.037 072	9.170 744	.109 042
34	29.806 944	274.351 848	.003 645	.033 549	9.204 293	.108 645
35	32.936 673	304.158 792	.003 288	.030 361	9.234 654	.108 288
36	36.395 024	337.095 466	.002 967	.027 476	9.262 131	.107 967
37	40.216 501	373.490 489	.002 677	.024 865	9.286 996	.107 677
38	44.439 234	413.706 991	.002 417	.022 503	9.309 499	.107 417
39	49.105 354	458.146 225	.002 183	.020 364	9.329 863	.107 183
40	54.261 416	507.251 579	.001 971	.018 429	9.348 292	.106 971
41	59.958 864	561.512 994	.001 781	.016 678	9.364 970	.106 781
42	66.254 545	621.471 859	.001 609	.015 093	9.380 064	.106 609
43	73.211 272	687.726 404	.001 454	.013 659	9.393 723	.106 454
44	80.898 456	760.937 676	.001 314	.012 361	9.406 084	.106 314
45	89.392 794	841.836 132	.001 188	.011 187	9.417 271	.106 188
46	98.779 037	931.228 926	.001 074	.010 124	9.427 394	.106 074
47	109.150 836	1030.007 963	.000 971	.009 162	9.436 556	.105 971
48	120.611 674	1139.158 800	.000 878	.008 291	9.444 847	.105 878
49	133.275 900	1259.770 473	.000 794	.007 503	9.452 350	.105 794
50	147.269 869	1393.046 373	.000 718	.006 790	9.459 140	.105 718
51	162.733 205	1540.316 242	.000 649	.006 145	9.465 285	.105 649
52	179.820 192	1703.049 448	.000 587	.005 561	9.470 847	.105 587
53	198.701 312	1882.869 640	.000 531	.005 033	9.475 879	.105 531
54	219.564 950	2081.570 952	.000 480	.004 554	9.480 434	.105 480
55	242.619 270	2301.135 902	.000 435	.004 122	9.484 555	.105 435
56	268.094 293	2543.755 172	.000 393	.003 730	9.488 285	.105 393
57	296.244 194	2811.849 465	.000 356	.003 376	9.491 661	.105 356
58	327.349 834	3108.093 659	.000 322	.003 055	9.494 716	.105 322
59	361.721 567	3435.443 493	.000 291	.002 765	9.497 480	.105 291
60	399.702 331	3797.165 059	.000 263	.002 502	9.499 982	.105 263

$S^n = (1+i)^n$	$S_{\overline{n}|} = \dfrac{S^n - 1}{i}$	$1/S_{\overline{n}|} = \dfrac{i}{S^n - 1}$	$V^n = \dfrac{1}{S^n}$	$A_{\overline{n}|} = \dfrac{1 - 1/S^n}{i}$	$\dfrac{1}{A_{\overline{n}|}} = \dfrac{i}{1 - 1/S^n}$

	1	2	3	4	5	6
YEARS	AMOUNT OF ONE	AMOUNT OF ONE PER PERIOD	SINKING FUND FACTOR	PRESENT WORTH OF ONE	PRESENT WORTH ONE PER PERIOD	PARTIAL PAYMENT
1	1.107 500	1.000 000	1.000 000	.902 935	.902 935	1.107 500
2	1.226 556	2.107 500	.474 496	.815 291	1.718 225	.581 996
3	1.358 411	3.334 056	.299 935	.736 154	2.454 380	.407 435
4	1.504 440	4.692 467	.213 108	.664 699	3.119 079	.320 608
5	1.666 168	6.196 908	.161 371	.600 180	3.719 258	.268 871
6	1.845 281	7.863 075	.127 177	.541 923	4.261 181	.234 677
7	2.043 648	9.708 356	.103 004	.489 321	4.750 502	.210 504
8	2.263 340	11.752 004	.085 092	.441 825	5.192 327	.192 592
9	2.506 650	14.015 344	.071 350	.398 939	5.591 266	.178 850
10	2.776 114	16.521 994	.060 525	.360 216	5.951 482	.168 025
11	3.074 547	19.298 108	.051 819	.325 251	6.276 733	.159 319
12	3.405 060	22.372 655	.044 697	.293 681	6.570 414	.152 197
13	3.771 104	25.777 715	.038 793	.265 174	6.835 588	.146 293
14	4.176 498	29.548 820	.033 842	.239 435	7.075 023	.141 342
15	4.625 472	33.725 318	.029 651	.216 194	7.291 217	.137 151
16	5.122 710	38.350 789	.026 075	.195 209	7.486 426	.133 575
17	5.673 401	43.473 499	.023 003	.176 261	7.662 687	.130 503
18	6.283 292	49.146 900	.020 347	.159 152	7.821 840	.127 847
19	6.958 746	55.430 192	.018 041	.143 704	7.965 544	.125 541
20	7.706 811	62.388 938	.016 028	.129 755	8.095 299	.123 528
21	8.535 293	70.095 749	.014 266	.117 161	8.212 460	.121 766
22	9.452 837	78.631 042	.012 718	.105 788	8.318 248	.120 218
23	10.469 017	88.083 879	.011 353	.095 520	8.413 768	.118 853
24	11.594 436	98.552 895	.010 147	.086 248	8.500 016	.117 647
25	12.840 838	110.147 332	.009 079	.077 877	8.577 893	.116 579
26	14.221 228	122.988 170	.008 131	.070 317	8.648 210	.115 631
27	15.750 010	137.209 398	.007 288	.063 492	8.711 702	.114 788
28	17.443 136	152.959 408	.006 538	.057 329	8.769 031	.114 038
29	19.318 274	170.402 545	.005 868	.051 764	8.820 796	.113 368
30	21.394 988	189.720 818	.005 271	.046 740	8.867 536	.112 771
31	23.694 949	211.115 806	.004 737	.042 203	8.909 739	.112 237
32	26.242 156	234.810 756	.004 259	.038 107	8.947 845	.111 759
33	29.063 188	261.052 912	.003 831	.034 408	8.982 253	.111 331
34	32.187 481	290.116 100	.003 447	.031 068	9.013 321	.110 947
35	35.647 635	322.303 581	.003 103	.028 052	9.041 373	.110 603
36	39.479 756	357.951 215	.002 794	.025 329	9.066 703	.110 294
37	43.723 829	397.430 971	.002 516	.022 871	9.089 574	.110 016
38	48.424 141	441.154 801	.002 267	.020 651	9.110 225	.109 767
39	53.629 736	489.578 942	.002 043	.018 646	9.128 871	.109 543
40	59.394 933	543.208 678	.001 841	.016 836	9.145 707	.109 341
41	65.779 888	602.603 611	.001 659	.015 202	9.160 910	.109 159
42	72.851 226	668.383 499	.001 496	.013 727	9.174 636	.108 996
43	80.682 733	741.234 725	.001 349	.012 394	9.187 030	.108 849
44	89.356 127	821.917 458	.001 217	.011 191	9.198 222	.108 717
45	98.961 910	911.273 585	.001 097	.010 105	9.208 327	.108 597
46	109.600 316	1010.235 495	.000 990	.009 124	9.217 451	.108 490
47	121.382 350	1119.835 811	.000 893	.008 238	9.225 689	.108 393
48	134.430 952	1241.218 160	.000 806	.007 439	9.233 128	.108 306
49	148.882 280	1375.649 113	.000 727	.006 717	9.239 845	.108 227
50	164.887 125	1524.531 392	.000 656	.006 065	9.245 909	.108 156
51	182.612 491	1689.418 517	.000 592	.005 476	9.251 385	.108 092
52	202.243 333	1872.031 007	.000 534	.004 945	9.256 330	.108 034
53	223.984 492	2074.274 341	.000 482	.004 465	9.260 794	.107 982
54	248.062 824	2298.258 832	.000 435	.004 031	9.264 826	.107 935
55	274.729 578	2546.321 657	.000 393	.003 640	9.268 466	.107 893
56	304.263 008	2821.051 235	.000 354	.003 287	9.271 752	.107 854
57	336.971 281	3125.314 243	.000 320	.002 968	9.274 720	.107 820
58	373.195 694	3462.285 524	.000 289	.002 680	9.277 399	.107 789
59	413.314 231	3835.481 218	.000 261	.002 419	9.279 819	.107 761
60	457.745 511	4248.795 449	.000 235	.002 185	9.282 004	.107 735
	$S^n = (1 + i)^n$	$S_{\overline{n}|} = \dfrac{S^n - 1}{i}$	$1/S_{\overline{n}|} = \dfrac{i}{S^n - 1}$	$V^n = \dfrac{1}{S^n}$	$A_{\overline{n}|} = \dfrac{1 - 1/S^n}{i}$	$\dfrac{1}{A_{\overline{n}|}} = \dfrac{i}{1 - 1/S^n}$

	1	2	3	4	5	6
YEARS	AMOUNT OF ONE	AMOUNT OF ONE PER PERIOD	SINKING FUND FACTOR	PRESENT WORTH OF ONE	PRESENT WORTH ONE PER PERIOD	PARTIAL PAYMENT
1	1.110 000	1.000 000	1.000 000	.900 901	.900 901	1.110 000
2	1.232 100	2.110 000	.473 934	.811 622	1.712 523	.583 934
3	1.367 631	3.342 100	.299 213	.731 191	2.443 715	.409 213
4	1.518 070	4.709 731	.212 326	.658 731	3.102 446	.322 326
5	1.685 058	6.227 801	.160 570	.593 451	3.695 897	.270 570
6	1.870 415	7.912 860	.126 377	.534 641	4.230 538	.236 377
7	2.076 160	9.783 274	.102 215	.481 658	4.712 196	.212 215
8	2.304 538	11.859 434	.084 321	.433 926	5.146 123	.194 321
9	2.558 037	14.163 972	.070 602	.390 925	5.537 048	.180 602
10	2.839 421	16.722 009	.059 801	.352 184	5.889 232	.169 801
11	3.151 757	19.561 430	.051 121	.317 283	6.206 515	.161 121
12	3.498 451	22.713 187	.044 027	.285 841	6.492 356	.154 027
13	3.883 280	26.211 638	.038 151	.257 514	6.749 870	.148 151
14	4.310 441	30.094 918	.033 228	.231 995	6.981 865	.143 228
15	4.784 589	34.405 359	.029 065	.209 004	7.190 870	.139 065
16	5.310 894	39.189 948	.025 517	.188 292	7.379 162	.135 517
17	5.895 093	44.500 843	.022 471	.169 633	7.548 794	.132 471
18	6.543 553	50.395 936	.019 843	.152 822	7.701 617	.129 843
19	7.263 344	56.939 488	.017 563	.137 678	7.839 294	.127 563
20	8.062 312	64.202 832	.015 576	.124 034	7.963 328	.125 576
21	8.949 166	72.265 144	.013 838	.111 742	8.075 070	.123 838
22	9.933 574	81.214 309	.012 313	.100 669	8.175 739	.122 313
23	11.026 267	91.147 884	.010 971	.090 693	8.266 432	.120 971
24	12.239 157	102.174 151	.009 787	.081 705	8.348 137	.119 787
25	13.585 464	114.413 307	.008 740	.073 608	8.421 745	.118 740
26	15.079 865	127.998 771	.007 813	.066 314	8.488 058	.117 813
27	16.738 650	143.078 636	.006 989	.059 742	8.547 800	.116 989
28	18.579 901	159.817 286	.006 257	.053 822	8.601 622	.116 257
29	20.623 691	178.397 187	.005 605	.048 488	8.650 110	.115 605
30	22.892 297	199.020 878	.005 025	.043 683	8.693 793	.115 025
31	25.410 449	221.913 174	.004 506	.039 354	8.733 146	.114 506
32	28.205 599	247.323 624	.004 043	.035 454	8.768 600	.114 043
33	31.308 214	275.529 222	.003 629	.031 940	8.800 541	.113 629
34	34.752 118	306.837 437	.003 259	.028 775	8.829 316	.113 259
35	38.574 851	341.589 555	.002 927	.025 924	8.855 240	.112 927
36	42.818 085	380.164 406	.002 630	.023 355	8.878 594	.112 630
37	47.528 074	422.982 490	.002 364	.021 040	8.899 635	.112 364
38	52.756 162	470.510 564	.002 125	.018 955	8.918 590	.112 125
39	58.559 340	523.266 726	.001 911	.017 077	8.935 666	.111 911
40	65.000 867	581.826 066	.001 719	.015 384	8.951 051	.111 719
41	72.150 963	646.826 934	.001 546	.013 860	8.964 911	.111 546
42	80.087 569	718.977 896	.001 391	.012 486	8.977 397	.111 391
43	88.897 201	799.065 465	.001 251	.011 249	8.988 646	.111 251
44	98.675 893	887.962 666	.001 126	.010 134	8.998 780	.111 126
45	109.530 242	986.638 559	.001 014	.009 130	9.007 910	.111 014
46	121.578 568	1096.168 801	.000 912	.008 225	9.016 135	.110 912
47	134.952 211	1217.747 369	.000 821	.007 410	9.023 545	.110 821
48	149.796 954	1352.699 580	.000 739	.006 676	9.030 221	.110 739
49	166.274 619	1502.496 533	.000 666	.006 014	9.036 235	.110 666
50	184.564 827	1668.771 152	.000 599	.005 418	9.041 653	.110 599
51	204.866 958	1853.335 979	.000 540	.004 881	9.046 534	.110 540
52	227.402 323	2058.202 937	.000 486	.004 397	9.050 932	.110 486
53	252.416 579	2285.605 260	.000 438	.003 962	9.054 894	.110 438
54	280.182 402	2538.021 838	.000 394	.003 569	9.058 463	.110 394
55	311.002 466	2818.204 240	.000 355	.003 215	9.061 678	.110 355
56	345.212 738	3129.206 707	.000 320	.002 897	9.064 575	.110 320
57	383.186 139	3474.419 445	.000 288	.002 610	9.067 185	.110 288
58	425.336 614	3857.605 583	.000 259	.002 351	9.069 536	.110 259
59	472.123 642	4282.942 198	.000 233	.002 118	9.071 654	.110 233
60	524.057 242	4755.065 839	.000 210	.001 908	9.073 562	.110 210

$$S^n = (1 + i)^n \qquad S_{\overline{n}|} = \frac{S^n - 1}{i} \qquad 1/S_{\overline{n}|} = \frac{i}{S^n - 1} \qquad V^n = \frac{1}{S^n} \qquad A_{\overline{n}|} = \frac{1 - 1/S^n}{i} \qquad \frac{1}{A_{\overline{n}|}} = \frac{i}{1 - 1/S^n}$$

	1	2	3	4	5	6
YEARS	AMOUNT OF ONE	AMOUNT OF ONE PER PERIOD	SINKING FUND FACTOR	PRESENT WORTH OF ONE	PRESENT WORTH ONE PER PERIOD	PARTIAL PAYMENT
1	1.112 500	1.000 000	1.000 000	.898 876	.898 876	1.112 500
2	1.237 656	2.112 500	.473 373	.807 979	1.706 855	.585 873
3	1.376 893	3.350 156	.298 494	.726 273	2.433 128	.410 994
4	1.531 793	4.727 049	.211 548	.652 830	3.085 958	.324 048
5	1.704 120	6.258 842	.159 774	.586 813	3.672 771	.272 274
6	1.895 833	7.962 962	.125 581	.527 473	4.200 244	.238 081
7	2.109 114	9.858 795	.101 432	.474 133	4.674 376	.213 932
8	2.346 390	11.967 909	.083 557	.426 187	5.100 563	.196 057
9	2.610 359	14.314 299	.069 860	.383 089	5.483 652	.182 360
10	2.904 024	16.924 657	.059 085	.344 350	5.828 002	.171 585
11	3.230 727	19.828 681	.050 432	.309 528	6.137 530	.162 932
12	3.594 183	23.059 408	.043 366	.278 227	6.415 757	.155 866
13	3.998 529	26.653 592	.037 518	.250 092	6.665 849	.150 018
14	4.448 364	30.652 121	.032 624	.224 802	6.890 651	.145 124
15	4.948 804	35.100 484	.028 490	.202 069	7.092 720	.140 990
16	5.505 545	40.049 289	.024 969	.181 635	7.274 355	.137 469
17	6.124 919	45.554 834	.021 952	.163 267	7.437 622	.134 452
18	6.813 972	51.679 752	.019 350	.146 757	7.584 380	.131 850
19	7.580 544	58.493 725	.017 096	.131 917	7.716 296	.129 596
20	8.433 355	66.074 269	.015 134	.118 577	7.834 873	.127 634
21	9.382 108	74.507 624	.013 421	.106 586	7.941 459	.125 921
22	10.437 595	83.889 731	.011 920	.095 808	8.037 267	.124 420
23	11.611 824	94.327 326	.010 601	.086 119	8.123 386	.123 101
24	12.918 154	105.939 150	.009 439	.077 410	8.200 796	.121 939
25	14.371 447	118.857 305	.008 413	.069 582	8.270 379	.120 913
26	15.988 235	133.228 752	.007 506	.062 546	8.332 925	.120 006
27	17.786 911	149.216 986	.006 702	.056 221	8.389 146	.119 202
28	19.787 938	167.003 897	.005 988	.050 536	8.439 681	.118 488
29	22.014 081	186.791 836	.005 354	.045 425	8.485 107	.117 854
30	24.490 666	208.805 917	.004 789	.040 832	8.525 939	.117 289
31	27.245 866	233.296 583	.004 286	.036 703	8.562 642	.116 786
32	30.311 025	260.542 448	.003 838	.032 991	8.595 633	.116 338
33	33.721 016	290.853 474	.003 438	.029 655	8.625 288	.115 938
34	37.514 630	324.574 489	.003 081	.026 656	8.651 944	.115 581
35	41.735 026	362.089 120	.002 762	.023 961	8.675 905	.115 262
36	46.430 216	403.824 145	.002 476	.021 538	8.697 443	.114 976
37	51.653 616	450.254 362	.002 221	.019 360	8.716 802	.114 721
38	57.464 647	501.907 978	.001 992	.017 402	8.734 204	.114 492
39	63.929 420	559.372 625	.001 788	.015 642	8.749 847	.114 288
40	71.121 480	623.302 045	.001 604	.014 060	8.763 907	.114 104
41	79.122 647	694.423 525	.001 440	.012 639	8.776 546	.113 940
42	88.023 944	773.546 172	.001 293	.011 361	8.787 906	.113 793
43	97.926 638	861.570 116	.001 161	.010 212	8.798 118	.113 661
44	108.943 385	959.496 755	.001 042	.009 179	8.807 297	.113 542
45	121.199 516	1068.440 139	.000 936	.008 251	8.815 548	.113 436
46	134.834 461	1189.639 655	.000 841	.007 417	8.822 964	.113 341
47	150.003 338	1324.474 116	.000 755	.006 667	8.829 631	.113 255
48	166.878 714	1474.477 454	.000 678	.005 992	8.835 623	.113 178
49	185.652 569	1641.356 168	.000 609	.005 386	8.841 010	.113 109
50	206.538 483	1827.008 737	.000 547	.004 842	8.845 851	.113 047
51	229.774 062	2033.547 220	.000 492	.004 352	8.850 204	.112 992
52	255.623 644	2263.321 282	.000 442	.003 912	8.854 116	.112 942
53	284.381 304	2518.944 926	.000 397	.003 516	8.857 632	.112 897
54	316.374 201	2803.326 230	.000 357	.003 161	8.860 793	.112 857
55	351.966 299	3119.700 431	.000 321	.002 841	8.863 634	.112 821
56	391.562 507	3471.666 730	.000 288	.002 554	8.866 188	.112 788
57	435.613 289	3863.229 237	.000 259	.002 296	8.868 483	.112 759
58	484.619 784	4298.842 526	.000 233	.002 063	8.870 547	.112 733
59	539.139 510	4783.462 310	.000 209	.001 855	8.872 402	.112 709
60	599.792 705	5322.601 820	.000 188	.001 667	8.874 069	.112 688

$S^n = (1+i)^n$	$S_{\overline{n}} = \dfrac{S^n - 1}{i}$	$1/S_{\overline{n}} = \dfrac{i}{S^n - 1}$	$V^n = \dfrac{1}{S^n}$	$A_{\overline{n}} = \dfrac{1 - 1/S^n}{i}$	$\dfrac{1}{A_{\overline{n}}} = \dfrac{i}{1 - 1/S^n}$

	1	2	3	4	5	6
YEARS	AMOUNT OF ONE	AMOUNT OF ONE PER PERIOD	SINKING FUND FACTOR	PRESENT WORTH OF ONE	PRESENT WORTH ONE PER PERIOD	PARTIAL PAYMENT
1	1.115 000	1.000 000	1.000 000	.896 861	.896 861	1.115 000
2	1.243 225	2.115 000	.472 813	.804 360	1.701 221	.587 813
3	1.386 196	3.358 225	.297 776	.721 399	2.422 619	.412 776
4	1.545 608	4.744 421	.210 774	.646 994	3.069 614	.325 774
5	1.723 353	6.290 029	.158 982	.580 264	3.649 878	.273 982
6	1.921 539	8.013 383	.124 791	.520 416	4.170 294	.239 791
7	2.142 516	9.934 922	.100 655	.466 741	4.637 035	.215 655
8	2.388 905	12.077 438	.082 799	.418 602	5.055 637	.197 799
9	2.663 629	14.466 343	.069 126	.375 428	5.431 064	.184 126
10	2.969 947	17.129 972	.058 377	.336 706	5.767 771	.173 377
11	3.311 491	20.099 919	.049 751	.301 979	6.069 750	.164 751
12	3.692 312	23.411 410	.042 714	.270 833	6.340 583	.157 714
13	4.116 928	27.103 722	.036 895	.242 900	6.583 482	.151 895
14	4.590 375	31.220 650	.032 030	.217 847	6.801 329	.147 030
15	5.118 268	35.811 025	.027 924	.195 379	6.996 708	.142 924
16	5.706 869	40.929 293	.024 432	.175 227	7.171 935	.139 432
17	6.363 159	46.636 161	.021 443	.157 155	7.329 090	.136 443
18	7.094 922	52.999 320	.018 868	.140 946	7.470 036	.133 868
19	7.910 838	60.094 242	.016 641	.126 409	7.596 445	.131 641
20	8.820 584	68.005 080	.014 705	.113 371	7.709 816	.129 705
21	9.834 951	76.825 664	.013 016	.101 678	7.811 494	.128 016
22	10.965 971	86.660 615	.011 539	.091 191	7.902 685	.126 539
23	12.227 057	97.626 586	.010 243	.081 786	7.984 471	.125 243
24	13.633 169	109.853 643	.009 103	.073 351	8.057 822	.124 103
25	15.200 983	123.486 812	.008 098	.065 785	8.123 607	.123 098
26	16.949 096	138.687 796	.007 210	.059 000	8.182 607	.122 210
27	18.898 243	155.636 892	.006 425	.052 915	8.235 522	.121 425
28	21.071 540	174.535 135	.005 730	.047 457	8.282 979	.120 730
29	23.494 768	195.606 675	.005 112	.042 563	8.325 542	.120 112
30	26.196 666	219.101 443	.004 564	.038 173	8.363 715	.119 564
31	29.209 282	245.298 109	.004 077	.034 236	8.397 951	.119 077
32	32.568 350	274.507 391	.003 643	.030 705	8.428 655	.118 643
33	36.313 710	307.075 741	.003 257	.027 538	8.456 193	.118 257
34	40.489 787	343.389 451	.002 912	.024 698	8.480 891	.117 912
35	45.146 112	383.879 238	.002 605	.022 150	8.503 041	.117 605
36	50.337 915	429.025 351	.002 331	.019 866	8.522 907	.117 331
37	56.126 776	479.363 266	.002 086	.017 817	8.540 723	.117 086
38	62.581 355	535.490 042	.001 867	.015 979	8.556 703	.116 867
39	69.778 211	598.071 396	.001 672	.014 331	8.571 034	.116 672
40	77.802 705	667.849 607	.001 497	.012 853	8.583 887	.116 497
41	86.750 016	745.652 312	.001 341	.011 527	8.595 414	.116 341
42	96.726 268	832.402 327	.001 201	.010 338	8.605 753	.116 201
43	107.849 788	929.128 595	.001 076	.009 272	8.615 025	.116 076
44	120.252 514	1036.978 384	.000 964	.008 316	8.623 341	.115 964
45	134.081 553	1157.230 898	.000 864	.007 458	8.630 799	.115 864
46	149.500 932	1291.312 451	.000 774	.006 689	8.637 488	.115 774
47	166.693 539	1440.813 383	.000 694	.005 999	8.643 487	.115 694
48	185.863 296	1607.506 922	.000 622	.005 380	8.648 867	.115 622
49	207.237 575	1793.370 218	.000 558	.004 825	8.653 692	.115 558
50	231.069 896	2000.607 793	.000 500	.004 328	8.658 020	.115 500
51	257.642 934	2231.677 689	.000 448	.003 881	8.661 901	.115 448
52	287.271 872	2489.320 623	.000 402	.003 481	8.665 382	.115 402
53	320.308 137	2776.592 495	.000 360	.003 122	8.668 504	.115 360
54	357.143 573	3096.900 632	.000 323	.002 800	8.671 304	.115 323
55	398.215 084	3454.044 205	.000 290	.002 511	8.673 816	.115 290
56	444.009 818	3852.259 288	.000 260	.002 252	8.676 068	.115 260
57	495.070 947	4296.269 106	.000 233	.002 020	8.678 088	.115 233
58	552.004 106	4791.340 053	.000 209	.001 812	8.679 899	.115 209
59	615.484 578	5343.344 159	.000 187	.001 625	8.681 524	.115 187
60	686.265 305	5958.828 738	.000 168	.001 457	8.682 981	.115 168

$S^n = (1+i)^n$	$S_{\overline{n}|} = \dfrac{S^n - 1}{i}$	$1/S_{\overline{n}|} = \dfrac{i}{S^n - 1}$	$V^n = \dfrac{1}{S^n}$	$A_{\overline{n}|} = \dfrac{1 - 1/S^n}{i}$	$\dfrac{1}{A_{\overline{n}|}} = \dfrac{i}{1 - 1/S^n}$

585

	1	2	3	4	5	6
YEARS	AMOUNT OF ONE	AMOUNT OF ONE PER PERIOD	SINKING FUND FACTOR	PRESENT WORTH OF ONE	PRESENT WORTH ONE PER PERIOD	PARTIAL PAYMENT
1	1.117 500	1.000 000	1.000 000	.894 855	.894 855	1.117 500
2	1.248 806	2.117 500	.472 255	.800 765	1.695 619	.589 755
3	1.395 541	3.366 306	.297 062	.716 568	2.412 187	.414 562
4	1.559 517	4.761 847	.210 003	.641 224	3.053 411	.327 503
5	1.742 760	6.321 364	.158 194	.573 802	3.627 214	.275 694
6	1.947 535	8.064 125	.124 006	.513 470	4.140 684	.241 506
7	2.176 370	10.011 659	.099 884	.459 481	4.600 164	.217 384
8	2.432 093	12.188 029	.082 048	.411 168	5.011 333	.199 548
9	2.717 864	14.620 123	.068 399	.367 936	5.379 269	.185 899
10	3.037 213	17.337 987	.057 677	.329 249	5.708 518	.175 177
11	3.394 086	20.375 200	.049 079	.294 630	6.003 148	.166 579
12	3.792 891	23.769 287	.042 071	.263 651	6.266 799	.159 571
13	4.238 556	27.562 178	.036 282	.235 929	6.502 728	.153 782
14	4.736 586	31.800 734	.031 446	.211 123	6.713 851	.148 946
15	5.293 135	36.537 320	.027 369	.188 924	6.902 775	.144 869
16	5.915 078	41.830 455	.023 906	.169 059	7.071 834	.141 406
17	6.610 100	47.745 533	.020 944	.151 284	7.223 118	.138 444
18	7.386 787	54.355 634	.018 397	.135 377	7.358 495	.135 897
19	8.254 734	61.742 420	.016 196	.121 143	7.479 637	.133 696
20	9.224 666	69.997 155	.014 286	.108 405	7.588 042	.131 786
21	10.308 564	79.221 821	.012 623	.097 007	7.685 049	.130 123
22	11.519 820	89.530 384	.011 169	.086 807	7.771 856	.128 669
23	12.873 399	101.050 205	.009 896	.077 680	7.849 536	.127 396
24	14.386 023	113.923 604	.008 778	.069 512	7.919 048	.126 278
25	16.076 381	128.309 627	.007 794	.062 203	7.981 251	.125 294
26	17.965 356	144.386 008	.006 926	.055 663	8.036 913	.124 426
27	20.076 285	162.351 364	.006 159	.049 810	8.086 723	.123 659
28	22.435 249	182.427 650	.005 482	.044 573	8.131 296	.122 982
29	25.071 391	204.862 898	.004 881	.039 886	8.171 182	.122 381
30	28.017 279	229.934 289	.004 349	.035 692	8.206 874	.121 849
31	31.309 309	257.951 568	.003 877	.031 939	8.238 814	.121 377
32	34.988 153	289.260 877	.003 457	.028 581	8.267 395	.120 957
33	39.099 261	324.249 030	.003 084	.025 576	8.292 971	.120 584
34	43.693 424	363.348 291	.002 752	.022 887	8.315 858	.120 252
35	48.827 402	407.041 715	.002 457	.020 480	8.336 338	.119 957
36	54.564 621	455.869 117	.002 194	.018 327	8.354 665	.119 694
37	60.975 964	510.433 738	.001 959	.016 400	8.371 065	.119 459
38	68.140 640	571.409 702	.001 750	.014 676	8.385 740	.119 250
39	76.147 165	639.550 343	.001 564	.013 132	8.398 873	.119 064
40	85.094 457	715.697 508	.001 397	.011 752	8.410 624	.118 897
41	95.093 056	800.791 965	.001 249	.010 516	8.421 140	.118 749
42	106.266 490	895.885 021	.001 116	.009 410	8.430 551	.118 616
43	118.752 803	1002.151 511	.000 998	.008 421	8.438 971	.118 498
44	132.706 257	1120.904 313	.000 892	.007 535	8.446 507	.118 392
45	148.299 242	1253.610 570	.000 798	.006 743	8.453 250	.118 298
46	165.724 403	1401.909 812	.000 713	.006 034	8.459 284	.118 213
47	185.197 020	1567.634 215	.000 638	.005 400	8.464 684	.118 138
48	206.957 670	1752.831 235	.000 571	.004 832	8.469 516	.118 071
49	231.275 196	1959.788 905	.000 510	.004 324	8.473 840	.118 010
50	258.450 032	2191.064 102	.000 456	.003 869	8.477 709	.117 956
51	288.817 911	2449.514 134	.000 408	.003 462	8.481 171	.117 908
52	322.754 015	2738.332 044	.000 365	.003 098	8.484 269	.117 865
53	360.677 612	3061.086 060	.000 327	.002 773	8.487 042	.117 827
54	403.057 231	3421.763 672	.000 292	.002 481	8.489 523	.117 792
55	450.416 456	3824.820 903	.000 261	.002 220	8.491 743	.117 761
56	503.340 390	4275.237 359	.000 234	.001 987	8.493 730	.117 734
57	562.482 885	4778.577 749	.000 209	.001 778	8.495 508	.117 709
58	628.574 625	5341.060 634	.000 187	.001 591	8.497 099	.117 687
59	702.432 143	5969.635 259	.000 168	.001 424	8.498 522	.117 668
60	784.967 920	6672.067 402	.000 150	.001 274	8.499 796	.117 650
	$S^n = (1+i)^n$	$S_{\overline{n}|} = \dfrac{S^n - 1}{i}$	$1/S_{\overline{n}|} = \dfrac{i}{S^n - 1}$	$V^n = \dfrac{1}{S^n}$	$A_{\overline{n}|} = \dfrac{1 - 1/S^n}{i}$	$\dfrac{1}{A_{\overline{n}|}} = \dfrac{i}{1 - 1/S^n}$

	1	2	3	4	5	6
YEARS	AMOUNT OF ONE	AMOUNT OF ONE PER PERIOD	SINKING FUND FACTOR	PRESENT WORTH OF ONE	PRESENT WORTH ONE PER PERIOD	PARTIAL PAYMENT
1	1.120 000	1.000 000	1.000 000	.892 857	.892 857	1.120 000
2	1.254 400	2.120 000	.471 698	.797 194	1.690 051	.591 698
3	1.404 928	3.374 400	.296 349	.711 780	2.401 831	.416 349
4	1.573 519	4.779 328	.209 234	.635 518	3.037 349	.329 234
5	1.762 342	6.352 847	.157 410	.567 427	3.604 776	.277 410
6	1.973 823	8.115 189	.123 226	.506 631	4.111 407	.243 226
7	2.210 681	10.089 012	.099 118	.452 349	4.563 757	.219 118
8	2.475 963	12.299 693	.081 303	.403 883	4.967 640	.201 303
9	2.773 079	14.775 656	.067 679	.360 610	5.328 250	.187 679
10	3.105 848	17.548 735	.056 984	.321 973	5.650 223	.176 984
11	3.478 550	20.654 583	.048 415	.287 476	5.937 699	.168 415
12	3.895 976	24.133 133	.041 437	.256 675	6.194 374	.161 437
13	4.363 493	28.029 109	.035 677	.229 174	6.423 548	.155 677
14	4.887 112	32.392 602	.030 871	.204 620	6.628 168	.150 871
15	5.473 566	37.279 715	.026 824	.182 696	6.810 864	.146 824
16	6.130 394	42.753 280	.023 390	.163 122	6.973 986	.143 390
17	6.866 041	48.883 674	.020 457	.145 644	7.119 630	.140 457
18	7.689 966	55.749 715	.017 937	.130 040	7.249 670	.137 937
19	8.612 762	63.439 681	.015 763	.116 107	7.365 777	.135 763
20	9.646 293	72.052 442	.013 879	.103 667	7.469 444	.133 879
21	10.803 848	81.698 736	.012 240	.092 560	7.562 003	.132 240
22	12.100 310	92.502 584	.010 811	.082 643	7.644 646	.130 811
23	13.552 347	104.602 894	.009 560	.073 788	7.718 434	.129 560
24	15.178 629	118.155 241	.008 463	.065 882	7.784 316	.128 463
25	17.000 064	133.333 870	.007 500	.058 823	7.843 139	.127 500
26	19.040 072	150.333 934	.006 652	.052 521	7.895 660	.126 652
27	21.324 881	169.374 007	.005 904	.046 894	7.942 554	.125 904
28	23.883 866	190.698 887	.005 244	.041 869	7.984 423	.125 244
29	26.749 930	214.582 754	.004 660	.037 383	8.021 806	.124 660
30	29.959 922	241.332 684	.004 144	.033 378	8.055 184	.124 144
31	33.555 113	271.292 606	.003 686	.029 802	8.084 986	.123 686
32	37.581 726	304.847 719	.003 280	.026 609	8.111 594	.123 280
33	42.091 533	342.429 446	.002 920	.023 758	8.135 352	.122 920
34	47.142 517	384.520 979	.002 601	.021 212	8.156 564	.122 601
35	52.799 620	431.663 496	.002 317	.018 940	8.175 504	.122 317
36	59.135 574	484.463 116	.002 064	.016 910	8.192 414	.122 064
37	66.231 843	543.598 690	.001 840	.015 098	8.207 513	.121 840
38	74.179 664	609.830 533	.001 640	.013 481	8.220 993	.121 640
39	83.081 224	684.010 197	.001 462	.012 036	8.233 030	.121 462
40	93.050 970	767.091 420	.001 304	.010 747	8.243 777	.121 304
41	104.217 087	860.142 391	.001 163	.009 595	8.253 372	.121 163
42	116.723 137	964.359 478	.001 037	.008 567	8.261 939	.121 037
43	130.729 914	1081.082 615	.000 925	.007 649	8.269 589	.120 925
44	146.417 503	1211.812 529	.000 825	.006 830	8.276 418	.120 825
45	163.987 604	1358.230 032	.000 736	.006 098	8.282 516	.120 736
46	183.666 116	1522.217 636	.000 657	.005 445	8.287 961	.120 657
47	205.706 050	1705.883 752	.000 586	.004 861	8.292 822	.120 586
48	230.390 776	1911.589 803	.000 523	.004 340	8.297 163	.120 523
49	258.037 669	2141.980 579	.000 467	.003 875	8.301 038	.120 467
50	289.002 190	2400.018 249	.000 417	.003 460	8.304 498	.120 417
51	323.682 453	2689.020 438	.000 372	.003 089	8.307 588	.120 372
52	362.524 347	3012.702 891	.000 332	.002 758	8.310 346	.120 332
53	406.027 269	3375.227 238	.000 296	.002 463	8.312 809	.120 296
54	454.750 541	3781.254 506	.000 264	.002 199	8.315 008	.120 264
55	509.320 606	4236.005 047	.000 236	.001 963	8.316 972	.120 236
56	570.439 078	4745.325 653	.000 211	.001 753	8.318 725	.120 211
57	638.891 768	5315.764 731	.000 188	.001 565	8.320 290	.120 188
58	715.558 780	5954.656 499	.000 168	.001 398	8.321 687	.120 168
59	801.425 833	6670.215 279	.000 150	.001 248	8.322 935	.120 150
60	897.596 933	7471.641 112	.000 134	.001 114	8.324 049	.120 134

$S^n = (1 + i)^n$	$S_{\overline{n}} = \dfrac{S^n - 1}{i}$	$1/S_{\overline{n}} = \dfrac{i}{S^n - 1}$	$V^n = \dfrac{1}{S^n}$	$A_{\overline{n}} = \dfrac{1 - 1/S^n}{i}$	$\dfrac{1}{A_{\overline{n}}} = \dfrac{i}{1 - 1/S^n}$

	1	2	3	4	5	6
YEARS	AMOUNT OF ONE	AMOUNT OF ONE PER PERIOD	SINKING FUND FACTOR	PRESENT WORTH OF ONE	PRESENT WORTH ONE PER PERIOD	PARTIAL PAYMENT
1	1.122 500	1.000 000	1.000 000	.890 869	.890 869	1.122 500
2	1.260 006	2.122 500	.471 143	.793 647	1.684 515	.593 643
3	1.414 357	3.382 506	.295 639	.707 035	2.391 551	.418 139
4	1.587 616	4.796 863	.208 470	.629 875	3.021 426	.330 970
5	1.782 099	6.384 479	.156 630	.561 136	3.582 562	.279 130
6	2.000 406	8.166 578	.122 450	.499 899	4.082 461	.244 950
7	2.245 455	10.166 983	.098 358	.445 344	4.527 805	.220 858
8	2.520 524	12.412 439	.080 564	.396 743	4.924 547	.203 064
9	2.829 288	14.932 963	.066 966	.353 446	5.277 993	.189 466
10	3.175 876	17.762 251	.056 299	.314 867	5.592 867	.178 799
11	3.564 920	20.938 126	.047 760	.280 511	5.873 378	.170 260
12	4.001 623	24.503 047	.040 811	.249 899	6.123 277	.163 311
13	4.491 822	28.504 670	.035 082	.222 627	6.345 904	.157 582
14	5.042 070	32.996 492	.030 306	.198 331	6.544 235	.152 806
15	5.659 724	38.038 562	.026 289	.176 687	6.720 922	.148 789
16	6.353 040	43.698 286	.022 884	.157 405	6.878 327	.145 384
17	7.131 287	50.051 326	.019 979	.140 227	7.018 554	.142 479
18	8.004 870	57.182 614	.017 488	.124 924	7.143 478	.139 988
19	8.985 467	65.187 484	.015 340	.111 291	7.254 769	.137 840
20	10.086 186	74.172 951	.013 482	.099 145	7.353 914	.135 982
21	11.321 744	84.259 137	.011 868	.088 326	7.442 240	.134 368
22	12.708 658	95.580 882	.010 462	.078 687	7.520 926	.132 962
23	14.265 469	108.289 540	.009 235	.070 099	7.591 026	.131 735
24	16.012 989	122.555 008	.008 160	.062 449	7.653 475	.130 660
25	17.974 580	138.567 997	.007 217	.055 634	7.709 109	.129 717
26	20.176 466	156.542 576	.006 388	.049 563	7.758 672	.128 888
27	22.648 083	176.719 042	.005 659	.044 154	7.802 826	.128 159
28	25.422 473	199.367 125	.005 016	.039 335	7.842 161	.127 516
29	28.536 726	224.789 597	.004 449	.035 043	7.877 204	.126 949
30	32.032 475	253.326 323	.003 947	.031 218	7.908 422	.126 447
31	35.956 453	285.358 798	.003 504	.027 811	7.936 233	.126 004
32	40.361 118	321.315 250	.003 112	.024 776	7.961 010	.125 612
33	45.305 355	361.676 369	.002 765	.022 072	7.983 082	.125 265
34	50.855 261	406.981 724	.002 457	.019 664	8.002 746	.124 957
35	57.085 031	457.836 985	.002 184	.017 518	8.020 263	.124 684
36	64.077 947	514.922 016	.001 942	.015 606	8.035 869	.124 442
37	71.927 495	578.999 963	.001 727	.013 903	8.049 772	.124 227
38	80.738 614	650.927 458	.001 536	.012 386	8.062 158	.124 036
39	90.629 094	731.666 072	.001 367	.011 034	8.073 192	.123 867
40	101.731 158	822.295 165	.001 216	.009 830	8.083 022	.123 716
41	114.193 225	924.026 323	.001 082	.008 757	8.091 779	.123 582
42	128.181 895	1038.219 548	.000 963	.007 801	8.099 580	.123 463
43	143.884 177	1166.401 442	.000 857	.006 950	8.106 530	.123 357
44	161.509 988	1310.285 619	.000 763	.006 192	8.112 722	.123 263
45	181.294 962	1471.795 607	.000 679	.005 516	8.118 238	.123 179
46	203.503 595	1653.090 569	.000 605	.004 914	8.123 152	.123 105
47	228.432 785	1856.594 164	.000 539	.004 378	8.127 529	.123 039
48	256.415 801	2085.026 949	.000 480	.003 900	8.131 429	.122 980
49	287.826 737	2341.442 750	.000 427	.003 474	8.134 904	.122 927
50	323.085 512	2629.269 487	.000 380	.003 095	8.137 999	.122 880
51	362.663 487	2952.354 999	.000 339	.002 757	8.140 756	.122 839
52	407.089 765	3315.018 487	.000 302	.002 456	8.143 213	.122 802
53	456.958 261	3722.108 251	.000 269	.002 188	8.145 401	.122 769
54	512.935 648	4179.066 512	.000 239	.001 950	8.147 351	.122 739
55	575.770 265	4692.002 160	.000 213	.001 737	8.149 087	.122 713
56	646.302 122	5267.772 424	.000 190	.001 547	8.150 635	.122 690
57	725.474 132	5914.074 546	.000 169	.001 378	8.152 013	.122 669
58	814.344 713	6639.548 678	.000 151	.001 228	8.153 241	.122 651
59	914.101 940	7453.893 391	.000 134	.001 094	8.154 335	.122 634
60	1026.079 428	8367.995 332	.000 120	.000 975	8.155 310	.122 620
	$S^n = (1+i)^n$	$S_{\overline{n}|} = \dfrac{S^n - 1}{i}$	$1/S_{\overline{n}|} = \dfrac{i}{S^n - 1}$	$V^n = \dfrac{1}{S^n}$	$A_{\overline{n}|} = \dfrac{1 - 1/S^n}{i}$	$\dfrac{1}{A_{\overline{n}|}} = \dfrac{i}{1 - 1/S^n}$

	1	2	3	4	5	6
YEARS	AMOUNT OF ONE	AMOUNT OF ONE PER PERIOD	SINKING FUND FACTOR	PRESENT WORTH OF ONE	PRESENT WORTH ONE PER PERIOD	PARTIAL PAYMENT
1	1.125 000	1.000 000	1.000 000	.888 889	.888 889	1.125 000
2	1.265 625	2.125 000	.470 588	.790 123	1.679 012	.595 588
3	1.423 828	3.390 625	.294 931	.702 332	2.381 344	.419 931
4	1.601 807	4.814 453	.207 708	.624 295	3.005 639	.332 708
5	1.802 032	6.416 260	.155 854	.554 929	3.560 568	.280 854
6	2.027 287	8.218 292	.121 680	.493 270	4.053 839	.246 680
7	2.280 697	10.245 579	.097 603	.438 462	4.492 301	.222 603
8	2.565 785	12.526 276	.079 832	.389 744	4.882 045	.204 832
9	2.886 508	15.092 061	.066 260	.346 439	5.228 485	.191 260
10	3.247 321	17.978 568	.055 622	.307 946	5.536 431	.180 622
11	3.653 236	21.225 889	.047 112	.273 730	5.810 161	.172 112
12	4.109 891	24.879 125	.040 194	.243 315	6.053 476	.165 194
13	4.623 627	28.989 016	.034 496	.216 280	6.269 757	.159 496
14	5.201 580	33.612 643	.029 751	.192 249	6.462 006	.154 751
15	5.851 778	38.814 223	.025 764	.170 888	6.632 894	.150 764
16	6.583 250	44.666 001	.022 388	.151 901	6.784 795	.147 388
17	7.406 156	51.249 252	.019 512	.135 023	6.919 818	.144 512
18	8.331 926	58.655 408	.017 049	.120 020	7.039 838	.142 049
19	9.373 417	66.987 334	.014 928	.106 685	7.146 523	.139 928
20	10.545 094	76.360 751	.013 096	.094 831	7.241 353	.138 096
21	11.863 231	86.905 845	.011 507	.084 294	7.325 647	.136 507
22	13.346 134	98.769 075	.010 125	.074 928	7.400 575	.135 125
23	15.014 401	112.115 210	.008 919	.066 603	7.467 178	.133 919
24	16.891 201	127.129 611	.007 866	.059 202	7.526 381	.132 866
25	19.002 602	144.020 812	.006 943	.052 624	7.579 005	.131 943
26	21.377 927	163.023 414	.006 134	.046 777	7.625 782	.131 134
27	24.050 168	184.401 340	.005 423	.041 580	7.667 362	.130 423
28	27.056 438	208.451 508	.004 797	.036 960	7.704 322	.129 797
29	30.438 493	235.507 946	.004 246	.032 853	7.737 175	.129 246
30	34.243 305	265.946 440	.003 760	.029 203	7.766 378	.128 760
31	38.523 718	300.189 745	.003 331	.025 958	7.792 336	.128 331
32	43.339 183	338.713 463	.002 952	.023 074	7.815 410	.127 952
33	48.756 581	382.052 645	.002 617	.020 510	7.835 920	.127 617
34	54.851 153	430.809 226	.002 321	.018 231	7.854 151	.127 321
35	61.707 547	485.660 379	.002 059	.016 205	7.870 356	.127 059
36	69.420 991	547.367 927	.001 827	.014 405	7.884 761	.126 827
37	78.098 615	616.788 918	.001 621	.012 804	7.897 565	.126 621
38	87.860 942	694.887 532	.001 439	.011 382	7.908 947	.126 439
39	98.843 559	782.748 474	.001 278	.010 117	7.919 064	.126 278
40	111.199 004	881.592 033	.001 134	.008 993	7.928 057	.126 134
41	125.098 880	992.791 037	.001 007	.007 994	7.936 051	.126 007
42	140.736 240	1117.889 917	.000 895	.007 105	7.943 156	.125 895
43	158.328 270	1258.626 157	.000 795	.006 316	7.949 472	.125 795
44	178.119 303	1416.954 426	.000 706	.005 614	7.955 086	.125 706
45	200.384 216	1595.073 729	.000 627	.004 990	7.960 077	.125 627
46	225.432 243	1795.457 946	.000 557	.004 436	7.964 513	.125 557
47	253.611 274	2020.890 189	.000 495	.003 943	7.968 456	.125 495
48	285.312 683	2274.501 462	.000 440	.003 505	7.971 961	.125 440
49	320.976 768	2559.814 145	.000 391	.003 115	7.975 076	.125 391
50	361.098 864	2880.790 913	.000 347	.002 769	7.977 845	.125 347
51	406.236 222	3241.889 778	.000 308	.002 462	7.980 307	.125 308
52	457.015 750	3648.126 000	.000 274	.002 188	7.982 495	.125 274
53	514.142 719	4105.141 750	.000 244	.001 945	7.984 440	.125 244
54	578.410 559	4619.284 468	.000 216	.001 729	7.986 169	.125 216
55	650.711 878	5197.695 027	.000 192	.001 537	7.987 706	.125 192
56	732.050 863	5848.406 905	.000 171	.001 366	7.989 072	.125 171
57	823.557 221	6580.457 769	.000 152	.001 214	7.990 286	.125 152
58	926.501 874	7404.014 990	.000 135	.001 079	7.991 365	.125 135
59	1042.314 608	8330.516 863	.000 120	.000 959	7.992 325	.125 120
60	1172.603 934	9372.831 471	.000 107	.000 853	7.993 178	.125 107

| $S^n = (1+i)^n$ | $S_{\overline{n}|} = \dfrac{S^n - 1}{i}$ | $1/S_{\overline{n}|} = \dfrac{i}{S^n - 1}$ | $V^n = \dfrac{1}{S^n}$ | $A_{\overline{n}|} = \dfrac{1 - 1/S^n}{i}$ | $\dfrac{1}{A_{\overline{n}|}} = \dfrac{i}{1 - 1/S^n}$ |

	1	2	3	4	5	6
YEARS	AMOUNT OF ONE	AMOUNT OF ONE PER PERIOD	SINKING FUND FACTOR	PRESENT WORTH OF ONE	PRESENT WORTH ONE PER PERIOD	PARTIAL PAYMENT
1	1.127 500	1.000 000	1.000 000	.886 918	.886 918	1.127 500
2	1.271 256	2.127 500	.470 035	.786 623	1.673 541	.597 535
3	1.433 341	3.398 756	.294 225	.697 670	2.371 212	.421 725
4	1.616 092	4.832 098	.206 949	.618 776	2.989 988	.334 449
5	1.822 144	6.448 190	.155 082	.548 804	3.538 792	.282 582
6	2.054 468	8.270 334	.120 914	.486 744	4.025 536	.248 414
7	2.316 412	10.324 802	.096 854	.431 702	4.457 239	.224 354
8	2.611 755	12.641 214	.079 106	.382 884	4.840 123	.206 606
9	2.944 754	15.252 969	.065 561	.339 587	5.179 710	.193 061
10	3.320 210	18.197 723	.054 952	.301 186	5.480 896	.182 452
11	3.743 536	21.517 932	.046 473	.267 127	5.748 023	.173 973
12	4.220 837	25.261 469	.039 586	.236 920	5.984 943	.167 086
13	4.758 994	29.482 306	.033 919	.210 128	6.195 071	.161 419
14	5.365 766	34.241 300	.029 204	.186 367	6.381 438	.156 704
15	6.049 901	39.607 066	.025 248	.165 292	6.546 730	.152 748
16	6.821 263	45.656 966	.021 902	.146 600	6.693 330	.149 402
17	7.690 974	52.478 230	.019 056	.130 023	6.823 353	.146 556
18	8.671 574	60.169 204	.016 620	.115 319	6.938 672	.144 120
19	9.777 199	68.840 777	.014 526	.102 279	7.040 951	.142 026
20	11.023 792	78.617 977	.012 720	.090 713	7.131 664	.140 220
21	12.429 326	89.641 769	.011 156	.080 455	7.212 119	.138 656
22	14.014 065	102.071 094	.009 797	.071 357	7.283 475	.137 297
23	15.800 858	116.085 159	.008 614	.063 288	7.346 763	.136 114
24	17.815 467	131.886 016	.007 582	.056 131	7.402 894	.135 082
25	20.086 939	149.701 483	.006 680	.049 784	7.452 678	.134 180
26	22.648 024	169.788 423	.005 890	.044 154	7.496 832	.133 390
27	25.535 647	192.436 446	.005 197	.039 161	7.535 993	.132 697
28	28.791 442	217.972 093	.004 588	.034 733	7.570 725	.132 088
29	32.462 351	246.763 535	.004 052	.030 805	7.601 530	.131 552
30	36.601 300	279.225 886	.003 581	.027 321	7.628 852	.131 081
31	41.267 966	315.827 187	.003 166	.024 232	7.653 083	.130 666
32	46.529 632	357.095 153	.002 800	.021 492	7.674 575	.130 300
33	52.462 160	403.624 785	.002 478	.019 061	7.693 636	.129 978
34	59.151 085	456.086 945	.002 193	.016 906	7.710 542	.129 693
35	66.692 849	515.238 030	.001 941	.014 994	7.725 536	.129 441
36	75.196 187	581.930 879	.001 718	.013 299	7.738 835	.129 218
37	84.783 701	657.127 066	.001 522	.011 795	7.750 630	.129 022
38	95.593 623	741.910 767	.001 348	.010 461	7.761 091	.128 848
39	107.781 810	837.504 390	.001 194	.009 278	7.770 369	.128 694
40	121.523 990	945.286 200	.001 058	.008 229	7.778 597	.128 558
41	137.018 299	1066.810 190	.000 937	.007 298	7.785 896	.128 437
42	154.488 132	1203.828 490	.000 831	.006 473	7.792 369	.128 331
43	174.185 369	1358.316 622	.000 736	.005 741	7.798 110	.128 236
44	196.394 004	1532.501 991	.000 653	.005 092	7.803 202	.128 153
45	221.434 239	1728.895 995	.000 578	.004 516	7.807 718	.128 078
46	249.667 105	1950.330 235	.000 513	.004 005	7.811 723	.128 013
47	281.499 661	2199.997 339	.000 455	.003 552	7.815 275	.127 955
48	317.390 868	2481.497 000	.000 403	.003 151	7.818 426	.127 903
49	357.858 203	2798.887 868	.000 357	.002 794	7.821 220	.127 857
50	403.485 124	3156.746 071	.000 317	.002 478	7.823 699	.127 817
51	454.929 477	3560.231 195	.000 281	.002 198	7.825 897	.127 781
52	512.932 986	4015.160 672	.000 249	.001 950	7.827 846	.127 749
53	578.331 941	4528.093 658	.000 221	.001 729	7.829 576	.127 721
54	652.069 264	5106.425 599	.000 196	.001 534	7.831 109	.127 696
55	735.208 095	5758.494 863	.000 174	.001 360	7.832 469	.127 674
56	828.947 127	6493.702 959	.000 154	.001 206	7.833 676	.127 654
57	934.637 886	7322.650 086	.000 137	.001 070	7.834 746	.127 637
58	1053.804 216	8257.287 972	.000 121	.000 949	7.835 695	.127 621
59	1188.164 254	9311.092 188	.000 107	.000 842	7.836 536	.127 607
60	1339.655 196	10499.256 442	.000 095	.000 746	7.837 283	.127 595
	$S^n = (1+i)^n$	$S_{\overline{n}|} = \dfrac{S^n - 1}{i}$	$1/S_{\overline{n}|} = \dfrac{i}{S^n - 1}$	$V^n = \dfrac{1}{S^n}$	$A_{\overline{n}|} = \dfrac{1 - 1/S^n}{i}$	$\dfrac{1}{A_{\overline{n}|}} = \dfrac{i}{1 - 1/S^n}$

	1	2	3	4	5	6
YEARS	AMOUNT OF ONE	AMOUNT OF ONE PER PERIOD	SINKING FUND FACTOR	PRESENT WORTH OF ONE	PRESENT WORTH ONE PER PERIOD	PARTIAL PAYMENT
1	1.130 000	1.000 000	1.000 000	.884 956	.884 956	1.130 000
2	1.276 900	2.130 000	.469 484	.783 147	1.668 102	.599 484
3	1.442 897	3.406 900	.293 522	.693 050	2.361 153	.423 522
4	1.630 474	4.849 797	.206 194	.613 319	2.974 471	.336 194
5	1.842 435	6.480 271	.154 315	.542 760	3.517 231	.284 315
6	2.081 952	8.322 706	.120 153	.480 319	3.997 550	.250 153
7	2.352 605	10.404 658	.096 111	.425 061	4.422 610	.226 111
8	2.658 444	12.757 263	.078 387	.376 160	4.798 770	.208 387
9	3.004 042	15.415 707	.064 869	.332 885	5.131 655	.194 869
10	3.394 567	18.419 749	.054 290	.294 588	5.426 243	.184 290
11	3.835 861	21.814 317	.045 841	.260 698	5.686 941	.175 841
12	4.334 523	25.650 178	.038 986	.230 706	5.917 647	.168 986
13	4.898 011	29.984 701	.033 350	.204 165	6.121 812	.163 350
14	5.534 753	34.882 712	.028 667	.180 677	6.302 488	.158 667
15	6.254 270	40.417 464	.024 742	.159 891	6.462 379	.154 742
16	7.067 326	46.671 735	.021 426	.141 496	6.603 875	.151 426
17	7.986 078	53.739 060	.018 608	.125 218	6.729 093	.148 608
18	9.024 268	61.725 138	.016 201	.110 812	6.839 905	.146 201
19	10.197 423	70.749 406	.014 134	.098 064	6.937 969	.144 134
20	11.523 088	80.946 829	.012 354	.086 782	7.024 752	.142 354
21	13.021 089	92.469 917	.010 814	.076 798	7.101 550	.140 814
22	14.713 831	105.491 006	.009 479	.067 963	7.169 513	.139 479
23	16.626 629	120.204 837	.008 319	.060 144	7.229 658	.138 319
24	18.788 091	136.831 465	.007 308	.053 225	7.282 883	.137 308
25	21.230 542	155.619 556	.006 426	.047 102	7.329 985	.136 426
26	23.990 513	176.850 098	.005 655	.041 683	7.371 668	.135 655
27	27.109 279	200.840 611	.004 979	.036 888	7.408 556	.134 979
28	30.633 486	227.949 890	.004 387	.032 644	7.441 200	.134 387
29	34.615 839	258.583 376	.003 867	.028 889	7.470 088	.133 867
30	39.115 898	293.199 215	.003 411	.025 565	7.495 653	.133 411
31	44.200 965	332.315 113	.003 009	.022 624	7.518 277	.133 009
32	49.947 090	376.516 078	.002 656	.020 021	7.538 299	.132 656
33	56.440 212	426.463 168	.002 345	.017 718	7.556 016	.132 345
34	63.777 439	482.903 380	.002 071	.015 680	7.571 696	.132 071
35	72.068 506	546.680 819	.001 829	.013 876	7.585 572	.131 829
36	81.437 412	618.749 325	.001 616	.012 279	7.597 851	.131 616
37	92.024 276	700.186 738	.001 428	.010 867	7.608 718	.131 428
38	103.987 432	792.211 014	.001 262	.009 617	7.618 334	.131 262
39	117.505 798	896.198 445	.001 116	.008 510	7.626 844	.131 116
40	132.781 552	1013.704 243	.000 986	.007 531	7.634 376	.130 986
41	150.043 153	1146.485 795	.000 872	.006 665	7.641 040	.130 872
42	169.548 763	1296.528 948	.000 771	.005 898	7.646 938	.130 771
43	191.590 103	1466.077 712	.000 682	.005 219	7.652 158	.130 682
44	216.496 816	1657.667 814	.000 603	.004 619	7.656 777	.130 603
45	244.641 402	1874.164 630	.000 534	.004 088	7.660 864	.130 534
46	276.444 784	2118.806 032	.000 472	.003 617	7.664 482	.130 472
47	312.382 606	2395.250 816	.000 417	.003 201	7.667 683	.130 417
48	352.992 345	2707.633 422	.000 369	.002 833	7.670 516	.130 369
49	398.881 350	3060.625 767	.000 327	.002 507	7.673 023	.130 327
50	450.735 925	3459.507 117	.000 289	.002 219	7.675 242	.130 289
51	509.331 595	3910.243 042	.000 256	.001 963	7.677 205	.130 256
52	575.544 703	4419.574 637	.000 226	.001 737	7.678 942	.130 226
53	650.365 514	4995.119 340	.000 200	.001 538	7.680 480	.130 200
54	734.913 031	5645.484 854	.000 177	.001 361	7.681 841	.130 177
55	830.451 725	6380.397 885	.000 157	.001 204	7.683 045	.130 157
56	938.410 449	7210.849 610	.000 139	.001 066	7.684 111	.130 139
57	1060.403 808	8149.260 060	.000 123	.000 943	7.685 054	.130 123
58	1198.256 303	9209.663 867	.000 109	.000 835	7.685 888	.130 109
59	1354.029 622	10407.920 170	.000 096	.000 739	7.686 627	.130 096
60	1530.053 473	11761.949 792	.000 085	.000 654	7.687 280	.130 085

$S^n = (1 + i)^n$	$S_{\overline{n}|} = \dfrac{S^n - 1}{i}$	$1/S_{\overline{n}|} = \dfrac{i}{S^n - 1}$	$V^n = \dfrac{1}{S^n}$	$A_{\overline{n}|} = \dfrac{1 - 1/S^n}{i}$	$\dfrac{1}{A_{\overline{n}|}} = \dfrac{i}{1 - 1/S^n}$

	1	2	3	4	5	6
YEARS	AMOUNT OF ONE	AMOUNT OF ONE PER PERIOD	SINKING FUND FACTOR	PRESENT WORTH OF ONE	PRESENT WORTH ONE PER PERIOD	PARTIAL PAYMENT
1	1.140 000	1.000 000	1.000 000	.877 193	.877 193	1.140 000
2	1.299 600	2.140 000	.467 290	.769 468	1.646 661	.607 290
3	1.481 544	3.439 600	.290 731	.674 972	2.321 632	.430 731
4	1.688 960	4.921 144	.203 205	.592 080	2.913 712	.343 205
5	1.925 415	6.610 104	.151 284	.519 369	3.433 081	.291 284
6	2.194 973	8.535 519	.117 157	.455 587	3.888 668	.257 157
7	2.502 269	10.730 491	.093 192	.399 637	4.288 305	.233 192
8	2.852 586	13.232 760	.075 570	.350 559	4.638 864	.215 570
9	3.251 949	16.085 347	.062 168	.307 508	4.946 372	.202 168
10	3.707 221	19.337 295	.051 714	.269 744	5.216 116	.191 714
11	4.226 232	23.044 516	.043 394	.236 617	5.452 733	.183 394
12	4.817 905	27.270 749	.036 669	.207 559	5.660 292	.176 669
13	5.492 411	32.088 654	.031 164	.182 069	5.842 362	.171 164
14	6.261 349	37.581 065	.026 609	.159 710	6.002 072	.166 609
15	7.137 938	43.842 414	.022 809	.140 096	6.142 168	.162 809
16	8.137 249	50.980 352	.019 615	.122 892	6.265 060	.159 615
17	9.276 464	59.117 601	.016 915	.107 800	6.372 859	.156 915
18	10.575 169	68.394 066	.014 621	.094 561	6.467 420	.154 621
19	12.055 693	78.969 235	.012 663	.082 948	6.550 369	.152 663
20	13.743 490	91.024 928	.010 986	.072 762	6.623 131	.150 986
21	15.667 578	104.768 418	.009 545	.063 826	6.686 957	.149 545
22	17.861 039	120.435 996	.008 303	.055 988	6.742 944	.148 303
23	20.361 585	138.297 035	.007 231	.049 112	6.792 056	.147 231
24	23.212 207	158.658 620	.006 303	.043 081	6.835 137	.146 303
25	26.461 916	181.870 827	.005 498	.037 790	6.872 927	.145 498
26	30.166 584	208.332 743	.004 800	.033 149	6.906 077	.144 800
27	34.389 906	238.499 327	.004 193	.029 078	6.935 155	.144 193
28	39.204 493	272.889 233	.003 664	.025 507	6.960 662	.143 664
29	44.693 122	312.093 725	.003 204	.022 375	6.983 037	.143 204
30	50.950 159	356.786 847	.002 803	.019 627	7.002 664	.142 803
31	58.083 181	407.737 006	.002 453	.017 217	7.019 881	.142 453
32	66.214 826	465.820 186	.002 147	.015 102	7.034 983	.142 147
33	75.484 902	532.035 012	.001 880	.013 248	7.048 231	.141 880
34	86.052 788	607.519 914	.001 646	.011 621	7.059 852	.141 646
35	98.100 178	693.572 702	.001 442	.010 194	7.070 045	.141 442
36	111.834 203	791.672 881	.001 263	.008 942	7.078 987	.141 263
37	127.490 992	903.507 084	.001 107	.007 844	7.086 831	.141 107
38	145.339 731	1030.998 076	.000 970	.006 880	7.093 711	.140 970
39	165.687 293	1176.337 806	.000 850	.006 035	7.099 747	.140 850
40	188.883 514	1342.025 099	.000 745	.005 294	7.105 041	.140 745
41	215.327 206	1530.908 613	.000 653	.004 644	7.109 685	.140 653
42	245.473 015	1746.235 819	.000 573	.004 074	7.113 759	.140 573
43	279.839 237	1991.708 833	.000 502	.003 573	7.117 332	.140 502
44	319.016 730	2271.548 070	.000 440	.003 135	7.120 467	.140 440
45	363.679 072	2590.564 800	.000 386	.002 750	7.123 217	.140 386
46	414.594 142	2954.243 872	.000 338	.002 412	7.125 629	.140 338
47	472.637 322	3368.838 014	.000 297	.002 116	7.127 744	.140 297
48	538.806 547	3841.475 336	.000 260	.001 856	7.129 600	.140 260
49	614.239 464	4380.281 883	.000 228	.001 628	7.131 228	.140 228
50	700.232 988	4994.521 346	.000 200	.001 428	7.132 656	.140 200
51	798.265 607	5694.754 335	.000 176	.001 253	7.133 909	.140 176
52	910.022 792	6493.019 941	.000 154	.001 099	7.135 008	.140 154
53	1037.425 983	7403.042 733	.000 135	.000 964	7.135 972	.140 135
54	1182.665 620	8440.468 716	.000 118	.000 846	7.136 818	.140 118
55	1348.238 807	9623.134 336	.000 104	.000 742	7.137 559	.140 104
56	1536.992 240	10971.373 143	.000 091	.000 651	7.138 210	.140 091
57	1752.171 154	12508.365 383	.000 080	.000 571	7.138 781	.140 080
58	1997.475 115	14260.536 537	.000 070	.000 501	7.139 281	.140 070
59	2277.121 631	16258.011 652	.000 062	.000 439	7.139 720	.140 062
60	2595.918 660	18535.133 283	.000 054	.000 385	7.140 106	.140 054

$S^n = (1+i)^n$	$S_{\overline{n}} = \dfrac{S^n - 1}{i}$	$1/S_{\overline{n}} = \dfrac{i}{S^n - 1}$	$V^n = \dfrac{1}{S^n}$	$A_{\overline{n}} = \dfrac{1 - 1/S^n}{i}$	$\dfrac{1}{A_{\overline{n}}} = \dfrac{i}{1 - 1/S^n}$

	1	2	3	4	5	6
YEARS	AMOUNT OF ONE	AMOUNT OF ONE PER PERIOD	SINKING FUND FACTOR	PRESENT WORTH OF ONE	PRESENT WORTH ONE PER PERIOD	PARTIAL PAYMENT
1	1.150 000	1.000 000	1.000 000	.869 565	.869 565	1.150 000
2	1.322 500	2.150 000	.465 116	.756 144	1.625 709	.615 116
3	1.520 875	3.472 500	.287 977	.657 516	2.283 225	.437 977
4	1.749 006	4.993 375	.200 265	.571 753	2.854 978	.350 265
5	2.011 357	6.742 381	.148 316	.497 177	3.352 155	.298 316
6	2.313 061	8.753 738	.114 237	.432 328	3.784 483	.264 237
7	2.660 020	11.066 799	.090 360	.375 937	4.160 420	.240 360
8	3.059 023	13.726 819	.072 850	.326 902	4.487 322	.222 850
9	3.517 876	16.785 842	.059 574	.284 262	4.771 584	.209 574
10	4.045 558	20.303 718	.049 252	.247 185	5.018 769	.199 252
11	4.652 391	24.349 276	.041 069	.214 943	5.233 712	.191 069
12	5.350 250	29.001 667	.034 481	.186 907	5.420 619	.184 481
13	6.152 788	34.351 917	.029 110	.162 528	5.583 147	.179 110
14	7.075 706	40.504 705	.024 688	.141 329	5.724 476	.174 688
15	8.137 062	47.580 411	.021 017	.122 894	5.847 370	.171 017
16	9.357 621	55.717 472	.017 948	.106 865	5.954 235	.167 948
17	10.761 264	65.075 093	.015 367	.092 926	6.047 161	.165 367
18	12.375 454	75.836 357	.013 186	.080 805	6.127 966	.163 186
19	14.231 772	88.211 811	.011 336	.070 265	6.198 231	.161 336
20	16.366 537	102.443 583	.009 761	.061 100	6.259 331	.159 761
21	18.821 518	118.810 120	.008 417	.053 131	6.312 462	.158 417
22	21.644 746	137.631 638	.007 266	.046 201	6.358 663	.157 266
23	24.891 458	159.276 384	.006 278	.040 174	6.398 837	.156 278
24	28.625 176	184.167 841	.005 430	.034 934	6.433 771	.155 430
25	32.918 953	212.793 017	.004 699	.030 378	6.464 149	.154 699
26	37.856 796	245.711 970	.004 070	.026 415	6.490 564	.154 070
27	43.535 315	283.568 766	.003 526	.022 970	6.513 534	.153 526
28	50.065 612	327.104 080	.003 057	.019 974	6.533 508	.153 057
29	57.575 454	377.169 693	.002 651	.017 369	6.550 877	.152 651
30	66.211 772	434.745 146	.002 300	.015 103	6.565 980	.152 300
31	76.143 538	500.956 918	.001 996	.013 133	6.579 113	.151 996
32	87.565 068	577.100 456	.001 733	.011 420	6.590 533	.151 733
33	100.699 829	664.665 524	.001 505	.009 931	6.600 463	.151 505
34	115.804 803	765.365 353	.001 307	.008 635	6.609 099	.151 307
35	133.175 523	881.170 156	.001 135	.007 509	6.616 607	.151 135
36	153.151 852	1014.345 680	.000 986	.006 529	6.623 137	.150 986
37	176.124 630	1167.497 532	.000 857	.005 678	6.628 815	.150 857
38	202.543 324	1343.622 161	.000 744	.004 937	6.633 752	.150 744
39	232.924 823	1546.165 485	.000 647	.004 293	6.638 045	.150 647
40	267.863 546	1779.090 308	.000 562	.003 733	6.641 778	.150 562
41	308.043 078	2046.953 854	.000 489	.003 246	6.645 025	.150 489
42	354.249 540	2354.996 933	.000 425	.002 823	6.647 848	.150 425
43	407.386 971	2709.246 473	.000 369	.002 455	6.650 302	.150 369
44	468.495 017	3116.633 443	.000 321	.002 134	6.652 437	.150 321
45	538.769 269	3585.128 460	.000 279	.001 856	6.654 293	.150 279
46	619.584 659	4123.897 729	.000 242	.001 614	6.655 907	.150 242
47	712.522 358	4743.482 388	.000 211	.001 403	6.657 310	.150 211
48	819.400 712	5456.004 746	.000 183	.001 220	6.658 531	.150 183
49	942.310 819	6275.405 458	.000 159	.001 061	6.659 592	.150 159
50	1083.657 442	7217.716 277	.000 139	.000 923	6.660 515	.150 139
51	1246.206 058	8301.373 719	.000 120	.000 802	6.661 317	.150 120
52	1433.136 966	9547.579 777	.000 105	.000 698	6.662 015	.150 105
53	1648.107 511	10980.716 743	.000 091	.000 607	6.662 622	.150 091
54	1895.323 638	12628.824 255	.000 079	.000 528	6.663 149	.150 079
55	2179.622 184	14524.147 893	.000 069	.000 459	6.663 608	.150 069
56	2506.565 512	16703.770 077	.000 060	.000 399	6.664 007	.150 060
57	2882.550 338	19210.335 588	.000 052	.000 347	6.664 354	.150 052
58	3314.932 889	22092.885 926	.000 045	.000 302	6.664 656	.150 045
59	3812.172 822	25407.818 815	.000 039	.000 262	6.664 918	.150 039
60	4383.998 746	29219.991 638	.000 034	.000 228	6.665 146	.150 034
	$S^n = (1+i)^n$	$S_{\overline{n}|} = \dfrac{S^n - 1}{i}$	$1/S_{\overline{n}|} = \dfrac{i}{S^n - 1}$	$V^n = \dfrac{1}{S^n}$	$A_{\overline{n}|} = \dfrac{1 - 1/S^n}{i}$	$\dfrac{1}{A_{\overline{n}|}} = \dfrac{i}{1 - 1/S^n}$

	1	2	3	4	5	6
YEARS	AMOUNT OF ONE	AMOUNT OF ONE PER PERIOD	SINKING FUND FACTOR	PRESENT WORTH OF ONE	PRESENT WORTH ONE PER PERIOD	PARTIAL PAYMENT
1	1.160 000	1.000 000	1.000 000	.862 069	.862 069	1.160 000
2	1.345 600	2.160 000	.462 963	.743 163	1.605 232	.622 963
3	1.560 896	3.505 600	.285 258	.640 658	2.245 890	.445 258
4	1.810 639	5.066 496	.197 375	.552 291	2.798 181	.357 375
5	2.100 342	6.877 135	.145 409	.476 113	3.274 294	.305 409
6	2.436 396	8.977 477	.111 390	.410 442	3.684 736	.271 390
7	2.826 220	11.413 873	.087 613	.353 830	4.038 565	.247 613
8	3.278 415	14.240 093	.070 224	.305 025	4.343 591	.230 224
9	3.802 961	17.518 508	.057 082	.262 953	4.606 544	.217 082
10	4.411 435	21.321 469	.046 901	.226 684	4.833 227	.206 901
11	5.117 265	25.732 904	.038 861	.195 417	5.028 644	.198 861
12	5.936 027	30.850 169	.032 415	.168 463	5.197 107	.192 415
13	6.885 791	36.786 196	.027 184	.145 227	5.342 334	.187 184
14	7.987 518	43.671 987	.022 898	.125 195	5.467 529	.182 898
15	9.265 521	51.659 505	.019 358	.107 927	5.575 456	.179 358
16	10.748 004	60.925 026	.016 414	.093 041	5.668 497	.176 414
17	12.467 685	71.673 030	.013 952	.080 207	5.748 704	.173 952
18	14.462 514	84.140 715	.011 885	.069 144	5.817 848	.171 885
19	16.776 517	98.603 230	.010 142	.059 607	5.877 455	.170 142
20	19.460 759	115.379 747	.008 667	.051 385	5.928 841	.168 667
21	22.574 481	134.840 506	.007 416	.044 298	5.973 139	.167 416
22	26.186 398	157.414 987	.006 353	.038 188	6.011 326	.166 353
23	30.376 222	183.601 385	.005 447	.032 920	6.044 247	.165 447
24	35.236 417	213.977 607	.004 673	.028 380	6.072 627	.164 673
25	40.874 244	249.214 024	.004 013	.024 465	6.097 092	.164 013
26	47.414 123	290.088 267	.003 447	.021 091	6.118 183	.163 447
27	55.000 382	337.502 390	.002 963	.018 182	6.136 364	.162 963
28	63.800 444	392.502 773	.002 548	.015 674	6.152 038	.162 548
29	74.008 515	456.303 216	.002 192	.013 512	6.165 550	.162 192
30	85.849 877	530.311 731	.001 886	.011 648	6.177 198	.161 886
31	99.585 857	616.161 608	.001 623	.010 042	6.187 240	.161 623
32	115.519 594	715.747 465	.001 397	.008 657	6.195 897	.161 397
33	134.002 729	831.267 059	.001 203	.007 463	6.203 359	.161 203
34	155.443 166	965.269 789	.001 036	.006 433	6.209 792	.161 036
35	180.314 073	1120.712 955	.000 892	.005 546	6.215 338	.160 892
36	209.164 324	1301.027 028	.000 769	.004 781	6.220 119	.160 769
37	242.630 616	1510.191 352	.000 662	.004 121	6.224 241	.160 662
38	281.451 515	1752.821 968	.000 571	.003 553	6.227 794	.160 571
39	326.483 757	2034.273 483	.000 492	.003 063	6.230 857	.160 492
40	378.721 158	2360.757 241	.000 424	.002 640	6.233 497	.160 424
41	439.316 544	2739.478 399	.000 365	.002 276	6.235 773	.160 365
42	509.607 191	3178.794 943	.000 315	.001 962	6.237 736	.160 315
43	591.144 341	3688.402 134	.000 271	.001 692	6.239 427	.160 271
44	685.727 436	4279.546 475	.000 234	.001 458	6.240 886	.160 234
45	795.443 826	4965.273 911	.000 201	.001 257	6.242 143	.160 201
46	922.714 838	5760.717 737	.000 174	.001 084	6.243 227	.160 174
47	1070.349 212	6683.432 575	.000 150	.000 934	6.244 161	.160 150
48	1241.605 086	7753.781 787	.000 129	.000 805	6.244 966	.160 129
49	1440.261 900	8995.386 873	.000 111	.000 694	6.245 661	.160 111
50	1670.703 804	10435.648 773	.000 096	.000 599	6.246 259	.160 096
51	1938.016 412	12106.352 576	.000 083	.000 516	6.246 775	.160 083
52	2248.099 038	14044.368 988	.000 071	.000 445	6.247 220	.160 071
53	2607.794 884	16292.468 026	.000 061	.000 383	6.247 603	.160 061
54	3025.042 066	18900.262 911	.000 053	.000 331	6.247 934	.160 053
55	3509.048 796	21925.304 976	.000 046	.000 285	6.248 219	.160 046
56	4070.496 604	25434.353 773	.000 039	.000 246	6.248 465	.160 039
57	4721.776 060	29504.850 376	.000 034	.000 212	6.248 676	.160 034
58	5477.260 230	34226.626 436	.000 029	.000 183	6.248 859	.160 029
59	6353.621 867	39703.886 666	.000 025	.000 157	6.249 016	.160 025
60	7370.201 365	46057.508 533	.000 022	.000 136	6.249 152	.160 022

$S^n = (1 + i)^n$	$S_{\overline{n}|} = \dfrac{S^n - 1}{i}$	$1/S_{\overline{n}|} = \dfrac{i}{S^n - 1}$	$V^n = \dfrac{1}{S^n}$	$A_{\overline{n}|} = \dfrac{1 - 1/S^n}{i}$	$\dfrac{1}{A_{\overline{n}|}} = \dfrac{i}{1 - 1/S^n}$

	1	2	3	4	5	6
YEARS	AMOUNT OF ONE	AMOUNT OF ONE PER PERIOD	SINKING FUND FACTOR	PRESENT WORTH OF ONE	PRESENT WORTH ONE PER PERIOD	PARTIAL PAYMENT
1	1.170 000	1.000 000	1.000 000	.854 701	.854 701	1.170 000
2	1.368 900	2.170 000	.460 829	.730 514	1.585 214	.630 829
3	1.601 613	3.538 900	.282 574	.624 371	2.209 585	.452 574
4	1.873 887	5.140 513	.194 533	.533 650	2.743 235	.364 533
5	2.192 448	7.014 400	.142 564	.456 111	3.199 346	.312 564
6	2.565 164	9.206 848	.108 615	.389 839	3.589 185	.278 615
7	3.001 242	11.772 012	.084 947	.333 195	3.922 380	.254 947
8	3.511 453	14.773 255	.067 690	.284 782	4.207 163	.237 690
9	4.108 400	18.284 708	.054 691	.243 404	4.450 566	.224 691
10	4.806 828	22.393 108	.044 657	.208 037	4.658 604	.214 657
11	5.623 989	27.199 937	.036 765	.177 810	4.836 413	.206 765
12	6.580 067	32.823 926	.030 466	.151 974	4.988 387	.200 466
13	7.698 679	39.403 993	.025 378	.129 892	5.118 280	.195 378
14	9.007 454	47.102 672	.021 230	.111 019	5.229 299	.191 230
15	10.538 721	56.110 126	.017 822	.094 888	5.324 187	.187 822
16	12.330 304	66.648 848	.015 004	.081 101	5.405 288	.185 004
17	14.426 456	78.979 152	.012 662	.069 317	5.474 605	.182 662
18	16.878 953	93.405 608	.010 706	.059 245	5.533 851	.180 706
19	19.748 375	110.284 561	.009 067	.050 637	5.584 488	.179 067
20	23.105 599	130.032 936	.007 690	.043 280	5.627 767	.177 690
21	27.033 551	153.138 535	.006 530	.036 991	5.664 758	.176 530
22	31.629 255	180.172 086	.005 550	.031 616	5.696 375	.175 550
23	37.006 228	211.801 341	.004 721	.027 022	5.723 397	.174 721
24	43.297 287	248.807 569	.004 019	.023 096	5.746 493	.174 019
25	50.657 826	292.104 856	.003 423	.019 740	5.766 234	.173 423
26	59.269 656	342.762 681	.002 917	.016 872	5.783 106	.172 917
27	69.345 497	402.032 337	.002 487	.014 421	5.797 526	.172 487
28	81.134 232	471.377 835	.002 121	.012 325	5.809 851	.172 121
29	94.927 051	552.512 066	.001 810	.010 534	5.820 386	.171 810
30	111.064 650	647.439 118	.001 545	.009 004	5.829 390	.171 545
31	129.945 641	758.503 768	.001 318	.007 696	5.837 085	.171 318
32	152.036 399	888.449 408	.001 126	.006 577	5.843 663	.171 126
33	177.882 587	1040.485 808	.000 961	.005 622	5.849 284	.170 961
34	208.122 627	1218.368 395	.000 821	.004 805	5.854 089	.170 821
35	243.503 474	1426.491 022	.000 701	.004 107	5.858 196	.170 701
36	284.899 064	1669.994 496	.000 599	.003 510	5.861 706	.170 599
37	333.331 905	1954.893 560	.000 512	.003 000	5.864 706	.170 512
38	389.998 329	2288.225 465	.000 437	.002 564	5.867 270	.170 437
39	456.298 045	2678.223 794	.000 373	.002 192	5.869 461	.170 373
40	533.868 713	3134.521 839	.000 319	.001 873	5.871 335	.170 319
41	624.626 394	3668.390 552	.000 273	.001 601	5.872 936	.170 273
42	730.812 881	4293.016 946	.000 233	.001 368	5.874 304	.170 233
43	855.051 071	5023.829 827	.000 199	.001 170	5.875 473	.170 199
44	1000.409 753	5878.880 897	.000 170	.001 000	5.876 473	.170 170
45	1170.479 411	6879.290 650	.000 145	.000 854	5.877 327	.170 145
46	1369.460 910	8049.770 061	.000 124	.000 730	5.878 058	.170 124
47	1602.269 265	9419.230 971	.000 106	.000 624	5.878 682	.170 106
48	1874.655 040	11021.500 236	.000 091	.000 533	5.879 215	.170 091
49	2193.346 397	12896.155 276	.000 078	.000 456	5.879 671	.170 078
50	2566.215 284	15089.501 673	.000 066	.000 390	5.880 061	.170 066
51	3002.471 883	17655.716 957	.000 057	.000 333	5.880 394	.170 057
52	3512.892 103	20658.188 840	.000 048	.000 285	5.880 678	.170 048
53	4110.083 760	24171.080 943	.000 041	.000 243	5.880 922	.170 041
54	4808.798 000	28281.164 703	.000 035	.000 208	5.881 130	.170 035
55	5626.293 659	33089.962 703	.000 030	.000 178	5.881 307	.170 030
56	6582.763 582	38716.256 362	.000 026	.000 152	5.881 459	.170 026
57	7701.833 390	45299.019 944	.000 022	.000 130	5.881 589	.170 022
58	9011.145 067	53000.853 334	.000 019	.000 111	5.881 700	.170 019
59	10543.039 728	62011.998 401	.000 016	.000 095	5.881 795	.170 016
60	12335.356 482	72555.038 129	.000 014	.000 081	5.881 876	.170 014

$$S^n = (1 + i)^n \qquad S_{\overline{n}|} = \frac{S^n - 1}{i} \qquad 1/S_{\overline{n}|} = \frac{i}{S^n - 1} \qquad V^n = \frac{1}{S^n} \qquad A_{\overline{n}|} = \frac{1 - 1/S^n}{i} \qquad \frac{1}{A_{\overline{n}|}} = \frac{i}{1 - 1/S^n}$$

	1	2	3	4	5	6
YEARS	AMOUNT OF ONE	AMOUNT OF ONE PER PERIOD	SINKING FUND FACTOR	PRESENT WORTH OF ONE	PRESENT WORTH ONE PER PERIOD	PARTIAL PAYMENT
1	1.180 000	1.000 000	1.000 000	.847 458	.847 458	1.180 000
2	1.392 400	2.180 000	.458 716	.718 184	1.565 642	.638 716
3	1.643 032	3.572 400	.279 924	.608 631	2.174 273	.459 924
4	1.938 778	5.215 432	.191 739	.515 789	2.690 062	.371 739
5	2.287 758	7.154 210	.139 778	.437 109	3.127 171	.319 778
6	2.699 554	9.441 968	.105 910	.370 432	3.497 603	.285 910
7	3.185 474	12.141 522	.082 362	.313 925	3.811 528	.262 362
8	3.758 859	15.326 996	.065 244	.266 038	4.077 566	.245 244
9	4.435 454	19.085 855	.052 395	.225 456	4.303 022	.232 395
10	5.233 836	23.521 309	.042 515	.191 064	4.494 086	.222 515
11	6.175 926	28.755 144	.034 776	.161 919	4.656 005	.214 776
12	7.287 593	34.931 070	.028 628	.137 220	4.793 225	.208 628
13	8.599 359	42.218 663	.023 686	.116 288	4.909 513	.203 686
14	10.147 244	50.818 022	.019 678	.098 549	5.008 062	.199 678
15	11.973 748	60.965 266	.016 403	.083 516	5.091 578	.196 403
16	14.129 023	72.939 014	.013 710	.070 776	5.162 354	.193 710
17	16.672 247	87.068 036	.011 485	.059 980	5.222 334	.191 485
18	19.673 251	103.740 283	.009 639	.050 830	5.273 164	.189 639
19	23.214 436	123.413 534	.008 103	.043 077	5.316 241	.188 103
20	27.393 035	146.627 970	.006 820	.036 506	5.352 746	.186 820
21	32.323 781	174.021 005	.005 746	.030 937	5.383 683	.185 746
22	38.142 061	206.344 785	.004 846	.026 218	5.409 901	.184 846
23	45.007 632	244.486 847	.004 090	.022 218	5.432 120	.184 090
24	53.109 006	289.494 479	.003 454	.018 829	5.450 949	.183 454
25	62.668 627	342.603 486	.002 919	.015 957	5.466 906	.182 919
26	73.948 980	405.272 113	.002 467	.013 523	5.480 429	.182 467
27	87.259 797	479.221 093	.002 087	.011 460	5.491 889	.182 087
28	102.966 560	566.480 890	.001 765	.009 712	5.501 601	.181 765
29	121.500 541	669.447 450	.001 494	.008 230	5.509 831	.181 494
30	143.370 638	790.947 991	.001 264	.006 975	5.516 806	.181 264
31	169.177 353	934.318 630	.001 070	.005 911	5.522 717	.181 070
32	199.629 277	1103.495 983	.000 906	.005 009	5.527 726	.180 906
33	235.562 547	1303.125 260	.000 767	.004 245	5.531 971	.180 767
34	277.963 805	1538.687 807	.000 650	.003 598	5.535 569	.180 650
35	327.997 290	1816.651 612	.000 550	.003 049	5.538 618	.180 550
36	387.036 802	2144.648 902	.000 466	.002 584	5.541 201	.180 466
37	456.703 427	2531.685 705	.000 395	.002 190	5.543 391	.180 395
38	538.910 044	2988.389 132	.000 335	.001 856	5.545 247	.180 335
39	635.913 852	3527.299 175	.000 284	.001 573	5.546 819	.180 284
40	750.378 345	4163.213 027	.000 240	.001 333	5.548 152	.180 240
41	885.446 447	4913.591 372	.000 204	.001 129	5.549 281	.180 204
42	1044.826 807	5799.037 819	.000 172	.000 957	5.550 238	.180 172
43	1232.895 633	6843.864 626	.000 146	.000 811	5.551 049	.180 146
44	1454.816 847	8076.760 259	.000 124	.000 687	5.551 737	.180 124
45	1716.683 879	9531.577 105	.000 105	.000 583	5.552 319	.180 105
46	2025.686 977	11248.260 984	.000 089	.000 494	5.552 813	.180 089
47	2390.310 633	13273.947 961	.000 075	.000 418	5.553 231	.180 075
48	2820.566 547	15664.258 594	.000 064	.000 355	5.553 586	.180 064
49	3328.268 525	18484.825 141	.000 054	.000 300	5.553 886	.180 054
50	3927.356 860	21813.093 666	.000 046	.000 255	5.554 141	.180 046
51	4634.281 095	25740.450 526	.000 039	.000 216	5.554 357	.180 039
52	5468.451 692	30374.731 621	.000 033	.000 183	5.554 540	.180 033
53	6452.772 996	35843.183 313	.000 028	.000 155	5.554 695	.180 028
54	7614.272 136	42295.956 309	.000 024	.000 131	5.554 826	.180 024
55	8984.841 120	49910.228 445	.000 020	.000 111	5.554 937	.180 020

$$S^n = (1+i)^n \quad S_{\overline{n}|} = \frac{S^n - 1}{i} \quad 1/S_{\overline{n}|} = \frac{i}{S^n - 1} \quad V^n = \frac{1}{S^n} \quad A_{\overline{n}|} = \frac{1 - 1/S^n}{i} \quad \frac{1}{A_{\overline{n}|}} = \frac{i}{1 - 1/S^n}$$

	1	2	3	4	5	6
YEARS	AMOUNT OF ONE	AMOUNT OF ONE PER PERIOD	SINKING FUND FACTOR	PRESENT WORTH OF ONE	PRESENT WORTH ONE PER PERIOD	PARTIAL PAYMENT
1	1.190 000	1.000 000	1.000 000	.840 336	.840 336	1.190 000
2	1.416 100	2.190 000	.456 621	.706 165	1.546 501	.646 621
3	1.685 159	3.606 100	.277 308	.593 416	2.139 917	.467 308
4	2.005 339	5.291 259	.188 991	.498 669	2.638 586	.378 991
5	2.386 354	7.296 598	.137 050	.419 049	3.057 635	.327 050
6	2.839 761	9.682 952	.103 274	.352 142	3.409 777	.293 274
7	3.379 315	12.522 713	.079 855	.295 918	3.705 695	.269 855
8	4.021 385	15.902 028	.062 885	.248 671	3.954 366	.252 885
9	4.785 449	19.923 413	.050 192	.208 967	4.163 332	.240 192
10	5.694 684	24.708 862	.040 471	.175 602	4.338 935	.230 471
11	6.776 674	30.403 546	.032 891	.147 565	4.486 500	.222 891
12	8.064 242	37.180 220	.026 896	.124 004	4.610 504	.216 896
13	9.596 448	45.244 461	.022 102	.104 205	4.714 709	.212 102
14	11.419 773	54.840 909	.018 235	.087 567	4.802 277	.208 235
15	13.589 530	66.260 682	.015 092	.073 586	4.875 863	.205 092
16	16.171 540	79.850 211	.012 523	.061 837	4.937 700	.202 523
17	19.244 133	96.021 751	.010 414	.051 964	4.989 664	.200 414
18	22.900 518	115.265 884	.008 676	.043 667	5.033 331	.198 676
19	27.251 616	138.166 402	.007 238	.036 695	5.070 026	.197 238
20	32.429 423	165.418 018	.006 045	.030 836	5.100 862	.196 045
21	38.591 014	197.847 442	.005 054	.025 913	5.126 775	.195 054
22	45.923 307	236.438 456	.004 229	.021 775	5.148 550	.194 229
23	54.648 735	282.361 762	.003 542	.018 299	5.166 849	.193 542
24	65.031 994	337.010 497	.002 967	.015 377	5.182 226	.192 967
25	77.388 073	402.042 491	.002 487	.012 922	5.195 148	.192 487
26	92.091 807	479.430 565	.002 086	.010 859	5.206 007	.192 086
27	109.589 251	571.522 372	.001 750	.009 125	5.215 132	.191 750
28	130.411 208	681.111 623	.001 468	.007 668	5.222 800	.191 468
29	155.189 338	811.522 831	.001 232	.006 444	5.229 243	.191 232
30	184.675 312	966.712 169	.001 034	.005 415	5.234 658	.191 034
31	219.763 621	1151.387 481	.000 869	.004 550	5.239 209	.190 869
32	261.518 710	1371.151 103	.000 729	.003 824	5.243 033	.190 729
33	311.207 264	1632.669 812	.000 612	.003 213	5.246 246	.190 612
34	370.336 645	1943.877 077	.000 514	.002 700	5.248 946	.190 514
35	440.700 607	2314.213 721	.000 432	.002 269	5.251 215	.190 432
36	524.433 722	2754.914 328	.000 363	.001 907	5.253 122	.190 363
37	624.076 130	3279.348 051	.000 305	.001 602	5.254 724	.190 305
38	742.650 594	3903.424 180	.000 256	.001 347	5.256 071	.190 256
39	883.754 207	4646.074 775	.000 215	.001 132	5.257 202	.190 215
40	1051.667 507	5529.828 982	.000 181	.000 951	5.258 153	.190 181
41	1251.484 333	6581.496 488	.000 152	.000 799	5.258 952	.190 152
42	1489.266 356	7832.980 821	.000 128	.000 671	5.259 624	.190 128
43	1772.226 964	9322.247 177	.000 107	.000 564	5.260 188	.190 107
44	2108.950 087	11094.474 141	.000 090	.000 474	5.260 662	.190 090
45	2509.650 603	13203.424 228	.000 076	.000 398	5.261 061	.190 076
46	2986.484 218	15713.074 831	.000 064	.000 335	5.261 396	.190 064
47	3553.916 219	18699.559 049	.000 053	.000 281	5.261 677	.190 053
48	4229.160 301	22253.475 268	.000 045	.000 236	5.261 913	.190 045
49	5032.700 758	26482.635 569	.000 038	.000 199	5.262 112	.190 038
50	5988.913 902	31515.336 327	.000 032	.000 167	5.262 279	.190 032
51	7126.807 544	37504.250 230	.000 027	.000 140	5.262 419	.190 027
52	8480.900 977	44631.057 773	.000 022	.000 118	5.262 537	.190 022
53	10092.272 163	53111.958 750	.000 019	.000 099	5.262 636	.190 019
54	12009.803 873	63204.230 913	.000 016	.000 083	5.262 720	.190 016
55	14291.666 609	75214.034 786	.000 013	.000 070	5.262 790	.190 013
	$S^n = (1 + i)^n$	$S_{\overline{n}} = \dfrac{S^n - 1}{i}$	$1/S_{\overline{n}} = \dfrac{i}{S^n - 1}$	$V^n = \dfrac{1}{S^n}$	$A_{\overline{n}} = \dfrac{1 - 1/S^n}{i}$	$\dfrac{1}{A_{\overline{n}}} = \dfrac{i}{1 - 1/S^n}$

	1	2	3	4	5	6
YEARS	AMOUNT OF ONE	AMOUNT OF ONE PER PERIOD	SINKING FUND FACTOR	PRESENT WORTH OF ONE	PRESENT WORTH ONE PER PERIOD	PARTIAL PAYMENT
1	1.200 000	1.000 000	1.000 000	.833 333	.833 333	1.200 000
2	1.440 000	2.200 000	.454 545	.694 444	1.527 778	.654 545
3	1.728 000	3.640 000	.274 725	.578 704	2.106 481	.474 725
4	2.073 600	5.368 000	.186 289	.482 253	2.588 735	.386 289
5	2.488 320	7.441 600	.134 380	.401 878	2.990 612	.334 380
6	2.985 984	9.929 920	.100 706	.334 898	3.325 510	.300 706
7	3.583 181	12.915 904	.077 424	.279 082	3.604 592	.277 424
8	4.299 817	16.499 085	.060 609	.232 568	3.837 160	.260 609
9	5.159 780	20.798 902	.048 079	.193 807	4.030 967	.248 079
10	6.191 736	25.958 682	.038 523	.161 506	4.192 472	.238 523
11	7.430 084	32.150 419	.031 104	.134 588	4.327 060	.231 104
12	8.916 100	39.580 502	.025 265	.112 157	4.439 217	.225 265
13	10.699 321	48.496 603	.020 620	.093 464	4.532 681	.220 620
14	12.839 185	59.195 923	.016 893	.077 887	4.610 567	.216 893
15	15.407 022	72.035 108	.013 882	.064 905	4.675 473	.213 882
16	18.488 426	87.442 129	.011 436	.054 088	4.729 561	.211 436
17	22.186 111	105.930 555	.009 440	.045 073	4.774 634	.209 440
18	26.623 333	128.116 666	.007 805	.037 561	4.812 195	.207 805
19	31.948 000	154.740 000	.006 462	.031 301	4.843 496	.206 462
20	38.337 600	186.688 000	.005 357	.026 084	4.869 580	.205 357
21	46.005 120	225.025 600	.004 444	.021 737	4.891 316	.204 444
22	55.206 144	271.030 719	.003 690	.018 114	4.909 430	.203 690
23	66.247 373	326.236 863	.003 065	.015 095	4.924 525	.203 065
24	79.496 847	392.484 236	.002 548	.012 579	4.937 104	.202 548
25	95.396 217	471.981 083	.002 119	.010 483	4.947 587	.202 119
26	114.475 460	567.377 300	.001 762	.008 735	4.956 323	.201 762
27	137.370 552	681.852 760	.001 467	.007 280	4.963 602	.201 467
28	164.844 662	819.223 312	.001 221	.006 066	4.969 668	.201 221
29	197.813 595	984.067 974	.001 016	.005 055	4.974 724	.201 016
30	237.376 314	1181.881 569	.000 846	.004 213	4.978 936	.200 846
31	284.851 577	1419.257 883	.000 705	.003 511	4.982 447	.200 705
32	341.821 892	1704.109 459	.000 587	.002 926	4.985 372	.200 587
33	410.186 270	2045.931 351	.000 489	.002 438	4.987 810	.200 489
34	492.223 524	2456.117 621	.000 407	.002 032	4.989 842	.200 407
35	590.668 229	2948.341 146	.000 339	.001 693	4.991 535	.200 339
36	708.801 875	3539.009 375	.000 283	.001 411	4.992 946	.200 283
37	850.562 250	4247.811 250	.000 235	.001 176	4.994 122	.200 235
38	1020.674 700	5098.373 500	.000 196	.000 980	4.995 101	.200 196
39	1224.809 640	6119.048 200	.000 163	.000 816	4.995 918	.200 163
40	1469.771 568	7343.857 840	.000 136	.000 680	4.996 598	.200 136
41	1763.725 882	8813.629 408	.000 113	.000 567	4.997 165	.200 113
42	2116.471 058	10577.355 289	.000 095	.000 472	4.997 638	.200 095
43	2539.765 269	12693.826 347	.000 079	.000 394	4.998 031	.200 079
44	3047.718 323	15233.591 617	.000 066	.000 328	4.998 359	.200 066
45	3657.261 988	18281.309 940	.000 055	.000 273	4.998 633	.200 055
46	4388.714 386	21938.571 928	.000 046	.000 228	4.998 861	.200 046
47	5266.457 263	26327.286 314	.000 038	.000 190	4.999 051	.200 038
48	6319.748 715	31593.743 576	.000 032	.000 158	4.999 209	.200 032
49	7583.698 458	37913.492 292	.000 026	.000 132	4.999 341	.200 026
50	9100.438 150	45497.190 750	.000 022	.000 110	4.999 451	.200 022
	$S^n = (1+i)^n$	$S_{\overline{n}} = \dfrac{S^n - 1}{i}$	$1/S_{\overline{n}} = \dfrac{i}{S^n - 1}$	$V^n = \dfrac{1}{S^n}$	$A_{\overline{n}} = \dfrac{1 - 1/S^n}{i}$	$\dfrac{1}{A_{\overline{n}}} = \dfrac{i}{1 - 1/S^n}$

	1	2	3	4	5	6
YEARS	AMOUNT OF ONE	AMOUNT OF ONE PER PERIOD	SINKING FUND FACTOR	PRESENT WORTH OF ONE	PRESENT WORTH ONE PER PERIOD	PARTIAL PAYMENT
1	1.210 000	1.000 000	1.000 000	.826 446	.826 446	1.210 000
2	1.464 100	2.210 000	.452 489	.683 013	1.509 460	.662 489
3	1.771 561	3.674 100	.272 175	.564 474	2.073 934	.482 175
4	2.143 589	5.445 661	.183 632	.466 507	2.540 441	.393 632
5	2.593 742	7.589 250	.131 765	.385 543	2.925 984	.341 765
6	3.138 428	10.182 992	.098 203	.318 631	3.244 615	.308 203
7	3.797 498	13.321 421	.075 067	.263 331	3.507 946	.285 067
8	4.594 973	17.118 919	.058 415	.217 629	3.725 576	.268 415
9	5.559 917	21.713 892	.046 053	.179 859	3.905 434	.256 053
10	6.727 500	27.273 809	.036 665	.148 644	4.054 078	.246 665
11	8.140 275	34.001 309	.029 411	.122 846	4.176 924	.239 411
12	9.849 733	42.141 584	.023 730	.101 526	4.278 450	.233 730
13	11.918 177	51.991 317	.019 234	.083 905	4.362 355	.229 234
14	14.420 994	63.909 493	.015 647	.069 343	4.431 698	.225 647
15	17.449 402	78.330 487	.012 766	.057 309	4.489 007	.222 766
16	21.113 777	95.779 889	.010 441	.047 362	4.536 369	.220 441
17	25.547 670	116.893 666	.008 555	.039 143	4.575 512	.218 555
18	30.912 681	142.441 336	.007 020	.032 349	4.607 861	.217 020
19	37.404 343	173.354 016	.005 769	.026 735	4.634 596	.215 769
20	45.259 256	210.758 360	.004 745	.022 095	4.656 691	.214 745
21	54.763 699	256.017 615	.003 906	.018 260	4.674 951	.213 906
22	66.264 076	310.781 315	.003 218	.015 091	4.690 042	.213 218
23	80.179 532	377.045 391	.002 652	.012 472	4.702 514	.212 652
24	97.017 234	457.224 923	.002 187	.010 307	4.712 822	.212 187
25	117.390 853	554.242 157	.001 804	.008 519	4.721 340	.211 804
26	142.042 932	671.633 009	.001 489	.007 040	4.728 380	.211 489
27	171.871 948	813.675 941	.001 229	.005 818	4.734 199	.211 229
28	207.965 057	985.547 889	.001 015	.004 809	4.739 007	.211 015
29	251.637 719	1193.512 946	.000 838	.003 974	4.742 981	.210 838
30	304.481 640	1445.150 664	.000 692	.003 284	4.746 265	.210 692
31	368.422 784	1749.632 304	.000 572	.002 714	4.748 980	.210 572
32	445.791 568	2118.055 088	.000 472	.002 243	4.751 223	.210 472
33	539.407 798	2563.846 656	.000 390	.001 854	4.753 077	.210 390
34	652.603 435	3103.254 454	.000 322	.001 532	4.754 609	.210 322
35	789.746 957	3755.937 890	.000 266	.001 266	4.755 875	.210 266
36	955.593 818	4545.684 846	.000 220	.001 046	4.756 922	.210 220
37	1156.268 519	5501.278 664	.000 182	.000 865	4.757 786	.210 182
38	1399.084 909	6657.547 183	.000 150	.000 715	4.758 501	.210 150
39	1692.892 739	8056.632 092	.000 124	.000 591	4.759 092	.210 124
40	2048.400 215	9749.524 831	.000 103	.000 488	4.759 580	.210 103
41	2478.564 260	11797.925 046	.000 085	.000 403	4.759 984	.210 085
42	2999.062 754	14276.489 306	.000 070	.000 333	4.760 317	.210 070
43	3628.865 933	17275.552 060	.000 058	.000 276	4.760 593	.210 058
44	4390.927 778	20904.417 992	.000 048	.000 228	4.760 820	.210 048
45	5313.022 612	25295.345 771	.000 040	.000 188	4.761 008	.210 040
46	6428.757 360	30608.368 383	.000 033	.000 156	4.761 164	.210 033
47	7778.796 406	37037.125 743	.000 027	.000 129	4.761 293	.210 027
48	9412.343 651	44815.922 149	.000 022	.000 106	4.761 399	.210 022
49	11388.935 818	54228.265 800	.000 018	.000 088	4.761 487	.210 018
50	13780.612 340	65617.201 618	.000 015	.000 073	4.761 559	.210 015

$S^n = (1 + i)^n$	$S_{\overline{n}|} = \dfrac{S^n - 1}{i}$	$1/S_{\overline{n}|} = \dfrac{i}{S^n - 1}$	$V^n = \dfrac{1}{S^n}$	$A_{\overline{n}|} = \dfrac{1 - 1/S^n}{i}$	$\dfrac{1}{A_{\overline{n}|}} = \dfrac{i}{1 - 1/S^n}$

	1	2	3	4	5	6
YEARS	AMOUNT OF ONE	AMOUNT OF ONE PER PERIOD	SINKING FUND FACTOR	PRESENT WORTH OF ONE	PRESENT WORTH ONE PER PERIOD	PARTIAL PAYMENT
1	1.220 000	1.000 000	1.000 000	.819 672	.819 672	1.220 000
2	1.488 400	2.220 000	.450 450	.671 862	1.491 535	.670 450
3	1.815 848	3.708 400	.269 658	.550 707	2.042 241	.489 658
4	2.215 335	5.524 248	.181 020	.451 399	2.493 641	.401 020
5	2.702 708	7.739 583	.129 206	.369 999	2.863 640	.349 206
6	3.297 304	10.442 291	.095 764	.303 278	3.166 918	.315 764
7	4.022 711	13.739 595	.072 782	.248 589	3.415 506	.292 782
8	4.907 707	17.762 306	.056 299	.203 761	3.619 268	.276 299
9	5.987 403	22.670 013	.044 111	.167 017	3.786 285	.264 111
10	7.304 631	28.657 416	.034 895	.136 899	3.923 184	.254 895
11	8.911 650	35.962 047	.027 807	.112 213	4.035 397	.247 807
12	10.872 213	44.873 697	.022 285	.091 978	4.127 375	.242 285
13	13.264 100	55.745 911	.017 939	.075 391	4.202 766	.237 939
14	16.182 202	69.010 011	.014 491	.061 796	4.264 562	.234 491
15	19.742 287	85.192 213	.011 738	.050 653	4.315 215	.231 738
16	24.085 590	104.934 500	.009 530	.041 519	4.356 734	.229 530
17	29.384 420	129.020 090	.007 751	.034 032	4.390 765	.227 751
18	35.848 992	158.404 510	.006 313	.027 895	4.418 660	.226 313
19	43.735 771	194.253 503	.005 148	.022 865	4.441 525	.225 148
20	53.357 640	237.989 273	.004 202	.018 741	4.460 266	.224 202
21	65.096 321	291.346 913	.003 432	.015 362	4.475 628	.223 432
22	79.417 512	356.443 234	.002 805	.012 592	4.488 220	.222 805
23	96.889 364	435.860 746	.002 294	.010 321	4.498 541	.222 294
24	118.205 024	532.750 110	.001 877	.008 460	4.507 001	.221 877
25	144.210 130	650.955 134	.001 536	.006 934	4.513 935	.221 536
26	175.936 358	795.165 264	.001 258	.005 684	4.519 619	.221 258
27	214.642 357	971.101 622	.001 030	.004 659	4.524 278	.221 030
28	261.863 675	1185.743 978	.000 843	.003 819	4.528 096	.220 843
29	319.473 684	1447.607 654	.000 691	.003 130	4.531 227	.220 691
30	389.757 894	1767.081 337	.000 566	.002 566	4.533 792	.220 566
31	475.504 631	2156.839 232	.000 464	.002 103	4.535 895	.220 464
32	580.115 650	2632.343 863	.000 380	.001 724	4.537 619	.220 380
33	707.741 093	3212.459 512	.000 311	.001 413	4.539 032	.220 311
34	863.444 133	3920.200 605	.000 255	.001 158	4.540 190	.220 255
35	1053.401 842	4783.644 738	.000 209	.000 949	4.541 140	.220 209
36	1285.150 248	5837.046 581	.000 171	.000 778	4.541 918	.220 171
37	1567.883 302	7122.196 829	.000 140	.000 638	4.542 555	.220 140
38	1912.817 629	8690.080 131	.000 115	.000 523	4.543 078	.220 115
39	2333.637 507	10602.897 760	.000 094	.000 429	4.543 507	.220 094
40	2847.037 759	12936.535 267	.000 077	.000 351	4.543 858	.220 077
41	3473.386 066	15783.573 025	.000 063	.000 288	4.544 146	.220 063
42	4237.531 000	19256.959 091	.000 052	.000 236	4.544 382	.220 052
43	5169.787 820	23494.490 091	.000 043	.000 193	4.544 575	.220 043
44	6307.141 140	28664.277 911	.000 035	.000 159	4.544 734	.220 035
45	7694.712 191	34971.419 051	.000 029	.000 130	4.544 864	.220 029
46	9387.548 873	42666.131 243	.000 023	.000 107	4.544 970	.220 023
47	11452.809 626	52053.680 116	.000 019	.000 087	4.545 058	.220 019
48	13972.427 743	63506.489 742	.000 016	.000 072	4.545 129	.220 016
49	17046.361 847	77478.917 485	.000 013	.000 059	4.545 188	.220 013
50	20796.561 453	94525.279 331	.000 011	.000 048	4.545 236	.220 011

| $S^n = (1+i)^n$ | $S_{\overline{n}} = \dfrac{S^n - 1}{i}$ | $1/S_{\overline{n}} = \dfrac{i}{S^n - 1}$ | $V^n = \dfrac{1}{S^n}$ | $A_{\overline{n}} = \dfrac{1 - 1/S^n}{i}$ | $\dfrac{1}{A_{\overline{n}}} = \dfrac{i}{1 - 1/S^n}$ |

	1	2	3	4	5	6
YEARS	AMOUNT OF ONE	AMOUNT OF ONE PER PERIOD	SINKING FUND FACTOR	PRESENT WORTH OF ONE	PRESENT WORTH ONE PER PERIOD	PARTIAL PAYMENT
1	1.230 000	1.000 000	1.000 000	.813 008	.813 008	1.230 000
2	1.512 900	2.230 000	.448 430	.660 982	1.473 990	.678 430
3	1.860 867	3.742 900	.267 173	.537 384	2.011 374	.497 173
4	2.288 866	5.603 767	.178 451	.436 897	2.448 272	.408 451
5	2.815 306	7.892 633	.126 700	.355 201	2.803 473	.356 700
6	3.462 826	10.707 939	.093 389	.288 781	3.092 254	.323 389
7	4.259 276	14.170 765	.070 568	.234 782	3.327 036	.300 568
8	5.238 909	18.430 041	.054 259	.190 879	3.517 916	.284 259
9	6.443 859	23.668 950	.042 249	.155 187	3.673 102	.272 249
10	7.925 946	30.112 809	.033 208	.126 168	3.799 270	.263 208
11	9.748 914	38.038 755	.026 289	.102 576	3.901 846	.256 289
12	11.991 164	47.787 669	.020 926	.083 395	3.985 240	.250 926
13	14.749 132	59.778 833	.016 728	.067 801	4.053 041	.246 728
14	18.141 432	74.527 964	.013 418	.055 122	4.108 163	.243 418
15	22.313 961	92.669 396	.010 791	.044 815	4.152 978	.240 791
16	27.446 172	114.983 357	.008 697	.036 435	4.189 413	.238 697
17	33.758 792	142.429 529	.007 021	.029 622	4.219 035	.237 021
18	41.523 314	176.188 321	.005 676	.024 083	4.243 118	.235 676
19	51.073 676	217.711 635	.004 593	.019 580	4.262 698	.234 593
20	62.820 622	268.785 311	.003 720	.015 918	4.278 616	.233 720
21	77.269 364	331.605 932	.003 016	.012 942	4.291 558	.233 016
22	95.041 318	408.875 297	.002 446	.010 522	4.302 079	.232 446
23	116.900 822	503.916 615	.001 984	.008 554	4.310 634	.231 984
24	143.788 010	620.817 437	.001 611	.006 955	4.317 588	.231 611
25	176.859 253	764.605 447	.001 308	.005 654	4.323 243	.231 308
26	217.536 881	941.464 700	.001 062	.004 597	4.327 839	.231 062
27	267.570 364	1159.001 581	.000 863	.003 737	4.331 577	.230 863
28	329.111 547	1426.571 945	.000 701	.003 038	4.334 615	.230 701
29	404.807 203	1755.683 492	.000 570	.002 470	4.337 086	.230 570
30	497.912 860	2160.490 695	.000 463	.002 008	4.339 094	.230 463
31	612.432 818	2658.403 555	.000 376	.001 633	4.340 727	.230 376
32	753.292 366	3270.836 373	.000 306	.001 328	4.342 054	.230 306
33	926.549 610	4024.128 738	.000 249	.001 079	4.343 134	.230 249
34	1139.656 020	4950.678 348	.000 202	.000 877	4.344 011	.230 202
35	1401.776 905	6090.334 368	.000 164	.000 713	4.344 724	.230 164
36	1724.185 593	7492.111 273	.000 133	.000 580	4.345 304	.230 133
37	2120.748 279	9216.296 866	.000 109	.000 472	4.345 776	.230 109
38	2608.520 383	11337.045 145	.000 088	.000 383	4.346 159	.230 088
39	3208.480 071	13945.565 528	.000 072	.000 312	4.346 471	.230 072
40	3946.430 488	17154.045 599	.000 058	.000 253	4.346 724	.230 058
41	4854.109 500	21100.476 087	.000 047	.000 206	4.346 930	.230 047
42	5970.554 685	25954.585 587	.000 039	.000 167	4.347 098	.230 039
43	7343.782 263	31925.140 272	.000 031	.000 136	4.347 234	.230 031
44	9032.852 183	39268.922 535	.000 025	.000 111	4.347 345	.230 025
45	11110.408 185	48301.774 718	.000 021	.000 090	4.347 435	.230 021

$$S^n = (1+i)^n \quad\quad S_{\overline{n|}} = \frac{S^n - 1}{i} \quad\quad 1/S_{\overline{n|}} = \frac{i}{S^n - 1} \quad\quad V^n = \frac{1}{S^n} \quad\quad A_{\overline{n|}} = \frac{1 - 1/S^n}{i} \quad\quad \frac{1}{A_{\overline{n|}}} = \frac{i}{1 - 1/S^n}$$

	1	2	3	4	5	6
YEARS	AMOUNT OF ONE	AMOUNT OF ONE PER PERIOD	SINKING FUND FACTOR	PRESENT WORTH OF ONE	PRESENT WORTH ONE PER PERIOD	PARTIAL PAYMENT
1	1.240 000	1.000 000	1.000 000	.806 452	.806 452	1.240 000
2	1.537 600	2.240 000	.446 429	.650 364	1.456 816	.686 429
3	1.906 624	3.777 600	.264 718	.524 487	1.981 303	.504 718
4	2.364 214	5.684 224	.175 926	.422 974	2.404 277	.415 926
5	2.931 625	8.048 438	.124 248	.341 108	2.745 384	.364 248
6	3.635 215	10.980 063	.091 074	.275 087	3.020 471	.331 074
7	4.507 667	14.615 278	.068 422	.221 844	3.242 316	.308 422
8	5.589 507	19.122 945	.052 293	.178 907	3.421 222	.292 293
9	6.930 988	24.712 451	.040 465	.144 280	3.565 502	.280 465
10	8.594 426	31.643 440	.031 602	.116 354	3.681 856	.271 602
11	10.657 088	40.237 865	.024 852	.093 834	3.775 691	.264 852
12	13.214 789	50.894 953	.019 648	.075 673	3.851 363	.259 648
13	16.386 338	64.109 741	.015 598	.061 026	3.912 390	.255 598
14	20.319 059	80.496 079	.012 423	.049 215	3.961 605	.252 423
15	25.195 633	100.815 138	.009 919	.039 689	4.001 294	.249 919
16	31.242 585	126.010 772	.007 936	.032 008	4.033 302	.247 936
17	38.740 806	157.253 357	.006 359	.025 813	4.059 114	.246 359
18	48.038 599	195.994 162	.005 102	.020 817	4.079 931	.245 102
19	59.567 863	244.032 761	.004 098	.016 788	4.096 718	.244 098
20	73.864 150	303.600 624	.003 294	.013 538	4.110 257	.243 294
21	91.591 546	377.464 774	.002 649	.010 918	4.121 175	.242 649
22	113.573 517	469.056 320	.002 132	.008 805	4.129 980	.242 132
23	140.831 161	582.629 836	.001 716	.007 101	4.137 080	.241 716
24	174.630 639	723.460 997	.001 382	.005 726	4.142 807	.241 382
25	216.541 993	898.091 636	.001 113	.004 618	4.147 425	.241 113
26	268.512 071	1114.633 629	.000 897	.003 724	4.151 149	.240 897
27	332.954 968	1383.145 700	.000 723	.003 003	4.154 152	.240 723
28	412.864 160	1716.100 668	.000 583	.002 422	4.156 575	.240 583
29	511.951 559	2128.964 828	.000 470	.001 953	4.158 528	.240 470
30	634.819 933	2640.916 387	.000 379	.001 575	4.160 103	.240 379
31	787.176 717	3275.736 320	.000 305	.001 270	4.161 373	.240 305
32	976.099 129	4062.913 037	.000 246	.001 024	4.162 398	.240 246
33	1210.362 920	5039.012 166	.000 198	.000 826	4.163 224	.240 198
34	1500.850 021	6249.375 086	.000 160	.000 666	4.163 890	.240 160
35	1861.054 026	7750.225 106	.000 129	.000 537	4.164 428	.240 129
36	2307.706 992	9611.279 132	.000 104	.000 433	4.164 861	.240 104
37	2861.556 670	11918.986 124	.000 084	.000 349	4.165 211	.240 084
38	3548.330 270	14780.542 793	.000 068	.000 282	4.165 492	.240 068
39	4399.929 535	18328.873 064	.000 055	.000 227	4.165 720	.240 055
40	5455.912 624	22728.802 599	.000 044	.000 183	4.165 903	.240 044
41	6765.331 653	28184.715 222	.000 035	.000 148	4.166 051	.240 035
42	8389.011 250	34950.046 876	.000 029	.000 119	4.166 170	.240 029
43	10402.373 950	43339.058 126	.000 023	.000 096	4.166 266	.240 023
44	12898.943 698	53741.432 076	.000 019	.000 078	4.166 344	.240 019
45	15994.690 186	66640.375 775	.000 015	.000 063	4.166 406	.240 015

$$S^n = (1+i)^n \qquad S_{\overline{n}|} = \frac{S^n-1}{i} \qquad 1/S_{\overline{n}|} = \frac{i}{S^n-1} \qquad V^n = \frac{1}{S^n} \qquad A_{\overline{n}|} = \frac{1-1/S^n}{i} \qquad \frac{1}{A_{\overline{n}|}} = \frac{i}{1-1/S^n}$$

	1	2	3	4	5	6
YEARS	AMOUNT OF ONE	AMOUNT OF ONE PER PERIOD	SINKING FUND FACTOR	PRESENT WORTH OF ONE	PRESENT WORTH ONE PER PERIOD	PARTIAL PAYMENT
1	1.250 000	1.000 000	1.000 000	.800 000	.800 000	1.250 000
2	1.562 500	2.250 000	.444 444	.640 000	1.440 000	.694 444
3	1.953 125	3.812 500	.262 295	.512 000	1.952 000	.512 295
4	2.441 406	5.765 625	.173 442	.409 600	2.361 600	.423 442
5	3.051 758	8.207 031	.121 847	.327 680	2.689 280	.371 847
6	3.814 697	11.258 789	.088 819	.262 144	2.951 424	.338 819
7	4.768 372	15.073 486	.066 342	.209 715	3.161 139	.316 342
8	5.960 464	19.841 858	.050 399	.167 772	3.328 911	.300 399
9	7.450 581	25.802 322	.038 756	.134 218	3.463 129	.288 756
10	9.313 226	33.252 903	.030 073	.107 374	3.570 503	.280 073
11	11.641 532	42.566 129	.023 493	.085 899	3.656 403	.273 493
12	14.551 915	54.207 661	.018 448	.068 719	3.725 122	.268 448
13	18.189 894	68.759 576	.014 543	.054 976	3.780 098	.264 543
14	22.737 368	86.949 470	.011 501	.043 980	3.824 078	.261 501
15	28.421 709	109.686 838	.009 117	.035 184	3.859 263	.259 117
16	35.527 137	138.108 547	.007 241	.028 147	3.887 410	.257 241
17	44.408 921	173.635 684	.005 759	.022 518	3.909 928	.255 759
18	55.511 151	218.044 605	.004 586	.018 014	3.927 942	.254 586
19	69.388 939	273.555 756	.003 656	.014 412	3.942 354	.253 656
20	86.736 174	342.944 695	.002 916	.011 529	3.953 883	.252 916
21	108.420 217	429.680 869	.002 327	.009 223	3.963 107	.252 327
22	135.525 272	538.101 086	.001 858	.007 379	3.970 485	.251 858
23	169.406 589	673.626 358	.001 485	.005 903	3.976 388	.251 485
24	211.758 237	843.032 947	.001 186	.004 722	3.981 111	.251 186
25	264.697 796	1054.791 184	.000 948	.003 778	3.984 888	.250 948
26	330.872 245	1319.488 980	.000 758	.003 022	3.987 911	.250 758
27	413.590 306	1650.361 225	.000 606	.002 418	3.990 329	.250 606
28	516.987 883	2063.951 531	.000 485	.001 934	3.992 263	.250 485
29	646.234 854	2580.939 414	.000 387	.001 547	3.993 810	.250 387
30	807.793 567	3227.174 268	.000 310	.001 238	3.995 048	.250 310
31	1009.741 959	4034.967 835	.000 248	.000 990	3.996 039	.250 248
32	1262.177 448	5044.709 793	.000 198	.000 792	3.996 831	.250 198
33	1577.721 810	6306.887 242	.000 159	.000 634	3.997 465	.250 159
34	1972.152 263	7884.609 052	.000 127	.000 507	3.997 972	.250 127
35	2465.190 329	9856.761 315	.000 101	.000 406	3.998 377	.250 101
36	3081.487 911	12321.951 644	.000 081	.000 325	3.998 702	.250 081
37	3851.859 889	15403.439 555	.000 065	.000 260	3.998 962	.250 065
38	4814.824 861	19255.299 444	.000 052	.000 208	3.999 169	.250 052
39	6018.531 076	24070.124 305	.000 042	.000 166	3.999 335	.250 042
40	7523.163 845	30088.655 381	.000 033	.000 133	3.999 468	.250 033
41	9403.954 807	37611.819 226	.000 027	.000 106	3.999 575	.250 027
42	11754.943 508	47015.774 033	.000 021	.000 085	3.999 660	.250 021
43	14693.679 385	58770.717 541	.000 017	.000 068	3.999 728	.250 017
44	18367.099 232	73464.396 926	.000 014	.000 054	3.999 782	.250 014
45	22958.874 039	91831.496 158	.000 011	.000 044	3.999 826	.250 011

$$S^n = (1+i)^n \qquad S_{\overline{n}|} = \frac{S^n - 1}{i} \qquad 1/S_{\overline{n}|} = \frac{i}{S^n - 1} \qquad V^n = \frac{1}{S^n} \qquad A_{\overline{n}|} = \frac{1 - 1/S^n}{i} \qquad \frac{1}{A_{\overline{n}|}} = \frac{i}{1 - 1/S^n}$$

	1	2	3	4	5	6
YEARS	AMOUNT OF ONE	AMOUNT OF ONE PER PERIOD	SINKING FUND FACTOR	PRESENT WORTH OF ONE	PRESENT WORTH ONE PER PERIOD	PARTIAL PAYMENT
1	1.260 000	1.000 000	1.000 000	.793 651	.793 651	1.260 000
2	1.587 600	2.260 000	.442 478	.629 882	1.423 532	.702 478
3	2.000 376	3.847 600	.259 902	.499 906	1.923 438	.519 902
4	2.520 474	5.847 976	.170 999	.396 751	2.320 189	.430 999
5	3.175 797	8.368 450	.119 496	.314 882	2.635 071	.379 496
6	4.001 504	11.544 247	.086 623	.249 906	2.884 977	.346 623
7	5.041 895	15.545 751	.064 326	.198 338	3.083 315	.324 326
8	6.352 788	20.587 646	.048 573	.157 411	3.240 726	.308 573
9	8.004 513	26.940 434	.037 119	.124 930	3.365 656	.297 119
10	10.085 686	34.944 947	.028 616	.099 150	3.464 806	.288 616
11	12.707 965	45.030 633	.022 207	.078 691	3.543 497	.282 207
12	16.012 035	57.738 598	.017 319	.062 453	3.605 950	.277 319
13	20.175 165	73.750 633	.013 559	.049 566	3.655 516	.273 559
14	25.420 707	93.925 798	.010 647	.039 338	3.694 854	.270 647
15	32.030 091	119.346 505	.008 379	.031 221	3.726 074	.268 379
16	40.357 915	151.376 596	.006 606	.024 778	3.750 853	.266 606
17	50.850 973	191.734 511	.005 216	.019 665	3.770 518	.265 216
18	64.072 226	242.585 484	.004 122	.015 607	3.786 125	.264 122
19	80.731 005	306.657 710	.003 261	.012 387	3.798 512	.263 261
20	101.721 066	387.388 715	.002 581	.009 831	3.808 343	.262 581
21	128.168 543	489.109 781	.002 045	.007 802	3.816 145	.262 045
22	161.492 364	617.278 324	.001 620	.006 192	3.822 338	.261 620
23	203.480 379	778.770 688	.001 284	.004 914	3.827 252	.261 284
24	256.385 277	982.251 067	.001 018	.003 900	3.831 152	.261 018
25	323.045 450	1238.636 345	.000 807	.003 096	3.834 248	.260 807
26	407.037 266	1561.681 794	.000 640	.002 457	3.836 705	.260 640
27	512.866 956	1968.719 061	.000 508	.001 950	3.838 655	.260 508
28	646.212 364	2481.586 016	.000 403	.001 547	3.840 202	.260 403
29	814.227 579	3127.798 381	.000 320	.001 228	3.841 430	.260 320
30	1025.926 749	3942.025 959	.000 254	.000 975	3.842 405	.260 254
31	1292.667 704	4967.952 709	.000 201	.000 774	3.843 178	.260 201
32	1628.761 307	6260.620 413	.000 160	.000 614	3.843 792	.260 160
33	2052.239 247	7889.381 721	.000 127	.000 487	3.844 280	.260 127
34	2585.821 452	9941.620 968	.000 101	.000 387	3.844 666	.260 101
35	3258.135 029	12527.442 420	.000 080	.000 307	3.844 973	.260 080
36	4105.250 137	15785.577 449	.000 063	.000 244	3.845 217	.260 063
37	5172.615 172	19890.827 586	.000 050	.000 193	3.845 410	.260 050
38	6517.495 117	25063.442 758	.000 040	.000 153	3.845 564	.260 040
39	8212.043 848	31580.937 875	.000 032	.000 122	3.845 685	.260 032
40	10347.175 248	39792.981 723	.000 025	.000 097	3.845 782	.260 025
	$S^n = (1+i)^n$	$S_{\overline{n}|} = \dfrac{S^n - 1}{i}$	$1/S_{\overline{n}|} = \dfrac{i}{S^n - 1}$	$V^n = \dfrac{1}{S^n}$	$A_{\overline{n}|} = \dfrac{1 - 1/S^n}{i}$	$\dfrac{1}{A_{\overline{n}|}} = \dfrac{i}{1 - 1/S^n}$

YEARS	1 AMOUNT OF ONE	2 AMOUNT OF ONE PER PERIOD	3 SINKING FUND FACTOR	4 PRESENT WORTH OF ONE	5 PRESENT WORTH ONE PER PERIOD	6 PARTIAL PAYMENT
1	1.270 000	1.000 000	1.000 000	.787 402	.787 402	1.270 000
2	1.612 900	2.270 000	.440 529	.620 001	1.407 403	.710 529
3	2.048 383	3.882 900	.257 539	.488 190	1.895 593	.527 539
4	2.601 446	5.931 283	.168 598	.384 402	2.279 994	.438 598
5	3.303 837	8.532 729	.117 196	.302 678	2.582 673	.387 196
6	4.195 873	11.836 566	.084 484	.238 329	2.821 002	.354 484
7	5.328 759	16.032 439	.062 374	.187 661	3.008 663	.332 374
8	6.767 523	21.361 198	.046 814	.147 765	3.156 428	.316 814
9	8.594 755	28.128 721	.035 551	.116 350	3.272 778	.305 551
10	10.915 339	36.723 476	.027 231	.091 614	3.364 392	.297 231
11	13.862 480	47.638 815	.020 991	.072 137	3.436 529	.290 991
12	17.605 350	61.501 295	.016 260	.056 801	3.493 330	.286 260
13	22.358 794	79.106 644	.012 641	.044 725	3.538 055	.282 641
14	28.395 668	101.465 438	.009 856	.035 217	3.573 272	.279 856
15	36.062 499	129.861 106	.007 701	.027 730	3.601 001	.277 701
16	45.799 373	165.923 605	.006 027	.021 834	3.622 836	.276 027
17	58.165 204	211.722 978	.004 723	.017 192	3.640 028	.274 723
18	73.869 809	269.888 182	.003 705	.013 537	3.653 565	.273 705
19	93.814 658	343.757 991	.002 909	.010 659	3.664 225	.272 909
20	119.144 615	437.572 649	.002 285	.008 393	3.672 618	.272 285
21	151.313 661	556.717 264	.001 796	.006 609	3.679 227	.271 796
22	192.168 350	708.030 926	.001 412	.005 204	3.684 430	.271 412
23	244.053 804	900.199 276	.001 111	.004 097	3.688 528	.271 111
24	309.948 332	1144.253 080	.000 874	.003 226	3.691 754	.270 874
25	393.634 381	1454.201 412	.000 688	.002 540	3.694 295	.270 688
26	499.915 664	1847.835 793	.000 541	.002 000	3.696 295	.270 541
27	634.892 893	2347.751 457	.000 426	.001 575	3.697 870	.270 426
28	806.313 974	2982.644 350	.000 335	.001 240	3.699 110	.270 335
29	1024.018 748	3788.958 324	.000 264	.000 977	3.700 087	.270 264
30	1300.503 809	4812.977 072	.000 208	.000 769	3.700 856	.270 208
31	1651.639 838	6113.480 882	.000 164	.000 605	3.701 461	.270 164
32	2097.582 594	7765.120 720	.000 129	.000 477	3.701 938	.270 129
33	2663.929 895	9862.703 314	.000 101	.000 375	3.702 313	.270 101
34	3383.190 966	12526.633 209	.000 080	.000 296	3.702 609	.270 080
35	4296.652 527	15909.824 175	.000 063	.000 233	3.702 842	.270 063
36	5456.748 710	20206.476 702	.000 049	.000 183	3.703 025	.270 049
37	6930.070 861	25663.225 412	.000 039	.000 144	3.703 169	.270 039
38	8801.189 994	32593.296 273	.000 031	.000 114	3.703 283	.270 031
39	11177.511 292	41394.486 267	.000 024	.000 089	3.703 372	.270 024
40	14195.439 341	52571.997 559	.000 019	.000 070	3.703 443	.270 019

$$S^n = (1 + i)^n \qquad S_{\overline{n}|} = \frac{S^n - 1}{i} \qquad 1/S_{\overline{n}|} = \frac{i}{S^n - 1} \qquad V^n = \frac{1}{S^n} \qquad A_{\overline{n}|} = \frac{1 - 1/S^n}{i} \qquad \frac{1}{A_{\overline{n}|}} = \frac{i}{1 - 1/S^n}$$

YEARS	1 AMOUNT OF ONE	2 AMOUNT OF ONE PER PERIOD	3 SINKING FUND FACTOR	4 PRESENT WORTH OF ONE	5 PRESENT WORTH ONE PER PERIOD	6 PARTIAL PAYMENT
1	1.280 000	1.000 000	1.000 000	.781 250	.781 250	1.280 000
2	1.638 400	2.280 000	.438 596	.610 352	1.391 602	.718 596
3	2.097 152	3.918 400	.255 206	.476 837	1.868 439	.535 206
4	2.684 355	6.015 552	.166 236	.372 529	2.240 968	.446 236
5	3.435 974	8.699 907	.114 944	.291 038	2.532 006	.394 944
6	4.398 047	12.135 880	.082 400	.227 374	2.759 380	.362 400
7	5.629 500	16.533 927	.060 482	.177 636	2.937 015	.340 482
8	7.205 759	22.163 426	.045 119	.138 778	3.075 793	.325 119
9	9.223 372	29.369 186	.034 049	.108 420	3.184 214	.314 049
10	11.805 916	38.592 558	.025 912	.084 703	3.268 917	.305 912
11	15.111 573	50.398 474	.019 842	.066 174	3.335 091	.299 842
12	19.342 813	65.510 047	.015 265	.051 699	3.386 790	.295 265
13	24.758 801	84.852 860	.011 785	.040 390	3.427 180	.291 785
14	31.691 265	109.611 661	.009 123	.031 554	3.458 734	.289 123
15	40.564 819	141.302 926	.007 077	.024 652	3.483 386	.287 077
16	51.922 969	181.867 745	.005 499	.019 259	3.502 645	.285 499
17	66.461 400	233.790 714	.004 277	.015 046	3.517 692	.284 277
18	85.070 592	300.252 113	.003 331	.011 755	3.529 447	.283 331
19	108.890 357	385.322 705	.002 595	.009 184	3.538 630	.282 595
20	139.379 657	494.213 062	.002 023	.007 175	3.545 805	.282 023
21	178.405 962	633.592 720	.001 578	.005 605	3.551 410	.281 578
22	228.359 631	811.998 682	.001 232	.004 379	3.555 789	.281 232
23	292.300 327	1040.358 312	.000 961	.003 421	3.559 210	.280 961
24	374.144 419	1332.658 640	.000 750	.002 673	3.561 883	.280 750
25	478.904 857	1706.803 059	.000 586	.002 088	3.563 971	.280 586
26	612.998 216	2185.707 916	.000 458	.001 631	3.565 602	.280 458
27	784.637 717	2798.706 132	.000 357	.001 274	3.566 877	.280 357
28	1004.336 278	3583.343 849	.000 279	.000 996	3.567 873	.280 279
29	1285.550 435	4587.680 126	.000 218	.000 778	3.568 650	.280 218
30	1645.504 557	5873.230 562	.000 170	.000 608	3.569 258	.280 170
31	2106.245 833	7518.735 119	.000 133	.000 475	3.569 733	.280 133
32	2695.994 667	9624.980 953	.000 104	.000 371	3.570 104	.280 104
33	3450.873 173	12320.975 619	.000 081	.000 290	3.570 394	.280 081
34	4417.117 662	15771.848 793	.000 063	.000 226	3.570 620	.280 063
35	5653.910 607	20188.966 455	.000 050	.000 177	3.570 797	.280 050
36	7237.005 577	25842.877 062	.000 039	.000 138	3.570 935	.280 039
37	9263.367 139	33079.882 639	.000 030	.000 108	3.571 043	.280 030
38	11857.109 938	42343.249 778	.000 024	.000 084	3.571 127	.280 024
39	15177.100 721	54200.359 716	.000 018	.000 066	3.571 193	.280 018
40	19426.688 922	69377.460 437	.000 014	.000 051	3.571 245	.280 014

$$S^n = (1 + i)^n \qquad S_{\overline{n}|} = \frac{S^n - 1}{i} \qquad 1/S_{\overline{n}|} = \frac{i}{S^n - 1} \qquad V^n = \frac{1}{S^n} \qquad A_{\overline{n}|} = \frac{1 - 1/S^n}{i} \qquad \frac{1}{A_{\overline{n}|}} = \frac{i}{1 - 1/S^n}$$

	1	2	3	4	5	6
YEARS	AMOUNT OF ONE	AMOUNT OF ONE PER PERIOD	SINKING FUND FACTOR	PRESENT WORTH OF ONE	PRESENT WORTH ONE PER PERIOD	PARTIAL PAYMENT
1	1.290 000	1.000 000	1.000 000	.775 194	.775 194	1.290 000
2	1.664 100	2.290 000	.436 681	.600 925	1.376 119	.726 681
3	2.146 689	3.954 100	.252 902	.465 834	1.841 953	.542 902
4	2.769 229	6.100 789	.163 913	.361 111	2.203 064	.453 913
5	3.572 305	8.870 018	.112 739	.279 931	2.482 996	.402 739
6	4.608 274	12.442 323	.080 371	.217 001	2.699 997	.370 371
7	5.944 673	17.050 597	.058 649	.168 218	2.868 214	.348 649
8	7.668 628	22.995 270	.043 487	.130 401	2.998 616	.333 487
9	9.892 530	30.663 898	.032 612	.101 086	3.099 702	.322 612
10	12.761 364	40.556 428	.024 657	.078 362	3.178 064	.314 657
11	16.462 160	53.317 792	.018 755	.060 745	3.238 809	.308 755
12	21.236 186	69.779 952	.014 331	.047 089	3.285 899	.304 331
13	27.394 680	91.016 138	.010 987	.036 503	3.322 402	.300 987
14	35.339 137	118.410 819	.008 445	.028 297	3.350 699	.298 445
15	45.587 487	153.749 956	.006 504	.021 936	3.372 635	.296 504
16	58.807 859	199.337 443	.005 017	.017 005	3.389 640	.295 017
17	75.862 137	258.145 302	.003 874	.013 182	3.402 821	.293 874
18	97.862 157	334.007 439	.002 994	.010 218	3.413 040	.292 994
19	126.242 183	431.869 596	.002 316	.007 921	3.420 961	.292 316
20	162.852 416	558.111 779	.001 792	.006 141	3.427 102	.291 792
21	210.079 617	720.964 195	.001 387	.004 760	3.431 862	.291 387
22	271.002 705	931.043 812	.001 074	.003 690	3.435 552	.291 074
23	349.593 490	1202.046 518	.000 832	.002 860	3.438 412	.290 832
24	450.975 602	1551.640 008	.000 644	.002 217	3.440 630	.290 644
25	581.758 527	2002.615 610	.000 499	.001 719	3.442 349	.290 499
26	750.468 500	2584.374 137	.000 387	.001 333	3.443 681	.290 387
27	968.104 365	3334.842 636	.000 300	.001 033	3.444 714	.290 300
28	1248.854 630	4302.947 001	.000 232	.000 801	3.445 515	.290 232
29	1611.022 473	5551.801 631	.000 180	.000 621	3.446 135	.290 180
30	2078.218 990	7162.824 104	.000 140	.000 481	3.446 617	.290 140
31	2680.902 497	9241.043 095	.000 108	.000 373	3.446 990	.290 108
32	3458.364 222	11921.945 592	.000 084	.000 289	3.447 279	.290 084
33	4461.289 846	15380.309 814	.000 065	.000 224	3.447 503	.290 065
34	5755.063 901	19841.599 660	.000 050	.000 174	3.447 677	.290 050
35	7424.032 433	25596.663 561	.000 039	.000 135	3.447 811	.290 039
36	9577.001 838	33020.695 993	.000 030	.000 104	3.447 916	.290 030
37	12354.332 371	42597.697 831	.000 023	.000 081	3.447 997	.290 023
38	15937.088 759	54952.030 203	.000 018	.000 063	3.448 059	.290 018
39	20558.844 499	70889.118 961	.000 014	.000 049	3.448 108	.290 014
40	26520.909 403	91447.963 460	.000 011	.000 038	3.448 146	.290 011

$$S^n = (1+i)^n \qquad S_{\overline{n}|} = \frac{S^n - 1}{i} \qquad 1/S_{\overline{n}|} = \frac{i}{S^n - 1} \qquad V^n = \frac{1}{S^n} \qquad A_{\overline{n}|} = \frac{1 - 1/S^n}{i} \qquad \frac{1}{A_{\overline{n}|}} = \frac{i}{1 - 1/S^n}$$

	1	2	3	4	5	6
YEARS	AMOUNT OF ONE	AMOUNT OF ONE PER PERIOD	SINKING FUND FACTOR	PRESENT WORTH OF ONE	PRESENT WORTH ONE PER PERIOD	PARTIAL PAYMENT
1	1.300 000	1.000 000	1.000 000	.769 231	.769 231	1.300 000
2	1.690 000	2.300 000	.434 783	.591 716	1.360 947	.734 783
3	2.197 000	3.990 000	.250 627	.455 166	1.816 113	.550 627
4	2.856 100	6.187 000	.161 629	.350 128	2.166 241	.461 629
5	3.712 930	9.043 100	.110 582	.269 329	2.435 570	.410 582
6	4.826 809	12.756 030	.078 394	.207 176	2.642 746	.378 394
7	6.274 852	17.582 839	.056 874	.159 366	2.802 112	.356 874
8	8.157 307	23.857 691	.041 915	.122 589	2.924 702	.341 915
9	10.604 499	32.014 998	.031 235	.094 300	3.019 001	.331 235
10	13.785 849	42.619 497	.023 463	.072 538	3.091 539	.323 463
11	17.921 604	56.405 346	.017 729	.055 799	3.147 338	.317 729
12	23.298 085	74.326 950	.013 454	.042 922	3.190 260	.313 454
13	30.287 511	97.625 036	.010 243	.033 017	3.223 277	.310 243
14	39.373 764	127.912 546	.007 818	.025 398	3.248 675	.307 818
15	51.185 893	167.286 310	.005 978	.019 537	3.268 211	.305 978
16	66.541 661	218.472 203	.004 577	.015 028	3.283 239	.304 577
17	86.504 159	285.013 864	.003 509	.011 560	3.294 800	.303 509
18	112.455 407	371.518 023	.002 692	.008 892	3.303 692	.302 692
19	146.192 029	483.973 430	.002 066	.006 840	3.310 532	.302 066
20	190.049 638	630.165 459	.001 587	.005 262	3.315 794	.301 587
21	247.064 529	820.215 097	.001 219	.004 048	3.319 842	.301 219
22	321.183 888	1067.279 626	.000 937	.003 113	3.322 955	.300 937
23	417.539 054	1388.463 514	.000 720	.002 395	3.325 350	.300 720
24	542.800 770	1806.002 568	.000 554	.001 842	3.327 192	.300 554
25	705.641 001	2348.803 338	.000 426	.001 417	3.328 609	.300 426
26	917.333 302	3054.444 340	.000 327	.001 090	3.329 700	.300 327
27	1192.533 293	3971.777 642	.000 252	.000 839	3.330 538	.300 252
28	1550.293 280	5164.310 934	.000 194	.000 645	3.331 183	.300 194
29	2015.381 264	6714.604 214	.000 149	.000 496	3.331 679	.300 149
30	2619.995 644	8729.985 479	.000 115	.000 382	3.332 061	.300 115
31	3405.994 337	11349.981 122	.000 088	.000 294	3.332 355	.300 088
32	4427.792 638	14755.975 459	.000 068	.000 226	3.332 581	.300 068
33	5756.130 429	19183.768 097	.000 052	.000 174	3.332 754	.300 052
34	7482.969 558	24939.898 526	.000 040	.000 134	3.332 888	.300 040
35	9727.860 425	32422.868 084	.000 031	.000 103	3.332 991	.300 031
36	12646.218 553	42150.728 509	.000 024	.000 079	3.333 070	.300 024
37	16440.084 119	54796.947 062	.000 018	.000 061	3.333 131	.300 018
38	21372.109 354	71237.031 180	.000 014	.000 047	3.333 177	.300 014
39	27783.742 160	92609.140 534	.000 011	.000 036	3.333 213	.300 011
40	36118.864 808	120392.882 695	.000 008	.000 028	3.333 241	.300 008

$S^n = (1+i)^n$	$S_{\overline{n}} = \dfrac{S^n - 1}{i}$	$1/S_{\overline{n}} = \dfrac{i}{S^n - 1}$	$V^n = \dfrac{1}{S^n}$	$A_{\overline{n}} = \dfrac{1 - 1/S^n}{i}$	$\dfrac{1}{A_{\overline{n}}} = \dfrac{i}{1 - 1/S^n}$

Appendix C

Mathematics in Appraising

Appraising requires the use of a wide variety of mathematical techniques ranging from simple arithmetic through algebraic formulas to the statistical techniques of multiple regression analysis. Adding, subtracting, multiplying, and dividing can be done with only a pencil and paper or a simple calculator. More sophisticated calculators are helpful for solving algebraic formulas and some linear regression analysis. Computers are required for almost all stepwise multiple regression analysis. Use of the more sophisticated techniques is increasing in appraisal procedures.

This section is a review of the mathematical techniques and language used by appraisers. Familiar processes and the rules that apply to each are shown.

BASIC ARITHMETIC FOR DATA PROCESSING

Data collected in the market is analyzed in the appraisal process to produce an estimate of value. Included are building dimensions, population figures, reproduction costs, rentals, and sales. The numbers that represent this data can be processed to produce other numbers leading to final conclusions or value estimates, which are also expressed in numbers. In addition to the fundamental operations of addition, subtraction, multiplication, and division, appraising involves the use of ratios, percentages, rates, and factors. Percentages, rates, and factors are usually expressed in decimals rather than as fractions.

Ratios

Ratios are the result of dividing one number by another number. A ratio may be expressed as a whole number (integer), decimal, or fraction.

Example: In a community school there is a ratio of 58 students to 2 teachers.

The ratio of 58 to 2 is 58 ÷ 2 = 29, usually expressed as a ratio of 29 to 1.

The ratio of 2 to 58 is 2 ÷ 58 = .0345 (rounded)

The ratio of 2 to 58 is $\frac{2}{58} = \frac{1}{29}$

Percentages

Percentages are ratios (decimal) multiplied by 100 (or expressed on a base of 100). When the numerator of a fraction is divided by the denominator, the ratio represented by the fraction becomes a decimal relationship to 1, the whole, which is 100%. Multiplication of the resulting figure by 100 translates this figure to a percentage relationship to 1.

Continuing the above example:

$\frac{2}{58}$ = .0345

.0345 × 100 = 3.45% of a teacher for each student

Rates

Rates are percentages expressed in terms of a time period. For example:

$8 interest per year on $100 principal = 8% interest per year

$.50 interest per month on $100 = .005 or .5% interest per month.

A rate expresses the relationship of one quantity to another. In the above example, 8% relates the $8 of interest return to the $100 of principal invested. In appraising, rates may be used to find an unknown capital amount when only the rate and the quantity of the annual return are known.

Decimals

Figures expressed in decimals are added, subtracted, multiplied, and divided similar to whole numbers (integers) with some additional rules for placing the decimal point.

When decimal figures are added or subtracted, the number of places to the right of the decimal point is equal to the largest number of places in any of the numbers being added or subtracted.

Example

```
      242.071
+      63.12
+       4.2
+       2.7983
      312.1893
```

When decimals are multiplied, the number of places to the right of the decimal point is the total number of places to the right of the decimal point in all the numbers being multiplied.

Example

$$3.23 \times 7.459 = 24.09257$$

$$17.31 \times 6.9 \times 41.27 = 4929.24753$$

The number can be rounded for practicality and still maintain the degree of accuracy necessary for the appraisal process.

When decimals are divided, the decimal points in the dividend (numerator) and divisor (denominator) are moved to the right to make the divisor a whole number (integer); the decimal point is moved the same number of places and in the same direction in both numbers.

Example

$$896.487 \div 57.31 =$$

$$57.31 \overline{)896.487}$$

$$\begin{array}{r} 15.64 \text{ (rounded)} \\ 5731 \overline{)89648.7} \end{array}$$

Reciprocals

The reciprocal of a number is 1 (unity) divided by that number. For example, the reciprocal of 4 is ¼, which may be expressed as 0.25.

When a reciprocal relationship exists between two numbers, 1 (unity) divided by either number equals the other number. This reciprocal relationship exists between certain of the compound interest table factors in Appendix B. For example, the present worth of 1 per period (Column 5) factors and the partial payment (Column 6) factors are reciprocals. These annual factors in the 10% tables for 10 periods are, respectively, 6.144567 and 0.162745. Since they are reciprocals,

$$\frac{1}{6.144567} = 0.162745$$

and

$$\frac{1}{0.162745} = 6.144567$$

When this reciprocal relationship exists, multiplication by either number is equivalent to division by the other.

Factors

Factors are the reciprocals of rates and may be similarly used in appraising to express relationships between income and capital value. Using I, R, and V to represent income, rate, and value, with F to represent factor, the relationships may be expressed as:

$$I = V \times R \qquad\qquad I = \frac{V}{F}$$

$$R = \frac{I}{V} \qquad\qquad F = \frac{V}{I}$$

$$V = \frac{I}{R} \qquad\qquad V = I \times F$$

These relationships may be shown

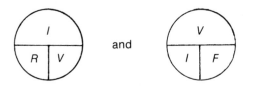

Commonly referred to as *IRV* and *VIF*, the formula for any single component is represented by the horizontal or vertical relationship of the remaining two components as one multiplied by, or divided by, the other.

The compound interest tables of Appendix B are at various rates applicable for specified numbers of compounding (or discounting) periods.

ALGEBRA

In algebra letters or symbols representing numerical quantities may be combined with numbers to state a mathematical relationship. These statements are expressed as equations. An equation is a statement that a number or group of quantities is equal to another quantity or group of quantities.

Example

$$6 + 10 = 16$$
$$12 - 8 = 3 + 1$$
$$44 + (5 + 4) = 53$$
$$15 + (6 \times 5) = 25 + (5 \times 4)$$

$$\frac{200}{20} = 10$$

$$\sqrt{36} = 3 \times 2$$

$$\left(\frac{12}{3} + 1\right)(11 - 1) = (7 \times 8) - 6$$

If one of the quantities is unknown, it may be represented by a letter or symbol in the equation. In solving equations every change in the statement of the equation must maintain the integrity or accuracy of the equation. One side of the equation must continue to equal the other side.

In the application of symbols:

1. The commutative laws state that, as with numbers in addition or multiplication, the sum or product is the same regardless of the sequence of the addition or multiplication.

   Example

$$2 + 4 + 10 = 10 + 4 + 2$$
$$16 = 16$$

   or

$$X + Y + Z = Z + Y + X$$

   and

$$8 \times 12 \times 5 = 12 \times 5 \times 8$$
$$480 = 480$$

   or

$$X \times Y \times Z = Z \times X \times Y$$

2. The associative laws state that when quantities are enclosed in brackets, the operations within the brackets are performed first. When two or more brackets are encountered, computation begins with the innermost bracket and continues successively outward.

   Example

$$18 + \left[(5 \times 9) - (18 - 3) + (4 \times 5)\right] =$$
$$18 + \left[45 - 15 + 20\right] \qquad =$$
$$18 + 50 \qquad = 68$$

3. The distributive law states that a number or symbol outside a bracket is multiplied by each number or symbol within the bracket.

   Example

$$8 (4 + 12) =$$

   can be solved

$$= 8(16)$$
$$= 128$$

but according to the distributive law may also be solved

$$8\ (4 + 12) = 32 + 96 = 128$$

or using symbols

$$X\ (Y + Z) = XY + XZ$$

The commutative, associative, and distributive laws are used to simplify equations in the process of solving for an unknown quantity contained in the equation.

Example of simplification using the commutative law:

$$10 + (2Y + 3Y + 6Y) = 10 + 11Y$$

Example of simplifications using the associative law:

$$(7 + 8X) + 3X = 7 + (3X + 8X)$$

This same equation can be simplified using the distributive law:

$$(7 + 8X) + 3X = 7 + (8 + 3)X$$
$$= 7 + 11X$$

Equations are mathematical expressions that relate one group of numbers and symbols to another group of numbers and symbols.
For example

$$X = 5Y$$

If it is known that Y equals 4, the equation can be solved to find that X equals 20.

$$X = 5Y$$
$$X = 5(4)$$
$$X = 20$$

Algebraic equations consist of two groups of quantities, expressed in terms of numbers, constants, coefficients, or variables, that are equal to each other. This is shown by an equal sign. The following are examples of types of algebraic equations in which the variables are unknowns and are represented by letters of the alphabet.

Reflective equation: $X = Y$
Symmetric equation: if $X = Y$, then $Y = X$
Transitive equation: if $X = Y$ and $Y = b$, then $X = b$

In solving algebraic equations it is axiomatic that both sides will remain equal after equal quantities are added to, subtracted from, multiplied by, or divided into both sides of the equation.

The effect of adding or subtracting equal amounts on both sides of an equation is equivalent to transposing items from one side to the other. For example

$$9X + 2 = 29$$

Subtracting 2 from each side of the equation results in:

$$9X + 2 - 2 = 29 - 2$$

and now

$$9X = 27$$

In effect, the $+ 2$ on the left side of the equation has been transposed to the right side with a change in sign from plus to minus. This procedure is applicable for addition, subtraction, multiplication, or division, provided the sign changes ($+$ to $-$, $-$ to $+$, $\times$ to $\div$, or $\div$ to $\times$). For example

$$3 (9X) = 81$$

To move the multiplier 3 to the other side divide each side by 3

$$\frac{\cancel{3} (9X)}{\cancel{3}} = \frac{81}{3}$$

$$9X = 27$$

This brief review of basic algebra illustrates techniques useful for the solution of simple equations of the type encountered in appraisal procedures. The illustrated techniques may be used in the solution of an equation containing one unknown quantity, X, as follows:

$$13X - 6X + 12 = -6X + 3X + 32$$

Step 1: Collect like terms

$$7X + 12 = -3X + 32$$

Step 2: Clear the negative terms by adding equal amounts to both sides.

$$
\begin{array}{rcr}
7X + 12 &=& -3X + 32 \\
+3X && +3X \\
\hline
10X + 12 &=& 32
\end{array}
$$

Step 3: Clear the equation by adding or substituting equal numbers to both sides.

$$
\begin{array}{rcr}
10X + 12 &=& 32 \\
-12 &=& -12 \\
\hline
10X &=& 20
\end{array}
$$

Step 4: Divide each side of the equation by equal numbers to find the value of the unknown letter (X)

$$10X = 20$$
$$\frac{10X}{10} = \frac{20}{10}$$
$$X = 2$$

BASIC STATISTICS

Statistics can be an effective tool for the interpretation of available data and the support of a value conclusion. In the language of statistics, a *population* refers to all the items in a specific category. If the category is houses in Chicago, the population consists of all the houses in Chicago. However, data pertaining to an entire population is rarely available and conclusions often must be developed from incomplete data.

The use of statistical concepts permits the derivation and evaluation of conclusions about a population from sample data. A *sample* is part of a population; the quality of conclusions based on a sample will vary with the quality or extent of the sample.

One item in a population is a *variate*. For appraisal purposes, one function of statistics is to identify attributes of the typical variate in a population. When observations about a population can be measured, the analysis may be *quantitative*. Observations about a population that do not permit quantitative measurement are *qualitative*, referring to attributes of the population.

A variate is called *discrete* when it can assume only a limited number of values on a measuring scale and *continuous* when it can assume an infinite number of values. A typical population of attributes would be house types—for example, one-story houses, two-story house, split levels. It is usually impractical to display or identify a population of variates because there are many.

One of the problems in statistics is to describe a population in universally understandable terms. For example, how does one describe all the houses in a community that have sold in the past year without an individual description of each sale?

One way is to use a single number to describe the whole population. This is called a *parameter*. One parameter that is used to describe a population is an *aggregate*, which is the sum of all the variates. All the house sales in a community in any given year can be described by the total dollar amount of all the sales. This is written in statistical language as

Σ = sigma = sum of

X = variate

ΣX = aggregate (summation of the variates)

Three commonly used parameters are the mean, the median, and the mode. These are three measures of *central tendency*. They are used in an effort to identify the typical variate in a population or in a sample.

The *mean* is commonly called the average. It is obtained by dividing the sum of all the variates in the population by the number of variates. The mean is by far the most commonly used parameter. In real estate appraising some common uses of the mean are average sale price, average number of days for sale, average apartment rent, and average cost per square foot.

The problem with the use of the mean to describe a population is that it can be distorted by extreme variates. A list of 36 house sales in a neighborhood is shown below.

$ 36,000
    37,300
    38,000
    38,600
    39,000
    39,500
    39,900
    39,900
    41,000
    41,000
    42,000
    42,800
    42,900
    43,000
    43,500
    43,600
    43,700
    43,900
    43,900 ←—median (Md.) = $43,900
    43,900
    44,000
    44,900
    45,000 ⎫
    45,000 ⎪ mode (Mo.) = $45,000
    45,000 ⎬
    45,000 ⎭
    45,300
    45,500
    45,500
    46,900
    46,900
    48,300
    48,500
    48,600
    49,400
$1,565,800

$$\text{Mean} = \overline{X} = \frac{\Sigma X}{N} = \frac{\$1,565,800}{36} = \$43,494$$

where ΣX = sum of the variates and N = number of variates

This same process can be performed with grouped data. This involves identifying the frequency with which a given sale price occurs and effectively weighting its contribution.

X	f	fX
$36,000	1	$36,000
37,300	1	37,300
38,000	1	38,000
38,600	1	38,600
39,000	1	39,000
39,500	1	39,500
39,900	2	79,800
41,000	2	82,000
42,000	1	42,000
42,800	1	42,800
42,900	1	42,900
43,000	1	43,000
43,500	1	43,500
43,600	1	43,600
43,700	1	43,700
43,900	3	131,700
44,000	1	44,000
44,900	1	44,900
45,000	4	180,000
45,300	1	45,300
45,500	2	91,000
46,900	2	93,800
48,300	1	48,300
48,500	1	48,500
48,600	2	97,200
49,400	1	49,400
	$N = 36$	$\Sigma fX = \$1,565,800$

$$\text{Mean} = \overline{X} = \frac{\Sigma fX}{N} = \frac{\$1,565,800}{36} = \$43,494$$

The "average" (or mean) price in this example—$43,494—might not give a fully accurate picture of the population of houses that have been sold if a few houses sold at prices substantially outside the indicated range.

The *median* is also used to describe a population or the average variate in the population. The median divides the variates of a population into equal halves. To compute the median of a population the variates are arranged in numerical order (as are the 36 sale prices in the example). If the total number of variates is odd, the median is the middle variate. If the total number of variates is even (as it is in this example), the median is the arithmetic mean of the two middle variates.

In the example of 36 house sales the middle two variates are $43,900 and $43,900. The mean of these two variates is $43,900, which is the median of the 36 sales. As many sales occurred above this figure as below it.

Like the median and mean, the *mode* is another parameter that describes the typical variate of a population. The mode is the most frequently appearing variate or attribute in a population. Of the 36 house sales, four sold at $45,000. No other sale price occurs with this frequency, so the mode in this sample is $45,000. If two prices were to occur with equal frequency, both would be modes and the sample would be bi-modal.

Here is another example, showing a population of types of condominium apartments available in a nine-unit complex:

```
efficiency
efficiency
efficiency
town house ⎫
town house ⎪
town house ⎬   mode (the most frequent attribute)
town house ⎪
town house ⎭
multi-bedroom
```

One of the problems in using statistics is to select the appropriate measure of central tendency to describe a population. The following single numbers can be used to describe the 36 variates in the group of house sales:

$$\bar{X} = \$43,494 = \text{the mean of all the sales}$$
$$\text{Md.} = \$43,900 = \text{the median of the sales}$$
$$\text{Mo.} = \$45,000 = \text{the mode of the sales}$$

The mean is often selected to describe a sample or population because the mean is a more widely understood concept.

Measures of Variation

The parameters mean, median, and mode are used to describe central tendencies of the population. Other sets of parameters are used to provide more information about the population being described. They measure the disparity among values of the various variates comprising the population. These parameters, called *measures of variation*, or *dispersion*, indicate the degree of uniformity among the variates and reflect the quality of the data as a basis for a conclusion.

One way to measure the disparity between the variates is known as the *range* (denoted by *R*). It is the difference between the highest and lowest variate.

R = maximum variate minus minimum variate

Using the figures in the example of 36 house sales

R = \$49,400 − \$36,000 = \$13,400

The range as a measure of variation is of limited usefulness since it considers only the highest and lowest values and neglects the variation in the remaining values. It also does not lend itself to further statistical treatment.

Average Deviation

Another parameter used to measure deviations between the variates is the *average deviation*, also known as the average absolute deviation because plus or minus signs are ignored. It is a measure of how much the actual values of the population or sample deviate from the mean (average). It is the mean of the sum of the absolute differences of each of the variates from the mean of the variates.

To demonstrate the average deviation the 36 sales are listed again.

Ungrouped Data

X Sale Price	$\|X - \overline{X}\|$ Absolute Deviation Between Each Variate and the Mean Sale Price of $43,494
$ 36,000	$ 7,494
37,300	6,194
38,000	5,494
38,600	4,894
39,000	4,494
39,500	3,994
39,900	3,594
39,900	3,594
41,000	2,494
41,000	2,494
42,000	1,494
42,800	694
42,900	594
43,000	494
43,500	6
43,600	106
43,700	206
43,900	406
43,900	406
43,900	406
44,000	506
44,900	1,406
45,000	1,506
45,000	1,506
45,000	1,506
45,000	1,506
45,300	1,806
45,500	2,006
45,500	2,006
46,900	3,406
46,900	3,406
48,300	4,806
48,500	5,006
48,600	5,106
48,600	5,106
49,000	5,906
$1,565,800 Total of sale prices	$96,048 Total deviation from mean $\Sigma\|X - \overline{X}\|$

Grouped Data

X	$|X-\overline{X}|$	f	$f|X-\overline{X}|$
$36,000	$7,494	1	$ 7,494
37,300	6,194	1	6,194
38,000	5,494	1	5,494
38,600	4,894	1	4,894
39,000	4,494	1	4,494
39,500	3,994	1	3,994
39,900	3,594	2	7,188
41,000	2,494	2	4,988
42,000	1,494	1	1,494
42,800	694	1	694
42,900	594	1	594
43,000	494	1	494
43,500	6	1	6
43,600	106	1	106
43,700	206	1	206
43,900	406	3	1,218
44,000	506	1	506
44,900	1,406	1	1,406
45,000	1,506	4	6,024
45,300	1,806	1	1,806
45,500	2,006	2	4,012
46,900	3,406	2	6,812
48,300	4,806	1	4,806
48,500	5,006	1	5,006
48,600	5,106	2	10,212
49,400	5,906	1	5,906
		36	$96,048

Total deviation from the mean $\Sigma f|X - \overline{X}|$

$$\text{A.D. (ungrouped data)} = \frac{\Sigma|X - \overline{X}|}{n} = \frac{\$96,048}{36} = \$2,668$$

$$\text{A.D. (grouped data)} = \frac{\Sigma f|X - \overline{X}|}{n} = \frac{\$96,048}{36} = \$2,668$$

A.D. = average deviation
Σ = sum of
f = frequency
X = observed value
$||$ = ignore the + or − signs
n = number of observations in sample (N = population)
$\overline{X}$ = mean of sample (σ = population)

This indicates that the average deviation of the individual values in the sample population from the mean is $2,668, or about 6%. This is a relatively small variation and suggests that the mean is an acceptable representation of this sample.

Like the range, the average deviation does not lend itself to further statistical calculations.

Standard Deviation

The *standard deviation* provides a way of describing a sample or a population that lends itself to further mathematical treatment. It permits application of rules of probability to draw inferences from samples concerning attributes of the population. In this method the square of the difference between each observation and the mean of the observations is used in lieu of the absolute deviation. This serves to magnify the effects of extreme variance from the mean.

In the example the mean sale price is $43,494; for a $41,000 sale the measure of deviation is $2,494 squared, or $6,220,036.

When the standard deviation of a *whole* population is being calculated, it is symbolized by sigma (σ). Expressed verbally, the formula is: *Standard deviation of a population is the square root of the sum of the squared differences between each observation and the mean of all the observations in the population, divided by the number of observations in the population.*

When the standard deviation of a *sample* of a population is being calculated, it is symbolized by the letter s. Expressed verbally, the formula is: *Standard deviation of a sample is the square root of the sum of the squared differences between each observation and the mean of all the observations in the sample, divided by the number of observations in the sample minus 1.*

The reason 1 is subtracted from the number of observations in a sample is to adjust for one degree of freedom that is lost when the mean is calculated. A set of data originally has as many degrees of freedom as there are observations. Every time a statistic is calculated directly from the data, a degree of freedom is lost.

Formulas for calculating the standard deviations follow.

For a population:

Ungrouped

$$\sigma = \sqrt{\frac{\Sigma\,(X - \bar{X})^2}{N}}$$

Grouped

$$\sigma = \sqrt{\frac{\Sigma f\,(X - \bar{X})^2}{N}}$$

For a sample:

Ungrouped

$$s = \sqrt{\frac{\Sigma\,(X - \bar{X})^2}{n - 1}}$$

Grouped

$$s = \sqrt{\frac{\Sigma f\,(X - \bar{X})^2}{n - 1}}$$

In real estate appraising samples are usually used, so the second formula is applicable, as in the example of 36 house sales for grouped data only (see Table C.1, p. 628).

The standard deviation is an important way to describe the variance of a population or sample. It tells how representative of the whole sample or population the mean is by describing a standard variance. It is a number that is used and understood in many disciplines. With the availability of electronic calculators, it now can be calculated easily. It undoubtedly will become more widely used by appraisers in the future.

When used for this purpose, the standard deviation can indicate what percent of the sample of the population may be expected to fall within selected ranges of *confidence intervals* (see page 633).

Approximately 68.26% of the sample or population will generally fall within plus or minus one standard deviation from the mean, provided the data meets certain tests of normal distribution (as explained later). Many types of real estate data conform to the pattern of a normal distribution when developed through appropriate sampling techniques.

In the example, assuming normal distribution, 68.26% of the house sales in the population will be between $40,080 and $46,908 ($43,494 − $3,414 and $43,494 + $3,414). Approximately 95.44% of the sales should fall within two standard deviations and approximately 99.74% should fall within three standard deviations from the mean.

Because the standard deviation lends itself to further mathematical treatment, it can be used for analytical purposes in addition to its use to describe a population.

Table C.1.   Standard Deviation for 36 House Sales

X	f	$(X-\bar{X})$	$(X-\bar{X})^2$	$f(X-\bar{X})^2$
$36,000	1	$7,494	$56,160,036	$ 56,160,036
37,300	1	6,194	38,365,636	38,365,636
38,000	1	5,494	30,184,036	30,184,036
38,600	1	4,894	23,951,236	23,951,236
39,000	1	4,494	20,196,036	20,196,036
39,500	1	3,994	15,952,036	15,952,036
39,900	2	3,594	12,916,836	25,833,672
41,000	2	2,494	6,220,036	12,440,072
42,000	1	1,494	2,232,036	2,232,036
42,800	1	694	481,636	481,636
42,900	1	594	352,836	352,836
43,000	1	494	244,036	244,036
43,500	1	6	36	36
43,600	1	106	11,236	11,236
43,700	1	206	42,436	42,436
43,900	3	406	164,836	494,508
44,000	1	506	256,036	256,036
44,900	1	1,406	1,976,836	1,976,836
45,000	4	1,506	2,268,036	9,072,144
45,300	1	1,806	3,261,636	3,261,636
45,500	2	2,006	4,024,036	8,048,072
46,900	2	3,406	11,600,836	23,201,672
48,300	1	4,806	23,097,636	23,097,636
48,500	1	5,006	25,060,036	25,060,036
48,600	2	5,106	26,071,236	52,142,472
49,400	1	5,906	34,880,836	34,880,836
				$407,938,896

$$s = \sqrt{\frac{\Sigma\, f(X-\bar{X})^2}{n-1}}$$

Mean: $43,494

$$s = \sqrt{\frac{\$407,938,896}{36-1}}$$

$$s = \sqrt{\$11,655,397}$$

$$s = \$3,414$$

Statistical Inference

Statistical inference is based on the assumption that the past actions in the market are a valid basis for forecasting present or future market actions. In the example past sale prices are used to estimate current sale prices. This technique can also be used to forecast rentals, costs, depreciation, and so on, using rules of probability.

The *normal curve* plots a normal distribution and is a technique to illustrate a distribution of data. Where original data may not be normally distributed, repeated random samples may be drawn with results that approximate a normal distribution. Sales are often treated as though they were normally distributed in competitive, open market situations. The normal curve is often graphed in a form known as a bell curve.

A major characteristic of a bell curve is that it is symmetrical. Both halves have the same shape and contain the same number of observations. The mean, median, and mode are the same value; and this value is the midpoint (apex) of the curve.

Figure C.1 (p. 630) is a bell curve and shows that 68.26% of the observations will fall within the range of the mean plus or minus one standard deviation, 95.44% within plus or minus two standard deviations, and 99.74% within plus or minus three standard deviations. It depicts an analysis of the probable population distribution for the 36 sales, assuming a normal distribution.

In this example the ranges for one, two, and three standard deviations are shown. The percentage of the population that will fall within any given distance from the mean or within any specified range can also be calculated. For example, the percentage of sales included within a range of $40,994 to $45,994 (the mean of $43,494 plus or minus $2,500) may be estimated by first calculating the Z value for this range (using the formula below) and then entering a table of areas under the curve of normal distribution with the calculated value of Z.

Z = the deviation of X from the mean measured in standard deviations

$$Z = \frac{X - \text{mean}}{\text{standard deviation}}$$

$$Z = \frac{\$45,994 - \$43,494}{\$3,414} = \frac{\$2,500}{\$3,414} = .73$$

Figure C.1.   Area Under the Normal Curve

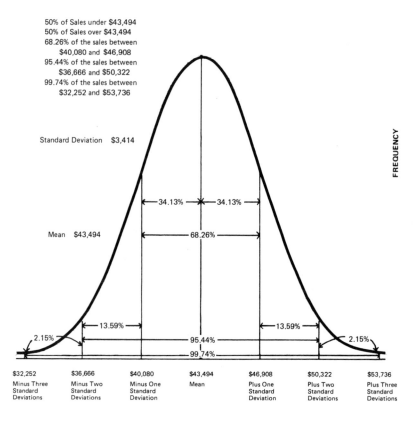

50% of Sales under $43,494
50% of Sales over $43,494
68.26% of the sales between
$40,080 and $46,908
95.44% of the sales between
$36,666 and $50,322
99.74% of the sales between
$32,252 and $53,736

Standard Deviation $3,414

FREQUENCY

34.13% ——✱—— 34.13%

Mean $43,494   68.26%

13.59%   13.59%

2.15%   2.15%

95.44%

99.74%

$32,252	$36,666	$40,080	$43,494	$46,908	$50,322	$53,736
Minus Three Standard Deviations	Minus Two Standard Deviations	Minus One Standard Deviation	Mean	Plus One Standard Deviation	Plus Two Standard Deviations	Plus Three Standard Deviations

SALE PRICE

This formula shows that $45,994 and $40,994 each deviate from the mean of $43,449 by .73 standard deviations.

The percentage of sales within this Z range of plus or minus .73 standard deviations can be developed from Table C.2 by first finding 0.7 under the Z column and then looking across the top of the page for the next digit. Accordingly, 26.73% of the sales are shown to fall between $43,494 and $45,994 or between $43,494 and $40,994; and 53.46% of the sales will be between $45,994 and $40,994.

Table C.2. Areas Under the Normal Curve

Z	.00	.01	.02	.03	.04	.05	.06	.07	.08	.09
0.0	.0000	.0040	.0080	.0120	.0160	.0199	.0239	.0279	.0319	.0359
0.1	.0398	.0438	.0478	.0517	.0557	.0596	.0636	.0675	.0714	.0753
0.2	.0793	.0832	.0871	.0910	.0948	.0987	.1026	.1064	.1103	.1141
0.3	.1179	.1217	.1255	.1293	.1331	.1368	.1406	.1443	.1480	.1517
0.4	.1554	.1591	.1628	.1664	.1700	.1736	.1772	.1808	.1844	.1879
0.5	.1915	.1950	.1985	.2019	.2054	.2088	.2123	.2157	.2190	.2224
0.6	.2257	.2291	.2324	.2357	.2389	.2422	.2454	.2486	.2517	.2549
0.7	.2580	.2611	.2642	.2673	.2704	.2734	.2764	.2794	.2823	.2852
0.8	.2881	.2910	.2939	.2967	.2995	.3023	.3051	.3078	.3106	.3133
0.9	.3159	.3186	.3212	.3238	.3264	.3289	.3315	.3340	.3365	.3389
1.0	.3413	.3438	.3461	.3485	.3508	.3531	.3554	.3577	.3599	.3621
1.1	.3643	.3665	.3686	.3708	.3729	.3749	.3770	.3790	.3810	.3830
1.2	.3849	.3869	.3888	.3907	.3925	.3944	.3962	.3980	.3997	.4015
1.3	.4032	.4049	.4066	.4082	.4099	.4115	.4131	.4147	.4162	.4177
1.4	.4192	.4207	.4222	.4236	.4251	.4265	.4279	.4292	.4306	.4319
1.5	.4332	.4345	.4357	.4370	.4382	.4394	.4406	.4418	.4429	.4441
1.6	.4452	.4463	.4474	.4484	.4495	.4505	.4515	.4525	.4535	.4545
1.7	.4554	.4564	.4573	.4582	.4591	.4599	.4608	.4616	.4625	.4633
1.8	.4641	.4649	.4656	.4664	.4671	.4678	.4686	.4693	.4699	.4706
1.9	.4713	.4719	.4726	.4732	.4738	.4744	.4750	.4756	.4761	.4767
2.0	.4772	.4778	.4783	.4788	.4793	.4798	.4803	.4808	.4812	.4817
2.1	.4821	.4826	.4830	.4834	.4838	.4842	.4846	.4850	.4854	.4857
2.2	.4861	.4864	.4868	.4871	.4875	.4878	.4881	.4884	.4887	.4890
2.3	.4893	.4896	.4898	.4901	.4904	.4906	.4909	.4911	.4913	.4916
2.4	.4918	.4920	.4922	.4925	.4927	.4929	.4931	.4932	.4934	.4936
2.5	.4938	.4940	.4941	.4943	.4945	.4946	.4948	.4949	.4951	.4952
2.6	.4953	.4955	.4956	.4957	.4959	.4960	.4961	.4962	.4963	.4964
2.7	.4965	.4966	.4967	.4968	.4969	.4970	.4971	.4972	.4973	.4974
2.8	.4974	.4975	.4976	.4977	.4877	.4978	.4979	.4979	.4980	.4981
2.9	.4981	.4982	.4982	.4983	.4984	.4984	.4985	.4985	.4986	.4986
3.0	.4987	.4987	.4987	.4988	.4988	.4989	.4989	.4989	.4990	.4990

Another question that can be answered using the Z value is the probability of a randomly selected sale falling inside a given range.

Continuing to use the population based on the sample of 36 sales, which has a mean of $43,449 and a standard deviation of $3,414, the probability of a randomly selected sale falling in any selected range of values can be calculated.

For example, the probability of a randomly selected sale falling between $43,449 and $44,449 ($1,000 over the mean) is calculated as follows:

$$Z = \frac{X - \text{mean}}{\text{standard deviation}} = \frac{\$44,449 - \$43,449}{\$3,414} = \frac{\$1,000}{\$3,414} = .29$$

Looking at the table of areas under the normal curve, a Z value of .29 corresponds to .1141. This indicates an 11.41% chance the sale will fall within $1,000 above the mean. Since the curve of normal distribution is symmetrical about the mean, the same probability exists that a sale will fall within $1,000 below the mean. Thus

Probability a sale will fall between $44,449 and $43,449	11.41%
Probability a sale will fall between $42,449 and $43,449	11.41%
Probability a sale will fall between $42,449 and $44,499	22.82%

If the range is expanded in the same example to $2,000 plus or minus the mean of $43,449, to $41,449 and $45,449 respectively, the probability of a randomly selected sale falling within this range would be increased.

$$Z = \frac{X - \text{mean}}{\text{standard deviation}} = \frac{\$45,449 - \$43,449}{\$3,414} = \frac{\$2,000}{\$3,414} = .59$$

Looking at the areas under the normal curve table .59 = .2224.

Probability a sale will fall between $45,449 and $43,449	22.24%
Probability a sale will fall between $41,449 and $43,449	22.24%
Probability a sale will fall between $41,449 and $45,449	44.48%

In the above examples the range being tested is equally above and below the mean sale price. However, the probability of a randomly selected sale falling between any selected range in the population can also be tested, for example, between $40,000 and $50,000:

$$Z \text{ area}^1 = \frac{X^1 - \text{mean}}{\text{standard deviation}} = \frac{\$40,000 - \$43,449}{\$3,414} = \frac{\$3,449}{\$3,414} = 1.01$$

$$Z \text{ area}^2 = \frac{X^2 - \text{mean}}{\text{standard deviation}} = \frac{\$50,000 - \$43,449}{\$3,414} = \frac{\$6,551}{\$3,414} = 1.92$$

Looking at 1.01 in the table for areas under
the normal curve tables gives   .3438

Looking at 1.92 in the table for areas under
the normal curve table gives   .4726

Probability   .8164

This indicates an 81.64% chance that a randomly selected sale in this sample will fall between $40,000 and $50,000.

Confidence Level

Using statistical inference and the laws of probability for a normal distribution, the previous examples have shown how *confidence intervals* may be constructed for a sample where there is an assumption (or approximation) of normally distributed data. These calculations may be valuable in a number of real estate decision-making situations, including loan administration, housing development, and appraising.

As seen in the previous examples, with 36 sales as a sample, an appraiser may say *with a 95% degree of confidence* that any sale randomly selected from the population will fall between $36,664 and $50,332. Similarly, there is a 68% level of confidence that the sample will fall between $40,080 and $46,908.

Such measure may be meaningful in connection with other statistical conclusions. However, because they are dependent on the accuracy of the estimated mean (as representative of the true population mean), some degree of confidence about the reliability of the mean must be established. Regardless of population size, there is a specific sample size that will permit a given level of confidence in the estimated mean.

In the continuing example of 36 sales the standard deviation for price has been calculated as $3,414. The arithmetic mean is $43,494, or about $43,500. If an appraiser wants to be 95% certain that the true mean is within $500 of the estimated mean ($43,494), or between about $43,000 and $44,000, calculation of the necessary sample size is:

n = Sample size required
z = Z statistic at 95% confidence level
s = Standard deviation of the sample
e = Required maximum difference in the mean

$$n = \frac{z^2 s^2}{e^2}$$

$$n = \frac{(1.96)^2 \, (\$3,414)^2}{(\$500)^2} = 179 \text{ sales}$$

Thus with 179 sales in a sample the required standard of confidence could be met. Similarly, for a confidence interval of not more than $750, calculations would be

$$n = \frac{(1.96)^2 \, (\$3,414)^2}{(\$750)^2} = 80 \text{ sales}$$

In the original sample of 36 sales, an appraiser may ask, "At a 95% confidence, what are the limits between which the true population mean may fall?" By substitution

$$e^2 = \frac{z^2 s^2}{n}$$

and

$$e^2 = \frac{(1.96)^2 \, (\$3,414)^2}{36} = \$1,243,760$$

$$e = \sqrt{\$1,243,760} = \$1,115$$

Thus the appraiser in this case may be statistically 95% certain that the true population mean falls between $42,399 and $44,609.

Although such calculations may seem to have an obscure relationship to day-to-day appraising, professional appraisers have a continuing interest in the availability of adequate data and in knowledge and understanding of the markets in which they appraise. Calculations such as these assist in quantifying change or in performing the neighborhood analyses essential to value estimation. They are also important for appraisal review, loan underwriting, and other analyses.

REGRESSION ANALYSIS

Simple Linear Regression Analysis

In estimating a probable sale price in the market, it is seldom sufficient to develop a sample of sales, calculate the standard deviation, and base an estimate on this evidence. The range of values is usually too great at the confidence level required to be useful. Appraisers recognize that the accuracy of the estimate can be substantially increased by considering one or more characteristics of each sale property, in addition to their sale prices.

Using the 36 sales in the earlier example, it may be demonstrated that there is an apparent relationship between sale price and the number of square feet of living area. The square footage of gross living area (GLA) for the 36 sales is exhibited in Table C.3. Typically, an appraiser might use only sales that have approximately the same square footage as the property being appraised and essentially ignore the others.

Note the appraiser's dilemma in appraising a 1,375 square foot dwelling. Sales 1, 2, and 3 are reported as $28.77, $32.07, and $27.98 per square foot respectively. Other sales may give a clue to the "right answer," but Sales 5 and 6 do little to resolve the conflict. Adjustments will probably be made for other differences, but complications may develop when multiple adjustments involve overlapping effects.

Sales 1 through 3 indicate a range of $27.98 to $32.07 per square foot, or when applied to the appraised property's 1,375 square feet, an indicated value range of $38,473 to $44,096. (These would be rounded in a report.) However, the remaining market information cannot effectively be applied to the analysis in traditional appraising except generally to reinforce the "appraiser's judgment."

Table C.3.   Comparable Sales Data Set for Simple Regression Analysis

Sale	GLA in Square Feet	Sale Price	Price per Square Foot GLA
1	1,321	$38,000	$28.77
2	1,372	44,000	32.07
3	1,394	39,000	27.98
4	1,403	37,300	26.59
5	1,457	42,900	29.44
6	1,472	43,700	29.69
7	1,475	42,000	28.47
8	1,479	42,800	28.94
9	1,503	36,000	23.95
10	1,512	38,600	25.53
11	1,515	41,000	27.06
12	1,535	39,500	25.73
13	1,535	43,900	28.60
14	1,577	45,500	28.85
15	1,613	45,000	27.90
16	1,640	39,900	24.33
17	1,666	45,500	27.31
18	1,681	39,900	23.74
19	1,697	43,600	25.69
20	1,703	43,500	25.54
21	1,706	44,900	26.32
22	1,709	45,300	26.51
23	1,709	46,900	27.44
24	1,720	46,900	27.27
25	1,732	41,000	23.67
26	1,749	48,600	27.79
27	1,771	48,600	27.44
28	1,777	43,000	24.20
29	1,939	43,900	22.64
30	1,939	45,000	23.21
31	1,939	45,000	23.21
32	1,939	45,000	23.21
33	1,939	48,300	24.91
34	1,940	43,900	22.63
35	2,014	49,400	24.53
36	2,065	48,500	23.49

Simple linear regression provides a technique in which more market data may be applied to this analysis—and avoids the zero intercept fallacy referred to in Chapter 15. For application in the simple linear regression formula, $Y^c = a + bX$, the 36 sales were analyzed by calculator and produced

a = $24,630
b = $11.29
r = .6598 (simple correlation coefficient)

Thus, for the 1,375-square-foot property appraised

Y^c = $24,630 + $11.29 (1,375)
Y^c = $40,154
(or $29.20 per square foot)

The calculated regression line and a plot of the 36 sales is shown in Figure C.2 (p. 638). Also shown is another statistical measure the *standard error of the estimate*, which allows construction of confidence intervals about the regression line. Calculations in this example produce a standard error estimate of $2,603. When applied to the property appraised, the appraiser may now state that the 36 sales in this market support an estimate of about $40,150 for the appraised property (based only on comparison of square footage). Further, at a 68% confidence level, the market price should lie between $40,150 ± $2,603 (or $37,547 to $42,753). At a 95% confidence level, price should lie between $40,150 ± (2) ($2,603), or $34,944 to $45,356.

Although other statistical measure such as the *standard error of the forecast* may be used, this analysis is generally considered sufficient and reasonably representative of most single family market situations. A more refined analysis of this data is possible, but this example illustrates simple application of a regression technique.

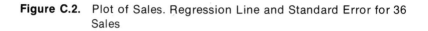

Figure C.2. Plot of Sales. Regression Line and Standard Error for 36 Sales

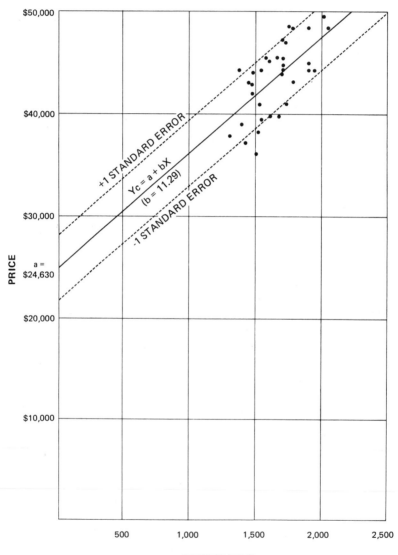

Example of Stepwise Multiple Regression Analysis[1]

An appraiser is asked to appraise a residential property located on a lot containing 7,575 square feet, improved with a recently constructed residence. The residence contains 1,720 square feet of living area with three bedrooms and two full baths. There are no porches and no swimming pool, although some swimming pools are found in the neighborhood. The dwelling has central air conditioning and physical characteristics that are similar to other properties in the neighborhood. There is an attached two-car garage.

After an inspection of the property and the collection and verification of comparable sales, a stepwise multiple regression analysis is selected for use in the market data approach to value.

Figure C.3 is a summary of information contained in a computer file of comparable sales. Based on the appraiser's selection of comparability factors that appear most important to this assignment, the computer selected these as most comparable from a list of available sales. The comparable sales printout is used by the appraiser to identify the comparable properties for inspection, to allow visual scanning of the data, and as a basis for a final screening of data to avoid including useless information.

Figure C.4 shows a computer printout of the 36 sales selected for initial analysis. These sales were randomly selected from the total file after the appraiser identified the independent variables involving the porch, number of bedrooms, lot size, garage size, living area, and any time parameters as the essential elements of the search. As shown in the last column, sale price was selected as the dependent variable for multiple regression analysis.

Figure C.5 is a summary of arithmetic means of each of the variables and their standard deviations. Also shown is a simple correlation matrix of the calculated interaction among each of the variables selected.

Each of the steps of multiple regression analysis applied to the comparable sales data set is summarized in Figure C.6. After the

---

1. The model illustrated in Figures C.3 to C.14 was developed by Valuation Systems Company, 1722 South Carson, Tulsa, Oklahoma 74119, and is used with permission.

initial regression equation has been computer-calculated (as shown in Step 5 of Figure C.6), the computer uses the regression equation to calculate the expected prices of each of the 36 comparable sale properties. By comparing actual sale prices with estimated sale prices for each, differences are shown in Figure C.7 as the "residuals," along with calculated percentages of error in estimate. In this projection of actual comparable sales information, only two sales were found to have more than a 10% error, and the majority involve less than 5%.

The percent of error in the residuals is shown in Figure C.8, which is a dynamic plot of residual error with the lowest amount of error at the left side of the plot and the highest error at the right.

A second run of the regression equation is made, deleting variables that produced the highest amount of error or were indicated by visual analysis to have the lowest degree of comparability with the property appraised. The results of this second run are shown in Figures C.9 through C.13. With the deletion of the least comparable variables, this second run produces a maximum residual error of 3.44% of actual price.

Recognizing and accepting the validity and statistical reliability of the analysis, the computer now may be employed to produce a final indication of value using the stepwise multiple regression analysis procedure. Final results of the projection for the property being appraised are shown in Figure C.14. The final projection indicates an estimated price essentially equal to the actual price of the property in a recent sale and establishes, for a 95% confidence interval, a range of approximately ± $2,000 as the reasonable price of the property appraised.

Figure C.3. Summary of Comparable Sales

COMPARABLE SALES
RESIDENTIAL PROPERTIES

SECTION - TOWNSHIP - RANGE :

PROP I.D.	ADDRESS	L AREA	BDRMS	BATHS	HT'NG	CL'NG	PARK'NG	L SIZE	C DATE	D SLD	PRICE	APPR I.D.
6358500000230	13129 93 AVE NO	1,666	THREE	TWO	CNTRL	CNTRL	2 GR'GE	8,100	1975	07 76	$45,500	421X
6358500000290	13152 93 AVE NO	1,457	THREE	TWO	CNTRL	CNTRL	2 GR'GE	8,100	1975	11 76	$42,900	422X
6358500000110	9290 132 ST NO	1,720	THREE	TWO	CNTRL	CNTRL	2 GR'GE	7,575	1976	10 76	$46,900	732Z
6358500000270	13196 93 AVE NO	1,749	THREE	TWO	CNTRL	CNTRL	2 GR'GE	9,936	1976	08 76	$48,600	987Y
6358500000120	9322 132 ST NO	1,709	THREE	TWO	CNTRL	CNTRL	2 GR'GE	7,568	1976	04 76	$46,900	7Z
6358500000150	13198 94 AVE NO	2,014	FOUR	TWO	CNTRL	CNTRL	2 GR'GE	10,002	1976	07 76	$49,400	325Z
6358500000100	9250 132 ST NO	1,709	THREE	TWO	CNTRL	CNTRL	2 GR'GE	7,560	1976	02 76	$45,300	681Y
6358500000070	13198 92 AVE NO	1,771	THREE	TWO	CNTRL	CNTRL	2 GR'GE	10,781	1976	01 76	$48,600	561Y
6358500000140	9376 132 ST N	1,479	TWO	TWO	CNTRL	CNTRL	2 GR'GE	9,033	1976	01 76	$42,800	552Y
6594300000220	12735 90 AVE NO	1,939	THREE	TWO	CNTRL	CNTRL	2 GR'GE	7,861	1976	03 76	$43,900	886Y
6594300000150	9153 127 ST NO	1,939	THREE	TWO	CNTRL	CNTRL	2 GR'GE	13,040	1976	08 76	$45,000	454Z
6594300000300	12744 91 AVE NO	1,940	THREE	TWO	CNTRL	CNTRL	2 GR'GE	7,700	1976	04 76	$43,900	941Y
6594300000250	9035 127LANE NO	1,939	THREE	TWO	CNTRL	CNTRL	2 GR'GE	9,800	1976	01 76	$45,000	630Y
6594300000010	9002 127LANE NO	1,706	THREE	TWO	CNTRL	CNTRL	2 GR'GE	8,400	1976	09 76	$44,900	666Z
6594300000100	12767 91 AVE NO	1,939	THREE	TWO	CNTRL	CNTRL	2 GR'GE	11,085	1976	08 76	$45,000	468Z
6594300000110	12745 91 AVE NO	1,939	THREE	TWO	CNTRL	CNTRL	2 GR'GE	11,022	1976	08 76	$48,300	486Z
6594300000080	12795 91 AVE NO	1,681	THREE	TWO	CNTRL	CNTRL	2 GR'GE	19,300	1976	01 76	$39,900	560Y
6268800040010	13625 CLARDON RD	1,475	THREE	TWO	CNTRL	CNTRL	2 GR'GE	9,191	1976	05 76	$42,000	305Y
6268800010070	13422 90 TERR N	1,515	THREE	TWO	CNTRL	CNTRL	2 GR'GE	8,500	1975	03 76	$41,000	874Y
6268800010120	13520 90 TERR N	1,697	THREE	TWO	CNTRL	CNTRL	2 GR'GE	8,800	1975	07 76	$43,600	28Y
6268800030090	9256 134 WAY N	1,732	THREE	TWO	CNTRL	CNTRL	2 GR'GE	7,700	1976	01 76	$41,000	477Y
6268800030060	13485 91 AVE N	1,613	THREE	TWO	CNTRL	CNTRL	2 GR'GE	8,580	1973	07 76	$45,000	320V

(Continued)

SECTION - TOWNSHIP - RANGE :

PROP I.D.	A D D R E S S	L AREA	BDRMS	BATHS	HT'NG	CL'NG	PARK'NG	L SIZE	C DATE	D'SLD	PRICE	APPR I.D.
6473900110150	11455 131 AVE N	1,777	THREE	TWO	CNTRL	CNTRL	2 GR'GE	11,000	1972	11 76	$43,000	16108
6473900110100	11450 132 AVE N	1,640	THREE	TWO	CNTRL	CNTRL	2 GR'GE	11,000	1972	10 76	$39,900	16105

SECTION - TOWNSHIP - RANGE :

PROP I.D.	A D D R E S S	L AREA	BDRMS	BATHS	HT'NG	CL'NG	PARK'NG	L SIZE	C DATE	D SLD	PRICE	APPR I.D.
6473900600020	11027 129 AVE NO	1,512	THREE	TWO	CNTRL	CNTRL	2 GR'GE	7,125	1972	02 76	$38,600	360Y
6473900300060	12740 110 ST NO	1,403	THREE	TWO	CNTRL	CNTRL	2 GR'GE	7,500	1975	07 76	$37,300	366Y
6473900700120	12853 112 ST NO	1,703	THREE	TWO	CNTRL	CNTRL	2 GR'GE	8,040	1974	06 76	$43,500	958Y
6473900300160	10907 126 TER NO	1,503	THREE	TWO	CNTRL	CNTRL	2 GR'GE	7,763	1975	04 76	$36,000	250X
6473900500140	11026 129 AVE NO	1,577	THREE	TWO	CNTRL	CNTRL	2 GR'GE	7,125	1974	09 76	$45,500	852X
6473900500080	10911 128 AVE NO	1,394	THREE	TWO	CNTRL	CNTRL	2 GR'GE	7,600	1976	10 76	$39,000	180Z
6473900500060	10919 128 AVE NO	1,372	TWO	TWO	CNTRL	CNTRL	2 GR'GE	7,410	1973	10 76	$44,000	750Z
6473900010570	11243 130 AVE NO	1,472	THREE	TWO	CNTRL	CNTRL	2 GR'GE	8,036	1972	04 76	$43,700	24U
6473900010020	10923 130 AVE NO	1,321	TWO	TWO	CNTRL	CNTRL	2 GR'GE	7,500	1973	03 76	$38,000	17493
6473900010250	11051 130 AVE	2,065	THREE	TWO	CNTRL	CNTRL	2 GR'GE	7,995	1976	09 76	$48,500	573Z
6473900010290	13119 11 LANE NO	1,535	THREE	TWO	CNTRL	CNTRL	2 GR'GE	7,500	1975	03 76	$43,900	747X
6473900020060	10914 126 TER NO	1,535	THREE	TWO	CNTRL	CNTRL	2 GR'GE	8,000	1974	02 76	$39,500	55X

Figure C.4. Selected Sales—First Analysis

```
STEPWISE MULTIPLE REGRESSION ANALYSIS


OBSERVATIONS
```

		INDEPENDENT VARIABLE					DEP
OBS	PROPERTY	1	2	3	4	5	VAR.
NUM	I.D. #	PORCH	BDRMS	LT SZ	GAR A	LIV A	PRICE
***	*************	*****	*****	*****	*****	*****	*****
1	6358500000230	1	3	8100	468	1666	45500
2	6358500000290	1	3	8100	484	1457	42900
3	6358500000110	1	3	7575	520	1720	46900
4	6358500000270	3	3	9936	448	1749	48600
5	6358500000120	1	3	7568	459	1709	46900
6	6358500000150	3	4	10002	501	2014	49400
7	6358500000100	1	3	7560	459	1709	45300
8	6358500000070	1	3	10781	449	1771	48600
9	6358500000140	4	2	9033	421	1479	42800
10	6594300000220	1	3	7861	444	1939	43900
11	6594300000150	1	3	13040	444	1939	45000
12	6594300000300	1	3	7700	444	1940	43900
13	6594300000250	3	3	9800	444	1939	45000
14	6594300000010	1	3	8400	459	1706	44900
15	6594300000100	1	3	11085	444	1939	45000
16	6594300000110	3	3	11022	444	1939	48300
17	6594300000080	1	3	19300	479	1681	39900
18	6268800040010	1	3	9191	441	1475	42000
19	6268800010070	1	3	8500	430	1515	41000
20	6268800010120	3	3	8800	441	1697	43600
21	6268800030090	1	3	7700	451	1732	41000
22	6268800030060	3	3	8580	524	1613	45000
23	6473900110150	0	3	11000	419	1777	43000
24	6473900600020	3	3	7125	422	1512	38600
25	6473900300060	3	3	7500	421	1403	37300
26	6473900700120	1	3	8040	454	1703	43500
27	6473900300160	1	3	7763	469	1503	36000
28	6473900500140	3	3	7125	458	1577	45500
29	6473900500080	3	3	7600	430	1394	39000
30	6473900050060	2	2	7410	455	1372	44000
31	6473900010570	3	3	8036	477	1472	43700
32	6473900010020	1	2	7500	460	1321	38000
33	6473900010250	1	3	7995	466	2065	48500
34	6473900010290	3	3	7500	471	1535	43900
35	6473900020060	3	3	8000	471	1535	39500
36	6473900110100	1	3	11000	427	1640	39900

Figure C.5.   Means, Standard Deviations, and Simple Correlation Coefficients of Variables—First Analysis

```
  MEANS

  VARIABLE NO.  1 - PORCH =        1.8055
  VARIABLE NO.  2 - BDRMS =        2.9444
  VARIABLE NO.  3 - LT SZ =    8,978.5555
  VARIABLE NO.  4 - GAR A =      455.5000
  VARIABLE NO.  5 - LIV A =    1,670.4722
  VARIABLE NO.  6 - PRICE =   43,494.4444


  STANDARD   DEVIATIONS

  VARIABLE NO.  1 - PORCH =        1.0642
  VARIABLE NO.  2 - BDRMS =        0.3333
  VARIABLE NO.  3 - LT SZ =    2,277.2125
  VARIABLE NO.  4 - GAR A =       25.0855
  VARIABLE NO.  5 - LIV A =      199.4894
  VARIABLE NO.  6 - PRICE =    3,414.0001


  SIMPLE   CORRELATION   COEFFICIENTS

      1        2        3        4        5     DEP VAR
    PORCH    BDRMS    LT SZ    GAR A    LIV A    PRICE

   1.0000  -0.0313  -0.1746  -0.0069  -0.2225   0.0224
            0.9999   0.1511   0.2596   0.5082   0.2909
                     1.0000  -0.0168   0.3232   0.0686
                              0.9999   0.0720   0.3210
                                       1.0000   0.6598
                                                0.9999
```

Figure C.6. Summary of Comparable Sales—First Analysis

```
                          STEP 3

*********** STEP NUMBER  1 ENTER VARIABLE  5 LIV A ***********

MEAN OF THE DEPENDENT VARIABLE . . . . . . . . . .   43,494.44
STANDARD ERROR OF THE ESTIMATE  . . . . . . . . . .    2,602.72
MULTIPLE CORRELATION COEFFICIENT  . . . . . . . . .    0.659848
CONTRIBUTION TO MULTIPLE CORRELATION COEFFICIENT . . . .659848
NUMBER OF VARIABLES IN REGRESSION EQUATION  . . . . . . .      1
DEGREES OF FREEDOM  . . . . . . . . . . . . . . . . . .       34
F RATIO  . . . . . . . . . . . . . . . . . . . . .      26.2195
CONSTANT TERM OF REGRESSION EQUATION  . . . . . .   24630.7425

VAR      BETA COEFF      S D COEFF      T VALUE      C COEFF

  5        11.2924        2.2053        5.1205       0.6598
```

```
*********** STEP NUMBER  2 ENTER VARIABLE  4 GAR A ***********

MEAN OF THE DEPENDENT VARIABLE . . . . . . . . . .   43,494.44
STANDARD ERROR OF THE ESTIMATE  . . . . . . . . . .    2,459.75
MULTIPLE CORRELATION COEFFICIENT  . . . . . . . . .    0.714532
CONTRIBUTION TO MULTIPLE CORRELATION COEFFICIENT . . . .054684
NUMBER OF VARIABLES IN REGRESSION EQUATION  . . . . . . .      2
DEGREES OF FREEDOM  . . . . . . . . . . . . . . . . . .       33
F RATIO  . . . . . . . . . . . . . . . . . . . . .      17.2118
CONSTANT TERM OF REGRESSION EQUATION  . . . . . .    8158.1402

VAR      BETA COEFF      S D COEFF      T VALUE      C COEFF

  4        37.4073       16.6174        2.2510       0.2748
  5        10.9533        2.0896        5.2417       0.6400
```

```
*********** STEP NUMBER  3 ENTER VARIABLE  1 PORCH ***********

MEAN OF THE DEPENDENT VARIABLE . . . . . . . . . .   43,494.44
STANDARD ERROR OF THE ESTIMATE  . . . . . . . . . .    2,421.98
MULTIPLE CORRELATION COEFFICIENT  . . . . . . . . .    0.734745
CONTRIBUTION TO MULTIPLE CORRELATION COEFFICIENT . . . .020212
NUMBER OF VARIABLES IN REGRESSION EQUATION  . . . . . . .      3
DEGREES OF FREEDOM  . . . . . . . . . . . . . . . . . .       32
F RATIO  . . . . . . . . . . . . . . . . . . . . .      12.5142
CONSTANT TERM OF REGRESSION EQUATION  . . . . . .    6120.3021

VAR      BETA COEFF      S D COEFF      T VALUE      C COEFF

  1       563.2193      394.6035        1.4273       0.1755
  4        37.1891       16.3630        2.2727       0.2732
  5        11.6240        2.1105        5.5076       0.6792
```

(Continued)

```
*********** STEP NUMBER  4 ENTER VARIABLE  2 BDRMS ***********

MEAN OF THE DEPENDENT VARIABLE . . . . . . . . .      43,494.44
STANDARD ERROR OF THE ESTIMATE  . . . . . . . . .       2,404.12
MULTIPLE CORRELATION COEFFICIENT  . . . . . . . .       0.748853
CONTRIBUTION TO MULTIPLE CORRELATION COEFFICIENT . . . .014107
NUMBER OF VARIABLES IN REGRESSION EQUATION  . . . . . . .      4
DEGREES OF FREEDOM  . . . . . . . . . . . . . . . . . . .     31
F RATIO   . . . . . . . . . . . . . . . . . . . .        9.8949
CONSTANT TERM OF REGRESSION EQUATION  . . . . . .       6332.8066

VAR       BETA COEFF       S D COEFF       T VALUE       C COEFF

 1         610.2820        393.6028        1.5505        0.1902
 2       -1790.3544       1473.0339       -1.2154       -0.1748
 4          42.5047         16.8208        2.5269        0.3123
 5          13.1522          2.4433        5.3829        0.7685


*********** STEP NUMBER  5 ENTER VARIABLE  3 LT SZ ***********

MEAN OF THE DEPENDENT VARIABLE . . . . . . . . . .     43,494.44
STANDARD ERROR OF THE ESTIMATE  . . . . . . . . .       2,401.97
MULTIPLE CORRELATION COEFFICIENT  . . . . . . . .       0.758756
CONTRIBUTION TO MULTIPLE CORRELATION COEFFICIENT . . . .009902
NUMBER OF VARIABLES IN REGRESSION EQUATION  . . . . . . .      5
DEGREES OF FREEDOM  . . . . . . . . . . . . . . . . . . .     30
F RATIO   . . . . . . . . . . . . . . . . . . . .        8.1413
CONSTANT TERM OF REGRESSION EQUATION  . . . . . .       7357.4683

VAR       BETA COEFF       S D COEFF       T VALUE       C COEFF

 1         565.1095        395.7003        1.4281        0.1761
 2       -1781.6589       1471.7387       -1.2105       -0.1739
 3          -0.1949          0.1897       -1.0274       -0.1300
 4          41.7828         16.8204        2.4840        0.3070
 5          13.8170          2.5254        5.4711        0.8073
```

Figure C.7. Comparison of Actual and Estimated Sale Prices of Comparables Showing Residuals and Percentages of Error— First Analysis

RESIDUALS LISTING

OBS	I.D. #	ACTUAL	ESTIMATE	RESIDUAL	% ERROR
1	6358500000230	45,500.00	43,572.00	1,927	4.23
2	6358500000290	42,900.00	41,352.77	1,547	3.60
3	6358500000110	46,900.00	46,593.18	306	0.65
4	6358500000270	48,600.00	44,655.44	3,944	8.11
5	6358500000120	46,900.00	43,893.81	3,006	6.40
6	6358500000150	49,400.00	48,736.92	663	1.34
7	6358500000100	45,300.00	43,895.37	1,404	3.10
8	6358500000070	48,600.00	43,706.24	4,893	10.06
9	6358500000140	42,800.00	42,319.52	480	1.12
10	6594300000220	43,900.00	46,387.87	-2,487	-5.66
11	6594300000150	45,000.00	45,378.19	-378	-0.84
12	6594300000300	43,900.00	46,433.07	-2,533	-5.77
13	6594300000250	45,000.00	47,140.06	-2,140	-4.75
14	6594300000010	44,900.00	43,690.15	1,209	2.69
15	6594300000100	45,000.00	45,759.33	-759	-1.68
16	6594300000110	48,300.00	46,901.83	1,398	2.89
17	6594300000080	39,900.00	42,055.36	-2,155	-5.40
18	6268800040010	42,000.00	39,592.11	2,407	5.73
19	6268800010070	41,000.00	39,819.90	1,180	2.87
20	6268800010120	43,600.00	43,865.95	-265	-0.60
21	6268800030090	41,000.00	43,851.60	-2,851	-6.95
22	6268800030060	45,000.00	46,216.18	-1,216	-2.70
23	6473900110150	43,000.00	41,927.86	1,072	2.49
24	6473900600020	38,600.00	40,842.47	-2,242	-5.80
25	6473900300060	37,300.00	39,221.52	-1,921	-5.15
26	6473900700120	43,500.00	43,509.97	-9	-0.02
27	6473900300160	36,000.00	41,427.31	-5,427	-15.07
28	6473900500140	45,500.00	43,244.76	2,255	4.95
29	6473900500080	39,000.00	39,453.72	-453	-1.16
30	6473900050060	44,000.00	41,447.90	2,552	5.80
31	6473900010570	43,700.00	42,410.24	1,289	2.95
32	6473900010020	38,000.00	40,369.49	-2,369	-6.23
33	6473900010250	48,500.00	49,021.91	-521	-1.07
34	6473900010290	43,900.00	43,134.51	765	1.74
35	6473900020060	39,500.00	43,037.03	-3,537	-8.95
36	6473900110100	39,900.00	40,934.29	-1,034	-2.59

Figure C.8.   Residuals Percentage of Error—First Analysis

```
                        RESIDUALS  AS  A  PERCENT  OF  ACTUAL
6358500000230 *                      4.23                                      *  1
6358500000290 *                    3.60                                        *  2
6358500000110 *      0.65                                                      *  3
6358500000270 *                                       8.11                     *  4
6358500000120 *                           6.40                                 *  5
6358500000150 *          1.34                                                  *  6
6358500000100 *                   3.10                                         *  7
6358500000070 *                                              10.06             *  8
6358500000140 *         1.12                                                   *  9
6594300000220 *                        -5.66                                   * 10
6594300000150 *      -0.84                                                     * 11
6594300000300 *                        -5.77                                   * 12
6594300000250 *                     -4.75                                      * 13
6594300000010 *             2.69                                               * 14
6594300000100 *        -1.68                                                   * 15
6594300000110 *              2.89                                              * 16
6594300000080 *                        -5.40                                   * 17
6268800040010 *                         5.73                                   * 18
6268800010070 *              2.87                                              * 19
6268800010120 *      -0.60                                                     * 20
6268800030090 *                           -6.95                                * 21
6268800030060 *          -2.70                                                 * 22
6473900110150 *             2.49                                               * 23
6473900600020 *                         -5.80                                  * 24
6473900300060 *                        -5.15                                   * 25
6473900700120 *    -0.02                                                       * 26
6473900300160 *                                            -15.07              * 27
6473900500140 *                       4.95                                     * 28
6473900500080 *        -1.16                                                   * 29
6473900050060 *                          5.80                                  * 30
6473900010570 *            2.95                                                * 31
6473900010020 *                           -6.23                                * 32
6473900010250 *        -1.07                                                   * 33
6473900010290 *          1.74                                                  * 34
6473900020060 *                               -8.95                            * 35
6473900110100 *          -2.59                                                 * 36
```

Figure C.9. Selected Sales—Second Analysis

STEPWISE MULTIPLE REGRESSION
ANALYSIS

OBSERVATIONS

OBS NUM ***	PROPERTY I.D. # **************	INDEPENDENT VARIABLE					DEF VAR.
		1 PORCH *****	2 BDRMS *****	3 LT SZ *****	4 GAR A *****	5 LIV A *****	PRICE *****
2	6358500000290	1	3	8100	484	1457	42900
3	6358500000110	1	3	7575	520	1720	46900
6	6358500000150	3	4	10002	501	2014	49400
7	6358500000100	1	3	7560	459	1709	45300
9	6358500000140	4	2	9033	421	1479	42800
11	6594300000150	1	3	13040	444	1939	45000
14	6594300000010	1	3	8400	459	1706	44900
15	6594300000100	1	3	11085	444	1939	45000
16	6594300000110	3	3	11022	444	1939	48300
19	6268800010070	1	3	8500	430	1515	41000
20	6268800010120	3	3	8800	441	1697	43600
22	6268800030060	3	3	8580	524	1613	45000
23	6473900110150	0	3	11000	419	1777	43000
26	6473900700120	1	3	8040	454	1703	43500
29	6473900500080	3	3	7600	430	1394	39000
31	6473900010570	3	3	8036	477	1472	43700
33	6473900010250	1	3	7995	466	2065	48500
34	6473900010290	3	3	7500	471	1535	43900
36	6473900110100	1	3	11000	427	1640	39900

Figure C.10.   Means, Standard Deviations, and Simple Correlation Coefficients of Variables—Second Analysis

```
MEANS

VARIABLE NO.  1 - PORCH =       1.8421
VARIABLE NO.  2 - BDRMS =       3.0000
VARIABLE NO.  3 - LT SZ =   9,098.3157
VARIABLE NO.  4 - GAR A =     458.6842
VARIABLE NO.  5 - LIV A =   1,700.6842
VARIABLE NO.  6 - PRICE =  44,294.7368


STANDARD DEVIATIONS

VARIABLE NO.  1 - PORCH =       1.1672
VARIABLE NO.  2 - BDRMS =       0.3333
VARIABLE NO.  3 - LT SZ =   1,605.3780
VARIABLE NO.  4 - GAR A =      31.2908
VARIABLE NO.  5 - LIV A =     202.1781
VARIABLE NO.  6 - PRICE =   2,739.9257


SIMPLE CORRELATION COEFFICIENTS

     1       2       3       4       5    DEP VAR
   PORCH   BDRMS   LT SZ   GAR A   LIV A   PRICE

 1.0000 -0.1427 -0.1895  0.1232 -0.2878  0.0431
         0.9999  0.1005  0.4261  0.4410  0.4014
                 0.9999 -0.3764  0.5334  0.1066
                         0.9999  0.0870  0.5390
                                 1.0000  0.7721
                                         1.0000
```

Figure C.11. Summary of Comparable Sales—Second Analysis

```
                              STEPS

*********** STEP NUMBER  1 ENTER VARIABLE  5 LIV A ***********

MEAN OF THE DEPENDENT VARIABLE . . . . . . . . . .   44,294.73
STANDARD ERROR OF THE ESTIMATE  . . . . . . . . . .   1,791.55
MULTIPLE CORRELATION COEFFICIENT  . . . . . . . . .   0.772143
CONTRIBUTION TO MULTIPLE CORRELATION COEFFICIENT . . .  .772143
NUMBER OF VARIABLES IN REGRESSION EQUATION  . . . . . .      1
DEGREES OF FREEDOM  . . . . . . . . . . . . . . . . . .     17
F RATIO  . . . . . . . . . . . . . . . . . . . . .     25.1007
CONSTANT TERM OF REGRESSION EQUATION  . . . . . .   26498.5669

VAR      BETA COEFF      S D COEFF      T VALUE      C COEFF

  5        10.4641         2.0886        5.0100       0.7721


*********** STEP NUMBER  2 ENTER VARIABLE  4 GAR A ***********

MEAN OF THE DEPENDENT VARIABLE . . . . . . . . . .   44,294.73
STANDARD ERROR OF THE ESTIMATE  . . . . . . . . . .   1,231.17
MULTIPLE CORRELATION COEFFICIENT  . . . . . . . . .   0.905826
CONTRIBUTION TO MULTIPLE CORRELATION COEFFICIENT . . .  .133682
NUMBER OF VARIABLES IN REGRESSION EQUATION  . . . . . .      2
DEGREES OF FREEDOM  . . . . . . . . . . . . . . . . .       16
F RATIO  . . . . . . . . . . . . . . . . . . . . .     36.5738
CONSTANT TERM OF REGRESSION EQUATION  . . . . . .    8357.6367

VAR      BETA COEFF      S D COEFF      T VALUE      C COEFF

  4        41.6297         9.3093        4.4718       0.4754
  5         9.9031         1.4407        6.8734       0.7307


*********** STEP NUMBER  3 ENTER VARIABLE  1 PORCH ***********

MEAN OF THE DEPENDENT VARIABLE . . . . . . . . . .   44,294.73
STANDARD ERROR OF THE ESTIMATE  . . . . . . . . . .   1,111.04
MULTIPLE CORRELATION COEFFICIENT  . . . . . . . . .   0.928963
CONTRIBUTION TO MULTIPLE CORRELATION COEFFICIENT . . .  .023136
NUMBER OF VARIABLES IN REGRESSION EQUATION  . . . . . .      3
DEGREES OF FREEDOM  . . . . . . . . . . . . . . . . . .     15
F RATIO  . . . . . . . . . . . . . . . . . . . . .     31.4893
CONSTANT TERM OF REGRESSION EQUATION  . . . . . .    7213.0588

VAR      BETA COEFF      S D COEFF      T VALUE      C COEFF

  1       511.2167       237.1465        2.1556       0.2177
  4        38.7790         8.5044        4.5598       0.4428
  5        10.7913         1.3639        7.9119       0.7962

                          (Continued)
```

```
*********** STEP NUMBER  4 ENTER VARIABLE  3 LT SZ ***********
MEAN OF THE DEPENDENT VARIABLE . . . . . . . . . .   44,294.73
STANDARD ERROR OF THE ESTIMATE  . . . . . . . . . .   1,050.50
MULTIPLE CORRELATION COEFFICIENT  . . . . . . . . .   0.941098
CONTRIBUTION TO MULTIPLE CORRELATION COEFFICIENT . . .  .012135
NUMBER OF VARIABLES IN REGRESSION EQUATION  . . . . . .      4
DEGREES OF FREEDOM  . . . . . . . . . . . . . . . . . .     14
F RATIO  . . . . . . . . . . . . . . . . . .          27.1122
CONSTANT TERM OF REGRESSION EQUATION  . . . . . .   11197.1810

    VAR     BETA COEFF      S D COEFF      T VALUE      C COEFF

     1       525.9293       224.3977       2.3437       0.2240
     3        -0.3516         0.2109      -1.6669      -0.2060
     4        31.0079         9.2946       3.3361       0.3541
     5        12.4101         1.6143       7.6873       0.9157
```

```
*********** STEP NUMBER  5 ENTER VARIABLE  2 BDRMS ***********
MEAN OF THE DEPENDENT VARIABLE . . . . . . . . . .   44,294.73
STANDARD ERROR OF THE ESTIMATE  . . . . . . . . . .   1,012.75
MULTIPLE CORRELATION COEFFICIENT  . . . . . . . . .   0.949381
CONTRIBUTION TO MULTIPLE CORRELATION COEFFICIENT . . .  .008282
NUMBER OF VARIABLES IN REGRESSION EQUATION  . . . . . .      5
DEGREES OF FREEDOM  . . . . . . . . . . . . . . . . . .     13
F RATIO  . . . . . . . . . . . . . . . . . .          23.7492
CONSTANT TERM OF REGRESSION EQUATION  . . . . . .   11015.6410

    VAR     BETA COEFF      S D COEFF      T VALUE      C COEFF

     1       495.1224       217.3957       2.2775       0.2109
     2     -1279.8154       891.0417      -1.4363      -0.1556
     3        -0.3353         0.2037      -1.6463      -0.1965
     4        36.8626         9.8442       3.7445       0.4209
     5        13.1415         1.6375       8.0251       0.9697
```

Figure C.12. Comparison of Actual and Estimated Sale Prices of Comparables Showing Residuals and Percentages of Error—Second Analysis

```
                    RESIDUALS  LISTING


OBS       I.D. #         ACTUAL    ESTIMATE   RESIDUAL   % ERROR
 2     6358500000290    42,900.00  41,943.43      956      2.22
 3     6358500000110    46,900.00  46,902.79       -2     -0.00
 6     6358500000150    49,400.00  48,962.46      437      0.88
 7     6358500000100    45,300.00  44,514.64      785      1.73
 9     6358500000140    42,800.00  42,362.46      437      1.02
11     6594300000150    45,000.00  45,146.33     -146     -0.32
14     6594300000010    44,900.00  44,193.49      706      1.57
15     6594300000100    45,000.00  45,802.02     -802     -1.78
16     6594300000110    48,300.00  46,813.39    1,486      3.07
19     6268800010070    41,000.00  40,580.90      419      1.02
20     6268800010120    43,600.00  44,267.78     -667     -1.53
22     6268800030060    45,000.00  46,297.27   -1,297     -2.88
23     6473900110150    43,000.00  42,284.91      715      1.66
26     6473900700120    43,500.00  44,090.49     -590     -1.35
29     6473900500080    39,000.00  40,282.86   -1,282     -3.28
31     6473900010570    43,700.00  42,894.22      805      1.84
33     6473900010250    48,500.00  49,305.18     -805     -1.66
34     6473900010290    43,900.00  43,680.73      219      0.49
36     6473900110100    39,900.00  41,274.54   -1,374     -3.44
```

Figure C.13.   Residuals Percentage of Error—Second Analysis

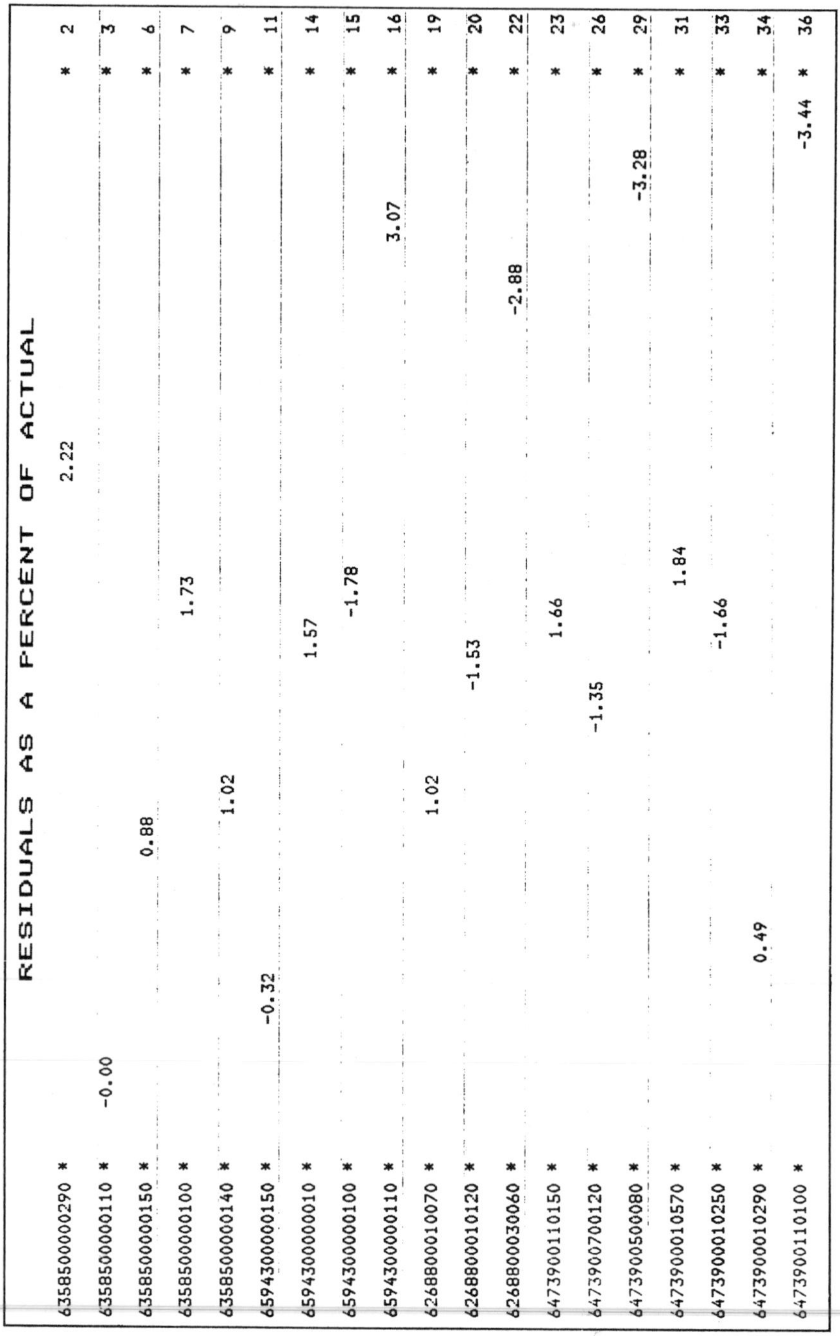

RESIDUALS AS A PERCENT OF ACTUAL

ID	Value	Value	Value	Row
6358500000290 *		2.22		2
6358500000110 *	-0.00			3
6358500000150 *		0.88		6
6358500000100 *			1.73	7
6358500000140 *		1.02		9
6594300000150 *	-0.32			11
6594300000010 *			1.57	14
6594300000100 *			-1.78	15
6594300000110 *				3.07	16
6268800010070 *		1.02		19
6268800010120 *			-1.53	20
6268800030060 *				-2.88	22
6473900110150 *			1.66	23
6473900700120 *			-1.35	26
6473900500080 *				-3.28	29
6473900010570 *			1.84	31
6473900010250 *			-1.66	33
6473900010290 *	0.49			34
6473900110100 *				-3.44	36

Figure C.14. Final Summary of Data Analyzed

```
        HOME  FEDERAL  SAVINGS  AND  LOAN
            MARKET  DATA  ANALYSIS


   PROPERTY ADDRESS   9290  132 ST  NO

   APPRAISER                                   DATE -

   PARAMETERS FOR COMPARABLES SEARCH:

   PORCHES      GENERAL  .  /  BEDROOMS    GENERAL    LOT SIZE    GENERAL ,
   GARAGE AREA  GENERAL      LIVING AREA  GENERAL


   COMPARISON GRID:
                                          COMPARABLE PROPERTIES
                         PROPERTY   ***********************************
        ITEM             APPRAISED       #1          #2          #3
   ****************      *********   **********  **********  **********
   DATE SOLD               10 76       09 76       11 76       10 76
   LOT SIZE                7,575       8,400      11,000      11,000
   CONSTRUCTION DATE        1978        1976        1972        1972
   PORCHES                 NONE        NONE        UNKWN       NONE
   BEDROOMS                THREE       THREE       THREE       THREE
   BATHS                   TWO         TWO         TWO         TWO
   LIVING AREA             1,720       1,706       1,777       1,640
   POOL                    NONE        NONE        NONE        NONE
   PARKING                 2 GR'GE     2 GR'GE     2 GR'GE     2 GR'GE
   COOLING                 CNTRL       CNTRL       CNTRL       CNTRL
   FINANCING               CNVTL       CNVTL       UNKWN       UNKWN
   EXTRAS                  N           N           N           N
   SALES PRICE             $46,900     $44,900     $43,000     $39,900


   ADDRESSES               # 1   9002  127LANE NO
                           # 2   11455 131 AVE  N
                           # 3   11450 132 AVE  N
```

(Continued)

```
        STEPWISE  MULTIPLE  REGRESSION
             VALUATION  ANALYSIS


SUMMARY DATA FOR ALL COMPARABLE SALES ANALYZED:
     TOTAL NUMBER OF SALES ANALYZED . . . . . . . . . . . .    19
     MEAN SALES PRICE FOR ALL SALES . . . . . . . . . .  $44,294
     STANDARD DEVIATION IN PRICE FOR ALL SALES . . . . .  $2,739

SUMMARY DATA FOR THE MULTIPLE REGRESSION ANALYSIS:
     MULTIPLE CORRELATION COEFFICIENT . . . . . . . . . . . 0.9493
     STANDARD ERROR OF THE ESTIMATE . . . . . . . . .  1012.7576
     NUMBER OF VARIABLES IN REGRESSION EQUATION . . . . . . .    5
     DEGREES OF FREEDOM . . . . . . . . . . . . . . . . . .    13
     F RATIO  . . . . . . . . . . . . . . . . . . . . .  23.7492

APPLICATION OF REGRESSION RESULTS FOR PROPERTY VALUATION:

   VARIABLE    SIGNIFICANCE    MULTIPLIER    DATA FOR    EXTENSION
     NAME       (T VALUE)      CALCULATED    SUBJECT    FOR SUBJECT
   ********    ************    **********    ********    ***********
    PORCH          2.2775       495.1224      1.0000         $495
    BDRMS         -1.4363     -1279.8154      3.0000      $-3,839
    LT SZ         -1.6463        -0.3353   7575.0000      $-2,540
    GAR A          3.7445        36.8626    520.0000      $19,168
    LIV A          8.0251        13.1415   1720.0000      $22,603


    CONSTANT TERM OF THE REGRESSION EQUATION   . . . . . $  11,015
    INDICATED VALUE FOR THE PROPERTY APPRAISED . . . . .  $46,902

CONFIDENCE INTERVALS FOR THE VALUE ESTIMATE:

   DEGREE OF      RANGE OF CONFIDENCE      REASONABLE VALUE INTERVAL
  CONFIDENCE    IN PERCENT    IN DOLLARS    MINIMUM   TO    MAXIMUM
  **********    **********    **********    *************************
    68.26%      +/- 0.0228    +/- $1,012     $45,890        $47,915
    95.44%      +/- 0.0457    +/- $2,025     $44,877        $48,928
```

Suggested Readings

BOOKS

American Association of State Highway Officials. *Acquisitions for Right of Way*. Washington, D.C., 1962.

Prepared as a training tool for trainees in right-of-way work; 46 chapters, by various authors, presented in three major groups: legal principles, engineering principles, and appraisal principles.

American Institute of Real Estate Appraisers. *The Appraisal Journal Bibliography, 1932-1969*. Chicago, 1970.

Author, title, and subject listings for articles.

American Institute of Real Estate Appraisers. *Managing an Appraisal Office*. Chicago, 1971.

Intended to lessen the appraiser's office-management burden, outlines basic planning and business management procedures; includes organization chart for a six-person office, budget flow chart, and other charts.

American Institute of Real Estate Appraisers. *Problems in Rural Real Estate Appraisal, with Suggested Solutions*. 2nd ed. Chicago, 1968.

American Institute of Real Estate Appraisers. *Readings in Real Property Valuation Principles. Readings in Real Estate Investment Analysis. Readings in the Income Approach to Real Property Valuation*. Chicago, 1977.

Collections of articles from *The Appraisal Journal* on three subjects described in titles.

American Institute of Real Estate Appraisers. *Real Estate Appraisal Bibliography*. Chicago, 1973.

Citations to approximately 4,000 items, largely articles in periodicals, published 1945 through 1972; arranged in subject categories.

American Institute of Real Estate Appraisers. *Real Estate Appraisal Practice*. Chicago, 1958.

Fifty-eight papers, presented at the Silver Anniversary Conference of AIREA, May 1957, devoted to fundamental principles and their application to the appraisal of specific types of property.

American Institute of Real Estate Appraisers. *Study Guide: AIREA Course I-B, Capitalization Theory and Techniques*. Chicago, 1977.

Twelve lessons on the income approach and methods of capitalization (direct, straight, annuity, mortgage equity).

American Institute of Real Estate Appraisers. *Urban Renewal and Redevelopment: Articles from The Appraisal Journal.* Chicago, 1963.
> Eighteen articles.

American Institute of Real Estate Appraisers. *Wide Divergencies in Right-of-Way Valuations.* Chicago, 1971.
> Report of a research study made for the Highway Research Board of the National Academy of Sciences.

American Institute of Real Estate Appraisers and Society of Real Estate Appraisers. *Real Estate Appraisal Terminology,* ed. Byrl N. Boyce. Cambridge, Mass., Ballinger Publishing Co., 1975.
> Contains several thousand definitions of appraisal terminology including areas of investment analysis, statistics, mathematics, and computers. Also contains sections of abbreviations, symbols, units of measure, basic formulas, and depreciation methods.

American Society of Appraisers. *Appraisal and Valuation Manual.* Washington, D.C., 1956-1972. 9 vols.
> Each volume is a collection of articles by various authors; articles on real property appraisal included with those on personal and intangible property, etc.

Babcock, Frederick M. *The Valuation of Real Estate.* New York, McGraw-Hill Book Co., 1932.
> Considered a classic of appraisal literature.

Bloom, George. *The Appraisal Data Plant.* Doctoral dissertation. Bloomington, Indiana University, 1953.
> Report on examination of specific collections of data, plus in-depth conclusions and recommendations for the improvement of this appraisal tool.

Bloom, George F., and Henry S. Harrison. *Appraising the Single Family Residence.* Chicago, American Institute of Real Estate Appraisers, 1978.
> An introduction to the theory and techniques of real estate appraising applied to the single family home.

Dombal, Robert W. *Residential Condominiums: A Guide to Analysis and Appraisal.* Chicago, American Institute of Real Estate Appraisers, 1976.
> Appraisal problems of entire projects, individual units, conversions, and resales.

Ellwood, L. W. *Ellwood Tables for Real Estate Appraising and Financing.* 4th ed. Cambridge, Mass., Ballinger Publishing Co., 1977.
> Tables, with explanatory text, for analysis and appraisal of income property.

Encyclopedia of Real Estate Appraising, ed. Edith J. Friedman, 3rd ed. Englewood Cliffs, N.J., Prentice-Hall, Inc., 1978.
> Various appraisal techniques and approaches plus the appraisal of specific property types covered in monographic chapters by individual authors.

Garrett, Robert L., Hunter A. Hogan, Jr., and Robert M. Stanton. *The Valuation of Shopping Centers.* Chicago, American Institute of Real Estate Appraisers, 1976.
> A guide to the elements the appraiser considers in valuing a shopping center; covers all types of shopping centers.

Gimmy, Arthur E. *Tennis Clubs and Racquet Sport Projects: A Guide to Market Analysis, Appraisal, Development and Financing.* Chicago, American Institute of Real Estate Appraisers, 1978.
> Study of tennis facilities from the standpoint of feasibility and investment.

Graaskamp, James A. *A Guide to Feasibility Analysis*. Chicago, Society of Real Estate Appraisers, 1970.
> A technical discussion of methodology, with applications.

Grier, Eunice and George. *Equality and Beyond: Housing Segregation and the Goals of the Great Society*. Chicago, Quadrangle, 1966.
> An analysis of segregated housing and recommendations for comprehensive planning to solve the problems created by it.

Grier, George and Eunice. *Privately Developed Interracial Housing: An Analysis of Experience*. Berkeley, University of California Press, 1960.
> Report of the findings of one phase of a broad study of housing problems involving minority and ethnic groups conducted for the Commission on Race and Housing.

Himstreet, William C. *Writing Appraisal Reports*. Chicago, American Institute of Real Estate Appraisers, 1971.
> A guide to good writing for reports of almost all types; does not treat preparation of appraisal reports specifically.

Institute on Planning, Zoning, and Eminent Domain. *Proceedings*. New York, Matthew Bender and Co.
> Papers delivered at sessions of the Institute, which is a continuing legal education program of the Southwestern Legal Foundation, Dallas, Texas; series started in 1959.

International Association of Assessing Officers. *Assessing and the Appraisal Process*. 5th ed. Chicago, 1974.
> The appraisal of real estate for assessment purposes; written as a text and reference work for the assessor and appraiser.

International Association of Assessing Officers. *Property Assessment Valuation*. Chicago, 1977.
> A presentation of the appraisal process and the approaches to value, written for tax assessors; includes a section on mass appraisals.

Kahn, Sanders A., Frederick E. Case, and Alfred Schimmel. *Real Estate Appraisal and Investment*. New York, Ronald Press, 1963.
> A textbook covering all phases of real estate appraising plus special sections on investment analysis of specific property types.

Kinnard, William N., Jr. *Income Property Valuation: Principles and Techniques of Appraising Income-Producing Real Estate*. Lexington, Mass., Heath, 1971.
> Introduces the income capitalization process, assuming reader familiarity with other appraisal principles and techniques.

Kinnard, William N., Jr. *Industrial Real Estate*. 2nd ed. Washington, D.C., Society of Industrial Realtors, 1971.
> Approximately 100 pages devoted to the appraisal of industrial property.

Kratovil, Robert. *Real Estate Law*. 6th ed. Englewood Cliffs, N.J., Prentice-Hall, Inc., 1974.
> A one-volume textbook on all phases of the law of real estate.

Laurenti, Luigi. *Property Values and Race: Studies in Seven Cities*. Berkeley, University of California Press, 1960.
> Report of the findings of one phase of a broad study of housing problems involving minority and ethnic groups conducted for the Commission on Race and Housing.

McEntire, Davis. *Residence and Race*. Berkeley, University of California Press, 1960.

Final report of a broad study of housing problems involving minority and ethnic groups conducted for the Commission on Race and Housing.

Murray, William G. *Farm Appraisal and Valuation*. 5th ed. Ames, Iowa State University Press, 1969.

All phases of farm real estate valuation including loan appraisals, assessments, inheritance tax appraisals, and condemnations.

National Cooperative Highway Research Program. *Reports*. Washington, D.C., National Academy of Sciences Highway Research Board.

A numbered series, each number on a single topic—e.g., Number 56: *Scenic Easements: Legal, Administrative, and Valuation Problems and Procedures;* Number 107: *New Approaches to Compensation for Residential Takings.*

Nichols' Law of Eminent Domain. 3rd ed. rev. Julius L. Sackman and Patrick J. Rohan. Albany, N.Y., Matthew Bender and Co. (looseleaf service).

Comprehensive, multi-volume work; national in scope, exhaustive in treatment.

Ratcliff, Richard U. *Modern Real Estate Valuation: Theory and Application*. Madison, Wis., Democrat Press, 1965.

The theory of market simulation, variant of the market approach, and its application to the valuation of specific property types; presented as a departure from traditional thought in appraising.

Ratcliff, Richard U. *Urban Land Economics*. New York, McGraw-Hill Book Co., 1949.

Based on the theory that the determination of urban land use is a market process; chapters on rights in land, demand factors with particular attention to housing, building, finance, and specialized markets.

Ring, Alfred A. *Valuation of Real Estate*. 2nd ed. Englewood Cliffs, N.J., Prentice-Hall, Inc., 1970.

Written essentially as a training and teaching guide for candidates who seek membership in one or more of the principal appraisal societies.

Rohan, Patrick J., and Melvin A. Reskin. *Condemnation Procedures and Techniques; Forms*. Albany, N.Y., Matthew Bender and Co. (looseleaf service).

Presents condemnation in its procedural setting and synthesizes recent developments; also intended as a supplement to *Nichols on Eminent Domain*.

Rushmore, Stephen. *The Valuation of Hotels and Motels*. Chicago, American Institute of Real Estate Appraisers, 1978.

Techniques for estimating the value of hotel and motel properties, including supply and demand relationships, projecting income and expenses.

Schmutz, George L. *The Appraisal Process*. 3rd ed. rev. Manhattan Beach, Calif., 1959.

Considered a classic of appraisal literature; author was President of AIREA in 1940.

Schmutz, George L. *Condemnation Appraisal Handbook*, revised and enlarged by Edwin M. Rams. Englewood Cliffs, N.J., Prentice-Hall, Inc., 1963.

Concepts, relationships, and analysis of the various problems involving compensation in eminent domain cases; includes case studies pertaining to takings for specific purposes.

Sutte, Donald T., Jr. *Appraisal of Roadside Advertising Signs*. Chicago, American Institute of Real Estate Appraisers, 1972.
> Prepared because of the increasing demand for appraisals of billboard and roadside signs resulting from implementation of the federal Highway Beautification Act; appendixes include Traffic Audit Bureau method of rating signs and typical lease forms and letter of permission.

Taeuber, Karl and Alma. *Negroes in Cities: Residential Segregation and Neighborhood Change*. Chicago, Aldine, 1965 (reprinted in paperback by Athenum, 1972).

Von Furstenburg, George M., ed. *Patterns of Racial Discrimination: Housing*. Lexington, Mass., Lexington Books, 1974.

Weimer, Arthur M., Homer Hoyt, and George F. Bloom. *Real Estate*. 7th ed. New York, Wiley, 1977.
> Textbook intended to provide introduction and decision-oriented approach to many facets of real estate activity.

Wendt, Paul F. *Real Estate Appraisal Review and Outlook*. Athens, University of Georgia Press, 1974.
> A text providing a review of the development of appraisal theory and practice and an evaluation of the state of the art and its future.

BUILDING COST MANUALS

Boeckh Building Valuation Manual. Milwaukee, American Appraisal Co., 1967. 3 vols.
> Vol. 1—*Residential and Agricultural;* Vol. 2—*Commercial;* Vol. 3—*Industrial and Institutional.* 1967 cost data base; wide variety of building models; built up from unit-in-place costs converted to cost per square foot of floor or ground area. *Boeckh Building Cost Modifier*, published bimonthly for updating with current modifiers.

Building Construction Cost Data. Duxbury, Mass., Robert Snow Means Co., annually.
> Average unit prices on a wide variety of building construction items for use in making up engineering estimates. Components arranged according to uniform system adopted by American Institute of Architects, Associated General Contractors, and Construction Specifications Institute.

Dodge Building Cost Calculator & Valuation Guide. New York, McGraw-Hill Information Systems Co. (looseleaf service; quarterly supplements).
> Building costs arranged by frequently occurring types and sizes of buildings; local cost modifiers and historical local cost index tables included. Formerly *Dow Building Cost Calculator*.

Marshall Valuation Service. Los Angeles, Marshall and Swift Publication Co. (looseleaf service; monthly supplements).
> Cost data for determining replacement costs of buildings and other improvements in the United States and Canada; includes current cost multipliers and local modifiers.

Residential Cost Handbook. Los Angeles, Marshall and Swift Publication Co. (looseleaf service; quarterly supplements).
> Presents square-foot method and segregated-cost method; local modifiers and cost trend modifiers included.

SOURCES OF OPERATING COSTS AND RATIOS

Only a few published sources are cited below. Attention is directed to the first item listed, the annotated bibliography issued by Robert Morris Associates.

Robert Morris Associates. *Sources of Composite Financial Data—A Bibliography.* 3rd ed. Philadelphia, 1971.
An annotated list of 98 nongovernment sources; arranged in manufacturing, wholesaling, retail, and service categories; subject index to specific businesses; publishers' names and addresses given for each citation.

Building Owners and Managers Association International. *Downtown and Suburban Office Building Experience Exchange Report.* Washington, D.C.
Annually, since 1920; analysis of expenses and income (quoted in cents per square foot); national, regional, and selected city averages.

Dun & Bradstreet, Inc. *Key Business Ratios in 125 Lines.* New York.
Annually; balance sheet, profit-and-loss ratios.

Harris, Kerr, Forster & Co. *Clubs in Town & Country.* New York.
Annually, since 1953; income-expense data and operating ratios for city and country clubs; the geographical data given are by four U.S. regions.

Harris, Kerr, Forster & Co. *Trends in the Hotel-Motel Business.* New York.
Annually, since 1937; Income-expense data and operating ratios for transient and resort hotels and motels; the geographical data given are by five U.S. regions.

Institute of Real Estate Management. *Income/Expense Analysis: Apartments, Condominiums & Cooperatives.* Chicago.
Annually, since 1954; data arranged by building, then by national, regional, metropolitan, and selected city groupings; operating costs per room, per square foot, etc. Formerly *Apartment Building Experience Exchange.*

Institute of Real Estate Management. *Income/Expense Analysis: Suburban Office Buildings.* Chicago.
Annually, since 1976; data analyzed on basis of gross area, gross and net rentable office areas; dollar-per-square-foot calculations; national, regional, and metropolitan comparisons and detailed analyses for selected cities.

Laventhol & Horwath. *Lodging Industry.* Philadelphia.
Annually, since 1932; income, expense and profit data; includes historical trend tables.

Laventhol & Horwath and National Restaurant Association. *Table-Service Restaurant Operations.* Philadelphia.
Annually, since 1976; income-expense data and operating ratios; superceded the Laventhol & Horwath *Restaurant Operations* report that began in 1959.

National Retail Merchants Association, Controllers' Congress. *Department Store and Specialty Store Merchandising and Operating Results.* New York.
Annually, since 1925; merchandise classification base used since 1969 edition (1968 data); geographical analysis by Federal Reserve Districts. Known as the "MOR" report.

National Retail Merchants Association, Controllers' Congress. *Financial and Operating Results of Department and Specialty Stores.* New York.
>Annually, since 1963; data arranged by sales volume category. Known as the "FOR" Report.

Realtors National Marketing Institute. *Percentage Leases.* 13th ed. Chicago, 1973.
>Based on reports of 3,100 leases for 97 retail and service categories in 7 U.S. regions. Data broken down by type of operation, area, center, and building; with regional and store averages given for average minimum rent, rent per square foot, average gross leasable areas, and sales per square foot.

Urban Land Institute. *Dollars and Cents of Shopping Centers.* Washington, D.C., 1978.
>First issued in 1961; revised every three years; income and expense data for neighborhood, community, and regional centers; statistics for specific tenant types given.

PERIODICALS

American Right of Way Proceedings. American Right of Way Association, Los Angeles.
>Annually. Papers presented at National Seminars.

Appraisal Digest. New York State Society of Real Estate Appraisers, a Division of the New York State Association of Real Estate Boards, Inc., Albany, N.Y.
>Quarterly. Primarily articles published elsewhere; some original material included.

Appraisal Institute Magazine. Appraisal Institute of Canada, Winnipeg, Manitoba.
>Quarterly. General and technical articles on appraisal and expropriation in Canada; includes information on Institute programs, news, etc.

The Appraisal Journal. American Institute of Real Estate Appraisers, Chicago.
>Quarterly. The oldest periodical in the appraisal field, published since 1932; technical articles on all phases of real property appraisal; section on legal decisions included as regular feature. Consolidated index covering 1932-1969 available.

Editor and Publisher Market Guide. Editor and Publisher, New York.
>Annually. Standardized market data for more than 1,500 areas in the United States and Canada; information includes population estimates for trading areas. List of principal industries, transportation, climate, chain store outlets, etc.

Journal of the American Real Estate and Urban Economics Association. New Brunswick, N.J.
>Quarterly. Focuses on research and scholarly studies of current and emerging real estate issues.

Journal of the American Society of Farm Managers and Rural Appraisers. Denver.
>Semi-annually. Appraisal articles included.

Just Compensation. Sherman Oaks, Calif.
>Monthly; reports on condemnation cases.

Land Economics. University of Wisconsin, Madison.
>Quarterly. Subtitle: *A Quarterly Journal Devoted to the Study of Economics and Social Institutes.* Good source of reports on university research; covers trends in land utilization; frequent articles on developments in other countries.

The Real Estate Appraiser. Society of Real Estate Appraisers, Chicago.
 Bimonthly. Technical articles and Society news; section on legal cases included as regular feature. Consolidated bibliographies for 1935-1960 and 1961-1970 available. Previously published as *The Review* and as *Residential Appraiser*.

Real Estate Issues. American Society of Real Estate Counselors. Chicago.
 Semi-annually.

Right of Way. American Right of Way Association, Los Angeles, Calif.
 Bimonthly. Articles on all phases of right of way activity; condemnation, negotiation, etc.; pipelines, electric power transmission lines, and other uses as well as highways; includes Association news.

Small Business Reporter. Bank of America, San Francisco.
 Irregularly. Each issue devoted to a specific type of small business; has covered, for instance, coin-operated laundries, greeting card shops, and restaurants.

Survey of Buying Power. Sales Management, New York.
 Annually. Population totals and characteristics, income and consumption data presented in various categories: national, regional, metropolitan area, county, city; separate section of Canadian information. A source for population estimates between the decennial United States censuses.

Valuation. American Society of Appraisers, Washington, D.C.
 Three issues per year. Articles on real property valuation included with articles on the appraisal of personal and intangible property; includes Society news. Previously published as *Technical Valuation*.

Index